Dancing Around the World

with Mike & Barbara Bivona

Order this book online at www.trafford.com
or email orders@trafford.com

Most Trafford titles are also available at major online book retailers.

Printed in Victoria, BC, Canada.

ISBN: 978-1-4269-2278-7 (sc)
ISBN: 978-1-4269-2279-4 (hc)

Library of Congress Control Number: 2009912296

*Our mission is to efficiently provide the world's finest, most comprehensive book publishing
service, enabling every author to experience success. To find out how to publish your book, your
way, and have it available worldwide, visit us online at www.trafford.com*

Trafford rev. 1/20/10

Trafford PUBLISHING® www.trafford.com

North America & international
toll-free: 1 888 232 4444 (USA & Canada)
phone: 250 383 6864 ♦ fax: 812 355 4082

CONTENTS

DANCING AROUND THE WORLD

IN 1998, MY WIFE Barbara began writing for the Long Island, New York Ballroom Dance Newsletter: "AROUND THE FLOOR." Her column covered our travels around the world and the many dancing experiences we've enjoyed. The newsletter evolved from a local paper into an international website with links around the world including China, England, Australia, South Africa, Korea and many Latin American countries. Some other links were Bridge to World Championships, Colleges and Universities, Swing dancing sites, and my favorite; Tango dancing sites. I soon had a column on the same website under the name, "Tangohombre," covering ballroom dancing on Long Island, with emphasis on the Argentine Tango. The stories that appeared in our columns and on the website were quite condensed from the original ones. I thought it would be fun to present the articles as they appeared in the newsletters and website, and then tell the full stories as originally experienced. In addition to the published articles, many of our dancing experiences were not presented for publication, so I thought, why not include those stories too? Where appropriate, I will update information that might help to clarify and bring the stories into current times.

Ballroom dancing has made an amazing resurrection. Dance studios are opening in every corner of the world to accommodate the demand for this wonderful activity. Unfortunately, our publisher, Adrian Cabral, did not benefit from this wonderful revival of ballroom dancing, as he had to give up publishing the newsletter and his website in 2004, due to poor health and the exhausting demands of maintaining a growing website and publication. If it all comes together successfully, this book should be interesting and enjoyable for the many readers who like dancing, or who intend to learn this art form, or who might just enjoy reading about the many wonderful experiences available to dancers who are out there expressing themselves in this manner. Dancing can also be a pleasant way to exercise, especially for those who prefer not to spend time at the gym, but would rather add this wonderful experience to their leisurely, somewhat sedentary, lifestyles.

ACKNOWLEDGEMENTS

I WOULD LIKE TO acknowledge the contributions of my many ballroom dancing friends and instructors, for their love, enthusiasm, patience, and camaraderie throughout the years. The bond that develops between people in a dance community is unique, in that a simple first dance with a stranger can develop into a lifetime friendship, a romantic beginning, or a wonderful social grouping of people with a common interest. In the social dance world it is not necessary to have a steady partner; all that is required is a willingness to go out to dance clubs, dance studios or other ballroom dance venues, and enjoy the music and feel comfortable dancing with people you know from that social group.

Our first dance lesson was at Swing Street Studios with the talented Elektra Underhill. We credit her with our passion for dancing, as her skill, patience and understanding nursed and nurtured us through our many dance lessons. Our first lessons were Tango and Swing. Barbara and I danced together for many years at weddings and other social events, but never got the hang of doing Swing or Tango very well. A problem I had was the thought of taking dancing lessons and being criticized by the instructor and, of course, my wife, an event that went against my macho persona. It took a lot of patience on their part before I learned how to behave myself when given constructive criticism. We decided to take a series of six lessons in Swing and Tango; if we were successful and enjoyed ourselves, we would take other dance lessons. Fortunately, with much difficulty, I got through the constructive criticism without too much damage to my ego, and did learn the dances, and totally loved the whole new experience. The pleasure of being able to get on a dance floor, and properly perform the routines we had learned, was worth the time and effort that went into our dance classes. Our next dance lessons, one at a time, were the Cha Cha, Mambo, Foxtrot and Waltz. Of course, it took many years of classes and practice to learn these challenging dances. Our most memorable dance lessons were the American and Argentine tangos. Elecktra introduced us to these passionate tangos and today, when we dance or perform the Argentine Tango, deep in my heart I thank her for the feelings of warmth and passion that comes with performing this dance of seduction and love.

Elecktra thought it would be a good idea to make video tapes of the perfected lessons. This allowed us to practice by viewing the tapes, which made for very pleasant and smooth routines that prepared us for our next lesson. It was amazing how quickly we learned the dances, thanks to the use of the video tapes. It certainly curtailed the friction that is usually created when partners have different recollections of how to perform steps and routines. We still refer to our tapes from time to time, to refresh our memories or clarify routines, and totally enjoy watching ourselves progress in the particular dance we were learning at that time. Elecktra had wonderful Sunday milongas (dances) at her studio which allowed us to practice and enjoy dancing with our new-found dancing friends. She also had dancing practice during the week for ballroom dance students, which went a long way to advance everyone's dancing skills. Sad to say, Elecktra passed away while I was writing this chapter. She is remembered throughout the dance community as one of the most dedicated dance instructors on Long Island. She inspired many of our younger dance instructors who were fortunate to have studied under her, to follow her lead, and has resulted in bringing ballroom dancing to its apex. It's amazing at the amount of dance instructors in New York who were influenced by her skills, passion, tutelage, and dedication. She was certainly instrumental in helping to make ballroom and social dancing a popular pastime in the 21st century, enjoyed by people in all walks of life. Thanks a million, Elecktra . . .

My office with Manchester Technologies was in Hauppauge, Long Island, New York. Fortunately, we had an office in Boca Raton, Florida, where I usually spent a couple of months during the winter. It was there that we were introduced to our next dance instructor, Dan Maloney, of the DanceSport Studio, in Delray Beach. We became interested in his dance technique when we saw some of our new Florida friends dance; it seemed all of the better dancers were taught by Dan. We approached him and asked if he would polish our dance routines, especially in the Hustle, Quickstep and Mambo. He agreed, and we began a life-long social friendship with him and fortunately, bonded with many of his students. Our friendship with Dan and his students, which began over 15 years ago, continues till today. His style of dancing was what we were interested in, he also had video equipment for our use, which made it easy to practice and refine our routines. Over the years, Dan has won many dancing awards and has placed first in many Hustle competitions. It was our hope that some of his talent would rub off on us. We thank him a million times over for his patience and expertise and for his friendship and all the many friends we met through the years at his dance studio. Especially beneficial were his Thursday night dance socials at his studio. It gave the students a chance to practice and dance with others, which helped everyone develop confidence on the dance floor. When learning new dances, it is very difficult to become comfortable right away because of shyness, uncertainty, or the feeling that everyone is watching you make mistakes. Dan's teaching puts students at ease and easily gets them past all these demons. When dancing is fun and relaxing, it's amazing how quickly the steps and routines are accomplished; if not exactly as taught, then at least well enough to enjoy them within the limitations of one's own ability. During the winter season, he has dances on Friday nights and occasionally Sundays, which are open to the public and include dance hosts in attendance to accommodate single ladies. Meeting new people at the socials is part of what dancing is all about, especially since it gives many single people an opportunity to meet and develop friendships in a comfortable and relaxed atmosphere.

Our next instructors were Alec and Tanya Koulik, teaching at Johnny Grant's Studio in Boynton Beach, Florida. They are from Siberia, Russia, where he was a practicing neurologist and she taught medicine at a local university. They are renowned ballroom dancers and use their talents to supplement their income, while studying to renew their medical licenses in the United States. Some of our friends took lessons from them in both the American Waltz and Foxtrot. We admired our friends' dancing so much that we were excited about taking lessons from such accomplished dance instructors. We rushed to their studio and asked if they would take us on as students. They asked us to dance the Waltz and Foxtrot. Being that we had a good understanding of these dances and showed promise for improvement, they agreed to take us on as students. Their method was quite effective. Tanya would teach me my steps and styling and Alec taught Barbara her part to the same dance routines. After an hour lesson, Alec would coach us and make sure that we performed our steps and styling correctly. He would tell us: "Unless you feel like you're flying, you are not doing your parts properly." After each 30-minute session of dancing together, it was amazing how much we learned with their technique. We were ecstatic how quickly we learned their dance styling, as we floated across the dance floor to the admiration of our friends. After six dance lessons, we accomplished the level of dancing we were aiming for, and till this day, as we perform, we silently seek our young mentors' approval. We are still friendly and watch them perform at various dance venues whenever we can, realizing how fortunate we were to have been trained by them and to have them in our lives.

One of our recent dance instructors is Louis Del Prete from Deer Park, Long Island, New York. He is a young man, in his thirties, who runs local dances at: Mirelle's Dance Club in

Westbury, Long Island, specializing in Latin, Hustle and West Coast Swing; the Suburban Jewish Center in Wantagh, Long Island, specializing in Ballroom Dancing; the VFW Hall in Deer Park, Long Island, featuring ballroom dancing, and Stony Brook University, Stony Brook, Long Island, for ballroom dancing and West Coast Swing. Each of these venues attracts 100 to 400 dancers of all levels, from beginners to polished professionals. We saw Louis perform the West Coast Swing and fell in love with his style and technique. It's such a unique experience when watching someone perform brilliantly, one gets the fanciful notion of: "This is what I should look like when doing that dance." After one of his performances, we asked him if he would teach us the dance and he said "ok." He was able to come to our home on Long Island, which is only ten minutes from where he lives, to give us lessons. We have a small dance area in our home where we were able to work, and it only took four lessons for us to be satisfied and confident that we could hold our own on the dance floor. Fortunately, many of the steps in West Coast Swing are similar to other dances we know, such as East Coast Swing and Cha-Cha, which helped us catch on quickly to this wonderful new dance experience. We plan on taking additional lessons with Louis in the future, as we would like to pick up some additional steps in the West Coast Swing to continue having great times on the dance floor when performing this very popular dance, which has developed an amazing following in the past couple of years.

We thank Louis for all the dance venues he hosts and the many free dance lessons that are given at these places and, mostly, for his dedication in encouraging newcomers to begin dancing. In May of 2008, we attended the Suburban Temple in Wantagh, Long Island, to see a special presentation that he sponsored featuring Dancing with the Stars professionals, Karina Smirnoff and Louie Van Amstel. This is the kind of promotional entertainment Louis is involved in; it keeps people interested in ballroom dancing and encourages newcomers to try this wonderful pastime. I discuss Karina and Louie's evening performance and their interplay with the audience in a subsequent chapter, "Dancing with the Stars."

Our current Florida instructor is Brian Smith of the Tower Ballroom in Pompano Beach. He holds many dance titles and is a dance adjudicator for USA Dance. Again we chose him because some of our friends, who are advanced dancers, had him as their dance instructor and raved about his expertise and the superior quality of his teaching. We are currently polishing up on Bolero, Rumba and Cha-Cha. Due to his intricate understanding of the dances we are advancing easily and having lots of fun with his easy going style. We plan to be with Brian for many years to come enjoying his coaching and his good nature.

It is our many friends, such as June and Misha Rudolph and Ellie and Sal Guarneri, that keep us fascinated and in love with ballroom dancing. We met the fabulous international dancers June and Misha over 15 years ago at Dan's DanceSport in Delray Beach, Florida, and it was their love of dancing and their dedications to promoting ballroom dancing that encouraged us to continue with this wonderful art form. Misha has voluntarily helped fellow dancers with their problems on the dance floor and encouraged many new dancers in the basics. He is responsible for helping many people who would have given up due to frustration, etc., to continue dancing. We met Ellie and Sal at the Kismet Hall in New Hyde Park, Long Island, about the same time we met June and Misha in Florida. They were single at the time and were introduced to each other by mutual friends at Kismet Hall. Soon they became dancing partners and then life partners. Sal is my role model. At 85, he is still dancing with all the passion of a younger man. He and Ellie do a Peabody in sweetheart position that captures everyone's attention on the dance floor. It never fails; all the dancers stop to watch their performances with utter admiration and some envy. In life there are times when "six degrees of separation" crosses one's path. With me and Sal, it was when we met at Kismet. He seemed very familiar to me; I kept searching my mind trying to figure out when our paths had crossed. I finally approached him and asked if I looked familiar to him. He said: "Somewhat, but he wasn't sure." So we searched our pasts and discovered we had many things in common. For instance, we both came from East New York, Brooklyn, living only a few blocks from each other, and he went to the same high school as my older brother and sisters. Then it hit home, we both worked for a company 50 years ago, named Appeal Printing, in New York City, at the same time. He was, in fact, my supervisor-- my idol. I was in my late teens at the time and looked up to him as an older brother and figure of authority. When I told him he accidentally locked me in the warehouse overnight, he knew exactly who I was, but he didn't recall if the lock-up was an accident or not.

CHAPTER ONE

The Language of Dance

THERE ARE MANY TERMS and expressions that are peculiar to dancing, and without some explanation it would be very difficult to understand much of my writing. The following are some common terms and phrases found in the dance vocabulary:

AMATEUR DANCER: A person who dances for pleasure and does not seek financial gain.

PROFESSIONAL DANCER: A dancer who teaches, performs, or competes for financial gain and, therefore, is ineligible to compete as an Amateur.

SOCIAL DANCING: Ballroom, Latin, Swing and Nightclub dances are done for enjoyment and relaxation and not meant for show or competition.

SLOW DANCING: A general term meant for dancing to very slow, romantic music, improvising moves, with a very close hold. No lessons are required, as there are no formulated steps or patterns involved.

GENERAL DANCING: Usually done at intermissions and between dance performances in competition dancing when the dance floor is available to the audience for social dancing.

Michael Bivona

LINE DANCING: Can be performed with or without a partner. Dancers form a line and repeat sets of patterns to the music. Some of the more popular line dances are: Country Western, Disco, Cha Cha's, Waltzes and even Polkas. Probably one of most popular line dances on the east coast is Zorba. The dance comes from the unforgettable movie, "Zorba the Greek," starring Anthony Quinn. He performed the dance as a single and then was joined by his friend to make it a duet. In Greece, the dance is usually done by men in a line formation. Oddly, in the United States, the dance is performed by women with very few men participating. In the United States, men dancing with other men is not considered macho, but in Europe and South America it is very common.

MIXERS: Women form a line and men pick the first person in the line as a partner; they dance once around the floor, and he then returns her to the end of the line and proceeds to his next partner who is first in line. This continues until the dance is over, which is about ten minutes. Mixers are usually done to Foxtrots and Waltzes, and are very popular where there are single people at a dance event.

FORMATION DANCING: Formation dancing allows dancers to show off their own techniques in addition to their ability to move as a team. Teams can be comprised of 4, 6, or 8 couples and will perform dance routines such as, Tango or Cha-Cha. Another popular format is a potpourri routine, which is often a mixture of dances in the same category, e.g., International Latin formation or International Standard formation. The latter format is used during the competitions of ballroom formation teams in such places as the British Dance Championships at the Tower Ballroom in Blackpool, England. (Blackpool competition is discussed in Chapter Fifteen.)

AMERICAN STYLE: A type of ballroom dancing, which evolved from social dancing and is now a fully-recognized competitive style of dancing. The smooth style allows the dancer to be in open or closed positions, allowing for a very beautiful "Fred &

2

Ginger" style of dancing. There are nine American style dances divided into two groups: Smooth and Rhythm.

Smooth style consists of:

Foxtrot

Waltz

Tango

Viennese Waltz

Rhythm style consists of:

Cha Cha

Rumba

East Coast Swing

Bolero

Mambo

INTERNATIONAL STYLE:

In International style ballroom dancing, couples remain in closed dance position throughout the standard dances. Many of the steps and routines are similar to American style dancing, but are performed in closed position for standard dances and open and closed positions for Latin. American style is performed in open and closed positions for all their dances. The ten International style dances are also divided into two categories: Standard and Latin.

Standard International style dancing consists of:

Slow Foxtrot

Waltz

Tango

Viennese Waltz

Quickstep

Latin International style consists of:

Cha Cha

Samba

Rumba

Paso Doble

Jive

ARGENTINE TANGO:

Argentine Tango and the above mentioned ballroom International and American tangos use very different techniques and vocabularies, which is confusing considering they are all considered tangos. In Argentine Tango, the body's center moves first, and then the feet reach to support the move. In ballroom Tango, the body is set in motion across the floor through the flexing of the lower joints (ankle, knee, and hip) while the feet are delayed. Then, the feet move to catch up to the body, resulting in snatching or striking action that reflects the staccato nature of the style of music.

Argentine Tango steps are more gliding, but can vary widely in timing, speed, and character, and follow no single rhythm. The dance is led and followed at a level of individual steps; variations can occur from one step to the next. This allows the dancers to vary the dance from moment to moment to match the music, fast or slow, and to match their mood. Improvisation and attitude are the essence of the dance.

The Argentine Tango's frame or embrace is not rigid, but flexible, allowing adjustments to the steps to come smoothly, and can go from slow and close to offset in a "V" frame to apart, as if dancing alone. The Ballroom Tango's frame is more rigid, higher in the elbows, and with tone in the arms. In Argentine

Tango, when in a "close embrace," there is continuous contact at the full upper body, but not in the legs. In Ballroom Tango, the "close embrace" involves close contact from the top of the ribs down to the upper thighs. In Argentine Tango, the ball or toe of the foot may be placed first, or the dancer may begin with the entire foot in a cat-like manner. Ballroom Tango steps stay close to the floor, while the Argentine Tango includes moves that can carry one's leg into the air, or hooking one's leg around the partner's leg or body, which results in the feet leaving the ground.

Ballroom Tango is performed in competitive dancing and consists of levels from Bronze to Gold with adherence to strict syllabus (steps and pattern) at each level that can be judged as to performance and style within the given syllabus. Argentine Tango has basic patterns, but can be combined, improvised, or mixed with the patterns of other dances, without adherence to the strict syllabuses of American or International dancing.

SHOW CASE DANCING: A dance exhibition, which can be performed by professionals or amateurs, or a combination of both. One of the more popular types is performed by a Professional/Amateur (Pro/Am) couple. It is usually a teacher and student that team up and compete against other Pro/Am dancers. It can be a local, national, or an international event and has gained increased popularity over the last several years. My friend June Rudolph competed in Buenos Aires, Argentina, in the 2008 World Champion Pro/Am, with her professional dance instructor, Thomas Del Flore, of Delray Beach, Florida. They placed third in that worldwide competition in three categories: Pro/Am International Standard Championship for contestants ages 50 to 70; Pro/Am International Standard Gold Championship for ages 50 to 70; and International Standard Gold Open Scholarship, which is open to all ages. Each of the categories required performing five dances: Viennese Waltz, Quickstep, International Tango, International Slow Waltz, and International Foxtrot. Not bad for a senior citizen.

Michael Bivona

MEDALIST SYSTEM: Is a uniform method of testing, used by dance schools to measure a student's progress. It offers structure in dance programs and gives students a standardized method of measuring their development.

BRONZE LEVEL: The first level of the Medalist System consists of specific basic dance concepts and movements. This level is represented in dance competitions and allows performers to compete within their level of expertise.

SILVER LEVEL: The second level in the Medalist System allows dancers to use continuity (open steps) in the American Style Waltz and Foxtrot. It also allows dancers to compete with others on their own level of expertise and to be judged accordingly. International Style Silver dancing has its own requirements that are similar to American but conform to their particular standards.

GOLD LEVEL: The highest level in the Medalist System; representing the most advanced figures and dance concepts; also used in competitions to measure the proficiency of the dancers on the highest levels.

DANCESPORT: The official name used in competitive Ballroom Dancing, relates to the more athletic form of Ballroom dancing as recognized by the Olympic Committee. As of this date, the committee has not included ballroom dancing as an Olympic event.

LINE OF DIRECTION: This is the direction that the flow of dancing should follow. It's a counterclockwise direction and it's considered proper dance floor etiquette for all dancers to move in the same direction in appropriate dances. The following illustration describes the flow and the alternative floor etiquette for dancers who dance different types of dances to the same music. A popular diagram is presented with permission of the artist, Ray Gerring:

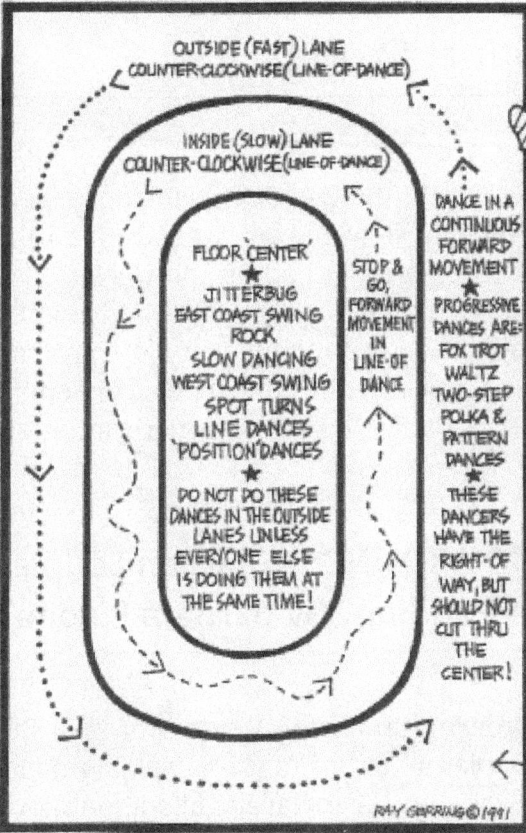

7

CHAPTER TWO

Three Short Stories

BEFORE WRITING ABOUT OUR dancing experiences while traveling, I thought it would be a good idea to present three articles that Barbara and I had on the website, "AROUND THE FLOOR." Although these articles only briefly discuss our travels and experiences with dancing, they do give insight to the dancing scene and the different types of people enjoying the various types of dancing, such as American, International and Social.

TRAVELING AROUND: "Chicken Soup and Chocolate Pudding" by Barbara Bivona

As a child growing up during World War II in Brooklyn, New York, the popular sound of that era was big band music. We listened to Swing and Jive, ballads alluding to loved ones who were far from home during the war, and patriotic music. Rumba was making a good showing on the dance floor, and the Andrew Sisters sang "Rum and Coca Cola" to a Rumba beat. I was young and innocent of the ways of the world, my memories of that time are not so much of the devastation and horrors of war, but growing up in Brownsville, my neighborhood in Brooklyn,

New York, and of my close circle of friends, going fishing with my dad and brother, and my mother's wonderful chicken soup and chocolate pudding. Mom collected records, the old 78 and 33 rpms, and was always buying the latest hits. We listened to Helen O'Connell, Buddy Clark and The Dorsey Brothers; I was amazed when Mom came home with the first LP (long playing) recording I had ever seen: Sing, Sing, Sing. Mom would take my hand and dance with me in our tiny living room. If she knew the words she would sing along and my brother, George, and I would soon join in. That's why, when I saw an ad many, many years later for Joe Battaglia and his New York Band at the Huntington Town House, in Huntington, Long Island, I made reservations for an evening of dinner and big band dancing.

I was fascinated with Joe's background. Until he retired, he worked in the garment industry in New York City. He started as a young man and after many years of hard work, owned his own business. After retiring, he decided to pursue a life-long dream of taking trumpet lessons. After just six years of lessons, Joe was ready to take on the big band sounds. He played trumpet with several bands and soon decided to form his own, fulfilling his life-long dream. His success was rapid, and soon Joe and his band were being booked for repeat engagements in New York's theatre district and supper clubs. The icing on the cake was a Grammy in the year 2000 for best instrumental recording titled: "Close Your Eyes," a tribute to Harry James and Ray Anthony. The band performs music from this album in clubs and is enjoyable either for listening or dancing. That night we danced to: "Embraceable You," "It Had to Be You," "Ain't That a Kick in the Head," and some more contemporary music, such as, "On a Clear Day" and "Misty." All of these and more are on his album. Joe has been compared to Harry James; however, he told me "He feels that he has his own sound." And, while he may be using some of Harry James' arrangements, this is definitely not what I would call a cover band. Joe's sounds are his own. True, they are inspired by the master, but they emanate from his own soul. They take me back in time to those wonderful days when my main concerns were homework and what Saturday matinee my friends and I would be seeing. They take me back to the days of Mom's chicken soup and chocolate pudding.

Tangohombre by Michael Bivona

When the publisher of "AROUND THE FLOOR" asked me to develop a column about Tango dancing and its popularity with today's dancers, I asked him: "Why me?" He said, being that my e-mail address is "Tangohombre," that I probably had some insight to the feel of Tango and its popularity on today's dance scene. Of course flattery can go a long way and I decided to give it a try.

When referring to Tango, you might wonder if we are talking about American Tango, International Tango or the original Tango, Argentine Tango. It just so happens that we are talking about all three styles of dancing. Discussing the technical differences of these incredible dances is beyond my ability, but I can discuss the differences from my point of view as a social dancer.

About 15 years ago, my wife Barbara and I decided to take dance lessons. We both loved Tango music and decided it would be a good starting dance for us. At the time, the most popular, and probably the only readily available lessons, were in American Tango. The choice of dance went from a whim to an infatuation and then love in a short time. We became so passionate with the feeling of the dance and the music that we encouraged many of our friends to take Tango lessons.

The image of the actor Anthony Dexter* portraying the great Latin lover Rudolph Valentino in the movie Valentino (1951) and dancing a passionate Tango was in my mind often as we progressed with our love for the dance. I recalled seeing him portray Valentino on screen and remembered how many times my teenage friends and I saw the same picture over and over again, totally absorbed with the music and the passion of the dance. *(There is a direct link to his website listed at the end of this column.)

Over the years, we observed the development of International Tango, enjoying the complexity of the steps, body and head movements, and strict syllabus. We tried to get into the dance, but for us it lacked the passion and freedom of movement that dancing the American Tango gave us. Last year we were invited to participate in an exhibition where the three tangos were danced to show their differences. We danced the Argentine Tango and were followed by a professional-amateur couple dancing the International Tango. The professional who was from Australia picked up the mike and said: "Well, you just saw how the Tango came to my country, full of passion and softness of movement, and now we will show you how we and the English took the sex out of the dance." Their performance was exemplary, the movements and precision were remarkable; certainly the right dance for competition dancing, but, as social dancers, we still preferred the Argentine Tango. Well how did we go from the American Tango to the Argentine Tango?

In 1989, the show "Tango Argentino" appeared off-Broadway in Manhattan. Our dance instructor, Elektra, of Swing Street Studios, Farmingdale, New York, thought that it would be a good idea to expose her students to this type of dancing, so we made group reservations and began our journey into the world of Argentine Tango. Little did we know that this Tango would take many of us to a new level of passion for the dance. We immediately took dance lessons from Elektra who was waiting for the opportunity to teach this original Tango dance that her father taught her so many years ago. She had such a passion for the dance and, thanks to the Tango Argentino show, was able to purchase a great Tango teaching tape.

Our lessons were difficult, as we had to learn new patterns that were not familiar from other dances we knew. Swaying cortes, body balancing, leg rubs, figure eights (ochos), kicks, and the most unusual, stopping to allow your partner to improvise and, in turn, to do the same.

Ten years later, I was reading a travel brochure, "Puente al Tango" (Bridge to the Tango), published by Dan Trenner with a website at www.BridgetotheTango.com. He was organizing a tour to Buenos Aires, Argentina, limited to 40 students. It was an eleven day tour and included daily lessons, dancing at different milongas (clubs) every evening, lectures and demonstrations by the world's great male and female Tango dancers and, most important of all, one instructor to for every two students. I booked the tour and gave it to Barbara as a birthday gift; luckily she was as excited as I was about our new adventure.

On our trip we learned new steps: cortes, turns, kicks, and fine-tuned improvising. But the most important and difficult thing we learned was emphasized by one of our renowned instructors, Mingo Pugliese -"ATTITUDE." He said, "There is no dance if you do not have the right ATTITUDE."

Barbara wrote a column about our dancing trip to Buenos Aires, Argentina. It appears in Chapter Three.

*There is an incredible website, "The Anthony Dexter Homepage," established for his memorial, 1913-2001. It includes the theme song for the movie Valentino, "Valentino Tango" and the history of this most fascinating and versatile man. The sophistication of the site is something to behold... Pure Enjoyment. Page two of the site is presented below with permission from Gilda Tabarez:

View Pictures and Facts about *Valentino* (1951)

Anthony Dexter Photo Gallery
Click on each image to view a larger version.

What a Lovely Way to Spend Two Evenings by Michael Bivona

Argentine Tango and Latin Tuesdays and Swing Plus Wednesdays, presented by the Long Island Dance Connection every week and hosted by George W. Morse, (DJ extraordinaire) is located at the 56th Fighter Group Restaurant, Route 110 at Long Island Republic Airport, Farmingdale, New York. A visit to the 56th Fighter Group transports you back to an era of Big Band music and unparalleled WWII patriotism. You begin to sense that there is something special as you enter "Checkpoint Charlie." Upon entering the parking lot, Big Band sounds of the 40s arouse your senses. At the pathway to the building, there is a vintage Red Cross ambulance and two WWII jeeps. Step through the doorway and you escape to this WWII French-style Allied Headquarters farmhouse, which sits on the site where P47 fighter aircrafts were built during WWII. There are three vintage WWII planes on display outside the restaurant. One is a P40 (known as the Flying Tiger, used in China by our pilots to fight the Japanese). It has fearful, large painted teeth on the front of the plane resembling the mouth of a tiger. There is a P47, built at this site by Republic Aviation, and a Corsair, which made military history for its effectiveness in aircraft carrier battles during WWII. The rustic timbered ceiling and cozy dining rooms boast seven fireplaces and a romantic view of the runway of Republic Airport in the heart of Long Island. Each dining booth has earphones to enable the diner to hear the Republic Airport Control Tower's conversations with pilots as they land and take off from the airport. There is an extensive collection of aviation and WWII memorabilia highlighting famous WWII air battles and ace pilots, which gives the place a museum atmosphere.

TUESDAY, OCTOBER 30, 2001

Time of arrival: 7:30 P.M. Atmosphere: Club setting with a wall of windows; has exceptional views of several WWII fighter planes situated 30-feet from the large viewing windows. Comfortable tables and lounge seating and DJ's Latin music filling the air with corresponding dance movements from the Tangueros (Tango dancers).

8:00 P.M: Argentine Tango dance lesson by Eddie Dorfer* and Randy Sherman. Their magic of the dance and their teaching skills are immediately reflected in the smiles and movements of their students. They gave a half-hour free dance lesson for beginners and one half-hour lesson for intermediate dancers; incredible excitement on both levels. After the lessons, when the students were practicing, Eddie and Sandy moved among the crowd to coach the dancers, where necessary.

9:00 P.M: The world renowned Buenos Aires Tango Trio began their special Argentine Tango musical magic. The sound from Jorge Anders on the piano, Hector "Tito" Castro on the bandoneon,** and young Thomas La Croze playing bass draws everyone to the dance floor to move and sway to the feeling of the dance and to practice steps they learned from Eddie and Sandy.

Lost track of time, but dance instructors Pietro Faccioli and Elena Bonini performed an authentic Argentine Tango with Latin moves that can only be described as pure sensual energy. The applause, during and after the dance, was from the hearts of the audience that were thrilled to see this young couple performing with such passion for the dance and each other.

A surprise appearance by two young male dancers from Argentina, Jose Delgadillo and Ivan Terrazas, set the audience on fire. They performed the 17th century dance, "Malambo," that originated in the Argentine Pampas region and was performed by the gauchos (cowboys) to show off their skills. Their use of bolas, in timing with the grazing of the floor with heels and soles of their high-heeled Latin shoes, resulted in a rhythmic marriage of music and dance. So gratified was the audience that they coaxed Jose and Ivan to do a second performance later in the evening.

Michael Bivona

The icing on the cake for the evening was an exhibition performance of the Argentine Tango by Eddie and Randy. This most remarkable couple performed with passion and perfection as they radiated around the dance floor performing Tango Ardonos (embellishments), such as, Ganchos (hooks), Ochos (figure eights), and Cuartas (prolonged embrace) to the applause and bravos of the audience. They also performed a Salsa routine that was spectacular in Latin rhythm, dance combinations and styling, which ended with overwhelming applause and bravos from the spectators. They were joined by many dancers who continued their flow, rhythm, feeling of the Salsa music, and the movements in their performance.

A hot buffet was presented consisting of salmon, spareribs, and a cold celery and carrot salad. Everyone sang Happy Birthday to our hostess, Theresa, when her surprise birthday cake appeared with ten candles. We all enjoyed the carrot cake for dessert and ordered drinks from the convenient bar, which was located in the same area.

While enjoying our dinner, Barbara and I were fortunate to be seated at the same table with Rick and Sherry Palencia. We watched them do the West Coast Swing and were impressed with their performance. They had watched us do the Argentine Tango and were also impressed with our interpretation of the dance. They asked us to teach them some Argentine Tango steps and we asked them if they could show us some of their steps in West Coast Swing, which we managed to accomplish during and after dinner. It is amazing how both these dances became popular in New York at about the same time. To make a long story short, Rick, who is Mexican born and works at Stony Brook University, and his Jewish wife, Sherry, continued with their love of the Argentine Tango and started a Club, "Argentine Tango Lovers of Long Island,"*** which today has over 150 members and is still growing.

Our evening ended after twelve midnight; we enjoyed singing and humming some of the different tunes we heard as we danced our way out of the club and to our cars..

*A footnote to this story is when I first saw Eddie Dorfer giving a Salsa lesson at the Kismet Dance Hall in New Hyde Park, Long island, New York. He is, without a doubt, one of the best Salsa dancers in New York. My wife, Barbara, and I agreed that this dark-haired, mustached Latino wearing a grey striped suit was the best Salsa dancer we had ever seen. We were introduced to him and told him how much we enjoyed his performance and asked if he learned to dance in his home country? He looked puzzled and said with a very Brooklyn accent that "he learned to dance in his neighborhood in Brooklyn and that he wasn't a Latino but was Jewish."

**The "Bandoneon" is a free-reed instrument, particularly popular in Argentina. It plays an essential roll in the Tango orchestra. Called bandoneon by its German inventor, Heinrich Band, it was originally intended as an instrument for religious music and popular music of the day. German immigrants in Argentina brought the instrument with them in the early 20th century, where it was incorporated into the local music. Like the accordions and concertinas, the banoneon is played by holding the instrument between both hands and either pushing in or pulling out the instrument, while simultaneously pressing one or more buttons. It's amazing that an instrument half the size of an accordion delivers such smooth and exotic notes, and when combined with the aforementioned instruments of the Buenos Aires Tango Trio, the bass and piano, the result is a dream-like rhythm that almost hypnotizes the audience. When dancers embrace, the affect of this music is reflected in the female's eyes, which are closed and lost in the beauty and comfort of the music and the magic of the Tango.

***Sherry devotes a great deal of her time promoting the "Argentine Tango Lovers of Long Island" organization. They run weekly Tuesday night Milongas (dances) at Mirelle's Restaurant in Westbury, Long Island. One hour of free dance lessons is given by local Tango dance instructors and, on occasion, by visiting world renowned Tango dancers. The venue usually draws between 50 to 75 people and the DJ is usually Sherry, another of her amazing talents. It's really a delight to watch Rick and Sherry do the Argentine Tango; they rank up there with some of the professionals. There is an evening buffet dinner that usually includes a salad, beef or chicken, vegetables and coffee or tea, and there is a convenient bar located along the side of the dance floor.

Every last Sunday of the month, the club has an Argentine Tango party, usually at a larger venue, such as the Knights of Columbus in Lindenhurst, Long Island. The party draws up to 200 dancers of every skill level, and usually runs from seven to eleven o'clock in the evening. The party includes a free dance lesson, frequently by a local instructor, and a performance of the Argentine Tango by local dancers or, on occasion, internationally famous Tango dancers. Dinner is also included and normally consists of a lot of home made food served buffet style with lots of desserts.

The club also holds practice lessons in Deer Park, Long Island, once a week and sponsors trips to Argentina to continue their romance with the Tango and the culture that created this warm and sensual dance.

WEDNESDAY, OCTOBER 31, 2001: SWING PLUS DANCING.

Time of arrival: 7:30 P.M. Atmosphere: Halloween costumes of cats, devils, angels, Latin gauchos (Argentine cowboys), female Latin dance companions, and just about every type of cartoon character imaginable.

DJ Cody's Swing music set the stage for the evening as everyone was on the floor doing their swing-things, jumping, turning, splitting, and some not-so-easily-described moves.

8:00 P.M. One hour of free West Coast Swing dance lesson by instructor Denise Coticchio. She began with basic patterns in West Coast Swing, which soon developed into nice combinations that everyone quickly mastered and enjoyed. She started with the basic steps and impressed the students with the importance of properly holding a partner when moving to the quick rhythm of West Coast Swing. It was difficult at first to get accustomed to the variations, as most of the people were used to dancing East Coast Swing which, although similar in many respects, allows for more free movement of the dancers. The main difference is that West Coast Swing requires that the dancers dance in the same direction and along side each other, as if they were on railroad tracks. East Coast Swing, which has been around for generations, allows for dancers to dance as they please in any direction, but is limited to the space required to perform so dancers don't collide, and is mostly done in a circular motion. Before long, everyone got the idea and the dance floor resembled a choreographed Broadway musical.

I lost track of time again, walked outside to view some of the WWII airplanes and, while standing near the P47 Flying Tiger airplane with its large tiger teeth in my view, I began laughing when I observed the dancers through the large windows dancing in their costumes: cats, devils, Latin gauchos and the other imaginative outfits, without the benefit of my hearing the music. This was a scary Halloween scene, to say the least; imagine cats, devils and all the other monsters jumping and gyrating around--but no music.

A hot buffet was presented, consisting of seafood and pasta with sausage and a lettuce salad. Drinks were available at the bar.

Dance instructors Denise and Rick Aubain performed a West Coast Swing showcase that had the audience clapping and stomping their feet to the music and their masterful performance. It is amazing how easy they made the dance seem. I got the feeling that I should be taking more dance lessons, but even if Barbara and I took lessons for the rest of our lives, we couldn't come close to the performance we just witnessed. Well, maybe we would come somewhat close if we paid attention and practiced.

A second showcase of the Hustle was performed by dance instructors Barry and Jeannie DeVos. It seems that every step from every dance is incorporated into the Hustle: Swing, Cha-Cha, Mambo, Foxtrot, and Waltz are all represented in one form or another. When danced by Jeannie and Barry, it appears that several dances are being performed at the same time--they have great talent. When I watch the Hustle being danced by professionals, I remember John Travolta in the 1977 movie "Saturday Night Fever," playing Tony Manero dancing with Karen Gorney as Stephanie Mangano doing their variation of the Hustle and the excitement that they and their dancing brought to the audience. These wonderful young actors started a dance craze unequalled since the Valentino phenomenon, brought about by his dancing the Tango in silent films. Many people started taking Hustle lessons after seeing the movie, and the dance today is still one of the most popular and a must to learn for members of the dance community.

In addition to Swing dancing, the evening was filled with Mambo, Cha-Cha, Tango, Bolero, Foxtrot, and Waltz dancing. We left at 11:30P.M., while the place was still jumping with costumed dancers enjoying a swinging night.

CHAPTER THREE

Dancing in Buenos Aires – Learning the Tango

I PREVIOUSLY DISCUSSED OUR trip to Buenos Aires, Argentina, to learn and fine-tune our Argentine Tango. It would be appropriate now, to continue our experience with the published article about our journey, which appeared in the Long Island dance newsletter. The rest of the stories won't be in chronological order as written by Barbara, but rather in the order of my mood; Paris, Rome, New Orleans, etc. So, if I'm writing on a rainy or cold day, I might indulge myself and write about sunny Hawaii or the New Orleans' Mardi Gras festival.

AROUND THE FLOOR: OCTOBER/DECEMBER 1999

TRAVELING AROUND By Barbara Bivona

Mike and I were drawn to the Argentine Tango in 1989, after we saw the first of many Tango shows that appeared on the American stage, originating in Argentina. About six years ago, we started taking Tango lessons with Elektra, at the Swing Street Studios, in Farmingdale, Long Island, and quickly became aficionados of the dance. So, when an ad appeared for a two-week trip to Argentina to study Tango dancing, Mike booked it before I could say no. The trip was run by Daniel Trenner of West Medford, Massachusetts. He called it "Puente al Tango" (Bridge to Tango), and his mission was to bring the true Tango form from Buenos Aires to North America and the rest of the world. He has been quite successful and has taken his "Puente" to Canada and Europe. A deciding factor for us to join him was the ratio of one instructor to every two students, so no one in our group of 40 was ever left without someone to help break down and explain the dance patterns. Our days consisted of four hours of Tango classes, divided into two hours of master class lessons by the most renowned dancers in the Tango world, one hour of practice, and a one hour interview and performances by these master teachers, who spoke about their love and personal experiences with the dance. We learned about the history of Tango, from one of the original Tango dances called "Canyengue," and its evolution to the current dance form. At night, we were picked up around eleven o'clock and taken to a Milonga, which is the Argentine name for a Tango ballroom. Dances at these halls are done in sets of three or four tangos, followed by a set of Argentine Waltzes or a Milonga dance (Tango walk), with brief intermissions between each dance. These three dances are the basis of the milongas and are danced at every ballroom, with occasional Meringues and Mambos. We even danced a Quickstep and Swing, as both dances are becoming popular in Buenos Aires. I danced with our teachers and the local tangueros, which was a bit intimidating at first because I am trained to do figure tangos; the locals dance the Salon Tango which has less movement and is done in a smaller area due to the crowded dance floors. The Salon Tango movements are straight forward and danced in the "line of direction" (counterclockwise); the way we learned the Argentine Tango, the movements are circular with lots of fans and turns, and it requires a lot of room to accomplish the dance moves. It was a whole different ballgame, but we soon learned to catch the ball. The dances lasted until about 5:30 A.M., however, Mike and I didn't, so we called it quits at around 4:00A.M. Each morning, after a late breakfast, we had a few hours to walk around the city, visiting a nearby pedestrian mall with wonderful shops, restaurants and parks, and then back to our classes and nighttime dancing.

Included in the trip was a beautiful Broadway type Tango show in which some of our teachers performed. In addition, Daniel Trenner hosted a party at his apartment one afternoon, which lasted until eight at night. He has a huge rooftop terrace overlooking the beautiful cupolas of Buenos Aires, where we were treated to a three-piece Tango band for our dancing pleasure and a professional Tango show. The elite of the Tango world were present and politely asked many of us to dance; what a wonderful experience to be floating on a strategically located rooftop in the heart of one of the most beautiful cities in the world, being led by world famous dancers, to the music of the seductive Argentine Tango. My OH MY!!...

We talked, lived, and danced Tango for eleven days, and remained in Buenos Aires for a few extra days after our group left so we could do some sightseeing. We went to the mausoleum of Eva Peron, the famous antique and street fair in San Telmo, and, of course, we went to the little street of Caminito, made famous by a song of the same name by the immortal singer, Carlos Gardel. Daniel helped us to realize a dream. We loved to Tango before we went to Argentina. We fell in love with it in Buenos Aires.

* *

The unedited version of our story begins with an advertisement appearing in the catalogue "Bridge to the Tango," published by Daniel Trenner of West Medford, Massachusetts. The picture of Tango dancers and the description of the trip to Buenos Aires took my breath away. The adventure was for eleven days of intensive studying and training with instructors whose ages ranged from early twenties to late seventies. The experiences and memories of the older instructors ranged from the beginning of the 20th century when Tango was in its infancy and danced mostly in brothels, through the reign of the infamous dictator Juan Peron and his wife the popular

Eva. The younger instructors were far removed from the hard times and challenges their ancestors experienced and were mostly interested in the rapture and passion of their profession as Tango aficionados and instructors. Part of the advertisement which appears below, shows the excitement of two dancers embraced in the Tango and gives the purpose of the tour and descriptions of the instructors that were the participants in that wonderful journey. The brochure also includes some exciting comments from former students who went on the tour, which added to the flavor, expectation, and romance that occupied my mind.

I showed my wife, Barbara, the advertisement; we reviewed the itinerary inch by inch. She still didn't know that I already booked the trip. The more we delved into the trip, the more excited we became. Famous Tango dancers, such as Gustavo Naveira, Olga Besio and Omar Vega were to be our mentors and instructors. Even Tango dancers we saw so many years ago in the "Tango Argentino" Broadway show were part of the group.

When I told Barbara that I already booked the trip she didn't say a word, she thought I was joking, as I often do. When I convinced her that it was for real, the hugs and kisses that followed are still felt by me when we dance the Tango. What a surprise birthday present for her, and what a chance for us to really get the feel of the Tango in the country where the passionate dance was originated. A copy of one of the pages of the travel brochure, "Bridge to the Tango" that captured our imaginations follows. It is reproduced with the permission of Daniel Trenner.

9th Dancer's Journey to Buenos Aires

Roberto and Vasina

"Never in my life have I experienced such uninterrupted joy, fun and excitement"
—TD, Oregon

"Ten days with Bridge To The Tango introduced me to the Tango community and culture of Buenos Aires, now I feel part of it! Bravo!"
—TD, Oregon

"I can't say enough about Jeff and his professional approach, he does an outstanding job".
—LG, Arizona

"With Bridge To The Tango you experience the very best. When you can have butter, why would you settle for margarine?"
—SM, Missouri

OUR PURPOSE

During our first tour to Buenos Aires in 1993, social tango and the great surviving milongueros were hard to find. Our job was to reveal this unpublicized world of clubs, or 'milongas.' Eight years later, our mission has changed. Tango's revival has given birth to a growing sprawl of events and schools, an intimidating maze to be navigated by a foreigner. Our staff dance year-round in Bs. As, and are in constant touch with the changing scene. From your first moment in BsAs, you will experience the best and most interesting clubs and teachers.

THE MASTER TEACHERS

An encounter with the living legends of Argentine Tango is at the heart of your trip. In our private studio spaces we organize daily group lessons and interviews with some of the most famous people in tango. Over the years our faculty has included: Pepito & Suzuki Avellaneda, Juan Bruno, Eduardo Arquimbau, Esther and Mingo Pugliese, Gustavo Naveira & Olga Besio, Rodolfo & Maria Cieri, Nito and Elba Garcia, Facundo and Kely Posadas, Puppy Castello & Graciela Gonzalez, Tete Rusconi & Maria Villalobos ,Teté & Sylvia Ceriani, Tommy O'Connell, Mariano 'Chico' Frumboli, Eduardo Cappusi & Mariana Flores, and many others.

OUR STAFF INSTRUCTORS

Our staff instructors are a cornerstone of our organization. They help gender balance the classes, providing one-to-one learning that enhances your experience and raises your learning curve, no matter what your level. They also go social dancing with you at night. Every staff instructor is a bilingual professional tango dancer, chosen not just for their tango but for their great personalities. Some of our staff have been working with us for many years, helping create a very relaxed and friendly environment. They have included: Lorena Ermocida (TangoX2), Omar Merlo (TangoX2), Pablo Pugliese, Gabriel Guerberoff, Florencia Toccetti, Luciana Valle, Damien Essel, Marcelo Solis, Valencia Batiuk.

OUR KEY STAFF

Jeff Anderson, Program Director for the past 3 years, has received rave reviews for his thoroughness and presence. He is a masterful translator and has an encyclopedic knowledge of rare and interesting things about tango in Buenos Aires. An actor, playwright, singer, and classical pianist, he lives in Buenos Aires, where he is exploring the creative possibilities of tango improvisation for performance.

Gabriela Entin and Robert Blank are our year-round staff in Buenos Aires. Gabriela has been Daniel's Administrative Assistant for 11 years. Robert, from Germany, has been living in Buenos Aires and working with us since 1994.

Zoraida Fontclara and Diego Alvaro are our "dance captains" since 1995. They coordinate the relationships between instructors and participants. They are internationally known teachers and performers, and run the famous mid-day classes and dances at the Confiteria Ideal in Buenos Aires.

Brooke Burdett, another American living the tango in Buenos Aires for the past 4 years, serves in a host of special roles for Bridge to the Tango. She also travels internationally teaching and performing tango.

Now the fun began. I had booked a March tour, which is summer/early fall in Buenos Aires, so we had to prepare the proper clothing for that time of year. We had to arrange for air transportation and research the best exchange rate for the dollar. Exchange rates can be very tricky; there can be a difference of ten to twenty percent if the right choices aren't made. Many travelers use their hotels or exchange stores to convert their dollars to local currency; a very costly mistake. We found that our Citibank ATM card was the fastest and least expensive way to convert dollars. There are many Citibank outlets in Buenos Aires, no lines, no forms to fill out, no passport problems; you can just walk into the bank as you would in the United States and go to the ATM machine, use your card and, behold, the local currency is in your hand at a very favorable exchange rate. Next we had to educate ourselves on available sightseeing and the history of Argentina and, especially Tango dancing in Buenos Aires.

Our tour had an optional airfare on coach with not much of a discount. The flight was 10 hours and, considering that we had to be at the airport two hours prior to take off, we decided to explore flying business or first class so we could use the special lounges provided for those classes and, of course, the extra comforts of flying business or first-class. American Airlines was the primary airline going to Argentina; its price for first class was more than the tour price. So we opted for business class, which worked out to be a couple of hundred dollars per person more than coach. As luck would have it, American Airlines was running a special for our time slot, which included the use of The Admiral's Club first class lounge at the airports. This turned out to be a blessing in disguise. Foreign flights require that passengers check in two hours prior to scheduled take-offs. Our plane was delayed for an additional hour, which meant killing three hours at the airport. What a difference having the use of The Admiral's Lounge made, as they served free coffee, Danish pastries, nuts and pretzels, and also had comfortable large spacious seats, with no crowds, plenty of reading material, private rest rooms, several television sets, and finger sandwiches. Not a bad way to spend three hours. Since then, whenever possible, we try to fly business or first class if the airline's lounge is included in the price. We left for Buenos Aires from Miami, Florida. Luckily we were wintering in Florida at the time, which made it convenient for us to take an airport limousine from Boca Raton, where we were staying, to the airport, without worrying about parking or the safety of leaving a car for two weeks at the airport garage.

Business Class on our ten-hour trip was exceptionally more enjoyable than our experiences with coach. There was more than adequate room for our carry-on bags in the overhead compartments and an area for hanging clothes or storing golf bags. Upon settling in, we were offered champagne, wine, refreshments, and finger snacks. The seats were spacious and reclined completely for sleeping, and were almost as comfortable as a bed. This became especially important as our flight left around midnight for a scheduled arrival at 10:00 A.M. By the time we boarded and got organized, a good night's sleep was a welcome friend.

The seats were two abreast with larger than coach windows, which gave us the feeling of spaciousness and made getting a good night's sleep a pleasant experience. The rest rooms were larger than what we were used to and were restricted to passengers in our section only, which cut down on waiting time and noise. Snacks were served without the usual annoying waiting period due to our section having fewer people to accommodate. Television was available with a choice of several current movies to choose from, which was nice; it certainly was better than not being given a choice of movies. Breakfast was served upon request. It was an event; we chose our meals from a menu, which included a good variety of hot or cold breakfast delights. Ten hours "flew by" very quickly, due mostly to the comfortable seats and the relative quiet in our restricted area, which allowed us to sleep without too much interruption.

While resting on my comfortable seat/lounge, I took the opportunity to read about the history of Argentina and to see if there were any places of interest that we might include in our sightseeing. I bought "Lonely Planet City Guide to Buenos Aires," by Wayne Bernhardson. While at home, we did extensive research on the internet, so reading the information in the travel guide became easy and familiar to us. Although Argentina dates back to 1536, when Spanish explorer Pedro de Mendoza made camp in Buenos Aires, the romantic history of Argentina actually began at the turn of the 20th century with the introduction of Tango dancing and a singer/writer named Carlos Gardel. To appreciate the passion that the people have for the Argentine Tango, a brief history of Tango and its first and foremost hero, Carlos Gardel, is in order.

The Tango originated in the streets around the capital of Argentina, Buenos Aires, about 1890, and was considered a vulgar dance practiced in houses of ill repute and other unsavory places. It combined gaucho (cowboy) verse with Spanish and Italian music. Carlos Gardel was also considered to have been born and nurtured in the streets, but not in Argentina. He was born to a single mother, Berthe Gardes, in Toulouse, France, in or around 1890. Today, being a single mother carries very little social stigma, and, in many cases, women travel that journey by choice preferring not to be tied down with a permanent partner, while enjoying the experience of motherhood. But in the late 19th century, Berthe and her young son were a disgrace to her family and community. When Carlos was three or four years of age, Berthe's lover paid for her and her son to relocate to Argentina.

They arrived in the capital alone and abandoned, and were immediately destined to live in the poor neighborhoods of Buenos Aires. So we have the arrival of Tango and Carlos at the same time, late in the 19th century, and the same place, Buenos Aires. These two forces were to become engaged in one of the most passionate dances of all time. It began in the lowest of places; brothels and tenement, and found its way into the homes of the rich and famous. Around the world it travelled-- New York, Paris, and Italy--making music, inspiring dancers, and finally the grand finale; acceptance of its passion in motion pictures.

Today wherever Tango music is heard, a picture or the sound of Carlo's voice is in close proximity. He has become almost mystical. When he died in an unfortunate plane crash in June 1935, it is said that a Cuban woman committed suicide in Havana, while a woman in New York and another in Puerto Rico tried to poison themselves, all over the same man whom they had never met but who were enamored with his voice and music. Below is a picture of Carlos Gardel playing the romantic in one of his few movie appearances.

Gardel with Mona Maris in the film "Cuesta Abajo", Paramount 1934

When listening to Carlo's music in Spanish, I always regretted not understanding the language, so I did some research and I'm presenting two of his famous songs; LA CUMPARSITA, written by Gerardo Rodriguez in 1917, and MANO A MANO, written by Celedonio Flores in the early 1920s, with Spanish and the English translations side by side:

LA CUMPARSITA Lyrics & Music: Gerardo Hernán Matos Rodriguez

LA CUMPARSITA

La cumparsa de miserias sin fin...
Desfile...
Enfermo de aquel ser
enfermo...
que pronto ha de morir
de pena;
por eso es que en su lecho
solloza acongojado,
recordando el pasado
que lo hace padecer.

Abandono a su viejita
que quedó desamparada
y loco de pasión,
ciego de amor,
corrió tras de su amada,
que era linda, era hechicera,
de belleza era una flor.
Que admiró su querer,
hasta que se cansó
y por otro lo dejó.

Largo tiempo después,
cayó al hogar materno
para poder curar su enfermo
y herido corazón,
y supo que su viejita santa,
la que el habia dejado
el invierno pasado,
de frio se murio.

Hoy ya solo, abandonado
a lo triste de la suerte,
ansioso espera su muerte
que bien pronto ha de llegar...
Y entre la triste frialdad
que invade al corazon,
sintio la cruda sensacion
de su maldad...

Entre sombras
se le oye respirar
sufriente...
al que antes de morir sonrie
porque una dulce paz le llega;
sintio que desde el cielo
la madrecita buena,
mitigando sus penas,
sus culpas perdono...

THE LITTLE MASKED PARADE

The masked parade of endless miseri
promenades
around that sick
being...
that soon will die
of sorrow;
That's why in its bed
cries mournfully
remembering the past
that makes it suffer.

He abandoned his mother
who remained deserted
and mad with passion,
blind with love,
he ran after his beloved one,
she was pretty, she was bewitching,
she was a flower of beauty.
She admired his love,
until she got tired of him
and left him for another man.

A long time later,
He went back to the maternal home
to be able to cure his ill
and injured heart,
and learned that his holy mother,
the one that he had left
last winter,
died of cold.

Today all alone, abandoned
on the sad side of luck,
he anxiously awaits his death
that should arrive soon..
And within the sad coldness
that invades the heart,
he feels the raw sensation
of his wickedness..

Among shadows
his suffering breathing
is heard
he smiles before dying
because a sweet peace comes to him;
he feels that from the heavens
his good mother,
mitigating her griefs,
has forgiven his faults...

MANO A MANO (Tango / 1923)
Música de C. Gardel & J. Razzano - Letra de C. Flores

EVEN [literally "Hand By Hand"] (Tango / 1923)
Lyrics by C. Flores - Music by C. Gardel & J. Razzano

Rechiflado en mi tristeza,
hoy te evoco y veo que has sido
en mi pobre vida paria
sólo una buena mujer.
Tu presencia de bacana
puso calor en mi nido,
fuiste buena, consecuente,
y yo sé que me has querido
como no quisiste a nadie,
como no podrás querer.

Crazy in my sadness,
today I remember you and I see you've been
only a good woman
in my poor recluse life.
Your refined presence
brought warmth in my nest,
you were good, consequent,
and I know that you have loved me
like you loved nobody,
like you'll never ever love.

Se dió el juego de remanye
cuando vos, pobre percanta,
gambeteabas la pobreza
en la casa de pensión.
Hoy sos toda una bacana,
la vida te ríe y canta,
los morlacos del otario
los jugás a la marchanta
como juega el gato maula
con el misero ratón.

Then came the game of sharpness
when you, poor woman,
were dodging poverty
in the pension home.
Today you are a whole rich woman,
life laughs and sings at you,
you gamble away
the fool's money
like the cowardly cat plays
with the miserable mouse.

Hoy tenés el mate lleno
de infelices ilusiones,
te engrupieron los otarios,
las amigas y el gavión;
la milonga, entre magnates
con sus locas tentaciones,
donde triunfan y claudican
milongueras pretensiones,
se te ha entrado muy adentro
en tu pobre corazón.

Today your head is full
of unhappy illusions,
you were deceived by the fools,
your friends, and the pimp;
the milonga, among magnates
with their crazy temptations,
were milongueras pretenses
are achieved and given up,
has gotten very deep
into your poor heart.

Nada debo agradecerte,
mano a mano hemos quedado;
no me importa lo que has hecho,
lo que hacés ni lo que harás...
Los favores recibidos
creo habértelos pagado
y, si alguna deuda chica
sin querer se me ha olvidado,
en la cuenta del otario
que tenés se la cargás.

I must thank you nothing,
we are even;
I don't care about what you've done,
what you do or what you'll do...
the favors I received
I believe I paid them back
and, if I inadvertently
forgot a small debt,
you can charge it to the account
of the fool you have now.

Mientras tanto, que tus triunfos,
pobres triunfos pasajeros,
sean una larga fila
de riquezas y placer;
que el bacán que te acamala
tenga pesos duraderos,
que te abrás de las paradas
con cafishos milongueros
y que digan los muchachos:
Es una buena mujer.

In the meantime, I hope your triumphs,
poor fleeting triumphs,
will be a long line
of riches and pleasure;
that the rich guy who maintains
you will have lasting pesos,
that you get away from the streets
with the milonguero gigolos
and that the chaps say:
She is a good woman.

Y mañana, cuando seas
descolado mueble viejo
y no tengas esperanzas
en tu pobre corazón,
si precisás una ayuda,
si te hace falta un consejo,
acordate de este amigo
que ha de jugarse el pellejo
pa'ayudarte en lo que pueda
cuando llegue la ocasión.

And tomorrow, when you'll be
deteriorated old furniture
and you don't have hope
in your poor heart,
if you need help,
if you need advise,
remember this friend
who will risk his skin
to help you in what he can
when the time arrives.

31

Our plane arrived at the Aeropuerto Internacional Ministro Pistarini de Ezeiza, simply known as Ezeiza (EZE), Buenos Aires, at 10:00 A.M., exactly on time and with no unusual surprises. The airport is located only 29-miles from our hotel, the Continental on San Roque Boulevard, downtown, in old Buenos Aires. Our luggage arrived at the airport unharmed, which was another surprise; we promptly took a shuttle bus to our hotel. We were surprised at how light the traffic in Buenos Aires was, considering its population of approximately three million residents. It appeared that most motorists obeyed the traffic laws. We arrived at our hotel promptly and, considering that it was rated as a four star hotel, we got another surprise, but this time an unpleasant one. We learned that foreign hotels are not rated the same as in the United States. Although the hotel was not up to the standards we expected, it was located in a great part of the city, and was only two blocks from Avenida Florida, which boasts every type of retail store imaginable: leather goods, women and men's designer clothing shops, shoe stores, etc. Also, the Avenue has every type of restaurant that exists: Italian, Spanish, American, French, South American, Russian, etc. We tried as many restaurants as possible in our short stay in Buenos Aires and, of course, Barbara tried as many of the shops as she could. Her only complaint was that she didn't have enough time and money to visit them all. Memorable sights on the Avenue were street dancers dancing the Tango, women wearing colorful designer dresses, men wearing Latin type hats, dressed in suits and ties; all of these views gave the avenue a very sophisticated European-Manhattan atmosphere.

Hearing Tango music while walking along the busy streets was absolutely enchanting. People just stopped and began dancing whenever their fancy dictated. Of course, Barbara and I also enjoyed a few impromptu Tango steps while we walked along, enjoying the feeling of our surroundings.

Our hotel was only a short walk to the historic area of San Telmo. It is one of the oldest neighborhoods in Buenos Aires, and was one of the wealthiest areas in the city until yellow fever took its toll. The wealthy abandoned their dwellings and this area became a haven for scoundrels and the immigrants of that era. Still unspoiled by the rampant modernization that seems to be going on all over Buenos Aires, San Telmo is an artist's quarter, where bohemians find large spaces to rent at low rates, very much like Greenwich Village, New York, right after WWII, where our GIs found an inexpensive lifestyle while attending local universities. It was here in the late eighteen hundreds that the Tango was born in the brothels and houses of ill repute, and it was in neighborhoods like this, in Buenos Aires, that Carlos Gardel grew up and turned the Tango into the nation's, and the world's, most popular music and seductive dance. Most of the Buenos Aires' nightlife is concentrated in this district, as well as some of the most interesting restaurants and bars. Street dancing is also practiced in this neighborhood and, again, Barbara and I took advantage of the great music heard everywhere to practice some of our new Tango steps.

Considering the location of these wonderful places and their close proximity of our hotel and the "Confiteria Ideal," where we would spend most of our time being taught Tango and listening to great lecturers, the fact that the hotel didn't meet American four star standards became less important or annoying. We spent very little time in the hotel, and only used our room to get some much needed sleep after long days at the dance sessions and milongas. Fortunately, the hotel had a restaurant with large viewing windows looking out at the street level, which became a great comfort station for drinking delicious dark Argentinean coffee and for "people watching." It's amazing how European the people looked; the men are inclined to wear European cut suits and the ladies dress in a very sophisticated and stylish manner. The viewing of the street activity and the beautiful Argentineans was very relaxing while we enjoyed an espresso or cup of local coffee. Breakfasts were included in our tour price, so we were able to enjoy many long moments at the corner restaurant, with large viewing windows, admiring the passing people traffic, as we leisurely enjoyed our extensive breakfasts.

We arrived at our hotel in the morning, which gave us an opportunity to unpack and settle into our hotel suite. It had a bedroom and a separate sitting room, with window air conditioners. Although the hotel and rooms were quite old, it was quaint and very comfortable. Our group leader, Jeff Anderson, welcomed us at the reception area set up for our group. Fortunately, he would be at our disposal for our entire trip. Jeff told us that some of our tour group were going to the Avenida Florida Boulevard for lunch, and then to a local shoe store to look at leather dancing shoes that were hand-made by a local shoemaker on site. We got a kick out of watching him make the dancing shoes we ordered, which were made of the finest soft Argentinean leather, almost tissue like to the touch. Needless to say, we wore our new shoes at every dancing opportunity; our happy feet enjoyed the feel of the soft tissue-like leather caressing them, as they didn't require a breaking-in period. In the evening, we joined our new friends in a cocktail party and were introduced to our fellow dance students. Our new acquaintances were from around the world; Germany, Italy, Canada, and many parts of the United States. Later that evening, at about 10:00 P.M., we were off to our first "milonga" at the Club Gricel. As always, we were escorted by our fantastic staff instructors. The club had a typical nightclub atmosphere and held a comfortable two hundred people. There was a DJ in attendance playing a variety of music for dancing, but most of the dancing and music was Tango. There is no such thing as a "no smoking" area in the clubs in Buenos Aires, so a smoke cloud filled the place and made it very uncomfortable to see and breath, especially since the club wasn't air conditioned, which is the norm for the city. But, the music and dancing made up for these short-comings. The men were all dressed in suits, as is the custom, and the women wore pretty, short-sleeved dresses. Considering it was summer/early fall in Buenos Aires, there was a lot of sweating going on. It's probably one of the reasons that the milongas start late at night and continue into the early morning, as it does cool down quite a bit between these hours.

The tradition at the dances is that, if a man wants to dance with a particular female, he makes eye contact and then nods his head. If the woman accepts, she will nod her acceptance; if she doesn't want to dance, she will turn her head away. It is customary for men to ask women to dance, even if the women are escorted by other men. Using the eye contact takes away all the embarrassment and doubt that goes along with verbally asking someone to dance. It's really a neat way to enjoy an evening without all the uncertainties that go along with approaching a stranger and asking them to dance. Our instructors made sure that everyone in our group had a partner to dance with. Many of us enjoyed dancing with the local people, once we got the knack of "eye contact" and its meaning. The dancing routine was that three tangos would be played, with about a minute intermission between each to talk and get acquainted with your partner. This also allowed dancers a chance to decide whether or not to continue dancing with the chosen person. If the partners decided to continue dancing, then, when the music resumed they would continue dancing in the "line of direction" (counterclockwise), being very respectful of the other dancers around them. No kicks, fans, or other dangerous moves are allowed on the dance floor because they could interfere or cause collisions with other dancers. Occasionally other dance music was played, more or less as an intermission between tangos. The students took advantage of these dances to show off their Swing, Cha-Cha, Mambos, etc. It is strange that the Argentines do not dance other dances than the Tango and its variations. Our night ended about 2:00 A.M., and we left exhausted from the excitement of this new experience and the incredible amount of dancing we had done. Many of the students stayed until closing at 5:30 A.M. God Bless them!

The next morning, which was Saturday, we woke up at about 9:30 A.M., and rushed to enjoy a buffet breakfast. The selection included many hot and cold dishes, which we devoured to replenish our energy that had been exhausted the night before. In the early afternoon, we had our first Tango lesson at one of the most picturesque salons in the city, Confiteria Ideal, which was featured in such movies as the 1997 "Tango Lesson," written by and staring Sally Potter and one of our dance instructors Gustavo Naveira, the 1998 movie "Tango," written by Carlos Saura and staring Carlos Rivarola, Cecilia Narova, and Mia Meastro; and the 1998 movie "Evita," written by Tim Rice, Alan Parker, and Oliver Stone, and staring Madonna and Antonio Banderas. The Confiteria was built in 1912 as a café-bar-nightclub and still carries the look of the turn of that century's art deco architecture, with its ancient wooden flooring, dark wood furniture, opulent marble staircase, and an ornate elevator. Some of the world's famous people, such as Maurice Chavalier, Marie Felix, Dolores del Rio, Vittorio Gassman, Robert Duvall, and many local and foreign dignitaries, have enjoyed the food and dancing of this one-of- a-kind establishment.

The emphasis on our first dance lesson was the relationship between dance partners and their responsibility towards each other. To emphasize the importance of each one knowing and respecting the other's movements, we were taught some of our partner's steps. The men danced the women's part and the women did the leading. Talk about confusion, yet it was very helpful in learning how difficult it is for a woman to dance backwards and to respond quickly to the male's lead. I learned to do ochos (figure eights), cortes, kicks, and many other sophisticated Tango steps while dancing backwards; it was different and easy to mix the steps up. It took a while, but the men seemed to get the routines down pretty well and translated the experience into holding and leading the ladies with a lot of consideration and appreciation for their role in the Tango. In Argentina, it is not uncommon to see people of the same gender dancing together. They are taught to dance both parts, as leaders and as followers. We did this for about two hours and then had a one-hour intimate interview session with a master teacher of the Tango. Our teacher shared with us his joys and heartbreaks with the Tango, and how dancing saved his sanity through the troubled political times in Argentina. After the session, we had an hour of practice with our partners, the dance instructors, and other students--male and female. It took a bit of getting used to dancing with a member of the same sex, but it worked well and we gained important knowledge--not only in dancing the Tango, but in dancing all other dances.

After the session, members of the tour paired and enjoyed dinner at one of the local restaurants, which was followed by walking around San Telmo and enjoying the street fair that was taking place. At about 10:00 P.M., we again boarded our bus for a night at Salon El Pial, another local milonga; however, fortunately, the club was air conditioned. We danced the night away and returned back to our hotel about 2:00 A.M., again leaving many of our group to dance on until closing.

After several lessons, our instructors concentrated on the meaning of improvisation, which is the essence of the dance. "It's easy enough to learn the many steps in the Argentine Tango, but the fun and passion of the dance is to improvise and to introduce new steps and feelings into the dance routines. To hear the music; to feel the music; to express the proper attitude; when this synergy is accomplished, then improvisation causes passion to radiate from the dancers' bodies and movements resulting in a 'dance of love'." Dan Trenner then interjected: "And isn't this why we all traveled from around the world to Buenos Aires, to learn and experience the dance of love?"

The rest of our trip was the same every day: morning buffet breakfast, dance lessons for about four hours at different venues, lectures by master Tango dancers, an afternoon nap when possible, dinner at a local restaurant, dancing at a different milonga late each evening, and then returning to our hotel, exhausted from the day's activities.

An exceptional day was a visit to our tour leader's apartment for a private rooftop dance party at La Cupula, a spectacular turn-of-the-century penthouse. Buenos Aires is often described as the "Paris of the South," and the view from the penthouse roof validated that belief. We got the same feeling when we visited Paris. The views were similar and absolutely breathtaking;

their church steeples, cupolas of every size and shape, and the brilliant affect of the sun's rays shining off the gold trim of many of the cupolas and steeples, were mirror images of the architecture in each city.

The party was exciting as the trio band consisting of guitar, bass, and bandoneon played beautiful tangos, which gave us an opportunity to meet and dance with many of our instructors, master teachers, and local dance aficionados. A buffet was set up with local finger foods and an open bar kept everyone refreshed and somewhat immune from the afternoon sun. There were several Tango exhibitions by our teachers, some local dancers, and teachers with students. It gave us an opportunity to dance in the sun with our instructors and made me feel as if I were dancing in the sky on a cloud. The afternoon turned into evening as we socialized and caressed our partners and our new-found friends to the sounds of Tango music. We drifted from the party and walked the enchanted streets of the magical city back to our hotel to prepare for another evening of Tango dancing at a local milonga.

One of the places we wanted to see while in the city was Eva Peron's burial place in the Recoleta Cemetery. The cemetery is in the trendy Recoleta area of the city, where there is an artisan market and the dwellings of the wealthy residents of Buenos Aires. The cemetery is enclosed by a high wall, but some of the monuments and statues can be seen from outside the wall. However, the message is clear; "private privileged property." Traditionally, only the wealthy and powerful aristocracy were buried at this cemetery, with Eva Peron being the exception. The remains of Eva are secured in the modest "Familia Duarte" subterranean vault, which irritates the upper class to no end. Her embalmed remains (embalming is not usual for the people of Argentina), rest there after being transported from South America to an obscure cemetery in Milan, Italy, where her husband, Juan Peron, lived, and then back again to Buenos Aires. Her family tomb is modest, but the floral arrangements at and around the tomb are breathtakingly beautiful; fresh, colorful, and by no means humble. When entering the cemetery, one is overwhelmed with the above ground splendor of monuments, mausoleums, and statues, ranging from modest to grand scale mini cathedrals. Many mini-buildings have gates and/or glass doors; their coffins and stairwells can be easily seen from outside, as if the viewers were being asked to look at the splendor within. The overall cemetery reminded me of the above ground cemeteries in New Orleans, only on a much grander scale.

Only a few blocks from Eva's tomb we found the tomb of her husband, Juan Peron, in the less exclusive graveyard of Chacarita Cemetery, which is not on the grand scale of the Recoleta Cemetery but is the home of many famous people who were not of the aristocracy. The cemetery was established in 1870 to accommodate the countless victims of the yellow fever plague. It has some tombs and statues to match the splendor of Recoleta; one of the most visited being Buenos Aires' "songbird," Carlos Gardel, who is held in a near Saint status by many Argentineans who feel a quasi-religious devotion to him. Plaques from people around the world cover the base of his life-sized statue, embroidered with flowers placed by the steady procession of people paying their respect to the great Tango singer; the abundance of beautiful flowers that decorate his tomb enhances the overall appearance of the cemetery..

The day before our dance tour ended, we had some free time to go shopping or sightseeing, and to walk around the nearby neighborhood. We chose to return to the leather shop to buy another pair of soft leathered dancing shoes. Our last class and farewell milonga was at the Sunderland Club, where we had a cocktail party, danced with our partners, other students, instructors, and some of our master instructors. I actually danced with two male instructors and enjoyed the dancing very much, even though dancing the female part was quite difficult and took some getting used to. One of our master teachers, Mingo Pugliese, and his dance partner-wife, Ester, approached us and said they liked our styling and passion for the dance. He said, "Michael, all of the teaching, demonstrations and lectures that you were a part of mean nothing if you do not develop the proper 'Attitude.' There is no dance, if you do not have the right 'Attitude' when doing the Tango." He praised our attitude and told us to "Continue dancing for the love of it, and to have a happy and passionate life with the Tango as he and his wife did."

The next morning we had our farewell breakfast and said goodbye to the many new dancing friends that we shared our wonderful vacation with. We extended our stay for three more days, and accomplished all the sightseeing that we had planned. The cemetery visits to see the final resting places of Eva, Juan, and Gardel will always be etched in my mind. We spent many hours just walking around the city, visiting neighborhoods and talking to as many locals as possible. Fortunately, Barbara has a great understanding of the language, which helped us to just relax and meet people on a comfortable level. While looking out the window of our airplane and watching the beautiful city of Buenos Aires fad away, Mingo Pugliese' words were still echoing in my mind: "Attitude, Attitude and more Attitude." What wonderful advice for dancing the Tango and for fully enjoying life.

There was one more place we wanted to visit, and we put the whole afternoon aside to satisfy our curiosity; it was the few blocks called "Caminito" in the La Boca district. We have been in love with the word "Caminito" for years as it's the name of one of our favorite Argentine Tango songs, sung by our favorite singer, Carlos Gardel. In the song, "Caminito" means "little path," and is the road to his lover. The last paragraph of the song goes something like this: "Little path covered with thistle, the hand of time erased your tracks. I would like to fall beside you and let time kill us both." As with many Tango love songs, the words are very dramatic and often fatal. So, with Carlos' music ringing in my ears, we headed for the area so romantically described in the song.

When approaching the small area, the variety of bright colors that the buildings are painted caused my eyes to dilate: bright yellow, shocking greens, many shades of blue and all the shades of red; these colors were on the sides and fronts of the buildings, steps and trim. Even the light posts were painted in rainbow colors. Although they were a menagerie of colors, they somehow blended to express the story behind that small area by the waters of La Boca, which mean mouth, as in mouth of the Riachuelo River. Millions of foreign immigrants entered Argentina between 1880 and 1930, turning Buenos Aires from a small town into a bustling metropolis. Many Italians migrated from Genoa to La Boca and settled in the Caminito area so they could work in the nearby shipyards, as they had in their home town of Genoa. They were poor and took scraps of metal or other usable materials from the shipyards to build their homes in Caminito and the surrounding area. The materials' finishes were ugly, so they decided to paint them with whatever leftover paint they could find at the yards. Although today no one lives in Caminito, the area is a testimonial to the ingenuity and hard work of its original settlers. The buildings are now occupied by shops, and restaurants, and the area is considered an open air museum, representative of the time when La Boca was the melting pot of Argentina.

Tango music filled the air throughout the area, giving motion to street performers, Tango dancers and musicians; Barbara and I immediately joined other Tango-lovers and showed off some of the wonderful routines that we learned from our great dance instructors. The whole scene seemed to be out of an "Alice in Wonderland" story; the street dancers were dressed in formal attire, the men wearing tuxedoes, and the ladies open-back short, beautiful dresses; musicians roamed the streets playing beautiful tango music, and Barbara and I dancing our recently learned passionate Tango. How much better could it get?

We found a second floor restaurant and sat on the terrace overlooking the square where we could view the surreal scene and enjoy a hearty lunch. We ordered pizza with cheese and pepperoni, which was a house specialty, and polished it off with a bottle of very sweet white Argentine wine, while we watched the street fill with tourists. By the time we finished our lunch, the streets were packed with people shopping, dancing, or just browsing the stores. We joined the crowd and couldn't help buy some Tango paraphernalia. I bought a great ceramic picture, 10 x 14 inches, depicting two Tango dancers with a Caminito sign in the background; Barbara bargained with a shopkeeper for a beautiful multi colored shawl and two fans with Tango dancers and Caminito's colorful buildings in the background. With our arms filled with our purchased prizes, we bid farewell to Caminito and its rainbow past, which is still etched in my mind as a fond memory of love and romance in the place where Tango was born.

While doing the Tango at different dance halls, Barbara and I have been approached on many occasions by people watching us dance and have been told that when dancing we seem to be telling a story of love and seduction. It makes us feel wonderful to have people enjoy our dance routines, and I often smile when I think of Mingo's advice of "Attitude." Maybe, in some way, we captured what he was telling us. In any case, we thank you Mingo for helping enhance our love for the passion of Tango. Some years later we were at Sherry's "Argentine Tango Lovers of Long Islands" milonga at Mirelles in Westbury, Long Island, and the dance master teaching the Tango and performing a show was none other than Mingo's son, Pablo. What a wonderful experience; certainly "six degrees of separation" in play, our being taught by the senior Puglieses, and now by their famous son, thousands of miles from Buenos Aires in a local Long Island club--what are the odds? He loved the story we told about our experience with his parents, and spent most of the evening telling us how much he loved Tango and his beloved Argentina.

CHAPTER FOUR

Paris - Dancing at the Moulin Rouge

AROUND THE FLOOR: JANUARY/MARCH 2000

TRAVELING AROUND by Barbara Bivona

MIKE AND I DECIDED to spend a week in Paris before meeting up with our tour group from the Smithsonian Institute for two weeks of exploring the Amalfi Coast area of Southern Italy. We kept putting off a trip to France because we had heard such negative reports about the French people's attitude toward Americans. However, the call of the Eiffel Tower, the Louvre and Notre Dame was strong so, putting aside our concerns, we flew off to Paris for a week of adventure. The French people surprised us; it seems that the main problem they have with Americans is that we do not communicate well with them. The people we met didn't speak English, and we, unfortunately, didn't speak French. Once we discovered a European language that they understood, things got more comfortable. I have a working knowledge of Spanish, and Mike understands and speaks some Italian. The French understand one or the other of these languages and readily spoke to us when necessary. An example is that one day, while trying to navigate a course on foot to the Champs Elysees with a walking map, I discovered that I was holding the map upside down and, after a very long walk, realized we were about two miles in the opposite direction.

We asked a passerby to help us get to the Champs Elysees in English with no luck, but Spanish and some sign language did the trick; she understood us, walked us to the Metro, and made sure we got onto the right train.

Mike found an ad for the Argentine show "Tango Pasion" that was traveling around the world and, fortunately for us, was performing in Paris; we bought tickets and rushed to see the show that evening. The Parisienne ladies were dressed in their finest silks and jewels, and the men wore suits and ties. The audience reacted very unexpectedly to the performance, with cheers, bravos, and enthusiastic applause. By the end of the show, the cheering rivaled an Army-Navy football game.

We wanted to go to the Moulin Rouge nightclub, but the cost for an evening of dinner, dancing and show was astronomical; $440.00 in American money. We decided to pass on the show, but Lautrec was calling us. So we decided, what the heck, this is a once-in-a-lifetime experience, let's go for it! Our seats were at the edge of the elevated dance floor. The orchestra was wonderful; they played Cha-Chas, Rumbas, and cheek-to-cheek music. After drinking a bottle of Parissienne wine, we felt like we were in heaven. Suddenly, the orchestra played an Argentine Tango. The dance floor cleared. Can't anyone Tango here? We didn't get up because we didn't want to be alone on the dance floor with a thousand people watching us. My heart was pounding. I wanted to Tango, but not as the only couple on the stage. Slowly, dancers drifted to the floor. No one could do an Argentine Tango, but they swayed to the music and enjoyed themselves. Now we were safe. We could dance and be inconspicuous in the crowd. As we danced to a few measures of the Argentine Tango, we became aware of the crowd thinning around us and soon we were alone on the stage dance floor. Our worst fears, we were the show! We moved toward the middle and performed our well learned routines. When we finished, the French gave us a rousing Army-Navy cheer.

* *

The unedited version of this story began many years before our trip to Paris. Our daughter, Laurie Jo, graduated college and decided to backpack through Europe with one of her friends so that they "could find themselves." I wasn't aware that she was lost, but being that she saved enough money by working odd jobs during her stay at the University, plus the many monetary gifts she accumulated during her lifetime, we couldn't refuse or interfere with her dream of being on her own and finding her identity while traveling through Europe with her closest friend. So we gave her our blessing and away she went with her traveling companion. Their main travels included London, England; Amsterdam, Holland; Paris, France; Rome, Italy; parts of Switzerland and, lastly, Athens, Greece. In Athens, they spent time with my nephew, Dennis, who lived in that city. He escorted them to some of the wonderful Greek Islands and, as they stayed a few days in my nephew's home, they were able to experience, somewhat, what living in a major European city was like. In all their travels they stayed at pensions; she told us they were not great residences, but at her age backpacking and living in extremely modest hotels while traveling through Europe was a once-in-a-lifetime adventure, so why not join the hundreds of other lost souls in search of themselves and fit in?

After spending a month traveling through the many European countries, she returned home to us a different person. She told us of the wonders that she had seen and the people she met, many of them young exploring backpackers from around the world. It seems that they all had one thing in common, "they were all lost and trying to find themselves." I was happy that her trip was a success and all she had dreamed it would be. We asked her what place she enjoyed the most and she said without a doubt, Paris. The people were friendly, the sightseeing awesome, and the other backpackers she met seemed to be in abundance with everyone hanging around, drinking espresso, and sharing their personal stories. The Parisians seem to encourage the young people, and have many public facilities to accommodate them, such as toilets, parks with ample seating areas, and many sidewalk cafes. Her choice of Paris as a preferred place to see remained in the back of our minds and, when we booked a trip with the Smithsonian Institute to tour the Amalfi Coast area in Southern Italy, we researched the possibility of visiting Paris first.

Our Smithsonian Institute trip began in Naples, Italy, went into the surrounding areas and then returned to Naples. So we had to figure out the best way to go from New York City to Paris and from Paris to Naples. We decided that while we were in Italy, why not make a stop in Barbara's favorite city, Rome; so a flight from Rome to New York City was contemplated. We decided the best way to travel from New York City to Paris was with Delta Airlines. We had many frequent flier miles and were able to book a business class passage to Paris; that was easy. However, Paris to Naples was another matter. The only convenient airline was Alitalia and a one-way ticket from Paris to Naples was almost one third more than a round trip from Paris to Naples. So we booked a round-trip fare and only used it to get to Naples. Unfortunately, we couldn't get a refund for the unused ticket. We figured we could get from Naples to Rome by train, which is what we did. Next we booked a flight from Rome to New York's Kennedy Airport with Delta Airlines as a return flight, and were able to use our frequent flier miles to complete our journey on business class.

We were so excited and nervous, as we had never traveled to Europe on our own; but we began our research with a passion. We decided to spend a week in Paris before our trip to Italy, and we made a list of the places we wanted to see, as well as all the places we had read about and seen in movies and fantasized about. We kept talking about the movies; "An American In Paris" (1951) with Gene Kelly, Leslie Caron, Oscar Levant, and Nina Foch singing and dancing to George and Ira Gershwin's lyrics and music. "Singing in the Rain" (1952) with Gene Kelly, Donald O'Connor, Debbie Reynolds, and Cyd Charisse falling in love in Paris and with Paris; and last, but not least, the great musical "Gigi"(1958) with Leslie Caron, Maurice Chevalier, Louis Jourdan, and Eva Gabor about life in Paris in the late 1800s and the passion of being part of Paris at that time. Gene Kelly's song, "Singing in the Rain," and Maurice Chevalier's singing of "Gigi" were ringing in my ears and bringing back all the warm memories from watching those great musicals about "Parie." So we compiled our wish list, humming the songs we remembered from those great musicals about the City of Love. We began making a list of the places we wanted to see and that's when the fun began: the Eiffel Tower, Notre Dame, Arc de Triomphe, the Louvre Museum, the Moulin Rouge, the Latin Quarter, the Sorbonne, the Pantheon, the Catacombs and, hopefully, Versailles. Wow, what a wish list!!! Hopefully, we would get to see most of them. Also, a walk along the "Avenue des Champs-Elysees" would be a must.

We booked our business-class flight on Delta Airlines, which happened to be running a special which included the use of their first-class lounge Crown Room at JFK Airport, which we took advantage of without giving it a second thought. What a difference comfort makes! We were able to lounge around for over two hours in pure luxury, enjoying drinks, snacks, sandwiches, magazines, newspapers, and the use of very sophisticated, clean rest rooms. The most memorable comfort was the lack of noise that we were used to hearing when traveling coach. We had an evening flight and were pleased when we were handed menus to choose our dinner; by this time we were famished and enjoyed the selections offered. After dinner we had a drink and then used the reclining seats to relax, sleep, and spend a very restful night dreaming to the hypnotic hum of the jet engines. Our sleep was broken at about 7:00 A.M., French time, by our stewardess; it was breakfast time and we were given menus to select our hot or cold breakfasts. Considering that France is six hours ahead of Eastern Standard Time in New York, we really weren't in the mood for any food, but we forced ourselves to have some coffee and Danish. The flight took about eight hours and we landed the following day around 9:00 A.M., French time, at Charles de Gaulle Airport, which is located just North of Paris. We were fortunate to get a cab with the help of a French policeman, and we were taken to the Hotel Ambassador Opera on Haussmann Boulevard. We chose this hotel because friends of ours had just returned from Paris and said it was an American four-star hotel, away from the hustle and bustle of the tourist areas on the Left and Right Banks of the Seine River. It sounded perfect, so we booked our stay at the contemporary style, air conditioned, boutique-type hotel. Well, that is why I thought we chose this hotel, but even before we unpacked, my wife was on the phone asking the concierge where the Galeries Lafayette and the Le Printemps department stores were located. Much to her delight, they were only a couple of blocks away on the same boulevard. I contemplated tying her up to stop her from leaving the room and running down the boulevard to explore the covered shopping streets, which were within walking distance of our hotel. But, being that it was early morning Eastern Standard Time, we decided to take a nap and plan our day when we awoke.

After refreshing ourselves, we explored the eight story hotel which had just been refurbished and seemed to sparkle. Air conditioning should never be taken for granted in Europe. Many hotels do not have that comfort and many more have air conditioning, but ration it during the day and evenings. Fortunately, Hotel Ambassador had an excellent policy and we were cool throughout our stay. The hotel had several restaurants and an up-to-date gym on the eighth floor, with large windows overlooking the city and an incredible view of the Eiffel Tower. We had our breakfast/lunch at their 16 Haussmann Restaurant, which was quite casual, with high ceilings, large windows, and a wooden deck overlooking the busy Boulevard Haussmann. If I had a valium pill, I would have slipped it into Barbara's drink, as she was kvetching and bobbing in her chair and rushing me to finish my meal. Finally, we finished eating and immediately exited the hotel and headed towards her targets; the covered shopping streets on and along the Haussmann Boulevard and, of course, Galeries Lafayette and Le Printemps department stores.

It's amazing that when we prepared our wish list, there was never any discussion about shopping being our first priority.

Choosing to travel in September is always a good choice in Europe. The weather in many cities is usually in the high 60s to mid 70s and is ideal for walking through neighborhoods for sightseeing and shopping. Barbara, evidently, had all of this figured out when we planned our trip. Boulevard Haussmann was a shopper's delight, very similar to the covered Ginza Market in Tokyo, Japan. Every imaginable vender was represented, selling wares from their stands which were decorated in very colorful patterns, giving one the feeling that they were inside a rainbow looking out. It didn't take too long for us to zero in on some nice inexpensive ballroom dancing CDs that would be difficult to find in the states. Especially precious were the CDs of French singers Edith Pilaf, the tragic songbird singing, "La Vi En Rose"; Maurice Chevalier, "the French Al Jolson," singing "Bon Soir, Good Night Cherie"; and the exotic and heroic American, Josephine Baker, singing songs in French, such as "Easy to Love," "The Loveliness of You," and "Goodnight, My Love." I was starting to enjoy walking along the Boulevard and the friendly French people we met along the way, while zigzagging through the streets leading up to the main events, which were the Galeries Lafayette and Le Printemps department stores. They are neighbors on the Boulevard and were built in the mid and late-19th century. They sprawl through several buildings and are considered the greatest emporia ever built. When they were constructed, they were among the first department stores and soon revolutionized Europe's way of retailing. Needless to say we left a considerable amount of unbudgeted funds in these beautifully decorated palaces. Shopping under an enormous stained-glass roof gives one the feeling that you aren't spending money but are having a grand time on a merry-go-round at a circus, trying to capture the brass ring. Loaded down with packages, we headed back to the hotel. I still had jet lag, or maybe I was hallucinating, but I could have sworn that Barbara was hopping, skipping and singing while traveling down the Boulevard with her conquests dangling from her extended arms. Later that evening we decided to walk along the Boulevard to find a local restaurant and have dinner. Through our many years of traveling around the world, we learned that some of the best restaurants are to be found by walking through local neighborhoods. That night was no exception. After walking about five minutes, we looked into a store front window restaurant and observed a person holding what looked like a boat oar, stirring what looked like food in a very large vat. Indeed it was a boat oar, and he was stirring the evening's special dinner, paella. Being that we both love paella, we sat down at a window table drooling in anticipation of a delicious meal. We ordered a pitcher of white sangria and were told that the evening's special could be ordered in a number of different ways. The price depended on the ingredients chosen by us, so Barbara, being a shell fish lover, ordered her meal with clams, mussels, lobster and sausage, the saffron rice came with peppers, peas, and some other green vegetable. I've never developed a taste for shell fish, so I ordered mine with sausage and pork and lots of vegetables in my rice. Voila! The meal was spectacular; we both agreed that the Spanish cuisine we just enjoyed in France was the best we had ever eaten, including the paella we had in Spain and Portugal.

The next day we got up early and decided to walk down Boulevard Haussmann, with a walking map of the area that our pleasant concierge, Pierre, gave us. He also gave us very explicit instructions on how to get to the Eiffel Tower. After strolling down the Boulevard for what seemed to be an eternity, we realized that the Eiffel Tower seemed to be disappearing in the distance. We stopped a young lady and tried to explain our predicament, but, unfortunately, she didn't speak English. We showed her the Eiffel Tower on the map and with Barbara's language skills in Spanish, told her where we were headed. She immediately turned the map around, as Barbara was holding it upside down and we were walking in the opposite direction. Needless to say, we were embarrassed, but the young lady smiled and walked us two blocks out of her way to the Art Nouveau entrance of the Metro train system. She pointed to the train number we had to take to get to our destination. The Metro needs some explaining as it's quite different from what we New Yorkers are accustomed too. To describe it briefly, it is first-class travel with very clear station signs and a very comprehensive color-coded Metro Map that can get you around underground Paris with little difficulty. When we went to buy a ticket to our destination, the clerk gave us a pamphlet in English, which explained the various tickets that are available for traveling around the great city. We bought a weekly pass (coupon he'bdomadaire) that was good for our entire stay. The station resembled New York's Grand Central Station and, with the comprehensive color coding, we had no trouble finding the track that our train ran on. We arrived at our station, which not only had its name on the platform tiled wall, but also some of the main attractions that were above ground. Considering that the population of Paris is over two million people and the metropolitan area about ten million, the trains were exceptionally clean, not too crowded, and the people were very polite--quite a difference from what we were accustomed to when riding the subways in New York City. We were so excited when we exited the train that we ran up the moving escalator to the street level. What a sight to see! The best known monument in the world, the Eiffel Tower, the symbol of Paris, was right in front of us. After taking a dozen pictures, we took the elevator to the top of the 1,000 + foot structure and hypnotically gazed at the magnificent city of Paris. The visibility was endless; we were told that on a clear day seeing 35 to 40 miles is possible. It was certainly, one of the most beautiful cityscapes in the world. It was now lunch time, and where else to enjoy some French cuisine but at one of the Tower's restaurants. We tried to get into Jules Vern's restaurant at the upper platform of the tower, however, reservations were required weeks in advance. But, the "Altitude 95" restaurant on the first platform was a good second choice. We took the elevator to that level and had a wonderful lunch while absorbing the view of the city. We made a mental note, that if we could, we would try to get reservations to the Jules Vern's restaurant for dinner so we could see the City of Lights in the evening in its entire splendor.

Where to next? Considering that Paris consists of twenty different neighborhoods, called "arrondissements," which are either on the Left or Right banks of the Seine River, we figured, being that we were already on the Left Bank, the best approach to sightseeing this magnificent city was to walk along the River and stop and explore whatever stimulated our interest.

We checked our wish list and decided that the first stop would be the Pantheon and then Notre Dame. The stroll along the Seine River is breathtaking to say the least; the effect of the three bridges crossing the Seine River is surreal, especially the Pont Neuf Bridge which has twelve arches; seven arches joining the Right Bank and another span of five arches connecting "Ile de la Cite" (this is the island that hosts Notre Dame Cathedral) with the Left Bank. It also boasts an equestrian statue of King Henry IV, who was responsible for its construction. The activity on the stone bridge is busy with people socializing and trading all sorts of small wares. The sun shining off the water, arches and bronze statues, and the beautiful 14th century towered palaces and ancient buildings in the background has the affect of a glorious dream-like halo above and around the bridge.

Le Pantheon is the burial place for the great souls of the Nation: Hugo, Zola, Rousseau, Voltaire, and many others. Originally, it was built as a majestic church and dedicated to the city's patron, St. Genevieve. When we entered, Barbara was immediately drawn to Foucault's Spinning Pendulum; she moved so fast, that I thought she spotted a designer store. Since her college days, she turned her studies in astronomy and geology into a passion. I had no idea what Foucault's Pendulum was and, quite frankly, wasn't too interested, but my curiosity peeked when I was told that it was in perpetual motion; I was fascinated by how it could keep moving without winding something. We located a docent who was lecturing on the pendulum and became fascinated and enthralled while she told of the history and its purpose. I was hypnotized by the slow movement, swaying to and fro beneath the dome of the former church, tracing its invisible path against the hour table below. On the ground, a large white ring surrounding the area of oscillation is marked with a series of numbers that reflect a period of 24 hours. A short video display was also available relating its story: it told visitors to "imagine for a moment that their feet were no longer touching the ground and consider that the pendulum's plane of oscillation, which also doesn't touch the ground, remains unchanged with respect to the stars, even as the earth rotates; this is proof that the Pantheon moves around the pendulum and not vice-versa."

Interesting, I'm still trying to figure it all out, but I enjoyed watching the hypnotic motion of the pendulum which made me relax, while trying to absorb all the information about its purpose. We exited the Pantheon and walked down the monumental steps to the street, which was crowded with pedestrians and people having late lunch or early dinner in the Latin Quarter of the Left Bank.

It was a short and pleasant walk to Pont Neuf Bridge and crossing on to the "Ile de la Cite," where the Notre Dame Cathedral is located. On the way, we stopped at a street-side café and had some wonderful espresso coffee, while admiring the Parisians and tourists busily moving about the Latin Quarter. Appearances of the Parisians are very similar to what we see in New York City, very serious in their demeanor and dress, the men wearing suits with ties and carrying brief cases; the fashionable ladies dress the same as their New York sisters and are just as beautiful to behold. All are very determined looking and seem to be in a rush to get to their destinations, as we were, so off we went to the historical Notre Dame Cathedral.

Crossing the beautiful Pont Neuf Bridge and absorbing Notre Dame Cathedral is mind boggling; one of the noblest monuments in the western world, its presence and French Gothic beauty dominates the Seine River, the "Ile de la Cite," and Paris itself. The location dates back to the Roman's Temple to Jupiter, which was followed by a Christian basilica, then a Romanesque church, and, finally, the Cathedral as it stands today. The building was under construction, so there was scaffolding around most of the upper portion, but the construction did not hide the famously grotesque gargoyles, the soaring elegance of the flying buttresses, the sculpted portals, the bell tower, and the water spouts. Looking at the Cathedral, I envisioned Quasimodo swinging from apse to gargoyles and ringing the famous Cathedral's bells, rising up and coming down while holding the bell's ropes, as his heart pounded and burst for the fair maiden, Esmeralda. I reflected on Victor Hugo's historical romance story, which was made into one of the most memorable movies of my youth, "The Hunchback of Notre Dame," (1939), starring Charles Laughton, Maureen O'Hara, and the evil Claude Frollo played by Cedric Hardwicke. Every time I hear "Notre Dame," memories of Quasimodo swinging and jumping from place to place flash through my mind.

The interior of the Cathedral with its graceful columns is impressive, and is dominated by three rose windows located to the West, North, and South. Their colors are spellbinding and a glory to behold as the sun shines through, accomplishing its designer's intention; to create unparalleled multiple colorful kaleidoscopes from all directions.

It was time to call it a day. Our jet lag was still playing havoc with our minds and bodies so we exited this incredible piece of history, walked across the bridge to the Left Bank, hailed a taxi-cab and returned to our hotel, where we had a quick dinner and retired after a rather long and exciting day. Before closing our eyes for the night, we decided that we would spend the next day at the Louvre Museum and explore the surrounding area of the Right Bank.

First thing in the morning we visited our concierge, Pierre. We had done some research before we began our trip and decided that we had better get some insider information about the "Musee du Grand Louvre" to guide us through the multitude of exhibits, architecture, and surrounding gardens. Considering that the museum displayed about 300,000 works, and warehoused an even greater number, whatever advice Pierre could give us would be greatly appreciated and put to good use. He suggested that we spend at least two hours exploring the outside of the museum and asked what exhibits we were interested in seeing. We had previously decided that the Egyptian exhibit was a must, as Barbara's interest in geology was attracting us to the mystique of the ancient Egyptians. He suggested that we spend from one to two hours at that exhibit and then explore whatever struck our fancy as we got the feel of the museum. He also suggested that we get a box lunch or eat at one of the many restaurants in the gardens, while enjoying the beautiful Carrousel and Tuileries Gardens adjoining the museum. Well, this gave us a plan, and we thanked Pierre and immediately went to the Metro and took the train to our next adventure. An impressive system is the turnstile revolving door (iron maiden) method the Metro has for entering their system with passes. One inserts the pass into a slot which opens the iron maiden turnstile (named after a medieval torture device), enters while retrieving the pass, and walks through. It's that simple and practical and, considering this system has been in place for a decade, it's surprising that so many American transportation centers are still using the coin method. We decided to have breakfast at a sidewalk café in the Latin Quarter and chose one right outside the train station exit.

We crossed the foot bridge to the Louvre Museum area where we were overwhelmed with the panoramic view that was bewildering in its complexity and beauty. To see so many places in person, for the first time, but to be intimately familiar with them in my mind's eye, was an experience in Déjà Vu. A video view from a high vantage point of the American architect I.M. Pei's glass paneled Pyramid in the courtyard, engulfed by rising water spouts and a glimmering pond; the Arc du Carrousel in the near background; the Place de la Concorde; the Arc De Triomphe de L'Etoile; the Grand Arch de la Defense; the Louvre Museum and the surrounding gardens, were a once-in-a-lifetime experience not soon forgotten. We took about an hour just taking pictures and admiring the amazing amount of statues, figures, friezes, and every other conceivable outdoor works of art. We had to close our eyes and quickly enter the museum, or we would have spent the whole day admiring the variety of masterful art work around and on the buildings.

We got a tour guide booklet with maps from the information center and were directed to the "Ancient Egyptian Art Exhibit." After getting quite lost, we finally found the exhibit and spent the remaining morning studying and admiring over 3,000 years of Egyptian history and artifacts, ranging in size from four-inch statuettes to over-life-size statues. Barbara was enthralled with the whole experience, especially the information and displays about its famous rulers: Amenhotep III, Akhenaten, Ramesses II (the Great), and our favorites, Tutankhamen (King Tut), and Cleopatra. A painted relief of Cleopatra in the time honored guise of a bare-chested male pharaoh giving a sacrifice to the goddess Isis absorbed our minds and imagination. We were amused, as she certainly was not the Cleopatra played by the beautiful actress Elizabeth Taylor, whose appearance we usually associate with Cleopatra. As I watched Barbara, who was fascinated and absorbed with the excavation exhibits, I could picture where her imagination was taking her; probably right to an Egyptian dig, maybe King Tut's, shoveling earth and examining stones and making a great discovery. It was past lunch time and we both decided to takes Pierre's advice and have lunch in the outside gardens.

We strolled to the Tuileries Garden (Jardin des Tuileries), which extends from the Louvre to the Place de la Concorde. We walked the central alley, lined with shady clipped chestnut trees and manicured lawns with ornamental ponds at each end, and surrounded by a multitude of beautiful flowers, dancing fountains, and statues. We stopped at the first restaurant and ordered some sandwiches and drinks to go. We were lucky and located two empty chairs, which we strategically placed at one of the ponds so we could enjoy the view of the gardens, statues, and an unusually surprising sight of children and adults at play around the pond. It's interesting to note that there are chairs throughout the park for the convenience of the public, which can be placed wherever one wishes to sit. Children were sailing and chasing their boats around the pond. Many of them had motorized remote-controlled boats, which they were having fun racing, but most were just enjoying a good sail and just horsing around. Taking in the whole sight of trees, flowers, statues, ponds, children and some grownups at play, and people promenading around was what we needed to end our perfect day in the park. It was our time to "stop and smell the roses." We enjoyed our sandwiches, took many great photographs, and decided to head back to our hotel as it was becoming overcast. Instead of taking the Metro back, we decided to take a city bus, which was, according to a helpful policeman, nearby and would drop us off close to our hotel. Unfortunately, it started to rain as we were waiting for our transportation and we got pretty wet. But, we figured, what the heck--we were in Paris and the ride to our destination would be short. We boarded the bus, inserted our Metro pass into the open machine, as we saw other passengers do, and away we went to our comfortable hotel.

The weather cleared and we decided to walk and discover a new restaurant, and whatever other surprises we might find along our journey. Our first stop was to the concierge, Pierre, to get directions to the closest restaurants. He said for us to go outside and walk in whatever direction we chose, and we would certainly find a restaurant that will satisfy our appetites. We did just that, and found a quaint Italian restaurant around the corner from the hotel. We entered and were greeted in French, seated, and given wine and meal menus. We were surprised that neither menu had an English interpretation. We asked for English menus, but the waiter didn't understand our language. I tried some Italian to no avail, but Barbara's Spanish did the trick. He told us that they didn't have an English menu and further explained that we were in a kosher restaurant, as were the other restaurants on the street. We decided to stay and try our luck by ordering pasta with eggplant and a bottle of local wine. The restaurant had about 20 tables, and while we were enjoying our wine and waiting for our meal to be served, a gentlemen and companion came in and sat at the table next to ours. They nodded hello, sat down, and both lit cigarettes. UGH!! The waiter saw that we were uncomfortable and asked them if they would mind sitting at the far end of the restaurant. They rose and sort of apologized to us and politely moved to their new table. Of course, we didn't understand French, but we assumed that the conversation went along those lines. The pasta and eggplant were absolutely delicious and the French wine, as usual, complemented the meal. We enjoyed the meal so much that we went back to the Italian Kosher French restaurant again before we left Paris. Before retiring for the evening, we decided to return to the Louvre Museum the next day to see the painting of Mona Lisa, the statues of Venus De Milo, the Winged Victory of Samothrace, and, if possible, the stele (stone) of Hammurabi's Code (the first written laws), which was done between 1795-1750 BCE.

We arouse early the next morning and decided to enjoy another breakfast at a street side café on the Right Bank. We entered the Metro station, went to the Iron Maiden, and inserted our passes; but the turnstiles didn't open. After several tries with no luck, we approached the cashier and tried to explain our predicament. He spoke some English, and asked if we had used the passes on a bus? I will never know how he knew, but I said "Yes" and he shook his head and said, "No good." It seems that the passes we had were only good for use on the train system of the Metro, and inserting them into the bus' turnstile voided them. I thought to myself, now we are in for it--what an opportunity for the notorious anti-American French to "zing" us. However, to our surprise, he took our passes, issued new ones (at no charge), and asked "where are you going?" I said, "The Louvre Museum." He exited his change booth and escorted us through the Iron Maiden, using our new passes, to the track that our train would be arriving at. We thanked him profusely as he disappeared from sight while returning to his office. What an surprising experience!!

After having another breakfast on the Right Bank, and enjoying the promenade of Parisians going about their daily routines, we rushed to the Louvre Museum, hoping to accomplish our goal of seeing all the exhibits we discussed the night before. In my mind's eye, I couldn't get the beautiful gardens out of my head and hoped that we would be able to spend some more quality time in them after finishing our tours. We were able to see all the exhibits and I was constantly reminded of the great baseball player and manager, Yogi Berra's, famous quote: "It seemed like déjà vu all over again." We recognized most of the displays and were familiar with their history from school studies, movies, magazines and posters, with many of them at one time or another being incorporated into my daydreams, especially Venus De Milo. We were satisfied with what we had accomplished and exited the great museum in the middle of the afternoon. We headed straight for the Tuleries Gardens and strolled through the Central Valley, again admiring all of man and nature's bounty. We ended up at the eastern end and entered the Garden Carrousel (Jardin du Carrousel), which is at the front of the Louvre. Its beautiful flowers and trim yew hedges complemented the oddly static buxom female nude bronzes by the sculptor Maillol. We left the grounds in anticipation of getting back to our hotel in time to refresh and dress for the Argentine show, "Pasion for Tango" (Tango Passion), for which I was able to get tickets through our concierge, Pierre. He advised us to dress up for the theatre as Parisians usually dressed very well when they attend shows. Barbara was ecstatic, she could wear and show off a new outfit that she had purchased at the Galleria Lafayette with complementing shoes. I would be able to wear a new tie that I had to go out and buy, under protest, for the occasion.

We took a taxicab to the Theatre des Champs-Elysees, which is not on the famous boulevard, but nearby. It is one of the few major examples of Art Nouveau remaining in Paris. The theatre is known for its contemporary music-making, dance, and opera; unlike the traditional and more conservative venues, such as the Paris Opera, which is featured in the play and movies, "Phantom of the Opera." We were pleasantly surprised at how fashionably dressed the ladies were; many of the gentlemen actually wore tuxedos, and all the others wore suits and ties; good thing I was persuaded to purchase a tie. We did fit in pretty well with the locals. An observation we made was that the Parisians appeared very reserved. Although they seemed to speak in a normal manner, with much feeling, they didn't seem to laugh out loud or smile much in public. It did seem that many of them smoked cigarettes and cigars, and no matter how we tried to avoid the smoke, we couldn't because there was always someone smoking in the public areas. We entered the auditorium and were ecstatic when we read the program. Music by some of our favorite composers was part of the show, including Carlos Gardel,* whose music we desperately loved to dance to. We had spent endless hours listening to his smooth, deep soul love and melancholy songs.** Part of the show also included Astor Piazzolla, the father of modern Tango or "Nuevo Tango." These two great Tango icons had a chance meeting when Piazzolla was a teenager and Gardel was touring New York City. Gardel was impressed with the boy's talent with the bandoneon, his love for Tango music, and some of his early compositions. He wanted Piazzolla to join his world tour, but the young prodigy's father thought he was too young to be traveling with a group of musicians whose reputation was known to be rowdy. Divine intervention played an amazing part in Piazzolla's life, as Gardel and all the members of his band were killed in an airplane crash while on that tour in South America. Piazzolla is considered one of the most important Tango composers of the 20th century. He was born in Mar del Plata, Argentina, in 1921, to Italian parents, but spent most of his childhood with his family in New York City, where he was exposed to jazz and the music of J.S. Bach. He returned to Argentina at the age of 16, and played in nightclubs and with various orchestras. His early compositions combined Tango with Jazz, and then graduated to a fusion of Tango with a wide range of other Western influences, such as baroque music from the 17th and 18th centuries. One of his first popular pieces,

"Adios Nonino," was being presented in that evening's show. This composition established a standard structural pattern for his works; a formal pattern of "fast-slow-fast-slow-coda," with the fast sections emphasizing gritty Tango rhythms and harsh, angular melodic figures, and the slower sections usually making use of the smooth string instruments and bandoneon. His "operita," "Maria de Buenos Aires," and other compositions established him as one of the world's foremost Tango classical music composers of the 20th century.

*Chapter Three has a brief history of Carlos Gardel. **Chapter Three has two popular songs in Spanish and English.

The curtains parted and the ensemble of beautiful dancers wearing the colors of "Tango" appeared; men wearing a variety of black outfits and high heeled Latin-style shoes, and the women showing off every color of the rainbow incorporated into their Latin-styled dresses and pants. The first dance was to the music of Carlos Gardel's and Julian Plaza's, "Mi Buenos Aires," a beautiful fast Tango performed by several couples doing their own interpretations and styles of Tango. The music was fast and required much coordination and confidence between the partners, especially when the girls performed kicks between the men's legs. This type of music is not considered romantic and it's not sensual in sound, but it does allow the dancers to show off their skills at a very fast pace with precision in their kicking, swaying and body balancing; more of an aerobic interpretation of the Tango.

My favorite Tango song, and very popular with dancers, was played halfway through the show: "La Cumparsita," by G.M. Rodriguez (the words to the song appears in Chapter Three in Spanish and English). This romantic dance was performed by one couple, slowly, with minor rhythm changes. The dance tells the story of seduction; the meeting, flirting, pursuing and finally, conquest of the sexes. It was done to perfection and Barbara and I found ourselves applauding wildly, but we seemed to be the only ones that appreciated the performance. The last three pieces of music played out of the 19 performed were by Astor Piazzolla, one of which was previously mentioned, "Adios Nonino." His music is also not of the romantic sexy type of Tango we picture when envisioning "the Great Lover, Valentino" romancing his conquest. His pieces are fiery and complicated and, as previously mentioned, a fusion of many types of Western music that has come down through the ages. His music gives the dancers an opportunity to show off their dancing skills at a very fast to slow pace, with precision being almost robotic in its accuracy. His music ended the show, and the Parisians, who up until this point didn't seem to be enjoying the show, as their applause didn't seem to be spontaneous or generous, arose in unison and blew the roof off of the theatre with their applauding, cat calling, and whistling. Of course, the entertainers did a couple of encores which received additional appreciation from the audience with some pretty loud sounds; I thought we were at a football game between the Army and Navy. I think we began to fall in love with the Parisians at that point. We left the theatre and had some difficulty finding a taxicab, as it was pretty late in the evening, so we walked towards Champs-Elysees and finally hailed a cab. The driver was the first Frenchman that we thought was downright obnoxious, but I closed my eyes and changed the location of the taxi to New York City and felt right at home. Being in a good mood, I rewarded him with a very gracious tip. Before retiring, we decided that the next day we would explore the Arc de Triomphe and the Champs-Elysees; we would also ask Pierre about getting us tickets to the Moulin Rouse, where I would finally get to see some real Can-Can girls.

The next morning we went straight to Pierre and asked if he could get us some tickets for the famous Moulin Rouse show that evening, preferably with seats as close to the stage as possible. He said that he had a cousin who worked at the box office and that he would contact him immediately. He told us to have some coffee and return in fifteen minutes and he would have the information for us. We decided to have breakfast at the hotel and return to Pierre's desk when we finished. He had all the information we needed. Did we want to see only the show? Did we want to see the show and have drinks? Or did we want to have a sit down dinner with wine at a good location? He gave us the price of each in American dollars, which put us in a state of shock. We certainly wanted to see the entire show with dinner included, but the price was $440.00 for the first evening show, which we thought was prohibitive. We told him we had to talk it over and went back to our room to discuss and investigate the pricing. We checked our travel guides and spoke to some other guests at the hotel that we met during our stay. All said that the prices we were given seemed to be the going price, being that the American dollar did not have a favorable exchange rate at that time. Well, the images in Toulouse Lautrec's paintings and posters of the Moulin Rouse's beautiful women were flashing through my mind, and the music from the movie resounded in my soul, so we told Pierre that we would like to see the show that evening, including dinner and wine. He told us that the price also included transportation to and from the cabaret, which certainly made the price a little more palatable.

We hurried to the Metro for another rendezvous with the "Iron Maiden" and had no difficulty finding the track that our train would arrive on to take us to the Arc de Triomphe station. Although I was anxious to see the sights we had planned for the day, my mind was really focusing on the evening show at the Moulin Rouge. That changed when we exited the train station; the sight of the Arc de Triomphe completely filled my eyes and absorbed every thought in my mind. It was so overwhelming! Not only was I viewing this magnificent structure, but I immediately saw the image of Adolf Hitler reviewing his troops, in a show of arrogance, marching through the Arc on that horrific day in history during WWII, when he occupied that great city. I shook the view from my mind's eye and thought of the more recent and happier event of Lance Armstrong as he rode through the Arc after his stupendous accomplishment of winning again, the "Tour de France" race. The race participants travel through the Alps for over 2,000 miles, and Lance Armstrong accomplished this feat after his miraculous struggle and recovery from cancer.

After clearing my mind, we attempted to cross the square in front of the Arc. This turned out to be a big mistake as we were almost run down by the insane car and scooter drivers. After crossing, an American tourist who watched our obstacle course maneuvers told us that there was an underground crossing that would have been a safer choice. It would have been nice if we met him before attempting our suicide mission.

We were immediately attracted to the grave of the Unknown Soldier from WWI, whose body was retrieved from Verdun in the region of Lorraine and buried beneath the Arch with a large and decorative flat headstone. Flowers in the shape of a horseshoe surrounded the site. Each evening at 6:30 P.M., the flame of remembrance is rekindled during a small formal ceremony in memory of the fallen heroes of that war.

The Arc de Triomphe was commissioned by Napoleon in 1806 to commemorate his army's victories, but it remained unfinished until after his death. It was completed in 1836 during the reign of Louis-Philippe. The design of the Arc is based on the Arch of Titus in Rome, but, of course, it is much larger (164-feet high and 148-feet wide). Surprisingly, it has the same proportions as its sister in Rome. It is the highest triumphal Arch in the world; adorned with many reliefs, most of them commemorating Napoleon's victories. So impressive are the faces in the sculptures that they seem to be staring back at you from their high vantage points. We climbed the steps to the viewing platform where I was amazed at the view. I thought that our previous experiences with the panoramic views of Paris could not be matched, but here it was, another marvel of French ingenuity. The integration of architecture and the beauty within the overview of this city is beyond belief; one has to see this sight to understand the complexity of the decision making by the city's fathers, and of the German generals who disobeyed Hitler's orders to destroy the magnificent city in WWII. Fortunately, their decisions not to have the city destroyed saved the "City of Lights," and left most of the city unscathed by the war, so that future generations could still marvel at the beautiful architecture and the talent of the French people who were responsible for the wonderful sights that everyone on the viewing platform was enjoying.

As you look in all directions, you see twelve avenues emanating from the "star" (center), as well as all the other phenomenal views of Paris. Looking eastward, down the Champs Elysees towards the Louvre, there is the Place de la Concord, the Tuileries Gardens, and the Arc de Triomphe du Carrousel, with the statue of four gilded bronze horses mounted at the top, shining in the sun light as they are being driven by the emperor (might be Napoleon) in all their military glory. Further down across the Seine River, the Eiffel tower beams in its height and splendor, and the golden dome, "Invalides," (Napoleon's resting place) sparkles in the sun. In the opposite direction in the business district, "La Grande Arche de la Defense," the newest of Paris' Arches and the surrounding avenues entering the "star" (roundabout) is too much to absorb all at once. We took a multitude of pictures and then descended the 200-plus steps to the street level. This time we did take the more cautious path out of the square and actually enjoyed the walk through the underground tunnel without being concerned about being run over and becoming part of the Champs-Elysees' road pavement. As I walked down the road, I looked back at the Arc and I recalled another happy occasion that took place at this monument; when WWII ended some of the soldiers of the victorious allied armies marched through "L'Arc de Triomphe" led by the towering figure of General Charles de Gaulle. I remembered the event from my childhood, when seeing movie newsreels and newspaper photographs of that historical day.

We decided to have a late lunch at a sidewalk café on the Champs-Elysees. The scene from our outdoor table on the street and the procession of people reminded me of a similar view in Rome, the Via Veneto, where some of the most fashionable women in the world parade their stylish wares. Of course, the French women cannot be outclassed by any of their foreign sisters, so there they were on the avenue promenading--so stylishly in what I'm sure were the latest in women's fashions and designs. What a beautiful sight! After lunch, we decided to walk back to our hotel and enjoy the beautiful day while window shopping and exploring the neighborhood. Unfortunately, after walking some distance, we decided to take a taxicab back to the hotel and, hopefully, get some sleep before our night out at the Moulin Rouge. Barbara was apprehensive about going into an area that had a reputation for its rowdiness and of being a red light district, but I assured her that the reputation was fictional and, being that we were going by bus and with lots of other people, that we would be safe.

A small bus holding about 20 people picked us up at the hotel and away we went to experience one of my fantasies, which was imbedded in my mind by the images of Henri de Toulouse-Lautrec's paintings and posters of exotic French girls doing the naughty Can-Can dance. The Moulin Rouge (French for Red Mill or windmill) is a traditional cabaret, situated in the red light district of Pigalle on Boulevard de Clichy on the Right Bank. Recognized by a large red imitation windmill on its roof, it went from a high-class brothel, where it's said that the striptease originated, to a fashionable spectacular cabaret, visited by the very best in French society. One of my most memorable movies was the 1952 "Moulin Rouse," adapted from the book of the same name by Pierre La Mure, and starring Jose Ferrer and Zsa-Zsa Gabor. The musical is about the 19th century painter, Henri de Toulouse-Lautrec, played by Jose Ferrer, and his battle with his deformity due to a leg injury as a child, which he could not deal with and resulted in his drinking, carousing in the red light district, patronizing the Moulin Rouge and, eventually, causing his early death. The film's musical score was by George Aurie and immediately hit the top ten charts. I remembered seeing the film on my newly purchased color television set and couldn't believe my eyes; I was actually seeing a movie in color in my own living room. Color television is certainly here to stay, I thought, which was one of my better predictions in life.

We entered the cabaret and were escorted to our table, which was right at the edge of the raised stage. I was in a position where the only way I could see the performers was by raising my head upward . . . lucky me. We were seated at a table with six other people from various parts of the world, but the table was situated so that everyone had an unobstructed view of the stage. Our waiter broke open a bottle of white French wine and allowed me to sample it before pouring. I have always been tempted to swish the wine sampling around in my mouth and then gargling, just for the fun of it, but Barbara saw the look in my eye and said, "Don't you dare!" What a mind reader she is. The dinner was adequate and the coffee and desserts just fine, but I couldn't wait for the show to start. Finally, the long-legged international ensemble of girls appeared--slightly dressed, or should I say almost undressed, and performed an exotic Can-Can. When the show ended I was not disappointed and, after a couple of glasses of fine French wine, was quite content with our experience at the Moulin Rouge. After the show there was general dancing on the raised stage. We did some shuffling to Foxtrots and Waltzes with about 50 other couples, and then they played a slow, seductive Argentine Tango. The stage cleared and we were the only ones left on the dance floor in front of 1,000-plus patrons. We decided to leave the dance floor as we didn't want to be the only ones dancing in front of such a large crowd, but soon other couples came into the arena, so we began to dance the beautiful Argentine Tango, which was being played by an amazingly talented band. I noticed that no one knew how to do the dance and soon all of the dancers cleared the floor to watch us; we had become the show. Not being bashful, we began to perform our routines; slow balancing, leg rubs, leg kicks, cortes, and all the other seductive moves we had learned through so many years of lessons and practice. The only problem we had was that the band wasn't ending the dance after the usual three minutes, so even though I felt that we could dance the whole night away, we came to our final step where Barbara kicks her leg between mine and leans way back. The music ended and the applause and howling was

Michael Bivona

incredible. I had that same feeling as the night we attended the "Tango Pasion" show; we were again at an Army/Navy football game with lots and lots of wonderful noise. We took our bows and left the brightly lit stage and returned to our table to be greeted by people surrounding us asking us where we learned to Tango. Considering that the crowd was of international origin, the scene became quite hysterically amusing. A person approached us, I think he was the manager, and asked if we would perform another Tango. I was ready, but Barbara was very reluctant. I sort of forced her onto the dance floor while the emcee announced our performance. The music began and we again fell in love with the dance and each other. The music was slow and we took advantage of the tempo to do many of our caressing sways and smooth kicks. This time we did lots of reverse slow dragging dips mingled with sways, which pleased the crowd as their applause and howls were stimulating and, if the band hadn't stopped playing, "We would have danced all night." Again, we bowed and acknowledged the audience's appreciation by taking several more bows. When we returned to our table, two beautiful showgirls were waiting for us, one with a bucket of ice and the other with a bottle of champagne. We were startled by the presentation and even more so by the double cheek kisses we received (especially on my part) from the gorgeous young girls. The shapely blond headed Can-Can dancer (the other one was a redhead), said in perfect English, "Compliments of the management and Moulin Rouge." They popped the cork and poured us the bubbly. I suggested that they also share the wine with our table guests, which they did and we toasted each other in our various languages: Good Luck, Arigoto, and Gracia. We received two more double cheek kisses; I got two great hugs, lucky me, and then the two gorgeous girls disappeared (sigh).

We left the "Rouge" and accepted the handshakes and pats on the back that many of the patrons so generously gave us. We boarded our bus and while resting I kept saying to myself, "What a night." I never expected in my wildest dreams to have an evening so filled with excitement and camaraderie with people from around the world, all going to the Moulin Rouge for an evening of fun and entertainment. Who would have imagined that we would be part of the night's program? We decided before retiring that we would spend the next day taking a boat ride on the Seine River and then explore the Left Bank. We kissed, said goodnight, and away I went into my Tango-dream-world.

Below is a picture of Barbara and me doing an Argentine Tango at the Fox Hollow Country Club in Woodbury, New York (not at the Moulin Rouge). The picture was taken by my son, Stephen Bivona, and I'm proud to present it here:

The next morning, we jumped out of bed, showered and dressed, and then I waited for an additional half hour until Barbara added finishing touches to her beauty. When she was satisfied that we were presentable enough to face the outside world, we left and went directly to the Metro for another rendezvous with the Iron Mistress. We paid the Maiden so often I was beginning to think of her as more of a Mistress than a Maiden. After inserting our train passes, the Mistress smiled, opened her arms, and allowed us into the railway station. We got off the train at the Tuileries

Station and quickly exited. It didn't take us long to find another wonderful sidewalk café to enjoy our breakfast. We relaxed and had a leisurely breakfast, knowing that as we watched the wonderful procession of tourists and Parisians parade by, we had plenty of time before we boarded our sightseeing boat for a morning cruise on the beautiful Seine River. We didn't rush our feast and just laid back and enjoyed the special sights and the clear Parisian morning air that surrounded us.

We boarded our glass covered ship, "le Bateau-Mouches," near the Eiffel Tower. The ship carries over 300 passengers, but is laid out so that everyone has a decent view of the waterway. We immediately found a seat that would give us a good view of the sights on the Seine River. Fortunately the weather was cooperating with our plans as it was one of those days where, "on a clear day, you could see forever." Our boat was equipped with a text display and an audio announcement system synchronized to the boat's movement and providing commentary, in several languages, on the passing sights through respective ear phones. The system informed us that the Seine River has been Paris' protein since the days the Parisii tribe first established a fishing village on the island, "Ile de la Cite," between 250 and 200 BCE. Since the days of the Roman Empire, it prospered through extensive river trading beginning in Northern France and linking the Loire, Rhine, and Rhone Rivers, extending almost 500 miles and finally flowing out to the English Channel. The area around the "Ile de la Cite" boasts some of the world's oldest and most majestic historical monuments, which we were about to see from the vantage point of 80-feet above sea level, which is quite different from our previous experiences from high structures with panoramic views; we were now going to enjoy looking at one building at a time as we traveled along the river. We were going to study the structures and neighborhoods from quite a different perspective--not from on high but from below.

Our voyage began at the Eiffel Tower and passed the Grand Palais, Concorde, Louvre, Musee d'Orsay, Notre Dame and my favorite, the Statue of Liberty. Wait a minute, "what is the

Statue of Liberty doing on the Seine River in Paris?" I asked Barbara. The information came forthwith from our high tech electronic docent. In 1889, Americans living in Paris donated a small replica of the New York Statue of Liberty (there are numerous other replicas around the world) to the city of Paris in appreciation of France's gift to the United States. The statue is identical in detail to her big sister, except it is about five times smaller (36-six feet, not including the pedestal of about the same size) than the New York version. What a glorious sight to see this world renowned symbol of freedom proudly displayed in the country that was instrumental in our success during America's Revolutionary War. The Lady is located on its own Isle de Grenelle, next to the Pont de Grenelle Bridge which connects the Right and Left Banks or 15th and 16th Arrondissements.

One of the highlights of the cruise was experiencing the same places and seeing the same landscapes where many of the 19th century artists did their most beautiful paintings. The 19th century Impressionist artists: Edouard Manet, Camille Pissaro, Edgar Degas, Alfred Sisley, Claude Monet, Berthe Morisot, and Pierre Auguste Renoir all loved painting outdoors and landscapes, with or without people. The Impressionist art movement started as a group of Paris-based artists began publicly displaying their paintings in the 1860s; the movement got its name from Claude Monet's painting, "Impression, Sunrise." We traveled some of the same routes that his famous boat studio floated by, while he painted the activity on the river, landscapes, and his famous painting "Le Bateau Atelier" (floating boat studio).

One of Monet's best friends was Pierre Auguste Renoir, with whom he worked closely during the 1860s. Renoir also loved boats, landscapes, nature, and portraits; they became painting buddies for many years, copying each other's styles just for the fun of it and defying anyone to tell the difference. It's amazing that all of these talented people arrived in Paris at about the same time, knew each other, learned from each other's styles of painting, and produced, in my opinion, some of the most beautiful paintings in existence. My favorite is one of Renoir's people paintings: "Bal au Moulin de la Galette, Montmartre" (Dance at Le Moulin de la Galette), an open-air scene of a popular dance garden on the Butte Montmartre. Evidently I'm not the only one that loves the painting as it recently sold for $78 million.

What a fulfilling day of sailing along a magnificent waterway, to actually see so many of the places that were stored in my memory come alive, with an added bonus of having the electronic docent's dialogue not only refresh my recollection of many of the sights and stories, but to add and fill in information that I forgot or wasn't aware of. What a wonderful learning experience. We disembarked the "Le Bateau-Mouches" and headed for the fabled Latin Quarter for lunch.

I wondered why an area in France would be called the Latin Quarter. I checked my French dictionary and found that it derived its name from the world famous Sorbonne University, where Latin was the common language for all students during the middle ages and, hence, the name Latin Quarter. We found a quaint sidewalk café with lots of pedestrian traffic on the rue Mouffetard Street, which is a primary artery where shops, international restaurants, student bars and cafes are in abundance. We enjoyed a wonderful French soufflé, a glass of wine, good conversation, and my favorite, watching the girls, oops, I mean, people go by. We spent a couple of hours walking around the neighborhood exploring the shops and admiring, up close, the incredible architecture and designs on the buildings. I was interested in the friezes on the building, while Barbara was more interested in what was inside them. We decided to spend the rest of the afternoon walking around and having dinner at a local restaurant.

For some reason, Barbara was pushing me towards the bridges that led to the Right Bank, and, although I was enjoying the left side of the Seine River, I acquiesced, as usual, and we meandered over to the Right Bank. As we were crossing the foot bridge, she began walking at a quicker pace and I began wondering what she knew that I didn't. Something was drawing her like a magnet to the rue du Faubourg St-Honore street, and then I knew. The great fashion houses of the world are represented in the stores along this street. Her secret designer city map identified all the stores in the area and the high-end clothing sold at each location; they were listed alphabetically in a directory order. She didn't tell me, but she had memorized most of the list for this expedition. She had all the information needed for her to spend the day in paradise. She said, "The entire world looks to Paris as the Grande Dame of Haute Couture and although Milan, London, and New York provide serious competition, the French designers are still every American girl's dream when it comes to clothing." I felt my wallet and bank account deflating at a very rapid pace. I didn't recall my wife as such a connoisseur when it came to clothing, but then I realized, of the 11 closets in our home, she occupies seven. She gave me a cryptic history of some of the designer clothing and of the latest fashions as we visited many stores, which featured designs by Hermes, Pierre Cardin, Louis Feraud, Yves Saint-Laurent, and Gianni Versace. She even knew that the popular Gucci had its Paris address in the neighborhood. Well, we spent the rest of the afternoon visiting many boutiques and buying some of the latest fashions. Barbara bought me a Gucci tie, which, to this day, I've only worn once. I was surprised when my wife told me that she was buying all the goodies with money she saved for this occasion--lucky me. Our afternoon ended in time for dinner, and we decided to eat at a local French restaurant and experiment with some more exciting French cuisine. After dinner, we entered what was becoming a "tunnel of love" due to its easy access and very clear train station directories, and inserted our passes for passage through the Iron Mistress to return to our hotel. Before retiring, we decided that our last day in the City of Lights would be spent at the Chateau de Versailles, which is a short distance from Paris.

We were up early in the morning and picked up our passes from Pierre to avoid the lines that he warned us would be at the

Chateau de Versailles. As usual, he gave us explicit directions using the Metro and RER (Reseau Express Regional), which was the train line that would get us to Versailles, located on the outskirts of Paris. Our plan was to see the Chateau first and then spend some leisurely time in the gardens. When we arrived, we were awestruck at the size of the Palace and its gardens, which seemed to extend as far as the eye can see. We immediately entered the Chateau through the marble courtyard and into the main Palace. Fortunately, audio head gear was available that explained in detail those parts of the Palace that we were interested in visiting; we put the equipment to immediate use. The audio docent boasted of the Palace being one of the largest in the world with more then 700 rooms, 2,000 windows, 1,250 fireplaces, 67 staircases, and more than 1,800 acres of parks and gardens. In its royal heyday, the Palace had entertained up to 3,000 princes, courtesans, ministers and servants. Among the main attractions are the royal apartments, which are so opulent it's difficult to comprehend that people occupied them comfortably. An amusing story is that the Royalty used the rooms in the winter, but had to abandon them intermittently in the summer months when the stench from their toilets became unbearable. Their toilet facilities were hidden behind decorated paneled doors and, although the servants serviced them regularly, when summer approached "all the king's men" and women left until the air cleared and it was safe to return. The Salon de Venus, like the Salon de Diane, preserved the austere, marble décor of the 17th century. An interesting statue of Louis XIV (the Sun God) as a Roman Emperor caught our attention and certainly reflected his future plans and ambitions. It's interesting to note, that with all his dreams of a glorious and spiritual reign, one of the things he is most remembered for today is his design of "high heels" for shoes that gave him more height, as he was unhappily only five-feet-three- inches tall. Currently, some women's high-heeled shoes are called French heels or Louis heels.

One of the most fascinating rooms in the palace is the Hall of Mirrors where the Treaty of Versailles was signed by the Allied and Associated Powers (mainly France, Britain, Italy, and the United States) with Germany in 1919 following WWI. This is the room where, due to the harsh terms of the treaty, seeds for WWII were planted. It's interesting that the magnificent Hall of Mirrors serves as a corridor between the Imperial War Room and the Peace Room; certainly an appropriate place to sign the Peace Treaty finalizing WWI.

Exiting the Palace, we both had stiff necks from viewing all the beautiful and decorative ceilings throughout the Chateau. We entered the Garden area, where we were overwhelmed with the size of the grounds; how do we begin to explore and enjoy 1800-acres-plus additional small palaces in one day? Well, the answer was simple. We boarded a little glass-sided train which ran through the gardens, making stops at the Grand Trianon and Petite Trianon Palaces and other points of interests. This allowed us the opportunity to appreciate the adventure, while sitting down and giving our feet and necks a well-deserved rest. The Garden's beauty is beyond description; when admiring them from the main Palace's upper floors, the panoramic view is breathtaking; but it appears as one large picture. When looking at the gardens from ground level, the perspective changes to one of individual beauty and artistic accomplishments. The grounds are laid out geometrically around a main axis, secondary axes, radiating pathways, and circular and semi circular pools known as basins. Everything is symmetrical and staggered on several levels. Trees are pruned to create a veritable architecture of vegetation. Closer to the Main Palace are flowerbeds, which complement the architectural features, especially when viewed from the upper floors of the Main Palace. One of our favorite sites was the Neptune Fountains and its water jetting scene; it's as if music is being played by the jetting water hitting the pond. While walking around the fountain, the sound of the music changes and, if one listens closely with a little imagination, a familiar melody will be heard in one's mind. The "Orangerie" garden is a gardener's delight. It was started in 1684 to protect the oranges and oleanders in cold weather. Six grassy lawns are defined around a large round basin by double hedges of boxes with multicolored flowers between them. What else can be said about the most beautifully created and maintained gardens in the world. It's no wonder that the king's head gardener and botanist, Le Notre, took 40 years to complete the formal gardens, fountains, jet waterfalls, statues, water flowers, Grand Perspective, and Grand Canal.

Our first stop on the glass train was the Grand Trianon Palace, built by Louis XIV as a hide-away for him and his family from the hectic court which he had moved from Paris to the Chateau de Versailles to escape from the unruly Parisians. After the demise of the French Monarchy, the Grand Trianon (called so after the Petit Trianon was built nearby by Louis XV) was occupied by Napoleon from 1805-1815 and today is used by the French President when entertaining foreign officials. As a matter of fact, the "Treaty of Trianon" between the Allied countries and Austria-Hungary concluding WWI was signed at this palace. Hungary lost over two thirds of its empire at the signing, which resulted in territorial adjustments establishing Romania, Czechoslovakia, the Kingdom of Serbs, Croats, and Slovenes. Although the gardens at this palace are not as elaborate as those of its big sister, the floral arrangement and decorations are certainly worth mentioning. The orange trees, floral flowerbeds, and the smell of jasmine combine to give a calming effect that sort of slow one's pace down to a slow stroll. It was getting late, so we didn't have an opportunity to explore and spend more time in the magnificent garden, but hurried on to the beautiful pink marbled Grand Trianon Palace. Our audio equipment came in handy, as we only stopped at places of interest and received all the information necessary to satisfy us. It's worth mentioning that Louis XV used this palace and its beautiful botanical gardens to rendezvous and stroll through the menagerie with his mistress, Madam de Pompadour. The madam eventually tired of the palace and convinced the king to build her a palace of her own. He agreed, and the Petit Trianon Chateau went to the drawing board. The Petit Trianon Chateau has a colorful romantic history. The idea for the chateau was conceived by Madam de Pompadour, but she never lived to see its completion. Instead it was subsequently occupied by her replacement, the king's new mistress, Madame du Barry. Upon his death and the accession to the throne by the 20-year-old Louis XVI, this Chateau and the surrounding park was given to his 19-year-old wife, Queen Marie Antoinette of Austria, whom he married at age fourteen. Our audio docent informed us that she used the palace to escape from the formality and burden of her royal responsibilities. She further alienated herself by making it difficult for anyone to enter the palace without her permission, which she gave very sparingly; this policy also applied to her husband, the king. She immediately began redecorating the Chateau to her own taste, with no cost spared, to make her feel at home in the "Little Chateau." In contrast to the formal, symmetrical French gardens that Versailles was renowned for, she commissioned a complete overhaul in these gardens, featuring meandering paths, hills and streams, and on an island, a small neo-Classical Temple of Love, commemorating her marriage to the king. A mock farming village, called The Petit Hameau (The Little Hamlet), completed this rustic area of the Versailles grounds.

The Petit Trianon is considered one of the most beautiful buildings in France. The exterior of the palace is simple and inviting. On the inside, it's difficult to determine the original decorating from Marie Antoinette's intrusion. The extensive woodwork and carvings are from the original building, but the most impressive site is her boudoir featuring mirrored panels, which can be raised or lowered to hide the windows. Her bedroom is quite simple, with more attention paid to securing her privacy than to artistic design. Time was limited, so we exited the Chateau, frustrated in not seeing more of it and the grounds, and headed for the train station. We promised each other that we would return to the magnificent palace in the future, and spend considerably more time exploring man's and nature's creations.

We arrived at our hotel in time to refresh, and quickly walked the few blocks to our favorite Italian, French, Jewish kosher restaurant. As it was our last night in Paris, we ordered an expensive bottle of wine; I intentionally went through the ritual of wine tasting at a very slow pace to savor the moment. We both ordered pasta smothered with egg plant; it was out of this world.

We arose early in the morning to catch our flight to Naples, Italy, to meet our Smithsonian Institute tour members and continue our adventure. As I looked out the window of the plane, I could see Paris in all its glory. We both promised her we would return. She smiled at us, and as we gained altitude and distance she disappeared from our sight, but not our minds or hearts. No doubt, we will surely meet again and, without a doubt, dance a Tango at the Moulin Rouge.

CHAPTER FIVE

Dancing in Italy

LOOKING DOWN AT NAPLES through the plane's window, I couldn't help but reflect that my mother's ancestors came from this city at the end of the 19th century. How times have changed. We were flying, at our leisure, by choice, to Italy for an extended vacation. They fled Italy in desperation to the United States in search of a better life, leaving behind generations of family history, traditions, and loved ones. I imagine that when they boarded their ship to the "Promised Land," their dreams of a better life, decent jobs, peace and security swelled their hearts with joy; while their tears reminded them of what they were leaving behind. Here we were two generations later, visiting the very country that my ancestors fled because they were unhappy with their circumstances. What a difference; our visit was one of pleasure and relaxation; their exodus was one of desperation, hardship and hope for a better life. Fortunately, the sacrifices they made by leaving their homeland for an unknown country resulted in most of their dreams becoming realities beyond their expectations.

We were able to locate the representative of our tour by the humongous sign displayed at the arrival waiting area: "Smithsonian Amalfi Coast Tour." What a relief to see our contact waiting for us. All the anxiety and uncertainty upon arriving at a new destination, especially in a foreign country, that traveler's experience, disappeared at the sighting of that very large sign. Our escort, Concetta, was standing under the sign with what seemed to be an equally large smile on her face. She directed us to the area where our specially-tagged luggage would be gathered by her assistant, while we waited. This was another nice experience. No searching for luggage; especially in a foreign airport where finding baggage is one problem, but communicating with someone if the baggage is misplaced or lost is, without a doubt, a nightmare. The assistant retrieved our luggage and placed it in a holding area, along with the baggage of several other tour members. Within an hour, we were on a small bus and on our way to our home for the next few days: the Bellevue Syrene Hotel, in Sorrento, Italia.

The hotel occupies a prime location at the seaside, on a cliff-top overlooking the Bay of Naples with a view of Isola di Capri. It's also next to the reconstruction of a Pompeii villa, which depicts a fascinating insight to the region's ancient history. The hotel's foundation was a Roman Villa dating back to the 2nd century BCE, and after several reconstructions it was transformed into the Bellevue Syrene Hotel. The name "Syrene" refers to the sirens from Homer's Odyssey, but certainly can be indicative of the serene atmosphere of the hotel and its surroundings. Getting to the hotel in our small bus was quite an experience. The driver had to maneuver it up a winding hill that could not accommodate our bus and a passing vehicle coming from the opposite direction at the same time. The Italian drivers have a system of horn blowing, utilizing every inch of the road while praying. While traveling up the winding road leading to our hotel, our driver would blow his horn when coming to a curve in the road. If there was no horn response from a vehicle coming from the opposite direction, then he would proceed up the hill. If there was a horn response, then by some magical signal, one of the vehicles would squeeze over to the side of the road allowing the other to proceed. The passengers did lots of praying, but the driver's skill got us to our destination safely. This whole scenario reminded me of some years ago when we were touring Rome, on a normal size bus, and the driver couldn't make a left turn into a side street because a small car was parked close to the intersection blocking the passage. He exited the bus and volunteered three male pedestrians to help him lift, with small jerking movements, the small vehicle onto the sidewalk until there was enough room for the bus to pass. When he passed the car, the driver exited again and he and his three helpers jockeyed the car back to its original place on the street. Italian drivers are without a doubt, amazing.

The hotel in Sorrento joins the Piazza Vittoria that complements its 18th century architecture which, fortunately, has not been damaged through its many restorations. Its 18th century antique frescos blend into the surroundings, enhancing its original style and justifying the hotel's listing as one of Italy's Historic Places, with terraces facing the Bay of Naples offering breathtaking views. A small elevator is provided for access to the beach area and a magnificent spa midway down the cliff. The spa includes a Roman Bath built into the rocks on the side of the cliff, a pool with hydro massages, and a relaxing sauna, which we put to good use in short order.

Before dinner we had a cocktail party for our group of 30-plus travelers and met our Smithsonian coordinator, docent, and driver. The tour leader-docent, Fran, briefly gave us an overview of our schedule for the Amalfi Coast trip and took the opportunity to have each member introduce themselves. The guide reminded us that this was primarily an outdoor tour and that we should be prepared for some strenuous walking and climbing. Just what Barbara wanted to hear! Her geological antennae was up as she couldn't wait to explore and dig; an amateur geologist's dream.

After the meeting, we proceeded to dinner at the hotel restaurant and were seated at a window with a view of the Bay of Naples, Mt. Vesuvius, fishermen attending their catch of the day and beautiful glimmering islands in the distance. We were fortunate to share a table with two members of our tour; Shirley and Dallas Peck, from the great southern state of Virginia. Dallas was the Director of the U.S. Geological Survey and one of the world's foremost geologists, specializing in volcanic eruptions- -one of Barbara's passions, in addition to her digging holes and discovering rocks. We became fast friends and spent most of the trip with them, enjoying their camaraderie and their wonderful ability to tell amusing and fascinating stories, such as: "They were both widowed and working for the U.S. Geological Survey. As he was the director of the organization, he had a privileged parking spot; number one in the parking field. After seeing Dallas at some business functions, and learning he was a bachelor, Shirley, the secretary, decided that he was the man for her, so she arrived very early one morning and parked her car in his parking space. She was immediately called into the personnel director's office and reprimanded for her poor judgment, and told to move her vehicle immediately to her usual place in the vast area at the back of the parking field. The next morning, arriving very early again, she parked in his number one spot again; this time Dallas told the security supervisor that he wanted to meet the perpetrator who had the audacity to park in his sacred spot, so he could personally discharge that person. So the redheaded Shirley, with a smile on her face and dressed for the occasion, entered Dallas' office to get her discharge papers. Instead, after salivating for a few seconds, he told the security guard to leave and asked Shirley if she would like a cup of coffee." The rest is history; her gamble paid off and a year later they married.

After dinner, our tour group met for additional orientation with Fran who addressed what to expect the next day on our visit to the ruins of the ancient city of Pompeii. She discussed in some detail the history, excavation, salvaging, and reconstruction of the one-time great city. The Smithsonian Institute's tours usually have an instructor with credentials accompanying them, which makes traveling to historic places all the more interesting. The hour lecture and distribution of material covering various topics of interest to the members of the tour, also gave us an opportunity to ask questions and to really delve into the next day's planned activities. After the meeting, we retired for the night in anticipation of awakening to an exciting journey the following day.

After breakfast, we boarded our tour bus for the short trip to the ancient city of Pompeii. While looking at the remains of this once great city, it's impossible to absorb or comprehend the complexity of the destruction immediately. It required much thought and imagination to envision the city as it once was before its earthquakes and volcanic eruptions. While we were pondering the unbelievable sites, Fran wisely recommended that we purchase an inexpensive book that was for sale at the entrance of the city square, which had overlay pages. The pages had the sites as we were experiencing them; when applying the overlay of the pages, we could see how the buildings and streets probably were prior to the time of their destruction beginning on August 24, 79 CE. The cobble-stoned streets seemed to be intact, laid out in the usual Roman straight line crisscross grid formation, making it easy to envision what the original city streets looked like. Walking on the stones of the streets where ancient Romans passed enhanced the feeling of being a part of the city thousands of years ago. The literature we received the previous night described how the "volcano collapsed higher roof-lines and buried Pompeii under many meters of ash and pumice." Pompeii, along with its sister city, Herculaneum, and other smaller cities located at the base of Mt. Vesuvius all experienced the same fate; total destruction. Fran guided us through the remains of the Forum, the Macellum (great food market), the Pistrinun (mill), the Thermopolium (a bar that served beverages), and Cauponae (small restaurant). We also visited an amphitheatre and two smaller theatres, but everyone's favorite was The Lupanara, from the Latin world "lupa" for prostitute; which was a two story brothel. Its rooms displayed frescoes depicting the services being offered to customers. We seemed to have spent more time in this building than we did on the whole day's outing. But it was lots of fun and amusing, to say the least. The most memorable sites were the mummified bodies of the Pompeiian's that were immortalized by the layers of molten ash from the volcano, which kept their remains almost intact, going about their daily routines and unaware of the calamity that was to befall them. The populations of the combined cities at the base of Mt. Vesuvius were estimated to be about 30,000 to 40,000 people. Fortunately, most of them escaped during the first signs of the impending destruction, as they had a similar earthquake scare in the year 62 CE, in which much of their infrastructures were destroyed. Still, it is estimated that thousands of people perished, many leaving permanent monuments of themselves in the form of well preserved skeletons. Fran's in-depth knowledge and explanations of the sites we visited made the whole experience exciting and helped us to envision what life was like during the heyday of this great ancient city, and of the day of its demise.

Considering that the event occurred almost 2,000 years ago, I asked Fran where all the detailed information about the destruction of the city came from. She had a ready answer: "Pliny the Younger, who was the 16-year-old nephew of Pliny the Elder, was eye witness to the two-day catastrophic volcanic eruption of Mt. Vesuvius that destroyed and buried the cities at the base of the volcano." She didn't go into detail about his two famous letters, as they were quite long and covered much detail of the event, but she gave us enough information so that we had a good understanding of what happened on those unfortunate days. Fran also distributed material to those who were interested in the details of the letters, which I was happy to receive. The contents of the two letters were written by the young man who witnessed an eruption column estimated to be 20-miles tall, from his perch on a hillside in the town of Misenum, across the bay from Mt. Vesuvius. I couldn't wait to read the details of what else he witnessed.

When we returned to our hotel in the late afternoon after a very fulfilling day, I read all the fascinating material that she gave me, and learned that Pliny the Younger, in addition to writing his two famous letters about the horrific event that took place in 79 CE, was also a prolific writer, poet and author of many books, and a natural philosopher of ancient Rome. He was counsel to Emperor Trajan, a Roman Senator, and held many high government offices throughout his life. His second letter about the eruption was written some 25 years after the event, focusing on his uncle's brave mission of discovery and rescue on those eventful days.

His uncle, Pliny the Elder, personified Roman intellect. He is regarded with the highest honors for literature; next to Homer, Cicero, and Virgil. His writing included "History of His Times," a 31-book collection extending from the reign of Nero to that of Vespasian; the "Naturalis Historia," a 160-volume encyclopedia, into which he collected much of the knowledge of his time; and 20 books on the History of the German Wars. He was a renowned author, naturalist or natural philosopher, and a naval and military commander of some importance. It was in his capacity as the Commander of the Roman Fleet at Misenum and his innate curiosity of nature that brought his life to a sudden end. During the volcanic eruptions, he took some of his ships to investigate and observe the phenomenon personally and to also rescue some of his friends from their perilous position on the shore of the Bay of Naples in the town of Stabiae. His nephew's second letter states: "The eruption can be compared in appearance to a stone pine tree; for it shot up to a great height in the form of a tall trunk, which spread out at the top as though into branches. Occasionally it was brighter, occasionally darker and spotted, as it was either more or less filled with earth and cinders. Several earth tremors were felt at the time of the eruption and were followed by a very violent shaking of the ground, the ash was falling in very thick sheets and then the sun was blocked out by the eruption, and daylight hours were left in darkness. Also, the sea was sucked away and forced back by an earthquake" (a phenomenon now called a tsunami). It was under these conditions that the Elder ventured out to "search, investigate, and rescue." The Younger continues: "He set off across the bay, but encountered thick showers of hot cinders, lumps of pumice and pieces of rock which, altering the shoreline and water depths, blocked his approach to the shore and prevented him from landing at his destination. The prevailing southerly wind also stopped him, but he continued South under it to Stabiae, where he landed and took shelter with Pomponianus, a friend. Pomponianus had already loaded a ship with possessions and was preparing to leave, but the wind was against him. Pliny the Elder and his party saw flames coming from several parts of the mountain, which would later destroy Pompeii. After staying overnight, the party decided to evacuate in spite of the rain of ash because of the continuing violent conditions threatening to collapse the building they occupied. Pliny, Pomponianus, and their companions made their way back toward the beach with pillows tied to their heads to protect them from falling rocks. By this time, there was so much ash in the air that the party could barely see through the murk and needed torches and lanterns to find their way. They made it to the beach but found the waters too violently disturbed from the continuous earthquakes for them to escape safely by sea. It is here that Pliny the Elder died." He is remembered in vulcanology, where the term "plinian" (or plinean) refers to a very violent eruption of a volcano marked by columns of smoke and ash extending high into the stratosphere. The term ultra-plinian is reserved for the most violent type of plinian eruptions. What an amazing piece of history; eye witnessed, written, and forwarded down through the ages so that we could understand and learn from that unfortunate event. With some imagination, while reading this material, I was transported back in time. I felt that I was a part of those two horrific days, if only briefly, occurring almost 2,000 years ago.

After dinner our group met for our evening orientation with Fran. She discussed what we would be seeing the next day at Herculaneum, the second largest city to be destroyed by the eruptions. After exploring the city, time permitting, we would then have an opportunity to scout around the base of Mt. Vesuvius. We retired to our room early after an exhausting day in the field, which gave us an opportunity to read the material that Fran had distributed at the lecture about the city of Herculaneum.

We woke early the next morning, and had our usual hot and cold buffet breakfast before boarding our bus for a short ride to Herculaneum. The city was established around the end of the 8th century BCE by the Oscan tribes from the Italian mainland. Although Pompeii and Herculaneum were destroyed by the same eruptions, the condition of Herculaneum after its partial excavation is quite different than its sister city. Whereas most of Pompeii's building's roofs were destroyed during the event, the buildings in Herculaneum remain almost intact. The reason is that the first eruption began spewing ash and volcanic stones into the sky. When it reached the boundary between the troposphere (extending 6 to 12 miles above the earth's surface) and the stratosphere (30-miles above the earth's surface), the top of the cloud flattened, leading Pliny to describe it as a "stone pine tree." The prevailing winds blew towards the Southeast, which caused the volcanic material to fall on the city of Pompeii and the surrounding area, causing the roofs in the city to collapse under the weight of the falling debris. Herculaneum lay to the west of Vesuvius, and was only mildly affected by the first phase of the eruption. Fortunately, the first event caused most of the inhabitants of this small city to evacuate, which, in turn, resulted in less loss of life than in Pompeii. It's believed that the loss of life in Pompeii was in the thousands and its smaller sister city in the hundreds. According to U. S. Geological Survey's research, "the amazing good state of preservation of the structures and their contents is due to three factors: (1) by the time the wind changed and ash began to fall on Herculaneum, the structures were already filled up; thus, the roofs did not collapse; (2) the intense heat of the first pyroclastic flow carbonized the surface of organic material and extracted the water from them, and (3) the deep dense tuff formed an airtight seal over Herculaneum for 1,700 years."

Excavation began at the modern city of Ercolano (a modern version of the original city's name) in 1738; however, excavation ceased once the nearby town of Pompeii was discovered, which was significantly easier to excavate due to the reduced amount of debris covering the site, 16-feet versus 60-feet. In the 20th century, excavation resumed in the city and, as it was submerged in a mass of volcanic mud that sealed and preserved wood and other materials, much of what was discovered was in situ (its original place and form). Although the city is much smaller than Pompeii, its intact remains make it a more dramatic sight; tourists walking around and exploring gave us a good idea of what the original living city must have looked like. Some of the excavated city lies about 60 feet below the modern city of Ercolano, giving the site a panoramic effect of a "before and after" picture; what the city looked like in all its glory at 79 CE and all its glory currently in the 21st century. In the meantime, the monster Mt. Vesuvius is still lurking in the background, smirking at the people who had the audacity to build on the very sight it destroyed almost 2,000 years ago. Many of our group discussed why people would build a new city at the very place that once was destroyed by a natural phenomenon, especially when the monster was still a living and breathing threat. We couldn't come up with a logical explanation, but we were not native Italians and didn't possess their passion for the land and country.

Fran guided us through what seemed to be a living city, with buildings, marbled floors, frescos, and furniture in situ. The most famous of the luxurious buildings, to date, is the Villa of the Papyri. It was given its name due to the 1,800 carbonized scrolls that were discovered in the early excavations, that are now located at the National Library in Naples for further evaluation. The villa was the seashore retreat for Lucius Calpurnius Piso Caesoninus, Julius Caesar's father-in-law. It stretches down towards the sea in four terraces. He was a literate man who patronized poets and philosophers, which explains the enormous library that was located in his villa, including the 1,800 scrolls. The most gruesome site of the city is the fornici (storehouses), where about 300 skeletons were excavated, all in their sleeping positions as they met their terrible demise. One interesting skeleton is called the "Ring Lady," named for the unusual rings still remaining on her displayed fingers extending from her mummified body.

Although Herculaneum had only a quarter of the population of Pompeii, with about 5,000 people, it was considered a wealthier resort, where the royalty lived and played, and, of course, had their own sports stadium. The large Palaestra was where a variety of ball games, wrestling matches, and other sports activities were staged and enjoyed by the populace. It's startling to see only a few of the estimated 20 peristyle columns of the sports arena, the remaining columns are still preserved under solidified volcanic mud beneath the city of Ercolano. One has to wonder how much of the ancient city will never be uncovered and remain buried and a continued mystery, beneath its modern counterpart.

After lunch we gathered for our planned visit to Mt. Vesuvius. Unfortunately there were heavy dark rain clouds over the monster, so Fran decided to detour to the Phlegraean Fields instead, which lies mostly underwater just west of Naples along the Bay. The field's name literally means burning fields, and refers to the highly volcanic nature of the area, a great place to stop and explore remnants of earthquakes and volcanic eruptions. Our destination was the town of Pozzuoli, where the Solfatara crater, mythological home of the Roman god of fire, Vulcan, is located. Solfatara is a shallow volcanic crater, and, although dormant, its ground is hot to the touch, emitting jets of steam and sulfuric fumes. The name comes from the Latin, Sulpha terra, "land of sulfur." Fumaroles, which are vents in a volcanic area that emit steam and hot gases, and the boiling pools of mud made the site surreal. When we reached the crater, Barbara and Dallas got so excited that they both raced ahead of our group, as if sprinting. I thought that they were going to jump into the mud pools and enjoy an unexpected bath, but they were saved by the yellow tape that cordoned off the boiling mud baths to prevent such ventures. The smell of sulfur was so overwhelming that most of our group remained at a distance, including me and Shirley; our reaction was to cover our noses and let out "eeews" sounds, while Barbara and Dallas inhaled the odor and responded with "ahhs." The smell was, without a doubt, the combination of rotten eggs and a football locker room after a strenuous game, plus some indescribable mixture of chemicals. The less adventurous members went into the 16th century Sanctuary of San Gennaro, built at the site of his martyrdom, which was near the entrance to the crater. Inside is a stone believed to have been stained with his blood that turns bright red and liquefies on his annual celebration in Naples. We then spent some time enjoying and taking pictures of the Greek and Roman ruins in the nearby surrounding area, which were, surprisingly, in disrepair. Due to the overwhelming odor of the place, we coaxed Fran to terminate the visit to Vulcan's home and head back to Syrene for well-deserved rest, aromatic baths, and showers to get the stench of the place out of our nostrils and clothing. After much persuasion, and some resistence from Barbara and Dallas, they decided to join the group for our return trip. On the bus ride back, Fran went over some details for the following day's trip to the Isle of Capri, and handed out literature, including street maps, about the history and geography of the "magnificent island in the sun." She then told us that we were free to have dinner on our own that evening. The four of us decided to give ourselves a relaxing evening in the town of Sorrento, which is a short walk from our hotel. The slow bus ride back to our hotel was a well-deserved respite, and gave me an opportunity to reflect on what I saw over the last couple of days. Although it's exciting to go from text book experiences to the actual places where ancient history existed and was written, visiting Vesuvius, Pompeii, and Herculaneum was bittersweet. All of the sites dealt with death and destruction, and I was happy that we were leaving behind those memories and continuing on to more pleasant adventures.

After refreshing ourselves, we met at the Piazza del Vittoria outside our hotel and strolled to Corso Italia, the main street in Sorrento, enjoying the sights along the narrow streets and the many touristy shops along the way. The town was buzzing with tourists, so we had to search for a sidewalk café with available seating and good views of the promenade of tourists shopping the varied shops and enjoying the abundance of restaurants. One restaurant in particular caught our attention; it was an English pub populated by English-speaking tourists enjoying themselves playing the game of darts, and for a moment I was transported from Italy to England. It was strange, but we all had the same experience. The predominant language heard while walking and reviewing the shops and restaurants was English, and it seemed that most of the tourists and locals spoke that language. We were pleased to find a sidewalk café playing local Neapolitan love songs where the waiters spoke Italian, and English only when necessary, giving us back the feeling of being in Italy. Both girls ordered gnocchi potato pasta with marinara sauce, and raved it was the best pasta and sauce they ever had. Dallas and I ordered pasta with local buffalo mozzarella spread over the top, complemented with eggplant in a meat sauce which was absolutely out of this world. We nursed our dinner with wine, espresso, and dessert so we could linger on and enjoy the music and festivities that were taking place in the square. Musicians were serenading the tourists and dancers were displaying their local talents and showing off their bright Neapolitan colorful outfits. Some dancers came to our table and coaxed us to join them in their festivities; Dallas wouldn't budge, but the rest of us ran out to join the dancing. We formed a circle with Barbara and Shirley at my side and danced to a Neapolitan Tarantella, which is a quick-motioned dance with lots of turns and kicks in 6/8 time. We truly "could have danced all night," but the half hour we did was out of a fairy tale, dancing and singing, and then singing and dancing some more. The whole experience was reminiscent of my family's parties when I was a young boy. Relatives would gather to celebrate a worthy occasion and, invariably, would end up singing and dancing in a circle led by my lively grandmother, Angelina, and my beautiful mother, Margaret. When the dancing in the square ended, the music continued and everyone around the square joined the chorus and sang

Michael Bivona

"Torna A Surriento" (Return to Sorrento). Few of us knew all the words, but humming the tune gave us the same wonderful exhilarating feeling. I loved the song so much that I had to find out what the lyrics were. After some passionate research, I came up with Italian and English versions, which were written by the brothers, Giambatista and Ernesto De Curtis, in 1902, as follows:

TORNA A SURRIENTO (De Curtis)	TORNA A SURRIENTO (Come back to Sorrento)
(Italian)	*(English)*
Vide 'o mare quant'è bello!	See the beauty of the waters!
Spira tantu sentimento,	How it plucks the very heartstrings!
Comme tu a chi tiene mente,	'Tis like you, whose glance seduces,
Ca scetato 'o faie sunnà.	though awake, to think we dream!
Guarda, gua', chistu ciardino:	Look, O look upon this garden,
Siente, siè' sti sciure arance;	smell the scent of orange blossoms,
Nu profumo accussì fino	scent so sweet it winds its tendrils
Dinto 'o core se ne va . . .	round about the inmost heart . . .
E tu dice: "I' parto, addio!"	Yet you say: "Farewell, I'm leaving?"
T'alluntane a stu core,	You'd desert these loving arms
Da sta terra de l'ammore . . .	and this very land of love . . .
Tiene 'o core 'e nun turnà?	Could you mean not to return?
Ma nun me lassà,	Go not away from me,
Nun darme stu turmiento!	break not my heart with sorrow!
Torna a Surriento,	Come back to Sorrento,
Famme campà!	that I may live!
Vide 'o mare de Surriento,	See the waves that lap Sorrento,
Che tesoro tene 'nfunno;	'tis in truth a jewel they cherish;
Chi ha girato tutto 'o munno	those who've never traveled far have never
Nun l'ha visto comm'a ccà.	seen its like in all the world.
Guarda attuorno sti Sserene,	See these sirens round about you,
Ca te guardano 'ncantate	gazing at you with enchantment
E te vonno tantu bene . . .	loving you so much and longing
Te vulessero vasà.	to bestow a fleeting kiss.
E tu dice: "I' parto, addio!" *ecc.*	Yet you say: "Farewell, I'm leaving!" *etc.*

We ended the festivities singing another Neapolitan favorite, "Funiculi Funicula." This song has always puzzled me. Everyone enjoys the liveliness of the music, but there seems to be much confusion as to the lyrics. While I was in the mood, I decided to research this song as well.

It was written in 1880 by Peppino Turco and set to music by the Italian composer Luigi Denza. It was written to commemorate the opening of the first funicular on Mt. Vesuvius. The Italian version, with English translation, is as follows:

FUNICULI FUNICULA (Denza) *(Italian)*
Coro:
Jammo, jammo, ncoppa, jammo ja, *(rip.)*
Funiculì funiculà funiculì funiculà,
ncoppa jammo jà, funiculì funiculà.

Solo:
Aissera, Nanninè, me ne sagliette,
tu saie addò? *(rip. dal Coro)*
Addò, sto core ngrato chiù di spiete;
Farme non pò! *(rip.)*
Addò, llo fuoco coce ma si fuje.
Te lasso stà. *(rip.)*
E non te corre appriesso, non te struje,
Sulo a guardà. *(rip.)*

Jammo, jammo, ncoppa, jàmmo jà *(rip.)*
Funiculì funiculà funiculì funiculà,
Jammo, jammo, jà, funiculì funiculà!

Coro:
Jammo, jammo, ncoppa, jammo jà, *ecc.*

Solo:
Se n'è sagliuta, oïe Nè, se n'è sagliuta,
La capa già; *(rip.)*
E ghiuta, pò è tornata, e po' è venuta . . .
Sta sempe ccà! *(rip.)*
La capa vota vota attuorno, attuorno,
Attuorno a te, *(rip.)*
Llo core canta, sempe no taluorno,
Sposammo, oïe Nè! *(rip.)*

Jammo, jammo, ncoppa, jammo jà *(rip.)*
Funiculì funiculà funiculì funiculà,
Jammo, jammo, jà, funiculì funiculà!

Coro:
Jammo, jammo, ncoppa, jàmmo jà *(rip.)*

Solo, poi tutti
Funiculì funiculà funiculì funiculà, *ecc.*

FUNICULI FUNICULA *(English)*
Chorus:
Come on, come on, to the top we'll go! *(rep.)*
Funiculi, *etc.*
To the top we'll go, funiculi.

Solo:
I went up this evening, Nanetta,
do you know where? *(rep. by Chorus)*
Where your hard heart can't reach
with scornful wiles! *(rep.)*
Where the fire burns, but if you run
you can escape it. *(rep.)*
It doesn't chase you nor destroy you
just by a look. *(rep.)*

Come on, come on, to the top we'll go! *(rep.)*
Funiculi, *etc.*
To the top we'll go, funiculi, funicula!

Chorus:
Come on, *etc.*

Solo:
It's climbed aloft, see, climbed aloft now,
right to the top.
It went, and turned, and came back down . . .
And now it's stopped!
The top is turning round and round,
around yourself!
My heart sings that on such a day
we should be wed!

Come one, come on, to the top we'll go!
Funiculi, *etc.*
To the top we'll go, funiculi, funicula!

Chorus:
Come on, come on, to the top we'll go!

Solo then All:
Funiculi, funicula funiculi funicula, *etc.*

Now we know that when we sing, or more likely hum, this song, it's about a sad romantic affair and a poor fellow trying to get some lost love out of his system, while traveling up and down in a mountain cable car. This rendition is sung by the great Italian tenor Luciano Pavarotti. There are many other versions of this song in Italian and English. The more popular

93

American version, "A Merry Life," which most school children learn, goes something like this:

> "Some think the world is made for fun and frolic, and so do I! And so do I!
> Some think it well to be all melancholic, to pine and sigh; to pine and sigh;
> But I, I love to spend my time in singing, some joyous song, some joyous song,
> To set the air with music bravely ringing is far from wrong! Is far from wrong!
> Listen, listen, echoes sound afar! Listen, listen, echoes sound afar!
> Funiculi, funicula, funiculi, funicula! Echoes sound afar, funiculi, funicula!
> Ah me! 'Tis strange that some should take to sighing, and like it well! And like it well!
> For me, I have not thought it worth the trying, so cannot tell! So cannot tell!
> With laugh, with dance and song the day soon passes, full soon is gone, full soon is gone! For mirth was made for joyous lads and lasses, to call their own! To call their
> Own! Listen, listen, hark the soft guitar! Listen, listen, hark the soft guitar!
> Funiculi, funicula, funiculi, funicula! Hark the soft guitar, funiculi, funicula!"
> Most people prefer the American upbeat version, and so do I! And so do I!

Our beautiful evening ended on a wonderful musical note, which we hummed as we journeyed back to our hotel for a well-deserved night's sleep.

Our bus ride to the ferry docks from Sorrento was brief, but gave me an opportunity to read the literature that Fran had given us the day before about the "Island in the Sun." She suggested that we pronounce the Island the Italian way "CAH-pree," instead of the American "Capri." If we did, she said "the natives wouldn't suspect that we were tourists." As we reached the docks, an unexpected rain downpour stranded us on our bus for about an hour, giving me time to catch up on my reading of the history of the Golden Island. It seems, but no one will swear by it, that the Island was first inhabited by the ancient Greek people of Teleboi, from the Ionian Islands (no dates available). The Etymology of the name is disputed between the Greeks and Italians. The Greeks insist it was named "Kapros," after the wild boars that inhabited the island, and the Italians claim its name was derived from the Latin "Capreae," after the goats that resided there. The tour members discussed the differences in the source of the name for about a minute and a half, and decided to enjoy the bus ride rather than exhaust the topic.

When the rain stopped, we quickly exited the bus and went to the departure gate for our ferry crossing to the magnificent island, which took about 40 minutes across the beautiful blue-green water of the Bay of Naples. Fran took the opportunity to review some history of the island and our scheduled day's activities. We settled into our comfortable seats and enjoyed some hot drinks, which helped to get the chill of the day's dampness out of our bones, while Fran gave us a brief history lesson about our destination. There isn't too much documented history of the Greek period, but the Roman era is filled with historically fascinating information, both actual and fanciful.

Caesar Octavius Augustus, the Roman Emperor, fell in love with his vacation island around 29 CE and, in short order, purchased it from the City of Naples, probably at a very reasonable price. His successor, Caesar Tiberius, moved his seat of power from Rome to the island, and spent ten years ruling the Roman Empire from this remote location. His claim to fame on the island is a cliff named for him called Tiberius' Fall, from which he and his successor, Caligula, deposited people that displeased them off the cliff from that high vantage point, onto the rocks and into the water. It's believed that Tiberius built 12 villas on the island, but only remnants of three remain. The most elaborate and his main residence, Villa Jovis, was one of our scheduled visits, time permitting.

Crossing the Bay of Naples was delightful and comfortable. The sun's beams reflecting and dancing off of the blue-green water were dazzling, and the smell of clean, fresh, saltwater air made my nostrils experience the same wonderful sensation as inhaling the fresh aroma of the first roses of springtime. One of the main features of Capri is the splendid geological formations of the three Faraglioni rocks along her jagged coast. In ancient Greek and Roman times, fires were maintained on the top of the rocks to assist their boats in navigating safely through the treacherous reefs surrounding Capri. They jut out of the water like pyramids. The largest, over 300 feet, is named Stella, or Star, and is attached to the island. The second, di Mezzo, or Middle, is over 240 feet high and has a natural tunnel, roughly 180-feet in length that passes through its center. Many boat tours sail through this large hole to the delight of their passengers. The third is named Faraglioni di Fuori, or Lo Scopolo (home of the blue-lizard), and is over 300-feet high. This rock is one of the few places in the world that has the blue-tinted lizard (Lacerta Viridens Faraglionesis) as a tenant, hence the name of the formation, Faraglioni. A fourth Faraglioni can be found away from this formation by itself, in front of the Port of Tragara, and is called Monacone, named after the sea lion or Monaca (Nun) seal that lived there long ago.

We disembarked our ferry at the port of Marina Grande. Looking back in the direction that we travelled, the mainland of Italy loomed in splendid contrast to the small idyllic island of Capri and its integral Faraglioni rocks, blue textured foliage, and surrounding reefs. Small white boats were zigzagging around the harbor, while hydrofoils and ferries created white lines in the blue-green water as they transported passengers to and from the mainland to the isolated destination. In the background is the ever present monster, Mt. Vesuvius, overseeing and monopolizing the panoramic view. We were quickly escorted to a nearby funicular, a cable car that would carry us upward to the Piazzetta of the village Capri Town, which is one of the two towns on the island, where the view of the island and surrounding waters are proudly boasted to transcend one's imagination of beauty. In short order, we were in the town square, window shopping and taking pictures of the decorative outdoor cafés, shops, people, and colorful assorted Italian flags, fluttering with the breeze, that were positioned around the square to generate excitement and smiles from viewers. We decided to do some shopping and then have lunch at one of the cafés, hopefully before spending our day's budgeted allowance in the inviting boutiques. Fran suggested that those of us who decided to have lunch in the square should try the renowned Capri Salad (Insalata Caprese), which is made of sliced tomatoes and buffalo mozzarella, and sprinkled with olive oil, basil and capers. It sounded good to us, and after shopping and almost staying within our spending allowance, we sat down at a beautiful outdoor café and had some local wine. It was white table wine for me and Barbara and red valley wine for Shirley and Dallas, accompanied by Italian delicious bread and plates of Insalata Caprese. My, oh my, how could we move from this imaginary place in paradise? Our stomachs made the decision for us, full past our expectations from a planned small lunch that seemed to never end, we dragged ourselves away to get a better view of the surrounding waters from our high vantage point.

We found a location that was truly a "Kodak moment" spot. Our cameras went wild, absorbing the surrounding spectacular scenery: turquoise/blue, crystal clear water, which seemed green/blue up close, but lightened from a distance; huge rocky cliffs with gardens interwoven and spreading their beauty in every direction; little white houses accenting the hills which seemed to be intruding on the flow of natural beauty that abounds in that extraordinary panoramic, dream-like setting. Of course, in the distance were Naples and the awakening sight of the monster, Mt. Vesuvius, which contrasted drastically with the natural beauty in our sights and made for a great backdrop in our photographs. After we calmed down from our idyllic experience, we had several choices of how to spend the rest of the day. Some in our group opted to visit Anacapri, the only other town on Capri. There are two ways of getting to this town, which lies above the town of Capri: walking up some 800 steps, which are believed to date back to Grecian times, or by motorized transportation. Considering the small winding size of the precarious road, which was finally built in the 20th century as an alternative to the steps, and looking at the endless steps, we decided to go back down to the Marina Grande and take a boat ride to the Blue Grotto.

Our return trip down on the funicular was much more fun than our first experience, when we were unsure of the safety of the cable cars. The passengers started singing some Neapolitan songs, prompted by the cable car attendant, which invariably ended the ride with our singing the American version of the song, "Funiculi, Funicula." We soon discovered that the Blue Grotto boat rides were best taken in the morning when the waters are calm. All the boats were staying in port for the afternoon, due to rough water conditions. What to do next? The four of us decided to find a scenic perch, get some drinks, and just enjoy the rest of the day by goofing off. We had no trouble finding a table at a nearby outdoor café and settled in for the remainder of the afternoon, drinks in hand, smiles on our faces, and good conversation. We decided that we would save the Blue Grotto experience for another time on a more extended vacation of the magical Island of Capri.

Our boat ride back, at about 5:00 P.M., was also more exciting than our original experience earlier that morning. We boarded a hydrofoil, which would get us back to our home port in half the time of our first crossing by ferry; 20 minutes versus 40 minutes. We decided to get seats on the upper deck so we could enjoy the magnificent scenery on our trip back; being an old salt, the wind in my face would be a welcome treat and considered heaven on earth to me. The hydrofoil moved forward and then up and out of the water as it increased its speed; we hadn't had time to settle in before we were disembarking. The calming affect that fresh saltwater air has on people is amazing; our short bus ride back was filled with yawns, and more yawns, with most of the passengers pleasantly napping. What a wonderful way to end our excursion to one of the most beautiful places on earth. We all promised that we would return, but for a much longer visit; like forever.

On our brief bus ride back to our home base, Fran reminded us that dinner at the hotel was included in the tour price, followed by an orientation of the next day's activities. After refreshing, we met Shirley and Dallas for cocktails in the lounge with views of the Bay of Naples and its tenants. We were joined by some of our tour members and enjoyed socializing and reminiscing about the past few days. We all agreed that the trip was as exciting as we expected, and more. It's human nature to be concerned about the next phase of a trip being as fulfilling as the current one, but invariably the new adventures are always just as exciting; so we toasted to tomorrow and all of the days to follow on our Amalfi Coast tour. We pried ourselves away from the camaraderie and strolled to dinner in the main dining hall, always startled at the magnificent view of the green/blue water scene and its varied occupants. We were reluctant to pick up our menus, as our clothes were starting to get a bit tight and there was a look of panic in the girls' eyes. Barbara and Shirley decided to have salads with no bread and no desserts for dinner, but Dallas and I couldn't resist the veal scaloppini with a side order of pasta in marinara sauce that our neighbors at the next table were having, so we ordered the same aromatic meals. The taste complemented the aroma and, if the girls were not with us, we would have devoured a second portion.

At orientation, Fran told us that we would be visiting The National Archaeological Museum of Naples the next day and handed out extensive literature explaining some of the more important exhibits that resided at the museum. The venue is considered one of the most important and leading archaeological museums in the world, containing extensive collections of Roman-Greco antiquities from the surrounding areas, including Pompeii,

Stabiae, and Herculaneum. The most famous and exotic exhibit is the Cabinetto Segreto (Secret Cabinet), containing artifacts of erotic or sexually explicit finds from Pompeii, which were deemed by the Italian authorities to be too obscene for public view. Therefore, they were collected and put in this mysterious chamber, under lock and key, and only viewed under certain strict conditions. We would find out what those restrictions were when we visited the Cabinet the next day, as they seemed to change daily. Of course, this information made everyone chomp at the bit to get the morning activities underway. We were told that our group would have a private docent who would guide us through the various exhibits and explain their significance and history. We were also informed that we would be spending the morning at the museum and had a choice of staying on unescorted for the remaining part of the day, or we could explore the city of Naples on our own. In any event, our bus would be ready for departure from the museum at 5:00 P.M. sharp, and it was strongly suggested that we leave promptly, as the city is not a safe place for tourists.

Before leaving for Naples, I asked our concierge, Vincent, if there was a place to do some ballroom dancing? He said he would gladly have the information for us by the time we returned from our trip. The four of us decided to spend the day at the museum, breaking for lunch at one of the outside cafés that we noticed on our bus ride through the city. We met our dark haired, olive skinned, beautiful, Neapolitan, thirtyish docent, Angelina, at the main entrance, on the ground floor. She briefed us on the exhibits we would be visiting, which included the world renowned Farnese Collection, the Egyptian section and, of course, the Gabinetto Segreto. She asked if there were any particular places of interest that we would like to see in addition to those mentioned, and most of the girls replied in unison: "The Farnese's Gem Collection." What a surprise; most of the guys were ecstatic at the prospect of their wives getting in the mood to buy jewelry, ugh!

We learned that the building we were in was built during the latter portion of the 16th century. It was originally the Royal Riding Academy, but, due to water shortages, it was transformed into the Palace of Royal Studies and the headquarters of the University of Naples. In the 18th century, when Naples was under the rule of the Bourbons, Ferdinand IV vacated the premises and established the Bourbon Museum and Royal Library. The Bourbons donated and are responsible for many of the collections at the museum today. When Italy became unified, the new regime took possession of the building, moved the library and art gallery to a new location, and gave the museum its current name. The most outstanding compilation is the Farnese Collection. It was begun by Alessandro Farnese, who became Pope Paul III in 1534. He started a new trend during his tenure; collecting antiquity and works of art for his private enjoyment. His predecessors' collections were primarily added to the holdings of the Vatican Museums in Rome. The ground floor of the museum displays many of his collections, including sculptures of the colossal statues of Hercules and the Farnese Bull, both uncovered from the excavation of the Baths of Caracalla in Rome. Both are Roman copies of ancient Greek antiquities, dating back to the 2nd century BCE. Of special interest is the spectacular Bull ensemble; a huge sculpture depicting the torment of Dirce, condemned to be tied to the horns of the Bull for eternity for her indiscretions and cruelty. His inscription and cameo gem collection are extremely impressive; the center of attraction is the Farnese Cup (Chalcedony Cup) made in Alexandria, which dates back to 150 BCE. It's made from sardonyx agate and is one of the largest cameos in existence. The girls were a little disappointed at the collection, as they expected to see diamonds, rubies, and other precious gems on display, such as those residing at the Museum of Natural History's gem collection in Washington, D.C., which includes the Hope Diamond. The Farnese's collection consists mainly of artistically- engraved intaglio and cameo antique jewelry, originally collected by such illustrious men as Cosmo and Lorenzo de' Medici, Pope Paul II, and Fulvio

Orsini. They include the aforementioned Cup, a cornelian of Apollo, Marsyas and Olympus, Artemis holding a Torch, and many other creative beautiful works of art.

The Egyptian section illustrated the relationship of the ancient world and Egypt, from the 4th century BCE. The main collection, begun by Cardinal Stefano Borgia in the 18th century, is the nucleus of the Egyptian sections. He was able to establish connections with Catholic missions around the world and was responsible for accumulating vast amounts of rare Egyptian antiquities from returning missionaries, resulting in one of the finest collections in the world. The second main Egyptian collection was accumulated by Giuseppe Picchianti, a 19th century traveler from Venice. He visited Giza, Saqqara, and Thebes in his quest for Egyptian antiquity. He collected many objects, but was mostly fascinated with funerary furnishings. Upon completing his journey, he sold part of his valuable collection to the British Museum and, after he died, the remainder was acquired by the Royal Bourbon Museum. Some of the fascinating collections are an embalmed crocodile; the funerary stele of the royal scribe Hui holding an ape; the statue of Anubis with a jackal's head; a statue of the God Serapis seated on his throne; and many mummies. We all rushed from these fascinating exhibits to explore the Gabinetto Segreto. The Secret Rooms should have been our first visit, as some people in our group were preoccupied with its contents, and became annoying in their anxiety and curiosity as they rushed Angelina through her well-planned dissertations of what we were viewing.

We expected to see a guard at the door of the Secret Rooms, but there was none. As a matter of fact, the door was open, and most of our group walked in past the signs stating that the rooms were a "restricted area for mature guests only" and a "special entrance fee was required to enter." Many of the ladies chose to remain outside of the chambers for obvious reasons, but one by one they eventually succumbed to the magnetism of the anticipated mysteries that awaited them. Before we entered,

Angelina gave us a history lesson on Roman morality and some background on the convoluted happenings of the venue throughout the ages. Although she did not join us in the Secret Rooms, she was well versed in its contents. Ancient Roman culture did not have the same standards that we have today in regards to sexuality; it was a normal part of their life and they chose to regard and display it with impunity. Different cultures viewed its openness in various ways, but in the 18th century, strict standards for obscenity developed into our modern day's concept of pornography. When the Enlightenment project for the excavation of Pompeii began in the 19th century, new methods of identification had been developed, enabling the experts to distinguish what was obscene and unsuitable for viewing by the general public; hence a definition of pornography was established in regards to the items uncovered. These precious relics were locked away in a Secret Museum, and the only people allowed visiting the stronghold were those with impeccable moral character. This excluded all women, and included mostly scholars and religious men. The nude statue of Venus Kallipygos, erotic to 18th and 19th century eyes, was included in the Holy sanctuary due to her partial nude body and the exposure of her "beautiful buttocks." To further the religious cause of morality, the doorway to the collection was bricked up in 1849. The stronghold was opened, closed, and reopened many times before its present day location at the museum. With this knowledge, we entered and began gazing and admiring the remnants of Pompeii's artwork, which was varied indeed, and included frescoes depicting sexual activity and sexually explicit symbols, depictions of the god Priapus doing his godly things, and even everyday household items, such as phallic oil lamps and kitchen utensils. The main male anatomy part was displayed in every imaginable way, doing the most unimaginable things. There was a lot of giggling going on from the females in the group and a lot of "no ways" coming from the male members. After seeing the contents of the rooms, I could understand why Angelina decided to remain in the outside corridor. After satisfying our curiosity, we left the popular area just in time for a late lunch. Before exiting, Angelina directed us to a large cork, wood, and paper model (scale 1:100) of the city of Pompeii, in its excavation stage in the mid-19th century. It's outstanding for its minute attention to detail, including the urban layout, monuments, and accurate watercolor reproductions inside the roofless replicated buildings. Thanks to this relief, there still exists today, reproductions of frescos and mosaics that have since been lost or destroyed. On exiting, I thought how incredible it is that relics, some dating back 2,000 years and more, have survived. Frescoes, sculptures, scrolls, pottery, gems, and other antiquities, have outlived not only the anger of the monster, Mt. Vesuvius, but the ravages of time, and are extant for civilization's perusal and enjoyment.

We said our goodbyes to Angelina with hugs and kisses, as if we were old friends or relatives. She strongly reminded us that the city of Naples was not safe and that we should be on guard for unusual happenings, and most of all to "travel in groups," as personal property was fair game for thieves in that populated busy city. The four of us felt pretty safe as we lived in large cities; Shirley and Dallas from the Washington, D.C. area, which is not only the capital of the United States but probably the crime capital as well. Barbara and I are from New York City, which is also known for its "misbehaved residents"; so away we went on our fearless journey to find a pleasant sidewalk café overlooking the center square of the city. We had our choice of several restaurants and chose one with a balcony view of the autos and bustling pedestrian traffic. It's shocking to walk the streets of a cultured metropolis and see the amount of litter scattered throughout; beggars were all over the place and approached people with impunity, hoping to either get a hand-out or to get their "hands-in" your pockets. We had to ward off several beggars and women carrying infants, who tried to get close to us to gain access to our valuables. Sitting in a restaurant and feeling safer than wandering around this noisy, crowded city, was a wonderful respite from our unpleasant experience on the streets of Naples. Watching the traffic moving at a snail's pace with inches in the back, sides and front of cars seemed surreal. Amazingly, the traffic did move, but ever so slowly.

We decided, being that we were in the city that boasts the invention of pizza, that we might as well enjoy one of the various types available, at somewhat reasonable prices. Their bragging that they make the "best pizza in the world" is well deserved; the aroma coming from the kitchen alone is worth the price of the pies. We shared two large pizzas with pepperoni, sausage, mozzarella cheese, and mushrooms. Italian Peroni beer was in order, so we ordered a few bottles and enjoyed the cool refreshing complementary flavor as we devoured our pizzas. We made a habit of ordering espresso after our meals; the coffee aroma was inviting and we quickly ordered the brew. There should be another proud boast in Naples; their delicious coffee, without a doubt, is one of the best I have ever enjoyed. It's strange, but back in the United States, Barbara and I avoid drinking regular coffee due to the hyper effect it has on us. But, in Italy, their regular espresso, which is somewhat stronger than what we are used to, gave us no concern, as we had no adverse reaction from its caffeine. After our leisurely lunch, we decided not to return to the museum, as it was getting close to our departure time. Instead we strolled through the crowded busy streets, window shopping, and being ever so cautious of our surroundings. While walking, another danger occurred, boys riding bicycles; they would come close to us and reach for the girls' bags, but being that we were from cities that have similar problems with street thieves; we stayed close to each other and away from the curbs, with the girls' bags tucked under their arms, away from the traffic flow. We were relieved to board the bus and return to our familiar comfortable place of rest. We were reminded that dinner was included in our tour price and there would be an orientation session covering the next day's relocation to the town of Amalfi.

Upon reaching the Syrene, Vincent approached us with a smile on his olive tan face and said he had two ballroom dancing venues for us to choose from. We took the information and returned to our room. One of the ballrooms was "The Foreign" Club in Sorrento. There was actually an excursion, "Evening under the Stars," going to the club that evening at nine-thirty, which gave us plenty of time to have dinner and get dressed, but we would have to skip the orientation. The brochure stated that the club is located in a big open piazza overlooking the Bay of Naples, with ample tables, surrounding a large dance floor paved with smooth stones; a live band would be delivering the music till the early morning hours. The price of admission included a first drink, a piece of cake, a glass of champagne, and ice cream. Not a bad deal. The only reservation we had was that the dancers, as the name indicated, would not be Italians. The second choice was another club in downtown Sorrento called the "Kalimera Club." It boasted three ballrooms, each large enough for ballroom competition. This seemed the more exciting and logical, as we would be at an Italian club dancing among the locals. We called Vincent and told him we would like visit the Kalimera Club, he said he would take care of the arrangements to get us there and make reservations for a good ring-side seat.

The four of us met for cocktails in the relaxing, beautiful lounge facing the Bay of Naples, and were joined by several other group members anxious to share their day's experience. One of the girls told us her pocket-book was stolen right off her shoulder by someone on a motor scooter, while she was walking and window shopping downtown with a group of friends. Fortunately the only things in the bag were comfort items, such as lipstick, wipes, etc. She made sure that her valuables remained in the room safe in the Syrene and her cash was in her pants pockets. We asked our comrades if any of them would like to join us at the dance hall. Arlene and Jack from Montana said they would love to, so we added them to our reservations with Vincent. After a couple of necessary drinks to calm us down from a stressful day in Naples, we went into the amazingly picturesque dining room, always smiling and enjoying the view from the large bay windows, of the serene waters surrounding the boats and islands on the distant horizon. Aside from the items listed on the menu, one of the main course specials for the evening were pesce de mare, consisting of shrimp, scallops, clams and other tiny shrimp-like fish, over linguine, in a red sauce. The second special was steak pizzaiola served with roasted potatoes. The girls decided to stick with the salad plates, while Dallas and I ordered both specials and shared them--what a delight. Of course, the girls managed to taste a little of each from our plates, satisfied that they were not betraying their diets by nibbling small portions from us. After dinner, we did have time for the orientation session, and joined our group in one of the conference rooms provided for that purpose.

Orientation for our next day's journey was exciting. We would travel north to the towns of Caserta, to visit the Bourbon's answer to Versailles, and to the town of Capua, to visit the scene of the great Roman rebellion by the famous gladiator, Spartacus. Fran handed out material which gave us some insight into both towns and their historical significance in their respective time periods. After our discussion, the four of us located Vincent in the lobby, where he was waiting hat in hand, to drive us to our destination. We were pleased that we were being escorted by someone we knew. He asked if he could join us at the dance hall. We were delighted to have this pleasant person with us; in addition to his good company, it also gave us an interpreter. We gladly accepted his request.

The place was only about 15-minutes away, but driving in the dark at night, along the winding roads bending around the mountain, lined with walls, in some places on both sides of the road, with only inches to spare on either side, is something I wouldn't want to personally navigate. Vincent's experience and familiarity with the terrain gave me a somewhat feeling of relief, but not entirely. Fortunately, the ride was short and, before we could wipe the sweat from our brows, we were at our destination in downtown Sorrento. The neon lights invited guests to enter this venue for happy times. Three large dance halls occupied the premises and loud disco music came from the basement, which had an unusually large dance floor enjoyed by happy young Italians dancing under the flashing, rotating overhead lights. The second hall was also quite large, and attracted dancers who preferred more subdued social dancing. The third hall extended partially outdoors for ballroom dancing. We sat in that room at a ring side table. There were about 60 other dancers and we were pleased to see that the patrons were well dressed. The ladies wore long dresses, most with slits down the sides of their legs, which enabled them to move around the dance floor easily. The men wore jackets or long-sleeved shirts and were impeccably groomed. We felt right at home, as Vincent had advised us that the dress code was not casual, so we dressed accordingly. The dancers were Silver International level performers, which is the preferred type of dancing in Europe, versus American Style, which is popular at home. They performed with the proper framing and footwork and were graceful and sophisticated in executing their dance patterns. International dancing is done in a closed position, with few fancy breaks. American style dancing is performed with more flowery open breaks, i.e., Fred Astaire's and Ginger Rogers' style of dancing. Whatever the preference, dancing with people at the silver level was an unexpected surprise. Arlene and Jack also danced at the same level, which made for a more enjoyable dancing experience, as no one felt intimidated by better dancers. The most obvious difference in a dance is Tango. There are basically three types: the International (in closed positions), which most of the patrons were dancing; the American (less rigid and allowing open positions), which no one on the dance floor was doing; and the Argentine Tango, which we do as a spot dance, staying in a small circled area, performing flowery and many improvised moves. Other couples on the floor doing the Argentine Tango performed the dance in salon style, which moves around the floor in the line of direction (counterclockwise) with the other dancers. The four of us were complimented on our dance styles in both Latin and Smooth dancing. The locals were very interested in how Barbara and I mixed our Tango between Argentine, American, and a little International; this is currently something new on the dance scene in the United States and is referred to as "crossover" dancing, where various dances are performed to the music of a specific dance, such as when Hustle music is played and Cha-Cha or Samba dances are performed. We also complimented many of the Italian dancers, of various ages from their 20s to 70s, on their interpretations. After admiring the locals' expertise and passion for dancing, it's understandable why so many Italians are world champion title holders in ballroom dancing. Many of the male dancers asked Barbara and Arlene to dance Latin, smooth Foxtrots and Waltzes. The smiles on the girls' faces expressed their delight with the performances that they were led into in the International style dances. Arlene remarked, "Now that's the way to dance." I didn't know if she was referring to the dancing or the handsome young Italian men who led her around the dance floor. Jack and I didn't miss out on dancing with many of the beautiful Italian ladies that gladly accepted our invitations. What a pleasure leading my partners around the dance floor with very little effort and lots of coordination between us. Whatever steps or styling that I led, they followed as if we had been dancing together for years instead of minutes. We made many acquaintances that evening and were invited to some of their homes the next day for dinner; unfortunately, we had to decline due to our busy schedule, but were tempted to find some way to visit with some of these most gracious and hospitable Italians. It was not to be, and after an amazing evening, we left the scene with lots of Italian hugs and kisses at 2:00 A.M., and headed back to our hotel to prepare for our next day's journey. We were fortunate to have Vincent with us; his understanding of the language made communicating with the locals enjoyable and put us at ease from the get-go.

An early morning start got us on our way to the town of Caserta. The bus ride wasn't long enough for us to get some much needed shut eye, as we were awakened several times by the loud speaker announcements from our constant companion and advisor, Fran. Her usual explicit dissertations informed us of what to expect at the Palace of Caserta, and the bus passengers' questions kept us awake and unwilling participants in the dialogue. But I did manage to snooze, as many of our comrades did, in between the sounds of chatter and loud speaker announcements.

The monumental complex at Caserta was created for King Charles VII of Naples in the mid-18th century to rival Versailles in France and the Palacio Real in Madrid, where Charles was raised as a child. Its primary purpose was to move the royal court's location from Naples, which was situated by the sea and exposed to the dangers of foreign invaders, to a more secluded and more readily defensible stronghold, with its own military barracks. The king was also determined to escape the tumultuous activity and filth of one of the largest cities in Italy, for the quiet and peaceful environment of this out-of-the-way inland location; bordered by mountains. The Palazzo was designed to bring together an extravagant palace, park, and gardens, surrounded by woodlands, hunting lodges, and a disguised industrial pavilion, for the production of silk. The plans called for approximately a half-million square foot fortress, with 1,200 rooms, two dozen state apartments, 1,742 windows, a national theatre, a 10,000 volume royal library, and a university; all insulated from the disorder, noise, and squalor of Naples. The plans were designed to emphasize the financial strength of the Bourbon's monarchy, but the king never spent a moment in his dream palace. He resigned his throne to become the King of Spain. It wasn't until the mid-19th century, that the palace was completed and occupied by Ferdinand II, and used as the royal residence and government administration offices, hosting countless balls, receptions, and hunting parties.

Several historical events took place in the Province of Caserta. In 1860, the famous "handshake" between Victor Emmanuel and Giuseppe Garibaldi took place. After spending most of his adult life fighting for the unification of Italy, including living in exile on Staten Island, New York, for many years, Garibaldi turned over his Army and authority to King Victor Emmanuel on October 26, resulting finally, in the unification of Italy under the House of Savoy. During World War II, the United

States' Fifth Army used the Palace as its headquarters and a rest and rehabilitation center for its troops. On April 29, 1945, the surrender of German forces to the Allies took place at this location. In the 1999 film, Star Wars Episode I: The Phantom Menace, and, again in the 2002 film, Star Wars Episode II: Attack of the Clones, the palace was used as Queen Amidala's and Queen Jamillia's residence, respectively. The same area was also used in Mission Impossible III as a holy room in Vatican City. The action scene where a Lamborghini is blown up is the square inside the Palace of Caserta.

I was unable to see the entire outside walls of the half-million square foot complex from the window of our bus. It is humongous in its size and incomprehensible in the synergy required to produce such a magnificent structure. It's the crown jewel in the midst of a 300-acre paradise, surrounded by protective esplanades, formal gardens, ornate fountains, a Large Fish Livery, a miniature Castle, an English Garden, an Open Air Theatre and a magnificent water fall, enriched with many sculptures. The park starts from the back facade of the palace, flanking a long alley with fountains and cascades fed by the incredible architect, Vanvitelli's Carolina Aqueduct, extending to the nearby mountains for about one and a half miles. When looking at the pools and alley way extending to the horizon, my field of vision was engulfed with the view; there was no room for anything else. Fran allotted an hour's time for us to visit the park and then return to the entrance of the fortress, where we were dropped off, to continue our visit into the Palace and its beautiful antiquated exhibits.

We didn't have much time, so we hired a covered horse-drawn carriage to carry us through the immense scenic park. We let our horseman, Antonio, decide which of the many beautiful places we should visit, while we sat back and enjoyed the ride. We were not surprised that Antonio spoke perfect English, as many Italians do, but he had a very pronounced Brooklyn accent. He explained that he spent most of his teenage years growing up in the Italian East New York section of that borough, which is where I was born and bred. It was precious to hear a mixed Italian and Brooklyn accent again; it reminded me of my relatives who came from Italy and spoke with the same inflection. It put a happy smile on my face all day, especially when he narrated the sights we were visiting. Closing my eyes, I was almost able to visit with my long-departed father, Luciano, and my grandparents. All came from Italy and had the same sounding voice as Antonio. He decided that due to our time limitation, the best approach would be to begin at one of the furthest sculptured fountains and work our way back to the entrance of the palace. The Fountain of Diana and Actaeon was our first stop. The ensemble is in a basin supplied by a water cascade with large rocks as a backdrop, fed by an impressive waterfall from above, which boasts 14 statues of huntsmen and huntswomen supported by balustrades. The group sculpture of Actaeon depicts hunting dogs attacking their master, Actaeon, who was turned into a stag. According to our narrator, one of the most prevalent myths surviving is: "Actaeon, a famous Theban hero, trained by the centaur Cheiron (master of many arts and science), suffered the fatal wrath of Artemis (Diana) when he stumbled across Diana bathing, thus seeing her naked. He stopped and stared, gazing at her beautiful body, which left him speechless. As punishment, she forbade him speech; if he tried to speak he would be turned into a stag. What retribution, all because he saw her sacred body; or because upon seeing her, he didn't take any manly action toward her. Subsequently upon hearing his hunting dogs, he called to them and instantly turned into a stag. The dogs immediately attacked him and tore him to pieces." Truly a Greek tragedy! We stared at the marbled presentation of this popular myth, which defies description. How such a depressing story could turn into a beautiful sculpture, depicting a pack of hunting dogs tearing a man-stag into pieces, is beyond my comprehension. The silvery pond surrounding this group, the rocks and cascade background, turn this horrific sight into one of mystery and beauty, so common in the works of Italian artisans. To balance this sculpture with a more pleasant beauty is a magnificent group of ladies: Diana surrounded by Nymphs, as she prepares to bathe. You could almost hear them singing while attending to Diana, quite an impressive sight and a more enjoyable vision than its neighbor. Antonio decided to restrict the remainder of the tour to some of the other fountains situated along the road back to our starting point.

We were frustrated, realizing that it would probably take more than a whole day to begin to appreciate what the park had to offer, not the mere hour we were allotted. While briefly passing the incredibly luxurious formal English Gardens, which we had no time to explore; Antonio described some of its exotic flora, glasshouses, a beautiful little lake with a statue of Venus bathing, a chalet, and groups of ruins, including a miniature Roman temple and a botanical garden. What a perfect place to bring a picnic basket, blanket and some music, and pass the time of day sipping on a bottle of local Italian wine. Next time, we will certainly devote more time to this incredible locale, which combines nature's beauty with the creativity of Italian artisans. Again the threatening Mt. Vesuvius was evident in the background; its majestic appearance put our cameras in action, as the film absorbed the beautiful scenery with the monster and the sky as wallpaper.

Our last stop was the Fountain of the Dolphins. Again I was looking at my watch and wishing we had more time to appreciate the beautiful sights we passed on our return trip. I would certainly make a point of mentioning to Fran, that spending only a half a day in Caserta exploring the park and palace is not conducive to a well-planned study sightseeing tour. Antonio was full of information about the spectacular Fountain of the Dolphins. It was a monumental aquatic fountain with three enormous dolphins protruding from rocks, spouting water from their mouths into a huge fishpond. The large curious fish inhabitants would follow our shadows on the water in whatever direction we were walking. In the days when royalty reigned, the pond supplied fresh fish for the tables of the elite and their guests. I could just envision an elongated dinner table, dressed with the finest accoutrements, being used by these privileged people, enjoying their delicious fresh fish, prepared by the finest Italian chefs. I could smell the aroma of the most gourmet food in the world and almost taste the cuisine. Unfortunately, we still had a couple of hours before our scheduled lunch stop on the way to the town of Capua. It wasn't easy pacifying my whetted appetite, but a packet of peanuts in my carrying bag took the edge off of my hunger. We hugged and kissed Antonio, thanked him for his friendly and informative guidance through the gardens, wished him lots of luck, and then joined our tour group for the next phase of our journey.

We were allotted an hour and a half on our own to explore the Palace. Electronic docents were at our disposal to explain the various places of interest we were visiting. Describing the appearance, after entering the facility, is beyond my capability, but the hand out pamphlet summed up what I saw precisely: "The entire complex suggests the idea of order and symmetry, but it also conveys strong integrations between central power and State administration, and between the court and its subjects. This relationship between the building and the park, created by means of the gallery-telescope and constituting an integral part of the fabrication, appears clear and rigorous against the emerald background of the lawns, which makes the white avenues stand out. The mass of trees, open in the middle, show the expanse of water in the distance, modeling itself to the contours of the land. In this sober austere picture, the spirited architecture of the Palace appears in all its monumental worth, in which space, colors, shapes and surfaces unite in unmatched unity of expression." Thanks to the creativity of the architect, Vanvitelli, and his benefactor's generosity, their plan to build one of the most magnificent palaces in the world was accomplished. The pamphlet continues: "One of the most delightful Vanvitellian innovations is the use of galleries and vestibules, which are aligned to the axis of the building, and the aesthetic and practical purpose given to them, intrinsically connected to the development of the main design. The internal circulatory system is perfectly achieved with radial passages which connect the vestibules to the courtyards and entrance halls, which, in turn, link the courtyards with each other and the exterior. A balanced network of passages and squares facilitate the performance of parades, balls, processions, and banquets, without confusion, blockage or conflicts. The vestibules are peristyle octagonal, capped by column-supported vaults. The central one is very wide and bright. On the right is the royal stairway; on the left is the statue of Hercules balanced on a podium. Opposite, against the green background of the hills, the waterfall glints in the sunlight; 'that crystalline obelisk, upright upon its fantastic base contrasted by the white ribbon of the avenues.' The courtyards, are as wide as squares and are seen through the arches of the gallery. They all have a function in accordance with the standards of Vanvitellian architecture. In the Royal Palace, the place of the courtyard is taken by the axial gallery, offering a deepened perspective. The four courtyards are sources of light, places of transit or for lingering; factors necessary in the playing out of the life at court." The dissertation must have been written by a poet. Not only did it describe the visual aspect of the setting, but it also captured the feeling and excitement of the moment.

The right side of the central entrance hall is the Stairway of Honor, which leads to an upper encircling line of columns, opening into a chapel and the Royal apartments. A brightly lighted stairway, made from a single piece of marble, leads to dual staircases guarded by two symbolic lion statues. The lions are there to greet all visitors and to remind them that they are in the midst of a powerful presence. Viewing the two parallel stairways on opposite sides of the hall, each guarded by a male feline, we proceeded with caution, ever aware that we were being watched by the two authoritarian cats. Barbara and Shirley took the right staircase and Dallas and I the left. The magnificent colors reflected from the various shades of marble throughout the hall leading to three arches at the top of the flights are picture frame perfect. I felt as if the view at the top of the steps was an enormously large painting, instead of the reality I was witnessing. The elegant vaults gathered together in a cupola, the arches and cornices and the three archways linked to the stairways gave testimony to the prolific genius of Italian artisans: truly, an unmatched, one-of-a-kind architectural delight.

We chose to continue on to the Hall of Nativity, where a three dimensional manger scene representing infant Christ and entourage are replicated in human size. The more important pieces are done in clay, while other statues have heads and limbs of clay, and bodies of wire and oakum. The statues and ornaments are placed on a bed of cork, in accordance with religious canon respecting scenes like the Nativity. The display of the Presepio (feeding through), signifying the Christ Child's initial resting place is a widespread custom throughout the Christian and, particularly, Catholic world. This tradition is traced to the 13th century, when St. Francis of Assisi celebrated mass before a sculptured group of the Holy Family, flanked by a living ox and ass (sometimes described as a "living Presepe," consisting of costumed people as well as animals) in a small village setting. An industry has developed in the Naples area that produces statues and figures that are displayed in manger scenes throughout the world at Christmas time; continuing a tradition established by the Bourbon Kings in the 18th century. Every year, the Royalty, princes, and even ladies in waiting, would participate in a joint venture, creating different presentations of the Nativity scenes, and proudly displaying their new creations for the Christmas season. The tradition is still carried out today. I remember as a youth, my grandfather, Peter, who was from the Naples area, building a Nativity scene from clay and a variety of stones, painted to present hair, eyes, and other appropriate bodily parts. Clothes were handmade to dress the entourage and decorate the manger. There was the Christ Child in a manger, watched by Mother Mary and Father Joseph, and three wise men and several animals breathing on the Child to keep him warm from winter's cold air. Then, I didn't realize the traditional significance of that scene and the love, patience and skill required to produce such a beautiful display for our Christmas seasons, but I do now.

A view of the Presepio with hundreds of terra cotta figures created in the 18th and 19th centuries is magnetic and overwhelming in its complexity. The figures are extremely realistic, inviting the viewer's imagination to enter and become part of the diorama. The manger scene is exquisite in its life-like presentation. A feeling of warmth ran through my body as I was drawn into the barn scene of which I was so familiar, recalling my religious lessons and the family stories told over and over throughout my life about that spiritual event. Another interesting scene is that of the journey of the Three Kings, detailed with a black woman suckling on a camel followed by their entourage consisting of small black children, a small camel, and a hand-traveling carriage decorated in the finest cloths. After glancing at my watch, I gathered my friends so we could visit some other places of interest before our remaining time ran out.

From the literature that Fran distributed, we decided to visit the controversial Queen Maria Carolina's rooms and her Palatine Library, which is home to over 14,000 books and documents. She was the daughter of Queen Maria Theresa of Austria and Francis I, Emperor of the Holy Roman Empire. Maria Carolina was one of 16 children; her younger sister was the extravagant and unfortunate Maria Antoinette, Queen of France, whose famous words after hearing of her subject's plight, supposedly remarked: "if there is no bread, then let them eat cake." Of course she and her husband, Louis XVI, were beheaded for their reckless administration and wasteful spending by revolutionary partisans. Her oldest sister, Maria Louise, became the second wife of Napoleon I, Emperor of France. Queen Maria Carolina was betrothed to Ferdinand I and married at the young age of sixteen; her husband's age exceeded hers by one year. The new Queen was able to dominate her marriage and the running of the monarchy as her mother did with Emperor Francis I. Her mother made sure that all her off-springs were educated and prepared for the rigors of Royal life. Her father was an enlightened Freemason member (believed in the Brotherhood of Man under the Fatherhood of a Supreme Being), and was very liberal in his actions and thinking. The young Queen Carolina immediately took charge of the administration and running of the Bourbon Kingdom. Over the years she replaced French and Spanish influence in the court and country with that of the English, going as far as appointing Sir John Action, an Englishman, as Minister of the Navy, Minister of Finance, and finally, Prime Minister. Sir John seemed to have dual roles as Minister: that of keeping the kingdom in England's sphere of influence and the more important role of administering to Maria Carolina's personal needs. Considering that her husband's father was King of Spain and abdicated his dominions in Italy to his third son Ferdinand I, and that her sister, Maria Antoinette, was Queen of France, it was a neat maneuver that she could accomplish a change in influence without going to the guillotine herself.

Being her mother's daughter, although ruling her domain was a full time endeavor, she still had time to do one better than her mom; she had 17 children. Most of the work on the Royal Palace was accomplished under the supervision of the two monarchs, including much of the landscaping and, in particular, the English Carolina Gardens. The garden designers were imported from England to create a beautiful formal setting that contrasted with the surrounding rural area, and was in keeping with her attachment to England, especially after the execution of her sister by French revolutionaries. The relationship worked to the monarch's benefit, as England's military came to their rescue on more than one occasion while they occupied their dual thrones. The queen was also her father's daughter in her belief in Freemasonry (Brotherhood of Man under the Fatherhood of a Supreme Being), although her acts were often criticized for not practicing her beliefs, as she was dictatorial and quite often cruel; particularly after the assassination of her sister, Maria Antoinette. Many of her accomplishments were due to her conviction in human progress and enlightenment during the New Golden Bourbon Age. We briefly visited her apartments which consisted of four rooms decorated in typical rococo taste. The first room (Work Room) is striking in its yellow satin walls and framed mirrors; a Stucco Private Room leads to a bathroom and private toilet, with Venetian mirrors and white marble baths. Passing her sealed Boudoir, which was closed for cleaning, etc., is the Company Room and Room of the Ladies in Waiting, decorated in bright friendly colors. Finally we arrived at the rooms we were interested in and were also part of the queen's apartment. Two reading rooms lead into the three rooms of the Palatine Library, which was considered her true "Kingdom." She again chose to import foreign artists to do extensive paintings and frescos; the German painter Friedrich Fugger chose classical images for the rooms assigned to him. The themes celebrated the new Bourbon "Era of Gold." He created a fresco, "the School of Athens," which emphasized the banishment of ignorance and the protection of the arts, in accordance with her beliefs in Freemasonry. His other paintings continued with the same theme. Outstanding is a rotating small mahogany and rosewood library case created according to her wishes, which were freshly stocked with books to facilitate what she was interested in reading, whether for Royal business or pleasure. A display of an ancient telescope and antique earth globe rounded out the impressive 14,000 volume library. An unusual painting done by the Italian artist Forgola, "The Inauguration of the Naples Railway" in 1840, which is out of the queen's time period, is proudly displayed in the Reading Room and captures the essence of what she was trying to accomplish: "Enlightened people do remarkable things." We found ourselves again racing against the clock, as our scheduled time was running out. We had just about enough time to visit The Court Theatre before joining our tour group, so we walked at a quick pace and entered the astonishing mini replica of the San Carlo Theatre in Naples.

The Bourbons established themselves in Naples in 1734 in an age where the French court influenced most of European culture with its levity, love for luxury and comfort, love for music, poetry and literature, and even for the sciences. It was at this time that King Charles had the 3,000-plus seat, San Carlos Theatre built to reflect the power of the Bourbon's and to show off his prize city of Naples, which at that time was considered the largest city, by population, in Europe. Till this day, the theatre is considered one of the most beautiful opera houses in the world, still drawing performers of the highest caliber, such as Luciano Pavarotti. When he decided to build the inland Royal Palace at Caserta, to escape the hazards of invasion by sea and the eruptions of Mt. Vesuvius, he subsequently added a small version of the San Carlos Theatre to his plans for the palace. The Court Theatre was not in the original plans by the architect Vanvitelli, but was the only project that he saw completed during his lifetime; most of the remainder of the construction was to be completed by his son, Carlo, and Charles' third son, Ferdinand, and his wife, Maria Carolina. The San Carlo Theatre was built in eight months, while its younger sister's 400-plus seat Court Theatre took over ten years. Supposedly, the smaller theatre is an exact reproduction of the San Carlo Theatre and was completed by the inauguration of the wedding between Ferdinand and Maria Carolina. There are three staircase entrances into the theatre of which two were closed; the Royal entrance in the middle and the second public entrance. We walked up the marble staircase to the opened entrance and were startled by the ambiance: the layout of the theatre was the usual horseshoe in shape, with 42 private boxes, finished in imitation marble placed in five rows, all decorated with cupids and floral festoons of various types. The royal box was the size of three boxes, with rich drapery in Bourbon blue with golden lilies. Looking directly ahead at the stage, the back curtains were open, giving us a surprising view of the park. We were lucky as there was a rehearsal going on for a flute concert; so we rested for a few minutes and enjoyed the music and the opulence of the venue. My mind drifted back to an earlier time, when the music hall would have been occupied by privileged Italians and guests attending a concert, opera or play, and taking pride in seeing their king and queen displayed in the royal box enjoying the performance. The Bourbons sure had the feeling of the period; luxury and comfort for us now, and worry about tomorrow later. Unfortunately, tomorrow would come sooner than expected, and the period of royalty in Europe would quickly fade away. It was time to catch up with our tour members, so we departed quickly to meet our bus and have a light lunch on our way to the town of Capua, which was just a few miles north of Caserta.

We stopped at a quaint Italian restaurant, decorated in bright Neapolitan colors: red, blue, gold and pink. There were many paintings on the walls showing off the seashore scenes along the Amalfi Coast, with emphasis on the blue-green water, small boats, and Capri in the background. There was also an attractive display that seems to be found throughout Southern Italy, especially Sicily: colorfully painted wagons referred to as Sicilian wine carts (carretti), ranging in sizes from six inches to two-feet. Traditionally, these carts were used to transport wine and food in the small villages. The scenes painted on the sides reflected the history of a particular village or location. Especially colorful were the carts depicting legends and historical events of their country or locale. It immediately transported me back to my youth; my ancestors displayed similar carts, usually in a prominent place; the art work, probably depicting the history of their towns or favorite legends. Unfortunately I didn't know the significance of the objects or I would have somehow made a point of inheriting one or all of them. Some of the carts also displayed painted mini-donkeys, which were done in colors representing the corresponding towns of origin. The restaurant's atmosphere is forever etched in my mind, especially the likeness of the carts to those proudly displayed by my relatives. We were the only patrons in the restaurant, as Italians don't eat their lunch at one o'clock; they prefer a 3:00 P.M., extended lunch and a very late dinner. We were expecting a light lunch, but a buffet of fish, veal, mozzarella, tomatoes, and antipasto was laid out and was too beautiful to pass up. We indulged ourselves as if it were our last meal on earth. Of course, we complemented the food with local Italian red and white wines. It was easy to forget that we had another stop before our trip to the Town of Amalfi, where we would be spending the rest of our trip. Fortunately, Capua was a short distance away, so after what seemed to be a never-ending feast, we reluctantly exited the hospitable restaurant, and bid farewell to the owners and staff in a manner that would suggest a long-standing relationship with them, instead of the two hours we spent enjoying the wonderful cuisine. I was wondering if the bus could accommodate the extra weight we were bringing with us from all the delicious food we had consumed.

I took the opportunity to read the literature Fran distributed the night before to familiarize myself with the ancient town we were visiting. Two historical events propelled Capua into prominence: its defection to Hannibal in 216 BCE, followed by its subsequent recapture and harsh punishment by Rome in 211 BCE, and the fact that it was the birthplace of the gladiators' revolt led by Spartacus in 73 BCE. The original city (Casilinum) was evacuated during an invasion in the 2nd century CE. The modern city of Capua was established a few miles north, while the ancient city was rebuilt and is now the modern city of Santa Maria Capua Vetere. Our destination was the former ancient city to investigate the Coliseum-amphitheatre that is one of the largest structures in Italy, second only to the one in Rome. Some experts believe that it predates its brother in Rome, while others claim that it was built 100 years after the more popular one in the Roman capital. Whatever the case may be, it did not exist when the Spartacus revolt took place in 73 BCE. Cicero wrote: "the amphitheatre seated up to 100,000 people," but this has been disputed by modern archeologists who claim that it could hold no more than 50,000 spectators. In either case, both numbers are a respectable representation of the size and complexity of the site. The structure is colossal in size and no better for the wear and tear that has occurred over the centuries. It is in worse condition than its bigger brother in Rome, but it does have enough remaining so that with a little imagination it comes to life easily. With an overlay booklet that I purchased at the entrance center, the coliseum is resurrected on paper and in my mind, with many extinct decorations and smaller buildings, shown in all their glory, and glory it was. The site was an architectural delight, high columns and arches surrounded the structure, created with sweat, blood, and whip lashes, and all handmade; certainly a testament to Roman ingenuity and their effective use of slave labor. The difficulty of running a sports arena of that size without the modern technology we have today, is to say, at the least, amazing! Throughout the structure there are stairways and ramps; animal and man-drawn elevators strategically located to bring the gladiators, scenery, and beasts to the arena's surface from the underground vaults, for their scheduled performances. Crowd control was accomplished much as it is today: numbered tickets were given to the spectators directing them to the gates, stairs, and levels where their seats were located. Most of the structure lies naked of its once beautiful marble and decorations, leaving the underlying brick exposed to the elements. The site could use some serious major renovating and, if done, would most likely bring enough additional revenue from tourists, who would spend more time at the location, to cover the costs of restoration. For instance, the grounds are covered with litter, and there are probably hundreds of friendly, well-fed stray cats and dogs wandering around, unattended, their droppings covering a good part of the walking sites. To compound the problem, it is very difficult walking around due to the many unsafe areas, in addition to many off limit ones. Although the main structure and surrounding area were worthy of further investigation, most of our group couldn't wait to leave.

On our bus trip back to the town of Amalfi, I read extensively about the gladiator, Spartacus, and his true story, versus the popular movie version. Spartacus was born in Thrace, which was probably, but not absolutely, a part of Greece. Today many countries claim it was a part of their territories, such as: Greece, Turkey, Bulgaria, and Macedonia. It's likely that he served as an auxiliary in the Roman Army and became a slave as punishment for deserting. The instigating reason for the revolt of the first 78 gladiators was probably their harsh treatment at the school of Lentulus Batiatus, near Capua. Upon scaling the walls of the training center, they were fortunate to come across an unguarded wagon loaded with weapons. This gave them the opportunity to begin supplying themselves and new recruits with sophisticated weapons and, thus, started what was to become an enormous slave army that would threaten the Roman Empire's existence. Initially, their objective was to flee Italy and the oppressive conditions that they were subjected to, but they became so successful at raising an army, estimated at its peak to be upward to 125,000, that they began systematically pillaging for profit and power, overcoming any opposition from Roman legions. During their peak, they made their headquarters at the base of the Monster, Mt. Vesuvius, winning all of their battles against Roman legions at and around that area. In the two years that they were plundering and roving most of Southern Italy, they defeated the Roman forces in at least eight battles, inflicting great losses of Roman soldiers, treasury, and pride. Needless to say, the loss of pride at being defeated by a slave army was too much for the proud Romans to bear. Fear spread through Rome in anticipation of the rebels attacking the defenseless capital and enlisting the large slave population of the city to their cause. Rome was vulnerable to attack by such a formidable force, as most of its seasoned armies were on foreign soils protecting and expanding their empire. After many defeats, the senate recalled Pompey's and Lucullus' armies from their foreign campaigns to put an end to Spartacus' victories, but they arrived too late to participate in the final battle. The Roman praetor, Marcus Crassus, was the only commander in Rome brave enough to volunteer for the task of facing and defeating Spartacus' army, but it was not an easy task. So cautious was he, that, when cornering the slave army in Southern Italy with its back to the sea, instead of attacking, he decided to build a 32-mile ditch across the peninsula. It was 15- feet-wide by 15-feet-deep and included a fence to keep the rebels isolated, hoping to starve them into submission. However, the rebels broke through and headed in the direction of Rome.

Upon hearing that the armies of Pompey and Lucullus were on their way and would arrive shortly, Spartacus decided to make a stand against Crassus' forces and, then, after winning, his troops would turn on the other two armies. He had his horse brought to him and killed it with a sword announcing: "victory or death, there will be no retreat." And so the rebels, who outnumbered the Roman legions, attacked in human waves hoping that their sheer number and passion would overwhelm and defeat the Romans, but it was not to be. Spartacus and most of his men were killed by the well-trained soldiers in the battle; some slaves escaped but were not pursued by Crassus, as his legions were decimated and had to return to Rome for rest and rehabilitation. It was left to Pompey to hunt down and slaughter the remnants of the brave army. The bodies of over 6,000 slaves were crucified and hung along the road from Capua to Rome as a testament to the strength of the Empire and the severe consequences of rebellion. Rome never forgot the anxiety and fear that this uprising caused throughout Italy, and went to great lengths to insure that gladiators never again had the opportunity to gather and form another rebellion. It took another 400 years of cruelty and bondage to gladiators and slaves before the sport of pitting man against man and beast would end.

Of course, the spectacular 1960 movie "Spartacus" told quite a different story. The extravagant movie follows the slave revolt of Pre-Imperial Rome in 73-71 BCE. The fantastic story (told with quite a bit of literary license), set in ancient times, had some outstanding acting from such renowned actors as Kirk Douglas (Spartacus), Laurence Olivier (Crassus, as general), Jean Simmons (Varinia, Spartacus' wife), Charles Laughton (Gracchus, as senator), Peter Ustinov (Lentulus Batiatus, as slave trader who purchases Spartacus), John Gavin (Julius Caesar, as Commander of Rome's Garrison), John Ireland (Crixus, as Spartacus' loyal lieutenant) and last, but not least, Tony Curtis (Antoninus, as Crassus' young slave and later Spartacus' comrade). The story traces the escape, and then the rise and fall of the leader of the rebellion. He is rescued from a brutally-run Libyan mine by Lentulus Batiatus to be trained as a gladiator. He learns his trade quickly and is allowed visitation rights with Varinia, whom he treats with respect by refusing to take the opportunity to sexually perform with her for the benefit of their overseers' viewing pleasure. So a relationship develops between them out of respect and admiration, and after his escape they eventually marry. But before that blessed event, Crassus takes a liking to Varinia, purchases her, and then takes her to his mansion for his amusement and pleasure, which of course, never happens. When Spartacus finds out, he is enraged and the beginning of the uprising is set in motion. He and some of his trusted friends overwhelm the guards and escape from their place of bondage.

As the rebels march through Southern Italy, looting and freeing slaves, Spartacus is chosen to lead the new founded army and to turn them into a fighting force, so they could fight their way out of Italy and return to their homes. Rome is upset about the slave army but not overly concerned, as they consider it only a minor uprising. They sent a small military party to uproot the upstarts and bring them to Roman justice. Of course, Spartacus' small army annihilated the unprepared Romans, which, in short order, gets the undivided attention of the powers in Rome. As the growing slave army moves through the southern part of Italy, there is much debate in the Senate about letting them escape from Italy. The consensus became, "It is bad business to allow an escape to go unpunished, especially of slaves." So they sent 19,000 troops to put an end to the rabble force; the soldiers march into a trap and are totally annihilated. During all this confusion, Spartacus and Varinia get together and consummate their marriage and quickly have a child to make the story more interesting. In the meantime, Crassus makes some overtures to his slave Antonius while getting a sponge bath, and is rejected; in short order, the slave decides to escape and join Spartacus and his forces. This scene perpetuates the belief that many of Roman elite were bisexual, in spite of their heroic manly conduct in battle.

The end of an era is in the making when Crassus raises an army and begins to hunt down the now fearless rebel forces. Only after being pursued and then cornered, does Spartacus give the order: "Meet the enemy head on in a fight to the end battle." The rebels are defeated and many captured in one of the most spectacular battle scenes in film history, the heroic

Spartacus and Antonius are spared the fate of their comrades, and survive. Crassus promises the defeated troops that if they surrender their leader, their lives would be spared. When he asks, "Who is Spartacus?" first Spartacus raises his hand and then, one by one, the slaves raise their hands and proclaim, "I am Spartacus." As a reward, Crassus has them crucified along the Appian Way, from the battlefield to the gates of Rome, all except, Spartacus and Antonius. Crassus, still not sure if Spartacus is dead or alive, has the two men fight to the death, the winner having the honor of being crucified with the rest of the rebels. Spartacus reluctantly fights, but only to prevent his friend, Antonius, from being nailed to a cross, so he now becomes his friend's Savior. Well, Spartacus wins the duel and is quickly crucified alongside his men. Varinia and her newborn are taken captive by Crassus and she is sent to his home as a love slave. She soon finds a friend in Gracchus, an influential senator, and escapes the grip of her new master. And that is the End.

There are considerable historical inaccuracies in the film, such as:

- The "I am Spartacus" scene never happened, as he was killed in the final battle and, therefore, the duel between him and Antonius never occurred.

- There are fewer battles in the movies than actually happened, including Spartacus' army escaping through the 32-mile ditch across the peninsula that Crassus built to contain them.

- It was not Crassus that crucified the remnants of the rebel army, but Pompey; Crassus' army was decimated in the final battle and was forced to return to Rome for repairs.

- In the film, Spartacus is born into slavery when, in reality, he was an auxiliary Roman soldier and was imprisoned for deserting.

- Antonius and Varinia (with a British accent) were totally fictional. Antonius played to the rumors that many Roman's were bisexual and Varginia's British accent predated Rome's contact with that barbarian island by many years.

But, all in all, the movie was one of the most exciting and technologically advanced shows I have been fortunate to see. I graduated college in 1960, the same year the movie premiered, and a friend of mine treated me to see the movie as a graduation present. It was certainly a surprise and appreciated treat.

We arrived at the Hotel Luna Convento, situated on a mountain cliff a short walking distance from the Town of Amalfi, where we would spend the next couple of days. It was dark, so we didn't get a chance at a daylight view of the area, but what we saw from the cliffside was a remarkable view of the Gulf of Salerno and the lights of boats at the distance, bobbing to the rhythm of the waves. I couldn't wait to get a better view in the morning. We were assigned our rooms, and I was sure that we would have preference over the other guests as to a choice of rooms, being that I had an Italian last name and the owner of the hotel had a similar name. Additionally, my grandparents came from the Naples region, which I informed them of upon our arrival. But, great ideas come and go, and mine went when I saw an exceptionally small room with a twin bed. Fortunately, it was clean and the toilet was adequate. We refreshed ourselves and went down to dinner. The restaurant was magnificent, with seascape paintings decorating the walls and colorful furniture highlighting the contour of the rooms; some with arches, others rectangular, and others square. The dining room was decorated simply but, as is so common along the Amalfi Coast, the water view was breathtaking. Shirley and Dallas Peck joined us for dinner and immediately raved about the wonderful first floor suite that they were assigned, with an additional alcove room and a court yard garden area--all their own. Well, my theory of having preferred treatment because I was Italian went right down the tubes; no such thing in Italy. We ordered some local

Italian wine and decided to eat family style. Each of us ordered main courses that we shared: pasta putanesca for Barbara, baked ziti for Shirley, egg plant parmesan for Dallas, and veal scaloppini for me. We all shared fried calamari for an appetizer and the last plate, as is usual in Italy, was a wonderful salad that no one could finish. I could never understand why Italians eat their salads last. As a youth, eating something I didn't like last was never a pleasant experience, but, if I didn't eat the traditional dish after a full course meal, "I wouldn't be able to digest my food," so I was told by those who knew better. After marrying Barbara, who is from a Russian Jewish background, I was introduced to eating salads before the main course. What a positive difference it made to the enjoyment of a meal. We decided that after the orientation, we would walk to the Town of Amalfi, which was a short distance from the hotel, to enjoy some espresso and dessert.

Fran handed out material for the following day's trip to the Royal Palace and the Museum of Capodimonte, which are located in a park bearing the same name. We were also reminded that the next day was the end of our tour, and that a farewell dinner and dance would take place at the Bersagliera Restaurant. We leisurely strolled down to the Town of Amalfi, enjoying the night view of darkness and peace and tranquility of the sea. We were led on our walk by the aroma of coffee, which we followed to a small street-side café that was crowded with patrons enjoying their after dinner espresso and sweets. We gladly joined the happy faces, and nodded recognition to some of the guests that we knew from our tour. We passed a pleasant hour drinking our caffe, munching on anisette cookies, and just enjoying watching people walking around the busy streets. We were all exhausted from the day's activities and decided to return to the hotel and get some R&R. We joined several of our tour members that were "expressorizing" at the café, and headed back to the hotel quite happy with the day's experience and how smoothly the trip was going-- so far.

We woke up in the middle of the night scratching ourselves intensely; I switched on the lights to find small black ants crawling all over our pillows and sheets. Barbara screamed as we pounded the pillows against the bed. I immediately called the front desk, and, of course, no one was there. I left my room and went directly to the owner's room and knocked on her door. She opened the door quite annoyed that we interrupted her sleep, even after I told her of our dilemma. All of a sudden she didn't understand English, even though when she greeted us upon our arrival, she spoke the language very well. Her son appeared and assured us that we really didn't have a problem; I suggested that if that were the case, he shouldn't mind exchanging rooms with us. He came with us to our room with fresh bed sheets and pillows, reassuring us that changing them would solve our problem. He also brought along a can of insect spray for good measure. We didn't sleep well that evening and were happy to see the sun come up so we could shower, dress, and get out of the room to escape the little critters; exacerbating our problem was the noise developing outside our window from the traffic below: tires squealing, engines revving, and horns honking. When we left, there were still ants in the room but not many on the bed.

When we saw the innkeeper at breakfast, I strongly suggested that she change our room to one without unwanted visitors and a lot less noise from the vehicle traffic. She said: "there were no available vacant rooms at the hotel and being that we were only staying another night, she would have our room fumigated while we were away touring, she also assured us that by the time we returned, the traffic noise would be less." The only redemption we had was the magnificent view of the Bay of Salerno from our terrace dining table. The sparkling blue-green water, with boats passing by and the surreal Island of Capri painted into the background, was just the calming influence I needed to get my blood pressure back to somewhere near normal. The view, smell of sea air, aroma of caffe, bacon and eggs and slightly burnt toast, was all that was needed as a turning point to begin our day anew and bring smiles back to our faces; especially when we were served blood orange juice, which is, without a doubt, Barbara's favorite drink. It's amazing how in such a short period of time, she went from screaming and pounding ants to purring as she drank her juice of choice. What a wonderful turn of events, from a horrific beginning, to welcoming a new day with anticipation and excitement of what was yet to come.

After breakfast, we had some time before our bus left for the Naples area to explore the former convent. The hotel is located in the commune of Amalfi in the province of Salerno, which is a part of the region of Campania, Italy. The town lies in a deep ravine at the foot of Mt. Cerreto (4,300-feet), surrounded by cliffs and beautiful coastal scenery. It's just over 20 miles from Naples, but is low keyed, clean, and a beautiful seaside resort location that many people from the overcrowded city of Naples escape to for fresh air and relaxation. The town is a main stopping place for tourists along the Costiera Amalfitana, which includes other hillside towns, such as Positano and Ravello. A huge cathedral lies in the center of town, which we noticed the night before while searching for a café. It was lit up with an abundance of lights that gave it a silhouette image. So large and spectacular was the church that it made the surrounding area disappear from sight, and all that could be seen was the electrified cathedral. It is dedicated to St. Andrew (as is the town itself) and is probably its largest man-made tourist attraction, both in size and attendance. St. Andrew's relics are preserved in this enormous church punctuated with the largest steps in width and elevation that I have ever seen, leading up to the large doors of the cathedral. The steps reminded me of the Aztec pyramids' stairway in Mexico City and those of the Mayan ruins in Chichen Itza, only there is no provision in Amalfi for human sacrifice. The Saint's remains were brought to the area in 1210 from Constantinople by Cardinal Pietro, and placed in the cathedral for safekeeping and religious worship. The former convent that we were residing at was founded in 1222 by St. Francis of Assisi and converted into the first hotel on the Amalfi Coast in 1821. Wow, what a history! I wondered how long the ants were occupants of our room and if they knew any of the people of that famous order. The hotel itself is perched on a cliff directly above the sea, with the most spectacular views of the coast, to be enjoyed from almost every window and terrace in this resort-like hotel. At sea level there is a spectacular infinity pool with comfortable lounge chairs and equipment that is easily accessible for snorkeling in the pristine blue-green waters containing an abundance of sea life. Oops, we forgot, it was bus time again, so off we went for our short trip to the Capodimonte area.

Although Naples is only a little over 20 miles from our hotel, it took more than an hour to get to our destination, due to the heavy traffic around and in the city. I put the time to good use and read material Fran so generously distributed the night before, on the history of Palazzo Capodimonte and the plethora of sights surrounding the palace. The monarch Charles VII kept himself pretty busy; in addition to having the Royal Palace of Caserta built, he decided at about the same time to have a summer residence built by another renowned Italian architect: Giovanni Antonio Medrano, who also built the beautiful Teatro San Carlo Opera House in Naples. One of his primary objectives was to house the fabulous Farnese art collection which he inherited from his mother, Elizabetta Farnese, the last descendant of her majestic family to carry that name. The enormous collection was transferred to Naples and consisted of paintings, drawings, statues, medals, coins, gems, cameos, and other archeological antiquities. The king also didn't remain in Italy to see this palace completed, as his father, the King of Spain, died and he inherited that superior, more prestigious, royal crown, passing the Kingdom of Naples and Sicily to his third son, Ferdinand. His son, who became one of the longest reigning monarchs in Europe, had the distinct honor of overseeing, with the assistance of his capable wife, Queen Maria Carolina, the completion of both monumental projects. The palace is located on top of a hill (Capodimonte) and is the largest open area park in Naples, sharing the park grounds with the former Capodimonte Factory (currently the

School of Ceramic), the Church of San Gennaro (built to provide services for the numerous colony of workers who lived in the park at that time), Casina dei Pincipi (Prince's House), Casina della Regina (Queen's House), and many statues and a maze of gardens with topiaries of every size and shape, especially arches.

There was so much to see and so little time to see it in. Fran's plans for the day were to spend one hour at the Palace Museum, one half hour at the former Capodimonte Factory, a leisurely hour exploring the Park, lunch, and then return to our hotel for an afternoon on our own. Again, we would have to prioritize which of the sights to see; it seemed that each, individually, could probably consume all of our day's allotted time. We decided to stick with Fran and follow her lead. We followed her into the park, exiting the hustle and bustle of the crowded city streets of Naples. The lush foliage seen upon entering is unexpected, due to the contrast between the serenity and silence of the park and the noise and squalor of the streets left behind. It reminded me of the feeling I always get when entering Central Park in New York City, except the streets there are a lot cleaner and the foot traffic less dense. We quickly located the palace which dominates the park and attracts everyone like a magnet, due to its large rectangular size and its pinkish appearance in the sunlight, contrasting the greenery of the surrounding foliage. Seeing this structure and recalling the Palace of Caserta and the Teatro San Carlo, one becomes cognizant of the complexity of King Charles VII and his passion for architectural beauty, appreciation of art and, eventually, his love for Capodimonte porcelain, which he developed in Italy.

The palace gained museum status after the unification of Italy, and is now the proud repository of Neapolitan and general Italian cultural heritage of the city. The ground floor is the showcase of the museum, displaying the elaborate Farnese collection of classical, mostly Roman, monumental sculptures. The first and second floors house the National Gallery, with paintings from the 13th to 18th centuries, featuring works of the great masters: Michelangelo, Raphael,, Titian, Caravaggio, El Greco, Botticelli, and many others. It is one of the few museums in Italy to feature classical as well as contemporary art, which is displayed on the third floor and is highlighted by Andy Warhol's Mt. Vesuvius (1985). A magnificent staircase leads to the royal apartments, where flashy ornate antique furniture and a staggering collection of highly decorated porcelain and majolica from the various royal residences are on display. The state apartments, located on the basement level, have room after room of gilded mermaids, Venetian sedan chairs, ivory carvings, a porcelain chinoiserie salon, tapestries, the Farnese armory, and a glass and china collection. After our briefing by Fran of what we would expect to see if we had a couple of days to explore the museum, she asked: "which of the exhibits would you like to visit in the one hour allotted to exploring the museum?" What an eclectic experience; what do we visit next? The four of us decided to use the floor plans that were distributed and wander around on our own to locate Michelangelo, Raphael El Greco, etc., and, time permitting, to study Andy Warhol's famous painting of Mt. Vesuvius. We located Michelangelo among the many incredible masterpieces. His drawing of the "Three Soldiers" is more of a sketch than a drawing. Raphael's "Moses and the Burning Bush," is also a drawing and is difficult to distinguish the burning bush without the benefit of color. We visited the "Crucifixion" by Masaccio, Botticelli's "Madonna with Angels," the "Gypsy" by Correggio, Giambellino's "Transfiguration," and the outstanding painting depicting the brother of Robert Anjou being crowned King of Naples by bishop of Toulouse, painted by Simone Martini. After leisurely gazing at the splendid collection of art work, we decided we had better hurry along and get to the top floor to see Andy Warhol's "Mt. Vesuvius." As is usually his style, the coloring and configuration of the mountain are distorted, but, surprisingly, I recognized the painting from its exposure in various publications. Next to the magnificent park; if only we had the rest of the day to explore this incredible venue, I made a note to return soon or in my next lifetime, whichever comes first.

The park's name, "Head of the Mountain" (Capodimonte), is not an Italian exaggeration. The park is on a high plateau over-looking Naples, its fabulous bay and the city of Sorrento jutting out just across the bay. In the background, the ever present monster, Mt. Vesuvius, looms in all its ugly glory, occasionally making sounds as if to remind the inhabitants of the surrounding area that it still has some fire in its belly. Walking through high gates brought us through the "Porta di Mezzo" (Middle Doorway), entering the largest expanse of open space one can imagine, hidden in a metropolis so far removed in its activity and appearance from nature, that it is hard to believe that this respite from reality exists. The scene is occupied by Holm-oaks, tall umbrella pines, and eucalyptus trees, and abounds with topiaries with arches enclosing statues in every direction. The large amount of people in the park, escaping from the stress and strain of the concrete city outside its green environment, was surprising, but understandable. Teens playing soccer, mothers and nannies pushing and attending to little ones, children chasing butterflies, joggers running in every direction along the wide paths (probably imagining that they were running a great marathon), and what has become a fixture in parks around the world, big or small men, young and old playing checkers or chess and discussing and solving the world's problems, momentarily at peace with one another. We leisurely strolled through the park and consumed the planned hour journey, while enjoying some espresso and cappuccino which was readily provided by road-side vendors.

We didn't have much time left before our rendezvous with the returning bus, but we thought we would visit the Capodimonte Factory, being that it was such an integral part of the history of the park and palace. Unfortunately, it was closed for renovation but there was a docent on sight that showed us some of the rooms being restored and was happy to tell us about the checkered history of the place. It was commissioned by the illustrious prolific King Charles VII in 1743. He married Princess Maria Amelia Christina of Saxony, who was the granddaughter of King Augustus II, who, in addition to being the monarch of Poland, also founded the first European hard paste porcelain factory in Meissen, Germany. Her dowry consisted of extraordinary examples of Meissen porcelain produced in her father's royal workshop, which King Charles immediately fell in love with. His love became a passion and he ordered the greatest of Italian artisans to duplicate the porcelain, which at that time was a royal secret held by Maria Amelia's family. The king set up a school to research and train students in the preparation of porcelain, but it took many years of experimentation to finally develop what is today known as Capodimonte Porcelain. The first pieces, which were considered on a par with the collection held by Maria Amelia, were fired in 1759. The king was allergic to flowers, but loved their beauty, so he commanded that the artisans create delicate floral arrangements, each a precious tribute to his love of nature. His passion became so profound that he built a porcelain room for his bride in their summer place at Portici. The ceilings, walls, and floors were constructed of porcelain and mirrors. This dazzling display of beauty also inspired his son, Ferdinand, to continue his father's passion for the art, but it didn't come easily. When his father left for Madrid to take his place on the throne of Spain, he dismantled the factory and took all the tools and molds with him, so that no one other than himself would have the pleasure of overseeing the production of such beauty. So the Capodimonte factory was operational for a very short period of time, 1759 to 1780. The king's son didn't get over his passion for the new art form and, upon his father's death, arranged to have the molds and paraphernalia returned to Naples. Ferdinand was an outdoorsman, and he made sure the artisans reflected this in their depictions of his frolicking and light hearted days in the porcelain designs. All was fun and games until at the turn of the century, when Napoleon invaded Italy and forced Ferdinand and his royal party to flee to Sicily. From that time on, the factory fell into disrepair and the ownership changed hands, scattering the production of Capodimonte throughout Italy. What a fascinating history lesson. Dong, the alarm went off and we rushed to our bus. Box lunches were waiting for us to enjoy on our tedious journey back to the Town of Amalfi, which consisted mostly of moving in slow traffic; but, at least we had an opportunity to have some food during the process.

We arrived at our hotel and quickly went to our room to change into bathing suits so we could enjoy the exquisite swimming pool at the seawater's edge. We spent the rest of the afternoon relaxing in the sun, drinking the local limoncello liqueur, snorkeling, and chasing little colorful fish that were in abundance 20 yards out in about four-feet of water, in the magnificent blue-green waters of Sorrento Bay. After doing some serious napping, we retired to our room to prepare for our farewell party at the Bersagliera Restaurant in the seaside area of Santa Lucia, Naples. Upon arrival, we were greeted by the current matriarch of the family that has been running the restaurant for three generations. We were led to our tables in a semiprivate room with views of the miraculous bay, especially from the terrace, where the stationary city's lights combined with moving automobile headlights gave me the feeling of being inside a giant Christmas tree, looking out. In route to our table we passed a signed picture showcase room of famous people that have enjoyed the cuisine of this renowned restaurant, such as Sophia Loren and Ingrid Bergman. The house specialties for the evening were clam and mussel soup, taglierini (fine ribbon pasta) with baby octopus, black olives and tomatoes or gorgonzola cheese. The one thing I learned about Italy in my several visits is, if there are house specialties, don't pass them up, because the chef obviously pays special attention to his creations, which have passed the tests of time and taste. So, we all ordered the house's suggestion and we were not displeased with the results. As usual, the local wines were not only palate-pleasing, but quite strong. After a couple of drinks, we were all feeling melancholy; unhappy to be leaving the incredibly historic and beautiful Amalfi area, and especially unhappy about leaving our new-found friends. There was pleasant background music playing, so many of us took the opportunity to visit the terrace, which had a surprisingly large dance floor, and danced under the hypnotic skies of Santa Lucia, inhaling and absorbing the sea air, the stars, the city lights, and the aroma of the moment. A dozen couples occupied the floor at any given dance, which left lots of room for us to dance without interruptions or collisions. There was a very sophisticated-looking couple, named Giovanni and Sophia, dancing a Waltz that turned the other dancers into spectators. We couldn't keep our eyes off of them; they danced the Waltz with great form and confidence. When they finished their dance we applauded and gave our verbal approval. They seemed embarrassed, but recognized our good taste with slight bows and enormous smiles on their faces. Barbara and I approached them and told them, in English, which they understood perfectly, how much we enjoyed their performance, especially a particular routine they did with exceptional style and grace. They were so flattered that they offered to teach us the steps; we accepted their offer without hesitation. They took us aside and showed us in ten minutes how to do the routine. Several other couples joined the class and they, too, were astonished at how easily they perfected the beautiful interpretation from the delightful couple. The routine went as follows: beginning with a Waltz basic in silver pattern we did quick-quick-quick; then, an open break (promenade) with a twinkle, into two double chasse' steps. Next, with partners facing each other, both parties open arms stretch out (sway), while looking to my left-forward direction. Then the male moves his partner back to his right, from the waist up, while the girl turns her head from forward to her left looking away from the male; at the same time the male turns his head from left-forward to his right, and looks passionately at his partner's turned away face. Then, both turn their heads forward while their eyes briefly meet and open into another twinkle and close in a basic box step. Giovanni asked the DJ to play another Waltz. We all performed our routines fairly well; in the meantime, other restaurant guests were attracted to our exhibition and rigorously encouraged us on with energetic applause and whistles. We danced the night away with additional bottles of wine, which our two new friends gladly shared with us. We couldn't have been more pleased with the dinner, wine, camaraderie and the addition of a new Waltz routine, which is, still today, an important part of our Waltz repertoire.

On our trip back to our place of rest, we were given mementos of our trip; Smithsonian pins and decorative majolica cups with the name of the restaurant imprinted on them. Neither would ever be able to take the place of the memories etched in our minds of this most incredible experience in and around the city of the birth of my mother's parents, Naples. We were looking forward to the next leg of our unescorted journey to Rome on our own, for three days of just relaxing and visiting some of the places we enjoyed on our previous trips to the Eternal City. We asked the hotel manager the best way to get to Rome from Naples and he said without hesitation, "take the very fast Eurostar train and you will be in Roma in just one hour and a half." He secured train tickets for us for 8:30 A.M., the next morning, which included reserved seats, which is mandatory when traveling on a busy train. Otherwise, there is no guarantee that there will be seats available. We bid everyone goodbye and exchanged addresses and telephone numbers, along with promises of keeping in touch. Shirley and Dallas Peck became our life-long friends who we would spend time with in Washington, D.C., and they would visit us in sunny Florida.

We took a taxi-cab to the station and boarded on schedule with our four pieces of luggage, ever so alert of our surroundings and keeping a close watch on our belongings, as we were told that pick pockets are rampant at railroad stations and on trains. We arrived in Rome's 30-plus platform train station, on time, with our luggage intact. Now the fun began. On our previous trips to Rome, traveling by train and intersecting at this major station was always confusing. The language was always a big problem, so getting a "red cap" to carry our property to the street was not an easy chore. We struggled with our suitcases and finally got to a taxi stand at the entrance, passing thousands of travelers on the way and noticing that a Tourist Station was available that we didn't recall from our previous visits. Unfortunately it was of little use to us, as the most difficult part of our journey was almost over. But, we both made a mental note of its location just in case we had to use the Termini in the future.

Our destination was the hotel InterContinental de la Ville on Via Sistina, at the top of the Spanish Steps in Roma, Italia. We researched staying at the renowned Hotel Hassler right next door, but the rates were more than double, even though they are both rated five stars (European standards). We were not disappointed in our choice. The excitement of approaching our hotel through busy, noisy, narrow Roman streets felt like a dream coming true; we were not used to staying at a fine hotel in the middle of so much activity. On our previous trips to the Eternal City, we were on economy tours and stayed at small hotels in out-of-the-way places, surrounded by extremely noisy traffic, without the benefit of air conditioning; usually three star hotels (European standards). We were now going to a choice hotel and couldn't wait to be pampered with its anticipated luxury and fine service for the next three days. The outside of the hotel was deceiving; it was not decorative and could have been mistaken for a one star hotel. Once inside the lobby, however, the feeling of the hotel's inadequacy was quickly dispelled. The beautifully furnished lobby, featuring oriental rugs and marble table tops, was a welcome sight. An elegantly appointed marble floor lounge, situated off the lobby, served refreshments and tea, which was more than a welcome sight as it was around lunch time and we were both famished. We had a leisurely lunch and discussed our game plan for our short visit in Roma. Utmost on our itinerary was a visit to the Sistine Chapel, which we had visited twice before: the first time Michelangelo's paintings were dark and covered with centuries of soot, which made much of the famous artwork's colors difficult to distinguish and appreciate. We recalled how upset we were when we saw the condition of the one-time heavenly ceiling, and spoke of it with frustration on many occasions after our first visit. Our second visit was in the midst of the Chapel's restoration and seemed like an epiphany; we saw about half of the ceiling restored with its original bright colors sparkling in contrast to the untouched dull parts of the ceiling; hypnotizing us as Michelangelo had intended. The incredible fete of painting religious stories on ceilings not only required his astonishing artistic talents, but his patience and stamina, which seems to be reserved for gifted artisans of his caliber. The restored art work couldn't be appreciated before the restoration, but now scenes that were not noticed, seemed like a revelation; radiant colors burst into life, decorating the holy scenes and enriching each story's message. What a contrast between the "before and after." Trying to get any meaning from the soon-to-be renovated remaining ceiling was an eye strain, as their true colors were mostly a dull gray, with many parts blurred. We were anxious to see the ceiling completely renovated so we could appreciate the artistic talents of the many artisans who were responsible for adding beauty to the glorious chapel.

Second on our list, or on Barbara's list, was to leisurely stroll to visit the shops on the Via Condotti at the bottom of the Spanish Steps, right below our hotel. Her fondest memories of Roma are visiting Gucci and Valentino, plus every designer-named clothing and jewelry store listed in her "wish book." Providing that we have disposable cash after shopping, we thought it would be nice to find a local place where we could do some dancing. We finished our lunch and immediately went to our mini-suite on the seventh floor facing the court yard, which we chose so the local traffic noise wouldn't keep us awake at night. The rooms with outside terraces had better views of the Eternal City, but we decided that forgoing the views for better sleeping conditions was worth the sacrifice. Views of Roma from the terraces throughout the hotel were almost mystical. In the distance is St. Peter's Basilica, the almost 2,000-year-old Pantheon, a monument honoring the first king of unified Italy, Victor Emmanuel, and the uneven tops of building, most predating the discovery of America in 1492, by the Italian explorer, Christopher Columbus. In the other direction are views of the "Borghese Gardens" and the hotel's beautiful central courtyard with gracious flower displays and a unique dancing water fountain. The most thrilling view to me is of the Spanish Steps when the azaleas lining both sides of the stairs are in bloom. Having seen many picture postcards of the colorful steps and its surroundings is just a tease to actually seeing them first hand; you feel as if you are drawn into the picture as one of the figures in this beautiful magical scenic view. Our room was what we had hoped for; quiet with a terrace view of the colorful courtyard, displaying an abundance of assorted colorful flowers.

After unpacking, we decided to stroll to the nearby shops that Barbara had dreamed of revisiting since our last vacation in the Eternal (shopping) City. Walking down the Spanish Steps is a treat; people were moving about with no purpose or just "hanging" with their friends, chattering away and enjoying that sort of camaraderie most people in Roma seem to take pleasure in. It was surprising to see the number of young backpackers that were hanging around the bottom of the stairs, just rapping and singing to their guitar music. It was a pleasant sight to see young people from all over the world getting along so well, while sharing their music with each other. Maybe all of the countries in the world should have young people in power who sing to each other when communicating; it might solve some of our major international problems. From the bottom of the stairs looking back is probably what the "stairway to heaven" looks like, so inviting and surreal in its colorful flowered splendor. Overwhelming in size, the French rose colored church (Trinita dei Monti) sits at the top of the steps; a protruding large obelisk in front of the cathedral is dwarfed by two large bell towers that are guarding the steps and the Piazza di Spagna below. The Cathedral's overwhelming size and beauty beckons those who believe, to journey up the 12 flights, consisting of 137 steps, to join the religious congregation worshiping within.

On our way to Gucci, we stopped to admire the statue of Fontana della Barcaccia (a small boat being filled with water); usually renderings of boats have them floating on water, but not this one; it commemorates the flooding of the Tevere River in 1598, where a small boat was stranded at this location after the water had returned to its home base in the river. I tried to kill some time admiring the art work, but Barbara wouldn't let me get away with wasting precious moments, when she could be putting the time to better use: "shopping," her words, not mine. After two hours of browsing and shopping, Barbara was satisfied with her new conquests, which meant we couldn't carry any more packages, so we gave up and looked for our favorite restaurant, Re degli Amici (Royal Friends), to see if it was still in business. This little restaurant, which is almost hidden from sight among the fashionable designer stores, is rumored to have attracted many young artists in the 50s and 60s. Some of these artists paid for their meals with paintings, which are festooned on the walls throughout the establishment. It was just where we remembered, so we made reservations for that evening. It was worth seeking out the trattoria; their buffet bar boasts 32 different antipastos, worthy of many helpings. Unfortunately, after indulging several times at the antipasto bar, ordering second, third or fourth courses, which is common in Italy, was out of the question. But I did find room for some orrechiette (ear pasta) smothered with eggplant, Sicilian style, and Barbara did force herself to enjoy her favorite pasta puttanesca. Sharing a bottle of local wine complemented the cuisine, and our waiter, Vito, who we asked for by name, was par excellence in charm, politeness and service, as he was in years past. He continued an Italian tradition, which rewards customers that waiters are fond of with a free pre-dinner drink and a complimentary (no charge), after-dinner refreshing limoncello drink.

After a great night's sleep, we enjoyed our sit-down breakfast at the hotel, which was part of the package rate for our visit. What is worth mentioning is that they served pancakes, which is very unusual in Italy, and their coffee, "Americana," was pretty good, not the usual watered down version. We exited the hotel and hailed a taxi for our journey to the smallest sovereign state in the world, The Holy Vatican City, official name, State of the Vatican City, or, in Italian, Stato della Citta' del Vaticano. It's a sovereign city-state whose territory consists of a walled enclave within the city of Roma, spread out over 109 acres, with a population of 800 people. It's an elected monarchy that is ruled by the Bishop of Rome, the Pope, who resides in his Apostolic Palace within the sacred walls. The Sistine Chapel is also located in the Apostolic Palace, and its purpose is for the use of papal religious and functionary meetings, most important being the Papal Conclave (election of new popes).

The restoration of the chapel was to be done in two stages: the walls first and then the ceiling. If the first phase was successful, then the ceiling's restoration would be tested as a precautionary measure and, if all went well, the whole ceiling would be restored to its near original renderings. Oddly, the restoration was not paid for by the Catholic Church but by Nippon Television Network and took approximately ten-plus painstaking years to complete. Having researched the history of the Chapel and its restoration made our visit all the more exciting, and we couldn't wait to see the completed accomplishments of so many talented artisans who worked on the chapel inch by inch for over ten years, to reestablish its artistic splendor. We had a lucky day, there weren't many people in the Vatican courtyard and very few in the chapel. Entering the holy place is like waking in the morning in a dark room and raising the window shades, allowing a burst of sunlight to envelop your senses. The colors in the chapel were bright and the backgrounds pristine; what a difference from our previous two visits, where darkness was prevalent throughout the venue, where walls and ceilings were dim, and the atmosphere of the chapel was dusty and smoky. Since the restoration, an air purification system has been installed to filter the enormous unwanted pollution that is imported by the million plus visitors a year entering and admiring the sacred place. With the use of electronic docents, we began our new adventure of exploring the incredibly creative endeavors of so many amazing artists, such as Pietro Perugino,

Sandro Botticelli, Luca Signorelli, and Michelangelo Buonarroti. The original wall frescos took less than a year to complete, and are divided into three epochs: before the Ten Commandments were given to Moses; between Moses and Christ's birth, and the Christian era. Some of the more profound frescos in artistic presentation and historical biblical meanings are in Perugino's "Christ Giving the Keys to St. Peter." The scene references the biblical story in which the "keys of the kingdom of heaven are given to St. Peter." The keys represent the power to forgive and to share the word of God with all people, regardless of race or creed, giving everyone access to the Kingdom of Heaven. Botticelli's three scenes of: The Life of Moses, The Temptation of Christ, and The Punishment of Korah, who was the leader of a rebellion against Moses, were also descriptive presentations of those events. We were fascinated by all of these presentations, but absorbed by "The Temptation of Christ" painting. This is a story that all Christians are taught at the beginning of their religious training, and frequently reminded of for the rest of their lives. In this scene, Christ's three temptations by the Satan, as described in the Bible, are in the background of the painting, with Satan disguised as a hermit. At the top left, residing on the top of a mountain, he is attempting to persuade Christ to turn stones into bread; in the center we see them standing on a temple, with Satan attempting to persuade Christ to cast himself down; on the right side, he is showing Christ the splendor of the world's riches, which he is offering to Christ for his capitulation. Christ finally drives away the Devil, who ultimately reveals his true form. In the middle ground on the left, Christ is explaining to three angels the activity that is taking place in the center of the fresco, which is a Jewish sacrifice signifying the crucifixion of Christ, who through His death offered mankind salvation. Christ's sacrifice is reconstructed in the celebration of the Eucharist, referred to by the gift table prepared by God's messengers, in the upper right side of the painting. The enjoyment I received in viewing these clear and easy-to-read paintings, right down to the minutest detail, can only be described as pure ecstasy. I was fortunate to have had a very religious upbringing, reinforced by detailed readings of the Bible. Seeing the stories of the Bible, which have been vividly imbedded in my mind for so many years, come to life with such clarity in these renderings, was extremely fulfilling, both intellectually and emotionally.

Behind the sacred Sistine Chapel alter wall is one of the most startling, in size and content, mural displays in the world of The Last Judgment, painted by Michelangelo, more than 30 years after he and his contemporaries finished painting the magnificent ceiling and wall frescos. His creation was done under duress, as he considered himself a sculptor, not a painter, and his last experience with the masters of the domain turned out to be anything but pleasant. He spent years painting the ceiling with papal interference and without proper compensation, and didn't want to repeat the experience. But Pope Paul III, Farnese, forced him to undertake that enormous project and, to placate Michelangelo, allowed him the freedom to paint the wall without supervision. It took him from 1535-1541 to complete The Last Judgment, which from a distance is heart shaped, as if engulfing the Biblical stories with divine love. When viewed by the papal entourage, their opinions were mixed and heated; some said the nude figures showing man in all his glory was the work of a genius, others said it was the work of a pervert and should be redone. Whatever, the work is enormous and spans the entire wall behind the altar. It's a depiction of the second coming of Christ and judgment day. At the center is the figure of Christ signaling people at the left side of the painting with his right hand, who are trying to rise to Heaven, that they are traveling in the wrong direction. His left hand is welcoming the chosen few to rise to their promised place in Heaven, including descriptive figures of those rising from their graves. The fresco rises from behind the altar in a threatening manner, instilling fear, piety and respect for the almighty, especially when considering his muscular presence. Even the Virgin Mary at the center seems to be trembling before God. The other figures in the various scenes are also muscular, very much as a sculptor would produce in a statue, and very much how Michelangelo saw humanity. Influential servants of the church began what was called the "Fig-Leaf Campaign," to have the genitalia in the fresco covered with paintings of fig leafs. This was eventually done by the artist Daniele da Volterra, whom history remembers by the descriptive nickname of "The breeches-painter." It's believed that Michelangelo used some of his friends as models for his figures; for sure he painted himself into the mural twice. The first being St. Bartholomew's displaying of his flayed skin, in his left hand is the face of Michelangelo (self-portrait of Michelangelo), and in a figure in the lower left hand corner, looking encouragingly at those rising from their graves and ascending to Heaven. A second known figure is that of that the Pope's Master of Ceremonies, Biagio da Cesena, who complained to the Pope that the mural should be covered over because the obscene renderings had no place in a holy sanctuary. For his complaining, Michelangelo gave him immortality by painting da Cesena's face on Minos, judge of the underworld. Over the years, many more figures were altered for what was considered justifiable sacred reasoning, and it is near miraculous that the restoration, to a great extent, restored much of the original content.

Michelangelo was first commissioned by Pope Julius II to repaint the vault, or ceiling, of the chapel, which at the time was a plain rendering of a blue sky with golden stars and not to the Pope's liking. It took him from 1508 to 1512 to complete the enormous undertaking, which originally was for painting the 12 apostles, and ended with over 300 bodies and heads. The massive scenes included the creation, Adam and Eve in the Garden of Eden, and the Great Flood. To successfully produce his stories on the ceiling, he made a flat wooden platform on brackets extending out from holes in the wall, high up and near the top of the windows, instead of from the bottom up, which would have required a monumental structure. The scaffold didn't extend the length of the room and had to be repositioned, as needed, to satisfy his needs. He stood, kneeled and laid on this platform to execute his creations, which resulted in painting 32 monumental figures, Sibyls, prophets and Atlases, all in frames with decorative accessories. In all, he executed approximately 370 figures in ever-changing situations and positions from his memory and deep religious beliefs. To complicate his task, the paintings were done on wet plaster to create a permanent color bond, which was mold resistant and, hopefully, more enduring than painting on dry surfaces. This reminded me of the Last Supper mural in the back dining halls at Santa Maria delle Grazie in Milan, Italy, painted by Leonardo da Vinci in 1495, which was commissioned by his patrons Duke Ludovico Sforza and his duchess, Beatrice d'Este. Leonardo did not use Michelangelo's wet surface method, instead he painted the Last Supper on dry surfaces, which resulted in deterioration of the colors and surface within a few years. When we saw the mural, prior to its "repainting," the scene was almost unrecognizable from the many pictures and mini sculptures we had seen of the famous painting. Leonardo knew of his nemesis technique, but chose to experiment with his own method, probably to show up Michelangelo, which turned out to be disastrous.

Michelangelo was able to maintain some sense of humor during the creation of the ceiling, and wrote a humorous sonnet and a sketch of his condition. The verse went:

"Here like a cat in a Lombardy sewer! I Swelter and toil!

With my neck puffed out like a pigeon, belly hanging like an empty sack.

Beard pointing at the ceiling, and my brain, fallen backwards in my head!

Breastbone bulging like a harpy's and my face, from drips and droplets, patterned like a marble pavement. Ribs are poking in my guts; the only way to counterweight my shoulder is to stick my butt out. Don't know where my feet are, they're just dancing by themselves! In front I've sagged and stretched; behind, my back is tauter than an archer's bow!"

The sonnet was accompanied by a sketch of his outstretched body reaching up to the ceiling continuing his painting and suffering.

The essence of Michelangelo's creations illustrates that God made the world a perfect garden and put Adam and Eve in charge to walk with him and flourish. But, humanity fell in disgrace and was punished by death. God sent Prophets and Sibyls to tell humanity that the Savior, Jesus Christ, would bring them redemption, if they behaved themselves and followed his rules. Michelangelo used bright colors and clear formats to describe these stories, which, thanks to the restorations, are still easily visible from below. On the lowest part of the ceiling over the windows, the ancestors of Christ are depicted by name. Above this, he displays male and female prophets, including Jonah who resides over the holy alter. On what seems to be the highest part of the ceiling, he painted nine stories from the Book of Genesis, the first book of the Bible. Trying to comprehend this vast undertaking without specific religious knowledge, and, my friend, the electronic docent, would have been an impossible task. Just looking up at the ceiling for long periods of time was a major physical effort making it difficult to focus on many of the scenes. The pictures fall into three main categories: God creating the Heavens and the Earth, God creating Adam and Eve, and thirdly, the plight of Humanity, in particular the family of Noah, the renowned Biblical navigator. Of all the outstanding scenes of the creation, God creating light and separating it from darkness was fascinating to me for its contrast in colors and meaning. In the central section of the ceiling is probably the most widely recognized painting in the world, that of God reaching out to touch Adam. It actually comes to life as if you are witnessing the actual birth or creation of Adam. While viewing this scene I couldn't help but remember the movie E.T., where the alien reaches out to touch the boy's finger in the same manner as the portrayal in the ceiling's rendering. The story of Noah in the final panels is outstanding in its rendering of the Great Flood, in which Noah, his family, and entourage, escape in the Ark while the rest of humanity tries to find safety from the flooding waters. When viewing the Sistine Chapel in all its glory, it is difficult to comprehend the intellectual complexity and depth of emotion that went into this astonishing achievement. It was best said by Goethe: "Without having seen the Sistine Chapel, one can form no appreciable idea of what one man is capable of doing."

When exiting the chapel, I felt euphorically dizzy; the overwhelming intellectual, artistic and spiritual journey enriched my soul. The experience is one that will stay etched in my mind forever. We didn't realize how much time we spent at the chapel, as it was well past lunch time. We decided to have some treats at our favorite outside café, "Doney's" on the Via Veneto, to enjoy some wine, and just goof off for the rest of the day. Walking along the Via is a treat in itself and just what I needed to clear my head from all the excitement of the day's enriching and mind-boggling experience. There are many sites that are within walking distance from the café that we were privileged to see on our former visits to the Eternal City: the ancient Aurelian Wall which surrounds the city of Rome, still pretty much intact (2/3 remaining); Villa Borghese; Trevi Fountain; Pincio Gardens and, one of our favorites, the Spanish Steps. We found a great viewing seat at "Doney's," as it was late in the afternoon but prior to the late afternoon onslaught of people watchers. We ordered some cakes with local Italian white wine and just enjoyed relaxing and watching the beautiful locals parading along the Avenue, just as in the Federico Fellini's 1960 movie "La Dolce Vita" (The Sweet Life), staring Marcello Mastroianni playing a newspaper paparazzo. After a couple of hours of relaxation, we strolled back to our hotel, following Barbara's traditional nosing into some of the better shops along the avenue. After such a grueling day, we decided to take a nap and have dinner at the hotel's restaurant, La Piazetta, which has a reputation of fine dining in a casual atmosphere. We enjoyed a small leisurely meal, which of course, included some pasta, and spent the rest of the evening hanging around the Spanish Steps, listening to the guitar music that filled the air, and songs from the young backpackers gathered at the bottom the steps.

I pictured my daughter, Laurie, and her friends in the group of young travelers, expressing themselves in song and music, in their quest to find themselves, which eventually most do.

The next day's schedule included the famous Rome Flea Market and an evening of dancing at the Alpheus multiclub. After an apple pancake breakfast, we walked to the Porta Portese Outdoor Flea Market; who can resist a flea market? This one put all the markets I've ever seen to shame in its size; over 4,000 merchants with every type of merchandise imaginable for sale. I visited the Tokyo Ginza Outdoor Flea Market, which is now enclosed, when stationed there while serving in the United States Air Force in the early 50s. It was considered, at that time, to be one of the largest in the world, but quite small compared to this never-ending Italian merchant's and shopper's marketplace. It's open on Sundays from 7:00 A.M. to 1:00 P.M., with peddlers from the surrounding areas setting up temporary booths and selling every imaginable type of merchandise, including antiques, second hand clothes, books, magazines, termite-eaten WWII wooden medallions, Etruscan hairpins, bushels of rosaries, and food products. It is located at the new gateway to the Roman wall, built in the 17th century by Pope Urban VII in response to the horrific sacking of Rome by German mercenaries. The present gateway replaced the original 3rd century ACE one built by Emperor Aurelianus, who decided to reinforce the existing Roman wall and include the strategic areas of Trastevere and Janiculum Hill within the wall's protection. It was a treat watching Barbara bargain with the Italian merchants; up and down they would go with their pricing, each trying to outsmart the other, knowing full well, that when the transaction was complete, the vendor would still be ahead of the game, and maybe Barbara would walk away with a bargain or at least with an item she convinced herself she couldn't find anywhere else at the bargain price. As far as I was concerned, shopping that takes more than five minutes is not my cup of tea, unless it's for golf clubs, cars or boats. I think most men would agree with me, shopping and "hondeling" are for girls, who have a lot more staying power than we do. So, when I saw the vendors' temporary booths extended for as far as the eye can see, I had to find a way out of the maze which had turned into a trap for me. The area was quite crowded and seemed safe, so I told Barbara that I was going back to the hotel to work out at the gym. She didn't mind, and seemed quite relieved to get me out of her hair so she could continue her favorite pastime, shopping and bargaining endlessly with merchants.

I took the opportunity to speak to our hotel concierge, Peter, to find out the best way to get to the Alpheus multiclub. He said "the only method is by taxi," as it was out of the downtown area where we were staying. Barbara knocked on the door to our room and woke me from a heavenly nap. Much to my surprise, she was only carrying two shopping bags, one with a small oriental multicolored reddish vase, and the other with leather lipstick holders for my daughter Laurie and daughter-in-law Donna, and, of course, one for herself. I told her that we would have to take a taxi for a short ride that evening and we should arrive at the venue early as, according to Peter, it gets very crowded around eleven o'clock. We decided to have a light salad dinner, as it is our habit not to eat too much food before we go dancing because it is very uncomfortable moving around the dance floor with full stomachs. We got to Alpheus early, but were surprised to see the crowds already building up. The venue is unique in that it's a multiclub building, with three main halls hosting every dance from Argentine Tango to Hip Hop. The favorite dance seemed to be the Salsa. The room with the Latin rhythm was already crowded with young people dancing and enjoying themselves. One of the dancers told us, in perfect English, that the Salsa craze reaches its crescendo when the annual World Salsa Festival is held in Rome, usually from the first week in July until the first week in September, attracting over a million and a half people from around the world, all coming to Rome to dance Salsa. Similar festivals are also conducted in many other major cities around the world. Rome also hosts the World Salsa Championship in the spring, lasting a few days and includes dance lessons, showcase dancing, Salsa performances by world famous dancers, and championship competitions on every level. Many are an open contest, which means anyone can enter regardless of their credentials or level of dance experience. We joined the dancers and felt right at home doing our Mambo-Salsa routines, which we've developed over the years, mixing steps from Salsa, Mambo and Cha-Cha. This method is called "cross dancing," where steps and rhythms from other dances are incorporated into the dance music being played. We usually dance both dances on the second beat, while many salsa dancers begin dancing on the first beat. For years there was much conflict in the Latin dancing community as to which method was correct, but fortunately, both have been accepted as the way to perform, and many dance instructors now ask their students which they prefer, dancing on the first or second beat? After exhausting ourselves with Salsa dancing, we moved over to the room that was featuring Argentine Tango, which is a lot less energetic, and danced the remainder of the night away in a less crowded, more romantic atmosphere. Some of the younger Tango dancers asked us where we learned our sophisticated routines. We told them about our trip to Buenos Aires and the fine instructors that we had who drilled the routines and attitude of the dance into our minds and bodies. They asked us for the name of the tour, which we gladly supplied: Daniel Trenner's "Bridge to Tango." We told them that he had several tours a year, including some to Europe, which they were excited to hear, as it meant that they could get great dancing instructions without traveling half-way around the world. They asked us to do one of our routines that they liked and we immediately accommodated them. We began with our balancing step, where I bend my knees and bring Barbara down with me and then we move from my left to right from our waists up. This sets the rhythm and pace of the dance. Then I step back with my left foot leaving my right leg extended in a corte position. I then throw my right leg around Barbara's extended right leg. She then quickly wraps her right leg around my right leg. We did this four times, and then I leaned forward and Barbara again wrapped her right leg around my right leg and held it there while I carried us back, which extended my right leg with her right leg wrapped around mine. The movement complete, I rotated our bodies from left to right several times, while Barbara's right leg was still wrapped around mine, this is done with her balancing herself on her left foot. We ended in a basic "Tango-close-step." Our friends loved the step and asked us to teach them the routine. We showed them the routine, but it took about 15minutes for them to get the general idea; it would take a lot of practice for them to perfect the complicated steps. It took us months of practice to finally get the patterns down pat.

To express their gratitude, our new friends bought us a couple of rounds of drinks. If we had time, we probably would have stayed, danced, and made merry into the wee hours of the morning with our Italian friends, but time was short and our drinking capacity even shorter, so we bid farewell to the Tango dancers and headed back to our hotel for a good nights rest. While waiting for a taxi, we noticed that the club had an active gay bar with people dancing and socializing without any friction between the various people in attendance at the other dance halls. We ended our last day in Rome totally satisfied with the entire trip and reminiscing about the good times and many friends we made on our three-week journey.

We made arrangements to fly from Rome to JFK with Alitalia Airlines, with a special business class program that allowed us to use Alitalia's first-class lounge. As fate would have it, our flight was delayed over an hour due to the baggage handling personnel threatening to strike. We put the first-class lounge to good use again; newspapers, coffee, finger food, TV, comfortable seats, and private toilets. Three hours passed rather quickly, and it was with regret that we boarded our plane and headed home to New York, humming:

> Arrivederci Roma, it's time for us to part, city of a million moon-lit faces,
>
> City of a million warm embraces; la-la-la-la . . .

CHAPTER SIX

Dancing in the Catskill Mountains of New York

AROUND THE FLOOR: JANUARY/FEBRUARY 1999

TRAVELING AROUND by Barbara Bivona

WATCHING JERRY PARRIS DANCE a showcase at his Dance Magic weekend at the Nevele Grande Resort & Country Club in Ellenville, New York, left us impressed with his styling. So much so, that we took classes in Waltz and Foxtrot patterns from him. At his master class, we learned a very beautiful step which we always admired others doing. At night, we were treated to the authentic live sounds of the Conjunto Imagen Band. The group is a favorite of Latin dancers, and we were thrilled that we would have an opportunity to dance to their music that evening. It was Latin music at its best.

A class in open variations in the Cha-Cha with Norton and Agi Hyman proved easy and uncomplicated; I learned three new steps in one hour. Best of all, I remembered them, and I'm still doing them with ease. Norty, as he calls himself, has a dance studio on Cangero Road in Monticello, New York. Paul Rubin, who has been teaching ballroom dancing for 42 years and is a well-known face on the Long Island dance scene, was also teaching at the Nevele. He is a past president of the New

York Dance Society and Fellow of North American DanceSport Teachers' Association. His Swing dance class seemed to be the most popular of all the classes. I'm sorry I had decided to merely "audit" this class, as he was teaching some steps I could enjoy doing. I will catch him on another dance weekend. I also audited Walter Montebianco's Rumba class and I was very impressed with the way he dances and his teaching method. I saw Walter doing a Mambo in the cocktail lounge and I couldn't tear myself away. He was sensational; one of the best Mambo dancers I've ever seen! When I asked him where he learned to dance, he told me he was originally from Peru, came to the United States, and eventually went to a dance club with friends. They were playing a Mambo, which he had never done, but he got up on the floor and faked it, moving to the rhythmic beat of the music. One of his friends entered him in a Mambo dance contest and, to everyone's surprise, he won. His prize was ten free dance lessons, and that's how he got started. Walter now teaches at the Progressive Dance Club in Nutley, New Jersey.

As luck would have it, sitting at our table we met a couple, Dee and Curt Anderson, who are neighbors of our friends, Dallas and Shirley Peck from Reston, Virginia. Now, on our annual trip to the D.C. area when we visit Dallas and Shirley, we have two new friends to see, thanks to a magical weekend with Dance Magic.

* *

Our adventure began when we met Jerry Parris at the Bennett's monthly Saturday night dance, held at the Suburban Temple in Wantagh, Long Island. He was hired to give a complimentary American Foxtrot dance lesson to about 200 dancers that were in attendance that evening. His method of teaching was painless and smooth, and the routines easy to remember. At the end of the hour-long lesson, he handed out pamphlets for a dance weekend (Dance Magic) at the Nevele Grande Resort & Country Club, located in the Catskill Mountains in the town of Ellenville, New York. This was a relatively new type of dance experience for us, so we asked him lots of questions about what the weekend would entail. He was just beginning to sponsor these getaway dances and the few he had already done were well attended by people from around the country; we were comfortable with the information that dancers of all levels were attracted to his Dance Magic weekends. The weekends consisted of three full days and two nights of dance lessons, given by experienced dance instructors, including Paul Rubin, who was at the Bennett's dance that evening and who we knew very well. He would be teaching Swing at the getaway. Norton and Agi Hyman, from upstate New York, who we also knew and admired for their Latin dancing skills, would also be two of the many instructors. We told Jerry that we would probably attend his next session and left the dance that night excited at the prospect of returning to the Catskill Mountains. We had spent a great deal of time there with our family, friends and children many years ago, during the heyday of the Borscht Belt.

Borscht Belt is a term for the summer resorts, cottages, and cabins in the Catskill Mountains in Sullivan and Ulster counties, upstate New York. Borscht is a beet soup, popular with people of Eastern European descent and, more specifically, of Jewish heritage; hence, the name, Borscht Belt. Due to the predominately Jewish population, the area was referred to as the Jewish Alps, and Sullivan County was called "Solomon" County. It was primarily a vacation place enjoyed by New York's Jews who escaped the city's hot summers by traveling, usually by car with an inordinate amount of traffic, to the cooler Catskills. Well-known resorts in the heydays of the 1940s, 1950s and 1960s included: Brown's, The Concord, Grossinger's, Kutsher, Nevele, Friar Tuck Inn, The Pines, Raleigh, Shawangha Lodge, and many more, not to mention the many cottages and summer camps that were spread throughout the region. The upscale places would host famous entertainers, such as Joey Adams, Woody Allen, Milton Berle, Mel Brooks, George Burns, Red Buttons, Sid Caesar, Danny Kaye, Jackie Mason, and Don Rickles. They were only the beginning of a long list of celebrities performing for the ever-gracious crowds. The area began to decline as a vacation haven with the availability of air conditioning and the popularity of jet planes, which allowed people to fly to faraway places in comfort in the same amount of time as it would take them to drive on the crowded highways to the Catskills. In addition, the decline of discrimination or "restrictions" in the hotel and travel industries in the 1960s allowed Jews access to other resorts and playgrounds around the world, so they joined the "jet set" and abandoned the Borscht Belt.

Jerry's flyer was very inviting; it gave a short biography of his accomplishments, including being called America's most talented teacher, dancer and choreographer of ballroom, social, nightclub, and exhibition dances. He is also credited with teaching celebrities and has hosted his own TV dance show. The scheduled continuous dance classes were: Quickstep, Merengue, Rumba, Tango, Cha-Cha, Foxtrot, Waltz, Hustle, Mambo, Swing, Argentine Tango, and Master Classes for advanced students. All meals were included in the weekend price and Nevele's sports facilities were also available, if anyone had the time to use them. The facilities, according to their brochure stated:

"Imagine a place, just a short drive from home, where the natural beauty and clean country air transports you to a state of serene exhilaration. Nestled in a valley bordered by the tranquil Shawangunk Mountain range, there are 1,000 panoramic acres called the Nevele Grande Resort and Country Club. Our 432-room resort offers an intimate estate of guest accommodations, conference facilities and recreational amenities. Whether you wish to exercise on our 18 holes of championship golf course, 8 outdoor or 5 indoor tennis courts, indoor/outdoor pools, or our state-of-the-art fitness center or play basketball, volleyball, softball, bocce, or shuffleboard; the Nevele Grande offers an extensive array of family and children's activities. A stay at the Nevele Grande includes comfortable accommodations, bountiful meals, exciting activities and nightly entertainment."

Well, there seemed to be a lot of activities going on for a three-day, two night adventure, so Barbara and I decided to add one night before the weekend and one night after so we could make a mini-vacation out of the trip and enjoy the hotel's facilities, as well as the great dancing that was anticipated from the program.

So we booked five days and four nights at the resort and got an early Thursday morning start, hoping to beat the horrific automobile traffic that was so common when traveling from Long Island to upstate New York. We arrived in time for lunch, checked into our room, and spent the better part of the afternoon enjoying the gym and indoor swimming pool. After a nice late afternoon nap, we went to dinner and ordered from an extensive menu. Unfortunately, none of the food was exceptional and the service mediocre, but we did pick and choose until we were satisfied and quite full. There was a show that evening in the large opulent theater, featuring no other then Jackie Mason, one of our favorite comedians. It was rare to see him since his dispute on the Ed Sullivan show, where he allegedly gave Ed the finger and was fired from the show, becoming persona non grata in the more upscale entertainment centers. His humor was spontaneous and "belly laughing funny"; his ability to poke fun at his Jewish heritage without being offensive is ingenious. After the show, we followed the direction of the music that was coming from the bar area, had a drink, danced a little, and headed for the elevator to our room. On our way, someone called out: "Hey meester, vate a minute." It was Jackie Mason taking a midnight stroll. He asked what our names were, "Mike and Bobby, nice names" he said. "What business are you in? An accountant," he said, "do I have a tax shelter for you. Do you like horses? You do? I have a stable that can make us a fortune........" He went on for half an hour, with his routine, serious as can be, plugging away at tax shelters. Wouldn't you know, the next evening his show had a whole skit on accountants and their tax shelters, specifically for horses and cows.

The next day the dancers started arriving, and the quiet resort began to jump with different music coming from the rooms assigned to us for our dancing classes. We visited the dance reception booth and received our weekend package of activities, including the various dance schedules, which were extensive and included the dances described in Jerry's brochure. Now we had to select the dance classes that we wanted to attend. It wasn't an easy task--the lessons were listed for beginners, intermediate and masters, for every hour, on the hour, of the day, beginning at 9:00 A.M., through to 5:00 P.M. We decided to select the intermediate level of dancing for Cha-Cha, the master level for Waltz and Foxtrot, and beginner's level for Mambo. We figured if any of the levels became too complicated for us, we would just switch to an easier one. It all worked out very well; Jerry taught both the Waltz and Foxtrot master classes, which we attended every day until we were comfortable with the new patterns. We had admired our friends performing these steps and were excited that we could finally imitate them. We learned one in particular that is still one of our favorite patterns in the Foxtrot, called the Grapevine. Jerry told us it was one of his favorite steps because it can be done in the Foxtrot, Polka, Electric Slide and Hustle. Starting with a basic pattern, slow-slow-quick-quick, we then did a full 360 degree spin turn. Then, with partners in a mirror position (facing each other) the Grapevine begins: partners move to the man's left (woman's right) with a sideStep, then a cross step in front of the supporting foot, then a side step, with a step behind the supporting foot, and then repeating the movement until it is convenient to enter another pattern, usually a basic slow-slow-quick-quick. We loved the pattern, going from a basic, into a full spin turn and then coming out into a Grapevine, repeating and then alternating steps at least eight times. It's probably one of the fastest Foxtrot steps in the dance syllabus and its lots of fun using the routine as crossover steps in the Polka and Hustle.

We also took Cha-Cha lessons in open variations from Norton and Agi Hyman, who operate a dance studio on Cangero

Road in Monticello, New York. We learned three new and very complicated open steps, which we still enjoy doing. Both instructors' teaching styles were painless and easy to remember, making the lessons a lot less intimidating then we expected. We learned a very popular, but slightly difficult step called the "New Yorker," which is also a crossover step that can be used in other dances, such as the Rumba, Mambo, and Samba. It goes like this: From a Cha-Cha basic, man's left forward, right back; then back, left-right-left. Then, man's right back and then left forward, followed by man's forward right-left-right. The man turns to an open right promenade (woman to her left) for 1-2, then turn facing each other (mirror position) for 1-2-3. It's important that there is a hesitation or eye contact at this point to make the routine look sharp. Next a turn to the man's left (woman's right) for an open promenade for Cha-Cha (1-2), and then turn to a mirror position for an in place cha-cha-cha (1-2-3). Now we add to the New Yorker by turning again to the man's right for cha-cha (1-2) and then mirror position for a swivel, in place, cha-cha-cha (1-2-3). Again open promenade to the man's right for cha-cha (1-2) and again to the mirror position for another swivel, in place, cha-cha-cha (1-2-3). It ends in a Cha-Cha basic, forward man's left and back right and then back left-right-left. We learned to do this routine in all our Latin dances, and even improvised the steps in the Foxtrot and Waltz.

I was fortunate to take some Swing lessons from Paul Rubin, while Barbara was auditing dance classes for her article in "Travelling Around." Swing lessons were given by Paul, who is from Long Island and well known for his dancing acumen and skill. He has been teaching ballroom dancing for 42 years and is a past president of the New York Dance Society and a fellow of the North American DanceSport Teachers' Association. His Swing dance class was always crowded, but he did manage to control the 40-plus dancers and get his dance patterns across to most of them. The beginner's class for Mambo was taught by a young man in his mid-20s named Walter Monteblanco. Mambo was a dance Barbara and I had lots of trouble with, so this gave us an opportunity to see if we could polish up with some new steps and styling. We saw him perform a Mambo in the cocktail lounge at the hotel and were spellbound by his styling and execution of the dance. He was, without a doubt, one of the best Latin dancers we had ever seen. Barbara asked him where he learned to perform the Mambo so well. He said he was from Peru and didn't have the faintest idea or interest in dancing when he came to the United States. A friend invited him to a Latin dance club, where he was asked by a young lady to do the Mambo. She was so pretty that he couldn't resist dancing with her, so he got up and faked the dance, moving to the beat of the music and shuffling around. One of his friends entered his name in the Mambo dance contest that night and, much to his surprise, he won. The prize was ten free dance lessons which he took with a passion. He is currently teaching Latin dances at the Progressive Dance Club in Nutley, New Jersey. We were able to pick up some nice underarm and double turn routines from him, but, most importantly, he corrected our posture, which, in Mambo, is quite different from many of the Latin dances. My posture is to stand straight and lean forward from the waist, always keeping the knees in a bent position. Barbara's position is to do whatever she wanted, as long as she kept her hips in motion and her arms swaying. Needless to say, she looked a lot better doing her Latin moves than I did.

Our dinners were open seating and, as advertised, music and a large area were available for dancing before, during, and after dinner. We sat at a table for eight; we all introduced ourselves and stated our home towns. Six degrees of separation came into play again in our lives when one of the couples, Dee and Curt Anderson, said they were from Reston, Virginia. We told them that we had dear friends in that town by the name of Dallas and Shirley Peck; they were shocked, as they are their dearest friends also and spend every New Year's Eve with them. We exchanged stories and were delighted when they asked us to share the upcoming New Year's Eve with them so we could surprise Dallas and Shirley. Unfortunately, we couldn't accept their offer, as we had already made plans for the holidays, but decided to do the next best thing. We took pictures, individually and together. They also planned on videoing Dallas' and Shirley's reactions to seeing the photos and would send us a copy, along with the pictures they took of our dance weekend. We usually plan our annual visit to Reston, Virginia, on our way from New York to Florida during the first week of January. We decided that would be a great time to get together and again view the video of Dallas' and Shirley's reaction to seeing the photos. We marked our calendars and made plans for the encounter, which turned out to be one of the most cherished experiences of our lives.

That evening, in the large cocktail lounge which had a nice-sized dance floor, we were introduced to the live sounds of the Latin Conjunto Imagen Band that was one of the hottest new and upcoming Latin bands on the music and dance scenes. Everyone was familiar with their music and was thrilled to meet and hear them in person. The bandleaders were Ernie Acevedo and Junior Rivera, who, with their compadres, compelled everyone to dance to their great Latin sounds in Mambo, Merengue, Rumba and Cha-Cha, until the dancers were exhausted. Considering that we all took dance lessons for the better part of the day, it was amazing that there was energy left in any of us to continue into the late evening, but when you love dancing, time and energy seem to be endless.

The short weekend came to a close after lunch on Sunday; we exchanged names, address, and telephone numbers with our new friends that we planned on meeting after the Dance Magic event. Barbara and I stayed on for another day and after lunch decided to do some toboggan riding down the slopes that were prepared for that purpose. We were a little leery about sitting in a small enclosed sled and zigzagging down an icy hill, until we saw children of every age and size having a great time with their toys. Down we went, exciting as excitement can be. The long ride down left us so breathless, we decided not to do a repeat performance. At the end of the run, we spotted snowmobiles that were for the use of the hotel's guests, so feeling our oats after our non-eventful but scary toboggan run, we rushed to the snowmobiles for another new adventure. There were only a few riders on the large acreage dedicated to snowmobiling; the thrill of flying on the snow was exhilarating and having Barbara holding me tight from behind and screaming in my ears because of my reckless driving and excessive speed (about 20 miles per hour) made the half hour ride all the more fun. I was just hoping that our drive back to Long Island would have the same clear roads, with as few obstacles as this snow field.

CHAPTER SEVEN

Dancing on the Mississippi Queen Riverboat and on to Mardi Gras

AROUND THE FLOOR: JULY/OCTOBER 2000

TRAVELING AROUND by Barbara Bivona

AS A YOUNG GIRL, I remember being fascinated with the adventures of Tom Sawyer and his friend, Huck Finn. So much so, that I would daydream about the Mississippi River and spending days on a paddleboat. Mike, on the other hand, told me he would daydream about Mardi Gras in New Orleans, so these became items on our "wish list" of things to do before we "kicked the bucket." One magical day, we received a brochure in the mail from the Delta Steamboat Company advertising a cruise on the Mississippi Queen Paddlewheel boat; the theme was big band dancing and Mardi Gras, while cruising the Mighty Mississippi, ending in New Orleans and being guests at a Grand Mardi Gras Ball. We couldn't ask for more; this was everything we both wanted in one great package. If you've never been paddle wheeling, this is like no other cruise experience. It is strictly Americana, the food is authentic Southern cooking, complete with great barbecues and with all you can eat chicken, fried catfish, corn bread, and lots of other delicious regional specialties from the heart of the Deep South.

We were given all the raw materials to create our own Mardi Gras costumes to dress up for an onboard celebration to the music of the great Guy Lombardo Band on the last night of the cruise. We were delighted by their dance music. Not just the playing of hits that made Lombardo famous, but for their good and very danceable arrangements for Swing and Latin. Earlier in the week, we were treated to the music of the Les Elgart Band, and we danced the evenings away to his music that has held its own with the passing of time. He enjoyed sharing stories about his big band days with anyone who cared to chat with him. We danced to his music the night of the dance contest. Most of the contestants were not really experienced "dancers," but that didn't stop them from having a great time while getting into the spirit of Mardi Gras. Trophies were awarded to all the participants, which put a smile on everyone's face after the competition. Following the cruise, we spent six days in the French Quarter of New Orleans, attending the parades and festivities, culminating with a Grand Mardi Gras Ball at the Fairmont Hotel, hosted by a Krewe from the Mardi Gras parade. The Krewes are organizations that put on the parade, which includes many floats, all with their own variation of the main theme. The year was 1992, which was the 500th Centennial celebration of the discovery of America. The theme of Mardi Gras and our Krewe's theme was "The Discovery." The Ball commenced with Queen Isabella, King Ferdinand, and their court being presented to the guests. In addition, Christopher Columbus, Amerigo Vespucci, and their shipmates circulated among the guests and introduced themselves, one by one, with chivalry and flare. I was shocked and delighted when Columbus came over and asked me to do the first dance of the evening with him, a spellbinding Waltz.

* *

While sorting through our mail, a colorful brochure stood out from among the other documents. It was a vacation invitation from the Delta Steamboat Company requesting our presence on one of their Mississippi River cruises. The one that caught my eye was a theme cruise featuring Big Bands, such as Guy Lombardo and his Royal Canadians and Les Elgart and his Manhattan Swing Orchestra. The cruise coincided with the annual New Orleans Mardi Gras and the 500th Centennial of the Discovery of America by Christopher Columbus, which was the main theme of the festival. Well, there it was: Barbara's childhood dream of traveling down the Mississippi River with Tom Sawyer and Huck Finn on a paddlewheel boat and my dream of going to a Mardi Gras festival in New Orleans. Both of our dreams of sailing on a Showboat (like the one in the great musical of that name) with Big Band music, and my passion and infatuation with collecting books on the Age of Discovery, especially concerning the great navigator, Christopher Columbus, were all in one package. Barbara and I couldn't believe that so many of the items on our "Wish List" could be satisfied in one vacation. We figured that we could take a riverboat trip on the Mississippi Queen Paddlewheel, for seven days, which began and ended in New Orleans, and then extend our trip to include six days in a centrally-located hotel around Bourbon Street, so we could really get into the Mardi Gras' spirit. We spent a previous vacation in New Orleans many years ago, but not at festival time; although it does seem that every day in New Orleans is a festival. We were familiar with the layout of the area and what would be the most advantageous location for our stay. On our prior visit to the city, we stayed at the Royal Sonesta Hotel in the Bourbon Street area, but the people and traffic noise made the stay less desirable then we hoped for. We did have occasion to enjoy a great dinner in an upscale restaurant at the 17 stories Hotel Monteleone in the French Quarter off of Bourbon Street, which was located in a less noisy place than the other hotel, especially in the rooms on the upper floors. It also boasted a rooftop swimming pool with spectacular views of the French Quarter and the historical city. We called our travel agent, Barbara, at Liberty Travel and told her what our plans were and asked her to put together a travel package for us. Considering that the trip would be quite extensive and somewhat complicated, we decided to leave all the arrangements and details in her experienced hands. Our decision turned out to be wise; within a week she laid out our itinerary, including all the sightseeing that we planned plus some extra goodies.

We flew American Airlines to New Orleans, and that's when the fun began. Our luggage didn't appear on the arrival carousel; the sinking feeling in my stomach got worst when we were the only passengers left waiting for our baggage to appear. After wasting a couple of hours with representatives of the Steamship Company and American Airlines, and filling out numerous forms describing our missing property, we left the airport and took a taxicab to the New Orleans Port where our ship was docked. The cab driver got lost in a rain downpour that restricted his visibility. I brought to his attention that what seemed to be the buildings of the city, were behind us; he said, "sorry, my mistake" and then turned his cab around to the right direction. We finally got to the embarkation point just as the rain stopped. There was a crowd of people on the dock in a covered area enjoying a small combo band's music, while they imbibed drinks provided by several waitresses from the ship. I immediately had a scotch and water, which was my drink of choice in those days, and before I knew it, down went several more, but to no avail. I was so hyper from the loss of our luggage and the prospect of going on a two-week vacation with little or no clothes, which was exacerbated by our getting lost on the way to the ship, that I was convinced that the whole journey was going to turn out to be a disaster. Barbara, although upset, tried to calm me down. She wasn't overly concerned, as the prospect of buying a new wardrobe for the trip wouldn't be an unhappy event for her. My mind formed prayers, hoping that the representative of the steamship company, who remained behind at the airline terminal, would locate our baggage. Until then, we just had to make the best of things. We boarded the paddlewheel and checked with the ship's coordinator, who informed us that due to our misfortune, they were upgrading our room, no charge, to a full suite. Well, maybe things were starting to turn around; in time my drinks did their job, and I calmed down quite a bit, returning to my optimistic, fun-loving self.

We went to dinner and felt the boat moving away from the dock, which brought back that helpless feeling that one gets when things happen that are out of their control; where was our luggage and what's next? How will we replace all of our personal belongings? The delicious French cuisine tempered my feelings of anxiety, somewhat; but sharing a bottle of wine with Barbara, was more effective. We hurried back to our cabin, opened the door, and miracles of all miracles, our baggage was staring at us. I lifted a piece and panic returned; the luggage was weightless. Now we had our bags, but there was nothing in them. Unbeknownst to us, our cabin steward had unpacked our bags and put our belongings in the dressers and closet. We both collapsed on the queen size bed and just remained silent and motionless for about 15 minutes. We regained our composure, freshened up, and journeyed to the lounge area for the tour orientation and to meet fellow passengers. When retiring for the evening, we both agreed that we should put this day behind us and erase the mishaps from our minds. Hopefully, we would continue with our wonderful journey with no further unhappy incidences. Mark Twain aptly said, "The face of the river, in time, becomes a wonderful book … not one to be read once and thrown aside, for it has a new story to tell every day." Well, we were hoping for a new story when we woke up the following morning.

And a new story it was. The sun peeked through our partially opened drapes; fresh Mississippi River air forced its way into our senses, while a whiff of bacon and eggs floating by got our attention, so we quickly dressed and hastened to the place creating the aroma. I would have been content to just sit on one of the outside chaise lounges and breathe in the fresh air and intoxicating smells from the food being prepared for our morning meal. What a wonderful beginning to a new day. After breakfast, the first mate took some of us on a guided tour of the Mississippi Queen. His dissertation was robotic, but precise as to the history and specifications of the paddlewheel. "The boat was built in 1976 in celebration of the bicentennial and, when built, was the largest steamboat in existence. It's 382-feet long, 68-feet wide, weighing 3,364 tons; has 208 staterooms accommodating 422 passengers and a complement of over 100 crew members and staff. The red circular paddlewheel itself weighs 70 tons; located forward of it, at the stern of the boat, is the largest steam driven calliope on the river, boasting 44 pipes, whose music is magical and can be heard for five miles, announcing the majestic ship's presence on the river. The décor of the boat is Americana, with floral wallpaper and matching fabric, beveled mirrors, crystal chandeliers and polished brass railings. The staircases are red carpeted with ornate wooden hand rails, chairs, and the accessories are in the Victorian style. The Grand Saloon is the center of activity and is used as a showroom and gathering place, its dance floor large enough to accommodate the swinging dancers on the ship." My favorite place, the wheel house, is forward; what a thrill it was to steer the ship, with the captain's permission of course, and under his watchful eyes. He let me navigate an easy part of the river for about five minutes. "The steamboats were finer than anything on shore – like palaces." Mark Twain was right when he wrote those words in his book, Life on the Mississippi. I was navigating a palace down the waterway, with images of the great river flowing through my mind from the Broadway musical Showboat. I was humming the river's song, "Ol' Man River" and, for a few minutes, I became a riverboat captain transporting my passengers and cargo to the far away towns along the majestic river during the heyday of the paddlewheel boats.

We spent a relaxing and friendly day traveling the river, making friends, and just enjoying the homey feeling that is prevalent on small river boats. A big difference with cruising on a large ocean liner is that the staff of this ship were all American, not what we had experienced while traveling on larger vessels, where most of the crew members are foreigners with difficult names to remember. It didn't take long to get use to the odiferous surroundings in the air of deep Southern fried cooking, and the comforting feeling of the sun resting on my body as I enjoyed reading some of Mark Twain's adventures, while spreading out on a chaise lounge, in the open air at the stern of the boat, lulled by the rhythm of the bright red paddlewheel and dozing into dreamland between paragraphs. The ship's small combo of four, plus two piano players, played music on and off all day. Their sounds floating through the air, mixing with the aroma of our next meal, gave me the feeling of being at a carnival. Dinner was a cholesterol nightmare; Barbara and I ordered the same food: Southern fried chicken, tons of biscuits, candied beans and, for dessert, Shoo Fly Pie. It took many turns around the boat to try to alleviate the guilt of overeating before we came to terms with the fact that we were on vacation and an occasional "pig out" wasn't going to kill us, at least not right away.

We followed the sound of music to the Grand Salon, where Les Elgart's Manhattan Swing Orchestra had guests busy on the dance floor doing a Cha-Cha. It was surprising how many single ladies were in attendance, but the cruise operators evidently anticipated this and provided some male hosts to dance and talk with the girls throughout the evening. Between sessions, the ship's smaller band entertained us with light jazz and singing from their female vocalist. We danced until the wee hours and returned to our upgraded suite, content that the forgettable mishaps we experienced were being replaced by "happy times." We were welcomed in our cabin by a complimentary bottle of champagne and chocolate heart kisses strewn on our bed. We decided to save the beverage for another time, but the temptation of the chocolates was too much to resist, so we munched while listening to the smooth lazy soft piped-in music, and concluded a relaxing, pleasant day on the Mississippi River as we entered from the beginning of a dream vacation into our evening's dreamland.

We were awakened the next morning by the ship's deafening steam whistle: toot-toot-toot, which announced to the town of Natchez and everyone else within its listening range, that we were coming to town to explore its beauty and meet the local folks. One of the pianists joined in on the calliope and began harmonizing with the whistle's tooting. We followed the scent of bacon and eggs and, after indulging in a hearty breakfast, including our favorite Southern biscuits, which I was becoming addicted to, we went to the stern of the boat to watch the ship maneuver into the town dock, greeted by longshoremen, who quickly secured its heavy lines. The crew magically extended a platform from the bow of the boat to the levee, which allowed for easy exiting from the boat. A committee of the town's people and a small brass band greeted us to their historic antebellum town. We planned on spending time exploring the town and visiting at least one of the plantations that were located in and around the quaint settlement. The area of the town dates back to the 8th century CE, when the Natchez Indians were masters of that part of the country. Built on the sight of an ancient Indian village, it takes its name from that tribe. Around 1730, after several wars, the French defeated the inhabitants and disbursed the Native Americans, keeping many as slaves. Today most of the remaining Natchez tribe has integrated with the Chickasaw, Creek, and Cherokee Indians, and are mainly in Oklahoma within the Cherokee and Creek nations, quite a distance from their ancestral lands. The town boasts a population of about 18,000 people including some Natchez Indians, who are probably the descendants of the French slaves. It is probably one of the oldest cities in North America; elegant, well preserved, and a showcase for antebellum homes and magnificent plantations. Walking through the town was a throwback to pre-civil war times, especially when viewing areas where town folks are dressed in period costumes; I'm sure for the benefit of tourists such as myself, who are totally captivated by the charade. Like many Southern towns, the fragrance of flowers, particularly magnolias, freely occupy the air to the enjoyment of its recipients. We couldn't avoid walking into Stanton Hall Plantation which occupies a full block in the town. Built in 1851-1857 for Frederick Stanton, a cotton broker, who went to great lengths to import building materials from Europe, such as moldings, marble fireplace mantles, wrought ironworks, and a great deal of the furnishings, some of which are still intact and displayed throughout the mansion. The entrance immediately impresses visitors with its 17-foot-high ceiling and 72-foot-long hallway. The parlor displays gilded French mirrors and the fireplaces and mantles throughout are stunning in color and glaze. While exploring the mansion, the smell of buttered biscuits caught our attention, we were pleased to learn that the mansion, which became a National Historic Landmark in 1974, had its own restaurant, The Carriage House. The stately gardens were inviting and spending a few minutes enjoying the colorful flowers and topiary, while sitting on a bench was refreshing and tranquil. The compelling "call of the biscuits" finally overcame us and we went with haste to the place where the aroma was being created. We had our favorite foods: biscuits with gravy, fried chicken legs, toasty fries, berry ice tea, and more biscuits. The steamboat's whistle, toot-toot-toot, announced that it was time for us to return. The picture below was taken when we disembarked the boat to explore the quaint town.

When we returned to our cabin, there were written instructions and competition rules for the dance contest that was to be held that evening. There was also fabric laid out on the bed for us to make costumes for the Mardi Gras party, which was to be held on the last day of the cruise while heading back to our last stop, in time for the live New Orleans' festival. Much to do and so little time to do it in! We were novice dancers at that time and were embarrassed to enter a dance contest, especially having seen some pretty good dancers on the floor the night before. The competition rules were trophies for first, second and third place in Cha-Cha, Rumba, Foxtrot, Waltz and Swing, and the same for best overall dancers. No professionals, dance hosts, or crew members were allowed to enter the contest. We only knew the basics to all the dances except Swing, which we took some lessons in over the last year. So we reluctantly entered the Swing contest just to get into the spirit of things.

The music of Les Elgart's Band could be heard throughout the boat. We followed his sound to the Grand Saloon, where many of the passengers were warming up their dance routines for the competition. We were both intimidated by the better dancers showing their stuff on the dance floor and were inclined to withdraw from the competition, but we gathered our courage and picked up our number 25, which we pinned to the back of our clothing. It wasn't long before we realized that we made the right decision to enter the competition, which resulted in our meeting new friends at a very rapid pace. Before the main event, everyone on the dance floor was having a great time moving and jumping around to the sounds of the band and changing partners on cue from the boat's dance master, which enhanced meeting many of the passengers. The various dance competitions had from 15 to 20 couples in each category: Cha-Cha, Rumba, Foxtrot, Waltz and Swing, ranging from beginners to somewhat good dancers, but absolutely no top-notch dancers, which made the atmosphere a lot less tense. The judges included some dance hosts and different ranks of crew members; all in all, they did a commendable job in judging the contestants. It seemed that everyone won a prize, including us for coming in third place in Swing dancing. The evening felt more like a jamboree then a dance competition; the atmosphere was relaxed and jovial without the stress that usually accompanies dance competitions. We ended the evening as champions (as previously mentioned, we won third place in Swing) and retired to our cabin, wishing our many new friends a "fond farewell until the morrow."

We woke again to the toot-toot-toot of the steam whistle, reminding us that today we had a mock race with the Mississippi Queen's older sister, Delta Queen, who was the undisputed current champion paddlewheel of the river. The Delta Queen was born in 1927, weighed 1,650 tons, is 285-feet long and 60-feet wide, and carries 200 passengers and 80 crew members. Quite a small ship compared to her younger sister, who is 3,364 tons, 382-feet in length, 68-feet in width, and carries 422 passengers and over 100 crew members. But the Delta is a feisty ship and has won the symbolic "Golden Antlers," which she proudly displays below her pilot house, attesting to the fact that she is the fastest steamboat on the Mississippi River (based on her pilot's expertise and having won its last annual encounter). The history of the Golden Antlers dates back to 1963 when the steamships, Belle of Louisville and the Cincinnati's Delta Queen, ran their first race. It was a 14-mile battle up and down the Ohio River, on the first Wednesday in May before the Kentucky Derby. Over the years, this race has been drawing as much attention from the locals as the Derby race. Since then, the boats race against each other every year prior to the Kentucky Derby, for the bragging rights of "fastest boat on the river" and for the coveted Golden Antlers. The antlers are from an elk and are sprayed gold, signifying the sleekness and speed of the animal and the purity of gold. Our race with the champion began at "Dead Man's Bend" and ended at "Washout Bayou." These names conjure up all kinds of images; stories have come down through the years and have been repeated so often that they are accepted as fact. According to Jeffery, our ship's historian: "Over 150-years ago, during the heyday of the rootin' tootin' steamboat era, the river landings were lawless and violent places to live. The most popular of these roughhouse places was the Natchez-Under-the-Hill Landing, located just below the bluffs overlooking the river at Natchez, Mississippi. There were brawls and knife fights daily, so violent that the local police would not venture down Silver Street, which stretched from the top of the bluffs down to the river's edge. It was a busy stop for the steamboats and a hangout for cutthroats, thieves, mustached gamblers, and ladies of the night. With all that violence, there were always dead bodies that had to be disposed of, and the river was a convenient repository. The bodies would float down to a bend in the river and accumulate there. Many of the bodies that were retrieved still had knives protruding from their decaying bodies, hence the name Dead Man's Bend." The crew members spent the morning decorating our boat with banners, and placed noise makers throughout the boat for our use to add to the festivities. The male members dressed in period costumes; many were mustached gamblers, gentlemen of the day, or savory looking characters. The girls wore riverboat attire from that era, which included frills on their beautiful dresses, fancy hats, and pom-poms for the cheerleaders. The calliope played continuous music, including some songs of Stephen Foster, such as: "Oh' Susanna," " Nelly was a Lady," " Nelly Bly," "Old Folks at Home," " My Old Kentucky Home" and, of course, "De Camp Town Races." The Delta Queen pulled alongside us and blew its challenging whistle loud and clear, "toot-toot-toot." Our response was a spontaneous, "toot-toot-toot," and back and forth they went with the whistle blowing and playing music from their respective calliopes battling each other for supremacy of the air and waterway. In addition to the Delta's jazz band playing on her bow, the passengers on board seemed to be having a post victory celebration, a little premature for our taste, so we also started singing, howling, and making all sorts of loud sounds with our noise makers.

The expected long whistle blast from the Delta signaled the start of the race; being the smaller and lighter of the two vessels, she was off and running ahead of us with ease. We struggled for what seemed to be an eternity to get our heavier craft ahead, but to no avail, even though our boat had more powerful engines. The little mistress moved ahead, its pilots evidently had more experience than ours, and found more of the slow water (slack water) which allows a boat to move with less resistance and, therefore, more speed. Near the end of the race, our boat's engines began to show their strength and started pulling up to her older sister; inch by inch we finally caught up, but it was too late. The Delta seemed to become jet propelled as we approached, and crossed the finish line ahead of us by several boat lengths. She would retain her title as queen of the Mississippi and hold onto her "Golden Antlers" until challenged again by a faster boat. The celebration noise became louder from her majesty as she sped away, whistle blowing and calliope singing, while the passengers swayed to the jazz band's rhythmic sounds waving goodbye to our losing vessel. Her bright red paddlewheel churned and splashed water far and high as the boat picked up steam and disappeared around the bend and into the horizon.

We retreated to the cheerful "Golden Antlers Bar" (not the actual antlers, but good enough), with floor to ceiling windows and displaying beautifully decorated table servings of coffee, tea, hot chocolate, and freshly baked cookies, which were available around the clock for the passenger's delight. We enjoyed our snacks as we listened to Jeffery, the "Riverlorian's" voice, coming gently from the loud speaker system, explaining the sights and history of the various places we were viewing through the large windows. He would be the river historian throughout our voyage, his pleasant manner and his knowledge of the Mississippi River greeted us every morning to explain the history of various places of interest on our scheduled stops, while we enjoyed a buffet breakfast. He was a young southern gentleman that relayed fascinating historical information to us in a very gentlemanly manner.

Our dinner was another unique Deep Southern treat, with biscuits. we both had side orders of steaks to complement the many biscuits we stuffed our faces with. We finished our meal with key lime pie, downed with a wonderful secret blended coffee with a light taste of hazelnut, which totally did us in, as getting off our chairs became a strenuous event. We headed to the Grand Saloon to exercise and stretch our legs by dancing; hopefully enough to lose some of the weight that we were rapidly gaining. There weren't too many people on the dance floor; our new friends all seemed to be sitting around complaining that they were eating too much and having a hard time moving, even if only to perform simple dance steps. We shuffled around the floor for about an hour, noticing that many of our friends were no longer in attendance. It didn't take too long for us to come to the same conclusion, so we retired for the evening, dragging ourselves away from the dance floor and slowly moseying along to our cabin.

The next day we were scheduled to visit the historic city of Vicksburg, Mississippi. The Confederate and Union armies fought for this strategic location during the Civil War, it was thought to be impregnable and was known as the "Gibraltar of the Confederacy." The battle resulted in the loss of many lives on both sides. Strategically it was considered the key to controlling the Mississippi River and, therefore, the outcome of the Civil War. It was imperative that General Grant capture the fortress city so he could divide the South and bring the war closer to its conclusion. After several battles lasting 47 days, the city surrendered to the union forces on July 4, 1863, giving control of the river to the Northern Forces. Vicksburg National Military Park was established to memorialize that battle and the brave men who fought and sacrificed their young lives for what they believed to be a just cause. The brochure I read states: "Today, the battlefield at Vicksburg is in an excellent state of preservation. It includes 1,325 historic monuments and markers, 20 miles of reconstructed trenches and earthworks, a 16-mile tour road, an antebellum home, 144 emplaced cannons, the restored Union gunboat-USS Cairo, and the Vicksburg National Cemetery." The town is another antebellum Southern hospitable place to visit and welcomes tourist to explore its antique shops and plantations or just to walk around and enjoy the friendly surroundings. It has a population of about 25,000 people and is quite a bustling place. We decided to visit the ship's library the next day and find a couple of interesting books to read, skip the sightseeing of the famous historic town, and just enjoy the boat's facilities.

The toot-toot-toot of the steam whistle and the exotic music coming from the calliope announced to all within listening range that the Queen was arriving at Vicksburg. Before reaching the town, Jeffery brought to our attention that we were passing the very place that the Union gunboat, U.S.S. Cairo, was sunk by confederate artillery. As the story goes, "The U.S.S. Cairo was one of the seven ironclad gunboats named in honor of the towns along the upper Mississippi and Ohio rivers. These powerful ironclads were formidable vessels and each carried 13 big deadly cannons. The North had hoped that these ships would help in gaining control of the Mississippi River and split the Confederacy in two. The Cairo saw limited action before meeting its destiny. Its captain, Lt. Commander Thomas O. Selfridge, Jr., was a daring and ambitious leader who decided, on December 12, 1862, to lead a small flotilla up the Yazoo River, north of Vicksburg, to destroy the Confederate's gun placements and clear the way for General Grant to mount his attack on the city. Although the gunboat had ironclad around its superstructure, which offered protection from enemy artillery, its hull was made of wood, and that is where fate decided to place two direct hits, from electronically detonated torpedoes. It sank in 36-feet of water in just 12 minutes and was to remain in its burial ground until 1965, when it was excavated and brought to local shipyards to be restored. In 1972, Congress gave its permission for the gunboat to be placed in the Vicksburg National Military Park, where it still remains as a reminder, that winners of wars still have losses."

The town's welcoming committee was there to greet us, band and all; its music along with our calliope's contribution reminded me of the sounds coming from the merry-go-round I rode as a child in Coney Island, New York. The horses and buggies on the landing brought to mind the many horses I rode on the carousel at my favorite childhood playground. It brought back the same warm feelings of my childhood that came with being with loved ones and enjoying the fresh sea air and the aroma of the surrounding carnival. Many of the passengers disembarked, while Barbara and I went to the library to fetch some reading material. I spotted "The Songs of Hiawatha" by Henry Wadsworth Longfellow, which I read many, many years ago and couldn't remember anything from the book other than "from the shores of . . . " I chose it as my companion for the day while Barbara thumbed through many books before finding "It" by her favorite author, Stephen King. We found our way to the Paddlewheel Lounge that had only a couple of guests relaxing and enjoying the view from its large floor to ceiling windows. We found two comfortable chairs and, caressing cups of coffee in one hand and our books in the other, we began what was to become a very quiet and relaxing reading experience, with a great view of the river to boot. While enjoying our "alone time," an announcement came over the public address system that the current Guy Lombardo Band (he died in 1977), was expected to board our boat within the hour. Although we enjoyed the music of the Les Elgart Band, we were thrilled that the Lombardo orchestra was going to join us for the remainder of the trip. His was the premier orchestra throughout my youth and into adulthood; New Year's Eve was meaningless without the sound of his music being played on the radio from the Roosevelt Hotel, and later on television from the Waldorf Astoria in New York City. He and his sweet saxophones bid the old year farewell and welcomed the birth of the new year with smooth sounds from his orchestra playing "Auld Lang Syne." As with the Les Elgart Band, the Lombardo Band was a smaller version then the original, which was appropriate, as the boat didn't have adequate room to accommodate a full orchestra. The name "Guy Lombardo" brought to mind when I was on a two-week furlough while serving in the United States Air Force. My buddies and I decided to be at Times Square, in New York City for the "dropping of the ball" to celebrate the turn of the year. The four of us chipped in and rented one room at an off-beat hotel that we could afford, just blocks away from Times Square. On that eventful evening, we waited with upward to a million jubilant people, who were crowding the streets in every direction. Revelers, hanging from windows of the surrounding buildings in Times Square, seemed to be directing the people below with the waving of their arms, throwing paper trailers, blasting noisemakers, and howling strange noises from above. At 11:59 P.M., the 1,070-pound, 6-foot-diameter Waterford crystal ball located at the top of a 77-foot flagpole, high above One Times Square was lowered, reaching the bottom at exactly 12:00 Midnight. The revelers became a humongous, well-rehearsed choir, singing in unison, on cue, to Guy Lombardo's "Auld Lang Syne." The performance was broadcast every hour throughout the world in each time zone, to the music of Guy Lombardo and his Royal Canadians; beginning from the International Time Zone in the South Pacific and ending in Western Samoa. So much a part of our lives was Guy Lombardo that, in our early years as owners of a 28-foot Chris Craft cabin cruiser, we would have to drive our car down Guy Lombardo Boulevard in Freeport, Long Island, and past his home to get to our boat, which was docked on the same bay. On many occasions we would pass him on his boat and get a "sailor's wave" from him and his mates. We also spent many a pleasant evening at the 15,000 seat amphitheater in Jones Beach State Park, which was built on a landfill surrounded by a moat, located in Wantagh, Long Island, New York, enjoying concerts and Broadway musicals, such as "Carousel" and "Showboat." His band played there often and, on other occasions during a performance's intermission, he would sail by on his large yacht with some members of his band to entertain the audience with his special music. His passing was felt deeply throughout the locale and, surely, the world.

While sailing down the busy Mississippi, I distinctly remember seeing a barge breaking through the light fog, carrying an enormous red derrick. As it approached our vessel, its large size dwarfed us and everything else within sight. It must have been over 40-feet in height and was propped on a floating barge that seemed too small to carry such a large structure. It reminded me of the uneasy feeling of watching a human pyramid, the small person on the bottom supporting layers of people above, and swaying as if preparing to collapse. All the viewers ran to the opposite side of our boat in anticipation of the crane falling and crushing our craft, along with its passengers. As it passed, the little red towing tug boat's pilot smiled and waved, he seemed to sense that we were in awe of his cargo and that his smile and wave would reassure us that all was well. An announcement over the public address system was welcomed and broke the anxiety that many experienced while passing the fearful cargo. "The kite flying contest will begin in one hour, from the deck at the stern of the boat, by the paddlewheel. The material for making kites is in the Grand Saloon. Whoever keeps their kite in the air for the longest time, will become the 'Kite Master' of the cruise and have the honor and privilege of wearing the boat's 'Kite Hat,' which is a large white hat with a small colorful kite sitting on top and entitles the wearer to a salute of respect from fellow passengers. We consider it almost as prestigious as winning the Golden Antlers." Barbara and I hustled to the Saloon and picked up our kite kits and began assembling them. She was a lot more successful than I, as putting together this child's kit was beyond my comprehension. One of the crewmembers had to assist me with the job, but we finally did get the 4-foot beauty assembled. Many of the passengers gave up trying to put their kites together and decided instead to watch the contestants vie for the title of "Kite Master." My kite, although there was sufficient wind to get it afloat, went straight down into the Mississippi River. Barbara was more proficient than me and got hers in the air with ease, being helped along by a nice stiff breeze. Everyone, sooner or later, lost their kites, which kept the boat's small skiff that followed, busy retrieving the remnants. An 80-year-old grandmother, Louise by name, took first place by having her kite stay airborne for three minutes, which was quite an accomplishment, considering most of the kites went straight down like lead balls. In addition to Louise being named "Mistress of the Kite," she was given an enormous complementary mint julep drink for her bravery and skill, in addition to the coveted "Kite Hat."

After dinner that evening, we meandered over to the Grand Saloon and joined some of our friends at a ring side table; we had the wine steward pop open our complimentary bottle of champagne and pour everyone at the table a glass, which we drank slowly while waiting in anticipation of hearing some great dancing music from the famous band. We were not disappointed. They played " Harbor Lights," " Red Roses for a Blue Lady," " The Anniversary Song," and "My Old Flame." They also played Swing: "The Music Goes Round and Round," "Hot Time in the Old Town Tonight," and the great "Beer Barrel Polka" (Roll out the Barrel). We danced ourselves into oblivion doing Foxtrots, Waltzes, Polkas and Swing. While dancing and reminiscing, I visualized the great Lombardo leading a much larger full orchestra at the Jones Beach Amphitheater and on his large yacht, floating around the moat surrounding the theater, making his special sound of music to the applause of his beloved audience. We returned to our cabin exhausted with euphoria. I quickly went into a deep sleep with the sweet sounds of big band music echoing in my mind.

One of the advantages of traveling on a small boat, rather than a large cruise ship, is that whatever is cooking in the kitchen fills the air throughout the vessel. That morning was no exception; a whiff of breakfast's fragrance sped our dressing, hastening us to our next feast. While enjoying our buffet, Jeffery informed us of the day's activities on board: "Bingo games in the morning and Cha-Cha dance lessons in the afternoon in the Saloon. Also a reminder that it was the last day of the cruise and everyone is invited to the Mardi Gras Ball and don't forget your costumes. After lunch, we will be arriving in Louisiana's capital, Baton Rouge, and spending a couple of hours ashore." We took advantage of the free Cha-Cha lesson given by a sweet Southern Belle named Mary. About ten couples attended the class, the men and girls were told to line up facing each other on opposite sides of the room, leaving enough room between sides for Mary to demonstrate the steps she planned on teaching us. She asked if everyone knew the basic steps in the dance, and, fortunately, the response was a hearty "Yes," which meant we didn't have to start with basic steps. She demonstrated an underarm turn followed by an open break, which most caught onto quickly and eventually everyone mastered. After a few moments of dancing with our partners, everyone was asked to rotate to the next person on their left and to repeat the steps again. After doing this several times, with the help of Mary for those of us having some difficulty with the pattern, we were all able to perfect the routines to the satisfaction of our instructor and to our own amazement. I couldn't wait to dance the new routines to live band music that evening.

The boat's whistle sounded its alarming toot-toot-toot accompanied by the calliope' blurting out, "On a Clear Day," as the Queen announced to "The City of Seven Flags," Baton Rouge, that she was preparing to pay it a visit. The colorful history of "The City of Seven Flags" got its name from the seven nations that occupied it over the centuries: France, England, Spain, the Florida Republic, the sovereign State of Louisiana, the Confederate States, and the United States. Of course, when you think about it, history invariably discounts the original inhabitants when compiling information of this sort. Considering that the area, according to archaeologists, dates back to 8,000 BCE, there must have been many other flags and tee pees of Native Americans that also inhabited this region that were not considered when the nickname was developed. Well, anyway, the city is quite different from the small towns we passed or visited on our journey. It's a metropolis of the first order, having as its occupants the tallest Capitol Building in the U.S., which is also the tallest building in the South; one of the largest Neo–Gothic castles in the U.S. (old Capitol Building); two universities--the Louisiana State University, home of the Tigers' football team, and the Southern University, home of the Jaguars' football team; several museums, a major zoo, and the state's two largest shopping malls: the Mall of Cortana and the

Louisiana Mall. These are just some of the inviting venues that the great city has for its populace and guests to visit and enjoy. The city boasts a population of over 800,000 people, which is the second largest city by population in Louisiana, second only to New Orleans. We decided that, due to the limited amount of time we were allotted in this historic place, we would visit the U.S.S. Kidd WWII Fletcher-class destroyer, which was docked close to our berth and currently in the water. At certain times of the year, due to the high tides and inclement weather, the boat museum is in dry dock on land. Time permitting, we wanted to also visit the old Neo-Gothic Capitol Building, which is currently a museum. It was replaced in 1934 under governor Huey Long's administration, by a new 450-foot-high art deco Capitol Building. If we got lucky and had enough time left, the Louisiana State University with its 250 buildings, which are done in Italian Renaissance style, and its stadium, considered one of the largest in the U.S., would be a nice addition to our touring for the day. We would have to forego seeing the many antebellum buildings and neighborhoods for another time, maybe on our next Mississippi River cruise.

With the assistance of electronic docents, Barbara and I began our tour of the famous ship and learned that "The USS Kidd is one of 175 Fletcher-class destroyers and was commissioned on February 28, 1943, in Kearny New Jersey. It is 376-feet long, 40-feet wide, had a complement of 330 officers and crew, and its top speed was 37 knots." I thought it was named after the infamous buccaneer Captain Kidd, who strangely was raised from age five in New York City, since it flies a Jolly Roger from its foremast. But, its name isn't that romantic. "It was named after Rear Admiral Isaac Campbell Kidd, Sr., who was killed aboard his flagship, the USS Arizona, on December 7, 1941, during the surprise aerial attack by the Japanese on Pearl Harbor. The Admiral's nickname was Capt'n Kidd, referring to the pirate, so his wife petitioned the powers that be to have a Jolly Roger displayed from the ship's mast. No other American naval vessel has ever flown a pirate's flag before or since, but due to the high regard that she and her husband were held in by officials in Washington, permission was granted to fly the infamous cross-skull flag. On her maiden voyage into New York harbor, the first American naval vessel ever to fly a Jolly Roger entered the harbor, giving honor to the Admiral and to a native New Yorker, Capt'n Kidd.

The ship earned 12 battle stars while in service in the Pacific during WWII and the Korean Conflict. During WWII, she was part of Destroyer Squadron 48, which was composed of nine Fletcher-class destroyers. These ships were small, fast fighting ships, and were used to screen task forces, escort convoys, bombard shore positions and deliver torpedo attacks. No aircraft carrier or battleship ventured into enemy waters without escorting destroyers leading the way. On April 11, 1945, during the battle of Okinawa, the ship suffered a kamikaze attack when a Japanese pilot targeted and crashed into her, killing 38 crewmen and causing major damage. After the war, all surviving destroyers were modernized, except for the Kidd, due to the poor condition of the vessel. Modernization consisted of replacement of the rear island of the ship with a helicopter platform, the addition of side launch torpedo tubes, and the installation of hedgehog depth charge launchers. Some of her officers, crew, and friends were granted permission to save the ship as a war memorial and had it towed from Philadelphia to her new home in Baton Rouge in 1982 for restoration, to bring the ship back to her original condition. The crew's quarters on these naval vessels always amaze me, as the area they occupy is quite small and in a bunk formation, one on top of the other. Not much room to spread out, but evidently adequate enough to get a decent night's sleep. The toilet facilities were also primitive, made of trenches with saltwater entering one side and flushing out the other end, very much like the ancient Roman's public latrines. One of the saving graces of being on naval vessels is their food, which I experienced many years ago when traveling from Oakland, California, to Yokohama, Japan, when I was fortunate to have a piece of plain vanilla sheet cake with chocolate frosting. The same delicious cake was being served to guests on our tour of the Kidd, the quality and taste hasn't changed one iota from my earlier experience. I was delighted that they let me have a second piece of the tasty cake, which brought back many youthful memories of my days in the military. We moved quickly around the ship so we would have time to visit the Old Capitol Building which was just up the street from the Kidd.

The sight of the Old Capitol Building, known as the Castle, looked strange in its setting. A 15th century Neo-Gothic building, set on a hill overlooking the majestic Mississippi River, with turrets, parapets, exterior stained-glass windows, and gables; the only things missing were a moat and drawbridge, to make it an authentic castle, as seen in many movies showing its European counterparts. A strange scene to find in the Deep South, but one that Baton Rouge is proud of, as it probably is the only castle of its size in North America. We entered the grounds through an iron gate and, unfortunately, not a drawbridge, and were overwhelmed with the beauty and size of the building. The stained-glass dome and spiral staircase leading to the upper level is equivalent in beauty and artistic design to any I've seen in cathedrals throughout Europe. We both plugged electronic docents into our ears and began our journey through history. We learned: "In 1846, the Louisiana state legislature in New Orleans decided to move the capital from that city of 102,000 people to Baton Rouge, which only had a population of 2,269. New Orleans at the time was the fourth largest city in the United States and many thought that it was getting too powerful, so they decided to move the capital to another location to spread the wealth and power around. So, Baton Rouge donated land high on a bluff, believed to be the location of the 'Red Pole,' or 'le baton rouge,' where Native Americans gathered to have their council meetings for many centuries. A New York architect, James Dakin, designed the building, but not in keeping with current trends, which copied the Federal Capitol Building in Washington, D.C. Instead, he decided to copy the styles of Neo-Gothic castles in Europe and make the new (old) Capitol Building a one-of-a-kind in North America, which it probably still is today. The great paddlewheel captain and writer Mark Twain said when he saw the structure: 'It is pathetic that a whitewashed castle, with turrets and things . . . should ever have been built in this otherwise honorable place.' Of course, many people don't agree with his assessment of the Castle. In 1862, a short time after its completion, it was occupied by Union soldiers, when the city's leaders abandoned it for a safer, and more defendable, location in Shreveport. In 1880, Baton Rouge was again the capital; the building had to be resurrected, as it was the victim of two fires during the war and in need of major reconstruction. It was restored beyond its former splendor in 1882, by architect and engineer William A. Freret, by adding a magnificent spiral staircase and a stained-glass dome, which has become the center of attraction in the castle." The staircase and stained-glass dome captivates the viewer with its dark polished curved wooden design and a kaleidoscope of colorful glass panes, which seems to be moving with sunbeams reflecting through them and bouncing off the hallway and staircase. At the distance the toot-toot-toot and music of the calliope beckoned us to return to the boat; any other touring would have to wait for our return, hopefully in the near future.

We were soon sailing on our way to New Orleans at what seemed to be a very slow pace, as the paddlewheel's churning of the water was quiet and not its usually loud, splashing, hypnotic self. The late afternoon event was a passenger calliope contest to determine who could play the mysterious steam instrument with some degree of skill. Barbara, who is proficient in playing the piano and guitar, couldn't wait to sit down and give it a try. About 15 passengers decided to master the instrument. They lined up in alphabetical order, Barbara Bivona being the first. She played Dixie and did a pretty good job stretching her small fingers over the large keys. After rising from her seat, she received loud applause from the audience and some hoorays from me. She finished with a bright smile on her face and very pleased with her accomplishment. The next lady was annoyed that Barbara played "HER" song and said so. She also played Dixie, to the amusement of the spectators, and received loud applause from the audience as well, but her playing, of course, didn't measure up to my wife's. All the contestants were surprised that they were able to get recognizable tunes out of the beautiful and melodic steam instrument. For everyone's effort, they all won first prize and were awarded a "Vox Calliopus" certificate, which made them members of the exclusive club of calliope players.

We finished making our costumes for the Mardi Gras Ball. Barbara created an outfit that looked like a large salmon; pinkish sequins, with drawings that resembled fish scales. The strange thing about it was her head sticking out from the fish's mouth and her little feet protruding from the fish's tail, but overall her walking fish was quite effective. I took the easy road and made a toga from a white sheet and wore a Roman laurel wreath painted gold on my head, which I put together with some of the material supplied by the crew. The ball was surreal, there was a variety of fish, many men and women dressed in togas, (but not as good as mine), mustached gamblers all over the place, and lot of girls dressed as ladies of the night. We danced and sang the night away, which wasn't an easy task, especially if your costume was bulky like Barbara's. Her fish's stomach kept getting in the way of our dancing close, and my toga had the habit of sliding off my shoulder and showing my hairy chest. But, all and all, the evening was delightful, especially the laughs at seeing such strange creatures jumping around trying to dance without tripping on themselves and their partners. We raised our champagne glasses to the music of Guy Lombardo and the Royal Canadians, and ended the evening singing "Auld Lang Syne." To help us with the words we were given an envelope marked "Don't Open till Midnight." An American version was written in clear large letters, so we could all enjoy singing the whole song. The words are somewhat bastardized from a poem written by Robert Burns in 1788, but here is the rendition we sang:

> "Should old acquaintance be forgot, and never brought
> to mind?

Should old acquaintance be forgot, and old lang syne?

For auld lang syne, my dear, for auld lang syne,

We'll take a cup o' kindness yet, for auld lang syne.

And surely you'll buy your pint cup! And I'll buy mine!

And we'll take a cup o' kindness yet, for auld lang syne.

We two have run about the slopes, and picked the daisies fine.

But we've wandered many a weary foot, since auld lang syne.

We two have paddled in the stream, from morning sun till dine.

But seas between us broad have roared since auld lang syne.

And there's a hand my trusty friend! And give us a hand o' thine!

And we'll take a right good-will draught, for auld lang syne.

For auld lang syne, my dear, for auld lang syne.

We'll take a cup o' kindness yet, for

Auld land syne."

CHAPTER EIGHT

New Orleans-Dancing at Mardi Gras

WE WOKE THE NEXT morning to a very quiet and new environmental aroma. The paddlewheel's relentless churning resonance was gone and the motion of the boat was still. Peeping out our porthole explained the reason for the changes, we had arrived and were docked in the "Laissez les bons temps rouler" (Let the good times roll) City of New Orleans. We dressed, packed our luggage, and spent extra time filling out the destination tags to make sure that our baggage would be sent to the right location, the Monteleone Hotel in the heart of the French Quarter. Check in time was 1:00 P.M., and considering our previous experience, we were very apprehensive about being separated from our suitcases. I was tempted to buy homing devices and place them in our luggage to ensure that they wouldn't get lost or misplaced, but I couldn't locate any devices on the ship, or anywhere else for that matter. I made a mental note to invent a device that could be used for that purpose. We hypnotically followed the scent of breakfast, which seemed to be extending an invitation to all the guests to join in a farewell feast, which we obligingly did. Once again, I devoured more biscuits and gravy than my stomach could bear, but, what the hell, it was vacation time so why not "let the good times roll." I assured myself that any discomfort would be quickly remedied by the ever present "Tums" that I carried in my pocket.

We had a few hours to kill before check-in time at the hotel, so we decided to explore the incredibly complex and beautiful New Orleans Riverwalk. It was developed to accommodate the 1984 World's Fair, and transformed a run-down industrial area consisting of railroad tracks, warehouses, and waterfront activity, to a world-class pedestrian promenade, marketplace, aquarium, and a host of other interesting tourist attractions. On our previous visit to the sleepless city, Barbara had made a mental note to spend some time at the Riverwalk Marketplace. I made some mind etchings that included the Audubon Aquarium of the Americas and the New Orleans Zoo, which I thought would be good places to spend some quality educational time. As usual, I followed the leader and we headed to the mall. In 1986, the Riverwalk Marketplace opened for business, featuring in excess of 200 merchants selling creative art works and keepsakes, in national and international stores, such as Brookstone, Nine West, Foot Locker, and The Body Shop. The great food options housed in the magnificent air-conditioned mall include The Café du Monde, serving their world famous beignets (hot French doughnuts), sushi stands, Italian bistros, Mexican delights, and French and Cajun cuisine. The indoor Marketplace is located at the foot of Canal, Poydras, and Julia streets, and is across the street from Harrah's Casino and adjacent to the spectacular glimmering, Hilton Hotel. We spent over an hour browsing through the women's clothing stores and, much to my surprise Barbara didn't find anything to buy. "Why?" I asked, "Didn't you like anything you touched and investigated? After all, you left your DNA on all those garments and shoes and nothing to show for it?" She whispered in my ear: "Wow, these prices are high." With a delightful grin on my face, we exited the Marketplace and headed for the Aquarium. The New Orleans Zoo was now out of the question, as the outside temperature was beginning to get uncomfortably warm and spending time outdoors was no longer an option. We would have to save that adventure for our next journey to New Orleans.

Walking along the Riverwalk is an absolutely pleasant experience. It is very visitor friendly, benches are conveniently situated and shade trees display beautiful designs of various colors of green and the scent of magnolia tickles and pleases the senses. We viewed the ever present magnificent sparking Mississippi River giving life to riverboats, cruise ships and people actually sitting near the river bank and wading their feet in the murky waters. Street musicians performed along the walk, adding to the ambiance with sweet music from their trumpets, saxophones, and tambourines. An interesting sight caught our attention as we moseyed along; a rather large barge was docked and had about twenty house trailers on its deck. Some of the trailer's awnings were open, sheltering the owners from the sun, while they enjoyed breakfast and drinks on their patios. We were fascinated and, knowing that boaters are friendly and ever ready to converse with anyone passing by, we struck up a conversation with Louise and Tom. They asked us to join them on their nautical patio, which we did without hesitation. Tom asked if we would like breakfast and, as I was still trying to digest the morning's biscuits, I only accepted a cup of coffee. Barbara, although she shops in the children's or women's petite sections of most stores, accepted the breakfast offer knowing that no matter how much food she devours, not one ounce will stick to her ribs. Tom and Louise, who reside in Michigan, told us of their barge trip on the Mississippi. They towed their house trailer from Michigan to Memphis, Tennessee, making their first vacation stop at Elvis Presley's Graceland and then on to the pier where their barge was waiting for them to board, which is done in a similar manner as boarding a large ferry. After securing their car and trailer, the house trailer was connected to electricity, fresh water and a waste system. The power is provided by onboard generators; the water tanks are filled at predetermined stops and the waste is disposed of frequently. All of these annoying tasks are done by the polite and pleasant crew members without inconveniencing the passengers. They travelled down the Mississippi River stopping at many of the same places we visited; the big difference was that when they docked at the various cities, they had the option of taking their cars to go sightseeing and exploring, usually doubling up with other travelers from the barge to save on fuel. Well, talk about a unique way of travelling; being on a boat, taking your vacation house and your car with you, and not worrying about driving long distances or finding first-rate trailer camp accommodations, which to say the least, is not an easy task. We wished them a continued happy "barge-house trailer-car" vacation and decided that we would, hopefully in the near future, try the same type of adventure and maybe talking some of our boating friends into join us.

The New Orleans Audubon Aquarium of the Americas is rated as one of the top five aquariums in the United States. When entering, there is an astonishing exhibit of a Caribbean coral reef that requires walking through a transparent plastic tube, which put us in the midst of a large number of stingrays, hammerhead sharks, turtles, and an assortment of sea life, all located above, in front of, and around us. Their Adventure Island Exhibit offers an action packed interactive play zone designed for persons of all ages. The main attraction is a 2,600-gallon pool, where people are invited to pet the cow nose rays. Guests are also encouraged to purchase feed to help fill the rays' stomachs at feeding time. There is an unusual penguin colony that features two species of warm water penguins: the African black-footed penguin and the Rockhopper penguin. I was expecting to see snow among the little birds, but there are only two species that live in the Antarctic, and the aquarium did not have adequate facilities to accommodate either of them. It is always fascinating to watch these birds meandering around; they seem to be busy talking to each other and are constantly in motion. But what is it that they are accomplishing? I wouldn't be surprised if they scrutinize the onlookers and make comments about their appearances, such as, "Wow, look at the size of that fat guy's nose," or "Did you see the terrible face lift on that blonde? HE HE HE!!" We learned that the African black-footed penguins were the most numerous in the colony and that the majority of them were born in captivity. The Rockhopper penguins are distinguished by their orange feet and bright yellow tufts of feathers above their eyes. Our next observation stop was the aquarium's White Alligator's habitat in the Mississippi River Gallery. The big guy's name is Spots and he is one of 18 rare white alligators found in the Louisiana swamps in 1987 during a preservation safari to save the animals. Although Spots is white, he is not an albino, he is Leucistic (a gene mutation), which gives him his white color and steely blue eyes. Spots and his all male siblings probably wouldn't have lived long in the wild since their white coloring wouldn't camouflage them from predators anxious to dine on their tiny hatching. Spots and his brothers are considered goodwill ambassadors for Louisiana and are celebrities around the world, having appeared on entertainment programs such as The Tonight Show, CNN, The Today Show, Nashville Network and CBS Morning News. Although their history is fascinating and their appearance rare, watching several alligators lying around doing absolutely nothing left much to be desired. So we moved on to the Seahorse Gallery. This exhibit has an unusual assortment of seahorses and sea dragons, both becoming rare and, unless the governments of their native homes become more proactive in protecting their habitats, many of the species will become extinct in the near future. There are only 32 known species of seahorses and, unfortunately, they live in some of the world's most threatened habitats, which is why aquariums throughout the world, in conjunction with the international organization called Project Seahorse, are working to ensure their survival by breeding them in captivity. The exhibit is one of the most beautiful in the aquarium. Watching them floating through the water, reflecting and then becoming part of the colored lights, is absolutely beautiful to behold. Added attractions are the sea dragons with their flowing appendages that resemble yellow and orange leafy plants and have the head of a seahorse. Only two species of these Australian dragons are known to exist; the weedy and the leafy, and both are represented in this amazing display. These little creatures conjure up thoughts of mystical sea monsters, which in their original size are quite beautiful, but on a larger scale, like 100-feet long, would be quite scary. We only had time to visit one more exhibit, although we probably could have spent the rest of the day exploring the rain forest, sea otters, the Gulf of Mexico Exhibit (which is supposed to be the centerpiece of this venue), the Jellyfish Exhibit, and the many other displays. We decided to visit the Jellyfish Exhibit, as it was close by and we were in a hurry to get to our hotel to see if our luggage arrived without incident. This exhibit always fascinates me when visiting seaquariums. Observing jellyfish hovering and dancing around the tank with the backlights reflecting through their various sizes, shapes, and colors is similar to watching a ballet while listening to a symphony orchestra playing smooth, floating music. Watching the performers' harmony in the water stage is reminiscent of the tranquil feeling I get when attending ballets and concerts, so relaxing and gratifying.

We exited the seaquarium post haste and headed to the Monteleone Hotel, which is off Canal Street and only a short distance from where we were. But, what can happen in a few blocks in New Orleans is absolutely bizarre. The streets were already busy with revelers celebrating Mardi Gras, drinks in hand and partying to beat the band. The city allows drinking in the streets as long as the cups are plastic. There were many plastic cups being chug-a-lugged; many held by two-fisted male and female owners. As we walked at a quick pace to avoid some of the rowdy activity, I got ahead of Barbara, as she decided to peek in one of the storefront windows. While her nose was pasted to a dress shop's window, a young, rather handsome, inebriated man approached her and asked, "Would you like some beads?" Barbara said: "How nice, I'd love them." He then said, "Then show me your tits." She screamed and ran over to me and said: "That man wants to see my breasts." I looked back at the smiling procurer and started to head in his direction, when a policeman appeared from a doorway on my right and said, "Don't be concerned, it is customary for men to offer girls beads to show their breasts at Mardi Gras time." At that moment, I saw several young ladies flashing their cannons and accepting gifts from their happy admirers. Barbara calmed down while I began daydreaming about our week's adventure in the city of "Laissez les bons temps rouler" (Let the good times roll). We reached our hotel at about check-in time and went straight to the reception desk, got our key for a "no smoking" room on the 7th floor facing the courtyard, and almost ran to the elevator, opened the door to our room and behold, our luggage was sitting in the center of our mini-suite. Two major surprises awaited us: our luggage was intact, and the steamboat company had arranged for a room upgrade, at no charge, to further apologize for the problem we had with our misplaced baggage.

We chose the right hotel for location; it was within a few blocks of Jackson Square, Canal Street shops, The Riverwalk, Harrah's Casino, an abundance of renowned restaurants, and lively Bourbon Street. The 16-story, family-owned hotel dates back to 1886 and boasts a striking "Beaux Arts" style (French for fine arts which was popular in the late 19th century). Two wonderfull, exaggerated examples are found in New York City: the New York Public Library, which stands out in all its splendor on Fifth Avenue as a testimonial to creative architectural excellence and lasting artistic beauty, and the Grand Central Terminal, which I consider one of the most imaginative and complicated architectural events of the 20th century. It was built to coordinate the multitude of trains coming into and leaving the city.

It's said that the "French Quarter starts at the lobby of the Hotel Monteleone," which is just one block from Bourbon Street. The 100-plus years of continuous ownership by the Monteleone family has resulted in a host of hard-earned awards for its restaurants, rooftop swimming pool, and a unique Carousel Piano Bar, with a wild circus design, that slowly revolves and completes its circle every 15 minutes, taking its riders on a childlike journey while viewing the dancing lights of Crescent City (another name for New Orleans). American authors, such as William Faulkner, Tennessee William, Truman Capote, and

Ernest Hemingway, who immortalized the hotel in his story "Night Before Battle," were all repeat residents of this illustrious venue when they visited fun city. For those of us who are "gymaholics," there is a modern 24/7 fitness center and spa.

It was time for a well-deserved nap, and before dozing off I picked up a booklet that was in the pile of paraphernalia on my night table about Mardi Gras. "Fat Tuesday, which in French means "Mardi Gras," begins on the 12th night of Christmas, January 6th, which is the day the three Magi presented Christ with gifts, and ends on Fat Tuesday, the day before Ash Wednesday. Ash Wednesday is 47 days before Easter and, therefore, varies from year to year. Carnival in New Orleans is a season of balls, parades (up to 28) and continuous festivities. Carnival, which is Latin for 'kiss your flesh goodbye' (loosely translated), builds slowly from January 6th until Mardi Gras Day (Fat Tuesday); the intervening weeks are filled with all the popular activities that have made this season attractive to the four million-plus visitors that attend the events. Mardi Gras applies only to the day before Ash Wednesday, but has become interchangeable with Carnival; locals refer to the long party as Mardi Gras-Carnival. Contrary to the impression that people get from mass media coverage, it doesn't take place primarily on Bourbon Street, nor does it consist mostly of drunken revelry and indecent exposure in exchange for cheap beads. Although many of the traditional celebrations are centered there, the majority of the historic parades don't even include Bourbon Street in their routes. Entire extended families stake out prime spots hours in advance, often the same location every year for generations, along each parade route, in order to have an up-close look at the passing themed floats and to collect as many "throws" as possible from the passing menagerie. Mardi Gras is a great time for families to celebrate and spend time quality together. Many thousands of King Cakes are baked and decorated in the official Mardi Gras colors of purple, green and gold, representing justice, faith and power, and are consumed each year by families and friends as a testament to their continued love and commitment to each other.

Parades are planned as much as a year or more in advance by Mardi Gras Krewes, who sponsor elaborate balls and parties to honor their organizations. Some balls are stylized and formal, complete with tableaux performances and royal marches, while others more closely resemble large dinner-dance parties. One party is even held in the New Orleans Superdome. The balls have become so popular that New Orleans is now one of the country's largest markets for formal wear, including tuxedos and floor-length evening gowns, which are required attire at many of the more exclusive balls. Thanks to popular singer-actor Harry Connick, Jr., and his many native New Orleans friends, all the Krewes organizations now are required to allow members from all walks of life, regardless of race, color or gender, to join their clubs. The majority of parades are held the last five days, Friday through Fat Tuesday, of Carnival, when all the streets in the area are cordoned off to accommodate the many enormous floats and the thousands of people participating in and celebrating the festivities. It's advised that folks stake out a spot on the street where the parade of their choice will be reviewing, get a prepaid balcony, or find restaurants that have views of the activities and will allow diners to hang around and visit a while; this should be arranged prior to the frenzy that occurs during the parades. A map of the parades' routes and time schedules is at the end of this brochure to assist people in choosing the parades they wish to view and those areas they wish to avoid."

We woke refreshed and ready to face the new challenges of the day, especially having at our disposal a clearly defined map of the French Quarter and surrounding area that would help us safely navigate the places we wished to see and those congested areas we wished to bypass. We decided, with map in hand, to just walk around the area and see what we would discover before the hectic activity started the following day, which was the beginning of the last five days leading up to Fat Tuesday and the start of major parades showing off their creations and occupying the streets in and around the French Quarter. Walking through the French Quarter is like visiting a foreign country. While strolling on Royal Street, there is a mix of French and Spanish architecture garnishing the beautiful buildings dating back to the 18th century. All through the 6 x 13 block area of the French Quarter that was laid out in 1722, the same feeling prevails. First, you're traveling through some of the quaint towns in France, where small buildings are lined up in a symmetrical row boasting their ornately decorative facades, and then you're visiting a small town in Spain where buildings are more irregularly shaped, decorated with wrought iron balconies and gates, and beautifully adorned with flower arrangements of every imaginable color. This is the atmosphere of the last remaining intact French Colonial and Spanish settlements in the United States. Our hotel is at the head of Royal Street, which is an antique shopper's paradise. I'm not a shopper and usually try avoiding visiting stores with Barbara; my usual position is at the outside of stores striking up conversations with other distraught husbands. But, I must say that these quaint shops drew my attention. The intriguing shops possess wares ranging from museum quality continental antiques, to art deco statues, to weapons used during the Civil War, to furniture from almost every period--all in like-new condition. We spent over an hour browsing the shops and questioning salespeople about the origins, history, and cost of many pieces of furniture and memorabilia. One of Barbara's favorite pastimes is her love of music; she plays the piano, synthesizer, and classical guitar. When she practices her instrument of choice, I often hear the hollow click, click, click sound of her electronic metronome resounding throughout the house, which is annoying to no end. But in one of the shops specializing in French antique furniture, I spotted the most beautiful, highly polished, wood grained antique metronome, made in Paris, France, dating back to the 19th century, that supposedly once belonged to a Miss New Orleans beauty contest winner. I wound it and heard the same click, click, click, but this time it was different; instead of the plastic tinny sound of the one at home, it made a soft, solid, vibrating sound; tick, tick, tick, that was pleasant to my ears. What a great Christmas present for her, I knew she would love it, and, if not, at least I would enjoy listening to the more pleasant cadence of the mellower tick, tick, ticks, instead of the hollow click, click, clicks. We decided to return to the hotel and see if our concierge, Jean Paul, could get us reservations at the Fairmont Hotel's restaurant for dinner, while their was still a chance of beating the crowds. Jean Paul said, "No problem monsieur, I will make sure you are seated tonight." We dressed and confirmed with Jean Paul that our reservations were in order. He said, "But of course, I have a friend . . . "

The world renowned Fairmont Hotel is only a ten-minute walk from our home base. A Carnival atmosphere surrounded us as the revelers were on the streets celebrating their good fortune at being in such a festive place. The smell of food mixed with the strong odor of liquor was pleasantly shocking to my nostrils. It was surprising to see that people were busy drinking on the streets at around seven o'clock. They all seemed to be sucking on straws while talking, smiling, and even eating, all at the same time. We were offered a drink called an "N'awlins Hurricane" by one of the store/street vendors. It was a tall plastic, tulip shaped pinkish drink consisting of (this is the vendor's recipe):

"½ cup of ice

2 fluid ounces of light rum

2 fluid ounces of passion fruit-flavored syrup

1 cup of lemon and lime flavored carbonated beverage

1 ounce of lime juice, and

1 fluid ounce of 151-proof rum;

Put everything into a shaker, except the 151-proof rum, and shake it well. Pour the mix into a Hurricane glass and then gently top it off with an ounce of 151-proof rum. It is important that the drink is consumed with a straw; the result being, as you get closer to the top of the concoction and near the end of the brew, the drink becomes more potent."

Well, what the hell, we were in "merry land" so why not try one. We continued our walk, becoming two of the merry makers. We became part of the party scene, with drinks in hand, smiles on our faces, and walking in a zigzagging pattern while attempting to walk a straight line to the hotel. We got there a little light headed, but it complemented the mood we were in as we entered the astonishing lobby of this famous hotel. It was like entering a mansion-museum-castle, all rolled up into one. We wanted to explore the venue, but decided to save it for our final Mardi Gras Ball night, which was being held in their ballroom.

Jean Paul made reservations for us at Bailey's Restaurant, which is quiet and laid back, as opposed to the other "hang out" eateries in the hotel, such as, the Sazerac Room, which is named after a renowned Southern potent drink and is quite busy, with a large bar and layers of patrons vying for the bartender's attention. Our dining room's atmosphere was perfectly subdued, with soft piano music which immediately took us out of a hyper-festive mood and into a more relaxed supper one. We were expecting a very pricey food menu, but were surprised that the prices were just slightly above average. For appetizers, Barbara ordered New Orleans' crabmeat and I went for the crawfish cakes, which we happily shared. Instead of ordering a bottle of wine, we thought we would go easy, especially after the Hurricane experience, so we each ordered a glass of the white house wine.

The special soup of the day was "Hearts of Palm, Asparagus & Endive," which we both ordered and consumed very slowly to savor its taste, which matched the white wine we were nursing perfectly. The wine seemed to be made for the food we were enjoying, so much so, that we decided to have a second glass. For the main course, Barbara ordered "Breast of Duck Andreas," while I opted for the "Veal Escalope Acadian." The food was divine, complementing the piano music and the soft delicious white wine. We found our glasses empty again and couldn't resist having them filled once more, which was really way beyond our limit, but we were on vacation and decided "what the heck." After finishing a perfect supper, in an exquisite restaurant, with beautiful soft piano music, I asked for the bill. The price of the meal was what I expected, but I never asked how much the wine cost. Well, it cost twice as much as the dinner. Shame on me! We swore never to order anything in a restaurant without first finding out the price before hand. Then again, if we would have known the price in advance, we certainly wouldn't have ordered the divine nectar and would have missed out on an exceptional dining experience. When faced with this kind of a situation, where we spend more than expected for something we enjoy, we have learned to pacify ourselves by saying: "It didn't cost us anything; we paid for it with our kids' inheritance." Uttering those words magically makes us feel better.

Walking back to our hotel through the Halloween neighborhoods was like being in an Alice in Wonderland fantasy. It seemed that everyone was insane; people's behavior was out of the ordinary to say the least. Girls were showing off their bare breasts, and then some, for trinkets; most men were in some sort of frenzy and groping everything in sight with impunity. We actually had to push our way back to our place of rest, UGH! All of this was going on while policemen were in sight, patrolling the area.

We decided to spend the next morning walking around the French Quarter and the afternoon trying to get a good spot to view the Columbus 500 Centennial float, which was named the King (Rex) of Mardi Gras. We again asked our friend, Jean Paul, where he suggested was a good place to have breakfast, and where a good starting point for a walking tour through the Quarter would be. He said: "Mon Ami, you must have breakfast at the Court of Two Sisters, the food is the best. If you would like to walk and see some of our great sites, start at Jackson Square, which is down the street, and then just walk and enjoy yourselves." So away we went to the Court of Two Sisters, a courtyard is exactly what it is; the largest in New Orleans, with a turn-of-the-century look (19th century), beautifully landscaped with flowers and plantings surrounding the outdoor dining area. A jazz combo band's music filled the air and seemed to carry the flavor of the food with it into my nostrils. It was brunch time, so I ordered Eggs Benedict while Barbara chose Oyster Bienville. While waiting for our delights, I read a brief history of the café that occupied the back page of the menu. "The restaurant is named for two sisters, Emma and Bertha Camors, born in 1858 and 1860, respectively; they belonged to a proud and aristocratic Creole family. Their 'rabais,' or notions shop, outfitted many of the city's finest women with formal gowns, lace and perfumes imported from Paris. These sisters died within two months of each other in 1944, but their restaurant, fortunately, still survives." The brunch more than lived up to its reputation and the strong French coffee and jazz combo made for a great start to a promising day.

Thanks to the walking map that Jean Paul gave us, we had no trouble finding Jackson Square, which was a short distance from the restaurant.. When approaching the Square, the scene filling the lens of my eyes and overwhelming my brain was that of the statue of Andrew Jackson on Horseback, the three enormous steeples of St. Louis Cathedral, the Cabildo (Council) Museum on its left, and its twin, the Presbytere (Priests' House) Museum on its right. After taking pictures of President Andrew Jackson in all his military glory, we headed straight for the three steeples accentuating the St. Louis Cathedral. The walking map had a brief description of the three buildings. "The Cathedral was first established in 1718 and is the oldest continuous operating cathedral in the United States. It stretches one block between St. Peter Street and St. Ann Street. It's not considered the largest or grandest of the city's Catholic churches, but it's the seat of the Roman Catholic Archdioceses of New Orleans." Its three cone-shaped steeples, a large one in the center flanked by two smaller ones, sparkled in the sun, which at certain angles look like halos. The Cathedral has survived fires, bombings, and hurricanes, and each time was restored more magnificently than prior to each tragic event. We entered and were immediately taken in by the beauty of the stained-glass windows, murals and alter.

I'm always surprised and proud when finding medieval beauty in the United States that favorably compares to its European ancestors.

To the left of the Cathedral is the Cabildo Museum (council building), built in the early 18th century by the new Spanish rulers. It is a three-story building designed in old Spanish colonial architecture, featuring arched columns on the first and second levels and tulip shaped windows on the top floor. In the center is a "widow's walk" overlooking the city and its waterways. This is an excellent perch as a lookout for hostile activity in the area and a great spot for photos and viewing some of the parades. The first exhibit we visited was the Native American section, which concentrates on the history of Louisiana's Indians prior to the European invasion. The artifacts and a mini-village are good representations of what life was like back in that more peaceful era. Next we visited the Colonial Exhibit, which outlines the first French settlement and how the intruders lived. A highlight is the Iberville Stone, which marks the founding of the first settlement in Louisiana by the French. There is a special place exhibiting the original plans for the building of the city of New Orleans. An especially interesting room was a reproduction of the place where the signing of the Louisiana Purchase occurred. It was complete with paintings of those present and copies of the colonial wooden furniture used on that historic occasion. A painting showing how the town square looked on the day of the signing is highlighted with spot lights and is amusing to behold, considering what the sophisticated city has developed into today.

Another room displayed many artifacts from the Battle of New Orleans, where Americans under the leadership of General Andrew Jackson, defeated the supposedly invincible British forces. An especially interesting artifact is a lock of Andrew Jackson's hair, enclosed in a well guarded case. Not to be outdone by Americans, the French somehow managed to send us the death mask of Napoleon Bonaparte (it is said that it was donated by the doctor who serviced Napoleon on his death bed). I could have sworn that I saw the mask in other museums around the world, so I guess someone made a nice profit in reproducing that sacred artifact, or maybe there was more than one Napoleon. The museum certainly gives a respectful historical picture of pre-colonial times and the development of the great state of Louisiana. We could have spent all morning at the museum, but were anxious to visit the Presbytere Museum before lunch.

The Presbytere Museum, on the right of the Cathedral, was built in the late 18th century to house the Capuchin monks, but was never used for that purpose. It was designed to match the Cabildo on the other side of St. Louis Cathedral. It was used for commercial purposes and finally housed the Louisiana Supreme Court. Currently, it is the foremost Mardi Gras museum in the state. It has five major themes: History, Masking, Parades, Balls and Mardi Gras. The exhibits trace the Festival from its ancient origins to the 19th century emergence of the New Orleans' parades and balls, and then to the present statewide celebration that attracts millions of visitors each year. There are three galleries filled with dazzling Mardi Gras memorabilia, including handmade gowns worn by kings and queens of some of the city's Krewes; magnificent crowns and scepters adorned by royalty; and costumes made by local Indian tribes with hundreds of masks worn by various Krewes, parade participants and street people. There is an area set aside for watching a parade from an imitation float, with parade watchers on a movie screen in front of the float, allowing you to pretend that you're throwing beads at the people below. It's so exciting imagining that you are on the float, almost as much as the comical restrooms in the museum that masquerade as Fat Tuesday port-a-potties. We were attracted to the unique gift shop and couldn't resist buying masks for our kids. They are a respectable representation of the skill of the local craftsman that has come down through the centuries from their ancestors, two of which were being held in my hands to bring home as play things for our children. We hoped our son and daughter would appreciate the significance and beauty of these masks.

We exited the incredible museum and headed for a spot a few blocks away that would allow us to see the "Columbus and the Age of Discovery" floats.

On the way to our spot, we noticed that many restaurants had street-side bars selling oysters on the half shell, grilled shrimp, crab cakes, and other kebab foods. It was surprising how many people were eating at these bars while downing hurricanes, dancing, making all sorts of loud noises and, most startling, women willingly showing their breasts. The scene was probably similar to the one that shut down Sodom and Gomorra in biblical times. We headed for a less busy bar and ordered oysters on the half shell and grilled shrimp. We totally enjoyed the treat that was so readily available from street vendors throughout the area. We devoured our food and rushed to find a spot where we could view the Columbus floats that were supposed to pass around 1:00 P.M. The three floats arrived as scheduled; the first one was a replica of Columbus' main ship, the Santa Maria. The original was built in Spain and was approximately 77-feet long, by 26-feet wide, with a complement of about 40 men. At the float's head was the costumed Columbus waving to the crowd and throwing beads and fake doubloons to the lucky recipients. Seated behind him were King Ferdinand and Queen Isabella in all their glory, waving, and also showering gifts to the peasants. The second float was a reproduction of the Nina, which was originally 67- feet long and 27-feet wide, with a complement of 20 men, and captained by the youngest of the three Pinzon brothers that sailed with Columbus, Captain Vincente Yanes Pinzon. All the brothers were from the small seaside town of Palo, Spain. He and his shipmates duplicated the actions of Columbus and showered trinkets on the onlookers. The third replica was the Pinta, originally 70-feet long and 22-feet wide, with a complement of 26 men. It was owned and captained by the eldest brother, Captain Martin Alonzo Pinzon. His brother, Francisco Pinzon, went on their voyage of discovery as Martin's pilot. It was befitting the Pinzon brothers that they were represented in the parade, Columbus and the Age of Discovery, as it was their combined efforts that enabled Columbus to secure the ships and men required to begin his journey. As a matter of fact, Columbus was required by the realm to put up 1/8 of the cost of the expedition, but he did not have the funds. Martin Alonzo Pinzon put up the required funds, again becoming instrumental in helping the expedition on its way. Unfortunately the flagship, Santa Maria, went aground while anchored off one of the Caribbean islands. Columbus used the smaller and faster Nina to continue on his journey and finally to return to Spain, overcoming unimaginable hardships, including what was considered to be one of the most severe hurricanes in recorded history at that time.

I couldn't stop taking pictures and videos of the ships and the other floats in the parades, and continued to do so up until Fat Tuesday. The highlight of the main parade on Fat Tuesday was the trumpeter Al Hirt, a son of New Orleans, as Grand Marshal of the Festival. This enormous man at the head of his float blasting his high, sweet notes from his trumpet caused the crowds to become ecstatic as they howled and screamed as his float passed by. His harmonizing partner, Pete Fountain, playing a smooth, high-pitched clarinet, made the event a perfect ending to the parade celebrations. I wasn't sure if I could get many of the pictures that I took of people misbehaving developed at our local camera store, but I was sure that the videos, which were more revealing than the photos, wouldn't be a problem. Exhausted, we returned to our place of refuge, searching out Jean Paul to get directions to Preservation Hall and reservations to a fine restaurant. Directions to the famous hall were easy, just a couple of blocks away, but reservations at a fine restaurant during Mardi Gras were out of the question. He suggested that we just walk along the French Quarter and try whatever restaurant that had vacant seats. We decided to get a quick bite at the hotel's bistro which had a table available. I ordered a soufflé stuffed with crabmeat and Barbara ordered blintzes filled with apples. We washed our meals down with strong French coffee, and again were surprised at the rich deep flavor of the brew. We were anxious to get to Preservation Hall before the crowds gathered. We visited the world renowned venue many years ago, when "Sweet Emma" Barrett was still performing there. She was in her 80s and had to be wheel-chaired to her piano to perform. She was the personification of Jazz, and carried her title as "the Bell Gal of Jazz" for over 50 years. I remembered so well her singing "Somebody Else is Taking My Place," and "Just a Closer Walk with Thee." She was so weak from her advanced age and many ailments, that she could barely finish both songs. But, her weak voice singing "Just a Closer Walk with Thee," had people in the audience pulling out handkerchiefs and wiping tears from their faces, including me and Barbara. The words of the song by an unknown author went something like this:

"I am weak, but Thou art strong

Jesus, keep me from all wrong

I'll be satisfied as long as I walk, let me walk close to Thee

Just a closer walk with Thee

Grant it, Jesus, is my plea

Daily walking close to Thee

Let it be, dear Lord, let it be

Through this world of toil and snares

If I falter, Lord, who cares?

None but Thee, dear Lord, none but Thee

When my feeble life is o'er, Time for me will be no more

Guide me gently, safely o'er

To Thy kingdom shore, to Thy shore"

What a memorable evening so many years ago, when we were not only fortunate to hear her sing, but also to speak to her and tell her how much we loved her singing. Barbara reminded me that the small decrepit room was packed with people and that the heat was oppressive, causing her to become faint, so we had to leave, but we did get to see the most cherished of Jazz singers, "Sweet Emma." We promised each other that we would return, hopefully on a cooler night, and enjoy the rest of the Preservation Hall Jazz Band's music. So here we were many years later, fulfilling our promise to return to the same small dilapidated room, which hasn't changed since its opening in 1961. We again were sitting on uncomfortable wood benches and it was "hot to beat the band." The charisma was still there; the smoky air, moldy smell, light jazz music, and humming patrons clapping and tapping their hands and feet. None of this had changed one iota from our last visit, except Sweet Emma was no longer a part of the New Orleans Jazz scene, as she made her last walk in 1985. The music coming from the 70 and 80-year-old musicians was still sweet and kept the audience humming along to "Hindustan," "Tishomingo Blues," "Put on Your Old Grey Bonnet," "Savoy Blues," and finally, "When the Saints Go Marching In." The last song was played just in time, as Barbara was again feeling the effects of the oppressive heat, which was compounded by the amount of people and smoke present in the small room. So away we went, satisfied that we had fulfilled a promise to ourselves and Sweet Emma to return to Preservation Hall. As we were leaving, they performed my all time favorite song, "House of the Rising Sun," as if to reward me for returning. One of the versions that has come down over the many years, of this mysterious blues song, that was first recorded in the 1920s, comes from a favorite story about a house of ill repute in New Orleans around the mid-19th century called the Rising Sun, named after its owner Madam Marianne LeSoleil Levant, whose name translates from French to "The rising sun." The story helps to give meaning to the words of the song, which I have loved hearing by singing groups, such as the Weavers and the Animals.

Following are the words that I prefer to this fascinating song:

"There is a house in New Orleans

They call the Rising Sun

And it's been the ruin of many a poor boy

And God I know I'm one...

My mother was a tailor, sewed my new blue jeans

My father was a gamblin' man, down in New Orleans

Now the only thing a gambler needs

Is a suitcase and trunk

And the only time he's satisfied

Is when he's all drunk

Oh mother, tell your children

Not to do what I have done

Spend your lives in sin and misery

In the House of the Rising Sun

Well, I've got one foot on the platform

The other on the train

I'm going back to New Orleans

To wear that ball and chain they call the Rising Sun

And it's been the ruin of many a poor boy

And God I know I'm one . . ."

We walked back to our hotel via Bourbon Street, which is lined with bars, jazz clubs, hotels, restaurants, "gentlemen's clubs" and boutiques. I'm sure if we looked long enough, we would also find "lady's clubs," but we didn't have the time or inclination. Somehow we were again holding Hurricane drinks and were enjoying music coming from the clubs. Jazz, blues, and rock 'n' roll flowed from the joints, mixing in the air as the sounds became part of the street scenery, accompanying people dancing as they drank their night away. We pushed our way through the crowd and finally arrived at our sanctuary, where we could get some relief from the street noise and heat. We decided to spend the next morning sightseeing and the afternoon viewing parades. This time, we would try to have Jean Paul reserve a table for us at one of the local restaurants.

In the morning, we immediately approached Jean Paul and asked, "What is the best way to get around the area and avoid the parade traffic?" He said to "walk to Jackson Square, hire a buggy and tell the driver where you would like to go, he will know how to avoid the busy parts of town." I responded with, "Great, now can you get us a reservation at a local restaurant?" "I will try, Mon Ami, come see me after breakfast." We had a light meal at the hotel's Le Café bistro and hurried back to Jean Paul. He still wasn't able to get us a table, but was sure that he could find us a suitable place to have dinner by the time we returned from our day's excursion. We walked to Jackson Square, which was busy with street musicians, fortune tellers, artists, jugglers, and plenty of tourists. We were intrigued by an artist painting portraits at a street-side setting; his work was quite good, so we decided to have a pastel painting of our heads put on paper. The rendering still hangs in our home back in New York; unfortunately, the painting has little resemblance to us today. While sitting for our portrait, we heard music and singing coming from around the corner and we asked our painter what was happening? He said: "There is a funeral procession in progress." We asked if it was alright if we interrupted his painting while we took a quick peek, he said "okay." What an amazing sight! A coffin being carried by six pall bearers, followed by a four- piece band playing "Just a Closer Walk with Thee," followed by a line of family and friends all singing that oh, so very touching song.

We hired a mule and buggy and asked the driver, Manuel, to take us around the area and point out places of interest. He suggested that the least crowded area would be around the waterfront, which was only a few streets away; we agreed and he headed for the river area and Woldenberg Park. Manuel told us that "The park replaced the run down areas along the river in the 1970s and 1980s, and is now a five-acre grassy open space with landscaped walkways, river views, fountains, a sculptured garden, and stages for live music. The park was named after a local philanthropist named Malcolm Woldenberg and its Moonwalk, is named after a popular New Orleans mayor,

Maurice 'Moon' Landrieu." A bronze statue of Malcolm is at the center of an informal sculpture garden along the riverfront. Near his statue is a stainless steel sculpture called "Ocean Song." It was created by a local artist, John Scott, and depicts the motion of water in eight narrow pyramids, polished to a reflective gleam which emphasizes the water flows. Further downriver is the elegant "Monument to the Immigrant," crafted in white Carrara marble by sculpture Franco Allesandrini. The structure faces the riverfront with a ship's prow topped by a female figure reminiscent of our Lady Liberty. Behind her stands a turn-of-the-twentieth-century immigrant family looking toward the French Quarter. A little downriver is a sculpture of Robert Schoen's "Old Man River," also made of Carrara marble and standing approximately 18-feet high. The statue reflects the river's power and majesty in its muscular body presentation. Street musicians could be seen along our path playing their saxophones, trumpets, and banjos in time with our mules clippety-clopping; their harmony and the increasing heat almost put me to sleep several times. The area also includes the Audubon Aquarium of the Americas, which we previously visited, and the Entergy IMAX Theater. Further up river is the Spanish Plaza, dedicated in 1976 during the U.S. bicentennial. The plaza was a gift from Spain as a gesture of friendship to its one time colony. It features a beautiful fountain inlaid with Spanish mosaic coat of arms tiles representing that country's provinces. There were vendors in the plaza serving food and drinks; we took the opportunity to stop and have some tacos and beer for lunch, picnic style, while sitting on the lush inviting green lawn. Exiting the mule-drawn carriage brought us a welcomed bit of fresh air and much needed shade from a beautiful tree that helped cool us off from the rising temperature. While eating, we relaxed and just enjoyed the view of the river's activity. Watercrafts of every size and shape traversed the mighty river. Small sunfish boats and sail kites were everywhere, zigzagging between the larger vessels. Back in our carriage, we noticed the Riverwalk Marketplace Mall that we visited on our first day, and were tempted to visit again just to get some relief from the ever-increasing heat. We told our driver it was time to end our excursion and head back to Jackson Square. He said we couldn't end the trip unless we saw the golden bronze statue of Joan of Arch, which was a short distance and resided in front of the French Market Place. The sculpture was remarkable, an exact copy of the famous 1880 Emmanuel Fremiet's equestrian statue of Joan, located at the Place des Pyramides in Paris, France. The statue was a gift from the people of France by President Charles de Gaulle, during his state visit in 1959, and is certainly one of the main centerpieces on the Riverwalk. If not for the increasing temperature and the abundance of tourists, we would have continued exploring the riverside walk as there was so much more to see, but it was getting hot and we hadn't seen the grandest parade of the Festival. We found a spot and synchronized our watches, right on the minute the Bacchus Parade passed our location. Bacchus is the Greek God of wine; while passing, artificial wine grape throws seemed to be coming from every direction. There were over 25 floats in the parade, including super floats with descriptive names such as Bacchagator, Bacchassaurus, and Bacca-Whoppa. Some of the illustrious celebrities portraying the Greek God have been William Shatner (Captain Kirk), Bob Hope, Dick Clark, Dom DeLuise, Charlton Heston, and Raymond Burr. The Krewes' large signature floats had mixed themes of grapes and its importance during the "Age of Discovery." It seemed as if all the participants dressed as Native Americans were squeezing, throwing, or imbibing the fruits of the grapes. The parade was endless, with music coming from every direction and, the organizations' members marching in front of, in between, in back, and on the sides of the floats. I think all of its 1,000-plus members were participating in the parade; marching, singing, acting, juggling, hula hooping, performing acrobatic stunts, and throwing beads plus other ornaments to the roaring crowds. When the last float passed, we were exhausted from jumping around, catching trinkets, and yelling at the top of our voices. And, then again, there was the heat, which was quickly overwhelming us, so we headed back to our cool hotel and went directly to the revolving Carousel Bar on the roof. Barbara ordered a tall Mud Slide and I ordered a tall, cool, frosty glass of Corona beer with a piece of lime. We decided it was a good time to change into our bathing suits and enjoy the rooftop pool. With refreshing drinks in hand, and our bodies in the cool pool water, we were able to enjoy Mardi Gras at a distance with some degree of privacy, as most of the hotel guests must have been on the streets enjoying the festivities or in their rooms getting over their excessive celebrating.

After a well-needed nap, which almost turned out to be an around-the-clock marathon sleep-in, we were awakened by our telephone ringing--it was Jean Paul. He said we had better hurry if we wanted to keep our nine-thirty reservations at the Broussard's Restaurant. It was just nine o'clock, so we quickly dressed and ran down to meet him and get directions to the restaurant. As usual, the place was a short walking distance from our hotel. Again, Barbara's advice saved the day. She had said, "I think you should wear a dinner jacket," which I reluctantly carried over my arm to the restaurant. Who knew that the Broussard's Restaurant was one of the most celebrated places in New Orleans to eat? Our reservations got us past the line that was forming outside and it was a surprise that we were seated immediately. The grand entrance was similar to a Parisian promenade; we were surrounded by beautifully hand-painted Italian tiles of cherubs and Napoleonic insignias. Our table was in a picturesque cobblestone courtyard; it seemed that soft French music was coming from the soothing water flow of the fountain and lush tropical foliage. I was happy to be wearing my dinner jacket, as the place certainly deserved customers that dressed well. Barbara ordered another Mud Slide while I was content with a refreshing tall glass of very cold tap beer. The smell of jasmine and magnolia in the courtyard turned our drinks into ambrosia. The menu was extensive, but we decided to stay simple and just order salads and main courses. We both ordered Valencia orange, fennel, and jicama salads, with blood orange vinaigrette and seasonal greens. For her main course, Barbara ordered Parasol of Shrimp Marcus, with jumbo gulf shrimp in basil lemon and sherry butter with a zesty seafood risotto cake. Not to be outdone, I ordered a simple Louisiana Bouillabaisse with plump oysters, gulf shrimp, and fish in a savory tomato broth, flavored with saffron and topped with crabmeat and rouille croutons. Well, our simple meals were consumed in short order; French cuisine is without a doubt one of the most delicious delights on earth, if prepared properly. And, I must say, the food was prepared to perfection by their chef, Gunter Preuss, whom I personally complimented for our exquisite meal. After dinner, we fought our way through the crowds back to the Monteleone and rushed to our room for a well-deserved night's sleep.

When on vacation, we often take a trolley or bus ride through the city to see the different neighborhoods and to get a feel of the place. So we had a quick breakfast and headed for the St. Charles Avenue streetcars. The conductor was very pleasant and gave us a brief description of some of the places of interest on his route. The trolley took us along the river past Audubon Park, which includes the Audubon Zoo and Tulane University, which dates back to 1834 and is the largest employer in New Orleans. Loyola University, which was founded in 1849 by Jesuit priests, is also on the scenic route and boasts a six-level Recreational Sports Complex. The RecPlex includes two floors of racquetball, tennis, basketball and volleyball courts, in addition to a natatorium with a diving pool, whirlpool, sauna and steam room, an elevated jogging track, and a weight room. The complex also houses a four story parking garage. There is an outstanding Confederate Museum that devotes itself to the Civil War and the outstanding efforts of the Confederate Army in that conflict. While we were taking in the views, a young couple came on board, dressed in country western outfits. He was dressed in fancy cowboy clothes, including boots and a high hat. She was dressed in beautiful cowgirl clothes, also with boots and a high hat. I asked them why they were dressed that way, and they said they were on their way to a Country Western Festival Dance. After speaking with them for a few minutes, they asked us to join them at the dance, which we accepted without any hesitation. The dance hall was about 3,000-square feet and was filled to capacity. It's probably one of the most festive dance sights that I have ever witnessed. The outfits alone were dazzling. The boots that the girls wore would stop a fashion show. They were high heeled and in every imaginable color: red, white, blue, green, two toned, and striped. Their outfits were just as spectacular; some wore short skirts while others wore long skirts or slacks, with matching shoes. There was an incredible variety of sequined colors in a variety of shapes on their clothes. What was interesting is that none of them were dressed exactly alike. On the other hand, the men all looked alike, although they wore different styled clothes; their boots were primarily black, their dungarees blue, and their hats either black or white. Everyone was dancing in a circle and in strict patterns, very similar to our line dances in New York. There was an instructor tutoring two gents on the sideline in the Western Two Step. He was repeating: one, two and three as they repeated their steps, with much difficulty. I immediately copied the pattern: one, close two and three, which is what I saw these guys doing. Barbara and I joined the dancers in the first Two Step that was played and had a great time. After our dance, the instructor, Jimmy, came over to us and introduced himself. He said we were doing the dance wrong, there is no close on the second step, which I replied, "But I'm doing the exact pattern that your student did." He said, "I've been trying for weeks to get them to stop closing on the two, but they just don't seem to get it." Well, the next Two Step, Barbara and I fell in with the crowd and did one, two and three, just like everyone else, except the two gentlemen, who evidently had four left feet. They were serving a buffet lunch, which we helped ourselves to, and were introduced to "jambalaya soup and gumbo." Hot, hot, hot, but, oh, so delicious! We spent a couple of hours dancing and socializing with the most pleasant, well dressed, and synchronized dancers in the world. We didn't want to leave, but we wanted to catch the Zulu Parade that passed our spot late in the afternoon. We hopped on a red trolley that took us back to the French Quarter, just in time to occupy our place and witness the Zulu floats. The music was what I expected, African jungle, and lots of great jazz, with very tall natives dancing and singing, while throwing gifts to the admirers that were lined up along the way and begging for trinkets. The Zulus appeared incredibly tall on the floats and almost gave the impression of being on stilts. They were dressed in their various native costumes. The tall lean men wore colorful headgear and rattled deadly looking spears. The women showed off their shapely figures and danced to their native rhythms. It was one of the most colorful parades that we were fortunate to see.

We were at a point where avoiding parades was more appealing than witnessing another one. The festive attitude and noise were fine for the first few days, but when combined with the heat and poor manners of the crowds, avoidance seemed to be in order. The days rushed by and before we realized it, we were preparing for our "Columbus and the Age of Discovery Ball," which was at the Fairmont Hotel's Grand Ballroom.

My dream of dreams was to become a reality in 1992. I was at Mardi Gras in New Orleans with a "Columbus and the Age of Discovery" theme and we were planning on going to Spain in October to join in the 500 Centennial at the 1992 World Expo, celebrating the landing of Columbus and his three ships on our continent. I have been collecting "Columbus and The Age of Discovery" books and memorabilia for over 20 years, and that night I was going to meet not only Cristobal but, Amerigo, Queen Isabella, King Ferdinand, and many of the illustrious members of their first voyage. I couldn't wait to get to the Fairmont to meet all my "historical heroes." For the first time on that trip, I didn't mind getting dressed in my Sunday best so I would make a good impression. The short walk found us in front of one of the most magnificent hotels that I have ever seen. The outside is lined with flags over the entrance and a red carpet lining the outside steps leading to what seems to be a mile long hallway-lobby, gave me the feeling that I was royalty entering an imperial palace. The enormous hallway was lined with flowers and large vases, filled with plants of every color and description. On the right is the famous Sazerac Bar and Grill, filled to capacity. On the left is the Court Bar, also filled to the hilt. We headed for the elevator and went to the roof- top to see the 40-foot pool, which is adjacent to two tennis courts and a fitness center, all designed with high-class clientele in mind. It was time for us to make our entrance at the ball. We were welcomed out loud by the Court's announcer: "Mr. and Mrs. Michael Bivona from New York." There were two reception lines; I couldn't believe that I was in the line to be shaking hands with Queen Isabella, King Ferdinand, Cristobal and Amerigo, what an unexpected surprise. I asked the Queen if she would save a dance for me, she responded with a big "YES." The reception lines lasted about an hour and then to the blasts of the Court's trumpets, the Royal party was announced as they paraded to their seats at a long table, at the head of the room, on a slightly raised platform. The ball had over 300 people; it was amazing that most were received by the Royals or their entourage, who were lined up opposite each other, in such a quick and orderly manner. The music began and Columbus came to our table and asked Barbara if she would like to dance a Waltz. She jumped out of her seat and danced with the Genovese around the large ballroom dance floor. He returned her to our table, bowed, and asked me to dance . . . Oh wait, I must have imagined that . . . I've never seen Barbara so happy! She spent the rest of the evening smiling from ear to ear and floating on the dance floor, with me in her arms. I did get a chance to dance a Waltz with Queen Isabella, and while circling the dance floor, I had the urge to ask her if she and Cristobal had something going in the old days. I guess the answer to that question will forever remain silent. A minuet dance was announced. We were told to line up on either side of the dance floor facing the royal table, forming lines of boy-girl, boy-girl. A slow Waltz was played and the Royal party and their entourage went to the front of each line. When the music began, they showed us the way to perform the dance by entering in the middle and dancing the Waltz through the lines and then remaining at the

Michael Bivona

end. Fortunately, not everyone participated in the line dance, or there would have been utter pandemonium on the dance floor, due to the large size of the people in attendance. There was much confusion, but everyone did get a chance to dance with some of the court's entourage or, if they were lucky, as I was, they danced with royalty. When the dance ended I'm proud to say that I danced with Cristobal and Amerigo. What fun!! In my wildest dreams, I never thought that I would ever dance with my two heroes; Christopher Columbus and Amerigo Vespucci. The ball ended with the orchestra playing "When the Saints Come Marching In." The song was originally published in 1896 and is probably one of the most recorded songs in existence. My research came up with the following lyrics:

"We are trav'ling in the footsteps of those who've gone before

And we'll all be reunited, on a new and sunlit shore

Oh, when the saints go marching in, oh, when the saints go marching in

Lord, how I want to be in that number, when the saints go marching in

And when the sun begins to shine, and when the sun begins to shine

Lord, how I want to be in that number, when the sun begins to shine

Oh, when the saints go marching in, oh when the saints go marching in

Lord how I want to be in that number, when the saints go marching in

Oh, when the trumpet sounds its call, oh when the trumpet sounds its call

Lord, how I want to be in that number, when the trumpet sounds its call

Oh, when the saints go marching in, oh when the saints go marching in

220

Lord, how I want to be in that number, when the saints
    go marching in."

That was not only the end of our beautiful Mardi Gras Ball, but also the end of an incredible vacation. Some years later, I was fortunate to donate my Columbus and the Age of Discovery Library to the Columbus Foundation. They are the sponsors of the annual New York Columbus Day Parade; my books are now a part of that organization, which is dedicated to honoring and keeping the memory of those brave explorers alive. A copy of an article acknowledging my donation follows:

Bivona Collection Donated

The Foundation has received an enormously generous and essential donation, the Michael Bivona Collection: Columbus, The Age of Discovery and Related Books. The collection, which Mr. Bivona acquired over the course of 30 years, contains approximately 300 books and immediately gives us an extensive group of works about the Foundation's namesake. It will reside in the Ambassador Charles A. Gargano Library.

"This remarkable donation, by Michael Bivona, vastly increases and improves the quality of our library's holdings," said President Louis Tallarini. " We are deeply grateful to Mr. Bivona for his donation, and we are proud that our Member Louis Mangone made the introduction that has brought the Michael Bivona Collection to the Foundation."

"The age of discovery was roughly 1400 to 1700, and of course Columbus was central to the period," said Mr. Bivona. "He had the audacity and the courage to venture out into unknown areas. At that time, very few people would venture out on the water beyond the sight of land. He had few navigational instruments to guide him when he became the first European to discover and record this unknown continent. He found his way back to Spain using his knowledge of celestial navigation, ocean currents and prevailing winds. The route he took is still being used today because of the favorable winds and currents. What he did was just amazing."

Mr. Bivona, 72, and his wife Barbara live in Dix Hills, Long Island and have two grown children and two grandchildren. Now retired, he was a CPA and co-owner and CFO of Manchester Technologies. His main hobbies are boating and ballroom dancing. He owns a 42-foot Cris-Craft boat, which they've taken to Block Island, Cape Cod, Nantucket and Plymouth, among other places, but, unlike Columbus, he said, "with very sophisticated electronic navigational devices."

Foundation News

Mr. Bivona and Foundation Member Louis Mangone belong to a dancing group that meets regularly. Several months ago, Mr. Bivona was in discussions with Brown University, in Providence, Rhode Island, about donating the collection to the school. "I mentioned to Lou Mangone that I was talking to Brown, and he told me that the Foundation would be interested in the collection." Mr. Mangone pursued the collection, which is now coming to the Foundation.

Book collector, philanthropist and ballroom dance aficionado Michael Bivona with wife Barbara in a tango

The Michael Bivona Collection has great depth in its holdings of books about Columbus, from his own letters and journals and contemporary accounts of his voyages to the works of later historians who interpret and comment on the lasting changes brought about by his explorations. Mr. Bivona acquired the books from every type of source imaginable, from specialized booksellers to bookstores and flea markets, and the books range in age from recent to over 100 years old.

"It is wonderful to know that my collection will have a meaningful place at the Foundation to honor a great explorer," Mr. Bivona said. ✦

CHAPTER NINE

Dancing in South Florida

AROUND THE FLOOR: JULY/SEPTEMBER 1999

TRAVELING AROUND by Barbara Bivona

I RECENTLY READ AN article in the USA Dance magazine which stated that Florida was the unofficial dance capital of the United States. This certainly is true for South Florida. There are so many places to dance from West Palm Beach to the Miami area that choosing a venue can become challenging. There are dances in the mornings, afternoons and evenings, seven days a week. It is such an active schedule, that meeting people we know from New York unexpectedly at these dance halls is not uncommon and never surprising. A favorite spot of ours is the Goldcoast Ballroom in Coconut Creek, which was built in 1997, specifically for ballroom dancing. Its dance floor is over 3,000-square feet and is constructed of floating oak, which is state-of-the-art flooring for dancers' delicate feet. It's owned and operated by Vinny Munno and Jeff Sandler; Vinny provides much of the DJ music, which is always the right rhythm and duration to satisfy customers. You can expect to circle the floor several times when doing a Quickstep, Foxtrot or Waltzes, as his music is never too short, but timed just long enough so that dancers can perform many of their routines. Vinny has a good ear for Latin arrangements, his selections are authentic and the tempo is good for the various Latin dances. Mike and I especially enjoy dancing to his Mambo-Salsa music. A plus is that he takes requests and will play most any dance music that is requested by his followers. On most dance nights the crowd thins out after 10:30 P.M., from over 300 people down to about 100 dancers, which gives us an opportunity to enjoy dancing the smooth dances. With less people occupying the floor, International Ballroom dancers can perform their fast, long stepped movements without much interference, and fortunately without bumping into anyone, which is a major problem on many dance floors. Goldcoast is located at 1415 Lyons Road, Coconut Creek, and is opened from Tuesdays through Sundays, with all day activities; from dance classes to tea dances, to evening dances of every type. What makes Vinny's music so popular is his understanding of what dancers require to perform properly, as he is a competitive dancer himself and has won many awards. I have found that the best DJs are those who are proficient dancers and know the kinds of music that allows performers to dance at their best.

When we returned to Florida as snow birds this winter and learned that one of our favorite dance spots for the last five years had closed, we were disappointed and asked our dancing friends where they were going on Saturday nights. The latest popular dance hall was "Dazzle Me Twice," located in West Palm Beach. So we joined our friends at the large hall that has a 2,000-square foot dance floor and were immediately comfortable with the place, and happy at being reacquainted with our dancing companions. They had showcase dancing, usually with professional instructors and their students (Pro-Am), and unique theme nights celebrating whatever holiday is current, such as Valentine's Day, where everyone is requested to dress in some form of red, or St. Patrick's Day, where green is the color of choice. Once a month is birthday night, where large cakes are presented and singing the world's most popular song, Happy Birthday, is enjoyed by everyone present. Another special event is the movie star look-a-like contest, where contestants dress and try to imitate such celebrities as

Charley Chaplin, Liza Minnelli, Frank Sinatra, and other famous personalities. A large Christmas celebration tree is a permanent fixture; decorations are changed with each holiday which puts everyone in the spirit of the occasion. Dances are Thursday and Saturday nights with music by DJ Gordon and free lessons by his lovely wife Pat, who is a proficient dance instructor with a following of some of the more advanced students in the area.

* *

I recently read in the USA Dance (formerly USABDA) Magazine, that Florida was the dance capital of the United States. I can attest to the fact that South Florida, from West Palm Beach to Miami, certainly fits that description. There are dances in the mornings, afternoons and evenings, seven days a week. It is never surprising when we unexpectedly bump into friends from New York at one of the dance halls, as it seems everyone is crisscrossing from one dance venue to another. There are so many places to dance that choosing one becomes a challenge. Our favorite dance hall is the Goldcoast Ballroom in Coconut Creek, which was built in 1997 as a showcase dance site. It has become the trend setting and nucleus of the ballroom dance world in South Florida. It was designed and built exclusively for ballroom dancing by its owners, Vinny Munno and Jeff Sandler. Most of the DJ music is provided by Vinny, who is not only a DJ aficionado but a competitive dancer, who has won many awards. He has the understanding and ability to play music that is appropriate for dancers, as the timing and duration of his music is perfectly matched, which enables performers to dance at their best. We thoroughly enjoy dancing to his Latin music, especially the Mambo or Salsa, which usually lasts for a full three to four minutes and gives us a chance to perform many of our hard learned steps. I have always been of the opinion that the best DJs are those that are proficient dancers, as they are aware of the kinds of music that keeps people's feet happy. Its dance floor is over 3,000-square feet, constructed of floating oak wood, which is state-of-the-art flooring for dancers' delicate feet. It is a pure delight to be able to dance a Quickstep,

Foxtrot, Samba or Waltz around the large comfortable dance floor several times before the music ends, which attests to Vinny's exceptional knowledge of what dancers require in music to adequately perform to the best of their abilities. The hall is busy seven days a week, with dance classes during the day conducted by the many exceptional dance instructors that teach all of the ballroom dances at every level. They have afternoon tea dances and evening dances every night of the week. We can be found at the dance hall on Tuesdays, Sundays and occasionally on Saturday nights.

Our favorite dance night is Sunday, which has Latin dancing from 5:00 P.M. to 8:00 P.M., and ballroom dancing from 8:00 P.M. to 11:00 P.M. The entrance fee is $15.00 from 5:00 P.M. to 11:00 P.M., and $12.00 from 8:00 P.M. to 11:00 P.M., and includes a sandwich with garnishes, cake, hot coffee, and hot and cold tea. Upon entering you are welcomed by a crystal chandelier; following a red velvet rope leads you to a carved wooden reception desk where smiling faces collect the admission fee and dispense entrance tickets. The view that greets you after you pay your admission is a Tiffany lamp casting its light on custom-designed carpeting that embraces the walls and accents the Art Nuevo mirrors. Dance themed paintings, photos, posters, tapestries and sconces fill in the wall spaces around the hall. Oriental screens are displayed as well as French doors, complemented by large silk trees and creative flower arrangements. The finishing touches are the assorted sizes of tables with candle lights and beautiful burgundy and mauve chairs that can comfortably seat hundreds of patrons; certainly an exquisite setting for a wonderful evening of dancing and socializing. Sunday nights are usually very crowded with several hundred patrons, many from as far as the Miami and West Palm Beach areas, gather to enjoy and dance to the best Latin music in Florida. The DJ is usually from the Miami area and is so well loved that he has a following that stays by his side at most of his performances. From 5:00 P.M. until 8:00 P.M., the dance floor is packed with many Hispanic dancers from the Miami area enjoying the Latin dances that they do so well, especially the Mambo-Salsa, Cha-Cha, Guajira, Tango and Meringue. The music and dancing is so lively and vibrant that just watching them performing their routines is entertainment for the evening. By 8:00 P.M., we are usually exhausted from dancing to the quick-paced Latin music, but save enough energy to dance the rest of the evening away doing smooth dances to Vinny's music, which, unlike Latin, is done in the line of direction, counter clockwise around the dance floor, and not in place as most Latin dances are performed. It is astonishing how two thirds of the dancers leave after the Latin session, which gives the more advanced dancers, especially those dancing International Ballroom style, the room that is required to move around the floor while taking long, quick steps, without interfering with other dancers and causing collisions, which can be a major problem on any dance floor. A Sunday evening session can only be described as delightfully exhausting and invigorating as you carry the energy of the atmosphere home with you, and then enjoy a great night's sleep.

We are also found at their Tuesday night ballroom dance, which draws a smaller crowd of about 150 dancers and is as much a social night as it is a ballroom dancing evening. We are usually seated with our dear friends: Eloise Cristo, Jerry and Mike Easter, Vinny Perrone and Molly Lee and the amazing dance couple; Doctors, Vi and Vic Chiong. The evening's fun is enhanced as we exchange dance partners with each other and enjoy doing mixers of Foxtrots and Waltzes. Mixers give the single ladies in attendance a chance to dance and socialize with single and attached male dancers. The ladies form a line and dance with the first partner in the men's line; dancers go around the floor once and then dance with the next person on the line. The evening is from 7:00 P.M. till 11:00 P.M., with Vinny providing the music, which is always appropriate for the level of the dancers in attendance. We were celebrating my birthday one evening, and, as it is customary at this venue, I had to dance with willing ladies who formed a line to dance with me. My choice was a Mambo-Salsa and I had to dance with over twenty ladies, one at a time, before Vinny decided to end the exhibition. It ended just in time, as I was about to collapse, much to the amusement of Vinny. We attend Saturday night dances on occasion, but it is just too crowded with many non-dancers who attend just to pass the evening away socializing and cluttering the dance floor. So we choose instead to travel to West Palm Beach to the "Dazzle Me Twice" dance hall for our Saturday night dance fix.

We are members of the Royal Palm Chapter of USA Dance (formerly USABDA: United States Amateur Ballroom Dance Association), as are many of our dancing friends. The first Wednesday of every month, our Chapter holds a dance at Goldcoast Ballroom from 7:00 P.M. to 11:00 P.M. The fee is $8.00 for members and $10.00 for non-members. First time guests can enter free if they join the Chapter. We serve snacks, coffee, cake and hot and cold tea. Approximately 100-plus dancers attend, which makes it an exciting evening, as there is plenty of room to maneuver around the floor. A free dance lesson is given by one of the local dance instructors. The club provides single male hosts to dance with the unattached single ladies, which not only gives the girls an opportunity to dance with different partners, but puts them at ease as they socialize with other single ladies. The highlight of the evening is a mixer of Foxtrots and Waltzes that all the girls participate in, which gives them a chance, if they are lucky, to dance with many of the guys who are more experienced dancers. This gives them an opportunity to dance with different partners and learn various styles of dancing. USA Dance encourages dancing in high schools and we give many students an opportunity to perform what they have learned, as a group, at our Wednesday night dances. The last teenage group that we saw, of about 20 students, performed an Argentine Tango, which was taught to them by one of our members, and made the audience go wild with appreciation and applause. Watching these youngsters dance with such devotion and skill gives us a peek into the future of ballroom dancing and the pleasure and excitement its popularity will bring to future generations.

New Year's Eve at the Goldcoast Ballroom is an event that most social dancers await with bated breath. The hall is decorated with additional lights and glittering decorations. The masterpiece of the season is an annual Christmas display that is created by Vinny and friends on a three-sided platform that features miniature ski slope activities, toboggan runs, Dicken's type villages, trains zigzagging, people in motion, snow all over the place, and even New York City's buildings, such as Radio City Music Hall and surroundings, the Flat Iron Building, and the famous skating rink at Rockefeller Plaza. We stare at the scenes every year in total admiration and astonishment at the synergy required by Vinny and friends to amass such an intricate assemblage of beautiful Christmas works of art. The elaborate display is complemented by a beautiful Christmas tree, garnished with stunning delicate decorations symbolizing the season. Barbara usually has to drag me away from the area that has a miniature of the Radio City Music Hall building; as I will capture anyone's attention within earshot and tell them that the building attached to it, 1270 Sixth Avenue, is where I met her. She worked for Rugoff Theaters (an art movie chain) at that time, as an administrative assistant to the treasurer; I was a junior accountant, right out of college and worked for their public accounting firm. My job was to check their books. Well I spent more time "checking out" Barbara than I did on the company's books, lucky me. Viewing that scene brings my memory back to those magical days, where in the winter we would have lunch at the indoor restaurant in front of the skating rink, spending our hour break admiring the skaters all bundled up to ward off the cold temperatures. In the summer months, we would have lunch by the outdoor golden statue of Prometheus Bound overlooking the skating rink, still admiring the hearty souls skating and doing their favorite maneuvers, but with a lot less effort, due to the favorable temperatures and the lack of heavy clothing.

The evening usually hosts a world renowned champion dance team that perform several dances for the enjoyment of the audience and who circulate and talk freely with the patrons after their exhibitions. It is a special feeling to be dancing with Barbara, who is dressed in her best evening gown complemented by my uncomfortable tuxedo, when I realize that we're sharing the same dance floor with world champion dancers, dancing in the same direction and doing the same dances that they are. Well, somewhat the same that is-- WHAT A DREAM COME TRUE NIGHT!!

I can go on discussing the activity of bellwether Goldcoast Ballroom indefinitely, but I think enough has been written to get a pretty good idea of the importance of this establishment and its owners, Vinny and Jeff to the dancing community of South Florida. In the next chapter I will discuss another of their more exciting endeavors; that of sponsoring a ballroom dance boat cruise. Until then, on to our alternate Saturday night rendezvous at "Dazzle Me Twice" in West Palm Beach.

When we returned to Florida as snow birds and learned that one of our favorite dance spots for the last five years closed, we were disappointed and asked our dancing friends where they were dancing on Saturday nights? The latest popular dance hall that they were gravitating to was, "Dazzle me Twice," located in West Palm Beach. So we joined our friends at the moderate size hall that boasts a 2,000-square foot dance floor and immediately felt comfortable with the place and happy at being reunited with our dancing companions. The owners feature showcase dancing, usually with professional male or female instructors and their students (Pro-Ams). There are fun unique theme nights celebrating whatever holiday is current, such as Valentine's Day, where everyone is encouraged to dress in red, or St. Patrick's Day where green is the color of choice. Once a month is Birthday Night, where large home-made birthday cakes are presented for consumption, while everyone sings the world's most famous song, "Happy Birthday." My favorite nights are when we do movie star look-a-like contests, where we have had people imitate Charley Chaplin, Lisa Minnelli, Frank Sinatra and many other famous personalities. The winners of the contests are given gold "Oscars" of sorts, about twice the size of the famous one. A six-foot Xmas tree is a permanent fixture; decorations are changed for each holiday, which puts everyone in the spirit of the occasion. Foxtrot and Waltz mixers are always popular, and due to the small crowd of about 60 people, friendships are easily made; many developing into permanent associations or even marriages. There is an open snack bar with candies, desserts and hot and cold drinks for the attendees' enjoyment. Dances are Thursday and Saturday nights, with music by DJ Gordon and free lessons by his lovely wife Pat, who is a proficient dance instructor with a following of some of the more advanced students in the area. The entrance fee is $12.00 per person and is well worth the trip to West Palm Beach to interplay with such friendly and hospitable people.

I have discussed what we do on Tuesday, Saturday, and Sundays night. Time permitting, one of our more casual evenings is Friday night at Empress Ballroom, in Delray Beach, where our Florida dance life began. Owned and operated by Dan Malone, one of our first dance instructors in Florida, it's located in a strip mall on Avenue L right off of Federal Highway. Its large clear storefront windows welcome people to enter and join in the festivities. The dance session is from 7:30 P.M. to 11:30 P.M., and is hosted by DJ Tommy Engler, dance instructor extraordinaire. He is responsible for teaching many of the young incredible dancers that have performed for us on Wednesday nights at the USA Dance evenings. He is also the coach and instructor for many of the youths that compete in the annual USA Dance National Competitions. He is affectionately known as "Hair," due to the amazing amount of youthful waves residing on the top of his head. We celebrated his "something" birthday recently and he now admits to being in the senior citizen range, but no one knows exactly where. The dance floor is rectangular and comfortably accommodates 50 people. This is where we met many of our friends: June Rudolph and Misha Bartnofsky, Patty and Less MacDonald (President and Secretary of our USA Dance Chapter), Jerry and Mike Easter, Doctors Vi and Vic Chiong, and so many of our other dear acquaintances. The entrance fee is $10.00 and includes a food bar of fruits, vegetable dips, desserts, coffee and tea. Many local single ladies attend the dance to socialize and dance with the male hosts. Foxtrot and Waltz mixers are very popular with the girls, as all the men attending the event try to give them a turn around the floor. The evening is very casual and gives everyone a chance to practice routines, learn new steps from one another, and catch up on the latest gossip. It's here where Barbara and I enjoy doing our Argentine Tango exhibitions to the cheers, howls, and whistles of our friends. Tommy will take requests from the patrons for any dances that they may prefer. One of the highlights of the evening is several line dances, such as Country Waltz, Samba, Sex on the Beach, and everyone's favorite and the most difficult to perform due to the quick pace of the dance, Zorba; which comes from the movie of that name starring Anthony Quinn. After the dance, we drive a few minutes to Dunkin' Doughnuts for a late snack and some great coffee, while gossiping and catching up on the latest happenings in our ever-growing dance community; certainly a lovely way to end an evening with our new and long time friends.

The list of dance venues is endless for South Florida and the best way to locate a place is by accessing dance information on the internet. The latest dance hall to join our family was opened in 2006, completely renovated with a fine private restaurant, a full service bar and a separate 2,000-square foot dance floor built in an atrium setting, next to a beautifully lighted small waterfall. It originally opened as a Wednesday night dancing affair, but due to the popularity of its music and friendly dancing atmosphere, it has expanded its entertainment to several nights a week. It is located in the Stonegate Bank Building at 301 Yamato Road in Boca Raton. The entrance fee structure is unique: $15.00 for admission to dancing for the evening, which includes snacks and one drink. Another $7.00 to take a group dance lesson or $27.50 for a three-course gourmet dinner, which includes admission to the dance area and a dance lesson. It is the only venue in South Florida that offers a full dinner, a dance lesson and four hours of dancing for such a reasonable price. The atmosphere is similar to the popular nightclubs of years gone by, except the music is provided by DJ Richard instead of a large orchestra; he seems to have a repertoire of every piece of dance music ever recorded and gladly takes requests from the patrons for dances of their choice. The management for the dancing and entertainment is done by Axel and Elyse, who seem to have been born taking care of their customers' comforts and requests. Although the place only catered to dancing on Wednesdays originally, its June 2008 schedule reads something like this:

Tuesday and Friday nights: The fabulous "Sensations" performing a Motown Review, which includes music of the Beach Boys and Jimmy Buffet, rounded off with Latin music.

Wednesday night: Dinner/Dancing from 7:00 P.M. till 11:00 P.M., with music provided by DJ Richard. Group dance lessons are scheduled. A price-fixed menu is also provided.

Saturday night: The Paul Anthony Band, performing contemporary and old-time dance music.

Their New Year's Eve Extravaganza is also worth mentioning. It's all inclusive; dinner, dancing, drinks and holiday favors, all for about $90.00 per person. This unique dance venue is a welcomed new place to spend an evening having dinner, with lots of dancing for any occasion, at a reasonable price.

On January 24, 2009, Goldcoast Ballroom hosted the 6th Annual Royal Palm Winter Frolic DanceSport Extravaganza in their beautifully decorated, for the occasion, ballroom. Barbara and I are members of the Royal Palm USA Dance Chapter and make it a point to attend the event every year. It was an all day affair that allowed competitors from ages 14 to 70 to compete in their chosen dances. It gives us a good excuse to join many of our friends in cheering for dancers that we know from our chapter and for the many competitors from as far away as Canada, such as our good friends, Claude Guay and Ginette Beaulieu. Although ranked as amateurs (never performed for money), Claude and Ginette graced the dance floor as if they were professional world champions, which is why they took first prize in almost all the competitions that they entered on that exciting day. The following picture, taken by my good friend Mike Easter and shown here with his permission, shows the handsome French Canadian couple at their best, floating around the floor doing an International Quickstep and enjoying every minute of it, while entertaining the hundreds of spectators who were cheering the dancers on and encouraging them to perform their magic on the dance floor.

The competitions featured all syllabus events in American Smooth and Rhythm and International Standard and Latin, as well as Novice, Pre-Champ and Championship. West Coast Swing, Argentine Tango, and Hustle were all new exciting entries. In between competitions there was general dancing for the non-performers, which gave the competitors a break and allowed everyone else to show off their dancing skills.

A couple of months after the competition, many of our friends were invited by Claude and Ginette to some wonderful French cooking at their new home in Delray Beach. We all brought a specialty dish and added them to the dinner table for one of the most pleasant, friendly, sunny days in March, in the sunny state of Florida. Just the thought of enjoying a meal outdoors in the month of March and sharing stories with so many friends is prompting Barbara and me to consider relocating in the Disney state permanently. The fact that it was snowing in my hometown on Long Island, New York, certainly is another consideration for migration to a place where we can go swimming in warm pool or ocean waters, while the sun's rays penetrate our bodies, instead of freezing our butts off in New York.

We are looking forward to the 7th Annual USA DanceSport event in 2010, and are already planning a get together with many of our dancing friends from around the country and Canada to enjoy and celebrate the camaraderie and good will that dancing brings to our community.

CHAPTER TEN

Dancing in the Caribbean –
On the Good Ship Costa Fortuna

THIS CHAPTER IS NOT a continuation of one of our articles, but an expansion of the important role Goldcoast Ballroom has in the South Florida dance community. Over the last few years, theme cruises have become very popular with dancers and non-dancers alike. Recognizing this, Stardust Dance Productions of Woodbourne, New York, (www.Stardustdancecruises. com) has extended their successful land dance adventures to the ocean. Under the auspices of Vinny Munno and Jeff Sandler of Goldcoast Ballroom, Coconut Creek, Florida, a dance cruise was organized from March 9 to March 16, 2008. Vinny and Jeff helped organize the cruise, which started in Fort Lauderdale and sailed to many of the islands in the Caribbean. Vinny was also one of the great DJs that provided music on the ship, while Jeff co-hosted the sea venture. Over 300 guests signed on for the sea adventure, from as far away as Russia, Hawaii, California, Texas and, of course, New York and New Jersey, just to name some of the many ports of call that were represented on the cruise. The night before sailing on the Italian liner, Costa Fortuna, dancers were transported by bus from Ft. Lauderdale, about a 30-minute ride, where many of the travelers resided in preparation of leaving the next morning for their new dancing journey, to Goldcoast Ballroom for a BON VOYAGE PARTY. Over 150 guests arrived at the ballroom dressed in nautical attire. The girls wore mini, maxi and every other type of white nautical outfits that one can imagine. Even the guys looked like real sailors; some wore bellbottom trousers and navy caps, others dressed as officers, all spit and polished. When they entered the hall, the place turned white from the color of their outfits; it seemed as if snowflakes blew in with the wind and engulfed the place. The white outfits mingled with the colors worn by the other 200-plus dancers making the dance floor look like a checker board in black and white. We danced the night away to Vinny's music: Foxtrots, Waltzes, Cha-Chas and Mambos-Salsas, all the wonderful dance tunes that helped create a pre-cruise camaraderie that was to last throughout our Caribbean voyage.

We boarded the Italian cruise ship, Costa Fortuna, in mid-morning. Its brochure stated that: "It's the largest ship ever built for an Italian company, 890-feet long with a 124-foot beam. Built in late 2003, it boasts, the elegant three-level Rex Theatre, four swimming pools, a spa and gym, tennis courts, 11 bars and a state of the art gambling casino. The four dining rooms are smoke free, as are most of the common areas of the ship. It accommodates 2,720 guests in 1,358 rooms and has a complement of 1,027 crew members. Its 18 elevators carry passengers to their destinations, from deck one to 13." All in all, a pretty sizable ship.

Stardust had an orientation booth set up for our group and distributed dancing and planned activities programs, which included information, on a daily basis, of dance classes and social events for the coming week. Everyone was required to choose their dance classes in advance, and after confirming the availability of the classes, were given information as to the time, place and dance instructors teaching the lessons. The dance classes were broken down into A, B and C, signifying the level of proficiency required by the students participating in each lesson: (A) for beginners, (B) for intermediate, and (C) for advanced dancers. The levels of proficiency were strictly monitored, as a beginner in an intermediate or advanced class can slow down the progress of the other students and can be embarrassing for everyone. There were eight dance instructors conducting over 80 classes during the eight-day trip. Seven dance hosts were provided for the ladies, in addition to the dance instructors. Music for general dancing was provided by five DJs, all with their own style of music, so the dancers had a choice of where to enjoy their favorite dances. All the dance lessons were restricted to our group and were closely monitored so strangers could not interfere with the private sessions.

Barbara and I decided that we would take classes with Donna DeSimone and George (Jorge) Maderski who we know from our New York dancing community. Donna was the Stardust dance director and is a renowned dancer and choreographer, with her own dance studios. She also won the 1986 "USBC American Rhythm Championship" in Florida. We had taken group lessons with her at various dances that we attended and were happy to have the opportunity to learn from her again. Most of her classes were on the advanced level and were usually attended by ten to 20 students. We signed up with her for two West Coast Swing lessons, two Mambo-Salsa lessons and one Lindy and Hustle lesson. She lived up to our expectations, as her teaching method gets to the core of a dance routine and with some practice is easily learned. A bonus was that I had the opportunity to dance with her in the evenings at the general dancing, performing many of the steps that I learned in her classes.

We know George (Jorge) Maderski from the many dance halls we attended since we began dancing many, many years ago. He was dance champion of the 1986 and 1987 American Star Ball Theater Arts competitions and the 1987 Harvest Moon Ball Professional Cabaret Champion. He gives lessons at many of the dance venues in New York that we attend. Although he is proficient in many of the popular dances, he is considered an aficionado of Argentine Tango, which he teaches with passion and a unique styling. Many years ago, we attended a dance in Westhampton, Long Island, at Alfonso's Touch Dance Studio. We were all just learning and loving Argentine Tango, which was the feature dance of the evening. We were glad to see Jorge there and happy to share our steps and stories about the popular up and coming Argentine Tango. Alfonso and his partner, Agnes, have been promoting the dance for many years and did an exhibition that thrilled everyone. After their performance, Jorge asked him to play another Argentine Tango and then asked Alfonso to dance. Well, it is common in Argentina for men to dance with each other, but that sight here in the U.S. was a bit unexpected. Jorge's leads were amazing, while Alfonso followed as if they were long time partners. Then Alfonso played another Tango and took the lead away from Jorge as a challenge. Their performance and improvisation of the dance was a once-in-a-life-time experience; both dancing at fast, slow and moderate steps to the uneven tempo and sway of the Argentine Tango. The attendees were ecstatic and couldn't stop applauding and howling in admiration of these two very talented dancers who seemed to be at war with each other on the dance floor. Alfonso can be seen on New York television channels 56, 17 and 20 at various times of the week, teaching a variety of dances at different levels. More information can be obtained at his website: www.mnn.org, or at www. touchdancing.com. We decided to take two Argentine Tango lessons, two American Tango lessons, and two Rumba lessons with Jorge. His teaching lived up to his reputation as we left his classes feeling that we had a pretty good understanding of what we were taught; all we had to do was get on the dance floor and allow his teaching to come through in our performances.

After departing Fort Lauderdale, our ports of call included San Juan, Puerto Rico; St. Thomas & St. John in the Virgin Islands; Catalina and La Romana Islands, in the Dominica Republic; and Nassau Island in the Bahamas. Included in our package with Stardust Cruise were:

Seven night's accommodations in an outside room with a balcony.

Five Theme Nights: Mediterranean, Tropical Calypso, Italian Festival, Captain's Reception and Roman Toga

Two formal dress nights

Fabulous meals, gourmet midnight buffets, and 24/7 room service

A separate dining area for our Stardust dancers in the Restaurant Raffaello

Three complimentary themed cocktail parties:

Jack n' Jill Dance Contest

Stellar Broadway shows in the Rex Theatre

A Stardust hospitality desk set up during the entire cruise

Dance classes every day at all dance levels in private areas

Over 30 practice workshops

Our primary concern was our luggage, which arrived intact to our small cabin. There was just about enough space in the room to hang our clothes and hide our suitcases. Outstanding was our balcony. It was small but had enough room for us to sit and enjoy the view; especially exciting was the departure from the pier which was on our side of the ship, so we waved to our imaginary friends on shore as the ship sailed off into the horizon. The ship line has a unique infrastructure; it has many small rooms, approximately 180-square feet, and few suites, thereby increasing its passenger capacity accordingly. Its common areas are also downsized compared to other ships we've sailed on, but overall the accommodations were adequate and the overall feel of the ship was new and pristine. Its best feature for me was, that being an Italian ship, pasta was served 24/7, and I didn't waste any time going right to the pasta bar for lunch on our first day and ordered "little ears" pasta in a marinara sauce, with lots of parmesan cheese, cooked to order and right out of the pan. I would have gone for seconds and thirds, but Barbara's watchful eyes always seem to know where I am and what I'm up to, so salad was her more sensible choice to round out my lunch. Exiting the lunch area, I dreamed of capturing the palliative aroma of the various Italian sauces being brewed and spreading them on a piece of semolina seeded warm Italian bread; what an interesting sandwich that would make. "Dream On."

We spent most of the afternoon exploring the magnificent ship and enjoying its "adults only" swimming pool, which was on the upper deck and quite secluded from the hustle and bustle of the rest of the ship. There were no lessons scheduled for the first day, but we had general dancing for our group from 6:30 P.M. to 8:30 P.M., on the Colombo Pool deck on the 9th level. Vinny was our DJ and his excellent music put us all in the dancing mood that would last for our entire voyage. Our group had the late dinner seating at the main dining room; Restaurant Raffaello. We were seated with Joan and Alice from New Jersey, who were traveling together and hoping to improve their dancing skills beyond beginner's level. Also, my dear friend, Louis Mangone, who was instrumental in placing my Columbus Book Collection with the Columbus Citizen's Foundation, rounded out our table. The surrounding tables were occupied by many people we knew from Goldcoast Ballroom, which made for a very relaxed and chatty dining environment. The menu was extensive and favored Italian food. I was determined not to gain any weight on that trip, so keeping it simple was the way for me to go. I ordered an appetizer of sliced tomatoes with olives, covered with balsamic vinegar and olive oil. Although simple, this was always my favorite salad and I still enjoy it so much that I had it for an appetizer each evening for our entire trip. Needless to say, I was delighted to order a different pasta every evening to the chagrin of my fellow diners who were enjoying a variety of fish, pork, beef, and enormous salads and desserts.

After dinner, we moseyed along to the three-level Rex Theatre which accommodates over 1,300 people and was full to the brim. The theatre is decorated in art deco which gives the impression that you're surrounded by metallic polished, glittering mirrors. It's built like an amphitheater, giving all the patrons good views of the stage from their comfortable cushioned seats, with armrests and small tables to accommodate drinks. That night, the ship's staff of about two dozen performers danced and sang many scores from Broadway musicals. This spectacular performance was on a par with the original shows, but more exciting because we didn't know what songs were coming next and they had their own spin to the music, costumes and settings. A major advantage was that the stadium-style seats were the same as those in a private stadium room, so no one's head becomes an obstruction, which is something I'm plagued with when attending a theatre. The one-hour show was timed perfectly for us to attend Stardust's "Welcome Tropical Cocktail Reception," which was held at the Colombo Pool area on Deck 9 and was reserved for our group.

The dress for the occasion was colorful tropical clothing, the louder the colors the better. Some outfits were so imaginative in their color combinations and brightness that they were traumatic to my eyes and kept me alert the whole evening, allowing me to do some pretty serious dancing. Again Vinny was our DJ and played lots of music from the Tropics; we even did a limbo dance that turned out to be hilarious as the movement of the boat made getting under the rod somewhat difficult and many participants ended up on their backsides. We struck up an acquaintance with a couple that we saw around the Long Island dance scene but never really had any conversations with. Christine and Peter are from our hometown and are serious dancers. When we saw them at various dance halls, we always admired their smooth and technical dance routines, which in many ways were similar to ours. So we became friendly and exchanged many dance steps that evening and for the remainder of the cruise and took many dance classes with them. The Tropical Night theme was complemented with Pina'

Calotas and a mysterious red colored rum concoction that had a slow sneaky side-kick. The evening flowed by while we danced: Cha-Chas, Mambos-Salsas, Meringues, Foxtrots, Waltzes, and tangos. Fortunately the seas were calm and we didn't have too much trouble keeping our balance while maneuvering around the deck; keeping our balance from the potent tropical drinks was an entirely different matter. We met many new dance companions and reacquainted ourselves with New York and Florida friends. What made the evening especially pleasant was that the dance hosts and instructors mingled and danced with many of our group. The music stopped around 1:00 A.M., while the camaraderie was at its height, so many of the dancers retired to the 24/7 coffee shop or went to the other dance venues that were provided by Costa Fortuna.

We woke around ten the next morning after a delightful night's sleep, which was enhanced by the fresh Caribbean Sea air in our room that came from our open balcony door and filled our nostrils and minds with clarity and serenity. What a delightful way to start our first full day at sea. We checked our dance schedule and were disappointed that we had already missed some classes that began at 9:00 A.M., and ran every hour on the hour until 6:00 P.M,; but we quickly adjusted ourselves and chose to eat at the elaborate breakfast buffet, instead of a time-consuming sit down breakfast at the more formal restaurants. Our Rumba class with Jorge was at 11:00 A.M. There were about a dozen people attending the class, which made it easy to understand and follow his instructions. As this was an advanced class, he spent most of the 50 minutes working on the proper look and posture of the dance, which Barbara and I were delighted with, as we always seem to lose our posture in the excitement of following the beautiful Rumba rhythm. Our next class was West Coast Swing at 12 noon with Donna DeSimone. The class was quite crowded, about 20-plus students, but thinned out after the first lesson when it was determined that there were many beginner dancers attending this advanced class; they were asked to step outside of the dance area to make room for the qualified dancers. They were allowed to stay and watch the lesson, but couldn't participate as they were colliding with everyone and disrupting the class. This dance is particularly confusing due to the speed and technical acumen required to perform the routines. It must be performed with couples facing in the same direction as if on "railroad tracks"; the girls travel the tracks back and forth while the men step aside and let them pass. All of this is done to a quick "country western/lindy" timing and can become dangerous if dancers are not proficient in this type of dancing, which was the case with the beginners that were asked to leave the dance floor. Donna always comes through with her special type of teaching; we left very pleased that we learned some nice underarm turns, which we subsequently put to good use. Finishing the lesson unscathed was a very pleasant experience and was due to Donna's strict monitoring of the dance participants' skill levels.

We chose the buffet lunch to save time as we wanted to attend one or both of the two dance sessions that ran between 2:00 P.M. to 6:00 P.M. One of our favorite New York DJs, George Morse (Cody), was playing ballroom music at the Grand Bar di Savoia on Deck 6, and DJ Johnny Ortiz was playing Salsa, Hustle, Swing and Argentine Tango at the Vulcania Disco on Deck 4. We walked quickly to the dining area, passing the magnificent swimming pools where the occupants were enjoying the blue-green water and sunbathing. Following the aroma of the various sauces being brewed by the Italian chefs, I visited the pasta bar and had the chef make two plates filled with my favorite pasta, ears and ziti, with marinara sauce for the pasta ears and meat sausage sauce for the ziti. I was able to accomplish this quickly, while Barbara chose the long lines at the buffet and didn't have an opportunity to scale down my meal. By the time she found me among the many tables scattered throughout the restaurant, one plate of pasta was already devoured and removed from my table by one of the ever present bus persons. What Barbara brought back from the buffet was astonishing: sausage, pizza, pepperoni, orzo with veggies and a variety of desserts. I said:

"Honey, what happened to your diet?" She said: "Honey I'm only sampling a little of each."-- End of story.

We went to the Vulcania Disco to sample some of the music by DJ Otiz. Many of our friends were floating between his hall and DJ Cody's. We spent over an hour dancing Latin, switching partners and practicing the new routines we learned that day. We then visited the Grand Bar di Savoia hall to dance and continue practicing some of the steps we learned that day to DJ Cody's music. We always enjoy dancing and listening to his great selection of dance music. Barbara, especially, enjoys when he spins her around the floor a few times; he is an exceptional Latin dancer and she cherishes dancing routines with him. Barbara surprised me some years ago with a birthday party in which he was the source of our music, much to the pleasure of our guests. The hosts and instructors were busy at both locations dancing with all the girls and making them very, very happy. Many of the single ladies looked forward to this as their favorite part of the day because they got to dance with very polite, proficient dancers, and learned a great deal about dancing from them. We stayed till the music ended at 6:00 P.M., and then joined some of our friends in the Pizza Parlor for a pre-dinner snack and some juicy gossip. The topic of the week, or maybe month or even year, was the romantic escapades of New York's Governor Spitzer. No one could fathom why such a well renowned crime fighter and governor of one of our most important states could conduct himself so recklessly and in such a stupid manner, embarrassing himself, his wife and children in the process. The consensus was that he certainly isn't the only fool that has gone astray in the past or present, but he certainly was the fool that got caught due to his arrogance and blatant disregard for the secrecy that affairs require. Stupid man . . .

That night was the Captain's Formal Night, which required that I wear my black double-breasted uncomfortable tuxedo. As a lark, I wore my famous bright red nautical suspenders, which were hidden under my jacket. I always get a rise out of people when I take my very formal jacket off and the bright red suspenders appear capturing everyone's attention, resulting in lots of laughing and joking around. The passengers met in the Rex Theatre for a Gala Cocktail Party where everyone toasted Captain Claudio De Fenza and his officers as they were presented, one by one on the theatre's stage. After the ceremony, the Captain was available for photo taking with the guests, which has become a very popular event on cruise ships. Being that we have so many photos from prior voyages, we decided to go straight to the dining room and order some lovely Italian wine before the festivities began.

The highlight of the Captain's Formal Night was a procession by the kitchen staff marching through the dining room, dressed in kitchen garb, carrying large Baked Alaska Cakes (ice cream lined with sponge cake and topped with meringue), with sparkling fiery candles aglow while singing: "What a Lovely Way to Spend an Evening." What a great way to begin an evening's dining experience. At this point many of the diners were table hopping and even changing seats for the evening with other willing guests. We had a visit from a beautiful blonde from the Russian Ukraine who couldn't stop raving about the wonderful time she and her friends were having on the cruise, dancing and meeting new people and hopefully making lifetime contacts. The dinner and camaraderie didn't seem to want to end and we had to drag ourselves away to catch the show at the Rex Theatre.

The show's theme was acrobatic; the feats performed by the cast, whose muscles seemed to be bulging from their bodies as they performed their intricate movements, defied description. They built an inverted human pyramid, one person at a time, starting with one individual at the bottom and growing to several layers, rising upward until it was unbearable to watch for fear of their crumbling down on each other and the astonishing anchor man at the bottom. However they didn't crumble and received an overwhelming reaction from the audience as they completed their surreal act. After the show we had a choice of dancing at the Colombo Pool on Deck 9 with DJ Chris Marcelle who is originally from Long Island, New York, and now resides with her husband, Larry, (one of the dance instructors) in Vero Beach, Florida. We have become good dancing friends of theirs over the years and make it a point to dance at many of their events whenever they are hosts. Tonight she was playing Salsa/Hustle/Swing and Argentine Tango music. The second late dance session was in the Grand Bar Conti di Savaoi on Deck 5 with DJ Michelle Friedman playing general ballroom dance music. Both sessions were from 11:00 P.M. to 1:00 A.M. We decided to join Chris for the rest of the evening and, as usual, enjoyed dancing to her music. She, too, is a proficient dancer, which makes her choice of dancing music right on the beat. There were many dance hosts and instructors dancing with the guests, while the moonlight shining off the water of the swimming pool created a romantic atmosphere as we danced around the water's edge. I removed my tuxedo jacket to expose my bright red suspenders and not only got some chuckles from the dancers, but was out maneuvered by some of the other guys who also exposed their suspenders; some of which were more outrageous than mine. Some were pink, purple and orange, while some boasted scenic decorations, such as Christmas, Halloween, and Thanksgiving. We decided that on the next cruise we should have a Suspender Contest and give awards for the most outrageous attire. Another delightful, exhausting night passed, and we slowly strolled back to our place of rest to enjoy another calm night's sleep, with fresh warm Caribbean air filling the room from our open terrace door.

Our destination on the third day was the Island of San Juan, Puerto Rico; estimated time of arrival 5:00 P.M., departing at midnight, which didn't give passengers much time to explore the island. Many decided to see a flamenco dance show in town; we had visited the beautiful island many times, so decided to stay on board and enjoy more general dancing. I'm always thrilled when we approach one of the major islands in the Caribbean; all the books that I collected on the age of discovery over the years and many of their stories pleasantly pass through my mind, reminding me of the courage and audacity of the many brave men who dared to venture out into the unknown, not quite sure of their destination, or if they would ever return to their homes or loved ones. The island was discovered by the first European, Christopher Columbus, on his second voyage in 1493. The island was inhabited by friendly Arawak Indians, known as Tainos, who thought that the sailors were Gods and treated them accordingly. After many years of abuse by the Spaniards, the Indians rebelled, but to no avail. They were disbursed throughout the Caribbean or enslaved by their taskmasters, almost to a point of extinction. One of Columbus' crew, Ponce de Leon, returned many years later to govern the island and was primarily responsible for the unfortunate fate of the indigenous people. He later left the island in search of the Fountain of Youth, which he thought was in Florida; however, he is responsible instead for what is now known as the Fountain of the Aged. Anyway, if Columbus was a little off course on his second voyage, he would have missed this island, and what is known today as America would probably be called Columbia. Puerto Rico became the Spanish stronghold for their conquered lands throughout the Indies, Central and South America, and built a formidable fort at the entrance in Old San Juan to sustain their supremacy of these new lands; the fort still remains pretty much intact today.

We decided to limited our dance lessons to no more then two a day as we also wanted to enjoy the ship's facilities and didn't want to make our days onboard stressful by taking too many dance classes. Many of our friends took several dance lessons every day and totally enjoyed the chance to learn new steps and routines from the accomplished dance instructors provided by Stardust. Today we had a 10:00 A.M. advanced American Tango lesson with Jorge. The class was very private, only about ten people, which made it easy to understand and learn the new steps and routines he taught us. One step, in particular, was fun and sexy. It's called a "Gaucho," where a basic Tango step is done and continues into a left-hand turn in place, with lead hands lowered, for two complete counts of eight; a sexy maneuver and real eye catcher. There were two afternoon workshops: Ballroom dancing with DJ Vinny Munno and Salsa/Hustle/Swing and Argentine Tango with DJ Cody. We wanted to take our second lesson and then do some general dancing to the music of these two great dance music aficionados and practice the steps we were learning.

After lunch we took our second dance lesson with Donna DeSimone in Advanced West Coast Swing. Her classes always draw large numbers of dancers because she is such a proficient and easy-to-follow instructor and the dances she teaches are very popular. Again, she had to weed out dancers that didn't qualify for the advanced lesson; it seems that many people think that because they buy a pair of dance shoes, they suddenly have the ability to dance like Fred Astaire and Ginger Rogers. So, after the weeding out, the class had about 20 students which made the lesson much more manageable. We learned a couple of underarms variations and the importance of dancing this very quick-paced dance in the same direction as everyone else, on an imaginary railroad track to avoid collisions or what we call "train wrecks." We hurried to Vinny's and then Cody's dance workshops and practiced the steps we learned; some came easily, others took quit a bit of practice, but when the sessions ended, we had the patterns under control. At least, that is, until the next time we tried the steps.

We arrived at the beautiful harbor of San Juan at exactly 5:00 P.M., tied up to the pier and dropped the ship's boarding steps, which allowed those passengers who wanted to visit the area a speedy exit from the ship. We joined our fellow dancers for general dancing with DJ Johnny Ortiz at the Leonardo Da Vinci Lounge on Deck 5. Many of our group disembarked the boat to go sightseeing or attend a Flamenco Dance Show, so the dance floor at the workshop was not crowded and we were able to do some smooth dances (foxtrots and waltzes) easily, without the usual interference from other dancers. After the session, a poolside nap was in order, so we moseyed over to the poolside, had the attendant set up chaise lounges, and quickly settled in, and, in short order, we were napping. A post-nap dip in the pool rounded out our relaxing day, and we headed to our cabin to dress for another exciting evening with our friends aboard this wonderful Italian liner.

After dinner, it was back to the Rex Theatre for an Amateur Hour Contest between passengers. The bold volunteers performed to the best of their abilities, some very good and others not as accomplished. The fun of amateur contests is that contestants always give it their all, but come up short. One participant, in particular, was outstanding. He sang "On a Clear Day," but got the words of another song mixed in, which made the performance belly-laughing funny. We hurried to the Colombo Pool area on Deck 9 where our group was having a Calypso night theme party. Our friends were already starting the activities without us and were one up on us, drinking red concoctions with floating mini-umbrellas stuck in pieces of pineapple. The umbrellas didn't taste good, but the drinks were excellent. We spent the evening dancing to mostly Caribbean Calypso music, and then went to the late night session at the Grand Bar Conte di Savoia on Deck 5 where DJ Michelle Friedman was playing general Ballroom Dance music till 1:30 A.M. The calm waters that we were having on the first days were starting to act up, making it a little difficult to hold our balance while dancing. But we adjusted as best we could and danced the rest of the evening away to great music, lots of laughing and exchanging dance partners, which is always fun and what dancing is all about.. When the music ended, some of our group decided to continue the camaraderie at the Pizza Palace. Our day had been quite full, and we opted instead for a good night's sleep, and looked forward to opening our terrace door, filling the cabin with the fresh Caribbean air, and being lulled to sleep by the sound of the waves gently transporting the ship to its next destination, Charlotte Amalia in St. Thomas, Virgin Islands.

We arrived at St. Thomas at 8:00 A.M., and remained in port until 5:00 P.M., which gave the passengers a full day at the beautiful island to water ski, snorkel at the beaches, parasail, scuba dive for treasure, catamaran sailing around the island, sail to the neighboring islands of St. John or St. Croix, swim and sunbath at one of the many beaches, visit duty free shops, or just stay on board and enjoy the scheduled activities that were planned for the day. These included a lesson in Italian, group exercise classes, a miniature golf tournament, tennis on a respectable-sized court, dance lessons, or just relaxing at the poolside reading one of the many books available in the ship's library. Of course, the gym and spa were also always available for use and relaxation. We decided to take a dance lesson with Jorge in Argentine Tango, and after lunch visit the many duty free shops in Charlotte Amalia. Barbara carried a map with her of all the jewelry stores in the town and which have the best discounts; she kept notes from our previous visits to St. Thomas tucked away in her traveling bag.

There are over 65 islands that make up the Virgin Islands. The U.S. Virgin Islands (USVI) consist of St. Thomas, which is 32-square miles, St. John, which is 28-square miles, and the larger St. Croix, which is 84-square miles. Columbus visited these islands on his second voyage in 1493 and named them after St. Ursula and her 11,000 beautiful virgins. The first residents of the islands were the Ciboneys, Caribs, and Arawaks, who Columbus called "Indians" as he was searching for a shorter route to India and thought he had found the elusive land; consequently, labeling all the indigenous people that he met "Indians." Being that the Carib Indians were hostile and cannibalistic, the islands were considered unfriendly and remained outside of Spain's dominance and sphere of influence. In the early 1600s, the Dutch, French and English conquered these lands and found that the indigenous Indians had all but perished from European disease, abuse, and bondage. The United States purchased the islands in 1917 for $25 million from the Dutch. Subsequently, St. Croix, St. Thomas, and St. John became the U.S. Virgin Islands, which gave the residents the opportunity to become U.S. citizens. However not all residents thought that the option was a good one, and so they remained on as guests.

After breakfast, most of the ship's passengers disembarked to take advantage of the many attractions of this Caribbean paradise. Christine and Pete went to the one-mile long heart shaped Magen's Bay Beach. It's without a doubt one of the most beautiful and well maintained beaches in the world. The sandy bottom slops down gently, which encourages snorkeling and swimming and playing among the many small fish that inhabit the blue-green waters. We were considering spending some time at this magnificent beach, but it would have taken a good part of the day, and, as we spent time there on a couple of other trips, visiting the town for a short period of time seemed to be a better alternative. Especially since the temperature was expected to reach into the 90s and my remaining red hair and fair skin has difficulty dealing with the sun or heat. Oh, for the good old days when nothing seemed to bother me. I recalled the last time we visited Magen's Beach and swam for hours among the local inhabitants living in the water; we were comfortable swimming out into deep water, knowing that we were under the watchful eyes of the lifeguard on duty. A big surprise, however, was when Barbara and I swam a short distance to a nearby beach and discovered that it was a NUDE beach. Barbara was shocked and dragged me away, under protest, as I always felt that people should do whatever their fancy dictates. Unfortunately, my wife didn't agree, so we left all those beautiful people who seemed so at ease with their choice of bathing and returned to the more traditional bathing area.

We took a morning class in Argentine Tango with Jorge, which was a pleasure as we were the only students in the class. The Argentine Tango takes some explaining as it is one of three types of tangos (discussed in detail in previous chapters). International and American tangos are competition dances originating from the Argentine Tango, which was a street and brothel dance in Argentina in the late 18th century. In time, it was accepted as a social dance and became popular through many movies featuring its passionate movements; especially when performed by the actors Valentino and George Raft. Over the years it was refined into the American and International styles which are performed in world-wide competitions. But the main differences are that the two competition dances are done in ballroom positions, straight backs, with the male looking to his left and the female leaning back with her eyes directed over the male's right shoulder. There are strict routines and patterns that are followed, and whichever couples perform these the best are chosen the winners of the competitions. The dances are done in a counterclockwise direction, with zigzag variations. The Argentine Tango usually begins in a cheek-to-cheek position with partners caressing each other rather than holding. As the dance progresses, certain established routines and steps are performed, but the beauty of the dance is in the improvisations that each does to the changing rhythm and pace of the dance. It is considered one of the most complicated dances to learn and requires, in addition to many dance lessons and practice, a feel for the music as this turns it from a dance of steps to a harmonious and coordinated work of beauty. In the Tango world, this is called dancing with the right ATTITUDE. Another major difference in this dance is that it can be done in the line of direction (counterclockwise), which is salon style, or in place as an exhibition style, which is the sexier of the two and allows for more improvisation.

Jorge was pleased that we were the only students taking a lesson as it gave us time to catch up with the events in our lives that brought us to the Goldcoast Cruise. He took the opportunity to dance with Barbara, which was a sight to behold. I didn't realize how beautifully she danced, as I'm always holding her close and don't ever get an opportunity to see her perform. She followed him perfectly and displayed an exemplary attitude for the music. He also danced with me and showed me some attitude steps that were fun, especially the steps where I look at Barbara with a matador stare and challenge, while she throws a couple of kicks between my legs. He concentrated on our styling and polished our routines to a point where he was happy with our performance and had us do a private show for him before the lesson ended. We headed for lunch and a change of clothing before we left the ship for Charlotte Amalia to visit the stores that Barbara had plotted for us.

The temperature was already nearing 90 degrees, so we dressed accordingly. There were several shuttle buses from the ship to the center of town--it was only a few minute's ride. Barbara led me to the first of several jewelry stores, looking for what I thought was someone named John Hardy. I couldn't understand why she was bargaining with the salesperson for John Hardy. Then, she let me in on the secret; she was looking for a John Hardy bracelet, which is a silver or gold wrist band with some sort of stones. We went into four different stores before she decided that the first store had the best price. So we went back and she bought the bracelet for herself and one for my daughter, Laurie. I didn't ask her how much it cost, as we have an arrangement, I don't ask what her jewelry costs and she doesn't ask me how much it costs to play golf or buy clubs. I spotted a Christmas shop and headed directly for an ornament that was in the store's window, a beautiful angel with shiny gold sparkles. I bought it without bargaining, which annoyed Barbara, as she is one of the world's consummate "hondlers" and I deprived her of one of her most enjoyable pastimes by not letting her conduct the transaction. The temperature was rising and the heat was beginning to get oppressive, so we grabbed a taxicab back to the ship and then headed for our cabin to put on our bathing suits. We spent the rest of the afternoon in and around the pool, reading, and taking delicious naps. There were no afternoon classes scheduled, as most of our group left the ship and took advantage of the beautiful sightseeing and sea sport activities available in St. Thomas and, of course, the duty-free shopping. The late afternoon workshop was in the Grand Bar Conte di Savoia on Deck 5, with Chris Marcelle playing her great ballroom music. We danced for a couple of hours on a pretty empty dance floor, as most of our crew was still exploring and making contributions to the local economy. It gave us an opportunity to practice, without too much embarrassment, many of the new steps we learned at our dance classes. We then returned to our place of rest to refresh and prepare for the ship's Fiesta Italiana Night.

After dinner, we headed to the Rex Theatre for the Fiesta Italiana Show with international headliner John Ciatta performing the best of Dean Martin, Frank Sinatra, and other popular Italian singers. I closed my eyes and listened to him sing "That's Amore," " My Way," and many other popular songs. I couldn't tell the difference between him and the original artists that recorded those renowned songs. We exited the theatre and went to the ship's Tarantella Dance party, which included a dance lesson by some of the ship's staff. The ship's instructors, who also participated in the dance shows, were just as accomplished as the teachers provided by Stardust. Learning the Tarantella was a real treat. As a young boy, it was a favorite dance of my family and their friends. At many happy occasions, someone would produce a guitar, harmonica, tambourine, and even a kazoo, and get the music going for the girls who loved to dance the Tarantella. It is very similar in many ways to the Polka. I remember the girls trying to coax the men to dance, but to no avail, so the girls would enjoy dancing with each other. I danced Barbara around the floor a few times, doing the steps we had just learned and having one heck of a good time, while reminiscing the fun I had dancing that dance in my youth with my older sisters, Anne and Mae. We then left to join our friends at the Stardust Late Night Dance Session at the Colombo Pool on Deck 9. Dancing under the stars to DJ Chris Marcelle's music was romantic, even though the ship rocked and rolled, and keeping one's footing was a challenge. But, we all somehow managed to balance ourselves and enjoyed the ending of another beautiful day at sea, dancing till the wee hours of the morning. Breathing in the intoxicating sea air seemed to enhance my sleeping senses, as when I rested my head on my pillows at the end of the day, sleep was immediately imminent.

We were awakened in the morning to the ratcheting sound of the anchor being dropped off the shore of the Island of

Catalina in the Dominican Republic. The island was baptized by Christopher Columbus in May 1494, on his second voyage while still seeking a shorter route to India than the long dangerous prevailing routes. The island is famous for Captain Kidd's sinking of his ship "Quedah Merchant" in the 17th century (which he captured with considerable booty from the Spanish), to avoid being captured as a pirate by several English man-of-wars that were pursuing him. While returning to the safety of his home port in New York City, in an inconspicuous sloop, it's said that he buried some of his treasures in Block Island, Massachusetts, and Gardener's Island, New York. The mythology and legend contributed to such literature as Edgar Allan Poe's "The Gold-Bug," Washington Irving's "The Devil and Tom Walker," Robert Louis Stevenson's "Treasure Island," and Nelson DeMille's "Plum Island." They also gave impetus to the never-ending treasure hunts on Oak Island in Nova Scotia; in Suffolk County, New York; Charles Island in Milford, Connecticut and in the Thimble Islands in Connecticut. The most exciting myth or legend is his attacking the island named Takarajima (Treasure Island) belonging to Japan. The pirates landed on the island seeking food and cattle from the inhabitants, which was refused and resulted in the pirates burning the village and its inhabitants. Legend has it that he buried his considerable treasure in one of the cave-grave sights that the bodies were cremated in. He never returned to claim his booty, as he was captured and brought to England for prosecution and finally his execution. His hanged body remained on display for two years as a warning to anyone else contemplating being a pirate instead of a privateer (for the benefit of the crown). As odd as it may seem, his shipwreck was discovered on December 13, 2007, in 10-feet of water just 70-feet off the beach, centuries after its sinking.

The plan for the afternoon was for passengers to be transported in the ship's launch boats to the island for a BBQ, Calypso music, dancing, lounging on beach chairs, swimming in pristine waters, sunbathing, or relaxing among the 1,000-plus passengers that chose to leave the ship for a day on a tropical island. But, before our new adventure, there was an early morning advanced dance class with Donna DeSimone in Salsa. As usual, the class was crowded, and, as usual, she had to weed out many students who were not proficient at that level. It became evident how important maintaining the proper levels of dancing is as witnessed in one of her West Coast Swing classes, where a beginning-level student got into an advanced-level class. He not only caused a major collision with other students, but also resulted in his partner falling and injuring her knee. Barbara and I consider Mambo-Salsa to be one of our better dances, and totally enjoyed a swivel and underarm routine that Donna taught us that we were not familiar with. Mambo-Salsa requires a lot of energy to really enjoy the dance; learning to improvise is paramount to really looking special while performing. It's amazing to watch good dancers doing completely different steps and routines, while looking equally proficient and enjoying their own motions and improvisations. Although it is an energetic dance, it seems that many people prefer dancing only the Mambo-Salsa all evening long, and go out of their way to attend the Latin workshops which highlight this dance.

We boarded the launch boats with about 100 other passengers and defied the choppy seas and currents to arrive at Catalina Island, which took about ten minutes from the ship to the beach. The island is uninhabited and approximately 1.5 miles from the mainland on the southeast corner of the Dominican Republic, near the islands of La Altagracia and La Romana. The highest elevation of the island is 60-feet above sea level and about four-square miles in size, with a diverse preservation of eco-systems including sand dunes, mangroves, and reefs. The seas around the island are rich in wildlife, with many species of birds; tropical fish can be observed by walking out into the waters safely due to the many shallow sandbars. It is a lot of fun to walk out 50 yards, while visiting the many small fish in their natural habitat and being accepted by them as part of their scenery. We paired off with Christine and Pete and secured some chaise lounges under a large palm tree, which allowed us to relax without getting too much sun exposure. The seven-piece Calypso band's music filled the warm air, while many of the passengers began their gyrations that almost resembled dancing, while kicking up powder-like sand with the motion of their feet. Most were just jumping around and having a good time, while others chose to play volleyball and others walked or swam the shallow waters, all in unison with the music of the rhythmic sounds from the steel instruments. The BBQ lines were quite long, so we decided to go for swims instead of fighting the procession and heat. Christine, who is blonde and quite fair skinned, and I, a fair-skinned redhead, poured suntan lotion on to protect us from the very strong tropical sun. The temptation of the blue/green water was too much to resist and we all ran in to enjoy the water; we had to run out pretty far before the water was deep enough to swim in. The run was worth it, as the water felt like a welcomed cool shower bringing my body temperature down by at least 15 degrees. I could have spent the whole afternoon in the water, but previous experience with the sun warned me to get out before it was too late. So out I went, dripping the delicious liquid from my body, and noticed that I was the only one exiting the gifted waters. Barbara is dark skinned and can tolerate the sun better then most, but Christine, who is really fair skinned, and Sal, who is a little darker, also decided to stay in and enjoy the refreshing experience, hopefully not to their regret. We finally got to the BBQ food and took our booty to our secluded, shaded palm tree and devoured all the food in short order. Hot dogs, hamburgers, spareribs, conch fretters, watermelon and papaya fruit; washed down with tropical pineapple drinks, some with and some without boosters.

We left paradise by reversing our direction, heading for the massive Costa Fortuna that was anchored some distance away; its white super structure contrasting with the blue/green water and the pale blue sky, featuring just the right amount of clouds to create a post card scene of the first order. We headed back to our cabin to get rid of the salt and sand that was imbedded in our suits and hair. There were two dance workshops at 4:00

P.M. Vinny was playing Salsa/Hustle/Swing and Argentine Tango, while Chris was playing general ballroom dance music, mostly smooth. We decided to dress comfortably and attend an hour of each session and then enjoy watching the ship pull into the next port of the city of La Romana, which is one of the largest cities in the Dominican Republic with a population exceeding 250,000 people. It's only five miles from Catalina Island. I'm always fascinated when pulling into a port, either on my own boat or on a large cruising ship. The feeling of accomplishment and the excitement of a new experience is invigorating, and gets my mind imagining all the wonders that will be awaiting us when we land. Kudos must be given to the captain and his crew for their ability to bring this humongous 890-foot vessel into a small harbor and eventually ease it into its birth; all in a matter of minutes.

There is always a reception committee waiting when we dock and La Romana was no exception. A small calypso band greeted us with the song "Yellow Bird," which automatically had everyone singing or humming the words to the song: "Yellow bird way up in banana tree, yellow bird sitting there just like me . . . " The passengers waved and made all sorts of happy sounds in anticipation of what was to come from visiting that beautiful city. One of the city's famous attractions is the "Teeth of the Dog" golf course, which is one of three championship courses at the Casa de Campo Resort. Many of the passengers brought their golf clubs with them in anticipation of playing this world-renowned championship course. Unfortunately I didn't, and had to resign myself to listening to the players tell of their great experiences and wonderful imaginary scores, after their return. Maybe the next time I visit the city, I'll be better prepared. We retired to our cabin for a well-deserved nap, and were lulled to sleep by the fresh sea air and soft magical sounds of the calypso band.

We arrived at the Rex Theater early to get good seats for the Grand Variety Circus Show featuring acrobats Duo Markov and Duo Errani. Their skill with the ropes that seemed invisible was astonishing; they actually extended themselves over the audience as if flying through the air, arms and legs outstretched and balanced on their stomachs, to the delight and fright of the spectators. Two other performers imitated the actions of snakes that wriggled and squirmed and then entered combat with each other. The whole scene was surreal, and gave me goose bumps to watch such large creatures in combat and then kissing and making peace. The ship's dancers performed some exotic routines as circus animals, lions, tigers, elephants and zebras, which received continuous applause from the audience. Much of their performance reminded me of the Broadway show, The Lion King, where the animals ran through the aisles toying with the guests, as the Costa Fortuna's dancers did.

There were two late dance sessions scheduled for the evening, both featuring general dancing: DJ Johnny Ortiz at the Colombo Pool on Deck 9, from 10:00 P.M. to 12:00 A.M., and DJ Michelle, playing in the more private Grand Bar Conte di Savoia on Deck 5, from 12:00 A.M. until 1:30 A.M. We decided to dance at the early session and leave the Grand Bar to the more hearty souls in our group. There was a particular technique that Barbara and I wanted to practice to Argentine Tango music, and John willingly accommodated us with a varied tempo song. When we took our lesson with Jorge, he emphasized the importance of the right "Attitude" for the dance, so we decided to experiment with some "Attitude" and see if we could capture the spirit of the dance. At the beginning, I approach Barbara as she retreats, dodges, and shies away. I follow her and abruptly cut her off and then hold her in my arms. We do a balancing move, turning our bodies from left to right with our feet in place. The music intensifies and we are wrapped in each other's arms, she reluctantly and me demanding. Slowly, to the music, we begin to dance as one, enjoying the passion of the moment and then caressing aggressively at the finale. We were told that Tango dancing tells a story, and that story must be relayed to those watching. If this can be accomplished, then the right "Attitude" for the dance is captured. We must have gotten the Attitude right because our friends applauded and did some hooting;

even Jorge came over and complimented us by saying: "You almost got it right." Satisfied that we "almost got it right," we continued dancing till the session ended and then joined our friends at the Grand Bar for a late night mix. We danced and socialized until we were exhausted and then moseyed along to our cabin for another great night's sleep; breathing in the fresh salt air entering through our terrace door, and being lulled to sleep by the hypnotic sound of the waves gently splashing our ship.

The following day was at sea, journeying to Nassau Island in the Bahama's chain before returning to our final port of call in Ft. Lauderdale, Florida. We squeezed in three dance lessons for the day: in the morning, Advanced Lindy with Donna DeSimone and Advanced American Tango with Jorge; in the late afternoon, we had an Advanced Hustle lesson with Donna. Having some spare time in the afternoon, we decided to take an Italian lesson given by one of the pretty crew members. We both decided to skip breakfast, which was becoming our largest meal of the day, and hold off for the famous Midnight Buffet, which features finger sandwiches, sushi, and every combination of dessert imaginable, we couldn't wait. My Pollyanna attitude figured that by missing breakfast, eating a variety of desserts at midnight would even the calorie score, especially if I ate lots of unsweetened fruit. Further supporting my Pollyanna reasoning, we decided to spend some holistic time at the gym and then get stone massages at the spa which would certainly enhance our health and probably help us lose some weight.

The dance lessons went according to our plans and we picked up some valuable dance routines to add to our repertoires in Lindy, American Tango, and the Hustle. The highlight of the day was the stone massage that we both had in their state-of-the-art spa. I was put in a private room with soft natural music playing the sounds of rain drops and animal calls. Stripped down to my birthday suit, heated basalt stones (black volcanic rock) that retain heat well were placed on top of my vertebrae. The stones were heated in 120 to 150 degrees of boiling water and, when applied, immediately penetrated my body, causing the most relaxed feeling imaginable. The therapist performs the same traditional Swedish massage strokes that I experienced when getting my regular massages at home, except that she holds these magical heated stones in her hands while plying her trade. When finished, my body not only seemed at peace with itself, but was mysteriously energized. After cooling down and dressing we headed for our Italian lesson in the Conte Rosso Lounge on Deck 5.

Although I'm of Italian descent and my older sisters told me that I was able to speak Italian very well as a child, the language somehow left my memory. Learning to speak the language as an adult has become a challenge to me. I've taken lessons with Berlitz instructors, listened to Berlitz tapes, and have written lessons until the wee hours of the day, all to no avail. I just don't have foreign language retention. On the other hand, Barbara has a good understanding of Spanish and Yiddish, which gives her great insight into many languages. When we visited Greece many years ago, it only took her several days before she deciphered that difficult language, and when we visited Italy on several occasions, she had no trouble grasping their language. So she coaxed me into taking an Italian lesson on the ship, and, as her suggestions are usually my commands, I followed her to the Conte Rosso Lounge for another lesson in Italian. The lesson went as follows: Buon giorno = Good morning; Buona sera = Good afternoon or Good night; Bene = Well; Grazie = Thank you; Si = Yes; No = No; Signore = Sir or Mr; Signora = Madam or Mrs; Signorina = Miss; and Scusi = Excuse me. Barbara gobbled the information up and I was surprised that I mastered these few words as well. Pleased with ourselves, we left the class room and went to the Vulcania Disco Room on Deck 4 to join Michelle for general ballroom dancing. I asked her to play some Argentine Tango music, which she did immediately. This gave us a chance to practice some more "Attitude" routines which were becoming second nature to us as we were really getting into the passion of the music. Many of our friends were pleased by our improvement with the dance and tried copying our moves. I told them if they wanted to get a passionate feel for the dance, they had to develop the right "Attitude." As the words left my mouth, I pictured Jorge saying the same thing to us. I guess "Imitation is the best form of flattery."

After taking a prolonged nap, we dressed for a formal evening which was dictated by the captain and, again, I was plagued with wearing a tuxedo in a tropical atmosphere. But I remember so well the pleasure I received from seeing Cary Grant in a movie wearing a tuxedo while smoking a cigarette on the deck of an ocean liner and telling his lucky leading lady how much he loved her; this scene so indelible in my mind, made wearing my tux a little more tolerable. I felt I was Cary Grant as I looked in the mirror remembering that scene; however, taking a longer look at the mirror quickly dispelled my fantasy.

Tonight our show time was prior to the formal dinner and featured "In Concert" performed by the crew's singers and dancers. There were lots of sing-along songs and fancy ballroom dancing choreographed by the cruise director, Max. He also did some very serious baritone love songs, such as "On a Clear Day," "Some Enchanted Evening," and "September Song." We exited the show singing and humming some of the songs we just heard, while moving on to the Raffaello Dining Room for our "Farewell Dinner," which strangely was two nights before the end of our journey. I had my usual pasta delight with trimmings, while toasting and congratulating Captain Claudio De Fenza and his crew for the splendid job they did in transporting us around the Caribbean Islands. As the champagne was gratis, there was lots of toasting going on around the dining room; passengers to crew, crew to passengers, tablemates to table mates, students to dance instructors and tour leaders, and on and on.

While Chris was entertaining our group with her special music, some of us decided to try DJ Jascin, the ship's music aficionado at the Disco Vulcania Lounge on Deck 4. His music equaled our DJ's; the only problem was trying to dance among so many non-dancers without colliding with them. Our experiment was short lived, and we swiftly joined Chris in the larger Colombo Pool area on Deck 9. The buzz from our group was about the midnight "Buffet Magnifico" and the exact time it would begin. Sounds strange, what time will the midnight buffet begin? Well, it was a good question because it didn't start until 12:30 A.M., in the Raffaello Dining Room.

It's amazing that the staff could put together such a display of ice art work and food in such a short period of time. The whole dining room was inundated with ice sculptures of swans, Roman female figures, Roman gladiators, and beautiful flowers. Tables were lined up with finger sandwiches, sushi, hors d'oeuvres, and every imaginable dessert, presented in artistic surroundings and designs. Fruits were presented in various art forms, such as watermelon fruit baskets, cantaloupe butterflies, and pineapple hats. Tropical flowers were artistically placed throughout the hall, emphasizing Birds of Paradise and an abundance of lilies. Chocolates and more chocolates were everywhere, and would certainly win first prize for the most consumed treat in the shortest period of time. The feast lasted till after 2:00 A.M., which gave passengers an opportunity to sit with their booty and enjoy cappuccino, espresso, or any other number of drinks, with or without boosters. Most people just sat around till the wee hours of the morning, mingling and just having a great social experience with other guests on an incredible ship.

Our last day at sea included a short visit, from 1:00 P.M. to 5:30 P.M., to Nassau Island in the Bahamas. The Bahamas is an archipelago with about 700 islands and almost 2,400 islands consisting of rocks, white sandbanks, and coral reefs, extending from Palm Beach Florida to the coast of Cuba. Only 40 islands are inhabited. It was on one of these, the Island of San Salvador, that Christopher Columbus made his first landfall. Nassau was one of our favorite vacations spots during the great "Jet Set" era. Right after tax season, April 15th, we would pack our bags, grab our kiddies, and fly off to this incredible turquoise/blue water paradise. On one of our visits, we witnessed the ground breaking and the beginning of construction for the Paradise Beach Hotel on Paradise Island, while sunning on the beach across the channel. We immediately booked reservations for an afternoon excursion to the Greek philosopher Plato's imaginary city, Atlantis, to explore the world-celebrated resort. We were anxious to see how the pristine white sand island we visited and enjoyed so many years ago looked after being developed and civilized. We invited Christine and Pete to join us for the exciting excursion; they gladly accepted the invitation.

We scheduled three dance classes in the morning: Advanced Salsa and Cha-Cha with Donna and Advanced Argentine Tango with Jorge. All the lessons were well attended and we added more routines to our ever-growing repertoire. Hopefully we would remember what we learned after leaving the ship. We decided to have a sit-down lunch at Restaurant Christoforo Colombo on Deck 9. We were lucky to get a window table and ordered some of the fish specialties, with pasta, of course. It was really a treat to sit down for lunch in an upscale restaurant with white gloved waiters serving us. My Pollyanna trait went into gear as I tried to convince Barbara that a hearty lunch would energize us for the exhausting trip we planned to Paradise Island.

We were transported by jitney to a waterfront depot in town and got on line to board the Paradise Island 50-passenger boat launch, which would take us to the dream island. Approaching the island was shocking; I never expected to see the extent of development that had taken place since we swam at the isolated white sand beaches, with few structures in sight. Townhouses were lined up along the shore, as well as a multitude of hotels, which were all dwarfed by the 97-acre Atlantis Paradise Island Hotel. Its Royal Towers joined by the bridge section is one of the most expansive hotels in the world. We were deposited on the fairy tale entrance of the hotel and couldn't figure out where to look first, due to the most unusual marine architecture imaginable. Fortunately, we were able to pick up a guided tour and followed the leader through the maze of water and marine exhibits, each with its own unique attraction. We went directly to the Aquaventure which opened in 2007. The 63-acre, 200-million gallon seawater display combines slides, lazy rivers, and rapids into one large waterscape. The centerpiece of the colossal attraction is the 120-foot Power Tower, which contains four waterslides and a rock climbing wall. The slides include: The Abyss, The Drop, The Falls, and The Surge. Next to these are the Mayan Temple Slides, consisting of four major slides: Leap of Faith, The Challenger Slides, The Serpent Slide, and The Jungle Slide. The five-story Mayan Temple has a 60-foot vertical drop that ends in a clear tunnel inside a shark filled lagoon. The Challenger Slides accommodate people who want to race down the water to the bottom and splash themselves into oblivion. Our next stop was the Dig, which is a series of aquariums located beneath the lobby of the Royal Towers and has the world's largest open air habitat. Hundreds of different aquatic species (angelfish, sharks, manta rays, and various types of colorful jellyfish) can be seen in various tanks. The floors of the different aquariums have wreckage and debris scattered about representing the remains of the "Lost City of Atlantis." The remnants are supposed to mirror what the legendary lost city looked like after its destruction. In other parts of the Dig were subterranean views of Atlantis-themed chambers that stretch the imagination as to what life was like during its "day in the sun." Our guided tour ended abruptly and we found ourselves in the casino. Wouldn't you know, another place to deposit our pocket money--it was just what we needed. We raced out of the area to take pictures of the amazing displays around the resort before our excursion ended.

The waterfalls and slides were a photographer's dream comes true; I took pictures of at least six different falls including the spectacular waterfall at Beach Towers and the two Mayan Waterfalls. We had to rush to catch our launch boat and didn't have an opportunity to explore the rest of this magnificent playground, but we promised to return in the very near future and finish exploring that incredible venue. We learned from our launch guide that the island also had two 18-holes par 72 golf courses and a 9,000-square foot nightclub. The Paradise Island from days of old no longer existed; what took its place is a "concrete playland," for better or worse, depending on one's point of view. I enjoyed both the uninhabited pristine island of yesteryear and the modern architectural genius that brought us the potpourri of personal delights that exists today. Originally I preferred the former, but I must confess, I was impressed with what I saw on our adventure. I think the best of both worlds would be the Atlantis Resort standing alone on a pristine island without any "Disney World" or "Coney Island" type neighbors, which are in such abundance.

We returned in time for a quick nap and found white sheets in our cabin to be used as togas for the Roman Night Festival. We did this once before on the Mississippi Queen Cruise, and I was unhappy then and uncomfortable now about wearing a sheet through dinner, a show in the Rex Theater, and then the Stardust Going Away Party. But Barbara suggested that I join in the spirit of the evening and, as usual, her requests become my commands. So, I wrapped myself like a mummy and somehow did resemble some sort of Roman citizen. We went to our final dinner and were joined by our traveling companions; to my surprise some of the group evidently were pre-warned about the toga dress and wore some pretty fancy toga outfits. Christine looked like a Roman Goddess in her white, gold trimmed gown highlighted by her golden hair supporting a tiara. Her red sunburned skin contrasted beautifully against her outfit, making her look like a glowing Sun Goddess. Pete, by far, had the best toga ensemble, also with gold trim and sash and sporting a golden Roman laurel wreath. Together they looked as if they stepped out of a time warp to join our party. There were many farewell toasts and a farewell speech from Captain Claudio De Fenza, trying to convince us that we were the best passengers he ever carried on his magnificent vessel. After repeating my dining preference with a couple of plates of pasta, we retreated to the Rex Theatre for Roman Night and the Guest Talent Show.

The show featured Cleopatra, Mark Antony, Caesar, Bacchus, and Centurions played by the cruise staff. Somehow lions appeared for a gladiator exhibition that was quite funny; the lion, consisting of two people, looked quite disjointed while stumbling all over the stage trying to look threatening. Cleopatra, Mark Antony, and Caesar relived their parts in history, from her meeting the great Caesar to her romantic disastrous interlude with Mark Antony, and her final meeting with a poisonous asp, which concluded the Greek Ptolemy's lineage to Egypt's royalty. The history of her lineage dates back to 300 BCE when Alexander conquered Egypt and left one of his generals, Ptolemy, behind to rule the country. Subsequently, all the leaders were from his line and spoke Greek as their main language, including Cleopatra and her younger brother. The amateur talent show was pretty entertaining. Somehow all the contestants won first prize, which they certainly deserved for their courage and good humored dispositions.

We were anxious to attend the Toga Stardust Farewell Cocktail Party in the Leonardo Da Vinci Lounge where DJ Michelle provided the dance music. Our group was already in full swing when we arrived. The scene looked like a meeting of the Roman Senate gone wild. Everyone was in good spirits thanks to the free spirits (pun intended) provided by our host, Stardust. There was a lot of showcase dancing throughout the evening, provided by the better dancers, and, after a few drinks, the "not so better dancers." We couldn't believe how many new friends we made and how many different people we danced with on the trip. Seeing everyone having fun at the party, emphasized how satisfying the dance cruise was to the participants, who were acting like life-long friends. We said our goodbyes with hugs and kisses and by dancing one last time with some of our new friends.

It was after 2:00 A.M. when we returned to our cabin, so we had to rush and pack, as we were scheduled to arrive after our 180-miles voyage from Nassau to Ft. Lauderdale, at 8:00 A.M., and begin disembarking immediately.

Vinny and Jeff have booked another eight-day dance cruise on the Royal Caribbean's "Independence of the Seas," for January 31, 2010. Needless to say, we already have reservations for that journey. A copy of their brochure is presented with the permission of Vinny.

Goldcoast Dance Cruise

Cha Cha Cha   Rumba   Tango   Salsa   Swing   Hustle

CHAPTER ELEVEN

Dancing at Waikiki Beach, Hawaii

AROUND THE FLOOR: SEPTEMBER/OCTOBER 1998

TRAVELING AROUND by Barbara Bivona

WE WERE IN HAWAII recently, visiting our son and daughter-in-law, who are both officers in the United States Army and are stationed at Schofield Barracks, about 20 minutes from Waikiki Beach, in Honolulu. We took the opportunity to go to the Ala Wai Country Club in Waikiki Beach several times for ballroom dancing. The enormous dance floor, which we were told is 12,000-square feet, is utilized to its full potential as there are no tables crowding the dance space; chairs are strategically located around the perimeter of the dance area so they do not interfere with the performers. The floor has one of the best surfaces we have ever danced on, which is constructed of eucalyptus, making it soft on dancing feet, which gives performers the feeling that the floor is floating. One of the evenings was hosted by the Hawaiian Ballroom Dance Association (HBDA). The HBDA members did various showcases in competition. All of the performances were done in group formations rather than featuring individuals. It must have taken months of training and practice for these groups of up to 20 dancers to perfect their routines. The performances were quite an unexpected treat.

During the week there are no-charge afternoon dances, where the ballroom is divided by portable walls into three sections, each one 4,000-square feet. The popular style of dancing in Hawaii is International. With these large dance areas, dancers have an opportunity to zigzag in the line of direction with little interference from others, always aware of the courtesies that are required when dancing the fast-paced smooth dances. In spite of the large crowds, when the ballroom is at full capacity, which is 700 to 800 people, there is very little bumping by the dancers. On the one occasion where we saw a slight collision, both couples immediately smiled while bowing, apologized, and then continued dancing as if nothing had happened.

We look forward to our next trip to Hawaii for the big event, which is the birth of our first grandchild; a boy is predicted. Of course, in between changing diapers and babysitting, we will be going back to the Ala Wai Golf Club to dance. We'll also check out the Latin dance club at the Hawaiian Regent Hotel, where we stayed many years ago on our first visit to Hawaii, and other venues that we were told are scattered around Honolulu.

RETURNING TO HAWAII and IAN CHARLES BIVONA

AROUND THE FLOOR: MARCH/JUNE 1999

TRAVELING AROUND by Barbara Bivona

Once again, Mike and I returned to Hawaii. This time, it was for the birth of our first grandchild, Ian Charles. Of course, he is the most beautiful baby we have ever seen and he definitely has dancer's feet! Although our days were occupied with this gorgeous child, our nights were free. So we returned to the 12,000-square foot Palladium dance hall at the Ala Wai Golf Club in Waikiki. One evening was sponsored by the HBDA and another evening featured two difference dance clubs: the Pan Pacific Dance Association and the Aloha Dance Club. For these two events, the floor was divided in half by a portable wall and I was surprised that the music did not filter from one side to the other. We chose to dance at the Aloha Dance Club because the floor was less crowded; the choice was a good one as we were able to dance smooth dances (Waltz, Foxtrot, and Quickstep) without any interference from other dancers. We were also able to finally dance a Samba, which, although a Latin dance, is done in the line of direction. It's very difficult to find dance floors that have enough space or are large enough to perform the many beautiful steps and routines that are part of this wonderful Brazilian dance.

Latin dancing by Salsa Hawaii at the Acqua Club in the Hawaiian Regent Hotel on Thursdays, Fridays, and Saturdays, starting at 10:00 P.M. was a treat. Featured was the seven-piece band led by "Rolando Sanchez." Rolando has been playing at the Regent for three years and is instrumental in organizing and participating in Latin festivals in Hawaii. He has been featured on TV shows and music videos in Hawaii and Tahiti. Although the dance floor is a small, nightclub-sized one, we were able to dance with plenty of space as Latin dancing doesn't require much room. We were able to do some good Mambo-Salsas, Cumbias and Meringues. Half of the fun was just listening to this great band; Con Mucho Gusto!

Rumours Nightclub is at the Ala Moana Hotel in Honolulu and features ballroom dancing on Tuesday and Sunday nights. Although there is no cover or admission charge on Tuesdays, we were amazed by the complimentary buffet, which included sliced steak, various salads and fruits, and Japanese appetizers, including some really good sushi. There is a $5.00 admission charge on Sunday evenings, which is well worth the unheard of price, considering that a meal and great dancing are included. For information, call the Ala Moana Hotel, 1410 Atkinson Drive, phone number: (808) 955-4811. Although we didn't go to the Hale Koa Hotel in Waikiki, they have ballroom dancing during the week to live music. Their phone number is: (808) 733-7380. Also, the Wahiawa Ballroom Dance Club, which is

Michael Bivona

on the north shore of the island, holds dances in their Town Center Gym. They have a monthly dance and weekly classes at all skill levels, plus midweek practice sessions in the daytime, which is open to the public. You can write for information to the Wahiawa Ballroom Dance Club, Town Center Gym, Wahiawa, Hawaii 96786. Jane Miura Odo, who is a member, volunteered her phone number; for information call (808) 637-4875. Aloha . . .

* *

Our love affair with Hawaii started when we spent our 25th wedding anniversary vacation cruising the Hawaiian Islands, with ports of call in Hilo and Kona on the Big Island of Hawaii, and Kahului, Maui; Nawiliwili, Kauai and Honolulu, Oahu. We sailed on the vintage S.S. Independence (built in 1951) from Honolulu, for a seven-day voyage around the most idyllic ensemble of islands in the world. The ship was the perfect size to sail the short distances between the islands; 682-feet in length with a 90-foot beam. She accommodated 1,000 passengers in Henry Dreyfuss-designed cabins (ultimate utilization of space), with large size suites and penthouses. She featured Fifth Avenue shops, for the ladies on board, handsome turn of the 18th century public rooms, and bars decorated in Hawaiian tattoo design. Most memorable were their collection of miniature cruise ships in bottles, including the Titanic. Picture windows in the observation lounge, spanning 125-feet, gave viewers' panoramic scenes of the islands and the surrounding waters. In the evening, it was a safe haven for viewing the bright red steaming lava flowing from the Kilauea Volcano and meeting the sea, on the Big Island of Hawaii. We made a stop on the Big Island to explore the Kalapana Black Sand Beach (a result of volcanic remnants), which resembles a scene from an outer space horror film; its course sand and strange odor is surreal. We knew we were on a beach, but absolutely wouldn't lay on the sand or swim in the water, although there were people sunbathing and swimming in the turquoise/blue water and enjoying themselves. Our most fascinating experience was visiting the Kilauea (spewing) Volcano, which is 4,091-feet above sea level, is the most active in the world (45 eruptions in the 20th century), and it's flanked by the much larger snow-caped Mauna Loa Volcano (13,677 feet). Barbara went berserk, she ran to the cordoned off area and took pictures of the bubbly stuff with smoke spewing from its crest. Kilauea is considered to be the home of Pele, the volcano goddess of ancient Hawaiian legends. Several special lava formations are named after her, including Pele's Tears (small droplets of lava that cool in the air and retain their teardrop shapes) and Pele's Hair (thin, brittle strands of volcanic glass that often forms during the explosions that accompany lava flow as it enters the ocean). In Hawaiian mythology, Kilauea is where most of the conflict between Pele and the rain god, Kamapua'a, took place. Since it was the residence of Pele, Kamapua'a, jealous of Pele's ability to make lava spout from the ground at will, covered it with the fronds of the fern. Choking from the smoke which could not escape, Pele emerged realizing that each could threaten the other with destruction; the gods had to call their fight a draw and divided the island between them: Kamapua'a got the windward northeastern side, and Pele got the drier Kona leeward side. Our dear friend, Dallas Peck, must have had the time of his illustrious life when working and doing research at the Hawaiian Volcano Observatory (HVO) in his early years as a geologist, specializing in volcanoes. On the 75th anniversary of HVO in 1987, when he was the Director of the U.S. Geological Survey, which manages the HVO, he wrote an article called, "The Celebration on a Volcano," which stated: "The Kilauea Volcano sure knows how to prepare for a party. During the two months prior to lasts week's festivities commemorating the 75th anniversary of the nearby HVO and the opening of its new facilities, the volcano added 18 acres of lava to the Island of Hawaii. And, since the eruptions began three years ago, Kilauea has produced a record-breaking 850-million cubic yards of lava. The amount could cover, to a depth of almost 31-feet, four lanes of an interstate highway from New York to San Francisco, approximately 3,000 miles." He writes on, "The new HVO building, perched on Kilauea's rim, is equipped with an elevated tower from which both Kilauea and the neighboring Mauna Loa Volcano can be observed. The HVO, which is the United States' first and oldest volcano observatory, has been responsible for the development of most of the volcano monitoring techniques now used worldwide." What an exciting and fulfilling life Dallas had during his 23-year tenure as the presidential nominee of the office of Director of the U.S. Geological Survey, and an additional 18 years as a scientist and researcher at that world renowned organization. He would say that "Working at a job he was totally infatuated and absorbed with, and being around all the mythical gods of the volcanoes and the Hawaiian Islands, was the world's greatest dream job; being paid for the work was the icing on the cake."

We made one more stop at the Captain Cook Monument in Kealakekua Bay to pay homage to the great sea captain who was the first westerner to discover the Hawaiian Islands. The obelisk lies a short distance from where Captain Cook was killed in a battle with the hostile local natives. His sailing master was the much maligned Captain William Bligh of the infamous ship, Bounty, whose crew chose to stay with the beautiful women and easy life of the islands rather then return to the hardship of a sailor's life on board the Bounty. It was Bligh that Captain Cook sent ashore to fetch fresh water and food for the crew, thereby making Bligh the first European to set foot on Hawaiian soil. Cook's men also enjoyed the readily available sexual favors of the local girls and the easy life of living among such bountiful beauty. He would have probably had the same mutinous results as Bligh had the local natives been more friendly; unfortunately for him, they were war-like and actually provoked fights with the intruders, which eventually resulted in the death of Cook and many of his men.

Back on the ship, we enjoyed evenings of delicious food that included many local fish. We indulged ourselves with mahi, swordfish, and lobsters, plus varied meat selections. After dinner, we would withdraw to the nightclub for big band music and dancing. They had a ten-piece band playing Hawaiian music and lots of ballroom dancing numbers. Lucky for us, very few people were dancers so we were able to request many numbers and do some pretty good dancing to the live music of the colorfully-dressed members of the Hawaiian band. Many evenings we were the floor show, doing Latin and smooth dances to the applause of the people in the club; we were embarrassed at the attention, but were really in heaven performing our hard-learned steps and routines in front of an audience that enjoyed watching us. We had a ukulele contest that was exciting and lots of fun. The passengers were given ukuleles and had three days to learn how to play songs that were assigned to them. I was one of the winners, playing "We Are Going to a Hukilau." While singing "We Are Going to a Hukilau, a Huki, Huki, Huki, Huki, Hukilau." I had to perform topless, wearing a hula skirt. When all the men performed together, it turned out to be hilarious the girls couldn't stop laughing at our hairy chests and legs and the disjointed exotic movement of our hips.

We sighted Humpback Whale pods while passing between the islands of Maui County. The sight of 100s of humongous creatures breaking the turquoise-blue sea water in choreographed harmony is certainly one of the most spectacular sea wonders of the world. The whales migrate approximately 3,500 miles from Alaskan waters each autumn and spend the northern hemisphere winter months mating and birthing in the beautiful warm waters off Maui. Unfortunately, these beautiful mammals are facing many dangers due to increased levels of pollution, the high speeds of commercial vessels, and military sonar testing. They are now considered an endangered species and are protected by the government. We spent a few hours swimming and sunbathing on a pristine soft, white sand beach while devouring conch soup and fritters that were provided by the ever-pleasant native attendants. It was difficult leaving the heavenly beauty of this island to return to our ship; surely there is no other place on earth to compare with its natural beauty and bountiful resources. That is until we visited the Island of Kauai, which is considered the tropical centerpiece of Hawaii.

It's carpeted with lush greenery, covered with flowers of every color, and has visible fresh fruit growing in abundance. There is even a comforting cool mist to relax the body and soul on hot days.

Kauai is the oldest of the Hawaiian Islands, and it was here that Captain Cook gave the islands their first western name: Sandwich Islands, named after his sponsor the Earl of Sandwich. Oddly enough, the Earl invented the sandwich as we know it today. He was an avid card player and, to keep the players at the card table instead of the food bar, he concocted the sandwich to ensure uninterrupted gambling. We visited Waimea Canyon, which is the largest canyon in the Pacific. It measures 10-miles long, one-mile wide and more then 3,500-feet deep. It was carved thousands of years ago by rivers and floods that flowed from Mt. Waialeale's summit. It's not as large as the Grand Canyon in Arizona, but certainly rivals its beauty and complexity. The lines of the canyon walls depict different volcanic eruptions and lava flows that have occurred over the centuries, and from certain points look like the colors of a rainbow. The canyon is in the Koke'e State Park which encompasses 4,345-acres of land, with 45 miles of trails that run through it and nearby swamps. This is certainly a place to revisit for a week to spend time exploring the trails and campsites while staying at the Hale Koa Cabins.

Our next stop was the Spouting Horn. This natural wonder occurs when water rushes under a lava shelf and bursts through a small opening at the surface. Every wave produces another spray, frequently 50-feet into the air. The phenomenon is especially exciting at sunset when the spray becomes incandescent with the colors of the rainbow. There are signs warning viewers to stay behind the cordon ropes, as injuries and even fatalities have resulted to people that wandered too close to the blowhole. Legend has it that the coast was guarded by a large mo'o (lizard) that ate anyone who tried to fish or swim in the area. One day, a man named Liko entered the water; when mo'o attacked him, he swam under the lava shelf and escaped through the hole. The mo'o followed him and got stuck and was never able to free himself. The groaning from the blowhole is his cry from hunger and pain as he remains still trapped under the rocks. I just love Hawaiian legends, they seem to be steeped in Pollyanna mystique that captures and stretches the imagination. Many years ago there was a much larger blowhole called Kukuiula Seaplume adjacent to the Spouting Horn. It shot water 200-feet into the air. However, as the salt spray damaged a nearby field of sugar cane, the hole was blasted away in the early part of the 20th century. Imagine trying to destroy such a natural wonder today, every environmentalist in the world would be up in arms. The island has such diverse beauties that over 60 feature films have been shot on it, such as the majestic Manawaiopuna Falls in "Jurassic Park." The Wailua River was used in the movie "Blue Hawaii," and the Anahola Mountains were used as the backdrop in the "Raiders of the Lost Ark." Again we had to drag ourselves away from another island in paradise and return to our ship.

Our last night of the cruise was a formal one. Out came my tuxedo, starched collared shirt, suspenders, and sash wrapped around my waist, which gave me the feeling of being prepared to be mummified. The dinner was spectacular; I again had freshly caught mahi (dolphin, not the playful ones with long snouts, but the blue finned type). Watching the tuxedoed waiters singing Hawaiian songs while serving food was amusing; the only distinguishing differences between their dress and the tuxedoed guests were that the waiters wore white gloves and were singing. Aside from those two differences, all of us looked alike. After dinner, I had to return to my cabin and take off the uncomfortable tuxedo and put on some clothing that would allow me to dance with ease. We spent the evening dancing to the wonderful music of the live band, which went out of their way to play our requests for ballroom dance music. It was the custom many years ago for many cruise vessels to have a different themed midnight buffet every evening. Barbara's favorite was the chocolate buffet on the last night of the cruise. We were used to seeing ice sculptures at these feasts, but they were replaced that evening with chocolate birds, flowers, tigers and an assortment of other little critters. I found it difficult biting into a chocolate canary, but my wife had no trouble devouring her favorite desserts; I thought she would eat herself into heavenly chocolate oblivion. The cruise ships today wisely do not have these buffets every evening, as they resulted in an unnecessary waste of food and added needlessly to the expense of traveling. Today they usually have just one night of "pigging out" with a buffet style extravaganza, which alleviates the guilt feeling that I always had when eating a late, unnecessary fourth meal.

We docked in Honolulu at the same pier we departed the populated island from. It's easy to understand why more than half the people in Hawaii live on this island in paradise; it not only has some of the most beautiful beaches in the world, but is also a metropolis of the first order, with cultural and educational facilities readily available. It even boasts the world's largest wind generator (20 stories with 400-foot blades), that is employed to create electricity for the island. We headed straight to the Sheraton Waikiki Hotel which is located on the main beach avenue with commanding views of Diamond Head Mountain, Honolulu, and Waikiki Beach. We planned on spending a few days exploring the sophisticated clubs and some of the local sites.

We decided to spend the day walking the main street, Kalakaua Avenue, and exploring Waikiki Beach. As luck would have it, we immediately stumbled onto the Waikiki Town Center. The name is deceiving, I thought it was a visitor's center, but it wasn't. It is a shopping mall with about 50 vendors, restaurants and lots of tourists. Barbara was ecstatic; it was just what she needed after spending a grueling week aboard a ship cruising the Hawaiian Islands, some quality in-depth shopping. Our first stop was an outside vendor displaying oysters. For a price you can buy one that might contain a pearl. Barbara got lucky and bought one that had a mini-pearl enclosed, and immediately made plans for mounting it in a ring. During our walk I noticed that everyone seemed to be as lucky as she, they all won pearls with their purchases. The center is dominated by a gorgeous fountain in an open courtyard with shops surrounding it having local names like Red Dirt Tees, Quicksilver Boardrider's Club, and Chin Lan. For the most part, the shops sold Hawaiian souvenirs and clothing. It didn't take long before we were out of the small shopping center and, wouldn't you know it, right next door was the International Marketplace with 130 carts, shops, and artisan stands. It seemed I wasn't going to have a good day, as shopping isn't one of my favorite pastimes, unless it has something to do with golf or boating. I must say, the local craftspeople were very friendly and volunteered tales of their heritage, especially if they were "real Hawaiians" (unbroken racial lineage), which they are very proud of. We got some nice photos of a small cascading waterfall from under a century old banyan tree. The large eccentric tree was fascinating; the twists and turns of its branches and the bulges in its trunk were an anomaly, as if its creator couldn't make up his mind in which direction the tree should travel; its distortions make the tree one of nature's special works of art. Another unusual attraction was the Swiss Family Robinson-style tree house, which was the original home of one of the locals, Donn the Beachcomber.

We previously made a mental note to visit the Royal Hawaiian Hotel, known as the Pink Palace, on the beach side of the street. The entire outside facade of this enormous hotel is bright pink, which illuminates the beach and sky when the sun sets in the evening. A pink color scheme prevails throughout the hotel, right down to the linens and plush towels. As guests of its sister Sheraton hotel, we had dining and beach privileges, so we brought along our swim suits and decided to spend the afternoon on its private, gorgeous beach. Upon entering the hotel, native girls greeted us with leis and pieces of banana bread. The overwhelming pink vaulted ceilings blended in with the huge Art Deco arched mirrors in the public areas and over the shops, which matched the pink outfits the staff was wearing. We were escorted to dressing rooms so we could change into our swimsuits and then proceeded to the beach, where bronze suntanned boys secured pink chaise lounges, pink striped umbrellas, and pink towels for our pleasure. This pink Pacific gem, which was built in 1927 on Waikiki Beach, has to be experienced to be believed. A BBQ was being prepared, while music filled the air from a live Polynesian band. We ordered Mai Tai drinks from the open-air Mai Tai Bar, where it is boasted that the drink originated. Small handouts were delivered with the drinks listing its ingredients:

"One ounce of dark rum

One ounce of light rum

One ounce of orange Curacao

Two ounces of orange juice

One-half ounce of lime

A dash of orgeat

A dash of simple syrup"

"Combine all of the ingredients, in the order listed, into an old fashioned-style glass and pour over shaved ice. Stir with a swizzle stick. Garnish with a slice of pineapple and a cherry and then drink slowly." We decided to order the concoction in a pineapple with a small pink umbrella on top, which certainly enhanced the drink and made it a truly Hawaiian experience. It was easy to settle in and enjoy the food from the BBQ; spareribs and roasted pork strips with pineapple trimmings, while sucking in the fresh sea air and the hypnotic aroma coming from the pits. Watching the four to six-foot afternoon waves beating the sandy shore quickly opened my heart to the magic of Hawaii as being one of my favorite places on earth.

We replenished our Mai Tai drinks and relaxed for the rest of the afternoon, enjoying hula exhibitions by gorgeous Hawaiians in their exotic hula skirts, and ukuleles serenading by handsome, young, colorfully-dressed Hawaiian men. We stayed until sundown, which is an experience not to be missed. The sky turns bright red with rainbows abounding, as the sun inches out of sight into the horizon to the moans and sighs of the viewing spectators. We returned to our hotel exhausted from the pleasures of the day and went directly to our room for a glorious night's sleep.

We woke late the next morning and decided to enjoy the exotic tropical breakfast buffet at the hotel. It was surprising to see the variety of Japanese food presented: miso soup, rice, and even sushi were scattered throughout the maze of food. Looking around explained the reason; about two thirds of the guests were Japanese who were enjoying sushi with all its trimmings. It's difficult, while looking around the city and dining room, to believe that the Japanese lost World War II. It seems what they couldn't conquer during hostilities they succeeded in conquering during peace time, as the sushi bars and menus in their language are equal to the English equivalents. Japanese food has always been one of Barbara's favorite indulgences and that morning was no exception. She couldn't stop raving about how wonderful the food was. I satisfied myself with cereal, eggs, and plenty of Hawaiian pineapple, which I couldn't seem to get enough of.

We picked up a walking map of the area and decided to walk in the direction of the Diamond Head Crater, which is a short distance from our hotel and part of the Kapiolani Park complex. The 500 acre park was created by King Kalakaua in the late 19th century and is home to the famous Kodak Hula Show, the world renowned 42-acre Honolulu Zoo, and the Waikiki Shell Amphitheater. It has tennis courts, soccer fields, an archery range, and a three- mile joggers' course, but the most spectacular jewel is its beach with the historic Diamond Head Crater in the background. We brought beach-mats with us and the first thing we did was spread them under the shady picnic beach area and spent the better part of an hour sipping our coffee and just absorbing the heavenly beauty of nature's gifts to us. This respite gave me some time to read the fascinating history of the Diamond Head Crater. "It's considered one of the most famous dormant volcanic craters in the world, located on the southeast coast of Oahu at the end of Waikiki, overlooking the Pacific Ocean. It was originally named Laeahi by the ancient Hawaiians. The name meant 'brow of the tuna' and looking at the silhouette of the crater from Waikiki you can see the resemblance. The current name was given to the crater by British sailors in the early 19th century. When they first saw the crater at a great distance, the calcite crystals in the lava rock appeared to glimmer in the sunlight. The sailors mistakenly thought there were diamonds in the soil and hence they named it Diamond Head. The crater has been extinct for over 150,000 years. It's 3,520 feet in diameter with a 760-foot summit." Here is what makes it one of the most unusual craters in the world: "When the United States annexed Hawaii in 1898, its harbor defense became one of the government's main concerns. A major defense fort, Fort Ruger, occupied the crater. A battery of cannons was located within the crater, providing complete concealment and protection from invading enemies. An observation deck was constructed at the summit in 1910 to provide target sighting with a four-level underground complex, built within the walls of the crater as a command post. A 580-foot tunnel was dug through the crater wall to provide easier access to the fort. With the advent of radar, the observation deck and underground complex has been abandoned, but evidence of the command post is still present along the Diamond Head Trail. The trail is paved almost its entire length, but is very steep in spots. There are two sets of stairs, one with 99 steps and the other with 76 steps. There is also a 225-foot unlit tunnel. A hike up the mountain is classified as easy to moderate in exertion, but is certainly worth the breathtaking, unparallel view of the entire west side of the island, from Waikiki to Koki Head." The history was fascinating to read, and even though walking up to the top of the crater was considered "easy," we decided to have a relaxing day and just hang around the lower part of the park.

We followed the sound of island music and arrived at the Kodak Hula Show, where we were greeted by beautifully dressed young girls in hula skirts, with leis around their necks and flowered tiaras sitting on top of their long, black, shiny hair. They greeted us with alohas and put leis around our necks while they wriggled their hips and waved their arms to the rhythm of the tropical music. The Kodak Hula Show has been a Hawaiian tradition since 1937. The fabulous outdoor spectacular is an historical look at the island through the beauty of the hula performed by Hawaiian native dancers. The show featured a cast of 40 entertainers from the Royal Hawaiian Glee Club. The dancers were dressed in traditional skirts made of green Ti Leaves, coconut bras, and fragrant flower leis in their hair. Performances were conducted at the Shell Amphitheater and are probably the most synchronized, harmonious, and beautifully choreographed dances that I have ever seen. The music seemed to be coming from within the dancers as they move around the stage performing soft, flowing sensual motions in harmony with one another. I must say that Hawaiian dancing and music is an integral part of why so many people love these beautiful islands and why I am so captivated with the magic of it all.

The world renowned 42-acre Honolulu Zoo is unique in many ways. It has an African Savannah with lions, giraffes, zebras, elephants and many other animals, as well as an abundance of birds. What makes it an unusual place to visit is that it features moonlight tours so that visitors can enjoy the wildlife in their evening environments, especially observing nocturnal animals that normally sleep by day, such as the skunk, toad, snow leopard, red fox, raccoon, possum, hedgehog, firefly, and badger. To make a visit more interesting, they have overnight camping on sites where participants bring their own camping equipment and set up for the evening in a designated area, very close to the Savannah. Supervised feeding of the animals is allowed. I heard one young girl that spent the evening with her family in the park talking about how she visited the hippo den and fed an apple to a 4,000-pound animal. She saw that I was interested in her adventure and excitedly told me of being escorted by the zookeeper to a hyena's home at feeding time and helped him feed the hungry family. I asked her what her most memorable experience was and she said: "Trying to avoid the toads at night, which seemed to be all over the walking paths and were attracted to everyone's flashlights. Her happiest experience was when Pizza King delivered pizzas, sodas, garlic nuggets, and doughnuts." Not an unpleasant way to spend a night-out with the family. If we ever return with our kids, we most certainly will give it a try.

We returned to our hotel for a nap, which was becoming a necessary, every day event due to our excessive walking and the soothing sea air that seemed to relax us and make us sleepy. We visited our concierge, Jackson, and asked if there were any good dancing venues close by. He suggested the Hilton Hawaiian Village Beach Resort and the Pink Palace. We asked him to make reservations at the Hilton for dinner and for whatever entertainment that was available for the evening, and do the same for the Pink Palace for the following evening. We headed to our room and immediately visited dreamland for a necessary nap; we were so exhausted that we didn't even whisper our usual pre-slumber niceties.

We arrived at the Hilton Hawaiian Hotel just in time to hear the loud horn-like sounds of conch shells, announcing the end of daylight and the beginning of the lighting of torches ceremony throughout the tropical area to the beat of island drums, singing, and fireworks. We were again greeted by beautiful girls, who pleasantly placed leis around our necks while gyrating their voluptuous hips to the rhythm of the native drums. That was certainly a great way to put me in the mood for an enjoyable time, especially when their second act was to put Mai Tai drinks in our hands. We were seated facing the man-made enormous Duke Kahanemoku Lagoon, and were startled to see a large canoe with about a dozen Hawaiian fisherman land on the Great Lawn in front of us, which signaled the start of the night's luau. The Hawaiian fishermen began to mingle with the guests, inviting them to learn and dance the "Hukilau," a traditional song and dance that tells about fishermen and their catch of the day. It was so spontaneous and exciting; we were actually imitating the men doing the "Hukilau" dance within a few minutes while trying to catch and sing the words to the Hukilau Song, which was originally written by Jack Owens in 1948. I think it went something like this:

"What a wonderful day for fishing in the old Hawaiian way, where the Hukilau nets are swishing down in Old Laie Bay. Oh we're going to a Hukilau, a huki-huki-huki-huki Hukilau. Everybody loves a Hukilau, where the laulau is the kaukau at the big luau. We throw our nets out into the sea, and all the ama-ama come a-swimming to me. Oh we're going to a Hukilau, a huki-huki-huki-huki-huki Hukilau."

What a great time we had imitating fishermen casting their nets upon the sea and then retrieving them with their catch of the day. We enacted this to the rhythm of the Hukilau Song as we swayed our hips and arms, trying to imitate the Hawaiian men's motions. We were escorted to the imu (underground oven) while we were still in motion to see the ceremonial removal of the cooked pig from the imu and its preparation for the forthcoming feast. The luau menu included kalua pig, poi, iomi-iomi salmon, and cold selections, such as island style macaroni salad and seasonal fruit. Other hot items included grilled huli-huli chicken, mahi-mahi with macadamia nuts, creamed spinach, rice, taro, and sweet rolls. Desserts included haupia, macadamia nut cream pie, coconut cake, and guava cake. To add insult to injury, where our diets were concerned, Mai Tais were included in the price of the feast. We tried to be very selective in our selection of food, but between the two of us, we couldn't help sampling everything on the menu.

We needed the long walk back to our hotel to work off the heavy meal and delicious potent drinks. We swore that we would never again consume such large quantities of food and beverages, and decided that the next day we would avoid any place that had elaborate or tempting food selections. So we spent the day hanging around the hotel's swimming pool and working out at the gym, hopefully working off some of the calories we forced into our bodies, so unwillingly, the night before (pun intended). We visited our concierge, Jackson, who reminded us that the dress code at the Pink Palace was not casual and that we had an eight o'clock reservation for dinner and dancing. We dressed accordingly and put on our most comfortable shoes for some serious dancing. Entering the large dining hall was a throwback to the WWII era. The large 17-piece band, its members dressed in tuxedoes, resembled scenes from some of John Wayne's war movies, especially when seeing the many naval officers dressed in formal U.S. Navy uniforms throughout the hall. The venue has been a naval hangout since the beginning of WWII and, evidently, continues to be a favorite of the sailors stationed in Hawaii. We danced, danced, and danced around the ballroom and on the enormous outside terrace overlooking the Pacific Ocean, surrounded by the distant flames of the torches, which not only kept the mosquitoes away, but provided a very romantic setting for slow dancing. The side views from the terrace of Waikiki Beach's glowing nightlights added to the ambiance and mood of the evening. I was surprised at the number of people, especially sailors, that were not only dancing acceptable smooth ballroom dancing and Swing, but were also quite good at Latin Mambo, Cha-Cha, and Meringue. We had a special treat that evening; Martin Denny was in the audience and was asked to play some of his popular music, which he did with a big smile on his face. He played the piano to perfection, entertaining us with "A Taste of Honey," "The Enchanted Sea," and "Ebb Tide." Unfortunately, he didn't have members of his band with him; if he did we would have heard some of his exotic Hawaiian music. His writings and performances with unusual percussion instruments brought life back to many old standards, such as "Flamingo" and "Sayonara." We ended the evening with a conga line dance, where the guests lined up in back of each other and moved around the floor to the music of "Locomotion." Somehow I found myself at the beginning of the line leading the 100-plus guests to the beat of the music, while everyone was singing the words to the song "do the locomotion" and moving their arms back and forth, imitating a locomotive train. The dance ended our evening and our 25th "Anniversary Waltz" with the heavenly Islands of Hawaii.

* *

When our son and daughter-in-law told us they were leaving Korea and would be relocating to the Army's Schofield Barracks in Hawaii, which is about 20 minutes from Waikiki Beach, Barbara and I began to immediately pack our bags for our second trip to the "heavenly wonderland." It had been over ten years since we promised the Hawaiian gods that we would return, and lo and behold, here we were flying first to Los Angeles for a plane change and then to Honolulu. One of the last memorable times we had with the kids was over four years ago in Washington, D.C. We were celebrating my daughter-in-law, Donna, receiving the "General Douglas MacArthur Leadership Award," which is bestowed on twenty Army officers annually for their leadership qualities. The awards were presented by Secretary of State Alexander Haag and the Chairman of the Joint Chiefs of Staff, General Reimer. We had no idea how important and prestigious the award was until we saw the high profile people that were honoring these young Army officers. They were individually presented with a bust of General MacArthur, a wrist-watch, and an inscribed pen and pencil set, in addition to a fancy gold medal. After the ceremony, we attended a cocktail party where Donna introduced us to her commanding officer, a two-star general whose name I don't recall. I asked him what she did to deserve such recognition, he said: "The best person to ask is your daughter." I asked her, and she said: "I don't know, I only did my job." Not the answers that I was looking for, so I nosed around and asked some more questions. The best information I could get was that she was in Desert Storm and, being that she had a law degree, they thought the best job for her in the Army would be as a body guard for a field general; this is very common reasoning in the military. She, evidently, did an exemplary job in Saudi Arabia and in her many years with the military. I was satisfied with whatever little information I gathered and as proud as can be, especially when we were given a private tour of the General Douglas MacArthur Museum in the Pentagon and saw a plaque with award recipients' names listed. There it was, Lt. Donna Bivona, listed on the honor roll. It was truly a seminal moment, seeing our family name "Bivona" in such a prestigious place of honor in one of our Nation's most celebrated buildings. We were primed for our next trip to the Hawaiian Islands and thrilled to be staying with our children in their home and getting a little taste of what it's like to actually live as a local on the Island of Oahu.

I decided to do some research on the customs of Hawaiians so we could be better prepared to live among them on our upcoming journey. "Aloha," "Aloha," "Aloha," is a word that is heard every minute of every day when traveling through the islands. What does it really mean? It certainly is one of the most beautiful words in the Hawaiian language and conjures up all sorts of beautiful images, such as hula girls dancing, waves embracing the beaches, palm trees swaying in the soft breezes, colorful dresses and shirts, and flowers of every description in bloom year round, lending their fragrances to receptive breaths of fresh air. The word "Aloha" has come down through the ages and doesn't have one meaning, but a combination of meanings that describe its use:

"A-means welcome, what I have you may have, share with me.

L-comes from the Hawaiian word "loko maikai" which means, what I have said comes from my heart and good intentions.

O-comes from the Hawaiian word 'oluolu,' meaning happy, this is part of their heritage-a happy people, happy doing for others.

H-comes from the word "haahaa" meaning humility and meekness; we welcome you, we do things for you because we are happy doing it and are very humble to serve.

A-All of these expressions mean Aloha and should only be used when you feel them in your heart."

Well, that certainly explains the pleasant attitudes of the Hawaiians that we met on our last trip. It will give us all the more reason to use the word with a lot more understanding and humility.

Another custom is the "shaka," which is a hand movement which means "hang loose, everything is cool bruddah." It is done using the thumb and pinky of your hand and doing a little wriggle. It's a friendly gesture and is done with good intentions, similar to our saying; "have a good day" while tipping your hat. It's believed that the traditional "shaka" originated in ancient times when a great chief lost his three middle fingers in an accident. Thereafter, he would greet his subjects by waving the altered hand at them. They, in turn, not to show any disrespect, would respond in the same manner.

Another tradition that is found throughout the islands is the ceremony of "Luau." It has significance far beyond its being considered a BBQ. A "Luau" means: "good food and drink, music and dance, conviviality and fun, usually set against a background of a blazing tropical sunset." To ancient Hawaiians it was all this and more, since luaus were also occasions to thank the gods for good fortune and to ask for future blessings. Among the ancients, the gods were involved in every earthly activity; ruling over birth, marriage, death, war, seasons, sports, skills and, indeed, all daily happenings. Major events in the life of a village were commemorated with a communal feast, which was originally called an "ahaaina" and is now called "luau." It was only natural that these celebrations should be dedicated to the particular god, or gods, who held primary influence over the event. For instance, a feast celebrating the gathering of crops would be especially sacred to "Lono," the harvest god. The gods had their favorite luau foods: Kalua pig, baked in an underground oven called an "imu," and chicken were traditional offerings. No luau could be complete without the Hawaiian staff of life, "taro." It's the tender young leaf of the plant called "luau," from which the current name of the feast is derived; it is cooked with coconut cream and the roots pounded into poi.

While Hawaiian gods now live mainly in myths and legends, many ancient luau traditions still survive. The pig is still ceremoniously baked in the "imu," and poi is still a favorite food, still eaten with people's fingers. Hula dancing may have modernized, but many implements used in the dance, such as the "ipu" or gourd, recall olden times. In ancient days, the hula was a sacred ritual performed for the gods. The dancers, who dedicated themselves to the goddess Laka, spent many years learning their art. Accompanied by gourd drums and chants, the dancers celebrated the heroic exploits and wondrous feats of the all powerful gods. Most importantly, the spirit of luau, creates a festive atmosphere of companionship, relaxation and enjoyment, and still remains the same as in the days of the ancients.

With a better understanding of Hawaiian customs, we were ready to journey part way around the world to visit our children and, hopefully, spend some time enjoying the camaraderie of the friendly natives. The kids' new home was in a town called Waialua on the island of Oahu. I looked the location up on the internet and found the following information: "Waialua is one of the communities that make up the north shore of Oahu. Recreational activities include snorkeling, fishing, sailing, scuba diving, swimming, surfing, and more. The Turtle Bay Resort, in Kahuku, with 36 holes of some of America's best golf, is nearby. Kaiaka Bay Beach Park and Haleiwa Aii Beach Park are both located in the Waialua area, and each is a great spot for parties, swimming, or just hanging out at the beach. Sightseers can visit rainforests, waterfalls, beaches, and art galleries, or take an amazing helicopter tour around the island. It is situated just 30 miles from downtown Honolulu and 20 minutes from Schofield Barracks." We couldn't wait to get there.

The kids were very mysterious about where they lived and wouldn't tell us anything about their new home. They said: "We want to surprise you." When we arrived at their home, we were certainly surprised. They were living in a three-bedroom, two-level house, with a 200-foot back yard, leading to the most gorgeous beach in the world. My heart doubled its pace when I saw the view. After unpacking, I laid out on the hammock hanging from the ceiling of the terrace facing the ocean, nursing a tropical drink, when my son Steve asked me: "Dad did I do the right thing in renting this house instead of living on the base at Schofield Barracks, which is a lot less expensive?" My answer was spontaneous. I said, "Steve, if I were your age I couldn't think of a more beautiful place on earth that I would rather be then right here, on this hammock, looking at this ocean. I don't know what could possibly make me happier." Then he said, "Dad we have another surprise for you." At that moment, I heard Barbara let out a scream from inside the house where she was hugging Donna, as she yelled: "You're pregnant!" That said it all, we hugged and kissed; our first grandchild was on its way. It was one of the happiest moments in my life.

Steve decided to have a cook-out on the beach that afternoon. They invited some of their Army buddies and neighbors for the feast. Steve has always been a great chef and especially enjoyed doing BBQs. About 12 of their friends arrived to the smell of hot dogs, burgers, and spareribs roasting on their oversized pit. I couldn't believe the whole scene, it was dreamlike. We came to see our kids, who were in the military and had just returned from tours of duty in Korea. We were expecting to see them in the drab surroundings of a military base, but instead, here we were on a beach in their back yard, enjoying the surf, their tropical fruit drinks, their spareribs, and the camaraderie of their friends; what an exquisite turn of events from what we expected. The food had a special flavor, which was enhanced by the smell of fresh sea air, the pale blue sky with an ensemble of various shaped clouds, the sound of the waves caressing the beach, pleasant company, and of course, my pregnant daughter-in-law. After our feast, as if rehearsed, everyone donned their swimsuits and ran pell-mell into the delicious turquoise/blue surf screaming and howling at the pleasure of the water splashing their bodies. While we were swimming and horsing around, we were joined by the neighbor's two Labrador retrievers who couldn't resist an opportunity to join the excitement and add to the splashing and clamor. The setting of the sun was another spectacular event. It made the sky look as if it were on fire-bright-red and orange coloring blending in with the clouds and then, very gently, disappearing out of sight beyond the horizon. Steve lit a camp fire and we started roasting marshmallows as we sang. One of the guys magically produced a guitar and began playing Hawaiian songs, including "Tiny Bubbles (tiny bubbles), in the wine (in the wine), makes me happy (makes me happy) . . ." What a memorable way to end our first day in Hawaii with our kids, their jovial friends, and the serendipitous surrounding of nature's landscape beaming with perfection.

Waking to the sounds of waves hitting the beach and the irresistible urge of rushing to take a swim was too much to bear; I ran as quickly as I could and dove, head first, into the surf, with my eyes wide open so I wouldn't miss any marine underwater sights. Exiting the water, eyes burning from the salt and my lungs consuming the fresh sea air, I thought I must have died and went to heaven; so exhilarating and enjoyable was the experience. Steve, who is one of the best chefs around, whipped up my favorite blueberry pancakes for breakfast, which we quickly devoured. He then asked what we would like to do for the day. Barbara and I agreed that we wouldn't mind hanging around their beach, as we still had some jet lag, and would need rest for the dancing we had in mind for the evening. We heard of a great dance hall at the Ala Wai Golf Club in Waikiki Beach from friends of ours in Florida who have a home in Oahu. We asked Steve and Donna if they would like to join us for an evening of dancing and they said yes. So, after dining on delicious leftover food from the BBQ, my son drove us to Waikiki Beach and the dance hall, which took about 45 minutes.

We couldn't believe the size of the dance floor; 12,000-square feet of open space. What is immediately noticeable is that there are no tables for the patrons to sit at in the hall; just chairs strategically located around the floor, so as not to interfere with the performers. As we are members of the Royal Palm Beach Chapter of the United States Amateur Ballroom Dance Association (USABDA), we were invited in for a discounted $3.00 charge and seated with some of the officers of the Hawaiian Ballroom Dance Association (HBDA). We were treated as if we were old friends by many of the HBDA members, and were bombarded with questions about dancing on the Mainland (USA). There were over 400 people in attendance, which we were told is a minimal crowd. The venue has functions that hold between 700-800 people, especially when competitions are held at the magnificent hall. The dance music is provided by a DJ, who is located on a small platform outside the perimeter of the dance floor, as not to interfere with the flow of dancers. They have a unique method of communicating the dance that is to be performed; a placard, which is about two feet by four-feet and located above the DJ's platform, is displayed announcing the current dance. This is the dance that everyone must do or they are chastised. We didn't notice anyone who was not conducting themselves properly or being reprimanded for not adhering to proper dancing etiquette. Their dance style of preference is International Style. It's a pleasure to watch hundreds of people dancing smoothly, in the line of direction, with few collisions and all doing the same dance. There were some people dancing American Style, but they followed the same rules and blended in nicely with the International Style dancers. That is, except for us. A Tango was flashed on the board, so Barbara and I decided to do an Argentine Tango. We immediately had a circle of people around us watching us do our sways, ochos, ganchos, boleos, and kicks. We received applause when we were in closed position. I moved slowly away from Barbara putting her in an outstretched position on one foot, the other foot raised half way up. When fully extended, I moved her around in a circle going about 180 degrees, and then gently facing her, closed the position with a caress. Most of the people had never seen Argentine Tango performed up close and were excited at our sensual presentation. We received many handshakes and polite bows. Steve and Donna couldn't believe the reaction we received, and joined in on the camaraderie that usually follows a dancing exhibition.

We especially enjoyed doing foxtrots and waltzes, as there was ample room to move around the dance floor and perform many of the steps and routines that we love so much. There is a routine that Barbara and I learned many years ago from our Russian instructor, Alec, that can be performed in the Foxtrot and Waltz. However, it requires a lot of space, which is not usually available at most dance halls back home. We did it several times on the spacious floating eucalyptus dance floor. It goes something like this: From a closed position, we open to a promenade, then do a feather (moving back with my left foot briefly touching the right), then into a syncopation (a bit of a smooth skipping step), and into a sway and an over-sway in the opposite direction. Then, we do another feather into an underarm turn for Barbara where she has an opportunity to extend her left hand and show off her rings. I, in turn, have my left hand holding her right, extended in the same direction towards her. She then reverses her turn towards me, and we go into a sweetheart position (her back to my chest with arms extended). We complete four turns in a circle, she does an underarm turn and extends her left hand to my right hand and does a developpe, (gracefully lifting her left leg). She then does a full turn towards me, and we close into a basic dancing position. This routine can be done in both the Foxtrot and Waltz, and is very gratifying when it can be done in its entirety on a spacious dance floor without interference from other dancers. It was amusing to observe one mishap on the floor between two couples; they briefly brushed into each other and immediately stopped and apologized, while bowing profusely. Considering that more than half the people in the hall were Japanese, it wasn't surprising to see bowing going on all over the place, while greeting people, apologizing, or just saying good night. I noticed that Steve and Donna were almost enjoying themselves dancing. Neither of them had much experience on the dance floor, but they were good sports about being with us, and didn't complain about hanging out with old timers.

The HBDA had a formation competition that evening. The clubs throughout the Hawaiian Islands came to perform their specialty dances. There were more than a dozen chapters present, each wearing their respective colors and parading their incredibly beautiful costumes. We were told that many of the outfits were hand-made and had significant traditions attached to them. Pom-poms were displayed on many of the outfits, as well as frills and sequences in every imaginable color and shape. The dancing began with the Maui Chapter performing their formation dance, which consisted of about a dozen dancers doing a Cha-Cha. It started very much like a line dance, with dancers in starting positions, and then proceeded into dance steps and routines with lots of partners changing. The dance was synchronized to perfection which, without a doubt, probably takes an inordinate amount of practice and patience to accomplish. We were pleasantly surprised at the different routines each team had for doing a Cha-Cha. Deciding the winning team was not an easy task for the judges, as they were all top-of-the-line dancers and incredibly proficient formation dancers. We ended the evening with refreshments, cake and cookies, and lots of bowing and handshakes from our new-found friends. We promised to return as often as we could and then bid our fellow dancers good night.

We woke up the next morning to the ever present sound of the waves dancing on the beach, but this morning I noticed another delicious delight. The smell of pineapples seem to fill the air. I asked Donna if she was preparing breakfast that included pineapples and she responded in the negative, saying that the aroma was coming from the Dole Plantation which was a few miles from their home. This was another pleasant surprise as I imagined smelling that delicious fragrance year round. Steve had the day planned for us; we were visiting the Polynesian Cultural Center (PCC), which is also located on the Northern part of Oahu and a short ride from their house.

The Church of Latter-day Saints (Mormons) own and operate the 42-acre Polynesian living museum. Each of the major Polynesian countries has its own area in the park centered on a replica of a traditional village. Hawaii, Samoa, Aotearoa (New Zealand), Fiji, Tahiti, Tonga, and Marquesas, all have models of living villages prior to the Western world's intrusion into their somewhat peaceful and uncomplicated existence. Each village is inhabited by native students who received scholarships and represent their respective island. They attend Hawaii's Brigham Young University, and work 20-hours a week during school days and full time between semesters. Working at the park allows the students to attend the university at no charge and to graduate debt free. Upon entering the PCC, there is an exhibit tracing the immigration of the natives to the islands and the history behind their migration. There were lots of zigzagging by the natives from island to island, and following some of the lineage of the tribes can get a little fuzzy. Just beyond the center is the Hawaii Temple of the Church, which was built from volcanic rock and concrete in the form of a Greek cross and is surrounded by beautiful reflecting pools, formal gardens, and royal palm trees. Both the Church and Brigham Young University were open to visitors, with guided tours available. The park also has an IMAX theatre and a lagoon where visitors can take rides from one end of the park to the other.

Okay, where do we start? We decided to purchase VIP passes, which included preferred seating at the evening luau. We were given Koki beads, which are black and are made from nuts, to identify us as VIP guests. Due to the size of the place and the limited amount of time we had, the best approach seemed to be a narrated canoe ride around the lagoon, visiting as many villages as possible. We also had to coordinate our visits to the scheduled show times of each village, which usually lasted from 30 minutes to one hour. In addition, we wanted to join the festivities of Hawaii's largest luau and the spectacular evening show, "Horizons: Where the Sea Meets the Sky." Samoa was our first stop. We were greeted by the beautiful natives with "talofa," which is their equivalent to the

Hawaiian's affectionate "aloha." The response to this warm greeting is "talofa lava." The Island of Samoa is located almost 2,500 miles to the southwest of Hawaii, and is in the middle of the Polynesian Triangle. It is sometimes called the "Heart of Polynesia." Their show consisted of demonstrations that take place on the "malae" (grassy area), surrounded by examples of Samoan "fale" (houses). A large, high roofed "Maota Tofa" (High chief's house), has distinctive carved beams and coconut-sennit lashings. All the other natives live in smaller houses called "Fale Nofo" surrounding a community kitchen (Tunoa). The natives invited us to learn how to make fire by rubbing two sticks together, how to crack open a coconut, and how to distinguish the difference between coconut juice and milk. In this society, the men do all the cooking and coconut picking, which was demonstrated by several men climbing 40-foot trees and retrieving as many coconuts as possible. Whoever got the most coconuts cracked and peeled won the competition. It was amazing to watch these men climb the trees and then strip the coconuts of their shells in a matter of minutes. They also performed a fire dance, where spinning a fire log up and around their bodies is done with amazing precession, highlighted by sucking the flames into their mouths. I actually had to close my eyes to avoid seeing any mishaps, fortunately there were none. Bravo to these brave lads!

The infamous Fiji Islands of days gone by were our next stop. The earliest European explorer to sight the island in 1643 was a Dutch sailor named Abel Tasman, after whom Tasmania would later be named. Due to the war-like greeting received from the locals, he quickly left the area. Captain Cook also reached the same conclusion when he visited the island in 1774. The greatly maligned Captain Bligh came closest to landing on the island, but left pell-mell when the natives' war canoes approached his vessel and chased him off. Although he never explored the island, the bay that he dropped anchor in is called Bligh's Water. They were all fortunate to have fled, as the natives were cannibals and notorious for dining on neighboring tribes or any ill-fated explorers who crossed their paths. The island is located about 2,500-miles to the west-southwest of Hawaii on the border of the Polynesian Triangle. About half of the population of modern Fiji is of East Indian descent, giving the island a unique cosmopolitan flavor. Our greeting, fortunately, was from friendly non-cannibalistic natives; "bula" is their greeting for good health, and "bula vinaka" is the appropriate response. The most dominant feature of the village is the "bure kalou" (spirit house). Its high-reaching roof is considered a landmark and one of the most unique structures at the PCC. The face painted Fijian warriors performed a war dance with spears, machetes, lots of leaps and noises, and the most unusual distorted facial expressions, which included extending their tongues out about 12 inches. All of this was intended to terrify their opponents in battle. While it may have worked in their war-like days, it was now very comical to the audience. The more intense their fearsome facial expressions, the louder the audience laughed. The warriors didn't seem to mind the opposite effect that their terrifying facial expressions had on the spectators; they seemed to rather enjoy our response.

The "Rainbows of Paradise" show is performed on the lagoon at two different locations, simultaneously. Just as we were leaving the Fiji Village, we decided to stay in the area, which is the wider section of the lagoon. The show started with a young Polynesian girl in an outrigger canoe throwing flowers on the water. It is said that each blossom becomes a memory of visits to Hawaii, and each blossom that returns to shore will insure that the visitor will also return. The sound of the conch shell signaled the arrival of the Hawaiian "alii nui" (High chief) and his followers. The chief proudly displayed a royal cape, helmet and sash, which were made from selected red and gold plumage of hundreds of birds, who are set free after a few feathers are taken. The chief's wife (Alii) wore a yellow dress, while her attendant's dress was red. The first dance aboard the double-hulled canoes was "Hula Kahiko," which is the ancient sounds of drums and chants. The music then shifted to the more modern island sound of the ukulele and guitar and the more familiar songs of Hawaii.

The Tongans appeared on their double-hulled canoe and greeted everyone with "malo e lelei" (good health) as they performed their traditional island dances; the audience's response was "malo aupito" (thank you). The dancers wore red, representing the beautiful red morning skies of their friendly island. The hip and hand motions of the natives were spellbinding and communicated their love and friendship to everyone watching. The natives are known for their aggressive drumming and rhythmic beats, which they performed with great energy and chanting, while the spectators followed the beats with clapping and feet stomping.

The call of "Tahiti e imua" was followed by the appearance of a large Tahitian canoe on the lagoon. The dancers were dressed in yellow and orange as a gift of honor to "Mahana," the Sun God. These beautiful women, whose ancestors were, without a doubt, partly responsible for the "Mutiny on the Bounty" saga, haven't lost their charming glow centuries after the event. It's no wonder that Mr. Christian and his mates chose to stay on the beautiful Island of Tahiti and comingle with its beautiful girls rather then spend additional years on the rat-infested Bounty. The magic of "Tahiti's Love Call" could be felt throughout the lagoon as the beautiful maidens danced and welcomed visitors with their hand motions to join in their festive mood.

The Maori warriors of Aotearoa (New Zealand) came out howling and chanting war cries, as their canoe zigzagged the lagoon. Twirling poi balls and spears, they shouted their "haka" challenges to any and all who would meet them in combat. They were dressed in green as a tribute to "Tane," the Maori god of the lush ferns and forests; precious "pounamu" (greenstone jade) decorated their necks and wrists. The soldiers were fearsome in appearance as they threatened the audience with their aggressive motions and chanting. I was glad when they left my sight of vision. The women on the other hand, sparkled in their colorful red skirts of reeds and beads and performed intricate maneuvers with balls attached to long strings, while

299

balancing their matching feathered head pieces. I was not happy to see them leave the stage.

The friendly Samoan's canoe was hard pressed to balance itself from the exuberance and energy of the hula dancers. The traditional "lavalava" of the men, and the "puletasi" of the women, were in shades of magenta and pink to honor the beautiful sunsets of their South Pacific island. The natives sang and danced to the rhythm of their drums and chants, and coaxed the audience to join in with the singing and hula dancing. The girls threw flower blossoms at the audience and into the lagoon, which had the affect of a blossom shower from the heavens.

"Tomai, tomai" is the call of the chief as he beckoned the Fiji warriors and their canoe. The fighters appeared, doing a dance ritual to the warrior deity "Dengei." The girls wore bark cloth bearing beautiful traditional patterns of natural tones. The men were fierce in their appearance and expressions. The soldiers' faces were painted with war paint and their spears and poi balls were displayed with aggressive motions. Many wore tattoos of threatening designs, and their war-like facial expressions, including extending and distorting their tongues, got the attention of everyone in the audience. I was glad when their noisy performance finally passed by, which was also the end of the Rainbows of Paradise Show.

We were greeted with "kia ora" (good health) at the Aotearoa (New Zealand) Village or "Land of the Long White Cloud" as the Maori call their homeland. This island forms the southwestern apex of the Polynesian Triangle and is the only one that experiences four seasons. This is immediately apparent by the different clothes that they wear and the type of buildings in their village, which are quite different from their tropical cousins. The appropriate response to the Maori's greeting is also "kia ora," which the spectators learned to respond each time the natives sent a greeting. The Maori put on a demonstration that explained the symbolic significance of their beautiful meeting house, unique carvings, facial tattoos, their ancient origins, and the meaning of sticking out their tongues and twirling poi balls. All revolved around their war-like society and their fierce warriors. We learned how to play "tititoea," a stick game designed to develop hand-eye coordination, and how to swing the poi balls. Many of the audience volunteered to receive temporary tattoos. Some tattoos were beautiful, such as those with flowers, but others not so artistic, such as those of dragons and demons. The village was a fortified compound that enclosed a "marae" (open area) that was surrounded by several key structures, including a carved entrance where fighting challenges are issued. The focal point was the "whare runanga" (meeting house), where most presentations and important events in Maori tribal life occur. The center attraction of the village was the Maori's 40-man war canoe which was humungous, but quite stable, as we witnessed during their war-like presentation in the Rainbows of Paradise Show.

We were greeted with "malo e lelei" (good health) by the natives when we visited their Tonga village. Our response was also "malo e lelei." The Kingdom of Tonga is an archipelago in the South Pacific Ocean comprising of 169 islands, 36 of them inhabited. They lie south of Samoa and are about one third of the way from New Zealand to Hawaii. It's the only surviving monarchy among the island nations of the Pacific, as well as the only island nation never to have been formally colonized. The Islands are known as the "Friendly Islands" due to their friendly reception of Captain Cook in 1773. They demonstrated their "ta nafa" (drumming presentation) and taught us the simple, yet graceful, motions of a "mauluulu" (sitting dance), which we practiced while strumming on their drums after the show. We were also invited to play "lafo" (type of shuffleboard game) and to try our accuracy at "tolo" (spear throwing). We tried both, and I must say we were better at shuffleboard then we were at throwing the long spears. The village consisted of a one-quarter scale model of the late Queen Salote's summer palace, of which she personally supervised the construction. A meeting house, a common family dwelling, a cook house, and a game house, which contained a version of the shuffleboard game, were included in the summer palace. The people of the village were so friendly and outstandingly beautiful that I felt like spending the rest of the day just hanging around and talking to them about their beautiful lifestyle.

We were greeted by our Tahitian hosts with their placing leis around our necks and saying in unison "laorana" (good health). We responded with "laorana" in return and felt immediately at home. I got lost in the dark brown, soft, eyes of the Tahitian girls, which was becoming a habit. The softness of their dark eyes and the inviting nature of Polynesian women gave me the feeling that I belonged among these beautiful people. Who could resist joining the mood of these happy, warm, and inviting natives? Tahiti represents 100-plus French Polynesian islands surrounding Tahiti. It is located about 2,400 miles southeast of Hawaii and is renowned for the infamous mutiny that took place on the much maligned Captain Bligh's ship, HMS Bounty, in the 18th century. The sailors chose to stay in paradise rather then return to the squalor of a sailor's life aboard a decaying wooden vessel. Since then, the island has represented the dream of escaping to a Polynesian paradise. Tahiti fits the description perfectly, with its beautiful mountains, balmy climate, emerald and blue lagoons, and warm, inviting people. The women demonstrated their quick hip movements in the hula dance while their hand motions invited us to join them in their sensual dancing. We joined them and learned some basic hula moves. It didn't take long to learn the hand movements, but it took me a while to get my hips moving in the right direction. They also demonstrated how they make flower and shell leis and invited us to try. So, we all joined in and made leis. Barbara made a beautiful fragrant flower lei and I made one from small irregular sea shells. Many of the guests stayed after the show to learn how to fish the Polynesian way, but we were hungry and decided to take part in an Alii (King's) Luau which was just beginning at the other end of the lagoon. We visited some of the Tahitian buildings on our way to the luau and were surprised at their similarity to some of the other Polynesian structures. The "fare" (chief's house), the large "heiva" (celebration house), and the "ututu" (kitchen), were surrounded by a plantation and gardens with a fishing hut at the edge of the lagoon. It certainly was a perfect and inviting setting for the undernourished and hard-working sailors of the Bounty to retreat to after many months at sea.

We followed the mixed scents coming from the Alii Luau and were right on the money by doing so. The sounds of drums and chanting, combined with the delicious fragrance and aroma of the food being prepared, led us right to the entrance. Our nut beads allowed us to bypass the lines and go directly to the beautiful, light-tanned hostess for our preferred seating as VIP guests. We were seated near the platform where the entertainment would be performed. Cousin Benny Kai, the PCC's "Ambassador of Aloha," invited everyone by saying, "Whenever you are at a Hawaiian luau, you are 'ohana' (family)." We accumulated other leis from the Hawaiians and couldn't be more receptive of receiving such fragrant flowers from the ever smiling and wriggling daughters of Hawaii. To make the event more memorable, we had a souvenir picture taken of me and Barbara with some of the natives. Thirst-quenching pineapple smoothies were available and were just the drinks to get us in the mood for the King's Luau. Live Hawaiian music filled the air as the sounds from steel guitars vibrated throughout the palace. Cousin Benny, who was also the master of ceremoney, explained the meaning of luau and its significance. The performers, wearing fascinating grass skirts, colorful beads and leis, began the program by singing a "pule" (The Queen's Pray), which was written by Hawaii's prolific song writer and last reigning monarch, Queen Liliuokalani, while she was imprisoned by the United States Government in her own palace. The song written by this very religious monarch is as follows:

"Your loving mercy is as high as Heaven and your truth so perfect. I live in sorrow, imprisoned. You are my light, your glory my support. Behold not with malevolence the sins of man, but forgive and cleanse. And so, O Lord, protect us beneath your wings and let peace be our portion now and forever more."

The perpetual motion of their hips and the flowing movements of their arms, combined with the inviting smiles on their faces, in harmony with the beat of drums and chants, made their entrance dreamlike. This was how they conducted themselves on a daily basis, before the uninvited Europeans entered their world and altered the way they lived. We were getting great pleasure in watching them perform their most stunning routines as exhibitions to please tourists; unfortunately, the spiritual meaning of the rituals are no longer a realistic part of their lives, but the pleasure of watching such splendor in motion still lives on.

Cousin Benny announced the procession of the Royal Court into the luau, consisting of a ruling Alii (Chief) and his entourage. He explained their ranks and the significance of their traditional colorful costumes, which included many feathered headbands and long, rainbow-colored robes. The Alii invited everyone to partake in the evening's feast and to watch the uncovering of the imu (underground oven) which contained a very large pig that was cooking throughout the afternoon and was ready for consumption. The imu is a steam oven made up of river rocks heated over firewood at 350-degrees for several hours. When the rocks are sufficiently hot, any remaining firewood is removed, and crushed banana stumps containing lots of water are placed on top of the hot rocks, creating aromatic steam. Then the food is added and covered until cooked to perfection. Multilingual hosts and hostesses directed guests at each table to the all-you-can-eat buffet stations. Cousin Benny announced, "You shouldn't eat till you're full; you should eat till you're dizzy." The music and hula dancing continued throughout dinner and special tropical drinks made our experience all the more enjoyable. I was starting to get a little silly and actually got up and danced what I thought was a hula with a charming, pretty Hawaiian dancer. We were told, "Every hula tells a story. Graceful hands depict birds, waves, flowers blossoming, rainbows and mountains; while the feet move around the island and hips sway in tempo. Whether the words are in English or Hawaiian, you will understand the meaning of the song as long as you keep your eyes on the dancer's hands."

Beginning to explain what was served on the luau buffet is best accomplished by listing the information from the Alii Luau Menu, and here it is:

"Poi is a traditional Hawaiian staple. It's a starch dish made by pounding boiled taro roots and mixing them with water until the mixture reaches a smooth consistency. Taro is one of the most nutritious starches on the planet; some eat their poi with salt, some with sugar and some even like it with soy sauce.

Poke is a raw fish marinated in soy sauce with a dash of seaweed, onions, and other condiments.

Lomilomi salmon: In Hawaiian, lomilomi means to massage, or, in this case, to break the salmon into small pieces, which are then mixed with tomatoes, onions and other small condiments, giving it a tangy taste that goes great with poi.

Pipi kaula is seasoned beef jerky which was first introduced to the islands by European sailors.

Kalua puaa is roasted pork, which is steamed to perfection in an imu and is usually seasoned with sea salt and green onions.

Moa is chicken, boiled in the old Polynesian way with Asian teriyaki sauce served over Asian bean noodles.

Deep-fried filets of flakey, white island fish with Hawaiian sweet potatoes are mixed for a nice cold salad. Taro rolls are baked daily and have a distinctive purple color, derived from the taro flour used in the recipe.

A variety of salads: tossed greens with carrots and cherry tomatoes, spinach salad, sweet potato salad, fruit ambrosia, and cucumber carrot salad.

Cold fruits: Ripe pineapple spears, watermelon, papaya, and other fruits in season.

Beverages (all decaffeinated): Passion-Orange-Guava, Coca Cola, Diet Pepsi, Root Beer, Sprite, Fruit Punch, and herbal teas. (As Mormons do not drink any caffeinated beverages, they are only served if requested by guests.)

Desserts include Haupia, which are sweet custard cubes made with rich coconut cream, guava cake, coconut cake, and chocolate macadamia nut cake."

I guess their menu says it all; a feast of feasts, Hawaiian music, tropical drinks, and beautiful Hawaiians dancers performing and mingling amongst the guests. I was tempted to get a nose rub from one of the Polynesian princesses, but Barbara's ever watchful eyes seemed to always be at my side. With full hearts and bellies we proceeded to the 2,800-seat Pacific Theater to see the evening show, "Horizons: Where the Sea Meets the Sky."

Our VIP tickets again came in handy as we were escorted in the amphitheater to up front, center aisle seats by a pretty Polynesian hostess, and again given soft, colorful, fragrant leis. The beautiful necklaces were starting to weigh me down, but it was worth every extra ounce around my neck to see the smiles on their stunning faces and the glimmer in their eyes as they placed the flowers over my head and around my neck. Distinguishing between the aromatic fragrances of the flowers making up the leis from the natural fragrance and the native girls was becoming difficult. The storyteller announced in a powerful god-like voice: "Komo Mai (come in) and set your course to Makalii (Southern Star) and sail through the horizon to the islands of paradise." As he was speaking, the lights in the huge amphitheater dimmed and a magnificent rainbow waterfall curtain, which I thought was a fixed part of the background, rose to the sound of aggressive drums pounding Polynesian music. All that remained when the water disappeared was the fury of a volcano, making thunderous and threatening sounds.

The Hawaiians were the first to greet us with "Ke Alaula," which is a contemporary hula by young girls that expresses the dawning of light and peace that accompanies the break of day. The storyteller announced: "Here is the procession of the Royal Court. The sounds of the distinctive moan of the conch shells announces the arrival of the King and Queen, accompanied by their entourage of attendants and bearers of the feathered royal standards called 'kahilis.' Notice how the members of the court are richly arrayed in brilliant capes, leis and feathered helmets, according to their rank. 'Aia La o Pele' (There is Pele), fire goddess of ancient Hawaii. We recall a time when man walked and talked with the ancestral gods in the 'kahiko,' which is an ancient style of hula and is done to haunting sounds of drums and chants. With 'kalaau' (dancing sticks), the men remember the love found by 'Kamohai at Mamala,' the shoreline between Honolulu Harbor and Pearl Harbor. 'Pihanakalani,' the sound of the nose flute beckons Halialaulani, the maiden, to the top of Pihanakalani, a mountain on the Island of Kauai. 'I Alii no Oe' (dancing with split bamboo rattles), men and women tell of how men enjoy being treated like kings. 'E Kuu Sweetie' and 'Pili Mau Me Oe,' start the men dancing, remembering their sweethearts and hoping they will be together forever. 'Ka Anoi,' dancing with the 'uliuli' (feathered gourds) and 'ipu' (hollowed gourds), men and women dance honoring beautiful maidens of Kauai. 'Ke Alaula' (Reprise), the strength of our cultural and spiritual past leads us to the dawning of a bright new day." As the god-like voice faded into the background, the Hawaiian portion of the entertainment ended. The dancing and chanting, harmonized with the music and the words of the storyteller, became less audible as the dream-like view evaporated.

The storyteller continued with: "My heart dances with the joy to the rhythm of the pounding 'nafa' (drums), as the dancers from the Island of Tonga perform their sensuous and energetic 'maulu ulu' and 'lakalaka' movements. They listen for shouts of Malie (well done) and Lue (move it), which increases their motion and jubilation. 'Ngaahi Ongo o e Nafa' calls the community together as the drummers reveal their unity and skill. 'Malui a e Atakai' calls the young men to form two opposing groups to demonstrate their skill with the 'kailao' (jabbing spear), in preparation to defend their people. 'Tavake Taumafua' calls the young women to honor and give tribute to the royalty with their graceful movements and beautiful costumes. 'Taumua Kuo Siumafua' beckons the community to sing and dance the 'lakalaka' in celebration of their unified culture and customs and their future destiny which lies just over the horizon." The music, dancers, scenery and the storyteller's voice fades, as the lights dim and the Tonga part of the show ends. The young girls' costumes remained in my mind, as they were not the usual hula skirts and leis, but colorful red and white knee high sun dresses with complementary accessories of dark beads around their necks. White vertical feather head pieces and wrist flowers completed their perfect appearance as children of their Sun God.

Our storyteller continued with: "Welcome to the land of the long white cloud, where mountains touch the sky each and every day in the island known as New Zealand (Aotearoa). Maori flutes accompany the 'karanga' as the women dancers welcomed everyone to their magical island of the long white cloud, as the island magically appears. 'Taiaha' is the challenging movements of the 'taiaha' (fighting lance), which welcomed visitors to enter the 'marae,' the ceremonial gathering place. 'Karanga' is the greeting voice of women calling 'haere mai' (welcome), to this enchanted place. 'Whaka Eke,' the performers seek permission to enter the dancing platform on the 'marae.' 'Haka ko te Puru,' is when the men and women transform from the ancient to modern styles of dance and music. 'Ko Tereo,' through their actions and songs, the men and women combine to invite us to enjoy the traditions of their unique world. 'E Tui,' young women are likened to the grace and the voice of 'tui' (beautiful indigenous bird), in the poi ball dance. 'Terina,' is the colorful rhythmic motions of the illuminated poi balls that form Maori patterns with a likeness of the famous glow worms of their islands. 'Titi Torea,' is the stick dance that teaches flexibility, rapid reflexes and quick coordination to prepare everyone for life's constant surprises." The performance was fast, aggressive, and somewhat scary when you consider the Maori warriors threatening facial tattoos, fierce swinging poi balls, their extended distorted tongues and grimacing facial expressions, while yelling and howling their traditional invitations to fight or flee. Fortunately, they were the first to fade into the night leaving an image of the beautiful Aotearoa women in my mind as their performance ended.

Intermission time introduced us to "Pineapple Deelites," which consists of half a pineapple with ice cream and island fruits with a colorful umbrella on top. Just what the doctor ordered to refresh us after a long day, enjoying the Hawaiian sun and activities.

The storyteller continued: "I hear my ancestors call me, they speak through the voice of the 'Lali' (log drum). Come back to my beautiful Fiji. 'Vakamalolo,' the chief and his young men welcome you with tokens of acceptance and respect. 'Vakarorogo Noda Tuaga,' is an aggressive chant and dance telling of warriors who have encountered and fought the enemy and fiercely and courageously defended their people. 'Raude,' through the fan dance, expresses gratitude for the land and its beauty, as ancestors who have departed to the land of the spirits are remembered and revered. 'O i Au Na Gone ni Wasa Liwa,' is a traditional war club dance and tells of the days of the earliest Fijian ancestors and their migrations across vast oceans seeking a new homeland. 'Bula Laie,' is when the Fijian men use colored war fans and the women their bamboo 'derua' to bid farewell with this vibrant and energetic number written for the Polynesian Cultural Center. When Elvis Presley filmed Paradise Hawaiian Style at the center in 1965, he had the song arranged in English as 'Drums of the Islands.' Come and sing along with us:

"Drums of the islands you're beating in my heart. You're with me no matter where I roam.

If ever I wander, if ever we're apart, I know that you will lead me home.

If I should journey across the deep blue sea, I'll never forget these coral shores.

Drums of the islands, I hear you calling me and I'll return forever yours.

I love each valley, each grain of sand, each hill, the flowers and the music of the isles.

These are the things I love and always will, though I may roam ten thousand miles."

The scene slowly faded as the performers and the musical number dimmed out of sight after performing their native dances.

The storyteller continued: "The exotic fragrance of the tiare flower on the night air, the soft glow of the black pearl, the pulsating drums to the rhythm of the tamure, and the magic of a Polynesian moon all whisper: Tahiti. Out of the mist, the sun breaks through and now we are on the mystical Island of Tahiti. 'Haere Mai na Tau Here' - villagers are led by torch bearers and join in a wedding ceremony as Hinakura and her mate, Tane Nui, are united by the chief in marriage. 'Otea Amui' - the marriage celebration begins; villagers rejoice in expressing their hopes of youth and love through a traditional dance, the 'otea.' 'Hinakura Vahine' - young maidens join Hinakura, dancing the 'aparima' with poise and elegance , followed by the young men and Tane Nui dancing with lively exuberance. 'Hinakura,' through the 'otui' (solo dance), shares her radiant beauty, while Tane Nui shows his strength and agility. 'Otea' - the final demonstration of energy, color and excitement of traditional Tahitian dances at times of celebration." The handsome, muscular Tahitian men serenading the gorgeous women of their romantic island are idyllic in every sense. The island, which is associated with "Escaping to Paradise" reflects that mysterious image, as these harmonious people end their affair with the audience by throwing flower petals and kisses, which I actually felt, across the theater.

The storyteller continued with his final narration: "When the Polynesian demigod Maui, who is known in all the islands, captured the sun, he discovered the power of fire and shared it with the people of Samoa. 'Lumanai' - the women are dancing a standing 'mauluulu,' which encourages the youth of Samoa to look toward the future by working hard for a better life. 'Sauniunia o le Aso' shows in the motions of the Salsa dance, which demonstrates the many activities that must be completed in preparation of an important celebration. 'Faataupati' - with rhythmic energy the young men burst into a traditional slap dance, which dazzles the eye and delights the ear. 'Nuu Laiti e' - these three men accept the challenge to conquer fear by playfully extinguishing fire. 'Taupou o Samoa' - the Princess does a solo dance, she is the daughter of the high chief and invites villagers to sing, clap and dance around her to show their happiness and love. 'Le Afi Lae Ua Mu' - a chant and dance inspired by a volcanic eruption and reminds us that adversity is part of life and that strength comes from unity in the face of danger. 'Siva Naifi Afi' - our warriors are showing courage, strength, and bravery as they perform the traditional Samoan fire knife dance." The fires from their sticks, swords, and knives diminish with the quick movement of their performances and, as they extinguish the flames, the show came to an end.

The extravaganza ended with the entire cast of over 100 performers entering the stage, fully costumed in their various native costumes. The god-like voice reminded us that: "Happiness is here in paradise and beyond the horizon . . . " What an end to a glorious day!!

I convinced Barbara to join me in what was becoming my morning ritual of running full speed ahead into the ever-so-sweet turquoise/blue saltwater. What a delightful way to start our day. We decided to spend the day just relaxing and maybe going for a ride to see some of the local sights, but nothing too strenuous, as we planned on returning to the Palladium

Dance Hall in the evening for more ballroom dancing. Steve suggested that we visit some of the North Shore's beaches and, hopefully, see some world-class surfing. We agreed, and after breakfast Steve, who is a bit of a historian, gave us some history about the beaches in the area. "The North Shore of Oahu is world renowned as the surfing capital of the world. During the winter months, gigantic swells generate in the North Pacific to produce the most reliable surfing waves on the planet. The two most popular surfing spots are Banzai Pipeline and Waimea Bay, where the Hawaiian Triple Crown is held during December, and transforms the peaceful and quiet area into a world-class championship location, with people from around the world flocking in to witness or participate in the daring sport and unique Hawaiian spectacle. During the summer months, the ocean is placid and safe for swimming, snorkeling, boogie-boarding, diving, and rather safe surfing." Our first stop was the Banzai Pipeline/Ehukai Beach Park, which probably has the most treacherous waves on earth that form a giant tube when they move from deep water on to shallow coral reefs. On days where the waves are 10-feet or more, they break in 6-feet of water, which is challenging and dangerous to the world's most experienced surfers. The pipeline is "an expert"only area in the winter, but is peaceful and safe in the summer months. Our visit was in the summer and I was very pleased to see that many surfers were enjoying themselves riding high, sideways, and then forward on their small tubes. It seemed like many of them were practicing under safe conditions, preparing for the more grueling challenges during the winter season when they search for the "perfect wave." I was surprised that the only hotel nearby was the Turtle Bay Resort, which has a renowned Sunday brunch with panoramic ocean views. We were planning on spending our next trip at a hotel, and although it's an incredible resort and near the kids, with many amenities, including a world class golf course, it's too far from Waikiki and the Palladium Dance Hall at the Ali Wai Country Club for us to consider. I did, however, make a mental note about the Sunday brunch and the golf course for our next visit. Steve's next stop was Waimea Beach Park, another legendary surf spot, where waves reach 30-feet in the winter and is also an expert-only surfing area in season. We spread our blankets on the beach, as we couldn't resist the temptation to stretch out and relax, and then try the inviting soft waves that beckoned us to come and play. And play we did, the water was so soft and cool that spending the day in it was tempting and not out of the question. I was beginning to get a clear picture of what Paradise is like: soft white sand, soft turquoise/blue water, soft white clouds pasted onto a soft blue sky, a soft tropical drink and a soft beach towel. Add them together and we had the closest thing to Paradise that I could imagine. The picturesque scene of people parasailing, surfing, paddle rowing, and just horsing around, was part of what makes this site a candidate as a contender for Paradise.

We arrived at the Palladium Dance Hall a little late, and found that the hall was divided in half by a portable partition hosting two different dances. I was surprised to see the "Hawaii Federation of Square Dance Clubs" occupying one of the halls to full capacity. We were coaxed to join them and sign up for their "Annual Aloha State Square and Round Dance Festival," which takes place in January. It is attended by square dance aficionados from around the world who compete for the many championship levels, which are very similar to ballroom dance championships. We were tempted to join the "squares" (as they are called), for a dance lesson, but decided instead to enter the other half of the hall to join the "Hawaiian Ballroom Dance Association" (HBDA) for some good ballroom dancing. I took some of their brochures for future reference, and to remind me to look into the square dancing activities when we returned in the winter, time permitting.

We were greeted by some of the same people we met on our last visit to the dance hall and were made to feel right at home. We sat next to an American, Jack, and his Japanese wife, Meiko, from Ohio, who were just married and on their honeymoon. She told us that it was her life-long dream to honeymoon in

Hawaii and that she was waiting to wake up from her dream, as she couldn't believe she was at the dance with her handsome American husband. It seems that many Japanese women have this dream, due to the good weather and beaches. But I think an underlying reason was the buying power of the Japanese yen, which makes Hawaii a buyer's paradise. In addition to her luggage containing her personal items, she came to the island with two empty suitcases, and had already started filling the second with goodies. If need be she said, "I could always buy more suitcases, they are so cheap." The Bolero music beckoned us to the dance floor. We began about 10 feet apart and approached each other at a slow and rhythmic pace, while staring deeply into each others' eyes. The Bolero is unique in that, although it's a Latin dance, the dance position is that of ballroom dancing: shoulders back, my head to the left, while Barbara, head back, looks past my right ear when we make body contact at our midsections. This position is maintained throughout the dance. Unlike many ballroom dances, this dance usually begins by our taking our first steps to the side, left for me and right for Barbara. I then go back, taking her with me, and then to my right. That is my part, and now I move my left foot forward and then Barbara aggressively moves me back. Many of the open breaks require sensual arm movements which end up being extended to our sides in the same direction. The embraces are soft but exact and the coordination between couples, if done properly, results in the culmination of one of the most satisfying and beautiful of the Latin dances. We danced the night away, enjoying the spaciousness of the dance floor, the incredibly good music, and the companionship of our new-found friends. We asked one of the locals if there were any other places to dance in the immediate area and were surprised to find several nearby. There was Salsa Hawaii at the Acqua Club in the Hawaiian Regent Hotel and the Rumours nightclub at the Ala Moana Hotel, just to name a couple. We couldn't wait to return in the winter and visit these "Hot Spots," as the locals referred to them. On the way out, we peeked in on the "squares." The energy from their dancing and the colorful western outfits were magnetizing; it drew us in and we found ourselves dancing along. Even though we didn't have much experience in square or western dancing, we were able to do a West Coast Swing and one Country Western Two Step.

Finally, our last day was upon us. After a morning dip in the ocean, the consensus was to just hang around and spend time on the beach and do a little barbequing. Steve said he needed to do some shopping at the PX (Post Exchange) and asked if we would like to come along, we immediately said yes. I always get a special feeling of pride when entering a military post. In my four years in the U.S. Air Force, the only more pleasant feeling that I can remember was upon leaving, especially if on furlough. The feeling was still the same as we entered the Schofield Barracks entrance gate. The facility is enormous, some 18,000-acres in Central Oahu. It was established in 1908 to provide mobile defense for Pearl Harbor and the entire island by the Army's 25th Infantry Division (Tropic Lightning Division). It houses almost 15,000 people in approximately 3,000 households. It lies adjacent to Wheeler Field, which put it in the path of the Japanese warplanes who were headed for that airfield to destroy the two pursuit fighter groups of P-36s and P-40s. Although the attacking planes passed through the mountains that run along KoleKole Path, which runs through Schofield Barracks, they only strafed Schofield Barracks and the installation sustained minor damage. Their main objectives on that infamous day were to destroy as many planes and ships as possible. Steve took us to an observation area that had a monument and information of the attack that took place over the Barracks, while the Japanese warplanes passed over on the way to their kill. In the darkness of that day, when Pearl Harbor, Wheeler Field, Hickam Field, Bellows Field, and many other military and civilian facilities were demolished, there is a story that brings some light into that most horrific day in American history. The day after the attack of December 7, 1941, the Japanese launched five, two-man mini-submarines against Pearl Harbor to complete the destruction of the American Naval Fleet in the harbor; all were sunk except one, which drifted out to

Bellows Field and grounded on a reef. The Air Force personnel captured the surviving seaman, Ensign Kazuo Sakamaki, and then dragged the mini-submarine onto the beach, recording the first prisoner of war and the first war prize.

Steve filled his car up with gas, at a very reasonable price, and then took us to the PX. I always enjoyed shopping at the military stores when I was in the service. The variety of items for sale exceeds anything found in our major department stores and at more reasonable prices. Steve bought some steaks, spareribs, and all the goodies that go along with a delicious BBQ. Steve and Donna invited some of their friends over for a farewell outing and we again enjoyed the beach, swimming, great food, wonderful singing and the camaraderie of our children and their friends. What a wonderful way to end an evening and a splendid way to end our vacation. Our last thoughts were of returning in the winter and meeting our first grandchild.

* *

We began planning our trip back to Hawaii as soon as we returned to New York. We had seven months before returning, and Barbara figured if we used only our American Express card for purchases, we would have enough frequent flyer miles to pay for two coach tickets. She was right, and in a few months we had enough frequent flyer miles to buy two tickets, which I immediately upgraded to first class by paying an additional fee, which would make the long flight a lot more comfortable. Our next challenge was choosing a hotel in Waikiki Beach that was centrally located and as close as possible to the Palladium Dance Hall at the Ali Wai Country Club. There seemed to be literally hundreds of hotels that would serve our purpose, but we chose the Hyatt Regency on Kalakaua Avenue, which is across the street from the breakwater at Waikiki Beach. It's also a short distance from the International Marketplace, Waikiki Aquarium, Honolulu Zoo, Kapiolani Park and, most importantly, the Palladium Dance Hall. With the "blink of an eye" it was January, 1999, and we were on our nonstop flight, from JFK to Hawaii.

Or so we thought. We boarded our American Airlines' plane and settled in for the take off, but there was a mechanical problem and we had to exit the plane and wait for another. Fortunately, as first-class passengers, we had the use of their Admiral's Club Lounge, which made things a little more tolerable. We boarded the next plane and were informed that it didn't have the fuel capacity to take us nonstop to Hawaii, we would have to land in Los Angeles to refuel. To make a very long story short, our 12-hour flight took 16-uncomfortable-hours. When we landed in Hawaii, we were exhausted and totally annoyed at the whole experience; what else could go wrong? We soon found out. I can't explain the gruesome feeling I had while waiting for our luggage at the carousel. There was no baggage left on the arrival conveyor. There we were, standing by the carousel, flat footed, totally exhausted from the long flight, and not knowing what to do next. We went to the American Airlines' office and waited in line with about twenty other people. Some of the people in line were frantic, as they had to catch other flights out of Honolulu and were totally stifled as to what to do. We finally filled out the appropriate forms and explained our dilemma to a very sympathetic young lady, who assured us that the luggage would be found within a few days. Ugh! I couldn't imagine being without our personal belongings for that period of time. What was most upsetting, however, was that we had lots of presents for our new grandson in our baggage.

Seeing beautiful Waikiki Beach again had a calming affect on me and eased my frustration, somewhat. Seeing the Hyatt Regency's two 40-story towers also recycled my anger and made me a little more comfortable. The final comforting scene was the three-story, open-air atrium with orchids, palm trees and cascading waterfalls plus to Barbara's delight, more than 60 oceanfront shops surrounding the atrium. We had been using the Hyatt Regency in Washington D.C. on our car trips to Florida and were card-holding members of the chain, which gave us another welcomed surprise, a free room upgrade, including breakfast. We got a room on the 38th floor which was very spacious and had a furnished balcony facing the ocean, a view to die for! A nice feature was a pillow-top mattress draped beneath earth-toned duvets and fine linens. The oversized bathroom featured granite countertops and was stocked with Portico toiletries, which Barbara wasted no time in adding to her international collection. There was also a laptop-sized safe, which accommodated my computer easily, with room to spare. We were exhausted from the day's mishaps and jet lag, so we immediately jumped into bed to get some much needed sleep and to get rid of some of the stress that we were carrying around.

Thank God we woke up to a whole new sunny day, a much relieved attitude, and famished. The breakfast buffet was still open, so we showered and made a beeline straight to the dining hall. What a pleasant surprise! The buffet was endless, with an overwhelming smell of pineapple and bacon filling the room. I didn't waste any time getting an omelet with mushrooms and ham and a large glass of pineapple juice. Barbara went to the Japanese food section and came back with an assortment of sushi and a large glass of pineapple juice. The Hawaiian Kona coffee was delicious beyond words and, after drinking a pot, the day began to get brighter. If we were lucky, our luggage would be waiting for us in our room. Another pleasant experience was our waitress; a beautiful tan-skinned, bright smiling wahine (girl) named Lois. She brought sunshine into the room and lightened our table when her colorful, flowered red and white dress appeared before us. She asked, in a soft, bubbly voice, if there was anything she could get us? I couldn't take my eyes off the Plumeria flower inserted on top of her ear. Barbara couldn't stop admiring it and we told her so several times. Our day started to perk up a bit after a wholesome breakfast and meeting Lois. We had no luck with our baggage arriving, so we prepared for the 45-minute drive in our rented Buick Regal to see our new grandson with only a couple of presents that we had packed in our carry-on luggage.

There he was; our seven-pound, nine-day old, bundle of chubby joy. We couldn't stop kissing Donna and Ian Charles

Bivona while telling them how happy we were with the new addition to our family. Steve, our little baby, all six-foot-two of him, was smiling so hard I thought that his smile was going to continue around to the back of his head. We spent the day holding, cuddling, and kissing Ian Charles' small body until it was time to change his diaper. At that point, I turned him over to the girls, who seemed to get a special delight from changing diapers "the right way," whatever that means. Steve prepared another of his wonderful BBQs that we so enjoyed eating on the expansive lawn, while watching the surf capturing the sand and replacing it in different locations along the beach. We were anxious to return to our hotel to see if any of our baggage had been discovered, which made the return drive seem a lot longer then the morning trip. No luck, no luggage. We asked the kids to join us for breakfast at the hotel and to spend the day with us and enjoy the amenities of the pool and spa. We decided to buy some swimsuits so we could at least enjoy the pool when the children arrived. The hotel had a nice beach clothing store, so we didn't have any difficulty finding suits that were very tropical looking; with lots of flowers and colorful designs.

The kids arrived for a late breakfast buffet at the outdoor Terrace Grill which overlooked the ocean. They were thrilled to be out of their house and at a place that felt like vacationland. It was just what the doctor ordered after spending several weeks isolated while preparing for and giving birth to our little Ian Charles. Barbara and I couldn't get over how delicious the Hawaiian Kona coffee tasted. The kids were already Kona fans, but said that they thought that the brew at breakfast was exceptionally good. We spent the day hanging around the rooftop pool, which is bordered by two spa tubs and overlooks Waikiki Beach. I took advantage of the hotel's diversified cardiovascular exercise equipment, in their state-of-the-art gym. Exercising has become part of my new life style since my heart bypass surgery in 1993, and I was looking forward to using their sophisticated equipment. We told the kids that we would watch the new package (Ian Charles), if they got the urge to wander around on their own. Before I could get the last word out of my mouth, they were gone. What a pleasure to be babysitting again; we haven't had that pleasure for over twenty years and enjoyed every moment of it. We told the kids to take their time and to enjoy themselves; they returned in the late afternoon, which was perfect, as it gave us a good part of the day to play and show off Ian Charles to the other hotel guests. We decided to have dinner at one of the local Japanese restaurants and had a choice of several along the main strip. It was a new experience for us to be spending time not only with our children but with Ian Charles, who required lots of attention and soft soothing sways to keep him happy. After dinner the kids left and we returned to our room anticipating finding our baggage, but no such luck. Numerous telephone calls to the airline were to no avail. They reassured us that, in time, they would locate and forward our luggage to us, but we just didn't believe them. We knew our baggage was somewhere in Davey Jones' Locker, and that our personal belongings were being sold somewhere on the black market.

Our telephone rang early the next morning and, lo and behold, our luggage had arrived. They were brought up to our room, I had had an overwhelming urge to hug and kiss the suitcases on sight. We examined all the bags and found that everything was intact, just slightly jostled around due to their long journey to God knows where and back. I wondered, where does lost luggage go? Is it left at the airport? Is it left on the airplane in some dark corner? Is it put on the wrong airplane? Is it put on the wrong conveyor carousel? Is it put aside and looked into for possible theft? There are so many possibilities; I decided to just be content with the fact that they were returned intact. We headed for our children's home with lots of presents for Ian Charles and a couple of niceties for our kids. We enjoyed lunch, and Donna suggested that, being that I was enjoying the aroma of pineapples in the air, we should go to the source and pay a visit to the Dole Plantation Pineapple Museum, which was just a few miles away in the town of Wahiawa.

Upon entering the plantation, we were immediately drawn to the world's largest maze that has eight rest stations in an area occupying more than two acres with a path in excess of three miles. It consists of over 11,000 colorful Hawaiian plants, including hibiscus, heliconia, croton, panax, and pineapple. The center of the maze is in the shape of a huge pineapple, which is made up of croton and has a crown of agapanthus (blue lilies). There is an ongoing contest for adventurers to search for the eight secret stations on their way to solving the mystery of the labyrinth. In each station there are maze cards directing the participants to possible paths to the next station; eventually, the cards and the adventurer's ability will lead them to the exit. The winner of the day has their name placed on the entrance and receives a special prize, usually pineapple related. The best time has been recorded at about seven minutes, while the average is between 45-minutes to one hour. Well, we all entered at the same time and eventually took our own paths through the network; Steve exited in about 15-minutes, with Donna right behind him. Barbara exited in about 25-minutes and I was dead last at 45-minutes. I got so lost I couldn't believe it. How can an accountant get lost in a maze when it's such an integral part of his life? Oh well, it was lots of fun, although slightly embarrassing for me , especially the ribbing I took when I exited and found everyone pretending to be asleep. We then took a two-mile tour around the plantation that showcased the legacy of the pineapple and its impact on Hawaiian agriculture. There were several acres of diversified farming, including specimens of lychee, banana, mango, papaya, cacao, and coffee. Along the route, we were treated to views of the Koolau and Waianae mountain ranges that monopolize the background and add to the overall splendor of the plantation.

A brochure at the center explained the purpose of this one-of-a-kind museum: "The plantation blends the traditional elements of Hawaii's plantation life and the early pineapple industry with the new breed of diversified agriculture currently being grown on the North Shore of Oahu. It's dedicated to perpetuating the agricultural heritage of Hawaii and its place in history and the progress of the islands and its people. The founder, James D. Dole of the Dole Food Company, came to Hawaii in 1899, after graduating from Harvard University with $1,200.00. He single-handedly began the pineapple industry in Hawaii with 60-acres of rich red dirt on the site of today's Dole Plantation." In addition to learning about the wide variety of fruits, vegetables, Hawaiian plants, and tropical flora, we participated in pineapple planting and picking. We learned how to pick the fruit, as well as how to safely and properly slice it for consumption. The museum center began as a fruit stand on the 60-acre Dole Plantation in 1950, and now has become a first-class museum telling a story of how the pineapple impacted Hawaii and its people. The plantation center features "Made in Hawaii" items, including a variety of goods and handicrafts from local merchants, to Dole logo items and pineapple-themed baked goods, snacks, Waialua chocolates, and delicious Waialua coffee. Antique tables, baskets, and traditional wooden bins displayed items reflecting Hawaii's plantation stores of days gone by. The objective is to present a traditional marketplace, a country store, and a series of building facades reminiscent of the Town of Haleiwa on Oahu's North Shore. We had a late lunch in their restaurant that featured a "Crown of Hawaii" menu and enjoyed their Teri Chicken, Kalua Pig, Mahi sandwiches, salads featuring ingredients from the islands and, of course, our drink of choice, freshly made pineapple juice.

We invited the kids over the next day to enjoy the hotel's facilities and just hang around at the pool or the calm section of Waikiki beach, which is just across the road from our hotel. We dropped them off at their home and gave our new bundle of joy kisses and squeezes; then returned to our hotel anxious to revisit the Palladium Dance Hall for some ballroom dancing.

We were pleasantly surprised to find that the Hawaii U.S. Amateur Ballroom Dancers Association (HUSABDA) was holding their weekly dance.. We showed our Florida USABDA cards and were given a hero's welcome. We were invited in at no charge and were shocked that an announcement was made over the public address system stating that: "Our friends and members of USABDA from Florida and New York are joining us tonight, please welcome Mike and Barbara Bivona." We received applause and cheers. All night long people came over to greet us with the famous Hawaiian "Aloha." Of course, for the entire evening people were watching us dance. At first this made us very uncomfortable, but as all ballroom dancers like to show off a little, we ended up totally enjoying the experience while doing our special and well-learned routines. We were surprised that a small crowd gathered around us when we did a Cha-Cha and praised our performance when we finished. I never considered it one of our better dances, but accepted the accolades with a great smile and receptive heart. The evening ended with our saying goodbye to many of our comrades and, to my delight, a very young, pretty, flower-smelling wahine, named Joanna, actually gave me a sweet nose rub.

The kids joined us for a Sunday brunch at the Terrace Grill. The overwhelming aroma from pineapples and the view of the ocean from the outdoor restaurant were a perfect setting for what was becoming for me, a realization of a fantasy vacation come true. It was wonderful to have a choice of whatever food my palate desired; a view of Waikiki Beach's surf; my beautiful and pleasant wife Barbara at my side; my good natured and excellent chef-son-Steve, smiling at his wonderful masterpiece, Ian Charles; and my beautiful daughter-in-law and mother of our new bundle of joy, all together in one place.. It was, without a shadow of a doubt, the realization of my perfect fantasy come true. We split the day between the pool and beach. It was winter, which is the time of year that the surf gets pretty rough and the waves high. Steve and Donna took advantage of some high waves and did some neat surf boarding, while Barbara, who is a very strong swimmer, swam out to meet some of the smaller waves and came back arms extended while riding the crests towards the beach. In the meantime, I got myself a Mai Tai and just lounged around on my beach blanket, enjoying the view of all the athletic souls challenging the elements. The kids left after an early dinner. I couldn't get over how quiet Ian

Charles had been all day, not at all like his father who, at that age, was quite a handful and required a lot of attention. I guess Steve is lucky. I always told him that he would have a son that would give him as much stress as he gave us growing up, but so far it was not to be.

We had the next day to ourselves, as Donna and Steve had to go to Schofield Barracks. Donna had a doctor's appointment for a checkup and Steve had some meetings to attend. So we decided to finally pay a visit to Pearl Harbor, which I was avoiding as I do not handle seeing the results of destruction and its resultant gravestones very well. Until this day, although I live only a short distance from New York City, I haven't been to see the remnants of the destruction at the Twin Towers on September 11, 2001. But, I just couldn't avoid visiting Pearl Harbor as it meant so much to all of us growing up during that period of time. Hopefully, in the near future, I will gather enough courage to also visit the Twin Towers Memorial in my home town, New York City.

I had my laptop with me, so I decided to go on the internet and do some research on the events that led to that "Infamous Day" on December 7, 1941. Growing up at that time, any information available was spoon fed to us to serve the immediate purpose of its authors. But, now that some 60-years have past, much of the data has been carefully studied by historians and eyewitnesses and, hopefully, clarified. The United States government was certainly not unprepared for this war; it developed contingency plans for an eventual conflict with Japan as early as the 1920s and began preparing Pearl Harbor for the transfer of our Pacific Naval Fleet and Headquarters from San Diego to that location. As a matter of fact, our own military conducted a surprise attack on Pearl Harbor in the 1930s to determine the adequacy of our defenses; the attack succeeded and our defense was deemed inadequate. In the early 1930s, Japan invaded Manchuria and began to expand into China, Indochina, and the oil rich Dutch East Indies. This expansion into the "Southern Resource Area" (the Japanese' term for the East Indies and Southeast Asia in general), caused U.S. Pacific bases and facilities, including Pearl Harbor and the Philippine Islands, to go on practice alerts many times before the attack of December 7, 1941. Our factories were already geared and producing military armament for our defense, and shipping a multitude of equipment to many of our soon to be allies. There we have it, how can a country that was expecting an attack from Japan get caught "flat footed?" There is ongoing controversy, due to allegations made by many historians, that some members of our government had advance knowledge of the attack and ignored the information in order to gain public and Congressional support for the U.S. to enter WWII. Whatever the case may be, when Emperor Showa gave Admiral Isoroku Yamamoto his approval to attack Pearl Harbor, it was up to our military to have been prepared to ward off any assault, which they failed to do. Looking back at the event, there was a combination of mismanagement and unfortunate circumstances that made the attacks devastating for us. In my opinion, one of the main problems was that on Sunday on the land of Paradise, most servicemen were in town having a good time, with only skeleton crews remaining to man the military installations. The Japanese knew this and, therefore, chose that day to launch their attack. Subsequent events became academic; we had the equipment to ward off an attack, but there were not enough personnel to man the defensive positions on land or sea. In addition to our ships being exposed and lined up like ducks in a pond in Pearl Harbor Bay, we made our aircraft easy targets on the airfields by lining them up wing to wing. Why did we do this? Because the "brains" in the Navy were afraid the Japanese living in Hawaii might sabotage them; this act alone undoubtedly supports the theory that we certainly were preparing for an attack of some sort from the Japanese Empire. The Japanese pilots' prayers were answered, sitting duck targets on land and sea and sophisticated defensive military equipment unmanned.

So it happened, on December 7, 1941, aircraft and midget submarines of the Imperial Japanese Navy began their "alleged surprise attack" on the U.S facilities in Hawaii from six aircraft carriers. Prior to the attack, two reconnaissance aircraft were launched from Japanese's cruisers to scout over Oahu to report our fleet's composition and location. Another four scout planes patrolled the area in order to prevent their task force from being caught by a surprise counterattack from us. So there were six aircraft flying over our military installations, all unseen electronically or by the human eye, or, if they were detected, nothing effectively was done to alert our military. At approximately 8:00 A.M., the first wave of 183 planes attacked our ships in the harbor concentrating on the large battleships. Air bases across Oahu were attacked, simultaneously, starting with Hickam Field, the largest, and Wheeler Field, the main Army Air Force fighter base. One hour later, the second wave of 171 planes attacked the Air Corps' Bellows Field and Ford Island's air field. Of the 402 American aircraft in Hawaii, 188 were destroyed and 159 damaged. None were ready to take off to defend the military installations or to protect our servicemen; they were not properly positioned on the air fields to take off and, in addition, most of the pilots were in town on weekend passes. The attack lasted 90 minutes and when it was over, 2,387 Americans were dead and 1,139 wounded. Eighteen ships were sunk, including five battleships. Nearly half the Americans killed were on the USS Arizona, when its forward magazine exploded after being hit by a bomb.

If there are any bright sides to that horrific day, it would be that our ships sunk or captured all five midget-submarines before they could do much damage, although the Japanese reported that one got into the harbor and successfully launched a torpedo at its target. A tactical error was made by Admiral Yamamoto in cancelling a planned third strike by Japanese aircraft to destroy our repair facilities and oil reserves. This enabled us to begin repairs to the damaged vessels immediately and to put them back in service. The valuable oil reserves were used to quickly supply our aircraft carriers with fuel to pursue the Imperial Fleet and, ultimately, engage them successfully in battle.

With all this information, we were prepared to visit the heart wrenching memorial with a somewhat better understanding of how countries are drawn into wars. At the entrance to the Visitor Center is the Arizona's 19,585-pound anchor. Upon entering the Center, we passed one of the battleship's two bells and were surprised at the size and complexity of the hall. It hosts the Pearl Harbor Museum, dual theaters, restrooms, a snack bar, and the Pearl Harbor Memorial Exhibit, complete with wartime memorabilia. The central room features seven large open windows on the walls and ceiling commemorating the date of the attack. We sat through an orientation film explaining the events leading up to the December 7th attack and the massive restoration that subsequently took place. I was anxious to see the USS Arizona Memorial, so we skipped the rest of the Center and went directly to that site. We were lucky to find a docent, Johnny, who was a survivor of the attack, to guide us through the Memorial. He pointed out the oil bubbles that were still surfacing from the ship (two quarts a day) and are called "Black Tears" or "Tears of the Arizona" in memory of the 1,000-plus sailors that were left buried in the ship and considered by the U.S. Navy to have been buried at sea. It is at this opening that visitors are permitted to pay their respects by tossing flowers and leis into the water in honor of the fallen sailors. The USS Arizona's deck lies six feet below the water line, with a pole attached to its mainmast flying an American flag and protruding skyward from the 184-foot long Memorial that encompasses the vessel. Every day a new flag is flown and the former one is folded in a triangular shape and given to a special person, sometimes a lucky visitor. The ship was built in the early 1900s and had a rather relatively uneventful history up until that horrific day. The ill-fated ship arrived at Pearl Harbor on December 6, 1941, the day before the attack, and had the honor of having the Battle Ship Fleet Commander Admiral Isaac Kidd (known as Captain Kidd) pay it an inspection visit. The ship and the Admiral both became history on the next day, but Captain Kidd put up a gallant fight; he gathered and organized his ships and men to give whatever resistance they could to the oncoming slaughter. He was awarded the Congressional Medal of Honor, posthumously, for his heroic conduct and, subsequently, had three destroyers named after him. Unfortunately, he was never asked why his battleships were all in port at the same time and lined up in such a precarious formation. A choking experience was when Johnny took us to the marble shrine that bears the names of seaman that went down with their ships. There were several men Johnny's age standing before the wall, hats in hand, heads bowed and crying, while others searched the list for lost comrades and relatives. These scenes always have a profound affect on me, as I find it difficult not to join in their sorrow and shed a tear with them. Leaving the Memorial was bittersweet; I was glad to pay my respect to those fallen Americans, but sad that hostility seems to be the only solution to many of the world's problems.

Next to the battleship USS Arizona Memorial is the battleship USS Missouri Memorial. Looking at the two structures reminded me of a mechanical vise: the Arizona being the fixed part of the vise and the Missouri (Big Mo) the parallel jaw that moves back and forward. It was on this ship that the unconditional surrender of the Imperial Empire of Japan was signed. Big Mo represents the United States' power that squeezed the energy and resources from the infamous Empire like a vise and brought it to the peace table with hat in hand to sign an unconditional surrender. The Big Mo overshadows it counterpart in size, which perfectly represents the overwhelming might of the United States once it entered the war against Japan. It's 887-feet long, 209-feet from keel to mast, and has a 108-foot beam. It had speeds in excess of 30 knots (35 mph) and is 279-feet longer and 11-feet wider than its sister ship. The Big Mo was the most formidable and the last U.S. battleship to be commissioned, it was launched in 1944. In addition to its massive firepower capabilities, she possessed thick steel armor plating from between 13.5-inches to 17-inches. It fought in most of our wars and conflicts: WWII, Korea, Vietnam, and Desert Storm. She secured her place in history when the unconditional surrender documents were signed between Japan and the

Allied Forces on September 2, 1945, on her deck. The image is etched in my mind of the Supreme Allied Commander, General Douglas MacArthur, signing the Formal Instrument of Surrender, which ended the final hostilities of WWII, and then handing the historical pen to General Wainwright, as a sign of redemption for his being a prisoner of war throughout the struggle. Wainwright's heroic efforts in the Philippine Islands in resisting the Japanese attacks, won him a fourth star and the Medal of Honor. Unfortunately, he spent three years of the war in various prisoner of war camps, ending up in Manchuria before his release.

We took a guided tour of the enormous ship with Jason, a Korean War veteran who served on Big Mo during that conflict. He was one of 2,700 officers and men who served honorably on the ship that delivered 2,000-pound shells from its nine 16-inch guns, which are approximately 67-feet long, at the enemy in support of our ground troops. There was a group of young children, 11 to 14-years-old, in an overnight Encampment Program. They were allowed to live aboard the ship, like real sailors, sleeping in the crew's berthing areas, storing their gear in navy lockers, eating Navy-style meals on the ship's mess deck, and using the restrooms and showers as if they were real seaman. What an exciting overnight campout for these young people; the experience was beaming from their faces. We moved along with Jason through the bridge admiring the sophisticated electronic equipment that the ship required to effectively perform its duty: radar, sonar, GPS, loran, electronic compass, auto pilot, plotting equipment, and a multitude of computers. It is amusing that with all the state-of-the-art equipment, they still have old fashioned manual steering and magnetic compasses on standby just in case of an unforeseen happening that could disable their electronics. The big guns, reaching 67-feet in length are frightening; they have the capacity of delivering up to 2,700-pound shells to their targets. In addition, the rocket launchers make the ship an impressive aggressive and defensive weapon. The crew's quarters on large ships have always startled me; the closeness of the living conditions certainly requires patience and a great deal of tolerance of human behavior. My favorite place on naval vessels is always the kitchen, especially if they are serving their delicious vanilla cake with chocolate icing, which they were. It seems that it is a tradition on all naval ships to have that wonderful cake available for visitors; I took a second helping with the blessing of the chef. We thanked Jason for his informative guided tour and left the enormous ship to visit her neighbor, the USS Bowfin Submarine at the Submarine Museum and Park.

We visited the museum that features the world of submarines, both past and present. The 10,000-square foot building exhibits an impressive collection of submarine related artifacts, such as weapon systems, photographs, paintings, battle flags, original recruiting posters, and an incredible collection of submarine models. An outstanding exhibit displayed a Poseidon C-3 missile; we were allowed to examine the inner and outer workings of the deadly projectile, but very carefully, as it still looked threatening. In the park stands a public memorial honoring the 52 American submarines and more than 3,500 submariners lost during WWII. We were given electronic docents to guide us through the Bowfin. The submarine was built on December 7, 1942, and was immediately nicknamed "the Pearl Harbor Avenger" because it was launched exactly one year after the ill-fated day in 1941. The submarine is 312-feet long with a 27-foot beam, and carried 24 torpedoes manned by 80 submariners. It lived up to its name "Avenger" as it sunk 44 enemy ships during its nine extraordinary war patrols. The crew's quarters are exceptionally small compared to the accommodations on Big Mo. I could never understand how men could live in such tight quarters without becoming claustrophobic or at least ornery. Everything on the vessel is scaled down compared to other ships, but the kitchen is unique as it acts as a meeting place and a compact restaurant. They, too, had the delicious vanilla cake with chocolate icing laid out for guests, and I didn't waste any time eating another large slice. The most fascinating part of the boat is the torpedo room. The large shiny torpedoes made the hair on the back of my neck stand out as they were so threatening in their appearance and size. I thought of the destruction they bring when discharged and the impact on their targets. I was glad to leave that area and go on board for a look at topside. WWII submarines are small and cramped for space compared to the modern spacious atomic subs of today. It's eerie that this small vessel successfully carried out its missions, with 80 crewmembers aboard, into the deep waters of the Pacific for extended periods of time, searching for enemy ships, and returned to tell their stories. They were all alone and for a good deal of the time submerged in the deep waters of the ocean for months on end; still, they gallantly carried out their almost suicidal missions. God bless those men. We were in a hurry to return to our hotel and find another place to dance for the evening, so away we went to our next adventure.

We called the Ala Moana Hotel in Honolulu to see if they were open for ballroom dancing. They said, "Yes, and that they were open Tuesday and Sunday nights and the music started at 10:00 P.M." There was no admission charge on Tuesdays and a $5.00 charge on Sundays, which surprised us for we were told that they served a complimentary buffet and all we had to do to reciprocate was to order drinks, if we so desired. The Ala Moana was typical of the hotels in Waikiki, its twin towers reflected the opulence that was on the inside. We went straight to the Rumours Restaurant and joined the 60-plus dancers that were already enjoying themselves on a nice-sized dance floor. We usually have light dinners on the nights we go dancing as it's a lot more comfortable dancing with less weight in our stomachs. It turned out to be a good choice for that evening, as they had a substantial complimentary buffet table set up consisting of sliced steak, various salads, fruits and Japanese appetizers, including some really good sushi. I very rarely go looking for food unless I'm hungry, but hungry or not, if it's around where I can see the food, I can't seem to control my hands from picking it up and quickly devouring whatever is in sight, even though my brain is telling me not to. Well, the buffet was delicious and didn't slow my dancing down too much. They played lots of Latin music, especially Salsa, which Barbara and I are very comfortable doing. We learned Mambo/Salsa from one of our first instructors, Electra, in Farmingdale, New York. I spent much of my youth (pre-Barbara days) at the Palladium Dance Hall in Manhattan, New York, which was world renowned for its great Latin music. So we put our talents together and did some serious Mambo/Salsa steps which impressed some of the other dancers, particularly the local Hawaiians. We were asked to teach a couple of our routines, which we did willingly. This particular Latin dance can get pretty sexy or even deemed vulgar by some people, so we refrained from any movements that would be considered either. We started in a basic position and then did an open body lead into a small grapevine and then an underarm turn, which most dancers had no trouble copying. Then we did an underarm turn from my left while holding each other's hands. Upon finishing the left turn, we did a reverse turn and then did it from the right side going into a sweetheart position, arms overhead and ending with arms moving over each other's shoulders, and then back into the basic position. The dancers had no trouble with that routine either, and thanked us profusely for showing them the steps. We were presented with Mai Tais as a reward, which we gladly drank while making many new friends, who insisted that we attend the Aloha Dance Club at the Palladium in two days. We told them we would try if we got back from our children's home in time. We bid our new friends good night and returned to our hotel, desperate for some rest after a very long and fulfilling day.

We rushed to our breakfast buffet where we were greeted by one of Hawaii's beautiful daughters, Lois, whose captivating smile and presence brought the morning sunlight deep into my soul. She presented Barbara with a beautiful, white gardenia-type Plumeria flower that she grew in her garden that emitted a sweet tropical floral aroma; it matched the head garland that she was wearing on which the flowers were also grown in her garden and she proudly displayed on her shiny-silk-like-black-hair. What a sweet gesture from a more than sweet wahine. What a great way to start our day. Off we went to visit our speechless, toothless, chubby, cuddly little bundle of happiness. We found the kids enjoying their beach and didn't waste any time changing into our bathing suits to join them. Steve had snorkeling gear ready for us to use, so we donned the masks and mouthpieces and went pell-mell into the water. After a few minutes, Donna, who was knee deep in the water, picked up a two by three-foot piece of white coral to show us; what a surprise when a green sea cucumber, which is a sea urchin and is in the starfish family, jumped off from underneath the coral. It was about 15-inches long with tiny legs and looked like a fat giant wriggly green worm. She put the coral back ASAP and did a quick u-turn for the beach, with us close behind.

I asked Steve if we could revisit Banzai Pipeline to see the winter surfers challenging the large waves we heard so much about. He agreed and said it would also be a good opportunity to play some golf at the Turtle Bay Resort, which was not far from the Pipeline. What a sight to see--expert surfers riding the giant tubes of water that turn into tsunami-type waves. What is spectacular to watch is their paddling out on their boards to what they anticipate are good locations to begin their journey back on crests of what they hope are "perfect waves." The name Banzai (suicide) Pipeline is certainly an appropriate name for the beach that attracts so many of the world's surf daredevils. It was surprising to see the large number of surfers challenging the waves and the great number of people spread out on beach towels, picnicing while observing the daredevils in action. Needless to say, none of the spectators ventured into the surf, including us. We drove over to the Turtle Bay Resort in time for their famous cornucopia brunch. The resort is located on Turtle Bay; its brochure says it all: "It's located on an 880-acre oasis on the North Shore of Oahu, set among swaying palms, quiet coves and rolling surf. The beauty of this tropical paradise can be seen from one of the 443 magnificent beach cottages and guest rooms. The resort features two lushly landscaped pools, one overlooking the azure Pacific, two championship golf courses, ten tennis courts, horseback riding, hiking and mountain bike trails, a surfing school, world-class dining, and upscale shopping. The Palmer course is an 18-hole championship golf course designed by Arnold Palmer and Ed Seay and hosts the PGA Champions Tour Event in October. The course has five tees, Black, Blue, Gold, White and Red. The smaller George Fazio Course hosts the LPGA Tour's Hawaiian Open and was the site of the first Senior Skins Game, which included Arnold Palmer, Chi-Chi Rodriquez, Gary Player and Sam Sneed." Talk about being intimidated, I wanted to play the smaller Fazio Course, but Steve insisted that we play nine holes on the Palmer Course. I gratefully acquiesced being that he was treating me and I didn't want him too feel that I was unappreciative. Steve and I rushed through our brunch; we left the girls and Ian Charles in the Palm Terrace Restaurant so they could finish their meal and then go to explore the Resort's facilities.

Steve brought an extra set of clubs for me, which we checked at the baggage drop off and proceeded to the check in for some real quality golf time. There were several Japanese men in front of us at the cashier; I couldn't believe how much they paid for a round of golf. I told my son it was too much to pay for a few hours of relaxation, but he said, "no sweat, Dad, everything is under control." I've heard him use that phrase many times when he was a young boy and immediately began to sweat. Little did I know that the military received a large discount and paid about a third of the going price. He paid for the nine holes and away we went. We had a choice of playing the front nine, which is nearly devoid of trees and shrubs and has lots of sand, water, wind and rolling terrain, or the back nine, which is a forest of ironwood pines and offers no less then nine craggy bunkers surrounding the landing area and extending all the way up to the green. We decided on the front nine, as it seemed a little easier, and teed off from the white, which is 5,574-yards versus the 7,199-yards distance from the black tees. My first shot was heavenly, about 180-yards right down the middle of the fairway. Steve hit his about 200-yards a little to the right. Unfortunately, those were our best shots for the day. I certainly was the more experienced player as I knew the most important rules of the game, which distinguishes a seasoned player from a novice. I knew all the reasons why I missed opportunities, such as, the club is bent, the grass is wet, the greens are wavy, unexpected winds, etc., etc., etc. The course was mind boggling and we were way over our heads as golfers, but we did spend some quality time together and did lots of laughing as we pretended to be serious players.

We found the girls lounging around the shops and joined them for drinks in the Lei Lei Bar and Grill. We spent a couple of hours relaxing and wandering around the spacious Resort, admiring the views of the turquoise/blue Pacific Ocean from our chaise lounges while nursing our tropical drinks. Steve and Donna said they wanted to take us to a small restaurant in the town of Haleiwa, located only a few minutes from their home, to enjoy some local food. They hadn't had an opportunity to dine there since Ian Charles' arrival and were anxious to enjoy the Hawaiian cuisine. We had some time before dinner so we walked around the quaint town of Haleiwa. There was an abundance of surf shops selling snorkeling equipment, surf boards, skin diving gear, and every imaginable type of aquatic equipment that anyone might need. The town boasts that it is the surfing capital of the world and rightfully so, as it is the first stop that the world renowned daredevils visit before seeking the "perfect wave" at the largest and most beautiful beaches in the world. There are also some nice antique shops, which we visited and admired some of the photographs of Hawaiian scenes and natives. We couldn't resist buying a beautiful 8 x 12 inch photo of a beautiful wahine with her mate, expressing their love story through a peaceful hula dance on a beach; the photo hangs in my office at home and helps bring comfort and serenity to the room. One of the antique shops had French music playing that was so beautiful that I asked the owner if I could sit a spell and listen to some of the songs. He was delighted and asked me to come back after dinner and he would have a surprise for me. He spoke English with a very heavy French accent, a Maurice Chevalier-type voice that was friendly and sincere and reminded me of the great French singer/actor.

The town had an old plantation character and was a throwback to the beginning of the 20th century. The building facades were quaint and there were many town folks sitting on benches outside the stores passing the time of day in conversation. On the north entrance to the town is a white twin-span "Rainbow Bridge" that got its name from the shape and the rainbows it seems to attract during the rainy season. Children can be seen diving off the lower part of the bridge, about 20-feet into the Anahulu River, and swimming to the rocky shore and then repeating the exercise. Another distinction that the town has is that on December 7, 1941, the only fighter plane that managed to scramble against the Japanese took off from the now abandoned Haleiwa Airfield. There are many tee shirts for sale in Haleiwa honoring that event.

We had dinner in Haleiwa Joe's, and chose to sit in the lanai so we could enjoy the view of the water and the setting sun. We all ordered Caesar salads with our Mai Tai drinks, which were a perfect combination; after a couple of those tropical drinks, everything seemed to "hang loose." We kept track of the number of drinks we had by the umbrellas that were accumulating on the table, which were inserted into the pineapples garnishing our hour-glass shaped drinks. The presentation of the drinks was so glamorous that it was difficult to disrupt their appearance, at least that's how it felt before having the first drink; after that it became a lot easier. The girls ordered steamed lobsters which were caught in local waters and came fresh off the Haleiwa fishing boats. They were served with lemon, butter, sautéed vegetable, and steamed white rice. Steve ordered a pound of Alaskan king crab legs, served with steamed white rice, sautéed vegetable, and drawn butter. I chose the fresh Atlantic salmon, grilled and topped off with a zesty dill sauce. It was served with sautéed vegetable and my favorite garlic mashed potatoes. I had my doubts as to how fresh the Atlantic salmon was but, as it is my favorite fish, I ordered it anyway. We devoured the meals as if it was our last supper and would have probably stayed for seconds, but Ian Charles was starting to get restless. By the time we finished, the sun, which seemed magnified, was setting and cast an orange-red glow over the whole area, bringing sounds of delight from all of the restaurants patrons, except for our little baby, who was starting to make some strange baby sounds. We went back to the antique shop to visit our French friend, Rene, who greeted us with double-cheek kisses and a hug. He presented me with a copy of his tape that I had enjoyed listening to that afternoon. There were songs by Edith Piaf, Maurice Chevalier, Josephine Baker, Jean Gabin, and Fernandel. I couldn't stop thanking this kind man for his considerate act and gave him an extra hug and handshake. We exchanged names and addresses, promising to visit each other if ever the occasion would arise. We drove the short distance back to the children's home listening to the French songs. We reminded them that they were spending the next day with us at Waikiki Beach and then continued our long drive back, humming along to the beautiful French music.

We spent the next day hanging around the pool and enjoying the hotel's facilities. Steve and I took the opportunity to work out at the gym and then we baby sat while the girls spent some quality time at the spa. We had a poolside lunch of hamburgers and hotdogs and enjoyed the Hawaiian band's music, especially the Hawaiian Wedding Song, which was written by Charles King in 1926. The song is one of my favorite and the lyrics go something like this:

"This is the moment, I've waited for. I can hear my heart singing, soon bells will be ringing. This is the moment, of sweet Aloha. I will love you longer than forever; promise me that you will leave me never. Here and now dear, all my love I vow dear. Promise me that you will leave me never. I will love you longer than forever. Now that we are one, clouds won't hide the sun. Blue skies of Hawaii smile on this our wedding day. I do love you with all my heart."

What a way to spend a day: a relaxing pool, the sun shining and bringing warmth to our bodies, delicious tropical drinks served by beautiful wahines, tropical music filling the warm air, coos coming from our chunky grandson, and my family at arms' reach. The kids had to get back early to prepare for a big BBQ that they were having in our honor the next day. So we had an early dinner at a quaint Japanese restaurant a couple of blocks away and then returned to our room to dress for another visit to the Palladium to join our Aloha Dance Club friends. We heard that at sunset there was a torch lighting ceremony across the street from our hotel on Kuhio Beach, at the foot of the statue of the island's champion surfer, Duke Kahanamoku. The detour was worth the time, as a procession of Hawaiian dancers and torch lighters sang and danced to the rhythm of the drums while lighting the torches and paying homage to the great surfer. No matter how many times I see hula dancing by the beautiful, pleasant Hawaiians, I'm overwhelmed with the showmanship and sensuality of their performances, and just enjoy watching while breathing the same fragrant air as they do. I was surprised at the large number of people that gathered to watch the event. Many came with beach blankets and refreshments and seemed prepared to spend the evening at the site.

The Palladium's dance floor was again divided in two. The larger group of dancers filling the hall to capacity was from the Pan Pacific Ballroom Dance Society of Hawaii. This is a world renowned International Style dancers' organization that holds many competitions and festivals throughout the world and can be reached by e-mail at wedanz@yahoo.com, or by telephone at 808-478-5803. We joined our friends of the Aloha Dance Club and were relieved to see that there weren't as many dancers in attendance as in the Pan Pacific dance section. We were at ease seeing many of the dancers from the Ala Moana Club and were asked to join their circle of friends sitting at the side-lines of the dance floor. They liked our Cha-Cha dancing and asked if we would show them one of our routines. We obliged them with a traveling step, which is done as follows: From a basic position, hands lowered, the male travels forward; cha-cha-cha, cha-cha-cha, cha-cha-cha, and cha-cha. The male then goes backwards, cha-cha-cha, cha-cha-cha, cha-cha-cha, and cha-cha, and then back to a basic position. That is the usual way to do the closed position traveling step; however, what they were interested in was the variation that we performed that is done in an open sweetheart position (Barbara's back is to me with both arms extended). We executed the same steps; 1-2-3, 1-2-3, 1-2-3 and then 1-2 forward and then the same pattern backward. This variation looks a lot nicer and is a lot more complicated to execute. It took a little coaching, but most of the dancers got the routine down pat. We were given the names of some other dance venues that we could attend, time permitting. The Hale Koa Hotel in Waikiki has ballroom dancing during the week to live music, and they can be reached at 808-733-7380. Also, the Wahiawa Ballroom Dance Club, which is on the north shore and close to where our kids live, holds dances in the Town Center Gym. They hold monthly dances and weekly classes at all levels, plus a midweek practice session in the daytime, which is open to the public. Their telephone number is 808-637-4875. After dancing for hours, we sadly bid our new-found soul mates farewell and went back to our place of rest.

Although we had two more days to spend in Hawaii, it was the last day that we were spending with our kids, as they had to report back to duty the following day. We decided to hang around their beach house and just coast along for the day, enjoying the expansive lawn, palm and coconut trees, soft sandy beach, swimming, and our little joy bundle, Ian Charles. The guests started arriving in the late afternoon, carrying their contributions to the BBQ, which was gratefully accepted by Donna and placed on ice for future enjoyment. Steve lit the half dozen torches scattered throughout his lawn to ward off any uninvited flying visitors, which set the stage and tropical mood for the afternoon. A couple of ukuleles and a guitar appeared and the music and singing began. Some of the girls actually did some exotic hula dancing, which was spoiled when the guys tried to show them the right way to wriggle around and move their hairy arms and legs, while puffing on smelly cigars. Steve's barbequed spareribs were amazing, as were his hamburgers. I think the fact that he loves to cook adds flavor to his cuisine. He picked some coconuts from the trees, split them, and made coconut juice tropical drinks, with lots of rum. Fresh coconuts are one of the most delicious fruits of a tree I can think of, especially when spiked with a little rum or crème de cacao. Saying goodbye was not easy. The quality time we spent with the children was over and after many kisses, hugs, and special squeezes for Ian Charles, we said adieu, hoping that we would see them in the near future. Another trip to Hawaii was not out of the question. As a matter of fact, the thought of returning to Paradise for a fourth time was a tempting possibility.

We had the day to ourselves and mapped out our itinerary so we could put every minute of our last day to good use. First, we decided to visit the Punchbowl and then go to the Hilton Hawaiian Village Resort to see one of our favorite performers, actress-singer-comedian-guitarist, Charo. After her show, we would go over to the Hawaiian Regent Hotel and spend the rest of the evening dancing some hot Salsa at their Acqua Club. The Punchbowl is the United State's National Memorial Cemetery of the Pacific and includes the Honolulu Memorials. It covers approximately 116-acres in the extinct Puowaina Crater; Puowaina means "Consecrated Hill" or "Hill of Sacrifice." It was the site of many royal burials and also the place where certain religious offenders were sacrificed to the Gods. By the end of WWII there were many temporary cemeteries scattered throughout the Pacific, which included 776 casualties from the December 7, 1941, attack on Hawaii. They were the first to be interred at the cemetery and, thereafter, 11,597 identified and 2,079 unidentified WWII soldiers were gathered from Guadalcanal, China, Burma, Saipan, Guam, Okinawa, Iwo Jima, and from prisoner of war camps in Japan, and laid to rest at this site. The cemetery is now filled to capacity with 33,230 gravesites which includes soldiers from WWII to Vietnam wars. The remains are of solders killed in action and whose next of kin decided not to have their bodies returned to the United States mainland. There is one other hallowed burial place for WWII soldiers at the Manila American Cemetery and Memorial, Fort Bonifacio, Manila, in the Philippines.

Viewing the gravesites is just too much to bear. The heart-wrenching experience is overwhelming and exhausting and demands lots of soul searching, when trying to rationalize why so many lives are always sacrificed in the fight for freedom. To compound the deep uneasiness of viewing the gravesites is the Honolulu Memorial, which features eight marble courts containing the names of 26,280 Americans missing in action from WWII and the Korean War. Two additional areas list the names of 2,503 soldiers missing from the Vietnam War. At the top of the marble staircase stands a towering 30-foot statue of the woman, Columbia, with a laurel branch in her hand, representing peace and liberty. Cradled on each side of the statue are walls etched with maps of the many military campaigns in the Pacific, including Pearl Harbor, Wake Island, Coral Sea, Midway, New Guinea, the Solomons, Iwo Jima, the Gilbert Islands, Okinawa, and Korea. At the center, behind the statue, is an interdenominational chapel which is available for those visitors, like me, who required some time to reflect on the human race's inability to refrain from wars that produced these two memorials representing over 60,000 missing and dead soldiers. I had the same bittersweet feeling here that I experienced at the Pearl Harbor memorials; pleased to be honoring our fallen heroes, and disappointed and frustrated that mankind has not found a more sane way to resolve disputes.

When we got back to the hotel, we made a beeline straight to the rooftop bar and had Mai Tais to take the edge off of the disturbing sights we saw at the memorials. We dressed and revisited the Hawaiian Village Resort, where we spent time on a previous trip enjoying a native luau and participating in some ceremonial dances. The hotel was as beautiful as we remembered, right on the beach with its own lagoon, probably one of the most beautiful of the beautiful hotels in Waikiki. While we waited for Charo's show to begin, we ordered more Mai Tais to erase the day's scenery from our minds and to put us in the right mood to enjoy this one-of-a-kind entertainer. I made good use of my laptop computer in the hotel and did some research on the Spanish, chameleon-type goddess. She was born in Murcia, Spain, in either 1941 or 1951, as Maria del Rosario Pilar Martinez Molina Baeza, the daughter of a lawyer who fled the country to Casablanca during Francisco Franco's dictatorship, while his wife remained behind to raise the family. She had a passion as a young child for classical guitar music and proudly claims that Andres Segovia was her instructor. She took lessons from him and other teachers from the age of nine and, as a result of her training and skill, she was named the "Best Flamenco Guitarist" in Guitar Player Magazine's readers' poll twice. As a young entertainer, she was discovered by the famous Latin bandleader Xavier Cugat and soon became his fifth, but not last, wife in 1966 at Caesars Palace in Las Vegas. They were married for 12 years and upon separating she gave him a Rolls Royce to express her gratitude for his guiding her successful career. Her talents were in such demand that she commanded the same salaries as Frank Sinatra, Ray Charles, and Dean Martin when she entertained in Las Vegas. I remember her so well on the Johnny Carson show where her complete lack of fluency in the English language had him and Ed McMahon rolling on the floor laughing, especially when she did her "cuchi-cuchi" routine. She was called the "cuchi-cuchi" girl from that time on. People would roar laughing at her attempts to speak the English language, starting the rumor that she learned English from the comedian Buddy Hackett. Well that is a little background on the blonde bombshell that was soon to appear. She made her entrance singing in Spanish and playing her famous flamenco guitar. The audience stood up and applauded and howled at her flamboyant stage presence and provocative outfit. Her voice was magical due to the way she whined and sighed while expressing her love or grief and expertly playing flamenco music on her oversized guitar. The arrangements made her performance a truly artistic and passionate one. Her attempt at the English language was so out of sync with its cadence that many in attendance had tears rolling down their faces from the spontaneous laughter that her words brought, including Barbara and me. The highlight of the evening was when she sat on my lap as she sang, in her unique

English, "you do me something" or "you do something to me," while running her fingers through my diminished hair and pulling on my pony tail. I still have pleasant nightmares about that incident, which always puts a smirk and then a very large smile on my face. In one of her last interviews, she expressed that she would love to be a contestant on "Dancing with the Stars"-- wouldn't that be earth shattering?

We wandered over to the Hawaiian Regent Hotel to hear Roland Sanchez and his "Salsa Hawaii Band" perform their magic. He has been playing at the hotel for three years and is instrumental in organizing and participating in Latin Festivals in Hawaii. He has been featured on TV shows and music videos in Hawaii and Tahiti. The dance floor was small but it didn't stop us from doing some great Salsa, Mambo, Meringue, and Cumbia dancing. Fortunately, most Latin dances do not require lots of room, as they are done in place without moving around the dance floor, so the small dance floor worked out very well for our purpose. Half the fun was just listening to the great maestro and enjoying the last of our Mai Tais before we left Paradise. Con Mucho Gusto.

While flying back to the mainland, I gave much thought to my grandson's future. Ian Charles was born in 1999, making him a millennium baby. Looking back now to the turn of the 20th century, and some of the incredible events that have already become a part of his life, I shutter at what his future might hold. His first years witnessed the fiasco of the Y2K scare, where the computer industry had the world convinced that at the turn of the century, computers were going to crash and that the infrastructure of the world would come to a startling halt; that is, if everyone didn't replace or enhance their equipment with the manufacturers' new "Bullet proof products . . ." Well it cost the people of the world billions, if not trillions of dollars for an event that didn't happen. Also, in the same year, the stock market broke all records in its climb to 11,497 for the Dow and 4,026 for NASDAQ. An unexpected stock market crash sent the Dow down to 10,200 and the NASDAQ to around

2,000. The following year witnessed the September 11, 2001, attack on the Twin Towers in New York City, by the terrorist Muslim group, Al Qaida, which turned the objectives of our dream world around 180 degrees and headed our economy from a direction of easy living to one of an endless war on terrorists. As I write this in the last quarter of 2008, the stock markets again are on a downward spiral. In fact, just this week the Dow was down 1,000 points with no end in sight to where the bottom is. Considering the world that Ian Charles was born into, and the unique problems facing us, I'm sure he will become tough skinned enough to handle whatever challenges the future might have in store for him.

CHAPTER TWELVE

Dancing & Cruising from Long Island's Wine Country to New England's Islands (Block Island, Martha's Vineyard, Nantucket, Hyannis & Newport)

AROUND THE FLOOR: APRIL/JULY 2000

TRAVELING AROUND by Barbara Bivona

THE ARRIVAL OF SPRING and longer days is a welcomed sight after a cold, gray winter. However, while my neighbors are busy planting their vegetables and flowers, I'm preoccupied with my coming summer vacation. That's not to say I don't pay spring its due. I plant the requisite impatiens and a few vegetables, but my thoughts are on distant shores. Block Island has been my favorite for many years. It's laid back and casual, with uncrowded beaches, beautiful marinas, and steaming succulent lobsters. This island has beckoned me for many years and I always heed the call. The days are lazy there, spending time on its pristine beaches or just walking around the town is always something we look forward to doing. The island comes alive in the evenings, and there are several places for dancing that feature rock to country music. There is also our favorite dancing hangout, Ballard's. Ballard's is a huge restaurant, specializing in seafood. You can dine inside or on their patio overlooking the ocean, day or night. Jim Kelly plays keyboard and entertains every evening, playing everything from Country to Swing. Caribbean music, Rumba, and the ever-popular chicken dance are always enjoyed by the crowd. I'm not ashamed to say I've gotten up many times to flap my wings, especially if my friends join in to share the embarrassment. Jim does lots of sing-along songs too, which rounds out a fun evening. He plays until about 9:00 P.M. on weekends, and then a band continues the entertainment. The bands vary; last year we were treated to Lois Greco's Band "Hotline." They played a good mix of dance numbers and had the dancers jumping until 1:00 A.M. I asked Lois for some Latin music, which he promptly played with good timing and excellent Latin rhythm. Some years ago, Ballard's was destroyed by fire. Mike and I were so disappointed that we cancelled our reservations and skipped going to Block Island that year. It was quickly rebuilt to look exactly like it did before the fire and we couldn't tell the difference. After Block Island, we like to spend a week on Cape Cod and the islands of Nantucket and Martha's Vineyard. For the past three years, we've been staying in Hyannis because it's closer to dancing locations. Through USABDA, we located a dance on Friday nights held at the Sons of Italy in Cotuit, on Route 28. The music was performed by a three-piece band called the Mel-Tones, with a nice variety of smooth, some Latin, and a few line dances. General admission was $10.00 for dancing only and $15.00 with the buffet. Coffee and cake were served to all in attendance. The dance floor was large enough for the crowd and it was easy to get around without interference. We were lucky to be seated with a group of friendly New Englanders, which made our visit a pleasant one; especially nice was exchanging partners and dancing with people with different styles. The phone number for the Sons of Italy is 401-540-2407 or 420-3172. Mike and I look forward to returning there for more dancing with our new friends this summer.

* *

We spend our summer vacations cruising on our boat, Mikara, from Long Island up to Plymouth, Massachusetts, enjoying stops at such places as Montauk Point, Long Island, New York; Block Island, Rhode Island; and then in Massachusettes; Martha's Vineyard, Nantucket, Hyannis and Falmouth in Cape Cod, and then on through Buzzards Bay to New Bedford, and through the Cape Cod Canal to Plymouth. From there we would turn around and travel back through Buzzards Bay and head for Newport, Rhode Island. Mikara is named for Mike and Barbara and is also a play on the Italian word "Micara" (my love). She is a 1988 42-foot Chris Craft cabin cruiser. Its beam is 15-feet and it draws 4-feet of water when our 400-gallons of fuel and 150-gallons of fresh water are at capacity. It has two 350HP engines, a 6.5KW generator, two state rooms, two toilets with showers, and a tub that Barbara's 5'2" just about fits into comfortably. It also has heat and air conditioning pumps that keep us comfy in all kinds of weather. When it was delivered in 1988, we experienced a life-long dream come true, mortgage and all. The following picture was taken the year she was delivered, and today, 20-years later, she is as beautiful as the day we first boarded her:

We bought our first boat, a new 18-foot Crestliner runabout, two years after we were married. We decided to take a trip to Italy and when we weighed the cost of the trip, which was about $2,500.00, versus buying a boat that we saw at the New York Boat Show that we fell in love with, the decision became a no brainer. We named our new Princess "Big One," because of its small size, knowing some day that we would have a "Bigger One." We had the boat seven years, and then fell in love with my friend's 26-foot Chris Craft, which Barbara and I decided would be the next right-sized boat for us. It had double bunks and could easily accommodate our two small children, Steven and Laurie. In addition, it had a somewhat private V-birth at the front of the boat for Barbara and me, which added up to a boat we could all sleep on and spend some quality time together. She sent me to Al Grover's Chris Craft dealership in Freeport, Long Island, which was the boating capital of the island at that time, to find our next dream boat. He had just the boat we were looking for and it was only a few years old. So I gave him a deposit, but before we signed the contract Al said: "Wait, I may have a 1970, 28-foot boat that just came in that you might want to look at. The owner must sell and you can get it for a great price." What a beauty it was, two years old, a fiberglass hull with a wood superstructure, a single 225HP engine, private toilet, a fresh water pump system, and a gas stove. Wow! What more could a body want and just for $500.00 more. I signed on the dotted line and became the owner of "Alice B," which was the name on the boat. The name stayed on the transom until we sold it seven years later. As long as we owned the boat, people that we met while cruising called my wife Alice. Our kids were getting older and sleeping on upper and lower bunks was getting a little complicated, so we looked around for our third boat and fell in love once more (how fickle we are) with a 35-foot all fiberglass Chris Craft. We were lucky to find the exact boat we wanted, a 1977 Chris Craft double cabin that was only two years old. It had twin 300HP engines, a 5KW generator, a toilet with a stand up shower, a heat and air conditioning pump, a private master bedroom, a V-birth for Laurie, and a folding bed for Steven. After a family meeting we decided to call our new member "Mikara." With the introduction of Loran C for pleasure boats, which we didn't waste any time in acquiring, we took our 35-foot beauty from Long Island, NY, to Plymouth, MA, on her first two-week cruise. What a pleasure it was to travel and to arrive at planned destinations without getting lost, thanks to the Loran's point to point accuracy. That boat was the first Mikara and was a part of our family for ten years. We currently own the second Mikara and just celebrated her 20th anniversary as a family member. She is still with us, but our children have departed for greener pastures, although my son just purchased a 24-foot Sea Ray and plans on using it in Maryland's beautiful waterways, with his wife and two beautiful children, Ian Charles and Princess Catie.

We have kept our boats at the Stirling Harbor Marina, on the North Fork of Long Island in the seaport Village of Greenport, for over 30 years and consider it our home away from home in the summer months. We chose the location after spending time in the Hamptons, on the South Fork, because it was low keyed and very close to good boating locations, such as Shelter Island, Sag Harbor, and Southampton. The water in the area is deep compared to the South Shore, which makes boating a lot safer and more relaxing. It's also one of the best jumping-off points for boating on the east coast, making Connecticut, Rhode Island, Massachusetts, and Maine within reasonable boating distances. Cruising to Connecticut, Block Island, or Sag Harbor for lunch are some of our favorite short trips.

What attracted us to the quaint town of Greenport was the laid-back attitude of its townspeople and farmers. It didn't have the crowded restaurants and traffic jams that its sister on the South Fork had. In addition, the inland boating area is less crowded and its islands from afar reminded us of the friendly islands of the Mediterranean. We always are amazed that on some days the only boats to be seen are some distance away, which is unusual in any popular seafaring area. The town itself has a rather checkered history; from whaling, shipbuilding, rum running, illegal whiskey trading, fishing, oyster harvesting and home of the America's Cup winners, including the Enterprise in 1930, Rainbow in 1934, and Ranger in 1937. Its history has made the village the quaint sophisticated place it is today. Needless to say, it no longer participates in any of the above illegal activities. The focal point of the village is Mitchell Park, which became fully operational in 2007. Its main attraction is an Antique Carousel that was built in 1920 by the Herschell-Spillman Company and donated to the town by the Northrop/Grumman Corporation in 1995. It's fully enclosed in a glass pavilion and boasts of having one of the few brass ring dispensers in use. Its hours during the season are from 10:00 A.M. to 9:00 P.M. These same hours apply on weekends and holidays during the off season, weather permitting. The park's amphitheater is connected to a harbor walk and is the site for seeing band concerts, shows, and special events. The harbor walk connects the park to the Long Island Railroad Station, which travels to New York City and also connects with the North Ferry that carries cars and passengers to Shelter Island. The park has an ice-skating rink for outdoor winter sports, which is also used as a mist walk in the summer months to cool the area. Its "Camera Obscura," a medieval optical device that projects a live image from the outside into a round projection table in its dark room, is one of the only camera obscuras in the world that is open to the public free of charge. The park also has a harbormaster's building, observation deck, public toilets, and over 80- transient boat slips.

Of special interest to us are the musical events that take place at the amphitheater during the summer months. Once a week the residents bring their chairs and sit on the lawn outside the theater to enjoy the Greenport Band, made up of approximately twenty musicians, playing popular and marching music. Dancing bands are scheduled throughout the season playing Dixieland, Jazz, Smooth, and Latin music. Our last dance session was to the music of the Mambo Loco Quartet of Brentwood, Long Island they are considered one of the hottest Latin combos around. We danced to their fiery Latin rhythms, including spicy salsas, fast cha-chas, soft Rumbas, and torrid tangos. The band lead is Wayne Burgess on the bass, Alfredo Gonzales on the trombone, violin, and percussion instruments, with Larry Belford on conga and lead vocalist, and Bill Smith on the keyboard. Together they play some great dancing music. We were doing a Mambo on the wooden floor in front of the band, trying to perfect a step I saw performed by a professional dancer, Mark James, when an old acquaintance cut in. It was our old friend Alfonso Triggiani from the Touch Dancing Studio in Westhampton. He finished the routine with Barbara and then joked that he couldn't help trying the step because it looked so sexy and he wanted to do it so as not to forget the movements. I was quite flattered, as he is one of my idols in the dance world. The step is quite simple; I turn Barbara in a half turn with her back facing me and her arms extended behind her. I remain in my position as she moves away, stretching her arms and doing lots of hip motions; then she come towards me, still with her back facing me and we join and do a little wriggle. It's always fun meeting fellow dancers at these events. I was lucky because Alfonso brought his dance partner, Agnes, with him and it gave me an opportunity to do several dances with her, while Barbara and Alfonso wore some of the leather off of their dance shoes.

Eastern Long Island has an abundance of dance venues. Our favorite Thursday night dance is at the new Raphael Winery on Peconic Bay in Cutchogue (available on the web at www.Raphaelwine.com). It has weekly dancing to the sounds of a local dance group, Sahara, from 7:00 P.M. to 11:00 P.M. There is no admission charge and most people bring their own dinner, which can be enjoyed in the Italian style Renaissance Room or on their outside terrace overlooking manicured vineyards that extend to the bay. The entrance to the vineyard has a Roman water fountain with statues sprouting water into a reflecting pool. Its backdrop is the Raphael building, which is a magnificent Mediterranean-style Chateau with a red tiled roof and circular driveway. The inside, which includes the dance floor, is a massive, open-spaced room with earth toned ceramic tiles, high ceilings, tall arched renaissance-style windows, and a circular tasting bar trimmed in oak to resemble a wine barrel. The building includes a number of spectacular chandeliers, elevators, stairways, and its own chapel. The feeling of the place takes me back to the Tuscany area of Italy; even the aroma of the wine and grapes are reminiscent of that beautiful Italian region. We usually order a bottle of Raphael's famous merlot wine and sit at a table on the outside terrace, overlooking the classic straight-lined grape trees extending to Peconic Bay, and enjoy our bagged dinner and the fruity dry taste of their merlot wine. While dining, we interrupt our bites to do some serious dancing to the sounds of Fred Miner's Sahara trio with Prentiss McNeil as soloist. There are many dance students from the Riverhead Dance Studio and many locals who come to enjoy a pleasant evening dancing or just to be entertained by the dancers and appreciate the music. The music is great for the students to practice their dancing and it's nice to see how seriously they take their routines and keep repeating steps until they get them right. We did an Argentine Tango, which impressed some of the students and they asked us to show them a balancing step that we perform at the beginning of the dance. We started our dance about 10-feet apart and approached each other slowly, while brushing our shoes along the dance floor. We caress, slightly bend our knees for the Tango position, and then turn slowly from my right to left and again from my left to right. While this is being done, Barbara raises her left foot and swivels to my continued turns. It's a simple routine, but looks very sexy, while putting the partners in synch with each other so they can capture the right attitude of this sensual dance.

I think back to the days when Eastern Long Island was a major potato producing area and how it has been transformed from dirt farms into a beautiful, modern, world class wine farming region, with over 60 vineyards ranging from two and a half acres to over 500-acres. It all started in the early 1970s, when Alex and Louisa Hargrave's dream became a reality and they developed the Hargrave Vineyard in Cutchogue, Long Island. This new industry is responsible for revitalizing the North Fork. The vintners boast that over one million people a year visit their vineyards, enjoying wine tasting, and dancing to music that they provided. Touring bus trips to the wine country have become very popular over the years and allows people traveling from far away, especially Manhattan, to enjoy a relaxing day, tasting the local wines and dancing, if they so choose.

A Friday night favorite dance spot is the TGIF (Thank God it's Friday)Dance sponsored by the Brookhaven National Laboratory (BNL) & Cultural Club at the massive facility in Upton, Long Island. BNL was conceived in 1947 by representatives of the following nine major universities: Columbia, Cornell, Harvard, John Hopkins, MIT, Princeton, University of Pennsylvania, University of Rochester, and Yale. Its purpose was to establish a new nuclear science facility at the Army Camp Upton Base on the North Shore of Long Island, in a university atmosphere. It has grown to be one of the foremost scientific research facilities in the world, employing a staff of approximately 3,000 full time and over 4,000 visiting research scientists. It has the distinction of having had six Nobel Prizes awarded for work done in its laboratories. In the middle of this multifaceted scientific complex is a spacious dance floor, where dances are held every Friday by the BNL Social & Cultural Club TGIF. Its strange website address is www2.bnl.gov/rudy/social/activities.html. The weekly dances are run by Rudy Alforque, a scientist at the lab, who also gives dance lessons. They are opened to the public from 7:00 P.M. to 11:30 P.M. The entrance fee is $15.00 for members and $20.00 for guests. The evening includes a cold buffet dinner and a workshop dance lesson by one of the many local dance professionals, including Donna Marie Portelli, Michelle Cernese, and Jack & Michele Cooper. Music is provided by DJs or local bands, including Kane Daily's Band and the Long Island Sound Orchestra. Both sources of music provide just the right type of rhythms to make the evening a memorable one. Throughout the year, on special occasions or holidays, the club holds special parties, such as a Christmas Party with a live 20-piece Big Band, Bill Wilkinson & the Long Island Sound Orchestra. On New Year's Eve they have a black tie affair with DJ music and dancing till the wee hours of the morning.

The BNL's collegiate atmosphere is modeled after SUNY-Stony Brook University's, which is another dancing venue of the first order. The renowned 1,100-acre university is located on the North Shore of Long Island in the town of Stony Brook and hosts a student body in excess of 22,000 students. It is also the proud recipient of Nobel and Pulitzer prizes. It has a modern dance curriculum, consisting of over 15 dance courses ranging from an "Introduction to the World of Dance Cultures" to "Jazz Dancing Techniques III." Their course outline states: "The curriculum offers courses which encourage students to embrace a life-long journey through intellectual, creative and performance challenges. The dance minor examines the practice and study of movement and dance, with the detail of technique, form, content, structure, shape, energy, creativity, craft, design, rhythm and dynamic quality. But the goal of the study is to enable students to become more fully human, with all of the intelligence, discipline, playfulness, and purpose necessary to inspire work in a number of disciplines and career paths." The Stony Brook University Dance (SBUD) Club is very active and holds dancing workshops several times a week, some of which are open to the public. Their website address is www.liballroom.com, and features an updated calendar of their dance schedules and of other Long Island dancing venues. In light of their dedication and passion for dancing, it is not surprising that the students' professional dance instructors include two of the most accomplished dancers in New York. The loveable Patti Panebianco is an independent instructor and teaches at some of the finest studios in Manhattan and Long Island. She is the recipient of over 25 titles in the International Latin Rising Star and Open categories. She is the featured Tango dancer on YO-YO Ma's CD, Soul of the Tango, and was a feature dancer/performer for "All My Children's Holiday Ball." She also choreographed and starred in the "Tribute to Gershwin Show" at the Pierre Hotel in Manhattan. On occasion, she also DJs at various dance events that we are proud to say we have attended and have danced to her great music. I even had the honor and delight of dancing with her on several occasions.

DonaMarie Portelli is also an instructor extraordinaire; she teaches at the club's workshops and guides her students in the art of dancing. She is the recipient of numerous titles and championships, including: U.S. Latin & Theater Arts, World Disco Hustle, U.S. Rising Star, and Cabaret. She has appeared in the road tours of "Phantom of the Opera," " Dance Fever," and "A Tribute to Andrew Lloyd Weber." The results of these two talented instructors are evident when their students perform at the monthly dances held in the Student Activities Center. The 3,000-plus square foot dance floor at the Center gives the young dancers an opportunity to show off their smooth dancing, which has long stretching steps and requires ample room to maneuver. We attend the monthly dances regularly and also enjoy the rare occasion when we can dance on such a spacious floor, which allows us to perform routines that are not possible on smaller dance areas.

The monthly dances are held on Saturday evenings from 8:00 P.M. to 11:45 P.M. The entrance fee is $14.00 and includes a dance lesson and a buffet of finger sandwiches, a cold vegetable platter, a salad, fresh fruit salad, mucho desserts, coffee and tea. The event draws approximately 200 to 300 dancers, which leaves a lot of room to spin around the large dance floor. Our last visit featured one of our favorite DJs, Louis Del Prete, who is also our private dance instructor for West Coast Swing. His music is always excellent for the various dances, as he is also a dancer himself and knows the proper music required for the performers to successfully dance their routines. His music made the dance lesson easy; it was slow with loud specific beats for the Rumba. DonaMarie gave the lesson, which was easy to follow. She broke the steps down to simple moves and was patient with those of us who didn't get the routines right away. From a basic box step we did an underarm turn into a walk around, with Barbara's right hand extended to my left hand. We moved in a half turn facing outward for a six count and then I turned her to my right and she positioned herself in back of me, both of us holding and extending our left hands for another six count. Then, she turned so that her back was facing my front for another six count and an underarm turn into the basic Rumba position, facing each other. A tricky routine to say the least, but with lots of practice we did remember the proper way to execute it. It's is always nice when we see many of our dancing friends who travel from as far away as Nassau Country (about a one hour plus ride) to dance on the spacious floor at the Student Center.

Another dance venue on Eastern Long Island is Alfonso's Touch Dancing Studios, located in Westhampton Beach, Long Island. I already discussed this amazing dancer in other parts of my book and couldn't miss the opportunity to further explore the importance of his teaching to the world of dancing. Alfonso Triggiani has been running his studio in the Hamptons since 1985 and has kept the "Hampton Set" on their toes throughout the years. He is an internationally-recognized expert in ballroom dancing, specializing in Argentine Tango. He has served on the executive committee of the Dance Educators of America, which is associated with the official United States governing body in the World Dance and DanceSport Council. As previously mentioned, he has his own morning television show, "Touch Dancing with Alfonso." The show's schedule appears on his website: www.Touchdancing.com. He hosts dancing events throughout Long Island; some are in Westhampton Beach, Sag Harbor, East Hampton, and Southold. We attended a social dance that he had in Sag Harbor at the Sugar Reef Restaurant, which has a nice-sized dance floor. To get there, we decided to take our boat and cruise over to Sag Harbor and dock at the town's marina overnight so we could attend the event and also enjoy a meal at one of our favorite local restaurants. We were greeted by the maestro with his usual hug and double-cheek kisses. We caught up on the local gossip in the dancing community and then he gave a lesson in Cha-Cha which took us quite some time to master. We are now successfully using it as one of our favorite routines. It went like this: From a basic Cha-Cha to an open New Yorker (open break to my right) with a hesitation, Barbara turns towards me contacting my left hand with her left hand. I gently push her around and she does a full turn back into the New Yorker position; we then do a reverse turn, simultaneously, finishing in a basic Cha-Cha position. The timing is quite tricky, but with considerable practice we finally got it down pat. We spent the rest of the session dancing with others, and lucky Barbara got to dance with Alfonso again. Not to be left out, I asked his associate, Agnes, to do some Latin dances and totally enjoyed being able to keep up with her speed and Latin motions.

It was late when the social ended, but we were able to grab a snack at the restaurant during the dance breaks, so eating at one of our favorite restaurants would have to wait for our return to the lovely town of Sag Harbor. We hugged and kissed those who were willing, and wished them a "good evening until we meet again" and retired to our boat for a pleasant night's sleep. Waking up in the morning after sleeping on our boat always gives me a special feeling of being in the right place at the right time. We enjoyed a perfect breakfast at one of the dockside restaurants while viewing the boating activity coming in and out of the harbor. There were many boats moored out on the water, bobbing around with the motion of the waves and the changing of the tide. It makes for a picture perfect seascape; blue water supporting the boats coming to and fro, boats at anchor, twisting and turning, a light blue sky encompassing the background, and bright, white clouds of various shapes, creating imaginary formations. After breakfast, we returned to our homeport in Greenport where I went through my ritual of washing down Mikara to eliminate any accumulation of salt and to allow her to show off her brilliant shine when she is clean.

There are many places for dancing on Long Island, and information is readily available on many websites, including those listed in this chapter. But what is unique in our area is that there are two dancing publications: "The Rhythm Express," with their website at: www.Dancin.com, and "Dance, Dance, Dance," with their website at: www.Danceschedule.com. Both list dancing events throughout the month and distribute their monthly publications at the many dance halls in the area. The following is a page from Robert Beer's "Dance, Dance, Dance" publication for September 2008, and is presented with his permission.

We usually take our summer vacations in the middle of July when the weather along the Eastern seaboard isn't so erratic. But there are no guarantees that traveling these waterways at that time of year won't get a sailor in trouble with inclement weather. So it becomes difficult making reservations at planned ports-of-call, without saying a prayer or two. Reservations are required months in advance to guarantee docking space at marinas, which makes a cruise totally reliant on weather conditions during a planned vacation. There are many foolish sailors who will travel under most any conditions and, somehow, live to tell of their ordeals as if they were gallant adventures. It's possible to plan a stay at a marina for two days and remain a week, due to unexpected inclement weather. But, if a person loves boating, as we do, they will throw caution to the wind, so to speak, and make early reservations, as we do every summer, and then carefully plot the courses to our destinations on our GPS and our old faithful Loran C as a backup. For that year, we made reservations at Montauk Yacht Club, in Montauk, Long Island; then on to Champlin's Marina in Block Island, Rhode Island; to the town dock at Menemsha on Martha's Vineyard, Massachusetts; with the next stops in that beautiful state at the Nantucket Boat Basin, in Nantucket and Hyannis, in Cape Cod. Leaving the "Bean State" we set course for Newport, Rhode Island, and then finally returning to our home port in Greenport. The following map shows the route of our approximately 350-mile round trip. The wide line is a car route and the thin line identifies our water voyage:

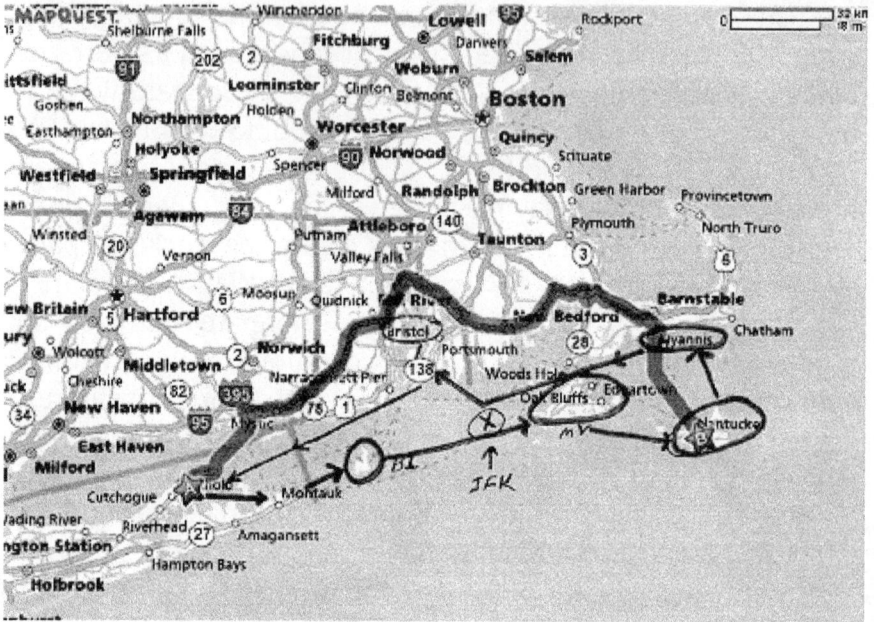

The furthest Easterly tip of the South Fork of Long Island is Montauk Point. This is always a good first stop because it gives me an opportunity to sea trial the boat and to do some preventative maintenance, before continuing on our extensive journey. Most of the islands on our itinerary do not have good repair facilities so it's important to check Mikara thoroughly before leaving Montauk Point. It's approximately 25 miles from Greenport to the Montauk entrance. It takes about two hours, from casting off to tying up, for us to reach this destination, weather permitting. If there is dense fog, it's imperative that we reduce our speed for safety purposes, from 18 mph to about 5 mph, which would result in our taking considerably longer than anticipated to reach our first port. Fog can be expected throughout our trip and the Navigation Rules of the Road must be adhered to implicitly. Regardless of the type of weather that might restrict visibility, mariners should follow these common sense safeguards:

1 - First order of a trip if poor visibility is present, or anticipated, is to put on navigational running lights.

2 - It's always a good idea to call the destination marina and boats in the vicinity of the planned route to get some "on the spot" weather information.

3 - It's important to determine from the National Oceanic & Atmospheric Administration's (NOAA) radio transmissions what the weather and tide conditions are on the planned route and destination.

4 - Life jackets should always be within reach when taking the boat from its slip, in the event of unexpected mishaps.

5 - When traveling, the boat's speed should be reduced to insure that there is enough time to react in case of any dangerous conditions that might present themselves. The rule of thumb is that a boat should be able to stop in half the distance of visibility. Further on in this chapter is a classic example of what happened when this rule was not followed. The collision between the Andrea Doria and the MS Stockholm sank Andrea Doria due to the negligence of both captains not adhering to Navigation Rules of the Road, as they sailed in restricted visibility.

6 - A fog horn, either a manual or electrical device, should be operational and sound a prolonged blast at least every two minutes if there is restricted visibility. I set my electric automatic fog horn at ten-second intervals when running in fog or heavy rain.

7 - Radar, if available, should be set to pick up any objects in the boat's path.

8 - If possible, a lookout should be posted at the bow of the boat when there is restricted visibility.

9 - Current charts for the area, referenced to previously written headings and distances of each point on the route to be travelled, should be readily available.

10 - Listening intently for any other fog horn sounds that may be coming from other vessels; especially useful is the use of an electronic hailer's receiving feature. If available, this will magnify the sounds of horns in the vicinity.

11 - Checking the engine's oil and water levels, as well as any evidence of hazardous fuel odor is imperative.

12 - Always fill the fuel tanks before making long trips as a two-hour planned trip could take twice the amount of time when unexpected situations arise, such as mechanical problems, fog, rain or accidents.

These safeguards should also be followed when there is heavy rain encountered on a voyage, as the wet, slippery conditions combined with diminished visibility can be more hazardous then traveling in the fog.

We like casting off around 10:00 A.M., which hopefully will give any fog in the area time to burn off. That was our plan as we began the first leg of our trip and it worked out well for us. As we entered Gardiner's Bay, the sun was burning through the fog as we settled in for a pleasant journey to the entrance of Montauk Harbor. It's always exciting and comforting when an inlet comes into view and we slow down to enter between the breakwaters. Upon entering this inlet, it's important not to make any wakes (waves) as there are people bathing on the left of the entrance and boaters are responsible for any damage caused by their wakes. On the right are some pretty threatening rocks, some visible and others underwater, so it pays to be cautious when entering this or any other inlet. To compound the already hazardous conditions, there are boats in front of you, behind you, and coming at you, so it's imperative that everyone obey established boating "rules of the road," which are very specific as to the conduct of boaters and their behavior while underway. Imagine all of this going on and there is dense fog to deal with. Further on in our trip we will encounter fog, fog, and more fog; I'll describe how we safely handled Mikara when we were faced with that unwelcomed visitor further on in this chapter.

We waited in line behind a couple of boats for the dock master of the Montauk Yacht Club to give us permission to enter the bulk headed marina. Native Americans called Montauk "the land of many winds." Fortunately there weren't any strong winds yet, and we were able to dock our boat in the assigned slip without incident. I always breathe a sight of relief when Mikara is tied up safely and the water and electricity are connected, which gives me an opportunity to wash the saltwater off of her body while I calm down from the anxiety that accompanies me on all of my trips. The marina can accommodate over 200 boats, and boasts at being one of the top ten marina destinations in North America. It can accommodate boats up to 225-feet and it's not uncommon to see several boats of that size docked at the marina. A great feature available to boaters staying at the marina is their use of the Resort's land facilities, which include an indoor heated pool, two outdoor pools, a spa, a gym, a small beach, an outdoor restaurant overlooking the pool and Lake Montauk, and a first-class indoor restaurant with an extensive wine list that serves local fish specials in addition to other delicious cuisine. In the evening, their indoor circular bar has a combo band for listening and dancing.

The resort was built by the famous master builder Carl Fisher in 1928, as a playground for the rich and famous. He had successfully developed Miami Beach and thought Montauk would be a great alternative for his "in crowd" to spend their summer months when it became too hot in Miami. To accommodate his friends' yachts, he dug a deep channel from freshwater Lake Montauk into saltwater Gardiner's Bay, making it the world's largest private harbor at that time. The members of his club included such dignitaries as Vincent Astor, J.P. Morgan, Nelson Doubleday, Edsel Ford, Harry Whitney, Thomas Eastman, John Wanamaker, and Harold S. Vanderbilt. According to legend, the Island Club became the most popular speakeasy and gambling casino on the East Coast. Unfortunately, the big stock market crash of 1929 put the kibosh on his plans, and the marina and resort soon fell into disrepair. It took many years to redevelop the "Montauk Yacht Club Luxury Resort Marina," and today it stands as the "Gem" of the East Coast, with its modern marine facilities and its world-class hotel resort amenities.

Montauk is considered one of the sports fishing capitals of the world, hosting more than 400 charters and fishing boats, many reeling in world record and prize winning catches of tuna, shark, striped bass, and fluke. It also boasts some of the best Atlantic Ocean beaches in New York, which draws over a million visitors a year to its shores. Walking through the pristine resort always gives me a feeling that the place was befitting my idea of where I belong in the scheme of things; just the right place for me and mine.

We took our traditional walk to Gosman's Dock, which is approximately one mile from the resort, walking through other smaller marinas and past some local restaurants to arrive at Montauk's most famous eatery, know only as "Gosman's." The restaurant is made up of three different eating locations, all on the same wharf. The largest is an indoor/outdoor sit-down restaurant facing the entrance to Montauk Point. The smallest is a counter "order and take out" eatery that provides outside seating for its patrons, also facing the entrance to the harbor. This area has many unwanted guests; "fat seagulls" or "baygulls" as many people call them as they are always hanging around the bay looking for a free handout. If diners aren't alert, these flying pirates will swipe the meal right off of their plates. Our favorite place to eat is the two-story restaurant with indoor/outdoor seating facing the busy harbor entrance. We'll get a table on the spacious terrace facing Gardiner's Bay and the entrance to Lake Montauk and spend a couple of hours eating sushi, mussels and lobster salad, washed down with white wine for Barbara and a cold Budweiser for me. The food, coupled with, in my opinion, one of the most beautiful boating scenes to be found in New York, makes for a perfect, relaxing afternoon far away from the stress and strain of our daily lives. Gosman's Dock also features a number of charming shops and boutiques selling nautical gifts, clothing, jewelry, fashionable women's wear (Barbara's favorite), home furnishings, a toy store and my favorite, an ice cream take-out window. The resort has a complimentary jitney that travels around the circuit for the convenience of its guests. After a long walk, large lunch, and some serious shopping by Barbara, it's a nice respite to return to our docking area by bus, instead of walking in the heat of the day. We spent the evening having a light dinner at the open-air restaurant, watching the night lights of the boats moving about, wandering in and out of our view as if they were horizontal traveling stars. The dance music from the bar area attracted us and we joined fellow boaters and hotel guests on the dance floor. We were quite exhausted from our busy day, but we managed to do some Cha-Chas, Rumbas, and Mambos before we retired for the evening.

Montauk also has a checkered history, from whaling to illegal liquor trading during the days of prohibition, with other diverse, questionable activities in between. The first English settlers from Massachusetts found the island inhabited by Native Americans of the Algonquian group, who were loosely divided into bands, grouped together into a confederation under the leadership of the Montauk, Sachem, who was considered to be the ruler from Montauk to the western end of the island. The friendly natives taught their new friends how to hunt wild game, such as deer and wild birds; how to fish, grow corn, squash and beans, and how to gather wild berries, herbs and roots. They taught the Europeans how to hunt whales from canoes and make use of all their body parts. Specifically, how to successfully extract oil from carcasses by burning them in large clam shells and on rock piles. Over the years, the Indians sold off or had their land stolen by manipulative land grabbers. The most notorious case was in 1910, when the railroad heiress Jane Benson won her lawsuit against the Montauk Indians stating that they were not a tribe and had no rights under the various treaties signed between the United States and tribal natives. The State Supreme Court ruled in her favor and the Montauk tribe was abolished, depriving them of any land rights. Eventually, the Benson family purchased Montauk for $151,000.00 from the state and opened the door to the evolution from a pasture culture into a resort area. One of the most important events at the Eastern end of Montauk was when President George Washington commissioned the Montauk Lighthouse in 1797. It was a Coast Guard station for many years and its signal light and foghorn warned ships to stay clear of the treacherous rocky shoals that extend outward from the point. Today the lighthouse is a museum and is visited by over a million tourists annually. Another interesting piece of history or legend has to do with our friend Captain Kidd, who purportedly buried treasure chests of pirate booty in what is now called "Money Pond." No one has ever discovered his buried treasure and, as a matter of fact, the only booty found on the beaches of Montauk have been bottles of liquor from the 13-year prohibition period that were buried on the beaches by bootleggers to be retrieved by their cohorts, when the coast was clear, to transport to New York City for the pleasure of their thirsty customers.

We took the resort's jitney for a 15-minute ride into the fishing and boating town of Montauk, where we had a delightful breakfast and then headed for the beautiful sandy beach, which is within walking distance from town. We spread out on our blankets, books in hands, determined to spend the better part of the day just relaxing and enjoying the tranquility that the sound of the ocean's surf and the saltwater air seems to bring to most people. We rented a large umbrella to protect my delicate light skin from the sun's rays and applied plenty of suntan lotion as an added precaution. Barbara relishes sitting in the sun, perfecting her beautiful dark skin, which makes me envious of her relative immunity to the sun's rays. But when I think about having dark skin and sporting my reddish hair, my envy disappears as it doesn't seem like an attractive combination. When we returned to Mikara, we immediately showered to get rid of the sand that seemed to have invaded every part of our bodies, dressed, and headed to one of our favorite restaurants, the Sea Grille, which is located at Gurney's Inn and features freshly-caught fish and Italian specialty dishes.

We've been visiting Gurney's for many years and always make it a point to have dinner at their oceanfront restaurant. But dinner is only one part of the pleasure we experience when visiting this seaside resort. Having a cocktail before our meal while walking their ocean view terrace, absorbing the Atlantic Ocean's dark blue water and salt air, and then moseying down to their 1,000-foot long beach and spreading out on a chaise lounge, is something we both look forward to during that part of the year when we dream of our next boating vacation at the same place. The surf picks up in the early afternoon from the "many winds" that visit Montauk due to its location. It's engulfed by water on three sides; to the south and east, the Atlantic Ocean pounds its beaches with long, large swells that relentlessly crash onto its shores. On the bay side, although it can get pretty rough at times, there is usually a calming relief from the ocean's intimidating activities.

By the time we sat down for dinner, the surf was pounding the beach with six to eight foot waves, which certainly is not a sailor's ideal boating condition, but does make a panoramic and exciting view of the sea's activity from the safety of the restaurant, which has large viewing windows for its customers' pleasure. We ordered their specialty salad of Prosciutto di Parma, salami, pepperoni, soppresata and Aurecchio, provolone & mozzarella di bufala. Barbara ordered rigatoni with mussels and clams in a red marina sauce; I ordered the world's best (next to my son Steve's), linguini and clams in a white sauce. A bottle of Australian Chardonnay perfectly rounded out the meal. As is customary in Italy, we left the restaurant and went to their coffee bar and ordered an espresso for Barbara and cappuccino for me with a large slice of Italian cheesecake, which we shared. We would remain seated at the booth in the coffee bar for the remainder of the evening. DJ Des and his vocalist, Linda, set up their equipment in the area right outside the bar. They played a variety of music, mostly Hustle and Swing, with some Latin in between. We had a chance to catch up on our Hustle steps, which we seemed to be losing for lack of use. There was enough room on the dance floor for us to spread out and do some of our arm stretching routines in the Hustle. The Hustle can be done in either a four or six count. The four count is a steady, 1-2-3-4, while the six count is 1-2 and 3. We usually do the more popular six count, but if the music is too fast for our old bones, we revert to the four count and enjoy the slower pace. We were able to perform a routine which we don't often have an opportunity to do, because it requires lots of room, but it worked well on that dance floor. It goes like this: we start with a basic 1-2 and 3, and then I swing Barbara to my right holding her left hand until she is shoulder to shoulder along side me. She then does a full turn in my direction, crossing in front of me and catching my left hand in her right, arms fully extended. I then take her right hand with my right hand and put her into a corkscrew (she does a full underarm turn), and we then both step back and return to the basic position. A tricky routine that requires lots of room, but we totally enjoyed doing it with no interference from other dancers. As a matter of fact, many of the people cleared the floor to watch us perform this exciting routine. We danced until the wee hours of the morning, and then returned to Mikara for a good night's sleep.

We rose early the next morning so we could leave on the next leg of our journey to Block Island, Rhode Island, which is about 20 miles East of Montauk, but takes us into some foggy and treacherous waters. Before traveling, we always check the weather reports from the NOAA to make sure that there are no small craft warnings (23 to 38 mph winds) in the area we're traveling to. If there are small craft warnings, we make it a practice not to leave our current location until the inclement weather passes. The report for us was clear sailing ahead, except for some fog and a reminder that there are many fishermen's lobster traps in the waters approaching Block Island. This is a major cruising problem as many of the bright colored markers are either faded or underwater. Hitting one can disable a boat when its line wraps around one or both of a boat's propellers. While cruising this body of water there is also a lot of sea traffic, including large ferries, coming to and from the North and West, and large cruise ships coming from or sailing out to sea.

There is commercial traffic zigzagging all over the place, but the most hazardous vessels to be on the lookout for are naval submarines that practice in and guard these waters. We have been hailed on many occasions by submarines while traveling in the fog, warned of their presence, and told to steer clear of them. So we started out very slowly, about 10 mph hoping to avoid any lobster traps and praying that the heavy fog would burn off. Well, as is common in this area, the fog stayed with us for the whole trip. As a sailor, I have always been fascinated with fog and the challenges and dangers it brings to travelers. A mariner's playground is the waters of the ocean, which also exists in other forms besides liquid, i.e., solid and gas. Liquid evaporates into the air above it as gas cools down and then condenses into rain or snow that falls back into the ocean and again reverts back to liquid. This gives us the atmosphere which protects us from the lethal rays of the sun. Fog occurs when the air around us begins to lose its ability to hold moisture. It's composed of minute water droplets suspended in the atmosphere. The amount of moisture that the atmosphere can hold is a function of temperature. The warmer the air, the more moisture it can hold. The temperature at which the moisture starts to condense is the "dew point." The amount of moisture that can be held in suspension before saturation is called "relative humidity." There are several types of fog, but sailors are mainly concerned with two:

ADVECTION FOG is the type that results from the horizontal movement (advection) of warm moist air over cold water areas. The warm air cools as it passes over cold water and reaches its dew point resulting in fog. The warm air usually emanates from a large source that can keep supplying moist air and is moved to cooler areas by prevailing winds. Therefore, the fog may last for long intervals resulting in low visibility. This type of fog will usually dissipate when the wind changes and the supply of warm moist air ceases. This fog is primarily caused by the drifting of warm, damp air over a colder land or sea surface.

PRECIPITATION FOG, which is also called "steam fog" or "sea smoke," is a special type of advection fog, occurring when cold air moves over warm water. The evaporating warm water is cooled, reaching its dew point, starting the condensation process which results in misty clouds of steam. This type of fog is caused by the addition of moisture to the air through evaporation of rain or drizzle.

We prepared for our journey by reviewing our checklist of "Things to Do Before Casting Off," which included all of the aforementioned Nautical Rules of the Road. Additionally, I had set my radar to pick up any lobster markers and periscopes that might be in front of us so we could avoid them. This slowed our travel down considerably and it took over two hours to reach the entrance of Block Island. Sighting the Red #2 entrance buoy was a relief from the stress of traveling under such uncomfortable boating conditions. The two main buoys when cruising are black and red. When returning from sea, the red buoy should always be on the right side of the boat (starboard) and the black on the left (port). Straying out of their invisible safety lines can cause a boat to go aground and trigger the beginning of a boating nightmare, which could result in the boat sinking or having to call the Coast Guard for a rescue mission. We entered the inlet doing about five miles per hour, which doesn't create a wake and prolongs the life of the rocks that are on either side of the entrance. There are beaches on both sides of the inlet, which makes it imperative not to send any dangerous waves at the bathers. Our destination after passing through the inlet and Coast Guard Station's beach, which are on the right side, was Champlin's Marina and Resort. This required navigating around many boats, anchored or on moorings. The mooring area is one of the most popular on the East Coast because it's considered a safe harbor for boats, has great clam beds for digging delicious soft (piss) clams, and its pristine beaches. An added bonus for the island is the 1,000-plus year-round residents who welcome visitors with their New England friendly and charming manners.

Champlin's Marina is a full-service facility, located in New Harbor on Great Salt Pond. It has gas docks, showers and laundry service, a marine chandlery, and an outdoor swimming pool with a restaurant and Tiki Bar. This renowned Trader's Tiki Bar, is famous for its mudslide drinks, music and aggressive dancing. It also boasts a picnic area, a private beach, an ice cream parlor, its own movie theater, and all the water toys imaginable. This is always a stop we look forward to visiting on our annual boating excursions, as it's without a doubt, a well thought out vacation spot and a boater-friendly resort. When our kids traveled with us, this was their favorite play land, as there is a never-ending amount of activities to keep children busy, especially its large pool and children's playground. After tucking Mikara into her slip and washing her down to show off her shiny hull, we embarked on our annual ritual of walking to the island's only town, New Shoreham, which is approximately one mile from the marina. Walking to town along the gorgeous Baby Beach, which is a favorite place for parents to bring their children, brings to mind how few unspoiled places remain in the world. Block Island is certainly one of them, which is why it was named by The Nature Conservancy as one of the twelve natural "Last Great Places" remaining in the Western Hemisphere. Exiting the beach at the Surf Hotel put us in the center of the bustling town.

The busy, little, three-block long town is lined with boutique shops, a supermarket, a couple of ice cream parlors, several Victorian-style hotels and, at the end of the strip, Ballard's Restaurant, which is next to the ferry dock in Old Harbor and a small, approximately 30 boat marina. If the boats raft to each other, this number can increase substantially. The amount of mopeds in and around town is distracting, as the riders didn't seem to think they were required to obey traffic rules. They reminded me of our visit many years ago, when my 16-year-old son, Steve, decided to rent a moped and roam the island. We caught up to him in town and Barbara immediately decided that he was too young to be driving the small vehicle and took it away from him (Barbara is 5' 2," Steve is 6' 2"). She sat on the seat, turned the gas handle, and, in an instant, crashed into a parked car, flying head over heals onto the car's roof. After returning the moped to the garage and bickering as to who was going to pay for the damages--my unlicensed 16-year-old son or the owner of the bike who rented it to an unlicensed driver--we decided to split the repair bill. We immediately went to lunch and I asked the waitress for some ice and a napkin to place on Barbara's swollen eye, which she was glad to do. Barbara was wearing an outstanding blouse, black with yellow butterflies; a combination that couldn't be missed from any distance. Well, the next day, on the front page of the local newspaper there was a cartoon of a lady flying through the air, wearing a black blouse with yellow butterflies. The headline read: "Should people over 40 be allowed to drive mopeds on Block Island?" To compound the embarrassment, flyers of the cartoon were posted all over town. We didn't realize that there was a movement on the island to ban mopeds because of the amount of accidents that they were causing and the noise coming from their motors; they used Barbara's mishap as an example of the carelessness that usually accompanies inexperienced moped drivers and the resultant accidents.

In 1524, the island was sighted by the Italian captain, Giovanni de Verrazano, who was an explorer in the service of France. He named the island Luisa after Louise of Savoy, the Queen Mother of France. At that time, it seemed all of the first explorers to this hemisphere were Italians. Columbus sailed for Spain, John Cabot (Giovanni Capoto) sailed for England, and Amerigo Vespucci sailed for Portugal and Spain. Although Verrazano was the first to sight the island, it was named after a Dutch explorer, Adriaen Block, who explored the area almost 100 years later in 1614. The Europeans found the Manissean tribe of the Narragansett's Indians living in peace on the island and quickly, through barter or manipulation, conquered the island and raised flags of conquest to prove their sovereignty. The Indians called the island Manisses, which means "Island of Little God," and lived for centuries within its unspoiled splendor of nature's bounty. Fortunately we can still find a major part of the island in the same condition that the Native American's enjoyed. On the Southeast part of the island is Mohegan Bluffs, still pretty much the same natural beauty as in the pre-European days, except for a stairway from the cliff down to Bluffs Beach. There are 141 wooden steps from the top of the stairs to the rocky bottom, and then on to a beautiful pristine beach, where nude bathers, although against the law in Block Island, are scattered throughout this isolated area. Mohegan Bluffs got its name from the unfortunate fate of the invading Mohegan Indians, who were defeated in battle by the Narragansett Indians on the cliff and were thrown down to their final resting places on the rocks surrounding the site (these were not the last of the Mohegans). Sharing the area is the Atlantic seacoast's brightest lighthouse, perched over 200-feet above sea level, which warns seamen of the perils of the many treacherous rocks surrounding the region. On a clear day from this high vantage point, you can see Montauk, New York, with the naked eye, just peeking out above the blue waters of the Atlantic Ocean; truly one of nature's visual delights. Many of the dunes surrounding the island are part of the Block Island National Wildlife Refuge, home to many species, including the Piping Plover and American Burying Beetle. Also, there is a 230-acre glacial outwash basin, Rodman's Hollow, near the Southern shore of the island that has several walking trails. The Northern section of the island is a great underdeveloped natural area that is often visited by birds making a stop along the Atlantic Flyway. On and on and on, the beauty continues. Hopefully, Block Island will remain an unspoiled natural region to be enjoyed by the never-ending visiting nature lovers.

We boarded Mikara for a well-deserved afternoon nap, and when we awoke the sun was setting and it was starting to get dark outside; what a great snooze. We dressed and took a cab over to Ballard's Restaurant for some dinner and dancing. Another delight of the island is its comfortable temperatures; in July the average high is 77 degrees dropping to 64 degrees in the evenings. This makes Barbara very happy, as she can wear a nice outfit while dancing without getting too uncomfortable.

How does one explain Ballard's Beach Club and Restaurant? It's truly a hybrid consisting of a hotel with a porch that welcomes visitors to sit and relax; an ice cream window; a spacious beach with a life guard on duty and volley ball nets; an outside Tiki Bar overlooking the Atlantic Ocean, where one can enjoy a sea breeze drink while enjoying the ocean breeze; a combo band filling the air with music; a large al fresco dining area; and an indoor circular bar that seems to accommodate up to 100 people. There is also an inside dining area that certainly services 100 diners, a piano bar, a dance floor and, in the evening, a variety of dance bands. A unique feature of the building is the collection of boats' name plaques that hang on the inside walls, such as, "Smuggler's Cove," "Our Dream," "SeaRest," "Our Home," "Trident," and "Mikara III" (our 35-foot Chris Craft). Well, all of this went up in smoke many years ago, which totally depressed us at the time. It took a couple of years to rebuild the facility exactly as it was before the fire, minus the old boats' name plaques that decorated the walls, have been replaced by newer and shinier ones. So we visited the new Ballard's and were pleasantly surprised to see a replica of one of our favorite entertainment places totally restored and swinging.

Ballard's is renowned for its family-style lobsters, cracked and in pieces and served at the dinner table in a hot pot, ready to be devoured. It boasts of serving more lobster plates than any other restaurant in the world. Looking around and watching the many people enjoying their meals validated their claim. Customers were eating inside and also enjoying al fresco dining to the sounds of music from the band harmonizing with the Atlantic Ocean's surf. Some of the diners seemed to be in somewhat of a trance, eyeballs rolling and making pleasant sounds while savoring their ambrosia. Although I'm not a lobster lover, I joined Barbara in ordering a pot full of the red pieces of crustaceans that seem to be universally loved by everyone, except me. She loves when I join her in this feast, as she can have all the pieces that I find difficult to eat. We strategically chose our seats so that after dinner we could be near the piano bar and our favorite robust piano man, Jim Kelly.

Jim was known as Ballard's Balladeer due to the many songs that he sang that have folk stories to them, such as: "Michael Rowed the Boat Ashore," "Good Night Irene," and "You Are My Sunshine." Everyone enjoyed singing along with him till 9:00 P.M., when his tour of duty ended. His famous Chicken Dance is a favorite of many customers. The dancers imitate chickens, including their clucks, while bending and raising their arms and squatting and walking around in that position like chickens. It has to be the most embarrassing display that anyone can perform, but we all did it, and totally enjoyed the fun, especially after a couple of drinks.

He also plays music for the Electric Slide line dance that all the girls love doing; occasionally a couple of guys will join the line and stumble along while trying to keep up with their friends. There are 22 steps in the dance, which are performed as follows: The group forms a line all facing the same direction, let's say "North" towards Jim. Everyone travels to the right for steps 1 to 4 and touches their left foot next to their right foot while clapping on 4. Traveling to the left, for steps 5 to 8 clapping and step touching the right foot next to the left on step 8 and clapping. Everyone walks back for steps 9 to 12, and then steps on the right, then left, then right and touch the left foot next to the right and clap on step 12. Stepping forward with their left foot for step 13, tapping the right toe at the left heel for step 14, and ending with a clap. On 15, step backward on the right foot and tap the left foot at the right heel for step 16, finishing with a clap. This sequence should resemble a rocking motion. Repeat the step touch sequence, dance steps 13 through 16, for steps 17 to 20. Use the left foot to step forward for step 21 and quarter-turn to the left ending with a hop for step 22. The group now faces "West" and is ready to repeat the steps starting with step one and continuing until the song ends. Everyone that does this line dance loves it and after a couple of sets the group started to look like a choreographed professional production.

We woke up the next morning to the call of "Andiamo, Andiamo." It was Aldo from the popular Aldo's Bakery selling morning treats, such as blueberry and cranberry muffins, danishes, and finger cakes, all freshly baked and being sold from his 18-foot Boston Whaler run-about boat. It's amazing how many boaters wait for his "Andiamo" so they can begin their breakfasts, especially sailors on their boats at anchor or on moorings that do not have easy access to restaurants. We ordered our favorite blueberry muffins and quickly demolished them while drinking our morning hazelnut-flavored coffee; what a great way to start a morning in the picture perfect marina at Block Island. We decided to take an alternate path into town by walking along the streets through the Block Island Boat Basin Marina and Payne's docks. Both docks accommodate ferries from the West and North mainland. Passing Smuggler's Cove brought to mind our old friend Captain Kidd who tried to negotiate his freedom when docked on this island, but was soon captured and returned to "Dear Old England" for his final appearance at the end of a hangman's noose. He is purported to have buried some of his treasure on this island, but none has ever been discovered, or if it was located, no one advertised the event. Walking along the water side of Water Street into town we stopped at the Victorian-style Surf Hotel, built in 1873, to enjoy a cup of coffee and sit down for a spell on their rocking chairs, which are located on their expansive porch and facing the center of town. This is a great spot to rock away while watching the promenade of people passing by, while playing a game of checkers. After drinking our coffee and congratulating Barbara for beating me without any mercy or sympathy, we proceeded to visit some trinket shops, trendy boutiques, a book store, and a couple of local craft stores. By the time Barbara was satisfied with her "daily shopping fix" it was time for lunch. There were many al fresco bistros to choose from, but one of our favorites is the Victorian-style Harborside Inn, which has an extensive lunch and dinner menu and dated furniture throughout its lobby and eating area. It has a great vantage point to view the comings and going of the ferry and boat traffic traversing Old Harbor. The Inn has a nice salad bar that we took advantage of to complement their New England clam chowder, which is served in a bread bowl and is delicious beyond words, especially when drinking their house specialty beer; a concoction called, Black and Tan, which is Guinness mixed with regular ale. When stirred briskly, it turns into beer malt. Umm!!

It is from the porch at the Harborside Inn, facing due east, that the submarine "Unterseeboot 853" was sunk by the U.S. Navy near the end of WWII. It had just been in a successful Battle of Point Judith, Rhode Island, and sunk the collier Black Point when American warships located her and sent her to the bottom of the ocean, just seven miles east of where we were sitting. This very submarine attacked the Queen Mary in the Atlantic, when she was carrying American soldiers and equipment to Europe. The sub was warded off by planes from nearby aircraft carriers, but not without damaging three planes before making its escape. So it must have been a celebrated day when "Unterseeboot 853" was sent down to the bottom of the sea to fulfill its destiny as an artificial fishing reef along with the two other German U-Boats that were sunk in the general vicinity earlier in the war.

While having lunch, we heard that John F. Kennedy, Jr.'s plane had crashed on his way to Martha's Vineyard. It happened on July 16, 1999; he was going to drop off his sister-in-law, Lauren Bessette, on the island, while he and his wife, Carolyn, were on their way to the Kennedy Compound in Hyannis, Massachusetts, to attend the wedding of his cousin, Rory Kennedy. His flight plan indicated that he was piloting a Piper Saratoga II HP single-engine aircraft from Essex, New Jersey, to the island, and then on to Hyannis. The Coast Guard and other naval crafts were in search for the wreckage and everyone was warned not to enter the area around Martha's Vineyard. It was determined that he didn't have much experience flying at night or in fog, and he probably became confused as to where the island was and crashed somewhere in the vicinity. We were scheduled to arrive at Menemsha, Martha's Vineyard, the next day, and immediately called to determine if the port was open; it was not, the whole area was off limits until further notice. Everyone on Block Island seemed to be in a state of shock at the news of the country's fair-haired JFK, Jr., having met such a sorrowful demise at the age of 38. It was inconceivable that another Kennedy could meet such a horrible fate at so young an age. The rest of the day we joined everyone on the island in a vigil waiting and praying for some good news.

We joined some friends for dinner and prayer at the Spring House Hotel, which is considered one of the island's most elegant historic landmarks. It's one of the oldest Victorian-style buildings on the island. Built in 1852, it has withstood over 150 years of natures challenges. Its wrap-around veranda, mansard roof, and distinctive cupola, rises from a 15-acre promontory overlooking the Atlantic Ocean and Block Island's foothills. The view is considered one of the most magnificent seascapes on the East Coast. Coincidentally, this picturesque location has provided the formal setting for some of the Kennedys' weddings. The atmosphere in the restaurant was solemn as religious services were being conducted for the recovery of the passengers of the plane crash. Their survival was no longer a possibility based on information from authorities at the search site, the best that could be hoped for was the recovery of their bodies. Everyone at our dinner table ordered modestly, as if semi-fasting in some way would change the events to a more palatable conclusion.

We left Block Island for Martha's Vineyard on July 18th, but were told by the Harbor Master of the island that the area was still under surveillance by naval vessels and helicopters and that we would have to bypass it. We headed for our next destination, Nantucket, Massachusetts, which is approximately 80 miles from Block Island. If we were lucky and had good weather with no unforeseen mishaps, it would take about five to six hours to reach "The Grey Lady," named after the intense fog that usually visits the island. The NOAA weather forecast was pretty good for the day, so we were off on the next leg of our trip by 10:00 A.M. That body of water can be very tricky as currents from several different areas meet along the route to Vineyard and Nantucket Sound. The strong currents from Buzzards Bay can cause some large broadside waves on the left (port) side of the boat, or the Atlantic Ocean's currents can cause some pretty big swells on the right (starboard) side of the boat. While approaching Menemsha Bight, our original destination, we spotted some debris in the water that looked strange and could possibly have been from the plane crash; my map of this area has an "X" on it, marking that location. We immediately called the Coast Guard and gave them our Latitude and Longitude so they could investigate; they thanked us and within minutes, boats were at the site. Unfortunately, it was debris from the aircraft which sent us into a depressed state causing Barbara to cry uncontrollably. We moved from the area slowly and had to do some tricky maneuvering to get past all the naval vessels in the water around the island. We called Nantucket Boat Basin and spoke to the dock master, George, who we have known for many years, and explained our circumstances hoping he would have an empty slip for us. He said to "come on in, very few people have been able to move their boats because of the restricted areas around the accident." We were delighted that he had available space for Mikara. It avoided our having to make an unexpected stop in Cape Cod, which meant we would then have to cross over to Nantucket and then back to the Cape again, passing some pretty nasty shallow waters, especially dangerous when pea soup (fog) is present. The currents were very strong as we approached Nantucket Sound; luckily for us, it was coming from behind us and pushed Mikara to a cruising speed of 22 mph which we had never achieved at 3,400 rpms, it usually takes the engines about 4,000 rpms to get her to move that fast. But we got to Nantucket much sooner then anticipated and just in time to avoid the strong winds from the Atlantic Ocean which were starting to pick up. There is a very narrow inlet at the entrance to Nantucket, so it's imperative that boats stay on the right side of the channel, especially if ferries or commercial crafts are coming toward you. After leaving the channel, Nantucket Boat Basin's bulkheaded marina is immediately apparent on the right side of the harbor. Waiting for permission to enter from the dock master, George, is always a tricky situation, especially when the wind starts to pick up, as it did. Mikara has a tendency to be pushed away from the entrance of the marina when it gets windy, so getting behind the bulkheaded sea walls took some nifty maneuvering. George gave us our docking assignment as soon as we called him on our VHF radio. I throttled up to get to the marina's entrance, but had to immediately throttle down upon entering as the steering area is very narrow and winding. After zigzagging past other boats, I finally reached my docking slip and backed in with the help of the prevailing strong winds. It was a long and tedious trip, and we were glad to be tied up at such a pristine and boater-friendly facility. We have been going to that marina for over 15-years and are always thrilled with excitement when tying Mikara up at our temporary home. The Nantucket Boat Basin Marina is at the end of town, which makes for a picturesque view when looking from the town at the marina or from the marina at the beautifully landscaped town. The Waterway Guide, Northern edition, describes the marina perfectly: "Nantucket Boat Basin sets an industry standard for service at its transient marina. You will find 243 slips to accommodate boats from 30 to 280-feet in length, as well as dockside electricity, water, fuels, ice, public phones and waste disposal, with individualized pump-out stations designed to reach virtually every slip. Ashore are restrooms and showers, a large 24/7 coin-operated laundry, rental cottages, rustic artists' studios along the wharves, and even a park for pets' needs. The Boat Basin's concierge, whose headquarters is located on the fuel dock, will arrange restaurant reservations, sightseeing trips, car rentals, medical appointments and baby sitting services." Well that just about says it all for this pristine marina whose staff is professional and boasts of having polite, experienced dock boys and dock girls to accommodate its guests.

Nantucket Island is one of the most natural and beautiful islands that I have ever had the pleasure of visiting. It has its own idyllic persona derived from its beaches and the abundance of beautifully landscaped designed and natural wild flowers. The island is only three and a half miles from North to South and 14 miles long, with miles of clean, well-maintained beaches. It's rich with Scotch broom, bayberry, beach plum, grape, holly, heather, huckleberry, bearberry and hundreds of wildflowers. Its Milestone Road cranberry bog is one of the world's largest and its aromatic flavor seems to flow throughout the island. We have seen deer, pheasants, cottontail rabbits and all kinds of birds on our walks around the island. As a bonus from nature, Harbor Seals are seen year round sun bathing and playing off the beaches. Whale watching is still viable by sightseeing boats that guarantee sighting them on every excursion. One of the islands biggest tourist attractions is biking; people travel from all over the country with their bikes, cross over on one of the ferries from the mainland, and spend days biking on the many excellent paths throughout nature's paradise. Some years ago, our son Steve and his wife Donna joined us on the island with their bikes. We thought we would spend some quality time with them, but we lost them for most of their visit to the "call of the wild," Nantucket. On each of their trips, Donna would gather wild flowers and return to Mikara with them. By the time they left the island, our boat looked like a florist's shop. Biking is one of several methods of transportation on the island; cars are discouraged and must pay exorbitant fees to cross over on the ferries, but there are many auto rentals on the island. Taxis are an alternative if other transportation is not available, but its shuttle bus system is most efficient and affordable. The Nantucket Regional Transit Authority (NRTA) provides an island-wide seasonal fixed-rate shuttle service and a year round "Your Island Ride" van service. In season, shuttle buses run every 15-minutes from the center of town. The fares are reasonable, from $1.00 to $2.00 each way with discounts for senior citizens and no charge for children under six. Our favorite method of transportation is by foot, as walking around the island can be a pleasant way to spend the day, if the temperature is in the low 80s. When it gets near 90 degrees, we prefer the shuttle buses.

We decided to have dinner our first evening in one of our favorite restaurants, The Harbor House, which also has dancing till the wee hours of the morning. After a light dinner, which we usually have when we plan on dancing, we entered the nightclub area which has a large circular bar and tables around the perimeter of the dance floor. The entertainment is provided by Phil on a synthesizer keyboard that he makes sound like a full orchestra and his beautiful, blonde, blue-eyed wife Elizabeth, whose voice can be ranked with that of Doris Day. When this young couple sees us entering the hall on our annual visits, they immediately play Barbara's favorite song, "Under the Sea." Over the years we have become friendly with them and some of the local ballroom dancers and, in addition to Barbara's favorite song, we are greeted with much ululation from our fellow dancers. Elizabeth and our friends joined together in singing the song, with our harmonizing:

"The seaweed is always greener in somebody else's lake.

You dream about going up there, but that is a big mistake.

Just look at the world around you, right here on the ocean floor.

What more is you looking for? Under the sea, under the sea.

Darling it's better down where it's wetter, take it from me.

Up on the shore they work all day, out in the sun they slave away.

While we're devoting full time to floating, Under the Sea, ha ha . . .

Down here all the fish is happy as after the waves they roll.

The fish on the land ain't happy, they sad cause they in the bowl!

But fish in the bowl is lucky, they in for a worser fate.

One day when the boss gets hungry, guess whose going to be on the plate?

Wo-no, under the sea, under the sea, under the sea.

Nobody beat us, fry us and eat us in frickazee. We what the land folks loves to cook.

Under the sea we off the hook, we've got no troubles, life is the bubbles.

Under the sea, under the sea, under the sea, under the sea.

Since life is sweet here, we got the beat here, naturally (naturally-ee-ee-ee).

Even the sturgeon and the ray, they get the urge and start to play.

We've got the spirit, you've got to hear it. Under the sea.

The lute play the flute, the carp play the harp, the plaice play the bass and they sounding sharp. The bass play the brass, the chub play the tub, the fluke is the duke of soul (yeah).

The ray, he can play the lings on the strings, the trout acting out, the blackfish he sings,

The smelt and the sprat, they know where it's at, and oh, that blowfish blow!"

Of course, the only one that knew all of the words is Elizabeth and maybe Phil, but we all somehow ended the song together. We joined some of our friends and spoke of the tragic Kennedy plane crash and the continuing search for the doomed passengers. We did some minor dancing that evening as none of us could get in the mood to jump around, so we spent most of the evening just discussing what happened in our lives since we last saw each other. Phil and Elizabeth joined us and led us in a prayer for the safety of the crew and the recovery of the wreckage. We ended the evening with lots of Amen's and made plans to join some of our friends at their weekly afternoon tea dance. We walked several blocks to Mikara, on cobblestone streets that usually play havoc with my feet. That night was no exception, as I was wearing dancing shoes with very thin soles and by the time we got to the boat, my feet needed a warm foot bath.

The next morning, we turned on the radio to get the progress of the rescue ships; the bodies still were not found, but some wreckage had been located. I'm sure the debris that we alerted the Coast Guard to was a part of that recovery, but nothing significant had been uncovered for sure. We decided to take advantage of the cool weather, about 80 degrees, and walk around the island ending our journey at the Nantucket Memorial Airport, which was the fictitious setting for the sit-com "Wings." But as the great Scottish poet, Robert Burns, wrote: "The best laid plans of mice and men gang aft agley." Truer words were never spoken, for we were in for some surprises on our journey. We mapped out our walkathon carefully, beginning at the cobblestone street outside our marina. These streets are inhabited by surprising colonial, Georgian, and Greek revival houses of ships' captains and whaling merchants, dating back to the 18th century and still remain intact. Many of the houses have engraved plates which identify the dates they were built and the original occupants' names. We stopped at the Nantucket Whaling and the Life-Saving museums, which gave us insight and a better understanding of the dangers that these mariners faced at a time when they had to go to sea to survive, but "didn't have to come back." To appreciate the importance of whaling on the lives of these brave seamen, some history of Nantucket is necessary. It wasn't until 1602 that Captain Bartholomew Gosnold of Falmouth, England, sailed his bark Concord past the bluffs of Siasconset and mapped out the territory for dear old England. The 2,500 native Americans living in peace on the island were the Wampanoag Indians; they called their home Nantican, Natocke, or Nautican, which is thought to mean "far away island" or "in the midst of waters." The island was deeded to Thomas Mayhew by the English Crown in 1641. Up until that time, Indians from Cape Cod and Martha's Vineyard sought refuge on Nantucket from the European interlopers and consolidated their energy and skills with the local natives to fish and harvest whales that washed up on the shore. The

Europeans didn't settle on the island until 1659, when Mayhew sold his interest to the "nine original purchasers," for 30 pounds and two beaver hats, one for Thomas and the other for his wife. English ingenuity brought whaling offshore and, with the help and skill of the Native Americans, Nantucket became the world's leading whaling port from the mid-17th and to early 18th centuries. Prior to the colonials' invasion, the natives harvested Drift and Right whales that were near the shore or washed up on the beaches. These whales were 30 to 60-feet in length and weighed upward to 60 tons. The English soon saw that a profit could be made by commercializing whale hunting. Whale oil for lamps, whalebones and ivory for ladies' corsets, buggy whips, parasol ribs and scrimshaw, proved to be a rainmaker and the main industry of the island. It didn't take long for the new settlers to man canoes, usually with up to six sailors, to seek out the V-shaped sprays of the cetaceans. Harpooning became an art form; the slow moving whales would surface and come up for air, making them an easy target for the whalers. They would throw their harpoons deep into the whale's blubber and then wait for the cetacean to play out the line that was attached to a log or large wood block. Dragging the heavy weight would soon exhaust the whale; its blubber would keep it afloat until the crewmen concluded their business. Many foolish whalers would have the end of their harpoon lines attached to their boats, which caused havoc in many cases, especially when the whale would submerge, sometime taking their boats into the depths of the ocean. The expression "Nantucket sleigh ride," came from the exploits of these brave seamen who foolishly chose to attach harpoon lines to their boats instead of safely attaching them to logs or heavy blocks of wood.

Walking along the bustling cobblestoned, three-block town, we stopped and browsed antique galleries specializing in scrimshaw, China trade porcelains, old hooked rugs, country furniture, weather vanes, English antiques, and maritime artifacts. The most fascinating items sold in many of the up-scale stores are whale ivory lightship baskets, which are decorated with nautical scrimshaw created by sailors of bygone days and lightship attendants. The starting price of these begin at around $800.00 and can cost into the tens of thousand of dollars if they are very old and designed by famous artists. Today it is illegal to use whalebones or ivory for artistic purposes, so these original baskets keep increasing in value. It's amusing to see many ladies walking around town with these baskets hanging from their arms, as if they were showing off trophies or badges of honor. I bought a miniature one decorated with a plastic design of a whale for my Xmas tree that cost 50 bucks and proudly hang it on my seven-foot artificial tree annually. We moseyed along and explored some of the art galleries that carry everything from inexpensive prints to expensive oil paintings. Nantucket is a haven for artists who find its natural and landscaped beauty ideal for expressing and challenging their talents. There are many paintings of the island's beaches, flower-laden houses and narrow, winding paths leading to the sea; all enhancing the character and charm of the area and for sale at reasonable prices. We visited some of the shops that featured gifts, trinkets, clothing, and many local craftsmen's artistic nautical carvings. I purchased small carvings of a Nantucket lightship and an old man of the sea. They both proudly appear on my Xmas tree every year.

During the summer season, the population of the island reaches 50,000-plus people from its year-round residency of 10,000. The influx of tourists and summer residents keeps the island's commercial establishments busy and the town's streets crowded, so it was a relief to head out of town away from the crowds to our final location; Nantucket Memorial Airport, which is located a little over three miles from the town. I was wearing comfortable sneakers, but my feet were killing me from walking on the town's cobblestone pavement. It was also close to noon, and the sun was starting to throw off more heat then we expected. From the town we headed South on Orange Street toward Gardener Court and walked a mile to the traffic circle. This is where we got into trouble. We stopped and asked a woman in a coffee shop how far the airport was. She said it was "just a few minutes up the road." So we purchased some large cold soft drinks, which we desperately needed as we were both getting weary from walking on the uneven roads and from the temperature rising to the upper 80s. We began our "Few minutes walk" and couldn't fathom why we weren't reaching our destination in that period of time. Well, evidently the lady we asked for directions thought we were traveling by car and her "few minutes" was in motorized time, not walking time. The two and a half mile walk took forever, we were sweating out of control and our feet were literally on fire. There was absolutely no place along the road to take shelter and when we finally reached the airport, I was tempted to run to it for shelter, but lacked the energy to do so.

We were facing the entrance to the three runway airport, expecting to see some resemblance to the fictional Tom Nevers Field in the popular sit-com "Wings" that ran from 1990 to 1997, but there was none. The show was one of our favorites; it was about the Hackett brothers, Joe and Brian, played by Timothy Daly and Steven Weber who were pilots and operated Sandpiper Airline from Nantucket airport. Joe plays a highly responsible but mildly neurotic and compulsively neat pilot who owns the one-plane Sandpiper Airline. He originally planned to launch the airline with Carol, his fiancé working behind the ticket counter, but his brother Brian ran off with her, causing a falling out between the brothers that lasted throughout the comedy's long TV run. Other cast members were Tony Shalhoub, of Monk fame, as an oddball cab driver, and Crystal Bernard as the on-again, off- again girl friend. We rushed into the air-conditioned waiting room and I almost collapsed with delight from the refreshing cold air conditioning caressing my overheated sweaty body. The inside of the airport was a replica of the sit-com, so we were immediately at home sitting on the small cafeteria counter seats and ordering extra large glasses of water to cool us off and large ice cream sodas to make sure our bodies would pleasantly recover from our uncomfortable walkathon. We decided then and there that, in the future, we would either ride bikes or take the shuttle bus or a taxicab for any walking distance of over one mile. Accordingly, we called a taxicab to take us back to Mikara, which took all of 15 refreshing minutes.

As soon as we got to Mikara, we showered, donned our bathing suits and went directly to the White Elephant Hotel, which is a few minutes from the marina, and jumped into their delicious swimming pool. I could feel my body sizzling as I swam underwater for the full length of the pool, coming up for air, and then submerging for a return underwater trip. The pool is one of our mandatory stops on our visits to Nantucket. Fortunately, it's owned by the same organization that operates the marina that Mikara is docked at which gives us unlimited use of the hotel and its facilities. We made previous arrangements to meet our dear friends Elaine and Austin Lyon, who are owners of the 48-foot Gulf Star, Sea Lyon. They keep their boat at the Nantucket marina for the whole summer, returning to our marina in Greenport for the winter months. This couple is so well liked that they are considered honorary citizens of Nantucket by the locals. We also enjoy their company in Florida where we have homes only a few miles away from each other. After lots of hugs and kisses, we spread out on our shaded chaise lounges and ordered refreshing drinks to sip while we caught up on the latest gossip. After a couple of hours, we decided to meet for dinner that evening. We said our goodbyes and headed back to Mikara for well deserved naps. There was still no news of JFK, Jr.

We met Elaine and Austin at the "Brotherhood of Thieves" restaurant which was only a short walk from our marina. The name of the eatery is taken from the title of an 1844 pamphlet written on Nantucket by Stephen S. Foster, in which he vigorously attacked those who continued to support slavery. The island has always been known for its tolerance. Even during the Revolutionary War, Patriots, Tories and Quaker pacifists coexisted on the island. The Quakers were the first to develop the island, and believed that all their children, male and female, should have the same education and nurtured independence and freedom as a way of life. That spirit provided fertile ground for abolishing slavery and encouraging women's rights. The island boasts of such distinguished women as Abiah Folger, mother of Benjamin Franklin, who was born on the island in 1667, and Maria Mitchell, a groundbreaker for women in American science, also born on the island, in 1818. Rugged individualism, personal liberty, and encouraging eccentricity are still alive and doing well on the "Grey Lady."

With this bit of history, we entered the bistro and found what I had hoped for; rustic brick, wooden beams, darkly stained furniture, and a roaring fireplace. It immediately gave me the feeling of what it must have been like during those historical days of yesteryear. We were in a Revolutionary War atmosphere and ready to order some "dark ale and pork loins." Everyone had different ideas of what food to order, but they all went for the fish dishes, except for me. Broiled Seasonal Scallops for Barbara, Fisherman's Stew for Austin, and baked Seafood Casserole for Elaine. Believe it or not, I ordered dark ale and crispy pork loin. Before leaving the Brotherhood of Thieves, we checked the status of JFK, Jr., and found there was still no news of any discovery.

The first thing we did the next morning was turn on the TV for an update of the naval search. Additional ships with sophisticated sensors had arrived and gathered offshore to continue probing for any wreckage of the aircraft. Investigators released new data that portrayed the final half minute of JFK, Jr.'s doomed flight as an "uncontrolled plunge into the sea." Although we expected that news, we were greatly sadden by the event and decided to do some sightseeing as a distraction.

A particular piece of the American history that we learned at the Brotherhood of Thieves Restaurant tweaked our curiosity, especially Barbara's, as she is an avid amateur stargazer. Maria (pronounced Ma-RYE-ah) Mitchell, astronomer, librarian, and 19th century intellectual; first cousin to Benjamin Franklin, four times removed, was born on the island in 1818. She earned international fame and was awarded a gold medal from the King of Denmark for discovering a telescopic comet. This discovery resulted in her being the first woman elected to a fellowship in the American Academy of Arts and Science, and the first woman Professor of Astronomy in the United States. She also promoted women's suffrage and higher education and, as President of the American Association for the Advancement of Women, she was able to forward her beliefs with authority. We headed straight for the Maria Mitchell Observatory & Museum to learn more about this incredible lady who also discovered that sunspots are whirling vertical cavities and not clouds, as previously thought.

We were surprised to see about 50 children, ranging from 10 to 15-years old, attending celestial demonstrations at the observatory. We joined in one of the classes and learned how to observe the sun by making a hole in a piece of paper and allowing the sun to shine through and reflect onto a table. We joined a tour and explored a scale-model of the solar system, a planar sundial, and even observed sunspots. Barbara couldn't wait to climb the ladder to the old telescope and sample some daylight sights of the distant sky. She was determined to return at night, time permitting, to further explore the solar system.

We decided to visit Elaine and Austin on their boat, which was on the side of the marina close to the entrance and bordered by half a dozen art shops. They invited us to join them for lunch, which we gladly accepted and decided that the best place in town on a hot mid-80 degree day was the pool at the hotel. We went there and spent the rest of the afternoon just lounging around and taking delightfully refreshing dips into the pool. We invited them to join us for some ballroom dancing in the evening and to swing and sway to the music of Sammy Kaye, but Elaine was having some trouble with her leg, so they had to decline. The latest update on the Kennedy tragedy was that more debris was found in the water off of Martha's Vineyard.

We took the shuttle bus to the quaint town of Siasconset, commonly known as Sconset, which took about 15-minutes. The dance was at the "Casino." It took its name from the Italian word "cascina" or "little house." Casinos were popular in the 18th century and were built for recreational and sporting activities; this club was anything but "little." This venue had a 2,000-plus square foot dance floor, in great condition for dancing. The facility, which includes tennis courts and conference rooms, was built in 1900 as a private club and has a patina of elegance, shingled buttresses, enclosed front and side porches, and dense landscaping. We were seated at a table for eight with four dancers from our Harbor House group and a couple of professional instructors that traveled from Cape Cod, Massachusettes, to see and dance to the fabulous music of Sammy Kaye's Orchestra. The band was directed by "the Professor," Roger Thorpe, trumpeter extraordinaire, and consisted of 16 musicians, including two vocalists. Their music filled the large hall and attracted the 200-plus patrons to the dance floor to do their thing. They played "It Isn't Fair," "Harbor Lights," "Daddy," "Sugar Blues," "The Angels Sing," and "You Made Me Love You." All of these, and many more, were the favorites of Maestro Sammy and made his band one of the most popular during the age of Big Band music, which is seeing an amazing revival today. We danced around the floor to Foxtrots, Waltzes, Quicksteps, and all the Latin dances with plenty of room to move around and enjoy the spaciousness of the venue. We introduced ourselves and asked Roger if he would play our favorite Tango, La Cumparsita. He said "No sweat," and played our Tango as the next number. Much to our surprise, he announced: "Mike and Barbara requested a Tango and here it is." Because of the announcement very few people got up to dance, so there we were, in the center of the large dance floor doing a Tango exhibition. Fortunately we were well trained in American Tango and performed doing some nice contra moves, close balancing rotations, and double cortes. We even threw in a couple of kicks, which received spontaneous applause from the folks in attendance. We quickly returned to our seats and spent the rest of the evening trying to be invisible, because we were slightly embarrassed at the announcement that caught us unprepared. Roger did something that was unique. In keeping with maestro Sammy's tradition, he announced: "So you want to lead a band? Okay, I need four volunteers to come up, one at a time, to take my place and lead the band, the winner will be awarded a prize." So, one at a time, the four conductors led the band for about one minute, when it was over each were presented to the audience to measure which director did the best job, whoever received the most applause would win. Wouldn't you know it, they all received the same response and each was awarded a music tape of the fabulous Sammy Kaye Orchestra. Our Nantucket friends reminded us that they were having a Tea Dance the next afternoon and invited us to join them. The evening ended with our exchanging telephone numbers with the couple from Hyannis, promising them that we would give them a call when we were in their town the following week.

The next morning, naval search teams announced that they were continuing to look for debris, but gave up hope of recovering any of the party alive. The flags in Nantucket were already flying at half mast and the buzz was, "Would John still be alive if he didn't detour his flight from Hyannis to Martha's Vineyard to accommodate his sister-in-law, Lauren Bessette? Would the bright lights from the larger city have guided him to safety?" Well, we will never know.

The next day we joined our friends for a tea dance at one of the churches in town. It had a small dance floor that easily accommodated the dozen dancers in attendance. Chris, who owns a Bed & Breakfast in town, supplied us with tea, coffee and his renowned homemade oversized blueberry muffins. I found it very difficult choosing between the muffins or dancing, so I held off until we did some dancing and then downed two incredibly large yummy delights. Chris supplied us with music from his large selection of tapes. We did a Samba, which caught everyone's attention; they were just learning this dance from an instructor that traveled from the Cape to teach them once a month. They asked us to show them some steps and we gladly obliged. We started with the basic step, with the men going forward and then back: one & two forward, three & four back, with hesitations on two and four. Then the same basic in a box step, with the same count: one & two forward, three & four to the right, five & six to the back, seven & eight to close the box, always with the same hesitations. Then we taught a Volta as follows: from a box or forward basic, you do a breakaway and then travel to the man's right sideways: one & two & three & four, then travel back to the man's left, one & two & three & four. After practicing for several minutes, everyone caught on. It was a pleasure watching these students accomplish the Samba dance routines; I've always admired the dedication and passion that dancers put into their lessons and practice drills and the resultant success that invariably follows. We said our goodbyes, as that was our last day in Nantucket. Hopefully, we would see each other in the evening at the Boston Pops Orchestra's "Great Social" that was to be performed at Jetties Beach and usually draws crowds in the thousands.

We left a half hour before the scheduled performance with our beach chairs and walked the short distance to the beach to find good locations; the beach was already crowded, so we had to settle for a spot that was quite a distance from the bandstand. We got comfortable and then applied anti-mosquito lotion to the exposed parts of our bodies to avoid becoming their evening BBQ. The program indicated that, during and after the concert, there would be fireworks by world renowned Grucci (officially called Pyrotechnique by Grucci, Inc.). The theme for the evening was "A Dedication to the Music of John Williams," conducted by the man himself, John Williams. He is considered the most prolific writer in the history of movie music and probably one of the most widely heard composers of the 20th and 21st centuries. His awards for music compositions are endless; he is the recipient of five Academy Awards, four Golden Globes, seven BAFTA Awards (British Academy of Film and Television Arts), and ten Grammy Awards. He was inducted into the Hollywood Bowl Hall of Fame in the year 2000 and was the recipient of the Kennedy Center Honors in 2004. Some of his movie compositions were in "Schindler's List," the six "Star War" films of George Lucas, Steven Spielberg's "Raiders of the

Lost Ark," the "Indiana Jones" sequels, "Jaws," "Jurassic Park," "Superman," and numerous other movie and TV pieces. The native Long Islander (born in Floral Park) was the conductor of the Boston Pops Orchestra (1980-1993) and also a guest conductor throughout the world during his illustrious career.

The orchestra played many of his compositions from famous movies and TV shows while the Grucci team displayed their expertise in producing state-of-the-art, spectacular fireworks. The evening ended with the orchestra playing "God Bless America" as the crowd of thousands joined in singing the beautiful lyrics. This was complemented by an incredible display of firework replicas of the American flag and atomic bomb like explosions. Multi-colored flares decorated and illuminated the sky, their sonic sounds and vibrations shook the surrounding beach front, which made the hair on the back of my neck stand straight up from the noise and the feeling of pride in singing one of our nation's favorite patriotic songs.

On our way back to Mikara, we stopped for a nightcap at one of the restaurants that had a great view of the harbor and shared its dock with our marina. We were still concerned about the JFK, Jr., crash and were sort of spooked about crossing from Nantucket to Hyannis because of the ever-present fog that seems to occupy the preferred traveling route across the Sound. We returned to Mikara and reviewed our charts carefully, highlighting any possible dangerous areas that might have rocks or shallow water. We decided that we should leave a little later then usual to give any fog a chance to burn off from the sun's rays.

In the morning we received news that JFK, Jr.'s plane and its occupants had been recovered. This upset us to no end, considering we were about to travel in the same general area of the crash. I said a silent prayer for JFK, Jr., and his companions and then remembered that in the area we were traveling there was also a major ship collision between the Italy's pride and joy cruise ship, SS Andrea Doria and MS Stockholm, a smaller passenger liner of the Swedish American Line. On the Andrea

Doria's 100th Atlantic crossing, it collided with, or to be more precise, was rammed on its right side by the Stockholm. On that fateful day, July 25, 1956, the Andrea Doria was heading west passing the shores of Nantucket on its voyage to New York, while the Stockholm was heading from New York, east toward the Nantucket Lighthouse, and then continuing across the North Atlantic Ocean to Sweden. The Italian liner had about 1,200 passengers and 500 crew members; the Stockholm had over 600 passengers and crew members. Deaths due to the infamous maritime collision were 46 on the Italian liner and 5 on the Swedish-American ship. What happened? What caused this horrific collision that sank Andrea Doria the next day? Well, it all boils down to "POOR VISIBILITY AND CARELESS SEAMENSHIP." The Italian liner was traveling at about 25 mph in fog and the Stockholm was cruising at about 20 mph. Both ships saw each other on their radar screens, but neither attempted radio communication with the other. The Stockholm followed International Rules of the Road and steered to the right to avoid collision; the Andrea Doria made a mistake and steered to the left, bringing the right side of the ship directly in front of the Stockholm. Neither reduced their speed prior to the collision and only slowed down after impact. Forty-six people were killed on the Italian liner and five on the Swedish-American ship; hundreds were injured during the impact and subsequent evacuation rescue. Fortunately, due to improved communication methods and the fact they were on a busy sea lane, where nearby ships responded to their distress calls quickly, most of the passengers avoided the horrific destiny of those on the Titanic.

How similar was the JFK, Jr. incident to the above collision? He was also traveling at night with poor visibility, although his GPS was on, his autopilot was off. If it were on, it would have kept his plane on course and upright, giving him an opportunity to safely follow the GPS heading. Again, "POOR VISIBILITY AND CARELESS SEAMANSHIP" caused an avoidable misfortune to become an unfortunate reality. The Air Tower at Nantucket's airport stated that seconds before the crash, his plane veered to the right and then suddenly went nose first into the ocean. The technical information that was gathered after retrieving the wreckage of the plane, unfortunately, resulted in a law suit for negligence between the Bessette family and the estate of JFK, Jr. The case was settled out of court for the benefit of the plaintiff without prolonged publicity.

We were concerned, but prepared, about traveling into some pretty unstable water and weather conditions for our short, and possibly nasty, 25-mile trip. Barbara suggested that we follow the twelve o'clock ferry from Nantucket to Hyannis and play it safe; great idea from my competent first mate (she calls herself the Admiral). After her suggestion, I was inclined to agree with her. We reviewed our pre-cruise checklist, filled our tanks with fuel, and followed the ferry out of the Nantucket inlet. The weather conditions and forecast were for clear weather, soft winds and the usual possible patches of fog, which is common in the area. We followed the ferry at a safe distance, as the large vessel created an undercurrent from its huge propellers. The first half of the trip went according to our plans, but dense fog soon encompassed Mikara, resulting in zero visibility. I immediately reduced our speed and put on the automatic fog horn and running lights. From that point on we were on our own, as the ferry continued full speed ahead to its destination. Our Loran and GPS got us to the entrance buoy of Hyannis Harbor and our radar guided us in. We traveled buoy to buoy until we reached the Hyannis Marina, where we had reservations for the next few days. It's so important to trust Mikara's instruments, which are necessary aids to navigation, and not to rely on one's own instincts when traveling under blind conditions. Only experience and patience can build the confidence that is required to trust inanimate pieces of electronics. Anyone traveling without the proper experience and confidence that's developed over time invariably gets into trouble, whether it's from piloting a boat or an airplane.

As we traveled from Hyannis Harbor into Lewis Bay our visibility improved considerably, and we were able to appreciate seeing yachts under sail, charter fishing boats, surf boarders, small sailfish boats, and the large ferries going to Nantucket and Martha's Vineyard. We could also see the Kennedy Compound with its flag flying at half mast, which quickly brought us back to the reality and sweet comfort of arriving safely at a planned destination. Hyannis Marina has been our preferred dockage when traveling to the Cape, as it has all of the comforts of home, plus some, including pristine private showers and toilet facilities, dockside water and electricity, cable hook ups, a marine supply store, a harborside swimming pool with Trader Ed's Cabana Bar at the poolside. It also boasts a full menu restaurant named Tugboat's, floating docks, and one of the best marine repair shops on the Cape. The resort-type location is an ideal place to spend a few days sightseeing, walking around Hyannis, relaxing at the pool, or spending time on the abundance of sandy beaches that are opened to the public. I gave Mikara her desalting bath while Barbara cleaned the stainless steel railings that were caked with salt from the moist salty air that accumulated from crossing Nantucket to Hyannis.

We took our annual 15-minute walk to the town of Hyannis, stopping at one of our favorite used book-stores to indulge in one of our pet pastimes, browsing. Barbara always manages to find novels by some of her favorite authors; this time she located two titles that she hadn't read by Dean Koontz and Michael Crichton. I, as usual, get stuck in the American and European History sections, looking for titles to add to my "Age of Discovery Library." I located two books to add to my collection; a book on Marco Polo's adventures and Amerigo Vespucci's voyages. We were both satisfied with our finds and proceeded to the John F. Kennedy Museum to get updates on memorial services and burial arrangements. Many of the stores in town were closed due the death of another young favorite son of the Kennedy clan. Store windows were draped with American flags and all flag poles were flying their colors at half mast. The details of the discovery were posted at the museum: "Navy divers recovered the bodies of JFK, Jr., his wife, and sister-in-law in 116-feet of murky waters off of Martha's Vineyard, seven and one half miles from shore." The atmosphere in the museum and town was solemn and surreal, as most of the people seemed to be in a trance and state of denial that there was yet another Kennedy death under tragic circumstances. I wrote a post card on that horrific day to my son, which is presented below:

NANTUCKET MARINA

These Charter Deep Sea Fishing and Sailboats await the arrival of visitors to embark on one of the many attractions of the Island.

Photo: Thomas P. Benincas Jr.   7/21/09

Hi,

OUR VACATION HERE WAS DAMPENED BY THE JFK, JR PLANE CRASH. TODAY THEY LOCATED THE CRAFT + THE UNFORTUNATE BODIES OF JR. CAROLINE + LAUREN THE PEOPLE HERE IN HYANNIS ARE DEVESTATED.

WE LOVE YOU ALL.

KISSES FOR IAN.

Mom + Dad

MR + MRS STEVE BIVONA + FAMILY

9 BROADWAY CT

DIX HILLS, NY 11749

We returned to Mikara, sharing the sorrow of the people we met in town, and decided that a refreshing dip in the pool would perk us up. We changed and walked over to the swimming area and ordered two margaritas, stretched out on chaise lounges, and sipped the edge off of our depressed states of mind. After enjoying the pool's cool refreshing water, we returned to Mikara and took well-needed naps.

While trying to nap, I read some history about Cape Cod and the surrounding area. It's a peninsula that opens to the waters of Massachusetts Bay on the north side, Nantucket Sound on its South Shore, the Atlantic Ocean on its east side, and Buzzards

Bay on the west. Its history parallels that of Nantucket, except for one big exception; Native Americans fled from the Cape Cod Peninsula to Nantucket for a short-lived respite from the cruelty of the European interlopers. The English also manipulated Hyannis and the surrounding area away from the Natives as they did in Nantucket, but for a lot less; 20 pounds and two small pairs of pants. They also share the same pirate myths. On the Cape, Captain Kidd is purported to have buried his gold at Money Head on Hog Island in Pleasant Bay, off the town of Orleans, just Northeast of Hyannis. Once a year, it's whispered by the town's people, that there is a chance of finding Captain Kidd's treasure, especially if the treasure seekers purchase maps to guide them, that are available at the local shops.

The Hyannis Marina has a courtesy car at the disposal of its boating guests, which we were able to secure for our trip to the Regatta Restaurant in the town of Cotuit, which is a short distance from Hyannis. The restaurant was recommended by friends who said, "It's beyond an eating experience, it's an event." How right they were. Two cranberry red, colonial-style buildings, the smaller one dating back to 1790, immediately transported my mind back to a time when our nation was struggling to become a democracy over 200 years ago. Its brochure "invites guests to enter through its fine Federal period front door and hear the laughter of patrons of a bygone era." The entrance hall is inviting with the "Good Morning Stairway" leading to a second floor and an entrance to the Adams Room on the left, which was used as Cotuit's first public library in 1872. On the right is the entrance to the Washington Room. Down the hallway to the right is the Jefferson Room, which was the original kitchen. Behind what was once the summer kitchen is the cozy Crocker Room with its low, beautifully carved, wood-beamed ceiling. To the left at the end of the hall is the Tap Room with a striking oak bar, where you can enjoy a before and after dinner drink. The Tap Room, as well as the Adams, Washington and Jefferson rooms, each employ one of the eight fireplaces found in this Federal twin-chimney Colonial. All construction is of hand-pegged posts and beams, which are most visible in the bar area where hurricane braces are also exposed, as are the 18 x 24-inch wide pine planking of the overhead exposed beamed ceiling. We decided to have our dinner in the Tap Room with a window view of the outside road and passing traffic.

The Tap Room menu was extensive; it took our enjoying a good part of an outstanding bottle of French chardonnay wine before we could choose our dinners. Barbara ordered "Fire & Ice Oysters" for an appetizer and "Crispy George's Bank Scallops" for the main course. I skipped the appetizer and ordered an extra plate so I could join Barbara with her delight. I ordered the evening's special, which we had never seen or heard of, "Shoulder of Swordfish." It was a daring choice, but I figured that swordfish has always been one of my favorite meals, so why not try a different part of the fish. We both made excellent choices. The oyster appetizer was beyond delicious. Barbara savored every morsel of the scallops, with small hesitations and deep breaths between each bite. The swordfish presentation, aroma, and taste were out of a culinary fairytale. It was above and beyond any fish I have ever tasted; thick, succulent, and exotically flavored. We decided it would be worth a return trip to Cape Cod just to dine at this "one-of-a-kind" bistro. We both finished our meals with espresso and a shared glass of black sambuca, which added to our unforgettable dining experience.

We drove back to Hyannis Marina and our floating vacation home, Mikara. We turned on the TV for an update on the memorial and burial status of JFK, Jr., and his party; the services and burials were planned for the following morning. At 9:00 A.M., the next morning, the ashes of John F. Kennedy, Jr., Carolyn Bessette Kennedy, and Lauren Bessette, were scattered at sea from the US Navy destroyer, USS Briscoe. JFK, Jr., son of the 35th president of the United States, was returned to the waters off the Massachusetts coast where he enjoyed sailing, sea kayaking, and searching for sunken pirate ships. His uncle, Massachusetts Democratic Senator Ted Kennedy, stated at the memorial services: "We dared to think that this John Kennedy would live to comb gray hair with his beloved Carolyn by his side. But like his father, he had every gift but length of years." And of his nephew's marriage he said, "Both his father's presidency and his marriage lasted 1,000 days." The incomprehensible death and final burial brought down the curtain on the life of one of America's favorite sons. Goodbye young John!!

Doing anything but mourning on that day seemed to be sacrilegious, but it was one of those situations that require keeping busy to distract one's attention from the deep sorrow that is being felt. So we decided to rent a car and leisurely drive to Provincetown, also known as P-Town, which is located at the furthest northern part of Cape Cod. Checking the local maps, we determined that the scenic Route 6A, originally called Old Kings Highway, would take us through many local towns and shops along the way, and would also give us intermittent views of the Atlantic Ocean on our right. The trip would be a "no rush event" to help shake off the depressed feeling we both were carrying around with us due to the inconceivable events of the past few days.

Barbara always likes to visit the Xmas Tree Shops whenever we are in the New England states. There is one located just at the edge of Hyannis, which was our first stop on our auto journey in a small, rental car. After many years of tagging along with her, I finally asked why she likes shopping there. She said: "It's fun; they have all sorts of unusual food products, glassware and household goods." Strangely, it has a very small selection of Xmas items, although the name would indicate otherwise. So we visited the shop and Barbara insisted that I take a shopping cart, just in case her purchases exceeded the limit of hers. We loaded up on all of the above mentioned items, which, fortunately, did fit into one cart.

We began our journey on Route 6A heading to our destination in Provincetown. The road runs the full length of Cape Cod; beginning at the foot of Sagamore Bridge on the west and traveling down through the horseshoe-shaped peninsula to Yarmouth at the shoe's bottom and extending upward to

Provincetown. Hyannis is somewhere left of the halfway point, so we had a long ride ahead of us on a very slow-moving scenic road. We passed many antique, gift and local craft shops, which we visited while stopping to stretch our legs and enjoying some refreshments, especially the delicious ice cream sugar cones--vanilla for me and chocolate for my beloved. Our first sightseeing stop was in Wellfleet, located just before our main destination. Of the many beautiful attractions of the town, such as pristine beaches, gorgeous sandy dunes and an abundance of boutiques, the main reason we chose to stop there was to visit the Marconi Wireless sight and explore the area where the infamous pirate, Black Sam Bellamy's ship, Whydah, was recovered in 1984.

The Marconi Station today is a far cry from the original four 210-foot transmitting and receiving towers that sparked the birth of global two-way wireless communication on January 18, 1903. On that day, Marconi's dream to send signals across the Atlantic became a reality. He chose the location because of its elevation and the writings of the great author Thoreau's description of the Cape as "A place where a man may stand and put all of America behind him." The location at Wellfleet was conducive to his plans for a quiet, secluded site to build his towers without interruption from the local residents. Marconi somehow convinced President Theodore Roosevelt to take part in a wireless experiment where a message would be sent from Cape Cod to the King of England. On that eventful day, President Teddy's message was tapped out in Morse code from South Wellfleet, Massachusetts, to King Edward VII in Cornwall, England. It was the first two-way transatlantic communication and the first wireless telegram between America and Europe. The message read: "His Majesty, Edward VII, London, Eng. In taking advantage of the wonderful triumph of scientific research and ingenuity which has been achieved in perfecting a system of wireless telegraphy, I extend on behalf of the American people most cordial greetings and good wishes to you and to all the people of the British Empire. Signed: Theodore Roosevelt, Wellfleet, Mass., Jan. 18, 1903."

Expecting a confirmation from the station in England, Marconi instead received a direct response: "From Sandrinham, Jan. 19, 1903. To: The President, White House, Washington, America. I thank you most sincerely for the kind message which I have just received from you, through Marconi's trans-Atlantic wireless telegraphy. I sincerely reciprocate in the name of the British Empire the cordial greeting and friendly sentiment expressed by you on behalf of the American Nation; I heartily wish you and your country every possible prosperity. Signed: KING EDWARD." And so the windows of Europe and the World were opened to communicating instantly with people around the globe, hopefully for the betterment of mankind.

The station was short lived, as it lasted only 16 years. Beach erosion, inclement weather, and new radio technology resulted in closing the site in 1920. Sand and trees covered both sides of the road and there are few traces of life remaining in the once important Marconi Station. There is an observation platform that looks out across the Atlantic Ocean toward England. To one side is an exhibit shelter, built to house a model of the station and various relative displays. This area has become part of the National Seashore and a habitat for many fragile species. There are many signs reminding visitors to be careful of the wildlife and the dangerous conditions of the sand that is slowly slipping into the ocean. Just outside the small shelter is a plaque honoring the message sent in 1903 to the King of England. Inside is a model of the station as it was at the time of the momentous transmissions, a schematic of the original spark gap transmitter, a map showing the original relay towers, a bust of Marconi, and some history about the famous inventor. Nearby are plaques commemorating the station that reads: "SITE OF THE FIRST UNITED STATES TRANSATLANTIC WIRELESS TELEGRAPH STATION BUILT IN 1901-1902." "MARCONI WIRELESS TELEGRAPH COMPANY OF AMERICA-PREDECESSOR OF RCA-TRANSMITTED JANUARY 18, 1903," and "THE FIRST U.S. TRANSATLANTIC WIRELESS TELEGRAM ADRESSED TO EDWARD VII KING OF ENGLAND BY THEODORE ROOSEVELT, PRESIDENT OF THE UNITED STATES."

In addition to Guglielmo Marconi's many inventions and improvements in wireless communication, one of his most significant contributions was the foundation he created for the developments in radio, radar, microwaves, and cellular communication. Upon his death in 1937, this Nobel Prize winner for physics was honored when all wireless radios around the world were temporarily silenced to pay homage to the man whose wireless invention was instrumental in rescuing over 700 passengers from the doomed ocean liner, Titanic, in 1912. That honor has not been repeated for any other person to date.

Down the coast from the Marconi Shelter is Marconi Beach, where pirate Samuel Bellamy's, aka "Black Sam Bellamy," ship, the Whydah, was shipwrecked in a violent storm on April 27, 1717, killing the notorious pirate and over 100 of his shipmates. He was one of the more successful pirates of his time, associating with such infamous pirates as Captain Benjamin Hornigold, aka "Horn of Gold," Captain Edward "Blackbeard" Teach, and our old friend, Captain William Kidd. He got his name "Black Sam" because he wore his black hair wild and in a pony tail instead of wearing the popular white wigs that gentlemen and sea captains wore. He is known to have captured and looted over 50 ships before he drowned with his shipmates at the early age of 28. He was leading a pirate flotilla of five ships from the Caribbean to Maine, where they intended to divide their booty and decide on their futures, when they were caught in a violent nor'easter storm with heavy rain and fog. He went aground and sunk, killing all but two of his 143 crew members and losing what is estimated to be around $400 million worth of loot. His companion ship, the Mary Anne, also went aground and sunk, killing all but seven sailors. His intention was to pick up his sweetheart Maria Hallet and their child in Cape Cod and to continue on their journey with their fortune and establish a place where they could live in peace and luxury. Unfortunately his young life ended when his ship sunk, joining the over 3,000 other ships that went to the bottom of the sea in the area. Due to the dangerous waters and the enormous number of sunken ships, the Cape Cod Canal was built to avoid the ocean side of the tip, turning Cape Cod from a peninsula into a man-made island. His most formidable conquest was the "Whydah Gally," a new 300-ton slave ship that had just finished the second leg of an Atlantic slave trade and was loaded with a fortune in gold and precious trade goods. The ship was new and was able to carry up to 600 slaves, which made it a prize catch for the pirate. He was affectionately known as "The Prince of Pirates." His men took pride in calling themselves "Robin Hood's Band," because of his mercy and generosity toward captains of the ships he plundered. He would usually let them retain possession of their vessels and their lives after asking them if they wanted to join his group. When he captured the Whydah, he offered the captain and crew of that ship a chance to join his league; when they refused he reprimanded them and then gave them his smaller ship, the "Sultana," with adequate provisions and sent them on their way, keeping the larger vessel as his new floating fortress.

From time to time after his death, his name would be resurrected, most recently in the movie, "Pirates of the Caribbean: The Curse of the Black Pearl." The piece of land on which Jack Sparrow was twice marooned by Hector Barbossa was "Black Sam's Spit" and was named after Captain Bellamy. Over twenty years ago, his name again was in the headlines when the wreckage of his ship was finally discovered in 1984 by underwater treasure hunter Barry Clifford. He spent over twenty years trying to locate the wreck to no avail, but with the help of John F. Kennedy, Jr.'s drawing of the underwater site, which he discovered and charted in 1982, Clifford was able to finally locate the Whydah. JFK, Jr., was a passionate treasure hunter and spent a considerable amount of time exploring the area with his friends. He is credited with making Clifford's dream a reality that uncovered over 200,000 artifacts, including coins, jewelry, pistols, and swords. Also found were skeleton parts, silk stockings, and the shoe of John King, who at 11-years-old was the youngest member of the ship's crew. Many artifacts are stored at the "Expedition Whydah Sea-Lab and Learning Center" in Provincetown, which is dedicated to Captain Black Sam Bellamy. Newly discovered cannons were found just 2,000-feet from the shore, ranging from 4-feet long and weighing 500 pounds to 8-feet long weighing 1,500 pounds. Clifford wholeheartedly gives Kennedy and his friends, who were specifically looking for the Whydah, credit for his success in uncovering the remains of the ship and his deepest gratitude for the many dives JFK, Jr., did with Clifford's teams.

On to Provincetown, aka P-Town, which is probably one of the most eclectic towns in the United States. How did it get that way? Well, the Nauset Indians originally settled the area and established a settlement known as Meeshawn. Other Indian tribes shared the waters in the summers and took advantage of the abundance of fish and the hospitality of the Nauset Indians. Unfortunate for the Indians, the English explorer Gosnold landed on the tip of P-Town in 1602, naming the area Cape Cod due to the great quantity of cod fish in the surrounding waters. The tip of the Cape was the first landing place of the Mayflower and Pilgrims in 1620. They didn't consider the region safe due to its exposure to rough waters on both sides of the tip and, therefore, sailed on to Plymouth where they established their famous colony. For the very reason that the Pilgrims didn't settle at the tip of the Cape, other unsavory types were attracted to the area. It presented a great escape route to sea and it was a safe distance from the mainland. The area attracted smugglers and privateers, including Captain Kidd, Captain Blackbeard, and Captain Black Sam. As law-abiding, English settlers migrated to the region, the more colorful shady characters moved on to more friendly shores.

Its sheltered harbor is the site where the Pilgrims signed the Mayflower Compact; this document would become part of the foundation of American democracy and nurture P-Town's growing reputation as a place of tolerance. Portuguese fishermen were attracted to the area due to the plentiful quantity of fish and easy access to whales. The Portuguese are still an important part of the fishing industry of Provincetown and surrounding areas. Another side of the town began to develop at the turn of the 20th century; Charles Hawthorne established an art school that attracted artists and writers from all over the world. Soon poets, novelists, journalists, radicals and dilettantes formed a colony and opened the Provincetown Players Theater in a converted fish house on an abandoned wharf. They turned the town into a mecca for the arts, which is currently the oldest art colony in the United States. Over the years, such famous artists and writers as Eugene O'Neil, Tennessee Williams, Susan Glaspell, Charles Hawthorne, Hans Hoffman, Norman Mailer, Michael Cunningham, John Waters, and a long list of others, called Provincetown their temporary home away from home. Known for its unique brand of tolerance dating back to the original Indian settlers and the marauding pirates, the unconventional population soon became a haven for gays and lesbians, and today is probably one of the most popular gay and lesbian resort towns in the world. The town's population is about 4,000 and grows to approximately 60,000 during the beautiful summer months, when people flock from around the world to enjoy its beautiful climate, fishing, whale watching, artists' colony, theater, miles of bike trails, and its pristine beaches.

The most striking structure in P-Town is the Pilgrim Monument, rising over 250-feet above the 100-foot hill that it sits on. Its cornerstone was laid in 1907, as president Teddy Roosevelt looked on. It wasn't until 1910 that President Taft attended its dedication and gave his blessing for the prosperity and peace of Provincetown. The granite tower looms over the city and acts as a compass and focal point, reassuring travelers of their location at all times. At the bottom of the tower is a museum featuring memorabilia of the history of P-Town from the Native Indian period to the present. There are exhibits showing Indian arrowheads, implements, tools and head gear; images of a Native American Wampanoag tribe; artifacts of a polar bear, musk ox and Inuit Indian's relics brought back by P-Town's native son, Donald B. MacMillan, who explored the Arctic with Commodore Perry. It also houses the town's first fire engine, built by an apprentice of Paul Revere in the 1830s; relevant furniture and decorative arts relating to the area's history; historical photographs, postcards, toys, clothing; magnificent scrimshaw carvings, holy relics, and many other items that are indicative to P-Town's earlier days. Ascending the 116 steps, with resting ramps in between them, was an easy climb leading to panoramic views of the jagged coasts and, in the distance, Boston, with a backdrop of New Hampshire's peeked mountains. We took lots of pictures from that high vantage point of the busy town and its people, traffic, shore-lines and skyway.

We were anxious to discover what artifacts were housed at the "Expedition Whydah Sea Lab and Learning Center" which opened in 1997 and was still developing as the foremost pirate museum in existence, with the first verified pirate shipwreck and its artifacts on display. It has a choice location on MacMillan Wharf right next to the ferry dock with a great view of the ocean. In addition to the relics rescued from the wreck, information about pirates heretofore unknown or questionable was being accumulated and verified. Pirates have always been depicted as "blood thirsty, murdering criminals," but the information gathered from the wreck and the history of the area seemed to prove that there was a more humane side to the buccaneers. At a time when seamen were shanghaied into the service of naval and merchant vessels and treated no better then slaves for years or "until death do we part," pirates had a whole different code of conduct for their members. The pirates, including ex-slaves, were, in comparison, free men living in a modified democracy, sharing equally in plundered booty and actually voting on important matters, such as who the captain should be or if a captured ship should be sunk or released. Many were convinced that they were fighting the corruption in autocratic governments and business institutions. Recovered artifacts confirmed many points made about pirates by contemporary observers, including important features of their society, such as their egalitarianism, internationalism, racial tolerance (there were more then 30 Africans serving as equal crew members on the Whydah), and their unique brand of democracy.

The most striking artifact at the museum is the 2-foot wide and 2 1/2-foot high ship's bell with the inscription "The Whydah Gally 1716." This discovery confirmed that the ship was truly Captain Black Sam's Whydah, thereby making it the first verified pirate's ship to be discovered. Since its discovery, there have been over 200,000 artifacts recovered. Some were suspended in tanks to show what they would have looked like in the sea. There were also gold coins from various parts of the world, and fascinating Akan gold jewelry from Africa. There is a wonderful children's hands-on section where kids can touch gold coins, utensils and pistols, and ask questions of the on site archeologist.

As I'm writing on this 2nd day of November, 2008, the Whydah "Real Pirates Exhibition" is on a five-year traveling tour; its first stop was the prestigious Franklin Institute and Museum in Philadelphia, Pennsylvania. The tour lasted from May 31, 2008, until today. It featured treasure chests of coins, gold, and a Weapons Gallery showing pirate's pistols, cannons, and knives, in addition to the famous Whydah ship's bell, a ship model of Whydah, and a full-sized replica of the stern of the ship. Of special attention are the slave shackles worn by some of the slaves that became crew members after the ship's slave-trading period. There is a lot of historical information throughout the Exhibition about the pirates of that era and in depth, detailed information about the salvage operation conducted by Barry Clifford. The "Real Pirates Exhibition" will continue its journey displaying and educating people about the meaning of the new-found information as it sheds light on the way pirates of the 17th and 18th centuries lived. An interesting observation that can be made from the new data is that Black Sam, the Prince of Pirates, was leading a flotilla of five ships. If he was commanding those ships, then it must be assumed that many of the pirates had the same beliefs as he did, which was: "Only plunder for profit and don't sink captured ships

Michael Bivona

or kill unnecessarily." Of course, this information is contrary to popular belief that "pirates are plundering, blood thirsty murderers." I'm sure that pirate aficionados and admirers will have many heated debates over this issue for many years to come.

Scheduled appearances of the "Real Pirates Exhibition" will be at the following locations: Chicago, IL, Summer/Fall 2009; Baltimore, MD, Winter/Spring 2010; St. Louis, MS, Summer/Fall 2010; TBA, Winter/Spring 2011; Denver, CO, Summer/Fall 2011; Phoenix, AR, Winter/Spring 2012; Cleveland OH, Summer/Fall 2012.

We decided to have a light dinner and then go to the Atlantic House for some dancing. Several of the town folks that we spoke to recommended it as the "in place" for music, dancing, and lots of fun. The oldest section of the complex was built in 1798 and is one of the oldest establishments in P-Town; it also boasts of being the oldest disco in the country. The "A-House," as it is called, turned out to be a lot more than a dance venue. It's more of a complex consisting of the Little Bar, with a jukebox; the Macho Bar, aka the "Leather and Levi Bar"; the Big Room, P-Town's #1 Dance Club, and a Patio Bar. The overall texture of the place is nautical with a fireplace and cozy sitting areas. When we arrived, the only bar open was the Little Bar. It was somewhat of a shock to see photographs hanging over the bar of Tennessee Williams strolling on one of the town's beaches in his birthday suit with some of his companions. We nestled in next to the roaring fireplace and watched gays, lesbians, and male and female couples dancing. We didn't know whether to stay seated or run for our lives. But after pleasant drinks and some sing-along songs from the juke box, we got up and did some nice Swing and Disco dancing; we even did a couple of Cha-Cha's and a Hustle. We struck up conversations with some of the patrons who were quite friendly and impressed with our Cha-Cha dancing. At about 10:00 P.M., the other bars opened and people started to gradually fill up the rooms. Within a half hour, the rooms were jammed packed with every combination of couples: male-male, female-female, and male-female. Many of the men were dancing without top shirts and seemed to be enjoying themselves while flexing and showing off their biceps. It was getting late so we bid our new friends good night and returned to our car for the long ride back to Mikara. We had a local map that indicated we should take the four lane highway, Route 6, back to Hyannis. It was a good choice, as it was well lit and got us to our home port in a lot less time then the scenic Route 6A.

It was comforting to see Mikara again. We didn't waste any time in preparing for bed and a delightful night's sleep to the familiar soft sway of Mikara, as she rhythmically followed the movements of the water. When we woke in the late morning, we were undecided on what to do for the day. Should we just hang around and enjoy the swimming pool? Do we take a train ride around Hyannis, or take a trolley car ride around the town? Or should we maybe take the Duckmobile for an amphibious ride around the town and harbor? We decided that we had such a good time the day before, traveling easterly along Route 6A and then up to P-Town, that we would try traveling in the opposite direction on the same road and see what we would discover. We didn't want to travel too far from our home port, as we made reservations to dance at the Sons of Italy's hall in Cotuit where the USABDA (USA Dance) Chapter was holding an open-house dance, so the short remaining part of Route 6A was made to order. Our local map indicated that Sandy Neck Beach was nearby; we thought that a box breakfast and searching for seashells on the beach would be a great way to begin our day. What a surprise when we arrived and saw a magnificent pristine beach playland. We picked up a brochure that had some interesting information about the beautiful peninsula: "Sandy Neck Beach extends six miles eastward from the Town of Barnstable on the north shore of Cape Cod. It varies in width from about 200-feet to a half-mile and, consequently, shelters Barnstable Harbor from Cape Cod Bay. This formation has allowed various types of soils and natural communities to develop, including migrating sand dunes, fresh and saltwater marshes, bogs and both deciduous and coniferous forests. The Nature Conservancy considers Sandy Neck one of the best barrier beach systems in the northeast eco-region, protecting at least eight species of threatened wildlife, including piping plovers and diamondback terrapins." In the middle of all this bountiful natural beauty, there are over 50 cottages on the beach where 4-wheel drive vehicles are allowed to roam in restricted areas, causing lots of stress to the residents and sun worshipers. We had our breakfast while watching people activity in the sand and water, then took one of the many walking trails along the beach while admiring the dunes and magnificent sea views. People were relaxing and enjoying the sun, while others swam or did other water activities, like parasailing. The beach activity was reminiscent of a wind-up Gadget and Gismos novelty store display. The difference was that what we were looking at was reality. It was reassuring to see lifeguards on duty and quite active in keeping kids from wandering too far out into the water. There were also adequate restrooms and food concessions which we used frequently while enjoying our stroll and seashell collecting. We like collecting unusual seashells and placing them in our rock garden at home, which really perks up its appearance and makes for interesting conversations with our friends.

Our map indicated that the "Heritage American Museum & Garden Plantation" of the Town of Sandwich would be an interesting stop, so we drove the short distance to the 106-acre plantation and again were surprised at the size and the sophistication of the place. It consists of three museums, an antique windmill, a maze of gardens, and clearly marked walking trails. It was close to lunch time, so we went to the Carousel Museum Café and had delicious vegetable wraps while we marveled at the activity and beauty surrounding the almost 100-year old working carousel. We didn't waste any time taking a free ride on the rotating menagerie, which is opened all day for the benefit of the guests at no charge. The carousel is housed in a tent-like room in the same building as the American Art Museum that has three galleries showcasing a wide variety of American art. The Folk Art Gallery features early shop signs, folk paintings, early American weathervanes, Nantucket baskets, and beautifully-carved scrimshaw. The whole texture of the building was a pleasant surprise and a fun place for kids. The children and some grownups were enjoying their endless free rides until dizziness or repetition persuaded them to exit the hand carved wooden, early 20th-century carousel.

An exceptional building was the Shaker Round Barn that houses an antique automobile museum. Unique to this location is a Model T Ford that welcomes visitors, including children, to sit in the car and take it on an imaginary journey. Some of the vehicles on display were a 1908 Waltham-Orient Buckboard Runabout, a 1909 White Steam Car (one of the first official cars of the White House, owned by President William Taft), a 1911 Stanley Steamer Model 62 Runabout with a 28-gallon water tank, a 1915 Milburn Light Electric Car (imagine, 100 years later and we haven't improved much on this automobile), and a 1930 Duesenberg Model J Derham Tourster, formerly owned by the actor Gary Cooper. These are just some of the many pristine cars on display at this amazing antique car extravaganza. An interesting feature was a children's map that guides the kids through an answer and question quiz that ultimately leads them to the autos in the test.

The American History Museum has four galleries housed within a replica of the "Revolutionary War Building," know as "The Temple in New Windsor, New York." There is a Cape Cod Baseball League Hall of Fame that features memorabilia from the local baseball league, dating back to the beginning of the 1800s. The American History Gallery included hand-painted lead solders wearing the uniforms, arms, and insignia of such famous military units as the Green Mountain Boys, the 4th Massachusetts Regiment, and the 53rd New York Volunteers. The history of some flags in America was nicely displayed with a detailed explanation as to their origin and a large antique firearms collection including a rifle belonging to

Buffalo Bill Cody. The Native American Gallery featured two cases of Indian artifacts, including basketry, hide containers, pottery, and beautiful native's carvings. The "Play Things of the Past Exhibit" was intriguing; it was fun seeing many of the toys of my childhood on display, such as large spinning circus tops. Many toys were from the early 1800s to the mid 1900s, with rare examples of iron and tin playthings, little trains, circus people and paraphernalia, including many little revolutionary war soldiers.

The gardens and grounds were breathtaking. Walking on the lush grass, smelling the flowers, listening to the birds singing, or just sitting on one of the many strategically located benches was a delightful way to enjoy nature's bounty. The care and layout of the grounds were impeccably maintained. While strolling through the maze of beautiful foliage, it was nice to see that many of the plants and flowers were labeled, such as, hollies, daylilies, hostas, and hundreds of trees and shrubs. The highlights of the gardens were the "Hybrid Dexter Rhododendrons" that were created and cultivated by the master gardener. The diversity of his creations almost defies human understanding. Some of Dexter's beauties are GiGi, a beautiful red rose colored hybrid; Scintillation, a magnificent pinkish hybrid; Wheatley, a ball-shaped red-pink charmer; Apritan or Honeydew, a fragrant apricot blush with large flowers; and Tom Everett, a superb lavender-pink mixture. These are just some of the 100-plus cultivars created by the genius hybridizer that are present throughout the 76-acre gardens. Leaving such a Garden of Eden wasn't easy, but all good things must have an ending.

It was getting late, so we headed back to Mikara for a refreshing nap and an update on the weather forecast for the next several days. The forecast for the next day was good for traveling, but not so great for the following days. There were heavy winds and rough seas expected, so we decided to cut our stay in Hyannis short by a couple of days and head for Newport, Rhode Island, which was the last port of call on our itinerary. It's imperative to heed weather forecasts when traveling in order to avoid the hazards that are always lurking around ready to test boaters' skills and experience. Wise seamen should always take a cautious approach. If stormy weather with rough seas are experienced, any number of unfortunate situations can develop which can't readily be resolved, such as, engine problems or physical personal accidents, while the boat is being pounded and tossed around. So we have learned through experience and many "hard knocks," to listen to weather forecasts and, if inclement weather is predicted, to take whatever steps necessary, to avoid possible unwelcomed problems. With the forecast we received, we decided to avoid a possibly bad situation by leaving Hyannis early and hopefully avoiding the poor weather conditions that were expected. We were disappointed, as we were looking forward to seeing a show at the Cape Cod Melody Tent where it is possible to sit 50-feet from some of our favorite entertainers, such as Kenny Rogers, Dolly Parton, the Beach Boys, and other first-rate performers. We also had planned to see a show at the famous Cape Playhouse in Denis, which is the oldest professional summer theater in America. It boasts as having had many illustrious entertainers acting in its theater, such as Betty Davis, who started there as an usher, Gregory Peck, Gertrude Lawrence, Lana Turner, Ginger Rogers, Humphrey Bogart, Tallulah Bankhead, Basil Rathbone, Henry and Jane Fonda, and on and on. We were fortunate to have seen Bonnie Franklin and Pat Carol in the stage play "Grace & Gloria," and Hal Holbrook in "Into the Wild" at this wonderful venue. However, as "Discretion is the better part of valor," we would have to save our visits for another more convenient and safe time.

The Sons of Italy's dance hall was quite large, easily accommodating the 100-plus guests in attendance. The La Sala Grande (Italian for The Great Room) had tables set up for the evening around the spacious dance floor, with plenty of room for dancing. USABDA (USA DANCE) arranged for a three-piece combo, the Mel-Tones, who were quite good and played all of the ballroom dance music that is expected at such

415

a fun event, which allowed everyone to enjoy dancing to their favorite tunes. We met many friendly New Englanders and, coincidentally, met a couple that we knew from our dance sessions in Nantucket. We were supposed to call them when we got to the Cape, but lost their phone number. As fate would have it, our serendipitous meeting was destined, so there we were hugging and kissing each other as if we had found long lost relatives. We were surprised that the reasonable entrance fee of $15.00 included a buffet with great Italian pasta and meatballs, and coffee and cake. There was also an optional $10.00 fee for those preferring to dance only and exclude the buffet, but also included the coffee and cake. We enjoyed dancing the night away while changing partners with many of our fellow USA Dance members. The fun with switching partners is that it sharpens dancing skills by requiring that each partner pay attention to the other's needs, especially if one is at the beginning stages of dancing. Our new friends saw us doing a Waltz routine and asked if we would show them how to perform the steps. It's common at dance halls for fellow dancers to request a quick lesson in routines they see and like, so we gladly accommodated them. From a basic Waltz in silver pattern we began a six count in two sets: one-two-three, four-five-six, with a rise on one and four and a fall on 2-3 and 5-6. From the basic we did a weave, still doing a six count: to my left, one-two-three and to my right, four-five-six. Holding the six, Barbara extends her body backwards and does a left leg lift (developpe) while I rise from my heels to my toes. We conclude with a double turn and then into the basic. It took a few practice sets but our friends quickly caught on and danced around the floor with enormous mirrored smiles on their faces. Fortunately many of those in attendance were pretty good dancers which made the evening all the more enjoyable.

We exchanged telephone numbers with some of our fellow hoofers with the usual promises of getting together and keeping in touch. The telephone numbers of USA Dance in Cape Cod are: 401-540-2407 or 401-402-3172, their website is: www. Capecodballroomdancers.org. The website for the Sons of Italy is: www.Sonsofitalycapecod.com. We headed back to Mikara for our final night's sleep in Massachusetts.

We woke up the next morning to a clear day and a great weather forecast for traveling. We decided to leave Hyannis at about 9:00 A.M. and, after fueling up and checking our pre-cruise list, we were on our way to Newport, Rhode Island. The trip is about 60 miles and usually takes between four to seven hours, depending on sea conditions and mechanical efficiency. We headed out of Hyannis Harbor and into Nantucket Sound, which is usually rough riding; that day was no exception. I set my GPS and Loran to take me past Falmouth, Woods Hole and into Vineyard Sound. The ride was bouncy, but with the aid of Mikara's autopilot, we held the course and were able to travel and average of 15 mph. Boating between the Elizabeth Islands on our right and Martha's Vineyard on the left calmed the water and wind considerable, which allowed Mikara to perform at her best, holding her course and riding the waves smoothly. Passing the protection of the beautiful tip of Elizabeth Islands, Cuttyhunk on our right and Gay Head in Martha's Vineyard on our left, brought us into the cross currents of Rhode Island Sound, Buzzards Bay, and the Atlantic Ocean. This is not a happy location for traveling. The rough and quick currents from Buzzards Bay and the waves and winds from the Atlantic Ocean gave us a plowing and bumpy ride for over an hour, until we were close to the Rhode Island shore. Buzzards Bay got its name from the Pilgrims in the early 17th century, when they mistook osprey for turkey buzzards; the name has stuck ever since. Considering the hazardous water conditions of the bay, due to its strong tides, undercurrents, shallow water, and winds, many an unsuspecting ship has gone down to "Davey Jones' Locker." It's also one of the few recorded places in Massachusetts where a shark attack resulted in the death of the victim. So, when traversing this area, we are always cognizant of impending dangers and keep our radio weather and alert stations on at all times, while both of us keep a very sharp eye out for any possible problems, like lobster traps, floating logs, general debris, and submarine telescopes.

To balance the frightening name of Buzzards Bay to the north, there is an island just passed Martha's Vineyard on the Atlantic Ocean's side named "Nomans Land." This island has a checkered history. It was discovered by Captain Gosnold in 1602 and named Martha's Vineyard after his oldest daughter. The name was subsequently transferred to the larger island to the northeast and took on the name Nomans Land. The name probably comes from the Wampanoag Sachem Indian, "Tequenoman." The U.S. Navy built an airfield there in 1942, which was used as a practice area for 53 years for its bombers. The field was abandoned, although its use as a target bombing range continued until 1996. It's now a Fish and Wildlife Sanctuary and is closed to the public due to unexploded ordinances still remaining there.

The fun history of the island is the "Leif Eriksson Runestone," which was discovered and photographed in 1927 by the writer, Edward F. Gray. He was researching the Norse voyages to North America for his book which was published in 1930 by Oxford University Press. Two lines of letters on a large black stone, which were only exposed at low tide, was translated to read, "Leif Eriksson, 1001." The lower lines could be interpreted to say "Vineland." Some scholars have disproved the possibility the Leif ever landed on this island or inscribed the above large black rock in runic (the written language of the Norse). There is no record of the stone being removed from the island, but because of restrictions imposed by authorities that closed the island to the public, due to the unexploded ordinances, further in-depth research has not been possible. It's also possible that U.S. Navy bombings of the island in its target practice drills may have destroyed the black stone. Hopefully, further exploration of the island will be conducted in the future to get to the bottom of Leif Eriksson's mysterious "Runestone."

Our destination was the coordinates of the old Brenton Reef Light, which was once a steel 87-foot high tower at the entrance to Narragansett Bay that leads to Newport and ends north at the state's Capital, Providence, Rhode Island. Seeing the tower when it was operative on our radar screen was always reassuring, especially when we would get a visual sighting which told us that our port of call was close by. The 87-foot structure has been replaced by a small red and white "NB" lighted horn buoy that flashes every four seconds, so navigating to the marker must be exact with little room for error. We found the buoy with no trouble, thanks to the clear weather, our GPS, and trustworthy Loran. We found that when we traveled this area, it was always a good practice to use both direction finders as the U.S. Navy makes a habit of jamming the airways for security purposes. If both electronic aids fail, Mikara's magnetic compass is always the final backup to lead us to our destination using "dead reckoning."

Narragansett Bay is New England's largest estuary, which functions as an expansive natural harbor that includes a small archipelago. The bay has over 30 islands of which Goat Island is one of our favorites and lies across from our preferred boating destination, Newport. Our usual morning walks to Goat Island from Newport take us over a suspension bridge that has panoramic eclectic views of the bay and the exciting, colorful, quilt like, nautical activity, including, lighthouses, sailboats, powerboats, gorgeous waterfront homes, and people bathing at the local pristine beaches.

It's about a fifteen minute ride from the wide opening of the bay to Newport, which is on Aquidneck Island. Passing two locations on the high cliffs at the right are sites that have made their place in history. The first is Hammersmith Farms, where Jacqueline Bouvier Kennedy Onassis grew up and had her wedding reception when she married the young senator from Massachusetts, John F. Kennedy. The 28-room Victorian mansion on 48-acres was built in 1887 by John W. Auchincloss, the great grandfather of Jackie's stepfather, Hugh D. Auchincloss. The place was often used by the Kennedy family and was referred to as the Summer White House during President J.F.K.'s time in office. We were fortunate to have toured the working farm when it was open to the public and was astonished at the size of the many small rooms and toilets in the mansion. One of our most memorable sights was the view of Newport Harbor and the surrounding waterways from atop their wide spread cliff. It is certainly one of the most beautiful nautical sights in America, incorporating large bridges in the distance, an abundance of large and small sailboats, power boats of every size, Navy vessels of every description, and the Ocean on the left and the expansive bay on the right showing off its beautifully scattered islands, including our destination, Newport. Also passing on the right at a strategic vantage point is the largest coastal fortification in the United States, Fort Adams. Active from 1824 to 1950, it has a six-acre parade field and breathtaking views of the harbor and surrounding areas. The fort is now a State Park and has tours of its massive (and somewhat scary) tunnel system, casements, and barracks. Today it hosts many spectacular events, such as the Summer Music Festival, the Annual Kite Flying Competitions, military reenactments, and antique car shows, among many other exciting open air events.

It's understandable that Newport is considered one of the boating capitals of the world. It's also considered the center of yachting in the Northeast, as just about every boat traveling the coast makes it a port of call. Large sail and power boats stop over for repairs in the many world-class yards or for provisioning and refurbishing. The harbor is well protected, has a wide mouth, and water depths of up to 100-feet, which is probably one of the main reasons that it's the home of the United States Naval War College, the Naval Undersea Warfare Center, and a United States Navy Training Center. Newport boasts that its Naval War College was the Summer White House of President Dwight D. Eisenhower who spent many hot summers enjoying the coolness of the constant breezes that visit the area.

It has come a long way since its discovery by Giovanni da Verrazzano in 1524 on his ship La Dauphine, after he successfully visited New York Bay. It took over 100 years before a European settlement was established by Pilgrim Roger Williams in the 1630s. Following the Pilgrims were the infamous pirates of the

17th and 18th centuries. Newport was considered one of the most notorious pirate havens during the Golden Age of Piracy. Pirates thrived under the protection of the government and the people; they were actually treated as celebrities. One of the most famous pirates was Captain Thomas Tew, who was so beloved by the people that they would celebrate his conquests with merriment and partying. Captains Blackbeard and Kidd were also frequent welcomed guests of the residents. In the early 18th century, colonial leaders, acting under pressure from the British government, arrested many of the pirates and sent them to their final resting places on Goat Island. Out of that checkered history, Newport has grown into one of the world's busiest and most beautiful waterways with some interesting nicknames, such as City of the Sea, Sailing Capital of the World, Queen of Summer Resorts, and America's Society Capital.

Approaching the Newport Harbor Marina, our final destination, required some patience and tricky maneuvering as the area is busy with boats in motion or on moorings and at anchor. It required moving through some pretty tight areas for at least fifteen minutes until the dock master and his aides could coordinate where and how we were to dock and secure Mikara. We have been docking at this marina for many years and are always relieved to be tied to the safety of their floating docks, with our ropes, electricity and water connected. I cheerfully gave Mikara her post cruise celebratory bath for a job well done, which always makes her shine with pride and produces an imaginary smile on her bow, which only I'm privileged to see. The marina is considered one of the best on the island and, fortunately, is attached to the Newport Harbor Hotel, that has a convenient indoor pool and sauna with excellent showers and a gym. Marina guests have hotel privileges, which we've used frequently, at no additional charge. The marina is located in the heart of Newport and a short walk to shops, restaurants, parks, and supermarkets. We usually spend our first hours in the city at The Visitors Information Center which is only a couple of blocks away. It's a pleasure going there, as it is very modern and spacious. It has a half a dozen people working behind its circular information kiosk ready to help with maps, hotels reservations, sightseeing tours, restaurant accommodations, and helpful hints about current entertainment in the area. It also has an electronic diorama featuring the town and its surroundings with push button displays that light up, giving information for chosen locations. Additionally, it houses a Dunkin' Donuts coffee and sandwich bar, which is located at the attached transportation hub next door. Public parking is available for those who want to spend time in town and have a safe place to rest their vehicles.

We gathered the information we needed to occupy our stay and were excited that the Newport Classical Music Festival was having their annual extravaganza. The annual Japanese Black Ship Festival was also appearing throughout the town, and one of our favorite entertainment places, the Newport Playhouse & Cabaret, was open for their usual dinner, stage show, and cabaret nights. While walking back to Mikara, we passed every imaginable type of retail store in existence, lined up one after another on each side of the street and around every corner, beginning at the Brick Alley and continuing through America's Cup Avenue. The Alley was one of the largest slave markets on the east coast in the 17th and 18th centuries and a notorious pirates' hangout. Today it has been extended and is filled with trendy boutiques, an overabundance of T-shirt and miniature lighthouse stores, a fudge factory, ice cream parlor, candy store, Xmas shop, children's clothing stores, and quality restaurants of every ethnicity. Just walking around the main street, America's Cup Avenue, is a treat, especially while devouring a giant ice cream sugar cone with chocolate sprinkles, or a freshly made candy apple or hot fudge. There are many marinas lined along the waterway just one block from the main avenue, each with its own personality, depending on the type and size of the vessels occupying their docks. Newport Shipyards can accommodate sail or power boats up to 315-feet, while the marina we stayed at handles boats from 20 to 180-feet. There is a place for every type of vessel in Newport, but it does favor sailboats, and proudly boasts being a sailor's haven.

The America's Cup races were one of the mainstays of Newport from 1852 till 1983. The New York Yacht Club's schooner-yacht, America, raced 15 yachts in 1851 that represented the Royal Yacht Squadron of England around the Isle of Wight and won by twenty minutes, forever changing the name of the trophy from the Queen's Cup to the America's Cup. The Club won 25 consecutive races over the next 130 years, making it the longest held championship in sports history. The Cup is the most prestigious regatta and match race in the sport of sailing and the oldest active trophy in international sports. The sport attracts top sailors and yacht designers from all over the world who put their seamanship and boats' designs through the tests and trials of the rigorous race. This competition made Newport the undisputed sailboat capital of the world for over 100 years. As all good things must come to an end, we lost the Cup in 1983 to Australia when "Australia II" took the prize from us, forever surrendering Newport as the Cup's homeport. The loss of pride and business due to the relocating of the Cup's home port brought hard financial times to the city. It took over ten years for it to begin the slow process of reinventing itself as a tourist attraction with world-class music festivals (Jazz and Classical) and sightseeing and entertainment at the opulent mansions (summer cottages) of the rich and famous American industrialists of the 19th century.

Our annual ritual is to spend the first night in Newport onboard Mikara enjoying a lobster feast that Barbara puts together. A short distance from our birth is the Aquidneck Lobster Co. on Bowen's Wharf. It's a unique lobster market in the heart of the bustling city that sells its products to commercial businesses as well as the ultimate consumer. We ordered a five-pound steamed lobster, cracked and ready for consumption earlier in the day, and picked it up at 6:00 P.M., ready for our dinner table. The market is huge, with lobster tanks racked as high up as 20-feet, each tank holding a specific size crustacean, some as large as 25 pounds. Our lobster, combined with Barbara's delicious Greek salad and a bottle of Pinot Grigio, transported us to an ambrosia paradise. We enjoyed our feast on the outside deck of Mikara with soft music in the background coming from our CD player and a small vase of daisies occupying the center of our round dinner table. Passersby complimented us on the wonderful aroma coming from the beautiful scene of our picturesque setting. Some even asked if they could join us; my reply was "maybe next time." After some espresso, we walked the marina's docks striking up conversations with some of the other mariners who were also enjoying the cool evening breeze and the fog that was overcoming the area. A wonderful day came to an end with our retiring to our place of rest on Mikara.

The next morning we had our breakfast on the outdoor dining table, which always seems to attract mariners who are walking along the docks enjoying the invigorating smell of the morning's fresh salt air. Quite a few stopped to inhale the coffee aroma coming from our table and spent some time chattering about how beautiful Mikara looked. This is a common boating ritual; walking the docks and meeting new fellow sailors and sometimes old friends, and passing the time asking: "Where are you from? Where are you going? How long is your trip?" And so on... just pleasant conversation with people that have a common love--boating. After breakfast we decided to visit one of the mansions and sit in on a concert sponsored by the International Newport Music Festival, on the web at: www. Newportmusic.org. The nonprofit organization has sponsored this festival for over 30 years and attracts some of the best musicians from around the world who are proud to be a part of this spectacular endeavor. They come from as far as the Czech Republic, Italy, France, Germany, Latvia, Canada, England, Sweden, Argentina, Spain, Romania, Ukraine, China, Greece, and, of course, all parts of the United States. They come to practice with each other and then entertain the abundance of classical music lovers who also travel from far and wide to enjoy their talents and partake in the glorious sounds of their interpretations.

The event usually covers 17 days with up to five concerts daily at the mansions, parks, and on evening boat cruises. Over 60 musicians perform as many as 600 pieces of music to the delight of their audiences, and can be found playing at morning, afternoon, evening, and even midnight concerts. Some concerts have box lunches included in the price of admission, which can be enjoyed on the luscious lawns of the palatial mansions. The dress code is rather casual because most of the venues are not air conditioned and wearing shorts is quite common. Many patrons dress well for the crowded performances; each attracts from 100 to 300 music lovers. The nearby Salve Regina University is gracious enough to extend their welcome and facilities to the multitude of musicians and staff, which makes coordinating such a complicated event manageable.

We decided to visit The Breakers Mansion, www. Newportmansions.org, for the 11:00 A.M. performance. It's the grandest of Newport's summer "cottages" and a symbol of the Vanderbilt family's social and financial preeminence in the 19th and 20th centuries. Commodore Cornelius Vanderbilt (1794-1877) made his fortune in the steamship business and later with the New York Central Railroad. His grandson, Cornelius II, purchased a wooden house situated on 13-acres overlooking the Atlantic Ocean at Ochre Point, called "The Breakers" in 1893. He immediately commissioned the world renowned architect Richard Morris Hunt to design a 70-room villa, of which 33 rooms were dedicated to his staff. His wish was to replicate the 16th century Italian Renaissance-style palaces of the seaside cities of Genoa and Turin. This was one of the many "summer cottages" built by some of the richest men in the world in Newport during the Gilded Age. Many lined the famous Cliff Walk along the ocean, where servants and common folks were allowed to view the privileged upper class. Our destination was The Breakers' two-and-a-half-story high Great Hall where the concert was to be performed.

The concert featured the piano compositions of Franz Liszt, Amadeus Mozart, Robert Schumann, Giuseppe Verdi, and Robert

Wagner. The individual interpretations were magnificent and kept me spellbound as I dreamt the morning away marveling at the profusion of talent from these young gifted musicians. Considering that the outside temperature was in the mid 80s, the breeze coming from the ocean, traveling through the maze of trees and over the spotless lawns of the spacious grounds, kept us quite comfortable as it combined with the sounds of music coming from the pianos, filling not only the Grand Hall but the whole palace with the beautiful floating sounds from their keyboards.

After the concert we walked around the well-maintained, landscaped grounds and gardens, absorbing the beauty of the panoramic scene into our hearts and minds. The view of the ocean from the cliff was surreal, something out of one of my ambitious fantasies that would hopefully one day bring me the pleasure of residing in a location that had such a magnificent view. The sight of blue ocean water caressing a sandy beach, while a soft haze blankets the horizon, with boats bobbing up and down and side to side as the sun is forcing its way through the light fog and haze are things that can't be owned, but can only be visually enjoyed and treasured. My compromise was to acquire a painting of such a scene from one of the local artists, which forever captured the feeling of the time I spent being part of the idyllic moment.

We walked down Bellevue Avenue, a few blocks above the water front and where many of the gilded homes and upscale stores reside. We were attracted by loud sounds of drums coming from the International Tennis Hall of Fame. We entered the renowned hall to find a Taiko Drum Exhibition in progress. This was part of the annual Black Ships' Festival commemorating the momentous signing of the Treaty of Kanagawa in 1854 between the United States and Japan which opened the doors for peace and trade with Asia. Rhode Island's Commodore Mathew C. Perry, USN, was selected to command an expedition to the Far East in 1852, with powers to negotiate a treaty with Japan that would hopefully initiate a "friendship, commerce and protection of shipwrecked people" relationship with that country. Japan was not receptive to having relations with any foreigners at that time and initially rejected our offer. What appealed to them were the two steam-powered black ships commanded by Perry. It was a technology that they had not yet developed and, based primarily on wanting to update their old world skills, they finally signed the treaty that established full diplomatic relations with the U.S.

The International Tennis Hall of Fame building, originally called the Casino, was built in 1880, and was Stanford White's first architectural commission. Its museum galleries chronicle the rich history of tennis through interactive exhibits, dynamic videos, and popular memorabilia from historic champions and superstars. Stanford White's architectural detail, as well as the state-of-the-art gallery, still shines as being unique, and houses in the "Enshrinee Hall," plaques commemorating the great players, coaches, administrators, and writers that have been inducted into the International Tennis Hall of Fame. The Hall was the site of the first U.S. National Championships in 1881, and still boasts as having the only grass championship courts in North America. It's the first American stop after Wimbledon, England, and hosts the world's top tennis players on its magnificent courts. It's on this grass that we luckily stumbled upon the Taiko Drum performance.

The Matsuriza Taiko Group from Disney's Epcot Center, one of the world's leading Taiko Drumming Groups, were mesmerizing the audience with their electrifying drums. Their awe-inspiring group beats on hand-made drums, ranging in height from six inches to six-feet, hypnotically filled the air with stylized and synchronized rhythms. They had a powerful performing style emphasizing speed, harmony and strength, which is "supposed to reflect the spirit of the Japanese people and the essence of their souls." It was exciting watching the dozen plus male and female drummers, dressed in their bright-colored native costumes, pummel their instruments with force, dedication, and synchronization. Although the harmony and sounds of the drums were foreign to my ears, I felt as if they were expressing the feelings in my heart and soul as I became enraptured by the beauty and mystique of the vibrating drums' rhythms. The cacophony of sounds and the body motions of the drummers resembled a lively wild ballet.

On the corner of the Hall of Fame are Memorial Boulevard and an outstanding statue of Christopher Columbus holding a globe in his right hand and a sword in his left pointing outward. The statue of the daring navigator divides the boulevard in half; he seems to be directing passersby in the direction of America's Cup Boulevard and the ocean which he is facing, inviting them to venture out into the unknown as he did. From one block away we heard some loud activity, so we moseyed on over to Touro Park which was hosting the main part of the Black Ship's Festival. Dignitaries were in the middle of a ceremony commemorating Newport's native son, Commodore Matthew C. Perry, and the signing of the Treaty of Kanagawa between Japan and the United States. Wreath laying at Commodore Perry's statue and speeches by American and Japanese diplomats were highlighted by the Navy Color Guard and Band. The ceremony was concluded with the Newport Artillery & Company's firing rifle and cannon salutes honoring the occasion. The park was transformed into a Japanese Culture Center, featuring demonstrations of Ninja martial arts, workshops teaching calligraphy, kite building, origami, tea ceremonies, Japanese language lessons, and other native artistic endeavors. We took the opportunity to sample some Japanese foods, especially sushi, which was being sold throughout the encampment. We had to drag ourselves away to catch a Sumo Demonstration at the Brick Alley Market, but before leaving we were drawn to a strange looking stone tower at the far side of the park. It's a 28 x 24 foot structure of uneven stones, built on eight tall pillars between the 11th and 17th centuries. The structure is considered one of the country's longest enduring architectural riddles. As all mysteries, it has many sources and names, such as the "Viking Tower," "Old Stone Mill," and "Mystery Tower." Much to the dismay of historians, who love exploring and theorizing about the source of myths, the fathers of the city decided to name the structure simply, The Newport Tower. There is much speculation as to its origin, ranging from the Norse, Chinese, Norwegians, and Swedes, but most archeologists are sure that the tower was built during Colonial times. Although there are many theories as to who built it, the two most prevalent are: (1) the Vikings built the Tower in the 11th century and is thought to have been their lookout tower. Unfortunately there are no inscriptions or documentation to substantiate this theory and, therefore, most scholars have discounted it; and (2) that Governor Benedict Arnold built a windmill in the mid-17th century to replicate the one in his home town in England. This Benedict should not be confused with his infamous great-grandson, General Benedict Arnold, whose illustrious career came to an unfortunate end when he betrayed his compatriots during the American Revolutionary War by changing sides, or by returning to his original side. It's surprising how passionate historians are over the origin of this structure, so much so, that there are organizations dedicated to researching and exploring any information that is available on the subject. One fascinating website is www.unexplainedearth. com.

On the way to the Market to see the Sumo Demonstration, which was just a few blocks away, we stopped at the oldest surviving Jewish Synagogue in North America that was built during the Colonial period. It's a beautiful Georgian-style building with much symbolism in its construction. The building faces the east toward Jerusalem, as does the Torah which is in the ark on the inside east wall. The interior is flanked by a series of 12 columns supporting balconies. Each column represents one of the tribes of Israel and is carved from a single tree. Above the ark is a mural of the Ten Commandments in Hebrew, painted by Newport artist Benjamin Howland. The Synagogue was built in the mid-18th century for the Jeshuat Israel Congregation under the leadership of Cantor Isaac Touro, who was held in such high esteem by the people of Newport that the aforementioned park was named in his honor. This temple of honor was visited by George Washington twice, in 1781 and 1790. After his last visit, he wrote the congregation a letter stating in part: " . . . the Government of the United States . . . gives to bigotry no sanction, to persecution no assistance . . . May the children of the Stock of Abraham, who dwell in this land, continue to merit and enjoy the good will of the other inhabitants; while everyone shall sit in safety under his own vine and fig tree, and there shall be none to make him afraid. May the father of all mercies scatter light and not darkness in our paths, and make us all in our several vocations useful here, and in his own due time and way everlastingly happy." In 1946, the Touro Synagogue was honored by being designated a National Historic Site and is an affiliated area of the National Park Service.

The Brick Alley Market was filled with kiosks of Japanese vendors selling wares, trinkets, and food. There were learning booths demonstrating kite building, calligraphy classes, Anime & Manga (animation & comic) art drawing lessons, Ninja classes of the secretive form of martial arts, and the main attraction, the Sumo Demonstration, with some history and explanations of that type of martial art. The history dates back to over 1,500 years ago when it was used in the Shinto religion and still includes many ritual elements, such as the use of salt for purifications. Sumo is a competitive contact sport where a wrestler (rikishi) attempts to force his opponent out of a circular area (dohyo) or to touch the ground with anything other than the soles of his feet. The sport originated in Japan which is the only place where it's practiced professionally. The wrestlers live in communal "sumo training stables" (heya) where all aspects of their lives, from meals to their conduct, are dictated by strict tradition. There are six divisions in sumo wrestling, going from beginners (Jonokuchi) to top professionals (Makuuch), the latter division has champion and titleholder ranks, the highest being the rank of Yokozuna. While sumo wrestlers compete in Japan only, the sport is open to foreign-born competitors. In the past, three Hawaiians rose to the top of the sport. One of them, Akebono, was the first foreigner to hold the top title. The current champion, Asashoryu, is a Mongolian.

The Brick Alley Market Place was packed with spectators waiting to see the Sumo wrestling exhibition. It consisted of two wrestlers and a referee. The wrestlers gave slow motion demonstrations of the various holds and moves, while the referee explained the essence of the sport. The awesome size of the competitors was astounding; they were each at least 300 pounds and wore nothing but thongs and cloth belts. The match lasted about ten seconds, which is considered a long time for this sport, but the reaction from the crowd for such a quick event, was positive and spontaneous. The wrestlers stayed after the match to answer questions from the spectators, which was a nice gesture considering the large amount of people in attendance. We continued walking around the Market Place, munching on Japanese treats as we visited the various booths and shops. It was getting late, so we decided to head back to Mikara for a quick nap and to make plans for the evening.

We slept a little longer then we had planned and decided to spend the evening walking up America's Cup Boulevard in the direction of the ice cream and fudge factory, where we treated ourselves to some fat-fee yogurt. Barbara enjoyed a cup of chocolate with dark sprinkles and I had a very large, vanilla, wrap-around sugar cone. We licked our way up and down the Boulevard visiting the T-shirt shops, clothing stores, and my favorite, the Xmas shop, where I managed to add some additional trinkets to my tree collection. We were exhausted from the busy day, so we headed back to Mikara, watched some TV, and decided to get to bed early and get some rest for our next busy day at the wonderful seaport.

We chose to attend a morning concert at the Elms Mansion, which was held in a large tent on their luscious expansive green lawn. The Elms is another "summer cottage" built by the coal baron Edward Julius Berwind, who was fortunate to have won a contract with the U.S. Navy to supply all their steam-driven ships with coal, which elevated him to the ranks of the rich and famous; he was considered one of the most powerful and influential men in America at that time. The estate was built between 1899 and 1901 by the Philadelphia architect Horace Trumbauer, at a cost of approximately $1.5 million. It was built to resemble the Chateau d'Asnieres in Asnieres, France. Like most mansions in the area, it was constructed with a steel frame, brick partitions, and a limestone facade. The first floor has a grand ballroom, a salon, a dining room, a breakfast room, a library, a conservatory, and a grand hallway with a marble floor. The second floor contains bedrooms and a private sitting room. The third floor contains bedrooms for the 40-plus servants that were in service at any given time. Considering that the Berwinds only spent six weeks a year during the summer months in residence gives testament to their wealth and to the affluence of their neighbors who built similar estates during the Gilded Age.

Berwind was a technology maven which resulted in The Elms being one of the first homes in America to be wired for electricity, including the first electric-ice-maker. The 11-acre site includes one of the most beautiful landscaping and statuary ensembles in Newport. The grounds were designed to replicate an 18th century French estate, complete with a sunken garden, bronze and marble statues, fountains, terraces, topiaries, and gazebos scattered throughout the elaborate site. On the edge of the property is a large carriage house, which is currently used as a café and offers reasonably priced lunch menus. The carriage house and stables were converted into a large garage to accommodate Berwind's many automobiles; it's said that the head coachman, in order to keep his job, became the family driver, but he could never learn to drive vehicles in reverse, so a large turnstile was installed in the garage to compensate for his problem.

An enormous white tent was erected at the center of the lawn to accommodate the 100-plus guests attending the concert. It looked quite out of place, a white Egyptian-style pyramid protruding out of the greenery surrounded by a menagerie of concrete statuary, topiary and the limestone facade of The Elms. Fortunately, the outside maze didn't carry to the inside of the tent; the seats were comfortable and the white tent seemed to cool the hot outside sunrays. The musical program for the morning was "Amoricana," which included some movements by Charles Ives for the piano; George Gershwin's preludes for the piano highlighted with Rhapsody in Blue; Virgil Thomson's Sonata for violin and piano, and Gian Carlo Menotti's, Ricercare and Toccata on the piano. The big surprise for the day was a jewelry display of the Buccellati Collection of rare works of jewelry art which was exhibited in the Elm's grand ballroom.

Barbara went berserk at intermission, much to my embarrassment. She raced out of the tent, knocking over several folding chairs, and headed for the exhibition inside the palatial building. After a few minutes, I was able to catch up with her; she had her nose inches from a glass show case, which made her look a part of the display. I asked her what was going on? She said, "You don't understand," and I didn't, "jewelry made by the Italian Buccellati family is equivalent to Renoir' paintings." Wouldn't you know, a handsome Italian with dark wavy hair, graying at the sides, said in a perfect Italian-American accent, "Signora, you make me glow with pride for you to say such a thing about my work." Barbara's knees wobbled and I thought she was going to join the ancestors of the Elms, but she held up while he bowed and kissed her hand while introducing himself and his wife Andrea Buccellati. He insisted on giving us a personal tour of his exhibit, which filled two of the large side rooms of the mansion, explaining as we went along each of the pieces that Barbara showed an interest in. My wife is an amateur gemologist and, as a matter of fact, knows a lot more about precious stones then most jewelers we have met over the years. He was thrilled at her knowledge of gems and jewelry design. He asked her if there was a particular piece of jewelry that she was interested in. She answered, "How can I chose from so many beautiful works of art?" The pieces on display were not on sale but were just being shown for public relations purposes. He told Barbara she could chose one of the small pieces as a memento of the occasion, at a much discounted price. She chose a silver seashell-shaped dish, which caused a commotion with his sales manager, as he didn't know what to charge. After calling the home office he told us it was $500.00. Barbara said she wasn't looking to spend that much, but appreciated the gesture. Andrea asked how much cash we had so I checked my wallet and said: "$250.00." He said, "Okay, if you like the shell, it's yours."

Returning to the tent, we continued our relaxing, pleasant musical journey to the sounds of the pianos and violins being played by the talented musicians. Leaving the elaborate gardens tests one's imagination as to the creativity and talent that went into developing the statuary and topiary that is in such abundance on the grounds. The era that produced such works of art was not only the Gilded Age but America's Renaissance Period, as it combined old world artistic beauty with modern day technology. Imagine what would have been accomplished by Michelangelo and Leonardo da Vinci if they had access to 20th century technology? It's understandable that The Elms was designated a National Historic Landmark, which will preserve its timeless beauty for many years to come.

We decided to have lunch after the concert at the Viking Hotel, which has a rooftop restaurant with a small jazz ensemble and is a short distance from The Elms. The hotel was built in 1926 to accommodate the overflow of guests from the "summer cottages." The mansion contained many rooms for entertainment and its service staff, but not adequate rooms for its many guests, so the "Barons" got together and had the Viking Hotel built. A contest was held to name the new hotel. It was decided to pay tribute to the Norsemen, who purportedly landed in Newport in 1000 AD and built the Old Stone Mill located in Touro Park several blocks from the hotel. The hotel is proudly a member of the prestigious Historic Hotels of America as it holds a special place in the history of Newport and New England. Entering the hotel lobby was exciting; above the front desk is a clock depicting ancient Nordic Ruins and an antique 1926 brass letter box that welcomes guests' mail. It boasts of past guests being such luminaries as President John F. Kennedy and his beautiful wife, Jacqueline; President Dwight D. Eisenhower and Mamie; members of the Vanderbilt clan; and most of the family members and guests of the "Captains of Industry" of the 19th and 20th centuries that went to Newport to enjoy the somewhat cool weather and their "summer cottages."

The rooftop restaurant overlooks Newport with views of old colorful colonial buildings, church steeples that glitter in the sunlight and, if binoculars are handy, some of the ships' masts bobbing to the rhythm of the ever-moving tide down at the water's edge. The four-piece combo played some neat Swing music which we didn't hesitate to take advantage of as we Jived around the dance floor. Between dance sets we ordered and shared our lunch which was quite delicious and unusual. Barbara ordered a plate of oyster mushrooms, smoked gouda, caramelized onions, with a 1,000 island dressing, wheat rolls, house fries and lobster "sliders." I ordered a creamy maytag blue cheese fondue with avocado, pancetta, mayonnaise, tomato and home fries. A bottle of Pinot Grigio wine rounded out the lunch nicely. We dipped our way through lunch, in between dancing to the sweet Swing music, with a perfect Lindy beat, for a better part of the afternoon. While sharing the dance floor, we met some locals who told us that there was an evening show at the Newport Playhouse & Cabaret Restaurant that evening, which included an extensive buffet. They convinced us that the three to four-hour experience was the best night's entertainment in the area. They asked us to join them for an evening of fun and relaxation; we immediately accepted. They gave us directions to the theater and asked us to meet them there at 6:00 P.M. We said our so-longs and headed back to Mikara for a well deserved nap.

The Playhouse was a short fifteen minute ride from our marina. It's a stand-alone white building with red trim and awnings with ample parking. The inside is set up to accommodate the three evening functions: a buffet dinner, a theatrical production, and a cabaret show. The main room is set up with tables that easily house up to 150 people. We were seated with our friends at the center of the room, with a good view of the cabaret stage. At about 6:30, the buffet stations, which were conveniently located in an adjacent room, were opened, and I was pleasantly surprised at the variety of food that was presented. I helped myself to a mixed salad, some lasagna and meatballs, a little bit of hot and mild sausage, some flounder filet and, my favorite, roasted crisp potatoes. Barbara had some roasted and barbequed chicken, sugared sweet potatoes, spareribs, and roasted crisp potatoes, which seemed to be favored by everyone on our food line. Passing the dessert table was not an easy thing to do, as there were over a dozen types of goodies laid out for our pleasure. I did manage to carry a slice of coconut custard pie with me and Barbara balanced a large slice of chocolate cake on her tray. The food was delicious, and we enjoyed eating every morsel. So much so, in fact, that I went back for sausage seconds and Barbara went back for some BBQ spareribs. Before leaving the main area to head for the adjacent theater, we placed our liquor orders, which guaranteed that they would be waiting for us when we returned for the cabaret show.

The show was held in a small theater that sat about 150-guests with excellent views of the stage from all the seats. The presentation was an Andrew Lloyd Webber's musical, "Joseph and the Amazing Technicolor Dreamcoat." The tale is based on the biblical story in the book of Genesis about Jacob and his favorite son, Joseph. As the story goes, Joseph's brothers are jealous of his ability to interpret dreams and their father's favoritism toward him. So, they plot to get rid of him by selling him to an Egyptian merchant and then tell their father that he was killed. They produce Joseph's goat's blood-stained colored coat as proof of his death. After many years in Egypt, including some time in prison, Joseph became the second most powerful person in the country due to his ability to interpret dreams accurately. His precise interpretation of the Pharaoh's dreams saved Egypt from a famine. The famine reached his family in Israel and brought his brothers to him looking for food for their tribe. Joseph isn't recognized by his brothers and he tricks them by having the youngest, Benjamin, wrongfully arrested for stealing a golden cup. He tells them to bring their father to him so that he might pass judgment on their younger brother's theft. When the whole family is gathered in his presence, he shows himself, and everyone joins in singing a happy ending to the play. That is the beginning of how Jews ended up in Egypt, and ultimately in bondage, but that's a whole other story. The singing throughout the production was of Broadway quality and the closeness of the stage and the performers to the audience made for a very exciting and surprisingly enjoyable experience.

After the show we retired to the cabaret area where our drinks were waiting, as promised, on our table. We toasted and thanked our new friends for the great evening we were having and promised them that when we returned to Newport the following year, we would look them up and repeat the evening with them. The cabaret show was performed by some of the same actors and singers that were in the musical production. The comedy was primarily one liners and slapstick which kept us laughing throughout the show. They mixed the jokes with lots of happy songs and some sing-a-long numbers. After the show, we stayed and had some drinks and pleasant conversation with our new friends and some of the performers who had joined us. One of our friends decided to play the piano and encouraged everyone to sing-a-long, which we did. We sang "Happy Days are Here Again," "Sunny Side of the Street," and "Auld Lang Syne." As the clock struck twelve, we decided it was time to end the memorable evening. We had spent six hours enjoying good food, a brilliantly performed musical, jolly cabaret follies, and the camaraderie of some very special people. We exchanged telephone numbers with our new friends and bid everyone a farewell--"Until we meet again."

Barbara was the designated driver which gave me a chance to reflect while riding back to Mikara. I was getting the feeling that our vacation was certainly "as good as it gets." It reminded me of one of my favorite quotes by Mark Twain: "Twenty years from now you will be more disappointed by the things you didn't do than by the things you did do. So throw off the bowlines, sail away from the safe harbors, and catch the trade winds in your sails and Explore, Dream, Discover." We were trying to accomplish the gist of what he said and were enjoying every bit of it.

The next morning was another cool, foggy experience at the marina. We had our usual morning breakfast on the outside deck and decided to spend the day doing some local sightseeing. We headed for St. Mary's Roman Catholic Church on Memorial Boulevard, just a few streets away, to visit the place that Jacqueline Bouvier and John F. Kennedy were married on September 12, 1953. The church was designed by Architect Patrick C. Keeley of Brooklyn, New York, in 1828, and has since been designated a National Historic Shrine. It's a quaint, red stone church of the second period Gothic design with a very high steeple and sits on top of the hill at Spring Street and Memorial Boulevard, proudly proclaiming it magnificence. It was the first Roman Catholic Church built in Rhode Island. Its guests included such famous people as members of the Kennedy Clan and many of America's 19th and 20th century "Captains of Industry." Upon entering the holy place, I was transported back to the wedding day of the Kennedys, as if I were one of the 800-guests in attendance.

I could see the bride, Jackie, walking down the isle in her ivory tissue silk gown with a portrait neckline, fitted bodice, and a bouffant skirt embellished with a band of more then 50 yards of flounces. Her rose point lace veil, worn first by her grandmother, Lee, was draped from a tiara of lace and orange blossoms. She wore a choker of pearls and a diamond bracelet that was a gift from her husband. Her bouquet was of pink and white spray orchids and gardenias. I could almost touch and smell her sweetness as she walked down the path to her destiny. I snapped back to reality and said a few prayers in support of her "Passion for peace on earth in our time . . . "

Rough Point, the home of Doris Duke, was our next destination. I fell in love with her spirit when we visited her 2,700-acre

Duke Farms in Hillsborough, New Jersey, which she donated to her foundation and is now a museum open to the public. Her love of nature and all living things captured my attention and then my heart. The most impressive feature, among the many artistic and cultural displays at the farm, was Planet Earth's enclosed gardens. She traveled the globe seeking specimens and ideas to complete her creations in keeping with the ethnic backgrounds of her various gardens. The indoor displays were housed in elegant turn-of-the-century glass conservatories, each representing a different country. The designs replicated various classic garden settings from around the world, spanning centuries of human culture. A mini tour of Planet Earth consisted of eleven gardens, including a romantic Italian courtyard containing playful and exotic statues surrounded by lush overgrowth. There was a South Atlantic United States garden showing off Camellias, Azaleas, Magnolias and Crepe Myrtle; an Edwardian garden where the intoxicating aromas of specimens from the oldest existing orchid range overwhelms the senses; an American desert with huge Barrel Cactus, Giant Aloe and Crown of Thorns that captures the imagination with pictures of expansive open desert ranges; a Chinese Garden with beauty and serenity surrounding the crooked paved steps that keep evil spirits from entering, as they can only traverse in straight lines; and, finally, the ultimate natural botanical expression, a tropical rain forest with a semi-tropical garden adjoining it. In completing the tour of the exotic gardens, I felt totally connected with Doris' soul and her philosophy that states: "While plants may seem to have a low profile in our society, they are, both biologically and culturally, the basis of life."

It was with those feelings that we ventured to her estate on Bellevue Avenue that lies at the waters edge of the Atlantic Ocean. An important distinction between her and the other "summer residents" who visited Newport for only six to eight weeks is that she actually lived in her manor from May to November and considered herself a local native. My feeling of our being kindred souls increased when she began to invest

Michael Bivona

in the perseveration of Newport's colonial past by funding the not for profit Newport Restoration Foundation. One of the purposes of the organization is to buy and restore buildings throughout Newport to their original state. Since its inception, it has restored or preserved 83 buildings, some of which are rented as private residences and are maintained by a full time crew of carpenters and painters who keep the properties in pristine colonial condition. To fully appreciate her noble efforts to maintain the colonial neighborhoods of Newport, we have to go back to over twenty years ago, when our travels through the city was limited to two or three blocks in either direction of the marina where we docked our boat. The perimeter past those streets was run down and derelict. The city was a Navy town and there were many bars lining the streets and unsavory characters walking and lying about all over the place. With the relocation of many of the Navy's operations to other shores, and the loss of the America's Cup which transferred its yachting activities elsewhere, the city began to settle down a bit. Doris' foundation took advantage of the circumstances and began successfully recycling and restoring many dilapidated buildings throughout the city. With the help of many of her friends, such as Jackie Kennedy, Newport began to reinvent itself and now is one of the colonial showplaces of New England, with strict ordinances that will enable it to maintain its 18th and 19th centuries' architectural heritage.

Doris was born in 1912. She was the only child of James Buchanan Duke, the founder of the American Tobacco Company and the Duke Power Company, as well as the benefactor of Duke University. When he died in 1925, he left his 12-year-old daughter an estate of about $80-million, making her one of the richest girls in the world. At a young age, she decided to carry on with her father's passions for charity, environmental preservation, fine art and furniture collecting. She spent much of her time traveling the world, amassing countless treasures; notably collections of Islamic and Southeast Asian art, as well as, European fine art and furniture. During her life-time, she donated over $400-million to various causes and, upon her death, she left her fortune to the Doris Duke Charitable Foundation which supports the performing arts, environmental conservation, medical research, and the prevention of child abuse. She was an accomplished pianist and enjoyed inviting talented musicians to her home for jam sessions that would last for days on end. She was also an excellent athlete, playing tennis regularly, and enjoying a swim in the Atlantic Ocean that was a part of her back lawn at Rough Point. She was one of the few American heiresses that had a greater fortune at her death than she inherited.

Rough Point was built in 1889 for Frederick W. Vanderbilt on the dramatic windswept promontory of Newport's Cliff Walk; part of the 10-acre site is a beach on its back lawn caressing the Atlantic Ocean. It's an English red sandstone and granite Manorial-style home designed by the architectural firm of Peabody & Stearns. Subsequently, Mr. Duke had architect Horace Trumbauer add two new wings to the home and redecorated the place to resemble a subtle homey atmosphere rather than a gilded-type mansion that was so popular at that time. A tour of the premises required advanced reservations and parking away from the main building, which meant taking a shuttle bus to the manor's entrance. Tour guides await guests to escort them through the premises. The docent was very informative about the history and the artifacts throughout the building and kept us interested through the one-hour tour with details of the life of Doris and her philanthropy. An interesting story is about her love of animals. She allowed her many large dogs the freedom of the house and her two camels, Baby and Princess, the freedom of the outside grounds--much to the dismay of her housekeepers and gardeners.

The outside landscaping and view of the ocean pounding on the estate's rear lawn is beyond picture perfect. We were immediately drawn to topiaries of the life-sized camels, Baby and Princess. I must have taken a half a dozen photos of the replicas from every possible angle, with Barbara horsing around in each photo (no pun intended). The picturesque landscaping enhanced the natural beauty of the rocky shoreline, especially a section that is indented toward land with a bridge crossing over it and the rough surf pounding its shore. The more than 100-beautiful, different colored varieties of dahlias in the garden, and the rose arbor with its spectacular American Pillar Roses display, are breathtaking in their multitude of colors and creative designs. In keeping with her love of nature is the Kitchen Garden that supplied her with her daily vegetable and cut flower requirements. The produce is still used by the NRF staff and for educational and experimentation purposes. Barbara had to drag me away from the Shangri La atmosphere by reminding me that we had to attend a Big Band Dance at the Astor's Beechwood Mansion that evening, and that we had better take a nap if we hoped to attend and participate in the festivities. I made a mental note to visit Doris Duke's home in Hawaii, which she named "Shangri La," if we ever are lucky enough to return to that beautiful island. If she gave it that name, I could only imagine the magnificence that she gathered there to satisfy her creative artistic, intellectual, and humanitarian passions.

The Astor's Beechwood Mansion, www.astorsbeechwood. com, also located on the miracle strip, Bellevue Avenue, is situated on five pristine acres along the famous Cliff Walk, with expansive views of the Atlantic Ocean. It's one of the few remaining privately owned Gilded Era mansions in Newport; most of the others are owned by the Preservation Society of Newport County. The property was purchased in 1881 by William Backhouse Astor, Jr., as an anniversary gift for his wife, Caroline; know as "The Mrs. Astor." She hired the renowned architect Richard Morris Hunt to turn the mansion into a place worthy of America's highest society dame. Hunt, who designed the Beaux Arts façade of the New York's Metropolitan Museum of Art, created a stunning Victorian-styled mansion for her, with a gilded ballroom featuring mirrored walls, water-drop crystal chandeliers, ornate brass sconces, bas-reliefs depicting Poseidon and Aphrodite, and French doors that open to expansive lawns and the glittering sea beyond. Inspired by the Hall of Mirrors at Versailles, France, the ballroom became the center of American Society for more than twenty-five years and played host to Mrs. Astor's famous annual "Summer Ball," where only guests included on her private list of the most important 400 people in New York and Newport society were invited. The palace is approximately 20,000-square feet with 39-rooms, including 15-bedrooms, befitting the grandson of John Jacob Astor, the German immigrant who made himself the richest man in America by investing in fur trading and real estate. As of 1999, he was considered the fourth wealthiest American ever (Microsoft's Bill Gates is fifth). The estate is small compared to the mansions that were subsequently built by other Barons, but still it remained the "In" place to be for the privileged upper class while she remained the undisputed Queen of New York and Newport society.

Today, the mansion still reflects the beauty created by its illustrious former owners. Every member of the Beechwood staff, from kitchen maids, butlers, footmen and tenants, were represented by talented actors portraying them, the Astor family, and other notables of the period. All were dressed in historical character, which made our visiting the Gilded Age mansion a believable experience. Today it hosts many social events, such as "Murder Mystery Theater," "Xmas Festivals," "Roaring Twenties Swing Time," and "Big Band Nights." We were welcomed at the entrance by actors dressed in period outfits, the men wore WWII Army and Navy uniforms and zoot suits, and the girls wore 1930-40s-style outfits, some even wore bobby socks. The sounds from the 18-piece tuxedoed band acted like a magnet and we were immediately drawn to the rhythm as we swayed to its beat on the way to our table. We were seated with a young couple from Kennebunkport, Maine, named Jill and Jason. They arrived the day before on their 44-foot Viking Cabin Cruiser, and planned on spending a week in Newport enjoying the abundance of fun activity in the area. Our waiter was none other than a tuxedoed Cole Porter, who introduced himself by singing a few lines from his love song, "Night and Day." He told us that he wrote the song when he was a guest of the Astor's at Beechwood. The Swing music got us on our feet and we lindy hopped at a very fast pace, which I wasn't happy about as I usually like warming up with a slow Foxtrot or Waltz. But I finished the dance without too much trouble; it was either finish or listen to Barbara tell me how out of shape I am. We settled in with some drinks and traded our seafaring stories with our new friends. We switched partners in a Waltz and I was pleasantly surprised at how well Jill followed me. When dancing with a new partner, it's customary to start with very basic steps, and as they are successfully performed, to increase the complexity of the routines. She had no problem following me and it was a pleasure moving her light 5-foot, 4-inch frame around the dance floor. It's surprising that some female dancers, regardless of their size or shape, can be extremely light on their feet, which makes it easy to lead them into almost any step without struggling. On the other hand, there are many girls that are clingy and require a lot of pushing and energy to get them to move around the floor. When that happens, dancing becomes an exhausting experience for me. There is no rhyme or reason for this. Some people, regardless of their dancing experience, are just easy to move around, although the more dance lessons a person takes, the easier it is for them to maneuver around the dance floor. This does not, however, guarantee that they will be light on their feet and easy for me to move them around. Jill was the exception, she didn't have much training but followed my leads to perfection and we both ended our Waltz with very satisfying grins on our faces. I danced with her several times during the evening to a Foxtrot, Rumba and Cha-Cha, all done very well and gratifying. Barbara danced the same dances with Jason and totally enjoyed the change of partners, especially that his style of dancing was mostly International Standard (done mostly in closed positions) which is a lot different from the American Style that she is accustomed to, which has many open breaks.

Approaching our table was a beautiful, well dressed young lady with long dangling curls hanging softly from her head, who introduced herself as "The Mrs. Astor." She asked me if

I would like to accompany her in a Viennese Waltz. I jumped at the opportunity to dance with the Queen of New York and Newport society. I told her that her royal purple velvet gown was gorgeous and she stopped for a moment to explain the different items in her dress ensemble. The gown had point lace and was embroidered in silver. She wore many of her famous jewels; a diamond tiara, a diamond stomacher, and a necklace brimming with large glimmering diamonds. Considering the weight and size of the full soft velvet gown, she was able to move around the floor quite nicely to the beat of the Viennese Waltz: left turn, 1-2-3, 2-2-3, 3-2-3 and 4-2-3 with a hesitation, 1-2-3 and then to the right, 1-2-3, 2-2-3, 3-2-3 and 4-2-3. We did a breakaway facing each other three times, hands touching and arms raised and then went into a propeller position, side by side, with our left arms extended and turning, imitating the motion of a turning prop. We both ended the dance hugging each other with delight for a job well done. In the meantime, I saw Barbara dancing with Cole Porter. She said he was a fabulous dancer and had put her into a running Waltz step that she had never done before. The ball ended with the actors doing a Waltz exhibition to Cole Porter's "Dream Dancing," and we were then asked to join them in a finale, which we did; ending our dreamy evening with a dreamy song.

The next day was our last in Newport. As is customary when traveling the waterways, I took the opportunity to review my pre-check list to make sure that all the basic parts of the boat are operating properly. I have always tried to follow Ben Franklin's advice: "An ounce of prevention is worth a pound of cure." This is especially true when considering winds, currents, fog, and any number of unexpected unpleasant calamities that await unprepared seamen. So, I occupied the morning checking the oil and water levels of the two engines and generator; checking her many hoses for leaks; checking for loose wires; checking my instruments and, of course, checking the weather forecast for the following day, which was predicted as "five-miles per hour winds and two to three-foot seas," a perfect weather report for our journey back to New York. The weather conditions are extremely important, as the trip back to New York can be treacherous as it is a highly traveled waterway, and fog can always be expected to pay a visit for a good part of the journey. I made the necessary repairs, reviewed my charts and was confident that with a little bit of luck, we would have a safe five to six hour journey across the busy shipping channels. We spent the rest of the afternoon goofing off and enjoying the swimming pool at the hotel, anxiously awaiting the Closing Gala of the Newport Classical Music Festival at the Breakers Mansion that evening.

It is always thrilling to approach the five-story 130,000-square-foot Breakers Mansion. Walking to the entrance requires some neck stretching to absorb the height and width of the structure. The entrance hall is 45-feet high and leads into the Great Hall, where our Gala Music Finale was being held, accommodating up to 300 guests. The evening's entertainment included: "Romantic Pearls from Russia," highlighted by the works of Sergei Rachmaninoff; "Waves of Emotions," with compositions of Carlos Paredes and Astor Piazzolla; and "Porky and Bess," the works of George Gershwin. The compositions were performed by a Latvian Soprano, a Dutch Saxophonist, and an American Pianist. The highlight of the evening was the "Dynamic Duo," the Latvian Soprano and the Dutch Saxophonist performing a duet, where the saxophone imitated the soprano's voice from her low to high notes. The musician made sounds that seemed to be coming from an entirely different instrument, matching her every note while playing in complete harmony. It was quite an amazing performance from two young talented artists and befitting the conclusion of a wonderful Classical Music Festival.

After the concert the guests were invited to join the performers on the outside terrace facing the Atlantic Ocean for a Champagne Salute to the event's successful ending. Hors D'oeuvres and finger sandwiches were provided, and we were able to munch, drink, and speak with many of the friendly artists. A cool refreshing breeze filled the air and reminded us that the next morning we had to awaken early and begin our journey back to our real world in Long Island, New York. We left, promising ourselves that we would return the following year, God willing.

The next morning's weather was clear as predicted. I started Mikara's engines, dropped my dock-lines, and headed for the opening of Newport Harbor to enter the waters of the Atlantic Ocean. We hit fog for about an hour, but eventually the sun burned it off and we continued with calm seas and the wind to our backs to Block Island Sound and then on to Gardiner's Bay. We passed many sailboats with full-sheets-to-the-wind, fishing boats with extended cross-like nets extended from their sterns, and many powerboats traveling in every direction to their happy destinations. We arrived at Stirling Harbor Marina in mid-afternoon, tied Mikara to her berth, connected her to fresh water and dock electricity, and washed her down with lots of soap suds. When she was as clean as a whistle, I smiled at her for a job well done and gave her a satisfying eye wink; she in turn, winked and smiled right back at me.

CHAPTER THIRTEEN

Dancing at the Kentucky Derby Ball and on the Mississippi Queen

ONE OF OUR MORE memorable trips was a vacation we took that began with dancing at The Fillies Derby Ball at the Galt House Hotel in Louisville, Kentucky. It was two weeks prior to the May Churchill Downs Kentucky Derby Race, and we boarded the Mississippi Queen Paddle Wheel Boat for a Derby-themed cruise from Cincinnati, Ohio to Memphis, Tennessee and then returning to Louisville, Kentucky for what is known as "The longest two-minute race in sports," at the Churchill Downs Race Track. We intended to conclude our trip by attending the Grand Gala Ball, which was also hosted at the Galt House Hotel. Although this story was never published, I thought it would be an interesting story to add to our other traveling adventures.

On the flight from JFK Airport in New York City, to Louisville, Kentucky, I took the opportunity to read some of the city's history. Louisville, pronounced "Loo-e-vel" by the locals, was named for King Louis XVI of France in appreciation of his support in supplying us with French troops which was instrumental in our winning the Revolutionary War. The city was founded by the Virginian General, George Rogers Clark, in 1778. He was the older brother of the famous William Clark of the Lewis and Clark Expedition that was sent west by President Thomas

Jefferson to explore and map the Western Territories. The city's growth was slow, but the introduction of the steamboat in the early 1800s and the city being one of the slave-trading centers in the country, expedited its development into the largest city in Kentucky. Owing to its strategic location at the Water Falls of the Ohio River, Louisville became a major commercial center.

During the Civil War, it was a major Union military supply center and played a critical roll in the Northern Forces winning that conflict. It's situated in North-Central Kentucky on the Kentucky-Indiana border at the only natural obstacle in the Ohio River, the Water Falls of the Ohio. Although considered a Southern state, it's influenced by both Midwestern and Southern cultures, and is commonly referred to as either the northernmost Southern city or the southernmost Northern city in the United States. Some of its notable residents have included inventor Thomas Edison, U.S. Supreme Court Justice Louis Brandeis, boxing legend Muhammad Ali, and writers Hunter S. Thompson and Sur Grafton. Notable events occurring in the city include the first public viewing place of Edison's incandescent light bulb, as well as many medical advances, including the first human hand transplant, the first self-contained artificial heart transplant, and the development site of the first cervical cancer vaccine. So there seems to be a lot more to the city then its annual Kentucky Derby Race, which is the first race in the Triple Crown of Thoroughbred Racing.

We arrived at our hotel, the Galt House, in the late morning, which gave us plenty of time to unpack and decide how we would spend the next few days in that metropolis. The hotel is located in downtown Louisville, Kentucky, on the Ohio River waterfront. It has two 25-story towers with a skywalk that connects it to the Kentucky International Convention Center. The towers are linked by a three-story glass-domed conservatory that houses a café, a cocktail lounge with a gathering area, a bird aviary and greenhouse space on level one, with large trees and foliage extending to the third floor. The conservatory offers panoramic views of downtown Louisville and the Ohio River. The original

Michael Bivona

Galt House, built in the early 1800s, was the residence of Dr. W.C. Galt, is now a 1,300-room hotel featuring traditional décor furnishings highlighting cherry wood armoires, desks, and armchairs. It's the pride of Louisville and, from the start of the two-week Kentucky Derby Festival to the final call to the posts at Churchill Downs, serves as the headquarters for many of the Derby's events. This includes "Thunder Over Louisville," which is an air show and the world's largest fireworks extravaganza which marks the beginning of two weeks of Derby celebrations prior to the big race. It also hosts the Fillies Derby Ball, the Mint Jubilee Gala, the Derby Festival Fashion Show, and the Grand Gala.

The house has more than a checkered history. It was rebuilt several times due to destruction by fires, inclement weather and old age. Each time it was resurrected it improved on its beauty and reputation as being "The most charming Southern hospitable place to spend time." It boasts as former guests such notables as Jefferson Davis, Stephen Douglas, Charles Dickens, P.T. Barnum, and presidents Lincoln, Grant, Taylor, Hayes and Buchanan. In 1864, generals Grant and Sherman planned their military strategies at the landmark venue, which led to the capture of Atlanta, Georgia, and the eventual end of that war. The hotel was a popular meeting place for the Union's generals. One such meeting between General Jefferson C. Davis (not to be confused with the Confederate President Jefferson Davis) and General William "Bull" Nelson resulted in a dispute and dual in which the "Bull" was shot. It's still not clear what the dispute was all about.

We reviewed the activities that would be taking place for the next couple of weeks and were overwhelmed at the scope of the 100-plus planned events. The main attractions included "Thunder Over Louisville." Each year, upward to 800,000 people gather around the waterfront at 9:30 P.M., to watch the world's largest fireworks display, which is heralded as the opening act for the Kentucky Derby. On the same day and at the same location, from 3:00 P.M. to 9:30 P.M., an "Air Show" with over 50 different acts is conducted. A "Marathon and mini-Marathon," that have a 26-mile and 13-mile race, respectively, are huge and popular events among both residents of Louisville and its surrounding cities; the participants are both runners and walkers. A "Great Balloon Fest" at the Kentucky Fair and Exposition Center, that usually draws up to 70,000 spectators, consists of a balloon race and an evening balloon glow, among other minor events. The famous "Great Steamboat Race" gathers a crowd in excess of the Derby Race, where the Belle of Louisville challenges the Delta Queen of Cincinnati for the bragging rights of "The Fastest Paddlewheel" title. They race down the Ohio River to the delight and roars of the spectators, who line both sides of the waterway cheering them on. The grand prize is a pair of Golden Antlers, which is displayed in a place of honor on the front of the winning boat, attesting to the fact that it's the best and fastest paddlewheel on the river. The "Kentucky Derby Festival Pegasus Parade" is considered one of its biggest and best festival events. Parade participants march, walk, and roll down Broadway in Downtown Louisville with their floats, inflatable characters, marching bands, celebrities, and marching horses.

We were lucky that our 17th-floor room had a balcony which gave us a spectacular view of the river. So we decided to watch the Air Show, order dinner in, and enjoy the world's largest fireworks display from the comfort of our room. The Air Show lineup was extensive, up to 50 continuous performances and fly-bys from 3:00 P.M. to 9:30 P.M., including, Army, Air Force, Navy, and Marine flying exercises and acts. The show started with the Navy Leap Frogs' team parachuting from 10,000-feet and landing on a Great Lawn, which was set up to accommodate the daredevils. Soon after exiting the plane, they somehow managed to assemble and hold hands in a circular and star formation. The National Anthem blurted out over loudspeakers, while the attack submarine, USS Louisville, and a Coast Guard cutter floated down the Ohio River, each carrying a humongous American flag. Barbara and I couldn't contain our excitement at seeing such an incredibly, coordinated, unexpected sight, which was accompanied by patriotic music. I was glad that I listened to Barbara and brought two pairs of binoculars and my super Nikon camera with extra distance zooming features. During the afternoon and into the evening, Apache helicopters, F-15s, F-16s, F-17s and F-18s showed off their technical skills, impressing us with their pilots' flying abilities and the maneuverability of the jets. An advantage to viewing the show from our room was that we were able to go inside and do some serious snoozing when the urge to sleep overcame us. In between naps, we saw the world's original six-aircraft civilian formation team, The Lima- Lima Aerobatics, flying their restored T-34 Mentors in several complicated formations, from the six-ship wedge and double arrowhead to the basic finger four and diamond.

At about 7:00 P.M., while we were enjoying our steak dinners, eight 400-foot barges moved into position on both sides of the Second Street Bridge, which served as the staging grounds for the annual "Run for the Roses" kick-off displays. A formation of the "Trojan Horsemen's Sunset Show," consisting of six T-28 Warbird fighters, appeared in a "V" formation with smoke or steam (I could never figure out which of the two applied) streaming from their tails; this is always an exciting display that signifies not only the might of the aircraft but the optional peaceful beauty they can exhibit. They were followed by the "Lima-Lima Night Show" which was surreal; the noise from their six loud engines was deafening, while the glitter from their fuselages, flames from their tails, and glares from the bright spotlights below, turned the darkness of the night into a scene from an air raid over London, England, during WWII.

Just as we were beginning to relax and sit back for the fireworks extravaganza, two helicopters appeared, each carrying a large American flag; in the background a loud and clear voice could be heard reciting, "Proud to be an American." We were beginning to wonder what surprise was next when an aerobatic-pyrotechnic show started. The plane was piloted by the famous Bill Leff; I couldn't believe my eyes at the fireworks coming from his aircraft while it flew straight up into the sky and circled around and down while the fireworks blasted from its wings. What was next?

Before we could think the words, fireworks were exploding right in front of our faces. We could smell the incendiaries burning and felt the heat and vibrations from the explosions. The opening display featured fireworks of a water cascade coming from the bridge; it resembled Niagara Falls on fire. Instead of the usual rainbow that appears above the falls, a flashing, moving rainbow seemed to be coming from inside the firework's cascade display. Throughout the extravaganza, a medley of ethnic, classic rock, patriotic, and rap music reverberated and mingled with the flashing colors coming from the pyrotechnics, which resulted in a dazzling, dizzying, eyeball rolling experience. While all eyes were looking above at the sky, below the paddlewheel, Belle of Louisville, was prancing around the river all lit up like a Xmas tree and showing off her Golden Antlers. Designs of American flags and many other complimentary symbols burst into the sky, turning darkness into a colorful daylight. In the finale, the explosions coming from the bridge and the eight barges turned the night sky into a sparkling rainbow exploding in every direction. Combined with the noise, lights, and erratic vibrations, it seemed like a preview of our planet, first imploding and then exploding. The spectacular opening act for the Kentucky Derby Festival was produced by "the first family of fireworks," Zambelli International of New Castle, Pennsylvania. Included in their pyrotechnics were contributions from China, Italy and Spain, making the synergy an international effort.

I couldn't believe how tired and dirty I was from watching the air and firework extravaganzas. Again my wife Barbara came to the rescue, and insisted that we close the balcony doors before the performances began. How right she was, as we were covered with residual soot from the explosions, which resulted in our foregoing our morning shower for an evening scrub before retiring. In the quiet of the room, we both realized that we had diminished hearing from all the noise and vibrations of the rockets, fireworks blasts, and the persistent loudspeaker music and announcements. I went to sleep with both ears ringing and my eyes tearing from all the commotion and pollution generated that day, but the experience was well worth the little discomfort that quickly disappeared when I entered the silent world of dreamland.

The next morning we awoke refreshed and ready to face another exciting day. We were attending the Fillies Derby Ball in the evening, so we decided that a leisurely day of sightseeing was in order. We asked our concierge, Jonathan, for some guidance; he strongly suggested the Kentucky Horse Park in Lexington. He convinced us with his rationale, he said: "Louisville has the race, which is the heart of the Derby, but Lexington is the soul of the horse country. A visit to the horse park will help you fully experience and understand what the Derby is all about. Lexington is where many of the world's top racehorses are born, bred, trained, registered, bought, sold, retired and finally buried." A bus tour was leaving in an hour which gave us time for a quick breakfast and preparation for the full day's outing.

The bus ride gave me an opportunity to read about the park. Their brochure was very informative and stated: "The Kentucky Horse Park is a working horse farm and educational theme park that opened in 1978. The equestrian facility is a 1,200-acre park dedicated to man's relationship with the horse. Open to the public, the park has a twice daily Parade of Breeds, showcasing both common and rare horses from across the globe. The horses are ridden in authentic costume. Beginning with the 1979 arrival of Forego, one of the leading handicap horses of the 1970s, the park has been a retirement home for some of the world's greatest competition horses. The status of the park as a retirement center was further established with the 1985 arrival of John Henry, 'Horse of the Decade' and one of the top money-winning thoroughbred gildings in racing history. Alongside other racing greats, such as Forego, and his fellow 1970s champion Bold Forbes, is Cigar, voted 'Horse of the Decade' for the 1990s, and Da Hoss, the first of only two thoroughbreds to win the Breeders' Cup races in nonconsecutive years. In addition to many competitions and educational events, it also hosts the Bluegrass Classic Dog Show, the Kentucky Fall Classic Saddlebred Show, and the Alltech FEI World Equestrian Games. The park also has the International Museum of the Horse, the American Saddlebred Museum, horseback and pony rides, carriage rides and horse farm tours."

At the park entrance, we were greeted by the bronze life-size statue of "Man O' War" resting on a crypt of his fully embalmed remains; he was one of the world's greatest race horses, if not the greatest horse that ever lived. Surrounding his statue are the headstones of his famous off springs: War Relic (his most successful sire), War Admiral, War Kilt, and War Hazard. These are just a few of the more than 64 stakes winners and 200 other various champions that he sired. The big chestnut horse, nicknamed "Big Red," won 20 of his 21 races and set five world records in his short two-year racing career, which ran from 1919-1920. This super horse won a Belmont Stakes Race by 20-lengths and the Lawrence Realization Stakes Race by 100 lengths. He was forced into early retirement because other horse owners refused to race their stables against him. They insisted on his giving them a handicap by adding additional weight onto Big Red to slow the great horse down. He lived a glorious 30 years, producing an amazing amount of champions, while in retirement in the blue grass country of Kentucky. It's worth mentioning that the one race that he lost was due to the fact that he was turned around at the opening gate, but still managed to come in second at the Sanford Memorial Stakes; the victor was a horse named Upset; an appropriate name for the horse that defeated the "invincible one." Upset has been popularized as a phrase in sports which is still used today: "Upset," meaning "a lowly entry which comes forth beating the favorite." A heart wrenching story about Big Red is that his groom and pal, Will Harbut, died suddenly in October, 1947. Man O'War was so depressed that he pined away, and in less than a month, died of a broken heart.

Michael Bivona

Our first stop was the Visitor's Information Center where we viewed the wide screen presentation of "Thou Shall Fly without Wings," a 25-minute film that paid homage to horses and their importance in the world of entertainment and commerce. It was surprising to learn that they are not indigenous to North America, but were first introduced to our continent by the Spanish conquistadors. There are several ways to visit the park. The two most popular are walking or taking a horse-drawn carriage tour. It was a beautiful day and we were tempted to walk around the ranch and enjoy the vast green rolling hills accented with long lines of white fencing and horses leisurely enjoying the calmness of the day. Unfortunately, we were short on time and opted for the narrated horse trolley tour that visited many of the park's attractions in a short period of time. Our trolley was pulled by two large draft horses whose easy temperament is renowned. These horses are magnificent creatures; their tall stature, extremely muscular with upright shoulders that are more than necessary to meet the challenge of pulling appropriately-sized loads. In addition to their massive bone structure, the pair looked like identical twins: dark chocolate brown with a white stripe down their faces, flared tails, and beautiful feathering on their white lower legs. Draft breeds range from approximately 16 to 19 hands high (four inches to a hand) and weigh from 1,400 to 2,000 pounds. Petting their foreheads brought a rush of precious memories back to me of my early teenage years when I was in my "horse loving phase" and my ambition when I became an adult was to be a cowboy; even another Gene Autry or Roy Rogers. Although I lived in Brooklyn, New York, which is as far from horse country as a city can be, we did have several riding academies not far from where I grew up. For a while, my gang of friends and I would visit the stables at least weekly, to ride or just hang around with the older pseudo cowboys that attended the horses. We even had beach outings and sing-a-longs around campfires, while pretending to be on the open ranges herding cattle to their final destinations. My most vivid recollection was when I was about fifteen years old and I worked in Playland at

456

Coney Island as a horse riding attendant. My job was to hold the ponies and horses while children, and sometime adults, rode around our circular riding path. I was actually paid by the hour, plus tips, to be with animals I so dearly loved. At the end of the day, my job included brushing down the stock and cleaning the stables, which I did without any reservations. My job gave me an opportunity to meet many of the show people and workers along the strip. By the time my summer job ended, I was considered one of "the guys" by most of my new friends and seriously thought about making my life a part of the carnival. But, as most youthful dreams come and go, that dream followed its natural course and came to an end with the beginning of the cool fall weather. The only unhappy memory I have of the experience is that, upon entering my house after a long day's work, I had to remove all my clothing and jump into the shower before I would be accepted by my family as a civilized, decent-smelling person.

So to me, that trip became more than another sightseeing adventure, it was a visit down memory lane. The sight of those beautiful animals and the fragrance of the area put me into a pleasantly relaxed state of mind and body. As the horse-drawn trolley moved forward, the narrator brought to our attention the "International Museum of the Horse" which is the largest equine museum of its kind in the world, where the 50-million-year history of the horse is explored. It's the perfect place to learn about the more than 100-different breeds of horses, their impact on civilization through the ages, and how they fit into our modern world. It houses racing trophies, priceless artifacts, carriages, and more. "Make sure you visit this museum before leaving the park" our tour guide said, "It's an affiliate of the Smithsonian Institution and much of the research into the history of horses comes from their efforts." The next stop was the "American Saddlebred Museum," home of the largest collection of Saddlebred artifacts in the world, including: trophies, photographs, tack, artwork, and a library of over 2,400 volumes used for bloodline and genealogical research. The museum celebrates Kentucky's only native

Michael Bivona

breed of horse with displays on its history from the past to the present. The museum has an award-winning theater show, interactive exhibits, and the Saddlebred sidewalk. We passed groups of visitors riding horses and ponies and were surprised to see a Draft Horse show in progress. Although our pullers were chocolate brown, the horses in the show varied; it seemed that every color brown was represented, many were two-toned, but all were magnificently handsome.

Another surprise was the campgrounds that has over 250 paved campsites, with all the amenities, nestled amid the park's enormous acreage of bluegrass. Its residents seemed frozen in time, sitting around their campers and outdoor tables, eating, drinking, and sunning themselves. The area contained a grocery and gift shop, a laundromat, two bathhouses with modern conveniences, which came in handy, tennis and basketball courts, a junior Olympic swimming pool, a horseshoe area, and even a pavilion where square dancing was taking place. The campground also has a primitive area for tent campers who prefer roughing their outdoor experience without modern conveniences in their tents.

The hammering from the blacksmith's shop brought our tour to an end. We didn't have much time to visit many of the free attractions, so we chose the Hall of Champions Show as our farewell stop. We didn't realize how extensive the park was. It would probably take a few days to really see the place at a leisurely pace, which, to our regret, we didn't have. The theme of the show seemed to be "Not only well-bred horses are champions." It started with the showing of CH Gypsy Supreme, a saddle bred horse that was considered too small and untrainable to be a race horse. He proved his critics wrong by winning nine World Championships and five National Championships. The next horse, Cigar, was also considered too small to be a winner; plagued with an injury at a young age he was discounted as a contender. He fooled everyone by winning 16-consecutive races and being hailed as the 18th best thoroughbred of the 20th century, winning almost $10 million for his efforts. The last thoroughbred we saw was John Henry. He was also considered small, ugly, foul tempered, and not raceable. Well he fooled the experts; he was the highest purse winner of his time, at almost $7 million. He didn't showcase very long, as his spirited actions caused him to be withdrawn from the exhibition. We had to leave the show early to catch our bus back to Louisville, but we promised ourselves that if we were ever in that area again, we would pitch a tent, find a fire pit, roast hot dogs, and marshmallows, and spend a few days enjoying the park that bears evidence that man and nature can exists in harmony, for the benefit of both.

A made-to-order nap on the returning bus prepared us for The Fillies Derby Ball, which, fortunately for us, was at our hotel. We decided to bring formal wear with us as we were attending two balls in Louisville and one on the Mississippi Queen Paddlewheel Steamboat. The invitation to the Ball stated that dress was festive to formal. While struggling with my tuxedo, I was tempted to put on dungarees and a tee shirt and attend as a festive person, but I knew Barbara would not be happy and when she is unhappy she seems to do lots of shopping. So, discretion being the better part of valor, I put on my tuxedo and headed for the ballroom. The name of the Ball made us think that it was in honor of the female horses, or ponies called fillies, that have not reached their fourth birthday, however, we were mistaken. The Fillies of the ball is with a capital "F" and refers to the young women who were the Princesses and Queen of the Kentucky Derby Festival. More than 70 young college students were nominated for the year's Princess Program from students with at least a 3.0 grade point average, and are involved on their campuses and in their communities in extra curricular activities. An out-of-state panel of three judges selected the five princesses, who each received a $2,000.00 scholarship as a prize. All the girls are members of The Fillies, Inc., a volunteer group that works closely with the officials of the Kentucky Derby Festival that entertains more than 1.5 million people each year in the various activities preceding the Derby. The princesses can be seen at all the official events; from the Poster Premier in January until they grace the first float of the Pegasus Parade in May. They were presented wearing their royal white gowns with prized jeweled tiaras, sparkling from their well-groomed heads. The high point of the evening was choosing the Queen from one of the beautiful princesses. This was accomplished by spinning an oversized wheel. The lucky winner was then crowned, signifying the beginning of the Kentucky Derby Festival that leads to the eventual race at Churchill Downs. To round out the Royal Court, four handmaidens and two pages, between the ages of 8 and 12, were selected by the parents and grandparents of the Fillies, to help the Queen and princesses in their demanding jobs. The ball combined the excitement of the Queen's Coronation with entertainment and a dinner dance.

We were surprised at the number of people attending the ball. There were over 800-people present; many of the men wore black and white tuxedoes that made the assembly resemble a penguin's colony. Most of the men were dressed in formal attire or suits, lending an air of elegance to the occasion. The women outdid themselves. They were not restricted, as the men were, to pants, jackets, shirts and ties of limited colors. The ladies seemed to have a rehearsed fashion parade in motion. None of the gowns were the same and were presented in every size, shape and design imaginable with colors consisting of every shade and glitter devised by the world's most fashionable designers.

The cocktail party was a first-class affair. Hors d'oeuvre were in abundance and delicious, especially the enormous shrimp and small lamb chops. Liquor flowed and the music from a three-piece combo filled the air with soft pleasant non-intrusive tones, which assisted in keeping the noise of the crowd at a tolerable level. The only confusing sights were the waiters, who were wearing black tuxedoes and couldn't be distinguished from the male guests. It is befuddling to me that, after the never-ending formal occasions that require waiters, more appropriate attire has not been popularized to differentiate waiters from guests. I think it would be a good idea for them to wear red hats or hats with propellers protruding from the top. I asked someone where the bar was, thinking the tuxedoed person was a waiter; he did direct me to the liquor fountain, but it turned out that he wasn't a service person at all. How was I supposed to know?

The dinner arrangements were well organized and everyone was seated at their assigned tables without any confusion, considering the amount of people in attendance. We were seated at a table for ten; the other guests were from a group of travelers from California. After introducing ourselves, we settled in and began absorbing our surroundings. There were arrangements of ivory, black, and gold-toned flowers on our table and throughout the ballroom, which sent their sweet aroma into the air and our minds. There was an elaborate stage set up with a throne decorated with a colorful floral trellis of white roses, awaiting the arrival of the soon to be crowned Queen. After a half hour of relative calm, the speeches began, honoring the people responsible for making the Festival and Derby a success. In recognition of their tremendous efforts, they were appointed as Knights and Dames of the Derby Festival Court of Pegasus. The induction ceremony became the new Queen's first official act. High political officials were introduced. I don't remember their names, but I do remember that the main speaker did mention that one of the former Princesses, Martha Layne Collins, went on to become the Governor of Kentucky.

After the tributes ended, the full orchestra blasted their instruments in unison to welcome the unveiling of a huge "Wheel of Fortune." The Royal Court appeared, Princesses, Handmaidens, Pages, and even a Court Jester. All were in period costumes; their presence transformed the floral decorated hall into a Royal Ball. The Grand Master introduced the honored girls and wished them luck. At the turn of the wheel the audience fell silent, when it stopped its circular motion, a new Queen had been chosen. She stepped forward; her tiara was replaced by a sparkling peeked jeweled crown, which was placed on her Royal head as her face beamed with delight. She took her seat on the throne to the roar of the crowd and the loud trumpet blasts from the orchestra. The Grand Master announced: "Long Live the Queen," and the crowd repeated in unison: "Long Live the Queen." That ended the coronation of the Derby's Queen and the beginning of our dinner and dancing.

Considering that there were over 800-guests, the dinner preparation and service went very smoothly. We had a salad of mixed greens with water chestnuts, purple onions, artichokes, cherry tomatoes and sliced almonds, topped with pleasant honey mustard. The main course, which we previously ordered, was sliced tenderloins with Dijon mustard sauce or Sea Bass encrusted with Caribbean bread crumbs. The side dishes were mashed potatoes, corn pudding, asparagus, and watercress garnish. The coup d'état was the dessert of a top hat filled with crème-de-menthe mousse, plated with fresh blueberries, raspberries, strawberries, and fresh mint syrup. The cuisine was surprisingly good. Mixed with the agreeable conversations of our tablemates and the soft piano music in the background, the dining experience was quite enjoyable; much more than we expected considering the enormous size of the crowd. The real fun began when dinner ended and the full 17-piece orchestra started playing some great dancing music.

The first dance began when the Royal Court gathered on the large ballroom floor and formed a double circle with partners facing each other, the males backs to the center of the circle. The music was similar to "How Do You Do My Partner," which I last heard in my kindergarten class. As they danced, I recalled the words that went something like this:

"How do you do, my partner? (Boys bow)

How do you do today? (Girls curtsy)

Will you dance in a circle? (Boys and girls take right hands)

I will show you the way!" (Both join left hands under right and face Line of Direction LOD)

Everyone danced in the LOD, and after one complete circle, the girls move forward one place to a new partner.

This was repeated several times, and then the Royal Court disbursed and went into the audience and chose partners to dance to the Waltz music that resounded throughout the hall. What a lovely way to begin the evening's dancing session. We joined the dancing; it didn't take long before the dance floor was crowded, but we still managed to get around and finish the Waltz. We were lucky that our new table friends were from a dance group so we were able to switch partners and dance to most of the music that evening. One of our new friends was a dance instructor. When he saw that I was out of breath after doing a Samba, he asked me if I would mind a little constructive criticism. Well, at that stage in my life, when it came to dancing, I was getting use to lots of criticism, so what was a little more? He said: "Your steps are too big, shorten them and you probably won't get as winded." Sounded easy enough, so later on in the evening when the crowd thinned out, I asked the band leader to play another Samba, which he gladly did. Lo and behold, the smaller steps did the trick--I wasn't as tired as I usually got when dancing that aerobic dance. In the process, he admired a step that he wasn't familiar with and asked if we would break it down for him. I was delighted to accommodate him. The basic step in the Brazilian Samba for the man is: forward, 1 & 2, back, 3 & 4. This is done to the beat of slow, quick-quick. The dance is done in ballroom position, rather than Latin. The dance is taken around the floor in LOD and has lots of hip movements and open breaks. What he liked was a routine we did in closed position, in place, where we don't perform a basic step, but rather, I kept my right foot in place with no movement. Barbara's left leg also remained in place. We both moved our other leg back and forward while we swung our dangling arms in the same direction as our leg motions, back and forth; we then reverse our arm movements in the opposite direction of our legs' motion. It was an easy routine once the timing is understood, which took all of two seconds for him to pick up. We spent the rest of the evening rotating partners, which is the epitome of great dancing and social camaraderie. We ended the evening by giving hugs and kisses to our new dancing friends and exchanged home, e-mail addresses and phone numbers, with promises to keep in touch. We left the Grand Ballroom delightfully exhausted and ecstatic that our destination was a short walk away, in the same hotel. Although it was late in the evening, we had to pack our bags for our next day's trip to Cincinnati, Ohio, for what would, hopefully, be another great experience on the Mississippi Queen Paddlewheel.

We arrived at the Cincinnati, Ohio, piers late in the morning, just in time to join the other passengers in boarding the ship. All the wonderful memories flashed back into my mind of the last time we cruised on the American beauty, the Mississippi Queen, on our Mardi Gras adventure. We promised to return to the majestic lady and here we were looking at her red paddle wheel, stark white superstructure, high black smoke stakes, and the proud American flags fluttering in the wind at the top of Her Majesty. This time our cruise theme was "The Kentucky Derby. Steven Foster's, "De Camp Town Races" music welcomed us to the boarding steps. She was docked next to her younger sister, the American Queen, which was built in 1995, and replaced the oldest sister, Delta Queen, which was built in 1976. The baby sister is the largest steam paddlewheel in existence at 412-feet long, versus our ship's measurements from stem to stern of 383-feet. We were looking at two of the few remaining steam riverboats in existence. Before the Civil War, there were over 11,000 steamboats traversing the rivers of the United States, while today there are only a handful. As of this writing, the older sister, the Delta Queen, has also been retired from service as a riverboat.

The last time we boarded the Mississippi Queen, we were minus our luggage. This time, we made sure that our baggage never left our sight. So when we arrived in our cabin, our traveling companions were all present and accounted for. We didn't waste too much time following the aroma of biscuits that were being served for lunch. As this was our second trip with the Queen, we were familiar with the surroundings, so we were able to pay a little more attention to the details and the scheduling of events. Dining is the most important event on the ship, so we were pleased to learn that a new schedule was in place. Breakfast could be enjoyed several ways. For an easy and quick delight, the large front porch was available; a buffet arrangement in the Grand Saloon was an inviting option, with the choice of endless breakfast delights; or the elegant dining room was an option for a sit-down meal. Of course, there is always the option of having breakfast served in the cabin. Lunch could be enjoyed in the open area by the calliope bar with hot dogs, hamburgers, and other BBQ favorites available, or the main saloon was available for a sit-down lunch with an extensive menu to match the mood of the day. There are two Captain's nights for dinner; the second night and the last night. Both are formal events, but don't require tuxedoes or evening gowns. An addition to the menu from our last trip was that vegetarian meals were offered for those requiring restricted diets or for people, like Barbara and me, who like pigging out one night and use the vegan menu to relieve our guilty consciences on the alternate evenings. We chose the open buffet for lunch and couldn't stop going back for second helpings of Southern fried chicken legs and biscuits with gravy.

After lunch, we went to the Grand Saloon for an orientation session. Our Riverlorian (river historian) was Clara, who gave us a brief history of the steamship line and its importance on the rivers that they sailed. She briefly reviewed some of the stops we would be making on our cruise and told us as we reached each destination she would be having in-depth discussions about the ports-of-call. After the lecture, we decided to just walk around the ship and refresh our memories about the amenities and the location of the various places of interest. Just then, the whistle blasted: toot-toot-toot and the calliope began playing "Anchors Away" as the Queen moved from the dock, much to the delight of the passengers who began waving to their imaginary friends on shore, who in turn waved back a hearty bon voyage. We were off and running down the Mississippi River; the cool fresh sea air forcing its way into our bodies and senses. What a pleasure it was to be back on the majestic lady.

Above the Grand Stairway, the ceiling of cherubs can be seen dancing in and around clouds. The Upper Paddlewheel Lounge has Victorian-style couches and overstuffed chairs that are perfect as a comfortable place to relax, enjoy a drink and view the passing scenery. On the Observation Deck, the Grand Saloon welcomes passengers as a gathering place for daily activities and is the showroom and ballroom for nightly entertainment. The Golden Antler Bar was as I remembered it, with game tables and floor-to-ceiling windows. The gym had some new treadmills and bikes, which I planned on making good use of. After showering, I was planning on taking a dip in the bathing pool or maybe watching a film in the movie theater. The library was well stocked with books and magazines, so we decided to relax and sit there for a while and browse through the books to choose some reading companions for our trip.

Our first stop was Louisville, Kentucky, where we had already spent time and would be returning to at the end of our trip to witness the Kentucky Derby. So, we decided to crack open our books and just enjoy the day lounging on the Queen. The boat approached the city toot-toot-tooting, while the calliope blurted Americana music. I'm always fascinated by the method used to quickly get passengers off the boat; a large plank is extended from the bow of the vessel to the pier with the greatest of ease and within minutes the passengers are on their way to their chosen destinations. We found comfortable stuffed chairs in the Upper Paddlewheel Lounge, nestled in with our books and coffees in hand, and just let the morning float away, while occasionally viewing the outside blue sky and the river activity through the large windows. While we were enjoying our quiet time, we spotted the current smaller Russ Morgan Band board the ship along with the Four Lads singing group. Ross Morgan started his music career in the early 1920s as a piano and trombone player, and later became an arranger for such distinguished legends as John Philip Sousa and Victor Herbert. His was one of the first "sweet bands," sharing bandstands with such greats as Artie Shaw, Paul Whiteman, Charlie Spivak, Jimmy and Tommy Dorsey and Lawrence Welk. His band was taken over by his son, Jack Morgan, who is still playing his father's sweet music around America in the 21st century. His music in the Swing Era helped lift a nation's soul from a Depression and wars by putting people on the dance floor at the many hotels he played at, and by providing music through the many radio stations that he worked for, such as the Rinso-Lifeboy Show on NBC and the Philip Morris radio series on NBC and CBS. Some of his popular renditions and my favorite songs are: "In the Mood," "Dance with a Dolly (With a Hole in Her Stocking)," "Your Nobody Till Somebody Loves You," "Bye, Bye Blackbird," "I'm Looking over a Four Leaf Clover," and the very appropriate song, "Cruising down the River." I was hoping to hear these and many more of his famous swing time songs during our voyage. In recognition for his many contributions for recordings and musical arrangements, he was awarded a "Star" on the Hollywood Walk of Fame.

The Four Lads were also a pleasant memory from my youth. The songs I remember most were: "Moments to Remember," "No, Not Much," "Standing on the Corner (watching all the girls go by)," "The Mocking Bird," and appropriately, "Cruising down the River." We were hoping to hear these and the many other top hits from their "Hours in the sun." The group was headed by one of the original singers, Frank Busseri, and still performs throughout the United States for the faithful song lovers of the fifties and sixties. For their contribution to the enhancement of music, they were inducted into the Vocal Group Hall of Fame in 2003. Thrilled that the band and the singing group would be traveling with us, we were looking forward to some pretty good dancing and reminiscing of the days when Swing was "King" and singing quartets were the rave of the era.

Our second night out was the Captain's Night, which was a formal event. I found myself squeezing into my tuxedo again,

Michael Bivona

as my mid-section was beginning to get deformed from the abundance of delicious food I was consuming on our vacation. Barbara's 110 pounds didn't add an ounce or an inch; she still had the capacity to eat me under or over the table and stay slim and shapely, which she reminded me of when she heard me grumbling about my trying to get into my formal wear. The captain greeted us at the entrance of the Grand Saloon with a handshake and big smile. We exchanged names with him and the other officers of the ship and then joined some of our new friends at the cocktail hour. At dinner, Barbara and I couldn't resist the Southern fried catfish, which we longed for since our last visit. Finding a good catfish meal up North is almost impossible and, on the rare occasions that we were lucky enough to have it for a meal, it was always disappointing; Northerners just don't have the knack of preparing it as well as their Southern cousins. So we thoroughly enjoyed our meal, which was enhanced with buttermilk deep brown biscuits and mashed potatoes. At dinner the captain welcomed all the seafarers and promised that the journey up and down the Mississippi would be a memorable one.

We returned to the Grand Saloon for a night of entertainment. The ship's combo and vocalist started the evening off with some sweet jazz and were followed by the Russ Morgan 11-piece band. Their opening number was "Cruising Down the River," which got everyone to sing:

"Cruising down the river on a Sunday afternoon. With the one you love, the sun above waiting for the moon. The old accordion is playing a sentimental tune, cruising down the river on a Sunday afternoon. The birds above all sing of love, a gentle sweet refrain. The winds around all make a sound like softly falling rain. Just two of us together, we'll plan a honeymoon, cruising down the river on a Sunday afternoon."

It was surprising how many of the guests knew the words to the song; their harmony resulted in an almost choir-like sound. We danced the night away to "So Tired," "There Goes That Song Again," "Somebody Else is Taking My Place" and "Forever and Ever." We were able to get some Swing dancing in along with Foxtrots and Waltzes on the tight dance floor. The Four Lads were not to be out-done, their voices filled the room with some of their popular hits: "Moments to Remember," "Istanbul (means Constantinople)," "Who Needs You," "Enchanted Island," and "Happy Anniversary." We were happily exhausted when the show ended and returned to our cabin as exhilarated from the music as we were on our first trip on the Queen. It is common that when returning to a favorite place, especially on vacation, that the subsequent experience is usually a let down. Our second voyage was turning out to be equal to, if not better than the first, as we were currently on the scene versus our first voyage, although precious to our hearts, was a memory.

We woke the next morning to the mouth-watering aroma of sausage, bacon, ham and eggs that was coming from the breakfast area; the smell alone was worth the price of the trip. We were drawn to the area as if we were addicted to it and, in time, we would be, because after leaving the ship at our journey's end, we were constantly sniffing around for a breakfast fix of the same quality. Unfortunately, none of the substitutes were as satisfying. Breakfast coincided with the toot-toot-tooting of the boat's whistle and the Americana music coming from the calliope that announced our approaching the town of Grandview, Indiana. Southern Indiana is more culturally connected to Kentucky then to the Northern part of the state. The town has a population of fewer than 1,000 people and is known for having one of the most beautiful views of any river in the U.S., hence it's name, Grandview. Its claim to fame is that Abraham Lincoln spent his formative years, from 1816 to 1830, as a resident of the nearby area. His parents moved from his birthplace in Kentucky to Southern Indiana when he was seven years old. During that period, Lincoln grew physically and intellectually into the President that history has recorded. Our destination for the day was the Lincoln Boyhood National Memorial in Lincoln, Indiana, which was a short distance from the river town.

We were welcomed to the National Park by a life-sized stone structure surrounded by horizontal wooden planks with the head of a boy carved along side the theme of the park, "Lincoln's Boyhood National Memorial." We went directly to the Memorial Visitor Center and were surprised at the larger than life size of five sculpted limestone panels in the cloister wall between the two main buildings. I was transfixed at the artistic genius of the presentations that depicted the life of our 16th president. The first of the five panels, sculpted by E. H. Daniels, depicts Abraham Lincoln's years in Kentucky (1809-1816), showing him in the middle as a seven-year-old, surrounded by Nancy Hank Lincoln, Sarah Lincoln, Thomas Lincoln, Dr. Christopher Columbus Graham, Jesse Lafollette, and Caleb Hazel. The second panel shows Lincoln as a youth in the Indiana wilderness (1816-1830), surrounded by people he knew, including his stepmother, Sara Bush Johnson Lincoln, and friends Josiah Crawford, Aaron Grigsby, Dennis Hanks and Allen Gentry. The third panel depicts him in the years that he lived in Illinois (1830-1861) and is surrounded by his wife, Mary Todd Lincoln and six of his friends congratulating him after his election to Congress in 1846. The fourth carved panel represents his years as Commander-in-Chief (1861-1865), and shows him with General Ulysses S. Grant. They are surrounded by four union soldiers at Grant's headquarters in Petersburg, Virginia. The final presentation symbolizes Lincoln's influence on future generations, with the tribute engraved on the wall that Secretary of War Edwin Stanton uttered at Lincoln's deathbed: "Now he belongs to the ages." To his left are symbols of a farmer, a laborer, a family, and a freedman. To his right are the Muses of History and Columbia offering their tributes. We spent a considerable amount of time admiring and discussing the beautiful limestone carving by E. H. Daniels and Lincoln's influence on the 21st century. His dream of equality certainly has come to fruition, especially in light of the fact that, at this writing, the people of the United States have just elected its first part African-American as president, Barack Hussein Obama, and the country's most important state, New York, has an African-

American as its governor; both of these accomplishments in less than 150 years after Lincoln's death.

A museum and two memorial halls commemorating both Lincoln and his mother, Nancy Hanks Lincoln, are part of the visitor center. A short film, "Here I Grew Up," about Lincoln's boyhood in Southern Indiana, explained how his family moved from Kentucky when he was seven. His father, Thomas, was a carpenter and farmer and with the help of friends they built a log cabin; it was in their cabin that the young boy mastered his lessons by candlelight and remained, helping his father with carpentry and farming, until he was 21. It was also at that place that he lost his beloved mother, Nancy Hanks Lincoln, when he was only nine-years-old. She is buried at the site, which is now a memorial to her famous son. Leading from the visitor center is the Lincoln Boyhood Trail, which travels past the grave of his mother to their original cabin's foundation and on to the Lincoln Historical Farm. Rangers dressed in period costumes demonstrated farm life in the 1820s. The reproduction is complete with cabin, outbuildings, split rail fences, gardens, field crops, and farm animals. From the farm, the Trail of the Twelve Stones, leads back to the gravesite and the visitor center. The two trails form a loop of about a mile. A third trail, the Lincoln Boyhood Nature Trail, loops for a mile through a restored forest, with all kinds of critters enjoying their man sustained habitat.

It was getting late and I was imagining the Queen's whistle beckoning us to return and join in the mock Kentucky Derby Race that was scheduled for the late afternoon. The short bus ride back gave us an opportunity to relax and take a well-deserved nap, which didn't happen. We were so engrossed with the life of Abraham Lincoln that we continued speaking about his fascinating life and his intellectual versatility. From our visit to the Smithsonian Natural Museum of American History in Washington, D.C., many years ago, we learned while viewing his scale model, that he is the only United States president to hold a registered patent. It was for a device to lift

Michael Bivona

boats over shoals, especially riverboats; an invention which was never manufactured but was invented by him to alleviate the problems that boats carrying heavy cargo had when crossing over shallow areas along the rivers. He was considered a maven when it came to things mechanical, a talent nurtured by his father, Thomas, out of the necessity of being a farmer and carpenter. In his formative years, his life reads like Mark Twain's "Huckleberry Finn," even the timing was right as Lincoln was an older contemporary of Twains. Lincoln built rafts and canoes to travel down the Ohio and Mississippi rivers as a teenager and actually worked on a flatboat that traversed the rivers, thereby fine tuning his navigation skills. If Lincoln's life wasn't cut short, I'm sure that he and Mark Twain would have eventually met and would have become close friends, as they had much in common. They spent much of their youths as river lads and shared the same experiences while working on boats that serviced the mighty rivers. Although the two never met, they appreciated each other's writings and shared many of the same ideas. Mark Twain was a devout Freemason, and Lincoln, although not a professed Mason, certainly practiced their philosophy of: Faith, hope, and charity, belief in God, the equality of all people, and the ability of each person to improve--which are the foundations for Masons' beliefs.

We arrived at the Queen just in time to participate in a miniature Kentucky Derby Race. The track was set up with 19 entries and a large bingo bowl with the names of the horses running. It was a pot luck drawing for the 400-plus passengers with winnings for the first, second, third and fourth place horses. Barbara bet $5.00 (big spender) on her horse, Charismatic; I bet $10.00 on my pick, Three Ring. Well, as the saying goes, "Money goes to money." The Wheel of Fortune swung around half a dozen times and when it stopped, Barbara's horse, Charismatic was the winner. The second, third, and fourth horses were chosen in the same manner--none were mine. The wheel was spun 19 times, and my horse, Three Ring, came in so last that I could have had lunch and still finished before he ended his run. Barbara told me she would share her winnings by paying for large handkerchiefs for me to dry my tears, but I opted for a mint julep instead, which she gracefully paid for. The race is also known as "The Run for the Roses," because the winning horse is draped with a blanket of roses around its neck. Well, not to be outdone by horses, our first place winners were decorated with beautiful leis of roses, which brightened and matched the color of Barbara's red flushed face causing her beautiful smile to brighten threefold. The race was to repeat another night during our voyage, so I still had a chance to be a winner in the imitation of the "Most Exciting Two Minutes in Sports."

Our casual dinner turned out to be another "pig out." We just ate as much of the Southern fried cooking that we could stuff into our bodies. Fried chicken, spareribs, catfish, fried potatoes and, of course, plenty of biscuits. We rambled over to the Grand Saloon for some Russ Morgan Big Band music and the camaraderie of our new friends. We were all content with the day's happenings, but full beyond our control and exhausted from the various excursions that we chose during the day. None of us could stay till closing, so we danced a little, talked a little, laughed a little and then retired to hopefully sleep a lot and shake off the exhausted feelings from the day's activities. In our room, placed in the middle of our bed, was a woman's plain hat with instructions about the next day's contest and the type of decorations that would look nice on the hat. "The Hat Parade" during Kentucky Derby Festival is similar to the Easter Parade that is so popular in New York. It seems that during Derby Festival, the women's Hat Parade, which is held on the first Saturday in May, is just as popular as the Easter Parade, with as much brouhaha but it is a lot noisier. The tradition of wearing hats at the races dates back to the early 18th century. The world famous Royal Ascot Racecourse in dear old England started the tradition when it was decreed that: "All guests within the Royal Enclosure must adhere to a strict dress code. Male attendees must wear full morning dress including a top hat, whilst ladies must not show bare midriffs or shoulders and must wear hats." It didn't take long for the Royal Code to catch on at the major races in the United States. Many years later a less severe dress code was established at Churchill Downs and is still seriously adhered to today. Like the Royal Code, there are traditional Kentucky Derby fashion rules that are followed, whether sitting in the Clubhouse, Paddock, or the Infield. Men seated in Millionaires' Row or the Clubhouse are expected to wear solid color suites or tuxedos. Women seated in either location are expected to wear spring-themed hats and dresses in pastel colors. On the Infield, the same fashion rules exist but they're taken to new extremes. They are about as relaxed as the attendees who are bourbon-driven and in a "happy go lucky mood" in anticipation of winning some money and the bragging rights that go along with their prizes. Well, those are the quasi rules for the dress code at the Derby. I couldn't clearly imagine the sight of 100,000 people, men wearing top hats and women displaying their creative hats, parading around the race track without my getting a little light headed.

The next morning the girls were busy creating their Derby Hats, which, rumor has it, actually brings the best-looking hats good luck at the races. The whistle began toot-toot-tooting and the calliope again brought forth its astounding harmonic sounds as we approached our next destination, Dover, Tennessee. This is a small town of about 1,500 people who enjoy their laid-back life style and the magnificent view of the Cumberland River. Its claim to fame is that it was the first major battle that the Union Army won during the Civil War. To commemorate the battle and the heroic young boys who gave their lives for their respective causes, the state of Tennessee restored and preserved what is known today as the Fort Donelson National Battlefield and Cemetery. The closest large city is Nashville, which is about 70-miles from the town. Most of the girls decided to stay on board and create award winning bonnets, while the majority of men chose to visit the National Park. I was glad to get away from all the hats and women's chatter and went directly to the National Park Visitor center. There was a full-size cannon in the center of the hall, which was surrounded by displays of Union and Confederate soldiers' hand guns, rifles, shoes, and other military memorabilia. A 15-minute film told the story of the surrender of Fort Henry, which was twelve miles from the site (it is now under water) and Fort Donelson. The film explained in detail how the cannons were placed to defend the fort against the oncoming gunboats and the Army of the North. I took a self-guided tour of the battlefield and, with the help of an electronic docent, the site came alive in my mind. The landscape was well preserved with man-made trenches still in place for the defenders' protection. The cannons were still located in the same placements as during the war, strategically pointing out onto the river to destroy incoming gunboats. The docent went on to tell the story that went something like this: "On February 14, 1862, early in the afternoon, a furious roar broke the stillness and the earth began to shake. Flag Officer of the Union Army, Andrew Foote, approached the fort with a fleet of ironclads consisting of the St. Louis, Pittsburgh, Louisville and the Corondolet. They were escorted by the timberclads Conestoga and Tyler. They immediately began exchanging 'iron valentines' with the eleven big guns of the Confederate Army that were mounted on a hill waiting for a 'Perfect Invasion,' which the Union provided for them. During the one and a half hour battle, the Confederates wounded Foote and inflicted such extensive damage to the boats that they were all forced to retreat. The gunboats were covered with so much blood that the sailors had difficulty walking on the decks. Certainly, this was a very decisive victory for the South, or so the shouting victorious Southern soldiers thought. In the meantime, General Ulysses S. Grant was bringing his forces into battle with the Southern Army and at the end of the conflict, captured over 12,000 Confederate troops. With the capture of Fort Donelson and its sister, Fort Henry, the Union had won its first great victory and also established the reputation of young General Grant, who henceforth was known as "Unconditional Surrender Grant," due to his negotiating an unconditional surrender from the Southern Generals. After the surrender of the forts, the South was forced to give up Southern Kentucky and much of the Middle and West Tennessee. The Tennessee and Cumberland rivers and railroads in the area became vital Federal supply lines;

Nashville was soon captured and developed into a main supply depot for the Federal Army. The heartland of the Confederacy had been opened and the Federals would continue fighting until the 'Union' became a fact once again. In addition to the victory being a strategic success, the area also provided a welcome for thousands of enslaved African-Americans. Slaves from the area came to the forts seeking protection and work, many enlisted into the Union Army to forward their cause for freedom or to work as laborers in building roads and fortifications. In his success, Grant faced a difficult situation in regards to the slaves. He was in the middle of uncertain Federal policies concerning freedom-seeking slaves and had lots of pressure from the states of Tennessee and Kentucky, where slave owners wanted their property returned to them. He decided to give protection to the escapees and continued to do so as he moved South in his battles for unification. He was well rewarded, as slaves joined his forces and helped bring the war to an end, probably a lot sooner than if they were not accepted as free people." The cemetery's residents are both Union and Confederate soldiers of those historic battles; most of the 700 graves are unmarked, as most were disinterred from mass burial grounds making identification impossible. Many of the veterans of subsequent conflicts, along with some of their children and spouses, also occupy graves at the National Cemetery.

The howling toots from the Queen's whistle told us it was time to return. Barbara and many of her friends were still busy chatting and putting the finishing touches on their trophy hats. At dinner, many of the girls strolled through the dining room showing off their new bonnets and accepting the wows and applause from the audience, with style and grace and as a token reward for their efforts. The positive reaction of the diners reassured the girls that their creations would certainly entitle them to some of the prize money from the Derby Race. After dinner, we retired to the Grand Saloon to hear the incomparable music of the Russ Morgan Band and the singing of The Four Lads.

The band played some great Swing dance numbers at slow, medium and fast paces, which are always good for an aerobic workout. The highlight of the dancing was when they played the Tennessee Wig Walk and asked the guests to get on the floor and follow the caller's lead. He sang and we followed:

"I'm a bow-legged chicken; I'm a knock kneed hen, never been so happy since I don't know when. I walk with a wiggle and a giggle and a squawk, doing the Tennessee Wig Walk. Hear a tune on the fiddle and my heart's aglow, though I'm broke and weary and my back is sore, I walk with a wiggle and a giggle and a squawk, doing the Tennessee Wig Walk. Now, everybody put your toes together, your knees apart. Bend your back, get ready to start. Flap you elbows just for luck, then you wiggle and you waddle like a baby duck. Come with me honey, tap your toes and glide and we'll always be together side by side, I walk with a wiggle and a giggle and a squawk, doing the Tennessee Wig Walk."

The Four Lads entertained us with some of their hits: "Down by the Riverside," "No, Not Much," "Gilly, Gilly, Ossenfeffer, Katzenellen Bogen by the Sea" and "Got a Locket in My Pocket." They still had the magic touch and sang songs that were perfect for romantic slow dancing. It seems that we can never stay awake late when we are around waterways; whatever the reason, at about ten o'clock we start fighting dreamland's call. We ended our evening dancing to, "So Long its Been Good to Know You," a perfect song to end a more than perfect day.

We had been very lucky since the beginning of our voyage; the weather was perfect and the water calm. We were a little rattled when we approached the city of Paducah, Kentucky, and the Queen started to bounce around while fighting the choppy river conditions. Paducah is located at the confluence of the Tennessee and Ohio rivers, with the mouth of the Cumberland and the mighty Mississippi rivers just a short distance away; this accounted for the swift tides and rough water conditions that we experienced. The grinding sounds from the large red paddlewheel churning through the water at the rear of the boat, and the splashing sounds from the water coming at us from every direction, made the boat rock from side to side; making many of the passengers uncomfortable and some sea sick. Once we were near the town, the Queen's whistle began tooting along with the musical sounds from the calliope that not only announced our arrival to the citizens of Paducah, but magically seemed to calm the rough waters as we entered the quaint river port.

After another hardy Southern-style breakfast, we left the boat and almost ran into town. We were both very excited to be visiting a town that is mentioned in one of our favorite fun songs sung by the late Jimmy Durante, it goes something like this:

"Mention my name in Paducah; it's the greatest little town in the world. I know a gal there you'll simply adore, she was Miss Paducah back in 1904. So, mention my name in Paducah and, if you ever get in a mess; just mention my name, I said mention my name; but please don't give them my address. While the teletypes are talkin' and the sirens roar, I'll be hopping on a freighter for a foreign shore."

The song also mentions the towns of Sheboygan and Elmira. Paducah is one of the few remaining towns in Kentucky that still retains an Indian name. According to legend, Chief Paduke, most likely a Chickasaw, welcomed settlers that traveled down the Ohio and Tennessee rivers. His tribe was so hospitable and well liked that a new community was established across the river from his village and had no trouble living in harmony for many years, trading goods, services, and cultures. The settlers introduced horses and mules to the area, which they used to pull flatboats upstream to farms, logging camps, trading posts and other settlements along the river. The cultures lived peacefully until William Clark, the famed leader of the Lewis and Clark Expedition, arrived in 1827 with a title deed to the American Indian's land. He asked the chief and the settlers to move, which they did peacefully, and took possession of all their lands for the cost of processing a deed, which in those days was a mere $5.00. Clark admired the chief's peaceful attitude and honored him by naming the town Paducah. The city today has a population of about 26,000 residents and, because of the dynamics of the waterways and its valuable port facilities, is one of the major ports in Kentucky. It also boasts as having the country's largest Seamen's Institute, which is a training center that provides practical and relevant training, specifically for inland mariners. It has a state-of-the-art computer simulation system that is used to improve a mariner's navigational and bridge management skills in a risk-free environment. It also promotes a safer workplace and a greater environmental awareness of America's unique waterways.

While walking through the busy waterfront district, it was understandable why it's called the "Inland Waterway Capital." Loading equipment and neatly lined warehouses actively process cargo from the riverboats. In the downtown area we explored some of the century-old brick houses, many with signs stating that artists resided within. It reminded us of SoHo in Manhattan, New York, where shops and artists' booths are scattered throughout the neighborhood, giving it a colorful Bohemian atmosphere. We explored several of the beautifully-restored buildings to find working artists' studios and galleries displaying paintings of artists' and a variety of local crafts. One of the artists told us that she was from Seattle, Washington and moved to Paducah several years ago with the promise of owning her own home under the towns Restoration and Relocation Plan. She saw an advertisement in a newspaper inviting artists to relocate and help rebuild the run down areas in town; she responded and ended up buying a house for "One Dollar." The bank loaned her enough money, at a very low interest rate, to renovate the house, which she did in short order by using local trade people and a lot of her own muscle. She is one of almost 100 artists that took the challenge and changed the landscape from dismal abandonment to a thriving artists' colony, where they practice their skills and enjoy being a part of the artsy community that they helped create. After that tale, we couldn't help but purchase a gorgeous three by five- foot Paducah quilt of nautical scenes and a beautiful fog-bound waterfront painting done by local artists. The Queen's whistle was again calling us home, so we bid farewell to Paducah, "The greatest little town in the world," and boarded her majesty for the last time.

We returned to the Queen just in time for Barbara to enter the calliope contest. She remembered the last time she participated in the event and was accused by one of the contestants of playing "her song," so this time she went to the end of the line to make sure that there would be no hostilities in the fun contest. We heard some pretty good renditions of "Dixie," " Old Man River," "By the Riverside," and "Mammy." It was surprising how well the people played an instrument that is not commonly found outside of riverboats and carnivals. Barbara was the last person to play and play she did; she embellished Stephen Foster's "Nelly Bly," while some of the passengers mumbled along with: "Nelly Bly shuts her eye when she goes to sleep . . . " Of the half dozen participants, I thought that she outperformed everyone. A vote was taken, measured by the audience's applause, and for some reason the judges thought that it was a tie, so everyone received a large decorative Mississippi Queen glass filled with mint julep and an official certificate as proof of their membership in the Calliope Club. Pleased at the results, the crowd disbursed and went to the Grand Saloon to participate in the next Kentucky Derby Race. The ladies were asked to bring their hats for judging to determine who had the lucky bonnet. Up until that point, I hadn't seen Barbara's creation and was surprised at the detail and effort that went into the birth of her headpiece. It was a straw hat with small daisies around the upper rim, three roses in the middle, some Xmas tree firs around the brim; several small decorative multicolored Xmas balls complemented the roses, and a large Peacock feather stretched from the rear of the eclectic creation. She was sure to win first place and the resultant "good luck" that purportedly goes with it to win at the actual Derby Race. The ladies paraded around the hall in a fashion show-style showing off their Derby Hats of every size, shape and color. One of the ladies had a stuffed skunk (fake of course) surrounded by a variety of flowers on her headwear; while another had small golden antlers protruding from the sides of her hat with a shining red Rudolph the Reindeer's nose blinking. The judges decided to postpone choosing the winner because there were so many creative hats in the contests and they needed more time to select the best one. The results would be announced the next evening at the formal dinner; all the ladies were requested to wear their hats again at that time.

Off to the races again. The names of the 19 horses that were going to actually run at the Derby the following week were listed on a large Race Track Board, this time instead of picking names pot luck from a bucket, we were allowed to choose our own horses. Barbara picked the same horse, Charismatic; I felt lucky, so I chose Three Ring, hoping that the spin of the wheel would favor me with some good luck this time around. Barbara bet her usual five bucks,I splurged and bet ten. The wheel went round and round and wouldn't you know it, my wife's horse, Charismatic, won again; what are the odds? On the fourth turn of the wheel, Three Ring came in, so I got my money back plus a few extra bucks. I insisted that Barbara share her winnings with me, or at least buy me two drinks. Big sport that she is, she opted for the two drinks, which I gladly accepted as it was better than nothing. What really hurt was her telling me, "You should have listened to me and bet my lucky horse." As a token for winning, all the "Run for the Roses" winners received their beautifully decorated necklaces, which they wore as trophies throughout the day.

After refreshing naps, we went to dinner and had another relaxing meal, loaded with cholesterol, but tempered with a fine bottle of red wine that washed away some of the fat . . . at least, we hoped it did. After a heavy dinner, a walk around the deck a dozen times was in order, which we did at a very slow pace--probably because of the extra weight we were carrying around. The music from the Russ Morgan Band attracted us like magnets and we quickly followed their magical sounds to a ringside table and settled in. I ordered a mint julep, which my mate paid for as a consolation prize to ease my pain for not listening to her and betting on Charismatic. We danced the night away while listening to The Four Aces pouring their hearts out singing romantic songs. We changed dance partners several times during the evening and I was greatly surprised when a very attractive young blonde lady asked me to dance; I was happy to oblige. It's considered bad manners in the dancing community to refuse someone's offer to dance, regardless of their level of expertise. She was a dance instructor, which was quite evident when we flew around the floor doing a Waltz as if we had been dancing together for many years. It's so important for dancers to take dance lessons and familiarize themselves with the syllabus of the various dances. Once that is accomplished a dancer will be able to enjoy the experience of dancing with any other well-trained person. We received applause for our dance routine and bowed in appreciation with wide smiles on our faces. I danced with her several times during the evening and to balance the experience, Barbara happily danced with her husband, who was also an accomplished hoofer. The highlight of the evening was when the band played a Mambo and the four of us did a combination routine where we changed partners, doing underarm turns, spins and hip rotations, as if we had practiced with each other for years. All in all, the evening was a great dancing experience and lots of fun for everyone dancing or for those wishing they knew how to dance. We danced till the band ended its session and took the familiar path back to our cabin for a well deserved night's sleep.

I took advantage of the next day, which didn't include any stops, to go to the gym and work off some of the calories that were quickly making my clothes very tight. The treadmill and stairmaster are my favorite choices of equipment. I worked out for over an hour and worked up a good sweat before showering and then sinking into a hot tub on the deck for a good soak. The workout increased my appetite, which at that point was out of control, so I went to breakfast and ordered sausage and sunny side up eggs with three humongous blueberry pancakes and those addictive biscuits. The delicious cuisine went down softly and willingly with the three cups of amazing hazelnut coffee that I drank. I did this out of sight of Barbara, who would, without a doubt, throw me overboard if she saw me feasting. I immediately took my Zocor pill (cholesterol medication), which I usually take after dinner but I thought taking it in the morning with my last gulp of coffee would offset the damage I had already done to my body and blood circulation.

There was a late morning dance class in Merengue, which Barbara and I knew how to do, but thought it would be nice to pick up a couple of new routines. The Merengue is known as a fun dance and can be performed by anyone wishing to give it a try--no lessons required. It is the official dance of the Dominican Republic and also, to some extent, of Haiti, its neighbor sharing the island. There are many versions as to how the dance originated, but the two popular versions are: "Slaves who were chained together and, out of necessity, were forced to drag one leg as they cut sugar to the beat of drums." The second is, "A soldier that returned from fighting was wounded in the right leg in battle; a celebration was given in his honor and while dancing he had to drag his right leg; not to embarrass him, everyone else danced to the beat the same way, beginning the dance we know today as the Merengue." Whatever the case may be, we joined the class for a lesson in the great fun dance. The lesson that Jane gave was a basic, then a turn, then a ladder step. The dance begins with partners facing each other in a loose natural position. The beat is 1 & 2, 3 & 4. It is very easy to hear the beat of the dance and to keep time with the music. So we went, 1 & 2 to the man's left side, with a leg drag on 2 and then 3 & 4 continuing to the left with a drag on 4. The left turn was a tricky Samba-type turn in a rolling pattern to the beat 1 & 2 roll 3 & 4, roll again-- this is done several times for effect. The ladder step is 1 & 2 to the man's left and then 3 & 4 forward for the male and back for his partner. This is done several times and should give the effect of climbing a ladder. The hour lesson was enough to get the fifteen couples in attendance, dancing like pros. We ended the session satisfied that we picked up the turn and roll step, which we immediately added to our repertoire.

The Queen began taking on a colorful atmosphere that changed her usual placid mood into a more festive one. The rhythm of the river and its affect on the boat remained the same, but the colorfully-decorated assortment of ladies headwear and the variety of Derby Hats that the men were sporting, combined with the magnificently colored rose necklaces, turned the boat into a surreal conglomeration of people expressing their individuality in very strange ways. While the celebratory hype was being developed throughout the vessel, we heard the toot-toot-toot of another boat. It was the steamboat Belle of Louisville heading toward us; the Queen didn't waste any time in responding with loud deafening blasts from its high rise whistles. Everyone on board ran to the side of the boat that the Belle was passing us on and joined the cheers from the oncoming lady of the river. There were lots of waving and jumping up and down by the passengers on both vessels that melded with the duet coming from the calliopes that each boat was producing to form a rallying cry for a race between the two majestic queens. The whistles blowing, the calliopes singing, and the crowds cheering couldn't get a race going between the two "Ladies of the Rivers." Belle was on her way to Louisville, Kentucky, to her annual traditional race with the Delta Queen to determine who was to be hailed as the Crème de la Crème of the waterways. We waved wildly as Belle passed us and then showed us the full width of her great powerful red paddlewheel as she propelled forward to her destination with our good wishes for a successful race against our baby sister, Delta Queen.

Our last evening on the Queen required formal dress. Again I had to struggle to get into my tuxedo pants, the jacket was also starting to get a little tight around my shoulders. Tuxedo pants should have expandable waists to conform to the ever-growing circumference of a man's belly; especially useful when they are on vacation and out of control with their eating habits. Barbara wore a very beautiful lavender dress, cut at the knees and strapless, which she bought for the formal occasion; combined with her floral Derby hat which she proudly wore, she looked like an authentic Southern Belle. I was able to acquire a brown plastic man's Derby hat which rounded out my sophisticated look as a formally-dressed fool. Maybe if the hat were black it wouldn't have looked so uncoordinated, but brown was all the store had and I was stuck with it; at least it was the right size. We sashayed over to the dining room and joined our fellow revelers to celebrate the ending of our great voyage and to exchange the usual formalities of exchanging phone and e-mail information. The captain and his officers greeted everyone at the entrance and set us in position for a photograph. Barbara and I smiled, heard the clicking of the camera and blinked at the burst from the flashbulb, and then went directly to our table for our last supper aboard the magnificent Mississippi Queen. The specials for the evening were deep fried catfish with hash browns and filet mignon steak with bacon. As I was in the pig-out mode, I ordered both, much to the displeasure of my wife, who still managed to maintain her girlish figure regardless of her food intake. I couldn't make up my mind which I enjoyed the most, so I took alternate bites of each; at the end of the feast I decided that both were winners. Just in time for dessert, the kitchen staff and members of the crew made a grand appearance carrying Baked Alaska cakes with sparkles bursting from the candles, giving the procession a carnival appearance. Each cake had, sitting on the browned meringue that was covering the inside ice cream, a foot-long chocolate horse to remind us that in a few days the big race would take place. The delicious cake was served with pomp and grace and was a perfect ending to a delightful dinner and a farewell to a boating experience that is pleasantly remembered to this day. The captain thanked everyone for choosing the Mississippi Queen for their vacation and then asked the ladies to pass him, one at a time, so he and the three judges could finally determine who was wearing the best headwear for the Ladies' Derby Hat Contest. I didn't envy the judges, their task of deciding the winner was not easy, as all of the creations were unique and individually outstanding. The decision was made; all the hats won first prize, which entitled the ladies to a complimentary Mississippi Queen glass filled to the brim with a drink of their choice. But, the judges decided that a first and second prize should go to the most creative hats; the antler hat with Rudolph's shining nose won first prize and the skunk hat came in second. The diners' applause concurred with the judges' decisions as everyone seemed to be pleased at the way the contest ended. In addition to bragging rights, first prize was awarded a gold-plated Mississippi Queen pin. Second place prize was a Mississippi Queen Xmas ornament. I raved so much about the Xmas ornament, which was a replica of the paddlewheel, that Barbara gracefully surprised me with one for my birthday. I added the brass boat to my proud Xmas ornament collection and it still remains one of my favorites. When I place it on my Xmas tree every year, the wonderful times we had on both our trips on the Mississippi Queen pleasantly flash through my mind and put me in a positive Christmas spirit. Everyone left the dining room with happy faces and making mental notes that another visit along the rivers on the Queen was in their futures.

We rushed to hear the music of The Russ Morgan Band and the singing of The Four Lads for the last time. My trousers were bursting at the seams and Barbara remarked that I looked as if I were four months pregnant. Looking at some of the other men on the boat didn't make me feel any less guilty, although some of my fellow passengers did actually look as if they were carrying more than themselves under their jackets. When I danced the slow, close dances with my mate, I did get the feeling that we were further apart than usual and thought that I had better start behaving myself for the rest of our vacation. We danced the night away to the band's many tunes, including "So Tired," "Forever and Ever," "You, You, You, Are the One" and "Hoop-Dee-Doo." We sang and hummed along to The Four Lads' songs of "The Mocking Bird," "My Little Angel," "A House with Love in It" and "Who Needs You." What a wonderful way to end a wonderful day; we were gastronomically satisfied and at peace with the world.

The next morning we just had orange juice for breakfast and began diets that we hoped to maintain for the rest of our trip. With the cityscape of Memphis in view, my mind flashed back to my younger days as a CPA with an accounting firm that handled some of the more popular entertainers of that time. I was just married and beginning my own accounting practice. As I didn't have enough clients of my own, I worked three days a week on a per diem basis for them. They provided accounting and financial management services for such illustrious entertainers as Tony Bennett, Florence Henderson, Hank Williams, and Connie Francis. One of their major responsibilities was to make sure clients received the proper royalties for their recordings from the major recording companies. Almost as important was paying the clients' bills in a timely manner and maintaining accurate records for them. The firm had offices in Los Angeles, California, and Manhattan, and were contemplating opening an office in Memphis or Nashville, Tennessee, and expanding their services to the growing music industry that developed out of those two cities. They wanted me to visit both cities to locate advantageous office space, and then establish accounting and management services for the abundance of country western and rock and roll singers that were rapidly rising in popularity in those cities and across the country. I've looked back and thought about the opportunity that was offered, including a partnership in the firm and wondered what our lives would be like and where we would be today if I had taken that challenge. It certainly was one of "Life's turning points" for me. Would my children and grandchildren be speaking with Southern accents and have the gentle demeanor that seems to be prevalent in warm climates? Would our family still be whole after being exposed to the lives of so many glamorous people? Would we have survived all the temptations that seem to go with rubbing shoulders with the rich and famous? Well, at that time, we were just married and had put a deposit on our first house in Long Island, New York. Neither of those facts would have been detrimental in making the decision to uproot and become Southerners, but we were very close to our families and just couldn't bear to put such a distance between us. So, taking the advanced ages of our parents into the equation, we decided not to join the ranks of those who service the rich and famous. We chose to just continue with the course of our lives and become simple folks, along with the rest of our family. Looking back, we're happy for the decision that we made; it led to the chain of events leading up to our cruising the rivers and enjoying our Mississippi Queen experiences.

We tooted our way into the harbor leading to Memphis, Tennessee. It was not like the other small towns we visited on our trip. Memphis is a metropolis with a population of over 700,000 people, making it the largest city in Tennessee. It's located on a substantial bluff rising from the Mississippi River, making it a perfect safe harbor for developing a settlement, which the Chickasaw Indians did prior to the European intrusion by Hernando de Soto and others in the early 16th century. The city itself was founded in 1819 by no other than the soon to be president, Andrew Jackson and his compatriots. It was named after the ancient Egyptian capital on the Nile River, Memphis, which means "White Wall." Its high elevation above the majestic river made it a perfect transportation hub due to its flood-free location. It became one of the largest cotton centers in the South and a major slave market, which supplied farmers with strong African-American laborers that they needed to plant and harvest their crops. For a short time during the Civil War it was a Confederate stronghold, but in 1862 in the Battle of Memphis, the Union Army defeated the Southern forces and turned the city into an important Union supply center and bastion. Protruding from the skyline is the Pyramid Arena; this unusual structure complements the city's namesake in Egypt and is one of the largest in the world, rising 321-feet with a base of 591-feet. To put its size in perspective, it's 16-feet taller than the Statue of Liberty in New York City. To further advance its theme, its sister city in Egypt gifted a 20-foot statue of Ramesses the Great, which stands in front of the 32-story steel and glass structure as if to guard it and keep it safe from harm.

This city has more than a checkered past. It gave birth to many renowned musicians during the rise of the Blues and Rock and Roll era in the 50s and 60s. Elvis Presley, Muddy Waters, Carl Perkins, Johnny Cash, B.B. King, and Booker T. Jones, are just some of the many individuals who got their starts in the musical city. It's also where the St. Jude Children's Research Hospital is located, thanks to our late beloved singer and comedian Danny Thomas. He promised St. Jude that he would build a monument to the saint; it turned out to be much more than a statue. It is now one of the foremost hospitals in the country, providing help to children of all races, regardless of their ability to pay. It's also proud to be the city where the center of civil rights issues culminated into a reality, notably with the sanitation workers' strike in 1960, the downside of that event being the unfortunate horrifying assassination of the great Martin Luther King.

Exiting the boat, we made sure that all our luggage was present and accounted for before taking a taxicab to The Peabody Hotel in downtown Memphis. That is where we would be spending a couple of days before heading back to Louisville, Kentucky, for the Run for the Roses Race. The hotel is centrally located in Peabody Place and is known as the cornerstone of the renaissance in the downtown area. It boasts that the Mississippi Delta begins in its lobby and ends on Catfish Row in Vicksburg, Mississippi. It's surrounded by key attractions such as Beale Street, the Fed Ex Forum (home of the NBA Memphis Grizzlies), the Orpheum Theater and AutoZone Park (home to the AAA Memphis Redbirds), as well as more than 80 restaurants, including Texas De Brazil, Jillians, Bluefin, Hooters, and the Majestic Grill, just to name a few. The original hotel was built in 1869 by Colonel Robert C. Brinkley for the sum of $60,000.00. He named the hotel in honor of his dear friend and philanthropist George Peabody, who died while the hotel was being constructed. The hotel was rebuilt and designed by architect Walter Ahlschlager in the Italian Renaissance Revival style, and, due to its history and importance, it's listed in the National Register of Historic Places. Its furniture is antique-style with overstuffed chairs and dark wood trim. Its showpiece is an Italian Renaissance Fountain that is proudly displayed in the center of its palatial lobby. The 14-story hotel features four restaurants, ranging from deli style to fine dining at Chez Philippe, which is a four star establishment. Its Athletic Club has an indoor pool, weight room, treadmills, bicycles, a sauna and Jacuzzi, and tanning facilities. The Peabody is the site of the world famous ducks that spend part of every day swimming in the Grand Lobby Fountain. When not entertaining the crowds that come from far and wide to see their marching procession that ends in the fountain, they spend their time in a lavish Duck Palace on the hotel's Plantation Roof. This show has to be seen to be believed; the pomp and ceremony that goes into their performance is headed by a Duckmaster and is surreal. A red carpet is unrolled and the ducks march through crowds of admiring spectators to the tunes of John Philip Sousa. Their act is held at 11:00 A.M. and 5:00 P.M. every day and is witnessed by people coming from afar by bus to see the unusual event. Myth has it that, "In the 1920s, turtles and baby alligators each briefly graced the fountain. They were replaced in 1933 by three live duck decoys as a prank, but were so enjoyed by guests of the hotel that it became a tradition. Since then, Duckmaster Edward Pembroke, a former circus animal trainer, took over the job of overseeing the training and supervision of the ducks and the daily procession of the one mallard and four drakes that participate in the Duck March twice a day. Pembroke supervised the ducks for 50 years. In 1991, he retired and turned the job over to Duckmaster Jason Sensat." The Peabody is world renowned for the Duck March; what an interesting way to get recognition as a first-rate hotel. The Duck March has attracted such luminaries as President Jimmy Carter, Michael Jordan, Priscilla Presley, Nicholas Cage, Patrick Swayze, Oprah Winfrey and many other dignitaries; all of them curious enough to go out of their way to see the fantastic procession of a mallard leading four drakes.

After we spent an hour enjoying some cappuccino coffee in the hotel's lobby, the ducks made their morning appearance. The lobby was so crowded that we had to stand on our toes and stretch our necks to see the procession marching on the red carpet doing their duck walk and quacking away in harmony with Sousa's music. The only thing missing was a conductor with a baton to lead the band and direct the marchers. We were glad to get away from the crowded lobby and headed directly to Beale Street, which was only a couple of blocks away.

Beale Street has a remarkable history. It was the headquarters of General Ulysses S. Grant during the Civil War and has had such dignitaries as President Woodrow Wilson, Booker T. Washington and President Franklin D. Roosevelt speak in its Church Park Auditorium. From that illustrious past came a period of decay that witnessed an urban slum with vacant buildings and a decaying infrastructure. In the 1980s, Memphis' government partnered with private businesses and turned what was considered the epitome of urban decay into the number one entertainment tourist attraction in Tennessee, if not the country. The street was named after a forgotten Mexican-American War hero. Part of the street from Main to 4th is now a National Historic Landmark and was officially declared as the "Home of the Blues" by an act of Congress. Its heyday was in the 1920s when the area took on a carnival atmosphere and gambling, prostitution, murder, and voodoo thrived alongside the booming nightclubs, restaurants, stores, pawnshops and great music joints. Indicative of that era, The Monarch Club, which was known as "The Castle of Missing Men," was the foremost den of iniquity. Many of its customers, including gamblers, were shot and their bodies conveniently disposed of across the alley in an undertaker's parlor. From a more than checkered past, Beale Street has re-emerged as the focal point of Memphis and the heart and soul of Rock and Roll, Rhythm & Blues, and Jazz. With all this information in my memory, we approached the street with some trepidation, expecting to find unsavory characters lurching out at every corner. Well it wasn't that bad, but there were a lot of panhandlers pestering the visiting tourists. Being that we are from New York and are exposed to similar situations, it wasn't a sight that disturbed us. The street absolutely had a carnival flair about it; lots of neon signs, street vendors, artists displaying their wares, and musicians playing their favorite instruments hoping to be appreciated with a donation into their inverted hats. We were thrilled to be in such a colorful and musical environment, so much so, that we sort of walk-danced down Beale Street to the eclectic sounds of music coming from the clubs and the street musicians. We stopped often to admire the street musicians who seemed to be permanent fixtures on the sidewalks. We passed King's Palace Café, Beale St. Tap Room, Mr. Handy's Blues Hall, and then stopped at our final destination, B.B. Kings Blues Club, for lunch and to listen to some blues and jazz music. The mixture of smells from the club was exotic. The aroma from the Cajun spices in their food, mixed with the odor from tobacco, mixed with the age old musty smell, culminated into an inviting invitation to "Enter and explore." We entered and explored and had wonderful Cajun pasta for me and deep fried shrimp for my mate. We washed our meals down with large frosted glasses of tap beer while listening to the jazz and blues from the trio on the stage just twenty feet from our table. We spent a couple of hours just boozing and schmoozing with the musicians and some of the customers. We were told B. B. King himself would be at the club that evening, so we made reservations to be seated at the same ringside table so we could get close views of the action. We left the club, but felt compelled to go into the gift shop and buy a couple of B. B. King T-shirts, which we did with pleasure, as mementos of our visit.

We returned to the Peabody Hotel just in time to see the afternoon Duck Walk. It wasn't as crowded as the morning's parade so we were able to really get a good view of the show; from the rolling of the red carpet, to the sashaying down the isle, and finally the fountain bath. It seemed as if the ducks were swimming around with smiles on their faces. For sure, when they exited their act, they turned, smiled and took bows. Barbara said I shouldn't have had the third beer at B. Bs; maybe she was right, but it was fun watching them perform those mystifying deeds, that evidently only I could appreciate. A nap was certainly in order after our busy day, so we retired to our room and quickly dozed off.

Beale Street at night is a whole different place than in the daytime. It's bright with neon signs and street lights that turn the entertainment district into a bright night-time carnival playland. The street was packed with people in very festive moods enjoying their beverages and the music that was coming from every direction and of every type: Jazz from one club, R&B from another, Rock from the right, and Blues from the left. All the music joined overhead and made the area sound like teenagers' cars at a drive-in, with everyone playing a different station. Fortunately I'm quite deaf in one ear, so it was easy to block out the sounds; Barbara wasn't so lucky, so we rushed to B. B. King's Blues Club with the hope of a more sympathetic atmosphere. What a treat; B. B. himself was at the door greeting his customers with a hardy "Welcome, come on in." We were seated at our reserved table and immediately started tapping our feet to "Let the Good Times Roll," which the house band played in Rock time. The place hadn't changed much from our afternoon rendezvous, except there were more patrons, many of them dancing on the narrow dance floor in front of the bandstand. The B. B. King All Star Band consisted of vocalists, guitar, bass, drums, keyboards and horns. Their arrangements got the patrons up dancing and hopping around the small dance floor. Barbara and I joined the crowd and did some shuffle dancing in place, which required lots of gyrations from the hips and lots of overhead arms stretching. We couldn't wait to order our dinner, as the aroma from the kitchen was making me salivate. For starters I ordered a cup of the house special soup, "Gumbo YA-YA," which is supposed to be straight from the Bayou (hopefully not the water). The brew had smoked chicken, andouille sausage, crawfish, peppers, onions, diced tomatoes and dark roux with white rice. Barbara ordered a "Lucille's Chef Salad," named after B. B.'s guitar, consisting of a blend of romaine, iceberg, carrots and red cabbage with julienne ham and turkey, Swiss cheese, tomatoes, cucumbers, croutons and a hardboiled egg. For the main course, I ordered their "Lip

Smacking Hickory Smoked Ribs" with honey mustard, baked beans and cole slaw. Barbara ordered their "Cajun Carbonara," consisting of blackened grilled chicken breast tossed with a mixture of ziti pasta, bacon, sautéed onions, cream, scallions, crushed red pepper and parmesan cheese, served with garlic bread. We washed the ambrosia down with chilled glasses of cold tap beer.

Our feast ended just in time. B. B. himself appeared on the stage above the crowd and began to strum his Gibson electric guitar, Lucille, and hum one of his popular songs, "Blind Love." Looking up at the icon of Blues music whose career has spanned over 50 years, with more than 15,000 performances was a thrill of a lifetime for us. He and his family were Southern dirt farm pickers and lived from hand to mouth throughout his childhood, while the seeds of success were being planted for his future. Few musicians have received more recognition and awards for their accomplishments than B. B. (Blues Boy) King. Some of his more notable awards during an illustrious lifetime are: Honorary Doctorate in Music from Yale University in 1966; a more recent Honorary Doctorate in Music by Brown University in 2007; National Medal of Arts Award in 1990; induction into the Rock & Roll Hall of Fame in 1987; 15 Grammy Awards of which ten were for Best Traditional Blues Albums and The Presidential Medal of Freedom. These are just some of the many tributes he has been paid in his long career as a blues singer and musician. Watching this exceptional person was inspiring; his humility and his attitude towards the fans in the club were touching. He joked about being a licensed pilot, a vegetarian and the rotund shape of his body. Someone in the audience asked him why his guitar was named Lucille? He readily explained: "In the mid 1950s, while performing at a dance club in Arkansas, a couple of guys became unruly and got into a fight, knocking over a kerosene stove and setting fire to the hall. I raced outside to safety with everyone else; realizing that I left my $30.00 acoustic guitar inside, I rushed back into the burning building to retrieve it, almost getting myself killed. Later I found out that the fight was over a woman named

Lucille, and decided to name my guitar Lucille to remind me never to do crazy things in hast, like fighting over a woman." Ever since, each one of his trademark Gibson guitars has been called Lucille. The original Lucille was stolen from the trunk of his car in Brooklyn, New York (my birthplace). He put an ad in the paper offering a $20,000.00 reward for its return, but to no avail. Today he is willing to pay $100,000.00 for the return of his beloved Lucille.

We close danced and hugged to some of his popular blues music: "Everyday I Have the Blues," "Sweet Little Angel," "I'll Survive" and "Ain't Nobody's Business." While we were dancing he looked right at us and gave a big smile and wink, which made our evening a lifetime memory. He left to the screaming and applause of the crowd. The band took over and played lots of Rock and Jazz, which put juice into the crowd and got everyone up on the dance floor to show off their sexy moves to the swing and sway of Memphis' best music. The club stayed opened until 5:00 A.M., which was a little too late for our rapidly-aging bones, so around twelve midnight we moved on out of the club and said goodbye to the many people that we became friendly with while enjoying and jumping around to the great music of incredible musicians. The only regret that we had was that we were missing the annual "Memphis in May International Music Festival," which is held on the first weekend in May and lasts for the whole month. The Festival starts with a three-day music fair that has a mix of big name stars performing side-by-side with local musical acts. It's held in Tom Lee Park at the foot of Beale Street and draws crowds in excess of 100,000 people for each event. The festival culminates with "The World Championship Barbeque Cooking Contest" and a "Sunset Symphony." Unfortunately, the event conflicted with our day at the Kentucky Derby, so we made mental notes to return in the future and added the Festival to our "Bucket List," which details things we must do before we kick the "Bucket."

We woke early the next day and had a quick breakfast. Our plans were to visit the St. Jude Children's Research Hospital and

Elvis Presley's Graceland. We were excited about visiting the Research Hospital as it is high up on our list of organizations that we gladly donate funds to. We became interested in the organization when the singer-comedian Danny Thomas' fund-raising events brought their important work to our attention. The hospital was founded in 1962 and is a leading pediatric treatment and research facility that focuses on children's catastrophic diseases. Its premise is that "No child should die in the dawn of life." He named the hospital for St. Jude Thaddeus, the Catholic patron saint of hospitals, desperate cases and lost causes. Danny was a struggling young entertainer when he promised the saint that if he was "Shown his way in life that he would build a shrine to honor him." That promise has resulted in a 68-acre campus with extensive hospital and research facilities that care for more than 5,000 patients annually from across the United States and from more than 70 countries from around the world. Due to their great work, the survival rate for acute lymphoblastic leukemia, the most common type of childhood cancer, has gone from 4 to 94-percent. All eligible patients are accepted for treatment and are treated without regard of their ability to pay. With this heartfelt information, we journeyed to the campus to see first hand some of the great work that this organization has accomplished.

We visited the Danny and Rose Marie Thomas Memorial Garden which frames their burial crypts. The award-winning garden has two cascading waterfalls surrounded by an abundance of trees including dogwoods, white pines, blue cypress, elms, red oaks and crepe myrtles. Strategically placed between the trees are beautiful carrisa hollies, blue rug junipers and azaleas. Scattered among the shrubs and greenery are seasonal flowers that pulls the contemplative setting together and turns it into a haven for the weary, such as me and Barbara. We sat a while and discussed the important work the hospital and research facilities were involved in and their positive affect on humanity.

Adjacent to the garden is the Danny Thomas ALSAC (American Lebanese Syrian Associated Charities) Pavilion that is a memorial to the late entertainer and his far-reaching work. The building contains memorabilia of the St. Jude founder and is home to his Emmy Awards and the many accolades for the "Make Room for Daddy" television show that propelled him into stardom.

The architectural design of the pavilion emits a star-like shape with five alcoves surrounding the rotunda. It is considered a modern representation of the world that symbolizes the far-reaching scope of the work done at the St. Jude facility. Inside are marble sheathed columns that support a cupola, elaborately painted in blue and green with accents of red and purple. Arched panels inscribed in Arabic and translated into English sum up the hospital and their founder's mission: "He who denies his heritage has no heritage." "No child should die in the dawn of life." "Those who work for the good are as those who do the good." We took a self-guided tour with the assistance of an electronic docent. One of the alcoves is dedicated to Danny's life as a humanitarian, including a wall filled with hundreds of awards, honorary degrees, and keys to cities that he received from admirers over his life-time. Highlighted is the Congressional Gold Medal he received for his humanitarian work, which is the highest civilian award given by Congress. During our tour we learned about the history of the founding of St. Jude and the institution's accomplishments in the fight against catastrophic childhood diseases, as well as the important role that the ALSAC played in the fund-raising success that finances their goals. It was getting late, so we left to visit our next stop, Graceland.

As we approached the Graceland Mansion we noticed the newly renovated 128-room "Heartbreak Hotel," which is part of the Presley facilities. We couldn't resist stopping in to investigate the 'Heartbreak Hotel," which was named after Elvis' hit of that name. The lobby is furnished in retro 1950s-style furniture with bright colors, animal prints, and gold patterned walls forming a backdrop for Elvis' photos. There is a Jungle Room cocktail lounge decorated in gold lame and sequins; the outside pool is heart shaped and brought images to mind from his song "Heartbreak Hotel." We asked to see one of the rooms out of curiosity; the attendant was very accommodating and escorted us to a guestroom which was surprisingly spacious, with blond wood furnishings of the 1950s era. The room was accented with framed Elvis photographs and included a kitchenette with refrigerator, coffee maker, microwave and a nice-sized TV set. Not a bad place to stay overnight to get in the mood, while visiting the King's mansion. Across the way was the tan-columned colonial revival Graceland Mansion, which is listed in the National Register of Historic Places and has been declared a National Historic Landmark. It's now a museum that is dedicated to the life of Elvis Presley and his impact on American music. This was a very exciting experience for us, as he was our idol as a musician and actor when we were growing out of our teens and into adulthood. When Elvis purchased the mansion from Dr. Thomas Moore it was already called Graceland. The 14-acre site, which was originally built in 1939, was named after one of the former owner's daughters, Grace. It was purchased by the King for $100,000.00, and after extensive renovations, he and his parents, Gladys and Vernon Presley, and his grandmother, Minnie Mae Hood Presley, moved into their dreamland home. The mansion is constructed of tan limestone and has 23 rooms, including eight bedrooms with baths. Passing through the music-styled wrought iron gate began our journey into the home of the world-renowned entertainer. The entrance contains several Corinthian columns and two large lions perched on both sides of the portico; their main purpose seemed to be reviewing visitors and reminding them that they were entering hallowed grounds.

Upon entering, we were handed earphones and had our pictures taken against a painted wall of the music gate. An attendant gave a brief history of the place beginning with the origin of the mansion's name to the fact that Elvis was only 22-years-old when he bought his new home. Directly in front of the entrance is a white staircase, filled with reflective mirrors. To the right is a posh, mirrored Living Room with a white fireplace and Louis XIV furniture. Adjoining it is the Music Room, with an outstanding black shiny baby grand piano and a 1950s TV set that is seen through a portico with two floors to ceiling stained-glass peacocks on its sides. The Living Room had a large, maybe nine or ten foot, white sofa which was placed against the wall overlooking the front of Graceland's property through expansive windows, where Elvis spent many relaxing moments admiring his open-range property. Hanging on the walls are pictures of Elvis' parents and of Elvis and Lisa Marie. Past these rooms and the grand staircase is his parents' room, which is predominantly white, with a smooth-looking velvet dark purple bedspread that drapes onto the floor from their queen size bed. Stretching my neck past the cordoned rope, I was able to see a pink colored full bathroom which was beyond a sealed clear glass closet showing some of his mother's dresses. Passing the elongated dining room and kitchen got us to the basement where the media room is located containing three television sets, which he would watch, at times, simultaneously. A wet bar and billiards' room is conveniently located and in easy reach to accommodate Elvis and his many friends.

Explaining his Jungle Room would probably take a book in itself. He somehow tried to recreate his Hawaii movie experience by introducing a stone waterfall in between his animal menagerie of furniture that almost comes alive as your taking in the scene. The room is predominately furnished with Witco furniture; a blocky style of wooden carved furniture created by William Westenhaver that was very popular in the 1960s when Elvis was in his heyday. I was familiar with seeing one or two pieces of that style of furniture in homes, but to have a whole large room to look at was startling to my senses. The room was cluttered with furniture: a full couch, half a dozen chairs, tables, a cabinet and a tiki bar complemented with tiki stools. The whole room was carpeted in lime green shag, and what was really surprising is that the ceiling is also covered with the same lime green shag rug. Well, we loved Elvis, so anything he did was okay with us. The Jungle Room exits to the back yard past Lisa Marie's childhood swing set, and on to a small white building that was his father's office. Past the office is a small room containing a scale model of Elvis' two-bedroom birthplace home, built by his father, in the town of Tupelo, Mississippi. Continuing our self-guided tour, we passed his shooting range, where he spent many hours perfecting his sharpshooting skills. Onward down the sloping lawn, we passed several horses grazing behind the white fences. In a specially-built Trophy Room, we saw walls of his displayed records, movie posters, old time memorabilia, and even a 1950s Elvis doll. In a place of honor were his three Grammys, Priscilla's wedding dress, and Elvis' wedding tuxedo. As we moved forward, we saw Lisa Marie's toy chest and baby clothes and the famous hall containing manyof his gold records and awards. Further down the hall there was a display of his "68 Comeback," featuring his leather suit, his personal copies of movie scripts, many of the costumes he wore in his movies, and his not-to-be-forgotten famous trademark sequined jumpsuits. On past his beautiful kidney-shaped swimming pool, which he built immediately after acquiring Graceland, is the Meditation Garden and Pond, where Elvis, his mother Gladys, his father Vernon, and his grandmother, Minnie Mae Hood Presley, lie buried in peace. There is also a small stone in remembrance of his identical twin brother, Jesse Garon Presley, who died at birth. Oddly, his paternal grandmother, Minnie, outlived her son, daughter-in-law and grandsons. The Meditation Garden was originally built by him as a place for quiet contemplation. After their deaths, to protect the remains from vandals, his father brought their coffins to the Meditation Gardens and created a family plot as a memorial to his family. The rock star is buried beneath a life-size sculpture of Jesus on a large pedestal, with Elvis' loved ones by his side. The Meditation Garden was originally designed and built by Bernard Grenadier at Elvis' request. It features Italian statues and an elaborate pond and fountain with attractive special lighting. A brick wall behind the Grecian columns is inlaid with primitive stained handmade glass from Spain. Its original intent was to offer him a private and serene area for meditation and became one of his favorite places to relax. The gravesite has become a world famous tourist attraction with annual graveside services in memory of the one and only Elvis.

Elvis' Car Museum contained over 33 vehicles, including a 1975 Dino Ferrari, a 1956 Eldorado Convertible Cadillac, the red MG from his movie Blue Hawaii, and two official 1998 racecars with Elvis-themed designs. Additionally, the museum is home to the NASCAR that was driven by racing star Rusty Wallace and the Elvis NHRA "funny car" that was driven by John Force. His Harley-Davidson motorcycles, when viewed, brought back memories of his sitting in the front seat wearing a black leather jacket, white T-shirt and black cap, with a gorgeous blonde squeezing his body; what a great visualization!! There were also some of his favorite motorized toys, including a go-cart, dune buggy, motorized three wheelers, and a pedal car. The most famous car in the world was the center of attraction; his 1954 Pink Fleetwood Cadillac, which was a gift to his mother who refused to drive it because she didn't have a driver's license. The car was originally blue with a black top. He had the car painted with a secret formula rose pink so that it couldn't be reproduced; hence the name of the car: "Elvis' Rose."

We were running out of time, so our last stop was to view the collection of jets that he used for pleasure and business. A converted Convair 880 Jet that originally held 100 passengers was his pride and joy. He called it his "Flying Graceland." He named the plane "Lisa Marie"; it contains a luxurious living room, conference room, sitting room and private bedroom, as well as gold-plated seatbelts, suede-chairs, leather-covered tables, and 24-karate gold flecked sinks: "Way to go Elvis." His smaller plan was a Lockheed Jet Star which was customized with a yellow and green interior (again with that green color). He used it for short trips and for transporting his manager, Colonial Parker, around on business.

We should have spent more time there, as we didn't get to really see all of the beautiful grounds or get a chance to study and fully appreciate some of his memorabilia. After reviewing his life, it was easy to see why his estate was depleted when he died. His generosity to friends and charities and his exorbitant lifestyle certainly took their toll on his finances. But, his heirs certainly put his name and popularity to good use and have benefited financially from their having been a part of the King's life.

Back at the Peabody Hotel, the afternoon Duck Walk was over so we didn't have to fight the large crowds that gathered to see the procession. We had a light snack before packing for our trip back to Louisville, for the big race and retired exhilarated but quite exhausted from the day's outing. We caught an early bus back to Louisville and the Galt Hotel. It was the day before the Derby and the streets and hotel were buzzing with excitement. We missed the Great Steamboat Race by a couple of days. The race was between the Spirit of Jefferson steamboat, instead of the Belle of Louisville which was in for repairs, and the Delta Queen. It began underneath the George Rogers Clark Memorial Bridge and raced to Six Mile Island where they turned around to return to the bridge, which was the finish line, a distance of fourteen miles with an average speed of seven miles per hour. The Delta Queen nosed out her adversary by a whisper and won the bragging right of being the fastest boat on the rivers. She also proudly displayed her Golden Antler trophy high on the bow, where it shouts, "Look at Me, Queen of the Waterways."

We also missed the Pegasus Parade by one day and were witnessing the massive street clean up of one of the largest parades in the country. Pegasus was the magical winged white horse from Greek mythology that, with a stroke of his hoof, would bring forth rivers. Over the centuries, the winged beauty has taken on muse like qualities with ideas of poetic inspiration; an appropriate symbol for the pre-Derby parade. The parade dates back to 1956, beginning with four volunteers who are now numbered at over 2,000, and draws crowds of up to 300,000 spectators in its 1.7 mile extravaganza down Broadway. The current parade consisted of larger-than-life floats, many built by employees or volunteers of the sponsoring groups who vie for the best float awards in various categories.

The highlights of the procession were the humungous animated balloons and historical figures, such as an astronaut and popular entertainers, like B. B. King. Music was provided by high school marching bands from around the country. Clowns and celebrities were available to entertain the crowds with their clowning and singing. The theme for the parade was: "Music-That's Entertainment" with the popular Loretta Lynn heading the procession as Grand Marshall. Other celebrities enjoying the festivities were Mohammad Ali and B. B. King. Some of the past Grand Marshalls have been John Wayne, Michael Landon, William Shatner, and Lorne Greene, with such entertainers as Carol Channing, Liberace, Gladys Knight, and of course, Loretta Lynn. The most spectacular sight of the parade was the large white-winged Pegasus balloon that rose high above the other balloons that depicted animals and every day people. Now, how did I know all of this being that we missed the event? Well, the Pegasus Parade was rebroadcast on NBC on Derby Day, so we were able to enjoy the procession from the comfort of our hotel room without being there on the day of the event.

We spent the rest of the day joining the revelers partying in the streets and in our hotel. The Derby's traditional drink is the Mint Julep which has many different recipes, but one of the more popular recipes follows:

"Muddle mint leaves and syrup in a glass and fill with shaved or crushed ice, then add 2 ½ ounces of Kentucky Bourbon, and top with more ice and garnish with a mint sprig; add straw to a silver-colored glass and enjoy."

We collected quite a few straws during the day and, before things got out of control, we decided to have an early dinner and get to bed so we could rise early the next day and join the crowds at Churchill Downs. The race track usually accommodates a little over 50,000 fans, but for the Derby, over 160,000 people showed up with standing room only occupied by the many racing enthusiasts. Churchill Downs includes over 140-acres of pastures with stables and practice tracks, the main race track, a club house, and seating for over 50,000 spectators. The race is a "Grade I" stakes race for three-year-old thoroughbred horses and is held on the first Saturday in the month of May. The race is a one and a quarter mile event that includes colts and geldings and is considered, "The Most Exciting Two Minutes in Sports" for its approximate duration. It is also referred to as "The Run for the Roses," as the winning horse is draped with a lush blanket of over 500 red roses around its neck. The race is the first leg of the United States Triple Crown of Thoroughbred Racing and is followed by the Preakness Stakes, and then the Belmont Stakes races. The fastest horse to run the track was Secretariat in 1973, when he finished in 1:59.4 minutes; all other races, except one, have been over two minutes. In 2001, Monarchos ran at 1:59.97 minutes, still not fast enough to break the standing record of Secretariat--currentlyl the record holder.

The infield of the race track was mobbed with people that started arriving days before the event, some even brought pup tents with them for protection against the elements. Super Bowl tailgate parties have nothing on the Derby partying that was going, there were people everywhere, eating, drinking, and watching TV on their portable sets. It's recorded that over 120,000 Mint Juleps, served in souvenir silver plastic cups with all the previous Derby winners listed, are sold every first Saturday in May at the Derby. This is in addition to another traditional Derby treat, the burgoo, which is a thick stew of beef, chicken, pork and vegetables. The vendors certainly were kept busy serving all the hungry and thirsty Derby Race lovers when we were there that day. To contrast the peasants that were partying on the infield was "Millionaires' Row," where the rich and famous occupied expensive box seats for easy viewing of the race. Around the track, women could be seen showing off their fancy Derby headgear while prancing in front of the spectators and looking for recognition of their creative handiwork. The sight of tens of thousands of women walking around with colorful hats of every description has to be seen to be believed; I saw it and still have a difficult time comprehending that so many women could be persuaded to participate in such a mystifying event, but then I'm not of that gender, so that part of my brain probably isn't fully developed to understand such a passion.

Our seats were in the middle of the race track and were probably set up just for the Derby event. Unfortunately, when the horses ran passed us and around the turn, they were out of sight. But, luckily, we did see the finish line. Guess who bet on the right horse? My wife Barbara, her blessed horse, Charismatic, won and for the third time, her three-year-old came in first . . . what are the odds? My horse, Three Ring, came in last. When am I going to learn? When the wise-one tells me something, why don't I listen? For the third time I was subjected to, "I told you to bet with me." I should know better; I mean how lucky can a person get, after all she did luck out by marrying me . . . or is it the other way around? Well, it was over, the ceremonies began with the Governor of Kentucky placing a lush lei of roses around the neck of Charismatic, and accolades, awards and trophies given to the jockey, Chris Antley and owners Robert & Beverly Lewis. Also not to be forgotten were the breeder, Oscar Penn and trainer Wayne Lukas. All this excitement was going on to the roar and cheers of the crowd, while music which was especially written for the event by pop vocalist Dan Fogelberg, "Run for the Roses," was sweetly playing over the loud speakers. On cue, the sky darkened and the clouds overhead let forth their praise for the winner; thunder and lightening came forth and hailed Charismatic and playfully watered all the flowers that were displayed on the ladies' hats and around his neck. While he was being praised and the flowers watered, we were getting soaked but could barely move as the area was thick with spectators. So, we slowly walked out of the stands and into the parking field to board our bus. Despite the unpleasantness of being drenched, the crowd moved in an orderly manner and somehow still kept the spirit of the event flowing.

What a strange feeling entering the bus and then the hotel sopping wet with strange squishing sounds coming from our shoes with every step we took. Everyone was still smiling, some were actually laughing at the whole experience. I guess the Mint

Michael Bivona

Juleps, despite their heavy price, did what they were supposed to do, keep their hosts happy. After taking hot showers and changing clothes, we went back out to join those celebrating in the hotel's lobby and lounge. We still had to keep in mind that in the evening we had the Grand Gala to attend in the hotel's large ballroom. At about 5:00 P.M., after imbibing more drinks, we decided to return to our rooms for a nap before dressing for the final event. My concern was getting back into my tuxedo. I had an alternate plan, if it didn't fit or was uncomfortable, I was going to attend in a Mardi Gras-type outfit by putting together some of the colorful clothes that I didn't get a chance to wear on the trip, the finishing touch would be my brown Derby hat. We fell soundly into napland. I didn't remember hearing the wake up call, but I did jump out of bed for some reason, looking at the radio clock in disbelief. I shook Barbara and told her it was twelve midnight, we slept through the Grand Gala. We called the front desk and told them what happened, they assured us that they called our room and assumed that we heard the call. Not to fret, we were still tired so we went back to sleep, missing our dinner and for the first time on our trip, we retired with empty stomachs, "Thank God."

CHAPTER FOURTEEN

Dancing Thru the Panama Canal on the Good Ship Crown Princess

THE LAST UNPUBLISHED DANCE-TRAVEL adventure that I'll write about came quite by accident and was sponsored by Zoe's Cruises & Tours located in Sacramento, California. We were reviewing our "bucket list" and decided it was time to cruise through the Panama Canal. We had traveled on the Crown Princess for her "New Year's Eve Under the Stars" maiden voyage some years before, which was also an item on our "bucket list," and, as former guests, we received a flyer from them describing a trip through the Panama Canal that was scheduled at the end of January, 1998. As we were very pleased with our previous experience on the Princess, the tour through the Canal on such a splendid ship was a perfect winter vacation for us, so we booked passage for a ten-day excursion through the famous canal. As fate would have it, some weeks after we booked the cruise, I received a flyer from "Zoe's Dance Cruises" for a dance cruise on the same ship. I checked with Zoe and found that for the same price, their tour would include a free cocktail party at orientation the first night, a going away party, a group photo, and the most important consideration, daily dance lessons by the world renowned English International Ballroom Dance Champions, Jackie and James McVicar. So I didn't waste any time; I cancelled my booking with the Princess Ship Lines and re-booked the same cruise through Zoe's.

The cruise was round trip from Ft. Lauderdale, Florida, and would visit Aruba; Cartagena, Columbia; Panama Canal; Colon, Panama; Limon, Costa Rica, and the San Blas Islands. We began our journey with a stay at the seventeen story Hyatt Regency, Pier 66 Hotel & Marina that is on 22-tropical acres conveniently located in the heart of Ft. Lauderdale. When traveling in the winter months, we found it wise to always arrive at our destination a day before, just in case of inclement weather conditions which can cause delays or even cancellation of flights. In addition, it gave us an opportunity to visit one of our favorite cities, Ft. Lauderdale, and without a doubt, one of our favorite resort hotels, Pier 66. The hotel is a high rise and has the most spectacular views of the city and the magnificent homes along Florida's Intracoastal Waterway. The shipping activity of Port Everglades can be seen from the revolving sky lounge at the top of the hotel. It's one of our favorite watering holes to have drinks and relax while viewing, through the large glass windows, the boating activity that takes place in one of the busiest boating cities in the world. The city is called "The Venice of the United States," due to its complex and intertwining canal system that carries boats in every conceivable direction, including out to sea. We could see the cruise ships arriving and departing the port from our high floor hotel window, which made us anxious to leave on the following day for our new adventure.

When we arrived at the hotel, we checked in and then went directly to the sky lounge. When we visited Ft. Lauderdale in the past, we always made it a point to drop in at the Pier 66 resort to enjoy the view from the revolving lounge and to wander around the first-class marina that surrounds the hotel. We found seats with perfect views of the city and settled in with coffee and Kahlua. We enjoyed taking the rotating 360 degree journey around the top of the hotel, admiring the cityscape, beautiful homes along the Intracoastal Waterway, and the ships moving through Port Everglade's inlet. The three-piece combo band kept the music flowing and gave us an opportunity to shuffle a bit on the dance floor that surrounds a circular bar. What a great way to spend a couple of hours before taking a nap and having dinner in their steak bar. The Grill 66 & Bar is considered one of the best steak houses in the city; after eating there I had to agree with that assessment. I ordered barrel cut filet Mignon, medium rare, smothered with strips of bacon. It was absolutely out of this world--it was so tender and juicy that it melted in my mouth. I had a large Idaho baked potato and broccoli rabe to complement my steak, and a tall glass of Budweiser beer to wash down the treat. Barbara ordered twin wild South African lobster tails with a side order of potato al-forno and creamed spinach, and a glass of Pinot Grigio to round out the perfect meal. After dinner, we went up to the sky lounge for a nightcap. The view from the rotating bar in the evening is a whole different experience than the daytime one. The blackness of night as a backdrop to the city's lights sparkling and blinking, sort of put me in a trancelike state that induced relaxation; with the help of a delicious cup of coffee and Kahlua, it didn't take long before I was ready for a good night's sleep.

We had breakfast at their tropical outdoor swimming pool and relaxed the morning away sunning ourselves beside a gorgeous palm tree. Our ship was scheduled to depart at 5:00 P.M., so we had the morning and the better part of the afternoon to wander around the resort and enjoy the sights, especially the world-class yachts that vacation at the marina in the winter months. There are over 140 slips for boats up to 225-feet. We walked around the marina and stopped to admire some of the larger boats. The biggest was the Forbes family's 151-foot Highlander Yacht, which was originally purchased by the ever-popular man about town, Malcolm Forbes, in 1985. The boat is 29-feet, 3-inches wide with a draft of 9-feet, 9-inches. It is capable of worldwide sailing and holds the record for pleasure yachts sailing 5,000 miles, without refueling. The 1,800 horsepower diesel engines deliver a top speed of 14.3 knots. The ship has a water capacity of 5,300-gallons and its fuel capacity is almost 20,000 gallons. To me and Barbara, this emerald green lady is our lifetime dream of boating in heaven. We peeked through the aft Fantail Salon's expansive wrap-around windows at the luxurious furnishings and were transfixed at the five glass tables that revealed what seemed to be elaborate nautical dioramas. If only we could get a better look. Well, some one up there heard us and the first mate appeared on deck and asked us if we would like to come aboard for a closer inspection of the vessel. We were delighted and gladly accepted the invitation, which included unexpected cocktails that were being served to some of the ship's guests; Bloody Mary for the Mrs. and a Pineapple Daiquiri for me. A white bearded gentleman bagpiper in full dress, including a kilt, serenaded us aboard with a Scottish tune, while the casually dressed guests hummed along and laughed at the surreal event. The First Mate took us to the back of the boat where the dioramas were for us to get a closer look at the miniature works of art. There were five glass-enclosed tables in front of overstuffed wraparound couches. The first was called "On the Banks," the second, "First Day Out," and next was "Essex Shipyard." The fourth was called, "Watering," and the fifth and most compelling was a "Whaling Scene of the Small Whaling Brigantine 'Katy'."

Of interest were five scale ship models of the Highlanders, past and present, lined up vertically, in chronological order in an enclosed glass case. The first was a 1955, 72-foot converted Canadian Corvette. The second model was a 98-foot steel hulled flagship for entertaining corporate America during its heyday. A larger 1967 Aalsmeer, built in the Netherlands, was the third model. This ship went up in flames and was replaced by the fourth model, the Highlander IV, which was built by the same firm and marine architect as its predecessor. Finally, there was the 1985 Highlander, which is 151-feet long and boasts 5 guest state rooms, 6 salons, 6 state rooms for crew and 14 heads (toilets). The first mate mentioned that kings, queens and presidents have been guests on the magnificent green lady and that, in the course of one season, some 6,500 people visit the ship. The ship has a crew of 14, including the captain, and boasts of having a Bell Jet Ranger III helicopter sitting on it heliport accompanied by two tenders, a 19-foot Cigarette race boat, and 23-foot Donzi speedboat. The bridge of the boat was off limits, but I asked if we could see the engine room. He said okay and away we went into the state-of-the-art room. We were actually able to stand up in the twin engine compartment, with room to spare. The premises were spotless with white, high-gloss paint challenging dirt to dare enter the sacred walls. When considering the small, crowded engine room on my 42-foot Chris Craft, also known as the bilge, the Highlander's pristine basement looked like a mechanic's paradise. We were running out of time, so we thanked our gracious host for his hospitality and hurried back to our hotel room to pack and make our way to the dock where the Crown Princess was patiently awaiting our arrival.

We approached the giant ship, which was one of the largest ocean liners at that time, measuring 811-feet with a beam of 115-feet and 11 decks. It also had 9 elevators and approximately 1,000 cabins, with a crew of almost 700 and passenger capacity of 1,600 people. The officers were Italian and the crew was an International mix. By today's standards, it would be considered a moderately-sized ship. Our last sailing, in 2007, had a passenger list of almost 3,000 people. We were unhappy about relinquishing our luggage at the gangway to the attendants and said silent prayers that we would see our companions intact in our stateroom. Walking up the gangway is always an exciting experience, so much so, that I can usually feel what little hair that is left on the back of my neck rising. We had a rather small room, about 180-square feet with an outside balcony, which gave us the feeling that the cabin was a lot larger than its size. The whole scene was breathtaking--the ship, the ambiance, the view from our balcony and my companion Barbara--I couldn't ask for anything more.

A special table was set for our group with itineraries for the trip and a list of dancers, so we could familiarize ourselves with the names of the other hoofers that we would be spending our journey with. The tour director's name was Helmet; he gave us the necessary pamphlets and reminded us that we had a 6:00 P.M. orientation cocktail party for our group of 30 dancers in the top deck lounge. The dress for the evening was casual and made to order after our long day of relaxation. We were introduced to our dance instructors: Jamie & Jackie McVicar, who were from Great Britain and were ballroom dancing champions. After some cocktails we introduced ourselves one by one; our companions were from all over the U.S., including California, Colorado, New York, New Jersey, etc. Some were on the trip just to take lessons from the English couple. The scheduled program was for three hour dance lessons in the morning, one for beginners and the second for the more advanced students. In the afternoon, there was a one-hour dance practice session open to all students. The lessons were in Rumba, Waltz and Quickstep, at both beginner and intermediate levels.

Our group had the early 7:00 P.M. seating in a reserved area, which made dinner an exceptionally pleasant event as everyone was excited about the scheduled dance lessons and the ensuing practice sessions. Fortunately, the ship had a predominately Italian speaking crew, so ordering my favorite pasta dishes was something I looked forward to every day. I did this with delight, I might add, as there weren't any pasta combinations that they couldn't perfect in a short period of time. Meeting so many people from all over the country, in such a casual setting, with common interests was quite pleasant; it skipped the anxiety that often is present when interacting with new acquaintances, and resulted in meeting many amicable people in a short period of time. After dinner most of us went to the large lounge at the top of the ship for cocktails and to become more acquainted with our new friends who we would be spending lots of time dancing with at the lessons and at practice sessions. We didn't stay too long as we had a rather long day and we still had to unpack and settle into our cabin, so we left with lots of happy goodbyes and retired to our room.

We usually prefer buffet breakfasts when we are on vacations, the rationale being that we can pick and choose "The lesser of all the evils" when selecting food. But, for some reason, it never quite turns out that way, as returning to the buffet's spread is very tempting and almost impossible to resist. So after a rather large breakfast, we walked around the deck several times to get rid of some of the extra calories we had added and to kill time until our 10:30 A.M. dance class; and what a wonderful lesson it was. Our lesson was Rumba, and instructors Jamie and Jackie started the lesson with, "Rumba is a romantic dance of love and seduction, but unless you have the right beat you will never experience that sensation." So Jackie said to our group of about fourteen people: "Say after me; chick-chicky-boom, chick-chicky-boom, that is the Rumba beat, with a hesitation on the boom." They then played Desi Arnaz' rendition of the song, "Cuban Pete, the King of the Rumba Beat." We followed their lead to the four beats of the Rumba as follows: male's part; left side, together, forward left then stop; right side, together, back right then stop, continued in a box pattern, those are the basic steps of the dance. The song and the words to the music brought flashbacks to me that placed me at the Palladium Dance Hall in Manhattan, New York. In my younger days, as a bachelor, it was one of my favorite watering holes for dancing and a great place to meet glamorous New York City girls. The center of attraction was always, none other than, Cuban Pete, who was considered the best Mambo and Rumba dancer at the club and probably in the city. Many titles were bestowed upon this Puerto Rican dance giant, such as "King of the Latin Beat," "The Maestro of Mambo," "The prince of the Palladium" and of course, "Cuban Pete." Over 100 dance steps are credited to him, including: "The Latin Cross Body Lead," "The Susie Q," "The Porpoise," "The Savoy Turn," "The Prayer" and "The Kick Tap-Tap." His real name is Pedro Aguilar, born in Puerto Rico in 1927. He was given the nickname "Cuban Pete" by his Palladium friends; the name came from a movie "Cuban Pete" with Desi Arnaz that was made in 1947, where he popularized the song. Subsequently, Desi endorsed Pedro's nickname as he considered him the embodiment of Latin dancing. I was privileged to see him at the Palladium and fortunate to meet him many years later at the Goldcoast Ballroom in Coconut Creek, Florida, where he and his partner, Barbara, were regulars at the Sunday night Latin dances. He was still the Rumba and Mambo king and continued dazzling people with his unique style of dancing. I took great pleasure in his reassuring wink and wave when, on occasion, my wife Barbara and I would dance a Mambo-Salsa. I always took it as a sign that we were doing something right with the dance.

The dance lesson continued to the music of Cuban Pete with the words loud and clear:

"They call me Cuban Pete; I'm the king of the Rumba beat. When I play the maracas, I go chick-chicky-boom. Yes sir, I'm Cuban Pete, I'm the craze of my native street, when I start to dance everything goes chick-chicky-boom. The senoritas, they sing and how they swing with the rumbero. It's very nice, so full of spice, and when they're dancin' they bring a happy ring to maraquero, singin' a song, all the day long. So if you like the beat, take a lesson from Cuban Pete and I'll teach you the chick-chicky-boom, chick-chicky-boom. Si, senorita, I know that you will like the chicky-boom-chicky, cause it's the dance of Latin romance and Cuban Pete doesn't teach you in a hurry like Arthur Murray. You're now in Havana and there is always manyana, so senoritas please, take it easy, do it with ease and you'll love it when you do the chick-chicky-boom, chick-chicky-boom."

That was the rhythm; we learned the Cuban motion which required moving our knees and hips in a twisting sexy manner, to chick-chicky-boom. We added a simple underarm turn to our repertoire and then called it a day. Our legs, knees, and hips were killing us; what seemed to be a simple Latin dance lesson turned out to be an aerobic exercise. Lunch was a welcome respite; instead of a buffet we opted for a sit-down meal on some soft comfortable seats to help relax and rest our strained muscles. Our whole dance class had the same idea, we spent our lunch hour enjoying some salads and discussing the wonderful experience we had learning a dance from such pleasant and accomplished instructors. Lunch was short lived for we had to hurry to our practice session where all the dance students from both classes met to see if the morning's dance instructions would result in what looked like a Rumba. Jamie and Jackie had the boys and girls line up opposite each other and told us to change partners so we could practice with different dancers. Initially this was very confusing, as getting in tune with a strange person for dancing is quite a challenge, but we did manage to dance to a slow chick-chicky-boom, chick-chicky-boom. We spent the session dancing with different partners, while Jamie and Jackie gave individual instructions to each couple to improve their performances. The session ended sooner than we would have liked, but we did have some evening dancing to look forward to. A well deserved nap was in order to prepare us for the formal dinner and late show at the elaborate theater, and, if our energy levels allowed, we might be able to do some social dancing afterwards.

As far as I'm concerned, there are few greater pleasures in life then napping, especially on a boat with the balcony door open and comfortable warm, fresh sea air enhancing the event; the pitter patter of waves against the ship added their sounds of music to the air and helped lull me into a deep dreamy sleep, smiling all the while. Barbara, on the other hand, finds the balcony door being open and the sounds of the waves quite annoying, but being the good sport that she is, she snuggled up and joined me in slumberland. After a couple of joyous hours we were ready to prepare ourselves for the big formal night event. It has never been one of my favorite social happenings. I love the camaraderie and good food, but the tuxedo is always a struggling pot luck affair. I'm never quite sure if the suit will still fit me, although this time I was lucky. It was only slightly snug and I didn't have to contend with a bow tie as I decided to wear an all black shirt with a nice matching regular long clip on black tie. Barbara said I looked sheik, which made me feel a little more agreeable about the whole tuxedo affair.

The Italian captain and his officers greeted our group at the entrance to the dining room with a bow and a "Benevento a Bordo." It was comfortable sitting with our traveling companions. We had four tables next to each other, which enhanced the camaraderie and conversation, mostly about how badly we did at the practice session. I was quite pleased that the kitchen was staffed by Italian chefs and didn't waste any time ordering my favorite salad, which is; provolone, tomatoes and black olives. A main course of pasta primavera in a red marinara sauce put me in gastro-heaven. Everyone thought I was crazy considering we could order steaks, a variety of fresh fish or many dishes that were not listed on the menu. However, being from a simple Italian family where pasta was the Sunday, Tuesday and Thursday meal, I was on cloud nine being able to order and enjoy wonderful al dente, succulent pasta, with fragrant red Italian sauce, resplendent with precious memories that kept entering my mind's eye with every bite. After dinner we walked around the outside deck for a couple of turns to enjoy the warm evening breeze and the dazzling brilliant stars surrounding a glowing full moon. Looking at the evening extravaganza of a full moon, stars and what seemed to be an occasional star bursts, tempted us to take a couple of chaise lounges and lie back, remaining silent, while absorbing heaven's wonders. Barbara, an amateur astronomer, pointed out the Milky Way, the Seven Sisters, the Big Dipper, Orion, and the Southern Cross. She woke me from my nap and reminded me that there was a show at the theater, so we strolled over to meet our friends and take in some relaxing entertainment. The theme for the evening was "The Best of Broadway." The ship's theatrical cast sang and danced numbers from the musicals "Phantom," "On a Clear Day," "Showboat," "Chicago," and "Fiddler on the Roof." I'm always impressed with the talent of the many people who perform so beautifully and are relatively unknown in the entertainment world; hopefully these young, beautiful, hard working artists will someday reach their stardom and have their days in the sun.

Dancing on the dance floor of the ship's open air deck is always an interesting experience, especially if the ship is rolling. We spent about an hour dancing to great DJ music, sometimes stumbling along with the movement of the boat, but regaining ourselves just in time to continue whatever dance it was that we were attempting to do. After drinking a tasty Mai Tai concoction, we headed for our room, post haste, as I was sure that I was going to fall asleep while dancing in the warm sea air under the stars. The only thought I had before leaving reality was "delightful, delightful, delightful, what a delightful way to end an evening."

The next day we were scheduled to be at sea, so we had a light breakfast and lounged around until our dance class. We've learned that eating a heavy meal and then dancing can be a very uncomfortable experience, so we finally found a legitimate reason not to over-indulge while eating at the ship's elaborate, inviting dining venues. The Rumba music to Desi Arnaz's Cuban Pete was playing when we entered the spacious room that was reserved for our group, so we chick-chicky-boomed into the session ready to perfect what we had learned and to add some new patterns to our dance. Jamie and Jackie asked us again to line up, boys on one side, girls on the other, facing each other. Jamie said he wanted the men to move forward and the ladies backwards to the beat of chick-chicky-boom, while keeping the Latin motion in our hips, knees and legs. We then joined the person in front of us and began to do what actually looked like a Rumba. We practiced the box step, underarm turn and the new Cuban Walk that started the dance lesson. They suggested the Cuban Walk as a good opening for the Rumba as it puts people in the right mood and motion. The next routine was a slow propeller move that began with an underarm turn; a breakaway and then meeting at the sides; men's right side touching women's right side; arms extended, the men move in a clockwise direction for a four count beat four times, coming out of it with a fifth position break and then back into a basic box Rumba. After about fifteen minutes, everyone was asked to join their significant other and try the routines in the order that we learned them, with the help of Jamie calling out the steps. It was amazing that most of the group, including Barbara and me, actually got it right on our first try. We felt like professional Rumba dancers doing turns, open breaks, propeller motions and fifth position breaks. The lesson ended too soon, but just in time to ward off the severe pain I was starting to get in my legs that required me to find a comfortable place to sit down. We remembered the soft chairs in the formal dining room, so the whole group decided that our bodies were entitled to some comfort and headed straight away for another visit to cuisine-paradise for a sit down lunch. Barbara and I were determined to limit our weight gain as much as possible, so we both ordered salads with yummy biscuits and Italian espresso. We also ordered, in perfect Italian, Acqua senza gas (plain water no bubbles) to the surprise of our waiter and friends. I think it's the only phrase that I remembered from all the Italian lessons I've taken. After a brief relaxing walk around the deck, we headed for our practice session and hoped that what we learned so far in the Rumba classes would materialize into some semblance of experienced dancers enjoying themselves. Well, it worked; we felt the passion and rhythm of the dance and were praised by Jamie and Jackie for the smoothness that we performed our routines. That made our day, and we spent the rest of the day floating on thin air and dreaming of the days to come that we would be able to finally get on the dance floor and perform the Latin dance of love and seduction with feeling and meaning.

Our dinner, as usual, was delicious. I stayed with my favorite salad and pasta, while Barbara and our table guests enjoyed the steaks and fish that were made to perfection. After the meal, we went directly to the theater to see the ship's cast's interpretation of "Aida in the 20th Century." Our biggest problem with opera appreciation is that neither of us understands Italian well enough to enjoy the meaning of the words that are expressed to the beautiful music. The story is about "Aida, an Ethiopian Princess that is captured and brought into slavery in Egypt. A military commander struggles to choose between his love for her and his loyalty to the Pharaoh. To complicate the plot, the commander is loved by the Pharaoh's daughter." The Italian composer Verdi's music is always somewhat pleasant, which made viewing the show tolerable. After the show we went to the upper lounge with members of our group and spent the rest of the evening enjoying the DJ's ballroom music, especially the Rumba.

As I was writing this chapter, our dear dancing idol, Cuban Pete, went to his happy dancing ground on January 13, 2009, at the age of 82. We attended a "Tribute to Cuban Pete" a musical memorial that was held at Goldcoast Ballroom in Coconut Creek on Saturday, March 7, 2009, that began at 10:00 P.M., and ended at 2:30 in the morning. The music was provided by the famous Latin DJ Puerto Rican Pete. Cuban Pete's dance partner and business manager, Barbara Craddock, gave a eulogy honoring his accomplishments and spoke of his incredible life and his impact on Latin dancing. She mentioned his many prestigious awards for his work, and proudly announced that he is the only Latin dancer recognized in the Latin Jazz Exhibit at the Smithsonian Institution. She mentioned that in December, 2007, Pete and she were the recipients of the Latin Jazz USA Lifetime Achievement Award; they were the first Latin dancers to receive this award and it was one of his most cherished possessions. Also speaking about the great Latin Mambo dancer was Tito Puente, Jr., son of the great Latin band leader of the same name, who today continues with his father's music and leads his own band in the same Latin music tradition. He spoke of his father's friendship and love for the great dancer and quoted his Dad as saying: "Pedro 'Cuban Pete' Aguilar was the greatest Mambo dancer ever." After the eulogies there were two performances. The first was a performance by two male dancers doing the Mambo, Cuban Pete style. The message that they transmitted while performing their intricate rhythmic steps was that it takes two of us to perform the great dancer's routines. The second act was a formation dance done by six couples to many of Pete's dancing styles and moves.

What a wonderful tribute to a great dancing genius: great music, wonderful memories and people traveling from around the country to pay their respects and to celebrate the life of one of our national treasures. I took a couple of pictures at the memorial; one of Barbara Craddock standing under a poster of Cuban Pete and one of my wife, Barbara and Vinny Munno (owner of Goldcoast Ballroom) alongside the same poster, with DJ Puerto Rican Pete in the background playing his music. The picture of Barbara and Vinny follows:

We awoke the next morning to the comfort of the warm sea air enveloping our minds and bodies. We were determined to keep our breakfasts simple and light, so I had juice and corn flakes with some fruit and a cup of herbal tea. Barbara had juice and an English muffin washed down with aromatic strong Italian coffee. We strolled around the outside deck for a refreshing constitutional and were then ready, with light stomachs, for our next dance lesson, which was one of my favorite dances, the Waltz. The music was blaring from the hall, so there was no mistaking where our Waltz class was located. We entered to see Jamie and Jackie doing an exquisite Waltz around the room; their stomachs seemed attached, while their upper bodies formed a perfect "V" with their heads directed to their left sides. It was a picture perfect scene; two professionals, in love with the Waltz, radiating their effervescent feelings into the surroundings with beautiful style and grace. Barbara and I looked at each other and knew what we were thinking: if only, someday, by some miracle, we could look like the enchanted couple . . . "Dream On." The Waltz beat is one of the easiest to hear, so said Jackie. Well, it was easy to pick up the beat, but the timing was another matter. Jackie called out: "Quick-Quick-Quick and a 1-2-3; 1-2-3. The first beat of each measure is accented and this corresponds to an aggressive driving step that is taken on the count of one moving in the line of direction around the dance floor. The movement of the dance is characterized by the use of sways, rises and falls; the rising and falling actions should be very smooth with no bouncing. When done properly, the Waltz should be soft, gentle and romantic, with long sweeping movements, smooth turns and stylish poses." Is that all there is to it? I said to myself . . . Well, again my mind echoed, "Dream On."

The bronze level Waltz, like the Rumba, is also done in a box pattern, for the men's part: left forward, right to the right and left close; right back, left to the left, right close; it's important to hover on the second beat, which makes the appearance of the dance exceptionally attractive and rhythmic. It's important that the partners' stomachs are in contact, with shoulders and heads back and looking to the left. When the basic box steps are executed it should be performed while turning to the man's left with: 1-2-3; 1-2-3 or quick-quick-quick; quick-quick-quick. It took most of the lesson to get the feel of the dance and the proper body positions, but when the class was over, most of the students had a good understanding as to what was expected in the performance of the beautiful centuries old Waltz. "Stomachs sucked in (if possible) and in contact with each other, shoulders back, heads to the left, tight butts and begin dancing." That's what we heard Jamie saying as we were leaving the lesson. So, with stomachs sucked in and tight butts we walked in a rather strange fashion to the lunch buffet where people were looking at us with smirks on their faces, as if they were in on our special secret. While we were at our dance class, the ship made its first scheduled stop at the Island of Aruba.

The island was once a Dutch colony and part of the Netherland's Antilles. The first inhabitants, the Caquetios Indians of the war-like Arawak tribe, date back to 1000 ACE. What sets Aruba apart from the other Caribbean islands is its arid year round climate, it gets about 20-inches of rain annually and has an average 82-degrees temperature year round. A unique gift from nature on the white soft sand atoll is its Divi-divi tree, or large shrub, that is common throughout the island. The small, twisted trunk tree, which usually grows to an average height of 25-feet, also grows at a 45-degree angle due to the prevailing winds, and is used as a marker for lost tourists. "Follow the direction of the trees and you will end up at the hotel area along the beaches," so the locals claim. Aruba didn't escape the fate of the inhabitants of other Caribbean Islands; the first Europeans landed on its shores in 1499 when explorer Alonso de Ojeda and his cohorts decided that the Indians would make good copper mine workers in the Dominican Republic. They tricked and captured the natives and exported them to their slave enclaves. Fortunately, in 1636, the more civilized Dutch took possession of the island and remained in control for two centuries. It briefly lost possession to the British in 1805, but the Dutch regained it in 1816. Today, Aruba, with its 100,000-plus population, remains a part of the Kingdom of the Netherlands; however, it functions independently with its own government.

The Port of Aruba, which is located in its capital city, Oranjestad, was a short walking distance from our ship. We only had a couple of hours to explore before the boat left for the Island of Cartagena, Colombia, so Barbara thought it would be a good idea to visit the Royal Plaza Mall, which could be seen from our ship, so she could satisfy her never-ending shopping urge.

I decided to join her, just to get a better look at the beautiful island and possibly find a cap that had "Aruba" and a "Divi-divi tree" on it. I was lucky, there were hundreds of $10.00 hats throughout the mall; I chose a red one with four small Divi-divi trees and "Aruba" written in script gold letters. Barbara, on the other hand, was drawn to the designer clothing outlets like a magnet; fortunately she found a colorful native beach dress, reasonably priced and the right size, which she purchased. It satisfied her shopping mania without too much strain on my wallet.

Aruba was put on our "Bucket List" as a place that we had to return to. The white beachscape with its pastel-colored 19th century homes made a future visit enticing; its crystal pristine green/blue water made a future visit inevitable. We would have to wait another five years before returning to the paradise island for a week of relaxation and exploration. We were able to return to the ship in time to enjoy the tail end of the practice session that our group was enjoying. We certainly needed more practice in the Waltz and were able to fine tune what we had learned by dancing with other classmates. After the session we decided to take advantage of the cool, refreshing water in the large swimming pool on the upper deck, and then just lounge around with a couple of drinks and pass the time of day reading and relaxing. That was my plan anyhow, but when I spread out on my chaise lounge and opened my book, it wasn't long before the gentle warm ocean breeze did me in and put me into dreamland. Barbara, however, wasn't going to miss the opportunity to wear her new bathing suit and headed straight for the cool water of the pool. After a refreshing, hour-long nap, we went back to our room to prepare for dinner and a show at the theater.

At dinner we sat with a couple from Pennsylvania named Jill and Don. They were the youngest couple in our group, around fortyish, and without a doubt, the best dancers. We hit it off pretty well with them and were able to switch partners and enjoy their level of dancing while improving our routines. We had lots in common with them, the most exciting was that we all wanted to visit the Rainbow Room in Manhattan, New York, to dine and dance on their famous revolving dance floor. We promised each other that when we planned on visiting the Big City, we would get together and make one of our dreams a reality. Well, many years later, our friends Eli and Sal Guarneri invited us to join them for Sal's 70th birthday at the Rainbow Room. We immediately looked for Jill and Don's telephone number, but to no avail--we just couldn't find it. The girls decided that a night out at such a prestigious place required that the guys wear tuxedos. So, again, I retrieved my black suit of armor, put it on with much distain, and proceeded to drive everyone to the Big Apple.

The Rainbow Room is located on the 65th floor of 30 Rockefeller Plaza. It is part of the Rockefeller Plaza complex which was built between 1929 and 1940 in midtown Manhattan and consists of fourteen limestone skyscrapers set amid a series of outdoor spaces on twelve acres of land. Its pride and joy are the art deco Radio City Music Hall, which is the largest theater in the city; and the picture-perfect out-door ice-skating rink that is enjoyed by visitors and residents alike, including me and Barbara; and the NBC building, which is the tallest of the complex's skyscrapers and home to the Rainbow Room. The complex was sponsored by John D. Rockefeller as a testimony to his faith in the American economy; its construction and labor force were instrumental in helping the Big Apple through the Great Depression. The Rainbow Room was completed in 1934 as a formal supper club where the elite and influential of New York could gather and socialize while dancing to the music of the legendary big bands. It was considered the epitome of sophistication, and to complement its reputation as the "in place," gave the Cipriani family, owners of the famous Harry's Bars, the opportunity to run the kitchen. They still manage the Rainbow Room and are currently renegotiating their lease with the landlords; hopefully their efforts will result in the continuation of the establishment's success as the most sophisticated nightclub in New York City.

The Rainbow Grill is also on the 65th floor of the NBC building, and is one of the most expensive and popular watering holes in the metropolis; it has a smaller menu than the main dining hall and is available for patrons who do not want the formal sit down dinner that the Rainbow Room offers. A spectacular panoramic view of Manhattan can be seen through the vertical paneled windows that runs the length of the restaurant. The night-time views of the skyscrapers are mesmerizing, giving one the feeling of being a part of a heavenly body, enjoying the skyline and the sky full of blinking and shining stars. I'm sure the views are built into the high prices of their drinks and meals, but the price justifies the sights of the marvelous skyline from on high.

When we entered the Rainbow Room, I felt like royalty arriving at a crown court function. The 12-piece big band was playing a Rumba; it was unsettling to see people dancing with an up and down motion while the circular dance floor was rotating clockwise like a 78-rpm record. The scene was reminiscent of a carousel turning its occupants and riding horses around in a circle, while moving them up and down. Our white gloved, tuxedoed waiter escorted us to a ringside table where we nervously sat down and waited for the next event. From that point on everything went along smoothly, especially after drinking some of the champagne that Sal ordered in perfect Italian, with much gusto, to celebrate his birthday.

The Italian waiter also spoke the language fluently and held a long leisurely conversation with Sal about how beautiful Italy is; they both agreed that when the time came, they would return and retire to their fatherland. The menu featured Northern Italian cuisine which we ordered in haste as we were all famished after the long ride and suffering through heavy traffic from Long Island to the Big Apple. We all ordered Buffalo Ricotta Panzerotti with Black Truffles for appetizers. I ordered Dover Sole with Fresh Tomatoes and Olives. Everyone else decided to order Baby Rock Lobster Amoricaine. As we waited for our food to arrive we danced on the revolving dance floor, which took a bit of getting use to. In time, we established our equilibrium and danced to the sweet music of the big band to smooth Foxtrots and Waltzes. Needless to say the appetizers and main courses were spectacular; each of us raved about the presentation and taste of the delicious Italian food. So there we were, enjoying our meal, absorbing the panoramic view of the city's sky-line, and dancing to sweet big band music; what else could we possibly ask for? Well, from across the room we heard, "Mike, Barbara; Mike, Barbara." Barbara and I couldn't believe our eyes, it was Jill and Don, our dancing partners from the Panama Canal Cruise. After hugs and kisses we all blurted out the same scenario: "We couldn't find your phone number, we couldn't find your phone number." Well . . . life is strange! Here we were, Barbara and I, sitting with Sal, who I met at The Kismet Ballroom in a serendipitous event (or a kismet moment), over ten years ago and who I knew from my childhood, both of us taking part in another serendipitous experience, meeting Jill and Don at a preordained happening. Talk about six degrees of separation, what are the odds of people involved in a first-fated meeting being a party to a second-destined event. They joined us at our table for after-dinner drinks and to share the birthday cake we ordered for Sal. We spent the rest of the evening reminiscing and catching up on important highlights in our lives since we last met. The best part of the evening was being able to dance with Jill again who was an excellent dancer. Rumbas, mambos-salsas and smooth dancing; the night evaporated and we said our goodbyes with promises of keeping in touch. Our drive back to Long Island went by quickly as all we could talk about was the chance meeting between me and Sal, and then Sal being a party to one of life's mysteries or tricks of destiny, between Barbara and me and Jill and Don.

After another delicious dinner on the ship we went directly to the upper deck lounge where our host, Helmet, had arranged a party for our dancing group. We had free tropical drinks diced with lots of rum and some tasty fruit which no one could recognize; nevertheless, after one of the potent drinks, it didn't matter what the ingredients were. We danced the evening away under the stars to great ballroom music that was provided by the ship's DJ. Changing partners was the order of the evening, so I spent lots of time dancing with ladies that were at all levels of accomplishment. One of the rewards of dancing with different girls is that you must be very cognizant of their level of expertise and dance with them accordingly. It's very difficult and even embarrassing for the ladies when male partners perform steps and routines that are beyond their partners' level; so showing off is always out of the question when it is at the expense of the ladies. After satisfying our dancing needs, we walked back to our cabin. The one complaint that was heard onboard by most nonsmokers is that getting to many of the ships cabins required walking through the gambling casino which allows the players to smoke, and it seems that they all smoke, much to the discomfort of nonsmokers. We would not deprive them the right to indulge, but it should be in areas that are totally isolated from those who do not want to breathe in toxic air.

Our next stop was Cartagena, Colombia, the fortified seaside resort city of over a million residents, which was the bastion of the Spanish Empire in the Americas during their dominance of the Caribbean from the 16th through the 19th centuries. Colombia has a population of over 40 million people and shares its borders with Peru, Ecuador, Brazil and Venezuela. It's one of the most populated and important countries in South America. Archaeologists estimate that around 7,000 BCE, the formative Puerto Homiga Indians lived in the area. Before the European intrusion of South America in the early 16th century, the Karib, Malibu and Arawak Indians called the region their home. The natives were decimated and enslaved by the Spanish conquistadores; their wealth was confiscated and sent to Spain to enrich the conqueror's treasury, making Spain one of the richest and most powerful countries in the world at the expense of the South Americans.

The city was founded by Spanish conquistador Don Pedro de Heredia on June 1, 1533. Since then, Cartagena has had a more then checkered history; being the stronghold of the

Spanish Empire in the Americas, gold, silver, emeralds, and other treasures were gathered and warehoused in the city for transport to Spain, making it a target for pirates. During the 1560s, two of the most infamous pirates, John Hawkins, and his cousin, Francis Drake, were regular plunderers of the city and the surrounding area. The Spanish feared Francis Drake so much that they called him "El Draque," or "The Dragon," and fortified their city against his attacks. The walled city, which has been designated a UNESCO World Heritage Site, has a seven-mile-long fortified coastline and was considered impregnable at that time and a tribute to Spanish engineering. However, Francis Drake wasn't impressed and he attacked a caravan in route to the city and was successful in capturing all of its precious cargo. There was too much treasure to carry, so much of it had to be buried with hopes of future retrieval. Drake is considered one of the most important sailors of his time; he was the first Englishman to circumnavigate the globe, and subsequently helped defeat the Spanish Armada off the southern coast of England in 1588. Although a rich man from his plunderings, he returned several times as a privateer to the New World, to loot and sack Spanish ships and cities. On his last trip to the Caribbean, he contracted fever and died. His body is buried in a lead coffin in the waters off Nombres de Dios.

We had a choice of staying on board and take additional dance lessons or to leave the ship and see some local sights. We only had several hours to explore the city, so Barbara decided that a trip to the Volcan El Totumo would be a nice diversion from our sea voyage. After riding in a minivan for about 30-minutes through swampy lowlands and gravel roads, we passed a few rundown wooden huts before coming to a muddy incline that lead to a large lake. Was this the volcano? We couldn't believe it. There was a sign that verified that we were at the "Volcan El Totumo," so we got out of the van and looked up at a 65-foot high volcano. We were told to leave our baggage on board and strip down to our swimsuits, which we put on before leaving the ship, and hand our clothes to a young local girl standing at the foot of a strange looking dilapidated wooden staircase that led to the mouth of the volcano. Up we went and were surprised to see that the top of the volcano was filled with wet gooey mud; people were sitting and bathing themselves in the goop and seemed to be enjoying themselves. When it was our turn to enter the goop, I sort of had to force myself down to sink into the thick slop, which was warm and had gas bubbles popping all around us. After a few minutes we settled in and then the fun began. Attendants joined us in the pool and asked if we would like a mud massage. I said okay, but Barbara said no. What a mistake she made. It was one of the most enjoyable and relaxing 30-minute baths that I have ever experienced. After the mud bath, we stood up; the sight was surreal, we looked like creatures from outer space with dark grey goo oozing out of our bodies. We were carefully led down the stairs where local women carrying large plastic tubs filled with water attacked us and began washing the mud off of our bodies. We were led to the lake and literally thrown in and told to remove our bathing suits, which we did, and handed them over to another group of women who scrubbed our suits with a passion. In the meantime, the remaining mud on our bodies was gently removed by the attendants. In short order our suits were returned and we left the lake sparkling clean. What an experience!

We stopped at a small seaside fishing village for a late lunch. Barbara and I had some local fish with an unknown name that was steamed to perfection. A tropical papaya rum drink concoction completed our journey; our minds were totally relaxed and our bodies invigorated from the unexpected mud bath-massages. We sat down in our seats and immediately found ourselves in napland; unfortunately, the ride back was only 30-minutes, so our trip to dream-paradise ended all too soon. Our ship was getting ready to leave the dock, so we rushed to board her. As the ship left the harbor, it was dwarfed by the humongous fortifications of San Felipe de Barajas which extends for seven miles along the coast and is so high that it seems to be reaching for the sky. I promised myself that if I ever returned, I would spend time exploring every nook and cranny of the majestic Spanish fort and spend additional time visiting the many colonial parts of Cartagena.

We joined our friends for dinner and told them of our experience with the mud volcano. They thought we were making the whole story up and were jealous that they missed such a once-in-a-lifetime adventure. But, they did enjoy their dance lesson and tried to explain some of the new dance steps they learned that morning. After dinner we decided to skip the show and go directly to the lounge on the upper deck and do some ballroom dancing. Jill and Don tried to show us two of the new routines they learned that day, but we just couldn't seem to catch on, and satisfied ourselves by dancing for a couple of hours under the stars, switching partners whenever appropriate. We retired to our cabin in a very relaxed state of mind and body; remembering the mud-massage and the pleasure that I received from it, made my journey into slumberland very easy.

Early the next morning we approached the Panama Canal entrance. What could be said about the man-made engineering marvel of the 20th century that we haven't heard before? We gathered in the large auditorium to find out and to view films taken of the construction of the canal, accompanied by a lecture from our ship's historian about the trials and tribulations experienced by the brave souls that were responsible for the incredible waterway achievement. Our historian, John, began with: "The history of the Panama Canal goes back to the 16th century. After plundering the treasures of Peru, Ecuador, Mexico and the surrounding countries, Spain decided that transporting loot to their homeland would be easier and save a considerable amount of time, with less risks from pirate attacks, if they could cut out a piece of land somewhere in Panama or Nicaragua and connect the Atlantic and Pacific oceans. In 1529, Charles V ordered a survey of the isthmus and in short order, a working plan was drawn up. Due to the wars in Europe and the struggles for the control of the kingdoms in the Mediterranean Sea, the project was put on hold. In 1819, almost 300 years later, the

Spanish government formally authorized the construction of a canal and the creation of a company to build it. The discovery of gold in California in 1848 and the rush of miners stimulated the United States' interest in digging the canal. It wasn't until 1876 that an international company was organized; it took two years for them to obtain a concession from the Colombian/Panamanian government to dig a canal across the isthmus. The international company failed, and in 1880, a French company was organized by Ferdinand Marie de Lesseps, the builder of the Suez Canal to continue the project. He proposed a sea-level canal through Panama, similar to the Suez Canal in Egypt, which he had successfully built ten years earlier. His dream was to complete a water circle around the world by combining the Atlantic and the Pacific oceans. Time and mileage would be dramatically reduced when traveling between the oceans. For example, a trip from New York to San Francisco would save 8,000 miles and would reduce a 6 to 12-months journey to less than 30 days. The trip between the east and west coasts of Central and South America involved a 3,000-mile journey via the treacherous waters around Cape Horn; many treasure vessels went down to the bottom of the ocean trying to pass the unpredictable waters, and it's estimated that tens of thousands of Argonauts joined them. After twenty years of frustration, the Frenchman gave up his dream of a sea-level-canal; eventually the company sold all of their equipment and the rights to build the canal to the United States for forty million dollars. The United States and the new state of Panama signed the Hay-Bunau-Varilla Treaty, by which we guaranteed the independence of Panama and secured a perpetual lease on the ten-mile strip for the canal. Panama was compensated by an initial payment of ten million dollars and an annuity of $250,000.00 per annum, beginning in 1913. That strip is now known as the Canal Zone. It took the United States ten years and $387 million to complete the project, bringing the combined total of American and French spending to almost $700 million. The Americans decided to build a series of locks to connect the Atlantic and Pacific oceans. The project was completed in 1914, at a considerable loss of human life; thousands of workers died from the diseases that were rife in the swamplands that had to be cut through to build the canal, and many more died from accidents incurred while building the passage from the Atlantic to the Pacific oceans. Memorials for the sacrifice of over 30,000 French and American workers who lost their lives in the construction are moving counterpoints to the engineering achievements of over 80,000 workers who labored diligently to accomplish one of the Modern Wonders of the World.

The length of the Panama Canal is approximately 51 miles. The nine hour trip through the canal from east to west takes a ship through a seven-mile dredged channel in Limon Bay. The canal then proceeds for a distance of 11.5 miles to the Gatun Locks. The series of three locks raises ships over 85-feet to Gatun Lake. It continues through a channel for 32 miles to Gamboa, where the Culebra Cut begins. This channel through the cut is eight miles long and 495-feet wide. At the end are the locks at Pedro Miguel. These locks lower ships 31-feet to a lake which takes ships to the Miraflores Locks, which lower ships over 53-feet to sea level at the canals Pacific terminus in the bay of Panama. The average ship making a journey through the canal today pays up to $200,000.00 for the privilege of using the canal.

Our destination was to traverse the canal and be lifted 85-feet through the three locks that would deposit our ship on Lake Gatun, and then reversing the route on the down side locks and experiencing the ship being lowered 85-feet through the locks to the east entrance of the Panama Canal. Everyone was ecstatic about experiencing passage through the canal and when the land locomotives were tied to the Princess, the passengers began hollering and could be heard above the great ship's blasting horns. My concern was how they were going to fit a ship that is more than two times the length of a football field and 115-feet wide into what seemed to be a small opening to the canal. Barbara and I were at the bow of the ship and watched the pilot board from his launch to take charge of steering us through the channel to the first lock. She was soon tied to what looked like 12-miniature locomotive trains (mules) and slowly moved into position for her first climb up the mountain of water. The "mules" moved up an incline towing the Princess through three sets of locks. The ship's hull cleared the canal by a couple of feet on each side; evidently, when the ship was built her width had to be considered so it could squeeze through the locks. Today there are ships that are too wide to traverse the locks; steps are underway to widen the canal to accommodate those vessels. As sailors, we have traveled through pleasure boat locks with our various boats, but the experiences were nothing compared to going through the mountainous locks of the Panama Canal. The lock system resembles giant steps and consists of three elevator locks that raised the ship 85-feet to Gatun Lake. Watching the first gate open to let the ship inside its protective custody, and then close to allow water into the basin which caused the ship to take its first escalated rise was fascinating, especially being that we are mariners at heart and anything to do with the ocean is very enthralling to us. We followed the gate's openings and closings and taking on water three times before we were lifted to the beautiful artificial man-made Lake Gatun. The lake covers 164-square miles and is fed by the water from the Chagres River, which feeds the Gatun Dam. When built in the early 1900s, the dam and lake were considered the largest man-made wonders of their kind in the world. The dam incorporates a hydro-electric generating station that uses water from the lake to drive turbine generators that supply electricity to operate the locks, spillway machinery, and the lighting for the locks and the canal villages.

Once on the lake, we observed the comings and goings of every type of vessel that sails the ocean: large cruise ships, barges loaded with cargo, yachts of every size, and pleasure crafts that call the lake their home. After spending a few hours on the lake, we started our return trip through the opposite set of locks that transported us back to the opening of the eastern part of the Panama Canal. I had an uneasy feeling watching the water above us being retained by the large lock gates as we were lowered to the next level and said a silent prayer that the gates would continue to hold back the enormous weight of the water from coming down on us. It was decided to skip the dance class as everyone wanted to watch the ship being transported both ways through the locks, but we did have an opportunity to practice our dance routines at the afternoon session.

After dinner we went to the show at the theater and saw their rendition of the French author Victor Hugo's play, Les Miserables (the miserable ones). The show was done in Italian which seemed strange as we saw the English version several times, which made their version seem comical. We didn't stay for the whole show because it was difficult to follow the story in a foreign language that we didn't understand well. Our option was dancing on the upper deck to the music of the ship's excellent DJ. We spent the rest of the evening dancing and switching partners and making good use of the steps we learned at our dance classes.

The next day was at sea and we took the opportunity of rising early and going to the gym to relieve our consciences of the guilt we were laboring under from consuming too much of the ship's Italian irresistible cuisine. We both spent 30-minutes on tread mills and 15-minutes on stationary bikes. After lifting some minor weights, we retired to our room for quick showers and then proceeded, again, to the dining hall to get a great Italian-style breakfast. We made it to our next class just in time to join our fellow students in another Waltz lesson. Jamie and Jackie played a beautiful Waltz and watched all of us perform the dance; they visited everyone and gave pointers on how to better perform our routines, which is such a special treat for students learning to dance. One-on-one instruction goes a long way in improving a student's dancing technique. They had us line up again, the guys facing the dolls, and showed us how to make a left turn, which sounds easy but takes lots of concentration to get the steps and timing right. The count was 1-2-3, 4-5-6 turning to the man's left and continuing again, 1-2-3, 4-5-6. A rise and fall is unique to the Waltz and should be performed as follows: Taking long steps, on the first step forward for the man, the weight is taken on the left heel, then on to the ball of that foot. A gradual rise to the toes should be started at the end of the first beat and continued to the second and third beats, lowering to a normal position at the end of the third beat. This should be done while the male turns first to his left for a full turn and then to his right for another full turn. Jamie explained that the American Waltz is similar to the International style, except it has both open and closed dance positions, allowing the American style dancer a distinctive freedom of expression. Sounds easy, but watching us try the left turn and then a right turn looked like a comedy of errors. After lunch, the practice session, with the help of our instructors, saw us developing confidence and precision with the Waltz routines. A little bit of Rumba to the sexy Latin beat really got everyone enjoying the afternoon event. The dancers were changing partners more often as we were really getting the hang of both dances and couldn't wait to experiment with others.

Dinner, as usual, was exceptional Italian delights. We briefly visited the theater to see the American rendition of Les Miserables (in English), which we had previously seen several times in various playhouses, including Broadway. We went to bed early as we had an 8:00 A.M. tour the following morning at Limon, Costa Rica.

After breakfast, we boarded a bus that took us for a short ride to the main wharf where our Tortuguero Canal tour would begin. While riding the bus, I took the opportunity to read about the history of one of South America's smallest countries that has a population of a little over four million residents. Unfortunately, it was one of the first countries to be sighted by Christopher Columbus on his fourth voyage in 1502 to the "New World." He called it Costa Rica (rich coast), either for its magnificent beaches and flora or for the riches he expected to plunder from the natives. Whatever his reasons, the inhabitants suffered the same indignities and hardships as their neighbors throughout Central and South America from the harsh Spanish occupation. Costa Rica also shared with its neighbors a period of privateering that was second to none, especially from the British pirates Francis Drake and Sir Henry Morgan, both buccaneers for the British Crown. Sir Henry Morgan, who was also governor of Jamaica at the time of his escapades against the Spanish, is not only famous for his daring raid and capture of Panama, which was one of the richest colonies in the mid-17th century, but because he missed as much as 700 tons of treasure that somehow escaped his claws and was buried somewhere in the area. His story has stimulated searches for hidden treasure for hundreds of years throughout the Caribbean, and is responsible for the printing of millions of treasure maps for use by treasure hunters in their search for the missing loot.

Limon, which has a population of a little over 300,000 inhabitants, is home to what is known as Costa Rica's Amazon because of its surrounding rainforest and the Tortuguero Canal regions, which are rich with exotic flora and fauna. The first leg of our trip was a ride through the Tortuguero Canal on a small twenty passenger covered boat that conveniently was powered by a quiet electric outboard motor. While traveling through the jungle canal, our tour guide, who spoke English perfectly, pointed out howler monkeys hanging onto tree limbs, resembling stuffed fuzzy toys, in addition to three toed sloths that hung high up from the trees. They are considered the laziest of creatures, so much so that moss gathers on their fuzzy bodies. There were tropical colorful toucan birds all over the forest; their large colored beaks makes them outstanding creatures of nature; they looked at us from their safe perches and seemed to be monitoring our movement and telling us not to corrupt their habitat. Bats, aquatic birds, iguanas and huge crocodiles, as well as exotic flora, decorated our one-hour journey on our way to a rest stop on land. Especially memorable was the incredible amount of butterflies that inhabited the jungle; our guide made a point of stating that ten percent of all the flying wonders are located in Costa Rica. In fact, there are over 1,000 species that call that country their home. Of all the butterflies we saw, the Monarch is my favorite. To see so many of the large, beautiful, deep orange, black and white specked flying wonders in one place was reassuring that nature is still alive and well. I was very impressed with the white modern small boat that transported us through the jungle canal; it was made of fiberglass with comfortable seats and open sides and satisfyingly immaculate.

After a refreshing snack of tropical fruits, we took a 20-minute drive to Brisas de la Jungla (jungle breeze). We were excited and a little apprehensive about taking the next part of our canopy tour adventure into the rainforest. It required taking individual cable rides through the tops of trees to get a look at the jungle and its inhabitants from on high. There are 12 cables and 13 platforms stretched across the length of the rainforest. The platforms are arranged at different heights and levels. Up to platform five, all the cables are of similar lengths; however after that platform, the cables become more daring. It's at this point that everyone has an opportunity to return to the beginning of the "Zip Line" and relax at the lodge. The longest cable runs about 890-feet and the highest height is about 270-feet. Our guide tried to reassure us about the safety of the ride by stating: "Our tour guides are expertly trained in first aid and carry special packs to assist them in the event of an emergency. The "Zip Line" tour begins with an orientation discussion where rules and regulations for safety and security are explained thoroughly. And, by the way, make sure you put on lots of mosquito repellent." After that little speech, Barbara and I were convinced that we were better off spending the hour-and-a-half at the lodge, until we saw two women that had to be in their 80s get in line for the orientation. At that point we decided, what the hell, if they weren't afraid, why should we be cautious?

We nervously waited our turn in line to be strapped into the dangling seats that would take us, one at a time, on our journey over and through the forest to see the living tropical flora and fauna that occupies these high places. Until recently, little was known about life in tropical forest treetops because getting up there was nearly impossible. But today biologists explore the canopy via towers and suspension rafts that are lowered gently onto the tops by dirigibles and even construction cranes. Biologists have discovered that about 90 percent of all organisms in a rainforest are found in the canopy. I was given thick gloves to hold onto the overhead handles and away I went, gravity propelled to the first platform; I felt like Tarzan of the Jungle and actually gave out a Tarzan howl: AH-AH-AH. I was never so happy to reach a destination as I was to reach the first platform, where a very efficient attendant unstrapped my harness and where I quickly jumped onto the platform and held the handrails for dear life. Barbara was right behind me, but she seemed a lot calmer than I was when she joined me full of vim and vigor, ready to take the next cable ride to platform Two. Needless to say, I didn't notice any flowers or creatures on my first ride, as my eyes were shut for fear of falling off the swinging seat. Looking back I considered that a return trip was a lot closer than continuing on my journey but, for fear of Barbara's reaction, I looked around and took in the scenery and then got strapped into my seat again and continued to platform number two. This time my eyes were wide open and I enjoyed viewing the abundance or orchids that grew in the upper parts of the trees. Costa Rica has roughly 1,500 species of orchids, almost all of them epiphytes (grow on trees) which they export throughout the world for the pleasure of orchid lovers. An unforgettable experience was sliding down the cable. Butterflies seemed to be everywhere, some even landed on my shoulders and head. I didn't know whether to brush them away or hope for more to land on my shoulders. To brush them away meant letting go of the handrail, which there was no way in the world I was going to do, so I relaxed and enjoyed the pleasant visit from some of the most beautiful flying pets in creation. One disadvantage of riding the cables is that both hands are occupied holding the overhead handrail so that taking pictures was out of the question; this could only be done from the platforms when my feet were firmly planted on the floor and my hands were free. It didn't take long for me to feel right at home with the Tarzan experience of traveling through the trees while talking to birds, monkeys and butterflies, while making strange jungle sounds, expecting some kind of a response from the inhabitants. But, the only sounds I heard were the every day chatter from the birds and monkeys. I was happy to finally reach platform five where I jumped off and told the attendant that it was the end of the ride for me. Barbara was of the same mind, so we ended our excursion through the breezy jungle and returned to the main level rushing to the lodge to sit down, unwind, and have some lunch. What an experience! I was surprised to see that we didn't have much company from our group, as most of them were courageous enough to travel through the more difficult Zip Lines from platforms 6 to13. I asked our guide what "Zip Line" meant and got a vague explanation of: "A pulley for one person that is suspended and allows the person to move between two points by the action of gravity." Not satisfied with that explanation, I looked it up when I got back to the ship and found the rest of the definition. "Zip Line" is also called "Tyrolean Crossing" and when an angle is steep, it's sometimes called a "death slide." Good thing I didn't look up the definition before the trip or we would have gone on a quiet beach tour instead of the nature adventure.

The six-hour journey had us exhausted, so as soon as we returned to our cabins we opened the door to let in fresh sea air and immediately went to sleep. At dinner we exchanged highlights of our tours with our dining companions. Jill and Don chose to spend time at a beautiful white beach and to do some local shopping. When we told them about our exhilarating "Zip Line" experience, they regretted not joining us and said if they ever return to Costa Rica they would make sure that they spent more time in the rainforest and explore some of the natural wonders that the country is noted for. I promised if we ever returned to the beautiful country that we would spend more time at their pristine beaches and maybe do some nature walks. After dinner we went to the theater to see what was being featured; the evening's entertainment was "Passengers' Talent Night." We were not in the mood to sit through amateur night, so we visited our favorite night spot and danced the night away to the music of the ship's DJ.

The next day we were out to sea, so we headed for the gym again to lose some calories and firm up our bodies, before we started to resemble the whales that were visiting us along side the ship on a daily basis. A half an hour on the treadmill and 40-minutes on a stationary bike was all my lazy body could take. A steam bath and a massage seemed to be in order, so I gave into the temptation of being pampered while Barbara went for a swim in the clear blue water of the pool and to polished her suntan with some sun worshiping. After a light breakfast, we went straight to our next dance lesson. Jamie and Jackie were waiting for the class to assemble while some strange music, sounding like a Peabody and Foxtrot mixture, filled the air. We lined up on opposite sides of the room again, boys and girls facing each other, and were told that the music we were hearing was to get us accustomed to the beats of the Quickstep dance. Jamie asked how many students ever danced the Quickstep; there were no hands raised. Next she asked how many ever heard of the dance and only a few raised their hands. Well, our instructors had their work cut out for them. They gave an exhibition of how the dance should be done; my, oh my, if only we could do the dance with a fraction of their expertise. They floated around the dance floor with such style, grace and confidence; it was a sight to behold, two people doing intricate steps and tricky combinations at a very quick pace, never missing a beat. At that point, I wished I could just have a dream where I was dancing as well as the glamorous couple to get the feel of the dance. She explained: "The Quickstep is a combination of the Foxtrot, Charleston, Shag, Peabody and One Step. While it evolved primarily from the Foxtrot, the steps are quite different. The basic Quickstep for the male is; left foot forward, slow-slow; left quarter turn to the right then, side quick-close-quick. The female mirrors the move. It's done in 4/4 time with many advanced patterns including hops, runs and quick steps, with lots of momentum and rotations. The fun part of the dance is the use of syncopated or double-time steps with as many as eight note durations. The dance requires lots of space on the floor to accommodate the long quick runs and hops; dancers must always be aware of other performers' locations to avoid bumping and colliding. As you all saw in our exhibition, the dance is elegant like the Foxtrot and should be smooth and glamorous. Dancers should be light on their feet, very energetic and maintain intensive forms." After that bit of information and viewing their performance, there was no way that I could do the dance. I called Jamie to the side and told him I didn't think I could do the Quickstep and he smiled and said, "Why don't you just give it a go?" So I did, and returned to my place in the line with the other nervous male participants.

The dance is all about posture and moving about smoothly on the dance floor, so we had to get our backs straight with heads tilted to our left, arms at a relaxed but firm position, and then walk over to our partners and join bodies with very definite stomach contact. Knees must always be flexed and ready to go into action at the sound of the proper beat from the music. They played Louis Prima's "Sing, Sing, Sing" and told us to listen to the beat and just hold our partners in the proper position and imagine dancing around the floor to the quick-paced music. That done, we learned the basic move: male's left foot forward for slow-slow, then quarter turn to the right, left foot side for quick-close-quick. To complete the basic, the male makes a left quarter turn and leads left foot back; slow-slow and then left foot side quick-close-quick. That puts the dancers in the position to begin some quick forward moving steps. Of course, the female partner performs mirror steps of the basic moves while both maintain proper straight backs, heads to the left and stomachs in contact position. It took the whole lesson to finally get the basic steps right, but was worth the frustration of trying to move along the dance floor to the quick paced music of "Sing, Sing, Sing." The dance is, without a doubt, one of the most difficult and exhausting that Barbara and I have ever attempted, and to this day, we have a lot of difficulty performing the dance. A lunch break was in order and we again opted for a sit down meal in a quiet atmosphere with soft comfortable seats to rest our aching feet.

At our practice session, Jackie and Jamie told us we were going to join them in the show that evening at the theater for a Waltz demonstration. Not everyone had to participate, but most of the students were thrilled to show off what they learned from the two masters. The girls were especially excited as it gave them an opportunity to put on their best outfits for the occasion; the men were asked to wear their tuxedoes, which made me very unhappy, but I acquiesced due to my honey's persuasive nagging and agreed to go for it. Needless to say, we all did some pretty serious practicing that afternoon and spent most of the session rehearsing the Waltz with Jackie and Jamie for our show that evening.

Barbara wore her best outfit, a pink with black trim evening gown, I reluctantly squeezed into my black armor to prepare for the occasion. We had a light dinner for fear that being nervous and moving around the stage might play havoc with our stomachs. We rushed to the theater and sat in the center row so we could get a good look at the performances. The evening's entertainment consisted of the ship's dancing and singing performers doing some numbers from famous movies, and then Jackie and Jamie doing a Bolero, Foxtrot and Quickstep. They would end their exhibition by inviting their students to enter on the stage and join them in doing a Waltz.

The show opened with the ship's cast performing two songs from "Saturday Night Fever," which was a movie released in 1977 starring John Travolta as Tony Manero, a troubled Brooklyn, New York, boy whose weekend activities consisted of dancing at the 2001 Odyssey Club in his neighborhood. That movie started the disco craze that is still popular today. I recall Barbara and me going to Elektra's Dance Studio in Melville, New York, to take lessons in the Hustle right after we saw the flick. It took us forever to learn the dance that became the rave of the dancing community at that time. The movie was responsible for saving many dance studios from going out of business, as they were having trouble getting people interested in dancing. Interest in the Hustle kept the dance community alive for many years until other movies, such as the Japanese production of "Shall we Dansu" in 1996, and the American follow up version movie, "Shall we Dance" in 2004 with Richard Gere and Jennifer Lopez, revitalized ballroom dancing as one of the most popular social activities of the 21st century.

The first number by the ship's dancers from Saturday Night Fever was, "You Should be Dancing" which shows Tony dancing the famous routine that revolutionized dancing in the United States and put the Hustle at the forefront of the dancing scene, was almost as good as John Travolta's moves in that movie. It was equal to a full Broadway production. The dancing and singing brought tears to my eyes as I remembered the excitement that the song brought to us when we first became interested in dancing. The second number that the troupe performed was the toned down romantic music of "More Than a Woman." It was the dance contest performed by John Travolta and Karen Lynn Gorney in the movie which won them their dancing award and trophy. Knowing that a Latin couple outperformed them, Tony gives that couple the prize money and trophy. The parts of Tony Manero and Stephanie Mangano were performed on a par with the actors in the movie. As a matter of fact, the performers were John Travolta and Karen Lynn Gorney look-a-likes in appearance and performance.

The second part of the show was their version of the 1961 musical "West Side Story." The movie, starring Natalie Wood, Richard Beymer, Rita Moreno, Russ Tamblyn, and George Chakiris, is about New York City gangs, the Jets (American boys) and the Sharks (Puerto Rican boys) and their ethnic hatreds and sometimes loves. The company performed the incredible "Rumble" song and dance scene where the two groups of boys have an all out fight that included knives, chains, and any other available street weapon. As a result of the fighting, the leaders of both gangs are killed. The singing and choreography was as good as it gets, on a level with Broadway shows. Their second

543

number was the elaborate rooftop scene where the Puerto Rican boys and girls argue, sing, and dance their feelings about being in "America." The boys expressed their dislike for the country in their dialogue, their singing and their dancing; the girls expressed their opposing feelings with passionate words, more singing, and even more energetic dancing. The audience responded with loud standing ovations that lasted for quite some time.

Jackie and Jamie captured the stage with their appearance; she was wearing a beautiful yellow dress cut at the knees with complementary yellow high-heal shoes. He wore a black tuxedo with tails and a black tie and white shirt. Latin Bolero music played as they floated around the middle of the dance floor to the soft slow beat. It's one of the only Latin dances that requires a ballroom posture; straight back, arms stretched, knees bent, and heads to the left. Although their appearance at first seemed stiff, when they moved the stiffness melted and the passion and warmth of the dance took over. The Bolero, as done by Jackie and Jamie, is one of the more passionate and romantic dances in the ballroom curriculum; they had the ability to transmit their emotions and fervor to the spectators and draw us into the mood of the dance. They then did a smooth graceful Foxtrot, taking long soft steps to the rhythm of the dance beat. In contrast, their Quickstep looked as if they were jet propelled, same positioning as the Foxtrot, but their movements were quick and syncopated with lots of runs, hops, hesitations, and uneven turns. When they finished, the audience went wild with applauding and cheering, to show their appreciation for the professional performance of the two Brits. They announced that they would perform a Waltz and then invited their students to join them on the stage. What an experience! I felt shell shocked, my legs got numb and my breathing became rapid; I was almost forced to sit down and skip the performance. But looking at Barbara and drawing from her courage, I followed her to the stage platform and took my position along side the other ten nervous couples. We danced in the line of direction. First we did a basic Waltz pattern with a left turn, then an underarm turn and then a right hand turn; we performed in formation and were all pretty much doing the same steps at the same time. Then we danced without formation to our own routines, which after a few turns ended the demonstration. The audience was polite and applauded respectfully; we bowed and immediately exited the stage, my heart was pumping rapidly and my breathing was still very heavy. After a few minutes, my metabolism returned to normal. We joined our fellow entertainers at the upper lounge to continue our dancing and to discuss how we felt about performing in public. Most said they were as nervous as we were, but looked forward to performing in public again in the future. What a lovely way to end an evening; good ballroom music and dancing, spending time with our fellow entertainers, and the great feeling of having accomplished something useful with our formation dancing.

The Princess docked at Ocho Rios, Jamaica, early in the morning, which gave us an opportunity to explore one of the largest (population about 3 million) and most historically fascinating islands in the Caribbean. We had the better part of a whole day to enjoy, at a leisurely pace, the beautiful sand-dominated island that was once considered the "Sodom of the New World, where most residents were pirates, cutthroats, whores and some of the vilest persons in the civilized world." The native Tainos/Arawak Indians of the island date back to between 4000 and 1000 BCE. When Christopher Columbus arrived in 1494, there were over 200 villages with people living in relative peace and harmony. Columbus claimed the island for Spain and shortly thereafter the Spaniards occupied the island and decimated its inhabitants. It wasn't long before most of them were exterminated by the Spanish and had to be replaced by African slaves, who were stronger and more adept at working in the island's sugar fields and plantations. Spain ruled the island as Santiago and used it as a slave trading post and treasure warehouse. It was constantly under attack by buccaneers and pirates until its defeat in 1655 by none other then Admiral Sir William Penn (father of the founder of the state of Pennsylvania), and General Robert Venables at the battle of Ocho Rios. They immediately offered buccaneers and pirates a base of operations in Port Royal, with the provision that they pledge their loyalty to the English Crown and help deter Spanish aggression against the island. The authorities also sanctioned the outlaws attacking Spanish territories and ships and encouraged them to bring their bounty to the island and to spend it freely, with impunity and much praise from the residents for their free spending ways.

The island became a haven for buccaneers and pirates. The old Port Royal was located along the shipping lanes to and from Panama and Spain and was strategically located for attacks on Spanish shipping and settlements. The island was not only a place where the outlaws could live in relative peace and have their ships and equipment serviced, but actually had the most notorious buccaneer-pirate, Sir Henry Morgan, as the governor. Other notorious pirates that called the island home were Bartholomew Roberts, Roche Brasiliano, John Davis, and Edward Mansveldt. The island had one drinking house for every ten residents and boasted as having the most beautiful whores in the Caribbean. As its biblical namesake, it too was destroyed by an act of God. On the morning of June 7, 1692, three earthquakes and a tsunami struck Port Royal, sinking almost 70 percent of the city. Over 4,000 people died from the calamity and the ships anchored in the harbor were either sunk or washed ashore. The survivors were convinced that God destroyed the city because of its wicked and lawless ways. The city never recovered to its former infamous glory and today it's a poor fishing village with a population of about 1,800 people.

We disembarked the ship at Ocho Rios, which has a population of about 15,000 people, and headed for a day's outing at Dolphin Cove at Treasure Reef, which was a short bus ride from the ship. I'm always amazed at the natural wonders that are in the Caribbean. The Cove and Reef offer supervised swims with dolphins, sharks and stingrays; self-propelled mini-boats with glass bottoms, kayaking on the ocean, and a pristine beach, with soft turquoise ocean water that forces you to relax. This idyllic retreat is also surrounded by five acres of a lush tropical rain forest. Visiting the miniature Old Port Royal and drinking and singing with pirates is another unusual experience, along with being a sea keeper and studying and feeding dolphins, sharks and stingrays. Next to the Treasure Reef is the world famous Dunn's River Falls that tempts hardy souls to climb to the top and water slide down its beautiful water runoffs. Our problem was that we couldn't experience all of the sights, so we started off with swimming with the dolphins. There were eight people in our group; the trainer told us the names of the dolphins and which one we would be swimming with. We were told not to wear any jewelry as they could be harmful to the mammals; the jewelry can scratch them or the shine can get their attention and they will try to suck the items off our bodies. We were introduced to our playmates and received a big splashing wave from them. They swam past us, splashing as if they were introducing themselves and then they let us rub their smooth tummies as they swam on their backs. We were able to swim with the dolphins individually and let them pull us while we hung onto their fins as if we were doing a tractor trailer maneuver. The most exciting experience was when my partner came up behind me while I was floating on my back and pushed me forward by my feet and then lifted me out of the water. What a thrill to be treated by these intelligent mammals as if we were life-long playmates. At the end of our aquatic session our playmates splashed, dove in the air, and then came to us and gave each person in the group a kiss. We, in turn, were allowed to give them a big hug, which they seemed to cherish and gave us a big appreciative smile and squeal in return. What a once-in-a-lifetime experience!!

As we were already wet, we decided to swim at Stingray Lagoon with the long tailed fish. We were instructed not to walk around too much, as stepping on their tails could be uncomfortable and possibly dangerous. What was fascinating about the experience was how friendly the creatures were. They came right up to us and rubbed against our legs and shoulders with their light sandpaper skin. I actually had one surface and look me right in the eye, which needless to say made me feel very uneasy, but I didn't flinch for fear of showing weakness and maybe inviting the sea wonder to become a little too friendly. Barbara, courageous soul that she is, was swimming after the rays and playing tag with them; she has always been an aquatic person and could outdistance me when we would race. I would always manage to get ahead of her by a few strokes when beginning a race, but in time I would slow down and she would leisurely pass me with her beautiful magnetic smile expressing victory over her superman. Looking back to September 4, 2006, when Australian Crocodile Hunter Steve Irwin was killed by a stingray while snorkeling at the Great Barrier Reef in Australia, I don't know if we would have been brave enough to swim with the creatures had that event happened prior to our swimming with stingrays that were similar in size to the one that killed him. Life is interesting and certainly unpredictable considering he was "One with nature" and probably didn't give the chance of a calamity a second thought when he began his underwater research that fateful day.

Both swimming experiences were invigorating and my next intended stop was to swim and feed sharks. Barbara was not happy with that decision, however, and since it was lunch time and the smell from the BBQ was too tempting to pass up, we followed the delectable aroma, found the outdoor buffet, and quickly filled our plates with ribs, corn, plantains and delicious ripe perfumed pineapple. We found a couple of chaise lounges on the soft, white sand and devoured our treats in short order, while enjoying the view of the ocean's turquoise water and the waves that gently caressed the beach, leaving effervescent foam behind as a reminder of its visit. There is no greater feeling than watching ocean activity while sitting under the warm sun and running soft, almost silky sand, through one's toes and fingers. That was certainly a vacation wonderland, which would have to be included on our Bucket List of places to return to before we "Kick the bucket." As fate would have it, we did return after a few years to attend my daughter Laurie and her husband Clint's wonderful themed wedding.

We ran out of time, so the other attractions would have to wait until we returned sometime in the future. Our bus got us back to the ship just in time to walk the plank and get on board before the warning whistle blew announcing that she was ready to leave port and go out to sea toward the United States. Although we were exhausted from the day's activities, we didn't have time to refresh with a nice nap as it was close to dinner time and we were both famished. We joined our dining companions and shared our day's experience with them; they regretted not having joined us, but were satisfied with their shopping and beach adventures. They had a lot more energy then we did and were anxious to go to the lounge and spend the evening jumping around and practicing their new dance steps. Barbara and I had to drag ourselves to the top deck of the ship to join our friends, as we were totally exhausted from all the excitement of the day. For some unexplainable reason, it seems that when we do any activity in or near the ocean, like swimming, snorkeling or water skiing, a good night's sleep is always forthcoming; conversely, trying to keep our eyes open beforehand always becomes a pleasant bedtime struggle. We did manage to do some dancing while the boat was bobbing around from the sea waves. Our sluggish coordination from the exhausting day's fun in the sun, and the motion of the boat, made dancing a major effort. So, we wished our friends a good evening after about an hour of stumbling on the dance floor, and delightfully retired to our cabin for another Caribbean slumber event.

Our last day on the Princess was spent at sea. We took the opportunity to relieve our feelings of guilt for eating so much food by going straight to the gym before breakfast. After an hour workout we were ready for our last breakfast at sea, so we decided to have a leisurely formal meal in the dining room. We justified adding the calories from our large breakfast as an offset to the calories we were expending using the exercise equipment, plus, it was the last day at sea, so what the heck. I ordered a large, fresh squeezed glass of orange juice, eggs Benedict, and three well-done pancakes with several buttery biscuits. Barbara scolded me for being so careless and then she ordered the same juice and scrambled eggs with breakfast sausages and buttery biscuits. We washed down our meals with multiple cups of delicious Jamaican coffee. We walked very slowly to our next dance class, as the added weight from the food was already having an affect on our movements. The Quickstep music was playing and some of our friends were already warming up for the next lesson. Jackie and Jamie had us line up, facing each other again, boys on one side and girls on the other, and began explaining the "lock step," which looked impossible for me to perform. The male moves forward with his left foot slow, right foot slow, left foot quick and right foot in back of the left for a quick lock. So it's, slow-slow, quick-quick lock. Of course the ladies mirror the men's steps. We tried it with our partners without the music and it didn't seem too difficult. We practiced our basic box steps and then went into the lock step in that order. It seemed pretty easy until the music came on. The fast pace of the dance got everyone confused and Jamie had to slow the music down until we could finally get the movements right. So, with the music playing, we went with two basic steps with quarter turns, first to the male's right and then to the left and then into two lock steps. It was quite an accomplishment when we all finally got the routine done properly. The last step we learned was a "natural turn," which is necessary when making corner turns. Following the "lock steps," the male turns to the right, the timing of the steps are slow-quick-quick and should feel like an American Foxtrot natural turn; the last three steps are all slows. It took the rest of the session to put all the routines together and although we weren't perfect in our performances, most of us were happy that we would be able to get on a dance floor and enjoy performing the routines we learned at the workshops with some degree of accomplishment.

After a light lunch of tropical fruit, we went to the practice dance session for our last chance to have Jackie and Jamie critique our dancing. Everyone in our dance group received a T-shirt with a picture of the Crown Princess and the "Zoe's Ballroom Cruise" printed on them as a memento. We were asked to put them on so Helmet could take a picture of our dance troupe. Jackie and Jamie were also gracious enough to provide everyone with a picture of their dancing the Waltz; she wearing her famous yellow gown and he with black coat and tails. We still display their picture in our recreation room in New York. Our mentors corrected our dancing routines for the last time in their ever-friendly constructive manner. Over the years we have kept in touch with the sweet couple through e-mails. It is amazing how easy it is to keep in touch with people from one continent to another by simply stroking a few keys on a computer.

The evening was our last formal dinner, which again required my wearing a black suit that made me and all the men on the ship look like members of a penguin colony. But, good natured fellow that I am, I squeezed hard and put the suit of armor on, enjoying the fact that it would be the last time that I would be wearing the restraining garment. Barbara wore a silver silk gown that magically appeared out of her small suit case, where she stuffed all her clothing. It's a mystery to me how she can get ten pieces of clothing into a five-piece hanging bag. I think it must be a girl thing, and without a doubt a talent, to be able accomplish such a complicated feat.

The captain and some of his officers greeted us at the front of the dining hall with a hearty welcome and handshake for the men and a short bow for the ladies. After all the guests were seated, a customary Baked Alaska Ice Cream Cake procession began with lots of sparkles coming for the candles on the cakes that were carried by the Italian crew members as they sang "On a Clear Day" in their native language. After the commotion, we settled in and ordered our last suppers. I had a delicious plate of cheese ravioli and meatballs, while Barbara ordered Osso Bucco with a side order of her favorite Pasta Puttanesca.

We flavored the meal with some red and white Italian wine, compliments of our host, and toasted each other with: health, long life and hopefully . . . Till we meet again!

The theater that evening had a comedy show which included some of the passengers. Our group had a cocktail party arranged so we didn't stay to see the whole show. We had a private lounge for our use and enjoyment with a nice-sized dance floor. The drinks flowed and the music played as we danced and changed partners, showing off our hard-learned dance routines. There were adequate tables to comfortably sit and talk to our new dancing companions. Our conversation centered on dancing and the great time we all had aboard the Princess, learning to dance with different partners and sharing our lives with new-found friends. We all promised to continue dancing and to take dance outings in the future. As the clock approached midnight, excitement started to fill the air as there was a dessert buffet scheduled for the passengers. How anyone could eat more food after the enormous dinner was beyond my comprehension, but I joined everyone just to see what the buffet extravaganza looked like, promising myself not to participate in the eating orgy.

When we entered the dining room the first thing that caught my eye was the three to five- foot ice sculptures that were displayed around the buffet tables. Beautiful swans, naked ladies, butterflies and an assortment of flowers lit up the room with their artistic design and beauty. The only thing more beautiful in the room was the dessert, especially the assortment of chocolate cakes, candies, carved chocolate animals and flowers. Fortunately, the treats were small, but inviting; they were small enough for a good taste and allowed us to eat a variety without feeling full or guilty. Yes, I said we, although I had made a semi-promise not to indulge, I couldn't resist just tasting whatever sweets caught my eye. We filled our plates with a dozen or so of little pieces of desserts; filled our cups with cappuccino and espresso; found a quiet corner table and sat down and "Pigged Out." Having a serving of sherbet after the sweets eased my conscience somewhat, so when I went to sleep that night, the last thing on my mind was the sherbet, which seemed to negate the guilty feeling of eating all the delicious but toxic desserts.

When we awoke the next morning, we were docked in Fort Lauderdale. After a buffet breakfast, we disembarked the Crown Princess, retrieved our luggage and bid the memorable experience and all our new friends, adieu—Till we meet again . . .

CHAPTER FIFTEEN

Where Champions Dance

WITH THE POPULARITY OF ballroom dancing and such television shows as "Dancing with the Stars," " America's Ballroom Challenge" and "So You Think You Can Dance," people have become curious about how and where the champions earn their titles. There is an interest in dancing by people of all ages who wish to learn how to dance. To accommodate their many different needs, clubs and organizations have developed to promote dancing for anyone with an interest in this popular pastime. For the many people who wish to bring their talents to a competitive level, there are dance competitions for amateurs, professionals and professional/amateurs (Pro/Ams), International, Rock & Roll, Country Western, Line Dancing, and just about every type of social and ethnic dance. The categories in each of these competitions range from pre-teen to over 65 and include grade schools through colleges and even senior citizen's facilities. The apexes in the world of dancing are Professional American and International Ballroom dancing titles. To accomplish the competitions in a standardized manner, organizations have been established to monitor and govern the competitions and to define their purpose. Ballroom dancing refers to a set of partner dances, which originated in the Western world and are now enjoyed both socially and competitively around the globe. Historically, ballroom dancing referred to any form of formal social dancing as recreation. With the advent and popularity of DanceSport, the term has been globally refined and has become narrower in scope, usually referring to International Standard and International Latin style dances. In the United States, there are two additional variations: American Smooth and American Rhythm. Other dances that fall under the umbrella of ballroom dancing include Nightclub Dances, such as the Lindy Hop, West Coast Swing, Nightclub Two Step, Hustle, Salsa, and Merengue. The definition of ballroom dancing is currently loosely interpreted, with new dances and folk dances being added from time to time.

There are governing bodies that oversee DanceSport, which denotes a style of competitive ballroom dancing at events that are sanctioned and regulated by DanceSport organizations. The term DanceSport originally applied to International Style of competitive ballroom (often referred to as Standard or Modern) and Latin dancing. Today it includes any dance style that has achieved an internationally-recognized organized competition structure and has adopted a sports based culture.

At the top of the complicated dance structure pyramid is the World Dance & DanceSport Council (WD&DSC) at www.wdcdance.org. It's the world's authority for professional Dance and DanceSport, and oversees the World Social Dance Committee and the World Dance- Sport Committee. Its aim is to encourage and promote dancing through its worldwide membership. The policy of the council requires that each country should operate under democratic principles similar to those of the WD&DSC. There are over 60 countries represented in this organization, each having one member in WD&DSC that is responsible for their country's adhering to the practice of its competition rules and professional behavior. The Council has two subdivisions. The World Social Dance Committee (WSDC), which deals with and recommends to the General Council, business improvements for Social Dance professionals and their Dance schools. The standing committee deals with all matters of the dance profession that relate to the activities of

Dance Schools and Dance Teachers. Social Dance Committee Members are drawn from the Americas, Asia, Europe, East Europe and Oceana.

The second subdivision is the standing World DanceSport Committee (WDSC), which is responsible for "the allocation of World and Intercontinental DanceSport Championships and Titles and the continuous review of the Competition Rules that control them. An enormous undertaking is the preparation and maintenance of their calendar that includes every known recognized Professional DanceSport event in the world. It also requires all member organizations to use only registered professional adjudicators. Another enormous task is maintaining archives of all recognized title holders and their accomplishments." The responsibilities of this organization have become so overwhelming that a new governing body, The International Professional DanceSport Council (IPDSC), www.ipdsc.org, was created in 2006 to take over many of their professional level dance responsibilities.

Next in the pyramid is the International DanceSport Federation (IDSF) at www.idsf.net. "It governs the rules applied to, and the granting of, all International DanceSport Competitions. It represents 86 International Member Federations, 63 of which are recognized by their National Olympic Committees, although the sport has not yet been accepted as a participating event in the Olympics. It represents more than four million dancers throughout their National Member Federations on five continents."

The next governing body in the pyramid is The National Dance Council of America (NDCA) www.ndca.org. It's the governing Council of NDC's sanctioned events and is recognized by the World Dance & DanceSport Council (WD&SDC) as its sole representative in the United States. Its purpose is to: "provide a united inter-association agency to represent the interest of those in the dance profession and other dance related entities and organizations, and to act as the agency for the cooperation with similar councils in other countries. It also conducts a continuing campaign for the establishment and maintenance of high standards in dance education and to acquaint the public with the nature and benefits of these standards and to recognize the status of qualified dance teachers affiliated with member organizations of its Council."

So, considering the thousands of titles that are bestowed on competitors on every level of recognized dancing around the world, I'm restricting my discussion to the two most popular and prestigious of championship titles that are awarded to professional dancers at The Blackpool Dance Festival, www. blackpooldancefestival.com, in Blackpool, England, and The Ohio Star Ball Championship, www.ohiostarball.com, in Columbus, Ohio. The Blackpool Dance Festival began in 1920 in the famous Empress Ballroom at the Winter Gardens in Blackpool. It covers a period of nine days and is the largest of the five Blackpool Festivals, which includes: British National Dance Championships, Blackpool Sequence Dance Festival, Blackpool Freestyle Championships and the Blackpool Junior Dance Festival. In 2008, there were 1,863 couples representing 68 countries competing for titles in the various events under the IDSF rules. The top competitions include the International Standard, which includes competing in Slow Waltz, Tango, Viennese Waltz, Slow Foxtrot and Quickstep. The winners are awarded the title of Blackpool International Standard Ballroom Champions. There are also International Latin competitions that include Cha-Cha, Samba, Rumba, Paso Doble and Jive. The winners are declared the Blackpool International Latin Ballroom Champions.

In the United States, the Ohio Star Ball Festival of DanceSport is one of the most important dance competitions in the country. It's a 6-day event with 70 judges, 3 chairmen, 3 emcees, 7 scrutineers, 2 deejays, 9 deck captains, and a 300-plus page program. It's held at the Columbus Convention Center and the adjoining Hyatt Regency Hotel in Columbus, Ohio. There are a multitude of competitions, such as: States National Collegiate Championships, Professional/Amateur Championships, Open

Professional Championships and championships in four major dance styles: American Smooth, American Rhythm, International Standard, and International Latin. The focal point is the "Show Dances," in which each couple has the floor to themselves to express their individual style of dancing. At the end of the competition, one couple walks away with the "America's Best" crown.

The television show, America's Ballroom Challenge, which airs on the Public Broadcasting Service, has become part of the annual Ohio Star Ball Festival of DanceSport. Each season typically consists of competitions in five categories, with the first four categories devoted to each of the major styles of competitive ballroom dancing: American Smooth, consisting of Waltz, Tango, Foxtrot and Viennese Waltz; American Rhythm, consisting of Cha-Cha, Rumba, East Coast Swing, Bolero and Mambo; International Standard, consisting of Waltz, Tango, Viennese Waltz, Foxtrot and Quickstep; and International Latin, consisting of Cha-Cha, Samba, Rumba, Paso Doble and Jive. The fifth category is the "Grand Finale," where the four champion couples compete for the title of "America's Best" dancers. The 2009 hosts were actress-singer Jean Louisa Kelly and seven-time U.S. National Latin Dance Champion, Ron Montez. One of the American Rhythm champions (2006 & 2007) is the popular professional dancer on "Dancing with the Stars," Tony Dovolani, who has won numerous world titles in his young career. Another "Dancing with the Stars" professional, Maksim Chmerkovskiy, is the Ohio Star Ball Latin Champion for the year 2003.

The following are descriptions of some major dance organizations in the United States that have an impact on the dancing community:

USA Dance at www.usadance.org, formally the United States Amateur Ballroom Association (USABDA). Its primary goals are "To promote amateur DanceSport as a sport both nationally and internationally and foster its inclusion in the Olympic and Pan American games; to organize and support amateur

DanceSport events globally, including national, regional and local championships; and to select the top DanceSport athletes to represent the United States in the IDSF World DanceSport Amateur Championships and the World Games and finance their participation." It's the foremost amateur organization in the United States and strives to "promote social dancing as a healthful lifetime recreational activity, suitable for individuals, families, and for those who are so inclined, and is a stepping stone into competition dancing." Some of its famous former amateur members can be found performing on ABC's "Dancing with the Stars" as dance partners to the stars. The following are the professional dancers who were once amateur members of USA Dance: Inna Brayer; Julianne Hough, www.juliannehough.net; Edyta Sliwinska, www.edytasliwinska.com; Anna Trebunskaya, www.jonathanrobertsdancer.com; Ashly DelGrosso, www.ashlydelgrosso.com; Andrea Hales, www.centerstageutah.com; Cheryl Burke, www.cherylburkedance.com; Lacey Schwimmer, www.laceymaeschwimmersworld.com; Corky Ballas, www.corky.com; Mark Ballas, www.markballas.com; Derek Hough, www.derekhough.net; Alec Mazo, www.alecmazo.com and Brian Fortuna, www.brianfortuna.com.

Another formidable dance organization is the American Ballroom Company at www.unitedstatesdancechampionships.com. They sponsor the United States Dance Championships (USDC) which is recognized by the National Dance Council of America (NDCA) and the World Dance & DanceSport Council (WD&DSC) as determining the majority of the United States professional ballroom dance champions in all styles and divisions. Unfortunately, it's not recognized by the International DanceSport Federation (IDSF), the United States Olympic Committee (USOC), or the Amateur Sports Act of the United States Congress; they recognize USA Dance, formerly known as the United States Amateur Ballroom Dance Association (USABDA) as the National Governing Body in the United States for DanceSport (i.e., competitive ballroom dancing).

There are many other ballroom dancing Championships, such as the Emerald Ball, that add to the excitement and popularity of ballroom dancing throughout the world. As can be gathered from the above information, there are organizations, councils and committees in place around the globe that stand ready to accept the challenges from the growth of this amazing pastime, especially its expansion into the World Olympics and the Pan American Games. Some vital organizations that help the governing boards accomplish their objectives are:

DancesportInfo is at www.dancesportinfo.net. They provide photos from most major dance competitions.

World Pro-Am DanceSport Series, www.dancesportseriew.com. They hold over 70 dance competitions annually across the United States.

International Dance Teachers Association (IDTA), www.idta. co.uk. They provide examination services for the public, professional performers and teachers.

AccessDance is at www.accessdance.com. They provide a network site that finds dance lessons and venues for students and offer information on dance organizations, competitions, merchants and publications.

DanceBeat International, www.dancebeat.com. They provide periodical highlights from the competitive ballroom dance world.

International Dance Directory, www.dancedirectory.com. They provide a worldwide directory of dancers, with sections for locating teachers, studios and merchandise.

Ballroom Dancers is at www.ballroomdancers.com. This is a clearinghouse for ballroom dancing information, including worldwide dancing locations and a dance learning center for most of the recognized dances.

Dance Forums is at www.dance-forums.com, maintains a wide selection of dance forums for people in the dance industry.

Hopefully this chapter will shed some light on the complexity and the many challenges that are on the forefront in the ever-popular world of dancing and the organizations that are in place to guide the millions of participants on their journey in becoming a part of the 21st century's social and athletic phenomena.

CHAPTER SIXTEEN

Dancing with the Stars

BARBARA AND I WERE fortunate to have seen two shows sponsored by Louis Del Prete at the Suburban Center in Wantagh, Long Island, New York,, featuring couples from "Dancing with the Stars." We saw Karina Smirnoff and Louie Van Amstel on May 31, 2008, and the husband and wife team of Edyta Sliwinska and Alec Mazo on May 30, 2009. Needless to say, both shows were spectacular and played to full houses of over 350 dance lovers. Although the venue is small, the enthusiasm in which the audience received both events was quite large.

Karina & Louie go back to the year 2000, when they won the U.S. National Latin Championship, the Can-Am DanceSport Gala-Canadian Open Professional Championship in International Latin, the Japan International Dancing Championship for Professional Latin, and the Emerald Ball DanceSport Championship for Open Professional Latin. This was certainly a busy and rewarding year for the new dancing partnership. They were introduced by Louis and received a roaring welcome from the anxious audience. Their first dance was Jive. The speed of the dance and the aerobic moves that they performed seemed unreal as they moved in a circle in the middle of the dance floor. Karina's short white dress and flowing legs, against Louie's black suit, was a contrast in perfection as they Jived in perfect unison to the beats of the fast music. Their next dance was the romantic Rumba. They performed the "chick-chicky-boom" to the rhythm of the music with sexy sways and Cortes; the room heated from their sensual rubs and caresses; you could almost see the steam coming from her long white open-backed dress complemented by his tight black pants and black wide open shirt. When watching romantic performances and getting caught up in the heat of the moment, it's easy to understand why many people prefer to call ballroom dancing an "Art Form" rather then an athletic endeavor. My opinion is that it is half of both; an athletic event when required and an "Art Form" when desired.

To continue the romantic mood, they performed a hot romantic Tango. The heat again radiated from their movements and filled the hall; it seemed that energy burst from her body and through her long black semi-open shoulder dress, sparked by his shirtless tuxedo showing his chest, bordered by the jacket's velvet lapels. The smooth sways and caresses followed by the quick turns and kicks clearly transmitted the essence of the dance: flirtation, chase, seduction and then finally conquest. It all happened before our eyes; it appeared to be a dress rehearsal of a passionate affair, which the audience approved of and confirmed with their spontaneous oohs and aahs and then a standing ovation.

Their final dance was a Cha-Cha. They exploded onto the dance floor and went full speed ahead into the dance with arms flying and legs moving almost as fast as the speed of light. Their quick movements and acrobatic gyrations didn't resemble a conventional Cha-Cha, but then these were not conventional dancers--they were world champions and performed the dance as champions should, with moves that are far beyond ordinary. Their speed caused her yellow short sleeveless and backless dress bottom to swirl when she spun around, resembling a Hawaiian hula skirt. His open black shirt, showing his manly chest, added to the energy of the dance. It's commonly known that "a picture is worth a thousand words," so below are pictures of their performance. While looking at the photos, one can almost feel the energy of the dances radiating from the pictures. The photos are presented below, with Louis Del Prete's permission:

After the audience calmed down and Karina and Louie had a chance to rest, they returned for a "Question and Answer" session. The first question was directed to Karina:

"Which of the Mario's do you like best? Twenty three year old R&B star Mario Barrett, from the sixth season of DWTS, or the 33-year-old television heartthrob Mario Lopez, from the third season of DWTS?"

After blushing and snickering, Karina answered: "I've been seeing Mario Lopez for some time, and there is nothing and has never been anything but a professional relationship between me and the other young Mario."

Question for Louie: "How long does it take to make the beautiful girls' outfits and the men's clothing?"

Louie answered: "The designers are given their tasks on Tuesday and they must have the outfits fitted and completed by Friday, which is a major undertaking by a staff of exceptional designers and craftspeople."

Question for Karina: "Who chooses which dances are to be performed by the couples?"

Karina answered: "ABC has a special staff of knowledgeable dance professionals that choose which couples are to perform each of the different dances."

Question for Louie: "Who chooses the music for the dances that are performed on DWTS?"

Louie answered: "ABC has a special staff that chooses the music for the dances and are guided by some of the professional dancers in their choice of music that each couple will perform. In many cases, the music is not what is usually heard when dancing to specific dances, which makes performing the dances a lot more difficult."

Question for Louie: "Is it true that the performing celebrities receive $200,000.00 per season and an additional bonus if they win the Mirror Ball Trophy?"

Louie answered: "That sounds about right."

Question for Karina: "Who chooses the celebrities' professional partners?"

Karina answered: "ABC chooses the partners based on a random selection with no preference to an individual's talent."

Question for Louie: "Do you create your choreography?"

Louie answered: "Yes, I do many of the group's choreography for the show and I'm also the Creative Director. It's very challenging to get twenty or so professionals to dance as a group, but the outcome is always a rewarding experience. When performing, I'm also responsible for the dance routines for me and my partner. Each of the professionals is required to do the arranging for their own dance routines once they are given the music and their dance assignments from ABC. So the professionals, in addition to being champion dancers, must also be proficient choreographers."

Question for Karina: "How long are the contracts between ABC and the professional dancers?"

Karina answered: "Our contracts run through 2015, but that doesn't mean that all the professionals will appear on all the shows, we are actually on stand by."

Another question for Karina: "How much notice do the professionals get before they have to appear on the show?"

Karina answered: "One month."

Another question for Karina: "How much notice do the celebrities get from ABC to prepare for the show?"

Karina answered: "Two to three months."

After the question session, Karina and Louie were gracious enough to stay to meet with some of their admirers; Barbara and I didn't have the time to wait for the privilege of taking pictures with the beautiful couple, as we had an early morning appointment. But we hope to be included in the lucky group of fans the next time Louis has talent from the DWTS show at his dance hall. The couple stayed on for a few days and conducted private and group dance lessons on Long Island. We had other commitments and didn't have an opportunity to join their dance classes. Again, we plan on remedying that the next time around.

Almost a year to the same day, on May 30, 2009, Louis Del Prete was able to promote another DWTS team to appear at the Suburban Center. On this occasion, it was the recently married couple (September 1, 2007), Edyta Sliwinska and Alec Mazo. They both hold individual distinctions with ABC's dancing phenomenon; she is the only professional that has appeared on all of the eight shows through the spring of 2009. He and his dance partner, actress Kelly Monaco of the TV show General Hospital, were the winners of the Mirror Ball Trophy on the first season of DWTS.

The small center was packed tight, probably holding the maximum capacity for the venue. The approximately 400 patrons were hyper in anticipation of seeing the stunning husband and wife team dance. Prior to their performance, a 30-minute Salsa lesson, on the one beat, by Mark James and his partner, Karen Lupo, enticed over 100 dancers on the floor. Mark is one of the foremost dance instructors in the Metropolitan area and was instrumental in bringing the various dancing events on Long Island into an organized group, resulting in a minimum of conflicting dancing events being held on the same day. He hosts a monthly dance at the Wantagh Center in Wantagh, Long Island. He has one of the most advanced dancing websites on the East Coast, which lists many of his competitors, who advertise their dance schedules, making it easy to locate a dancing event in the area. His animated website is www.mjames.org. The dance lesson was on a beginner's level. The 100-plus students formed two lines, men on one side of the room and women on the other side, both facing each other. He started with the basic Salsa step. For the men, left foot forward, right foot forward, and then left foot in place to the beat of one-two-three. Then, right foot back, followed by left foot back and then right foot in place, again to the beat of one-two-three. So we all did one-two-three, in forward motions, and then one-two-three in a backward motion. Of course, the ladies mirrored the men in moving in the opposite direction, which made dancing the basic step easy and smooth to the music that was played. The position of the dance is, head held in a straight forward position; knees bent; from the waist up, slightly bending forward, and away we went to the one-two-three beats. The next step was an open break where the men and women step back for an open break, which prepares dancers for many of the complicated steps in the Salsa. While in the open break position, the male raises his left arm so his partner can turn under it ending in a face-to-face position. From there we learned the New Yorker step, which is the same in many of the Latin dances. Both partners turn to the man's right (woman's left) for one-two, and then face each other on three. Then to the man's left (woman's right) for one-two and then three puts both in a facing position ready for the next step. The Salsa music played, and in spite of the confusion from the large crowd, we somehow managed to get the new steps done reasonably well. Mark and Karen circulated among the dancers, instructing where necessary, and before we knew it, the dance lesson was over and it was time for a professional Salsa dance show by two internationally famous couples. They danced a quick-paced Salsa that made me feel quite inadequate as a Latin dancer; I'm sure many of the people in the hall had the same frustrated feeling. I promised myself that I would take additional dance lessons and try to focus and practice a little longer than my usual lazy practice sessions.

We were invited to help ourselves to coffee, tea, fruit and vegetable platters, and an abundance of cake, including delicious chocolate doughnuts. After our coffee break, the main event began. I told Louis to make sure we had seats near the side doors to the dance hall so we could see Edyta and Alec up close as they entered to perform their dances. Well, we got lucky; the stunning couple entered the hall at the entrance where our table was located for their last dance, the Jive, which enabled me to get an excellent shot of them preparing to conquer the dance floor. Although I got a nice close-up of the couple, Louis' professional photographer took some great action photos which were more exciting than the shots I took. With Louis' permission, two great photos are presented below. Louis announced that they would perform five dances: Cha-Cha, Tango, Paso Doble, Quickstep and Jive, followed by a 30-minute Question and Answer session, followed by a complimentary individual picture sitting for those patrons who wished to have their pictures taken with the gracious couple.

They burst onto the dance floor to the fast paced Cha-Cha music. Edyta wore a two-piece white bathing suit type of outfit which covered her top to perfection. Her lower costume was brief with laced twirl material that easily moved to the gyrations of her hips. She was a beautiful sight to behold. The white outfit complemented her perfectly-tanned flesh, bright white teeth, and smooth sparkling blondish hair. He on the other hand, wore black pants with a sleeveless T-shirt, accented by his shiny slick-black-hair and an unshaven face. Quite a contrast! They did a Cha-Cha that was fast and timed to perfection; their maneuvers were so fast and sexy that, again, I was overwhelmed by the feeling that more dancing lessons and lots of practice were in order for me and Barbara. An outstanding routine was an exhibition step where he easily lifts Edyta over his head, putting her in a face up horizontal position, then does several turns, and slowly brings her down head first, both facing the audience, till her hands reach the floor and she comes out of the routine doing a summersault. Truly an outstanding athletic maneuver!

Their next dance was an International Tango mixed with some sexy Argentine Tango kicks and sways. She wore a short-sleeved, tight, black, backless dress that ended about six inches above her knees. The outfit looked as if were glued to her picture perfect trim body. He wore black pants with a scarlet, long-sleeved red shirt. They both looked the part for the sexy hot Tango that everyone was waiting for. And hot it was! They danced and became part of the pulsating Latin Tango music. Their moves told of the love they had for each other and the passion that still existed between the stunning couple. For a moment I thought I saw some steam emanating from their bodies as they twisted, swayed, kicked at each other, and then made imaginary love on the dance floor. My OH my, what a privilege it was to watch those two young, talented performers express themselves in their own unique way, to the utmost delight of the audience. We couldn't stop applauding as they took bows and then left their hardwood bed behind them. The patrons were certainly pleased and many couldn't refrain from whistling and hooting their approval of the couple's expression of love.

After a well-deserved intermission, they returned to their stage to perform a Paso Doble. The dance is based on music played at bullfights during a fighter's entrance (paseo) or during the passes (faena) just before the kill. The male plays the part of the matador and his female partner generally plays the part of his cape or the bull. The social version of the dance usually begins with the woman as the cape, and at the end of the dance, when the matador goes in for the kill, she appropriately becomes the bull. The music is fast and was originally fashioned after a French military march with the name "Paso Redoble." Edyta filled everyone's vision with a spectacular purple, off the neck, open backed costume that ran down well below her right knee and was open on her left side exposing her gorgeous long, perfectly-shaped leg. Her purple high-heeled shoes completed the picture. He wore black pants and a white, long-sleeved shirt, which was opened in the front down to his waist. His slick-black-hair and stylish dark, unshaven face immediately transmitted to the viewers that they were both ready to conduct a hot Latin bullfight. The quick-paced Latin music set them in motion; he dared her to approach, which she did with fast stealthy moves, zigzagging as if she were a cape; he, in turn, circled her and caught her in his arms and moved her around the dance floor while imitating a matador's perfect exacting moves. She then transformed from a cape to an aggressive bull attacking him, but to no avail. He mysteriously took possession of the cape which was accompanied by a sword, which he put to use with gracious deliberate moves that tempted her into his realm. While she tried to destroy her agitator, he quickly rose on his toes; sword raised high and plunged the messenger of death into her beautiful body. She fell limp to the floor, arms extended and her body twisted; he bowed, expecting approval from the audience, but no one applauded; our sympathy was with the dead beauty that had fallen prey to the matador's magnetic weapon of death. After a slight pause, the audience responded with applause and happy sounds in celebration that the maiden (bull) lifted herself from the floor, took her antagonist's hand, bowed and quickly left the dance floor, both smiling at the charade that they so skillfully performed.

Their next dance was a Quickstep. As its name indicates, the tempo of the dance is brisk and includes hops, runs and quick steps with lots of momentum and rotation. The extensive use of syncopated steps with long note durations sets it apart from all other International dances. It originally evolved from the combination of the Foxtrot, Charleston, Shag, Peabody and One Step. Like the Foxtrot, the dance is smooth and glamorous, which gives performers an opportunity to show off their light-footed, energetic and form-intensive skills, which is required to properly perform the dance.

All eyes were again on Edyta; her bright red, two-piece costume, with a short flowing top and a low waist, ankle length skirt, caused most of the men's heartbeats to race, or in my case, to almost stop. The women on the other hand, pictured the outfit and body with their heads gracing her shoulders; this was in response to her exquisite dazzling beauty. Alec wore what seemed to be the same black pants and shoes, but this time he sported a long-sleeved black shirt, opened in the front to his waist. His full head of hair was still a shining black crown and his face was still occupied by stylish black hair growth, which in a man's world is called a "five o'clock shadow." The dance was fast, with running, hopping, and in a couple of instances, flying through the air steps. The most spectacular step was where they ran for at least eight beats and then jumped into the air, legs extended, as if to take off into a flying pattern. If there was any question as to whether ballroom dancing is an athletic event and belongs in the Olympics, their performance would certainly clarify the issue.

Again, all eyes were on Edyta; her short grey skirt, which was somehow attached to her hips and stayed in place for her whole Jive performance; and her smart matching top were highlighted by long green suede boots. Alec again favored a black outfit with a hanging strap T-shirt. The Jive dance evolved from East Coast Swing, Boogie-Woogie, the Lindy Hop and the Jitterbug. It's one of the five Latin International competition dances and is considered one of the most athletically challenging. They burst onto the dance floor and began their rapid high knee lifts and rocking of their hips. The dance is done in place rather than around the dance floor and their motions resembled the movements of car pistons, jumping and pumping up and down and sideways. My attention, and I think the attention of everyone in the audience was, "How long will Edyta's short skirt remain in place?" Well, it did, thanks to the magic glue used to hold the short skirt in its assigned position for the occasion; much to the disappointment of "Moi." Their performance was equivalent to an Olympic event; high speed, quick kicks, and acrobatic jumps that brought the audience to its feet applauding and cheering their satisfaction with the stunning couple. They took their bows and promised to return for a Question and Answer session after they refreshed themselves.

When they returned the first question was: "How long have you been married?"

Edyta answered: "We were married on September 1, 2007."

"How long have you been dancing together?"

Alec answered: "We started competing in the year 2000."

"Is it difficult to work and share a private life?"

Edyta answered: "Very much so. We were ready to give up competing just before Dancing with the Stars came into our lives. The stress of seeing each other every day and working under stressful conditions was taking its toll on our relationship."

"Do you plan on having children?"

Edyta answered: "Yes, as soon as our DWTS tour is over, we plan on having many children."

Question for Edyta: "Do you keep your outfits?"

Edyta answered: "No. They are recycled, sold to the professionals or to the public. So, if anyone is interested in buying a costume, they can contact ABC and try to purchase one. I think for the right price, they would be willing to sell many of the outfits."

Question for Alec: "Do you have a choice of the music you dance to?"

Alec answered: "No, but if we hate the music and explain why, they sometimes will let us choose from their list."

"Who picks your dance partners?"

Alec answered: "The producers."

"How are partners matched?"

Alec answered: "The producers match partners. For instance, one of the reasons that Edyta has been on all the shows is that she is very easy going. Unfortunately, that makes her a first choice for matching with difficult personalities."

"Why aren't more qualified stars chosen to be on DWTS?"

Alec answered: "If all the contestants were good dancers or athletes, then there would be no unexpected winners which would take lots of the fun out of the competitions. For instance, this season Gil was a wonderful surprise to us, as he had no prior experience with dancing and was not an athlete. He was probably one of the best male dancing stars that we ever had on the show."

"Is there a monetary incentive for the professionals to win?"

Edyta answered: "No, just the prestige of having won first place and winning the Mirror Ball. The stars do get a bonus if they win."

"Are there any problems with the professionals and stars getting too friendly?"

Edyta answered: "Not often. You have to remember that the professional dancers come into contact with people from all walks of life and are used to handling any uncomfortable situations. But, of course, there are exceptions."

After the Question and Answer session, Edyta and Alec stayed to take pictures with the guests. After hanging around for over half an hour, Barbara and I decided that the line wasn't moving fast enough, so we ended our enchanted evening by waving goodbye to the stunning couple and holding on dearly to my camera that recorded the wonderful event. The pictures of their dancing are presented with the permissions of Louis Del Prete:

I have become captivated with ABC's DWTS and the magic it generates as the television show to watch, enjoy, and to get a good understanding of the complexity of ballroom dancing. The underlying excitement of watching the show comes from the participants being judged by dancing professionals and then by TV spectators who take the time to telephone and text message their preferences to ABC's adjudicating committee. This determines who will continue on the show and who will eventually be the the winners of the Mirror Ball Trophy. The show is based on the British Broadcasting Corporation's (BBC), television series "Strictly Come Dancing" and is a part of BBC Worldwide International "Dancing with the Stars" franchise. The whole concept became so fascinating to me that I decided to do some research about the show and some of its major professional personalities.

The hosts are Tom Bergeron and Samantha Harris. Tom's background includes being a disc jockey at a local radio station, WHAV, in his home town where he was born in 1955, to such TV shows as "Hollywood Squares" (1998-2004), "America's Funniest Home Videos" (2001-present), fill-in host for "Who Wants to Be a Millionaire" and "Dancing with the Stars." He is from Haverhill, Massachusetts, and has the distinction of having won a TV Daytime Emmy.

The beautiful new mom, Samantha, who was born in 1973, is from Hopkins, Minnesota. She is a correspondent with "E! Entertainment Televisions E! News" and the host of the "THS Investigates Show." In addition to writing, producing, and reporting daily for E! News, she co-hosts the network's live award show coverage for the Oscars, Golden Globes, and Emmys. She also appears as a special correspondent on "Good Morning America" and is currently the co-host of "Dancing with the Stars."

The panel of judges is Len Goodman (head judge), Carrie Ann Inaba, and Bruno Tonioli. Len and Bruno are kept busy commuting weekly between Hollywood and London to judge both the American and British versions of the show. Len

Goodman has been the head judge on BBC's "Strictly Come Dancing" talent show since its inception in 2004. Its unique format has been exported to 30 other countries including "Dancing with the Stars' in the United States. In his youth he was a professional dancer and currently runs his own successful dance school in Kent, England, where he lives permanently. He specialized in a form of Ballroom dancing called "Exhibition Dancing" and has won the "British Exhibitions Title" four times and was runner up in the "Exhibition World Championships." He was also awarded the "British Rising Star Award" by the British Academy of Films and Television Arts and the "Carl Allen Award" which is considered the "Oscar of the Dance World" in England. Most recently he received the Lifetime Achievement Award for his outstanding work in advancing ballroom dancing throughout the world. He was born in 1944 in London, England, and started his dancing career by accident when he was advised by his doctor to take up dancing to strengthen his foot, which he injured while playing football. His exact judging style and keen sense of humor has made him a popular world renowned dance adjudicator, lecturer, TV personality and good will ambassador in the world of dancing.

Bruno Tonioli was born in Ferrara, Italy and is a renowned teacher and professional choreographer for some of the world's most famous entertainers. He was the leading dance instructor at London's acclaimed Dance Centre (www.london-studio-centre. co.uk), which is one of the most prestigious dance schools in England for courses in Ballet, Contemporary Dance, Jazz Dance Techniques, and Music Theatre. The dancing aficionado is fluent in English, Spanish, French and Italian, which puts him at ease with being a judge on the English speaking BBC's "Strictly Come Dancing" and "Dancing with the Stars" shows. He is a top choreographer and has worked in almost every level of contemporary dance. Some of his outstanding music video choreography has been with such renowned entertainers as: Elton John, Michael Jackson, Freddie Mercury, Tina Turner and Paul McCartney. In 2003, he had a cameo role in the French & Sanders Christmas Special, where the infamous kissing scene between Madonna and Britney Spears exploded onto television screens around the world, in their "Against the Music" skit. His amicable, passionate and effervescent personality has made him a favorite judge on DWTS and is sought after as an adjudicator on other dance shows.

The third judge on the DWTS panel is the beautiful multi-talented Carrie Ann Inaba, (www.carrieanninaba.tv). She was born in 1968 and raised in Honolulu, Hawaii, and is of Japanese, Chinese and Irish decent. After winning a Hula Skirt dancing contest as a teenager, she went to live in Tokyo, Japan, to continue her education and became a popular singer. She released three singles: "Party Girl," " Be Your Girl," and "Yume no Senaka." After returning to America, she appeared as one of the "Fly Girls," a dancer in the series "In Living Color." In 1993, she toured with Madonna as a dancer in "The Girlie Show Tour," which required her to shave her head bald and to perform topless. She was the "Pole Girl" who danced and slid down a pole to open each show. She also toured in Ricky Martin's "Living La Vida Loca" tour. She had minor parts in many movies such as "Monster Mash," "Showgirls," "American Virgin," Austin Powers in "Goldmember" (as Fook Yu), and in Austin Powers, "The Spy Who Shagged Me." Her fame and popularity can be traced to her choreographing several popular television series, including, "American Idol," "American Juniors," "All American Girl," "He's a Lady," "In Search of the Partridge Family" and "Who Wants to Marry a Multi-Millionaire." She also choreographed the Miss America Pageant for five years. She is the founder and President of EnterMediArt, Inc., a video production company. In addition to her busy schedule, she also directs, writes and edits films.

Recently she was invited to be a celebrity judge at the 2009 USA DanceSport National Championships in Baltimore, Maryland. This year, there will be more than 1,000 amateur DanceSport athletes vying for national titles and placements on the U.S. DanceSport teams scheduled to compete at the upcoming World Championships. Twenty DanceSport couples will be selected for 11 World Championship events. Competitors are expected to represent nearly every state in the nation in categories, including Pre-Teen (as young as age 7), Youth (to age 18), Adults (19 to 34), and Seniors (35 to 70 +). Carrie Ann will serve as an Honorary Judge and master workshop instructor; she will also provide additional critiques to the top dancers in overall artistic areas of performance, showmanship, and individual talent. USA Dance, along with Carrie Ann, will present the first annual Star Quality Award to twelve DanceSport Champions in the various divisions. Quite a busy lady!!

Watching DWTS aroused my curiosity about the professional dancers' credentials, so I decided to research the backgrounds of some of the regular professional performers on the show.

Karina Smirnoff is probably the most decorated female professional on the show. She was born in the Ukraine in 1978, where she studied ballot, gymnastics and skating at a very early age. She migrated to the United States when she was 12-years-old and her family settled in the Bronx where she spent her informative years. She eventually graduated from Fordham University with a double major in Economics and Information System Programming. Although she planned on studying law, her love for and skill in dancing led her on a different path. Her passion for dancing led her to winning the World Trophy Championship; the Asian Open two times; U.S. open three times, U.S. National Professional Championship and the Dutch Open five times. She came in second in the prestigious British Open Blackpool Dance Festival and is ranked second in the world in Latin dancing.

Karina made her acting debut in the movie "Shall We Dance," which was released in 2004. She was one of the choreographers and trainers for Jennifer Lopez, Richard Gere, and Stanley Tucci; they all miraculously learned their routines to perfection from her and the other professional teachers in a short period of time. She shared a scene with fellow DWTS professional Tony Dovolani in the movie and has since danced with him many times on the TV show.

She started on DWTS on its third season in 2006 and was partnered with movie heart throb Mario Lopez. They placed second in the competition but first in each others' hearts. After two years, she decided to leave him because of his philandering but soon found her true love in fellow countryman from the Ukraine, Maksim Chmerkovskiy, who is also a renowned professional dancer and also appears on DWTS. They recently announced their engagement and wedding plans. Her dance partner in the spring of 2009, Apple Computer co-founder Steve Wozniak, will give her away at what will probably be a spectacular wedding event.

Maxsim Chmerkovskiy (Max), at www.Maksimchmerokovskiy. com is Karina's soul mate and fellow countryperson. He was born in Odessa in the Ukraine in 1980. In his early teens, he was in a serious ski accident that almost severed his leg. After many surgeries and the insertion of a 12-inch metal rod in his leg, he was told to forget about dancing or participating in athletic activities. His stubbornness, perseverance, and many months of physical therapy proved the doctors wrong, and today he is one of the world's most popular ballroom dancers. His family moved to the United States in 1994 and settled in my original home town, Brooklyn, New York. It didn't take Max long before his dancing abilities started to bring him fame. He won titles in the Ohio Star Ball Latin Championships; Manhattan DanceSport Professional Latin Championships; Yankee Classic Professional Latin Championships; Nevada Star Ball Championships; Philadelphia DanceSport Festival Championships and the La Classique du Quebec Championships. He is the owner of three dance studios in the New York City area, one of which is the "Rising Star Dance Academy," which is the premier youth ballroom dance school in the United States. He is a board member of the non profit organization DanceTeamUSA, which works to promote DanceSport among the youth of America. His dance studio "Dance with Me" at (www.dancewithmeli. com) in Glen Head, Long Island, is just a short ride from where Barbara and I live in Melville, and has become a hot spot in the area for ballroom dance lessons and social dancing.

Max also operates Maksim Chmerkovskiy Productions that promotes and organizes dancing performances around the world. As if all of this activity isn't enough, he also appears as a dancing professional on DWTS. He appeared on the second season and immediately got into trouble disagreeing with the judges decisions of his performances. He actually showed hostility and even argued with them on several occasions. He has since calmed down and has learned to accept the judges decisions with a little more humility than in the past, and he is no longer called the "Bad Boy of Ballroom Dancing." I'm sure that Karina will add to his new-found inner peace after they get married.

Edyta Sliwinska, at www.edytasliwinska.com, is the only professional dancer on DWTS that has performed on all the shows since its beginning in 2005. She was born in Warsaw, Poland, in 1981, and came to the United States in the year 2000 to partner with her current husband Alec Mazo, who is also a professional dancer on DWTS. They hold first place titles in the Emerald Ball Latin Amateur Championships; 2001 International Grand Ball Championship (San Francisco); 2001 Holiday Ball Championship (Las Vegas, Nevada); and are five time finalists in the U.S. National Ballroom competitions. The gorgeous dancer with a picture-perfect figure also does modeling and played in the TV show "CSI: NY" as Tanta Love in "Rush to Judgment," where she played a Salsa dance teacher who was involved in a murder. She and Alec currently run the "Genesis DanceSport Academy" (www.genesisdancesport.com) in San Francisco and Los Angeles, and have just released an instructional DVD, "Dancing like the Pros," and a fitness DVD, "Fitness with the Pros."

Alec Mazo, at www.alecmazo.com, was born in Russia in 1980 and migrated to the United States in 1992 where he developed his dancing skills at his mother's newly opened dance studio in San Francisco, California. He is another professional dancer that took lessons to strengthen his body due to physical problems and to improve his social skills with girls. His success in overcoming his physical handicap subsequently led him to become a dancing champion. He danced with his wife, Edyta and won titles in the Emerald Ball Latin Amateur Competitions and took first place in the 2001 International Grand Ball Competition in San Francisco. They also took first place in the 2001 Holiday Ball Competitions in Las Vegas, Nevada. He was also a six time U.S. National Finalist, five times with Edyta. Shortly before appearing on DWTS, he dropped his amateur standing and became a professional dancer. He was the first winner of the Mirror Ball Trophy in 2005 on DWTS with his dance partner, General Hospital star, Kelly Monaco. Today he manages the largest youth dance studio in California and is a physical fitness advocate for the youth of America. Alec and Edyta have been traveling with the road tour of DWTS, which keeps them pretty busy between their other dancing activities.

Cheryl Burke, at www.cherylburkedance.com, was born in San Francisco, California, in 1984. Her father is Russian and Irish and her mother is Filipino, which accounts for her beautiful exotic features. She began taking ballet lessons when she was four-years-old and then trained in both standard ballroom and Latin dances which prepared her for competition dancing at the age of thirteen. She has won titles in the 2005 World Cup Professional Rising Star Latin Championships, 2005 San Francisco Latin Championships, 2005 Ohio Star Ball Rising Star Latin Championships, and in UK Championships. She was a two-time nominee for the Prime Time Emmy in 2006, for Outstanding Choreography in Paso Doble and Outstanding Choreography for Freestyle. In 2007, she won the Role Model Award at the 7th Annual Filipino/American Library Gala.

Of course, what we all know and love her for was her performances in winning back-to-back Dancing with the Stars championships in Seasons 2 and 3; first with "98 Degrees" member Drew Lachey, and then with retired football great, Emmitt Smith. In Season 8, she is teamed with Gilles Marini, best known for his role in the "Sex and the City" movie, and may be looking at her third Mirror Ball Trophy on DWTS. (After this writing, she came in second in the competition, but in my opinion should have won, as Gilles was without-a-doubt, the best male star dancer since the series began.) Cheryl keeps herself busy with the "Cheryl Burke Dance Studio" in San Francisco and her road tours with DWTS. Cheryl is currently dating model Maxwell Zagorski.

Corky Ballas, at www.corky.com, was born in Houston, Texas, in 1961. Where do you start writing about one of the most renowned ballroom dancing title holders in the world? He won his first title at the age of six as a flamenco dancer and has continued dancing while collecting some of the most prestigious titles in ballroom dancing. His parents owned and operated a 64,000-square foot dance studio called Dance City USA, in Houston, Texas, which was not only the largest studio in the world, but had 125 on-site dance instructors. Coming from a dancing family, it's understandable that while growing up, his attention and passion would be in that profession. His first love was flamenco dancing, which his mother, a flamenco dancer of some renown, taught him; then he went on to become a disco dancing champion and, when that style of dancing went out of favor, he began concentrating on ballroom dancing. Corky's accomplishments include winning titles in: Open to the World International Champions, 1995 and 1996; Open to the World British Champions, 1995 and 1996, which is the pinnacle of world ballroom dancing trophies; three times British National Champion; Dual of the Giants Champion and eight times undefeated United States International Latin Champion. He is the only American to win the "United States, Pro/Am Championship" (three years in a row) as the amateur, then winning the "World Professional Latin Title Pro/Am" as the professional in 2008. There are many other awards and trophies that he has received, which are too numerous to list, but can be found on his website at www.corky.com.

He also is the coach and trainer for many of the DWTS professionals and is remembered as the partner of the naughty 82-year-old comedian Cloris Leachman in the seventh season.

His winning smile and good humor made the comical conduct of Cloris tolerable on DWTS. He has a unique website where free dance lessons are given at www.learn2dance.com.

Barbara and I had a chance meeting with Corky and his wife, Shirley, in the New Yorker Hotel many years ago at a National Ballroom Dancing Conference. The hotel is across the street from Penn Station and Madison Square Garden, so it was easy for us to take a train from our home in Long Island to the station and walk across the street to the hotel. They were attending as guest speakers and we were there as social guests. The conference included lectures on dancing techniques and the dancing issues of the day. After the lectures, we attended a dinner and Grand Ball where we joined the professional and other social guests in a night of ballroom dancing to big band music. We attended one of the lectures that they gave on ballroom etiquette and the responsibility of dancers for their actions on the dance floor. They were followed by a group panel whose main topic was: "Should we allow same gender partners to compete in the National Ballroom competitions?" By the end of the conference, the consensus was a resounding--"NO."

We had two chance meetings with the famous couple; the first one was in the hotel's elevator on our way to the dinner and dance event. I stepped aside to let Shirley into the elevator and commented on her beautiful red hair and emerald gown. She sort of blushed and said "Thank you." We then accompanied them to the Grand Ballroom and wished them good luck in their future competitions. The second meeting was the next morning when we went to breakfast at the hotel's restaurant. We saw them sitting down at a table. I was about to comment on her beautiful hair again and then noticed she was a brunette that morning; so I just said "good morning." They responded with a friendly nod and asked us to join them for breakfast, which we did. I had difficulty ordering my breakfast as my throat passage seemed to have closed and I was unable to talk. Corky's mild manner and friendly smile lightened the atmosphere as he asked us questions about our reason for attending the conference. I was surprised that two such famous people were interested in strangers that they had just met and who had gone to the conference just to have fun and get an insight into the essence of ballroom dancing. The breakfast went quickly, with Shirley and Corky asking us a stream of personal questions about our families and our interests in ballroom dancing. We said our goodbyes and were thrilled to have met such famous down-to-earth people, who graciously gave their time and attention to two new dancing enthusiasts. The experience has been etched in my mind over these many years and has caused me to follow their dancing accomplishments to the top of the professional ballroom championship ladder, as noted above and on their website.

Corky and Shirley's son, Mark, at www.markballas.com, is also a professional dancer on DWTS. He was born in Houston, Texas in 1986 and didn't waste any time following in his father's footsteps. His grandparents were Spanish and Greek, which accounts for his handsome, dark, sharp features and his passion for music. He moved to London, England, with his parents and immediately began his dancing career. At the early age of ten, he won the British Juvenile Ballroom and Latin American Dance championships. In 2005, he was honored with the "Performer of the Year" award. He went on to win championships at the "British Open to the World," the "U.S. Open to the World," and the "International Open to the World," with dance partner Julianne Hough, who is also a professional dancer on DWTS. He won Junior and Youth World Championship titles and The Junior Olympic Gold, while living in England and under the tutelage of his famous parents.

In addition to being a champion dancer, he has performed in stage productions of the musicals: "Copacabana," as the lead, Tony; "Maria de Buenos Aires," as one of the lead dancers and "The Buddy Holly Musical," as the lead understudy. He also performed at the London Palladium. His current passion is the "BallasHough Band" at (www.ballashoughband.com), with his

DWTS friend, Derek Hough (brother of Julianne). He writes and sings many of the band's songs along with his four group members and, when they have the time, they head for the open road touring and playing their beloved music.

Season six of DWTS saw him and Olympic Gold Medalist figure skater, Kristi Yamaguchi, win the seasons Mirror Ball Trophy. He has maintained the highest average for a pro dancer on the show with a 26.71. With his eighth season's partner, Olympic Gymnast Shawn Johnson, who at age 17 is the youngest competitor on the show to date, he may see his average increase.

The beautiful Julianne Hough, at www.juliannehough.net, is the youngest pro dancer to star on DWTS to date. Born in 1988 in Salt Lake City, Utah, to LDS (Mormon) parents, she developed her love of dancing and entertaining from her four grandparents who were dancers, and her parents, who met while performing in a ballroom dancing team in college. She and her brother Derek, who is also a pro dancer on DWTS, are a testament to the Mormon's dedication to excelling in ballroom dancing; their dancing teams are ranked among the top performers in the world. Julianne began dancing competitively at the age of nine. She and her partner, older brother Derek, were noticed by Corky and Shirley Ballas at one of their performances. The famous dance couple were so impressed with their potential that they offered to coach the young siblings in London, where they lived. First Derek, at age twelve, took up the offer and then subsequently, Julianne, at age ten followed him on their new adventure. The young couple's parents were going through a divorce at the time and thought it best to spare their children the agony of the proceedings. Well, what was supposed to be a few months in London turned out to be five years for Julianne and eight years for her brother, Derek.

The Ballas' son, Mark and the two new additions to his family became close friends. The trio became students at the famous "Italia Conti Academy" where they were trained in song, theatre, gymnastics and other forms of dancing, including Jazz,

Ballet and Tap. When Julianne was twelve, the three formed their own pop music trio 2B1G (2 Boys, 1 Girl) and travelled and competed in the United Kingdom and the United States. In her spare time, at age fifteen, Julianne and Mark won both Junior World Latin championships and International Latin Youth championships at the Blackpool Dance Festival in London. Her brother also won those prestigious titles with his Polish dance partner, Aneta Piotrowska. Corky's and Shirley's dream of making the kids all-around entertainers in singing, dancing and acting was becoming a reality. To accomplish this, the trio had to train like Olympic athletes with no expense spared by Corky and Shirley. The three young champions travelled around the world and competed whenever possible; they lived lives of adults and gained experience that eventually shaped their successful entertainment careers. She and Mark also won the United States National Latin Youth Championship. Julianne is the youngest and only American to hold both the International Latin Youth and Junior Blackpool World Latin titles.

On DWTS she won two Mirror Ball Trophies; first with Olympic gold medal winning speed skater Apolo Anton Ohno in the fourth season, making her the youngest professional to win the prize. Her second trophy was with two-time Indianapolis 500 Champion Helio Castroneves in the fifth season. As I'm writing this, Helio, who was brought up on charges of tax evasion in the U.S., was recently exonerated and is again free to enter his next car race competition. Julianne was nominated at the 60th Primetime Emmy Awards in the category of "Outstanding Choreography" for her Mambo "Para Los Rumberos," which she performed with partner, Helio. Following her performance in the seventh season when dancing with actor Cody Linley of Hannah Montana, she was rushed to the hospital and had surgery to have her appendix removed. While on the operating table, she also had a cyst on her ovary, and scar tissue from her bladder and fallopian tubes removed. In spit of the traumatic experience, she was back on the show in a couple of weeks to continue her partnership with Cody, but unfortunately, was shortly disqualified.

In 2008, she announced that she was going to devote all of her time to singing country music and would not be returning to the DWTS show. However, she did return for the eighth season in 2009 partnering with her real life boy friend, country singer Chuck Wicks, but was eliminated in the final rounds. Her first country music single, "Will You Dance with Me?" was released to iTunes and Wal-Mart in 2007 to raise money for the American Red Cross. Since then, she has cut albums and has made many TV appearances. In 2009, she won the "Top New Female Vocalist Award" and went on to win the "44th Annual Academy of Country Music Award."

Corky and Shirley Ballas fulfilled their dreams with the three wonderful children that they nurtured by challenging their mettle, which resulted in their being at the apex of the entertainment world of music with their outstanding dancing and singing successes.

Julianne's older brother Derek, at: www.derekhough.net, was born in 1985, also right outside of Salt Lake City, Utah. He is currently a dancer, choreographer, actor, musician (guitar player), and singer. His informative years' experience paralleled Julianne's except that he chose to remain in England and, in addition to studying at the "Italian Conti Academy of the Arts," he also became one of their teachers. He also took the opportunity to develop his acting skills in such musicals as "Footloose," playing Ren, and as Jesus, in "Jesus Christ Superstar." In the process, he accumulated titles in: "The World Under 21 Latin American Championships"; was two time winner of "Open British Championships (Blackpool)"; two-time "International Open to the World Champions"; two-time "U.S. Open Championship" and "IDSF World Youth Latin Champion in 2002 for Poland" with his partner, Aneta Piotrowska, who appeared on Poland's version of DWTS. He also won the LA Outstanding Dancer of the Year and the New York Dance Alliance Outstanding Dance awards.

His appearance on season seven with partner model/TV host Brooke Burke resulted in their winning the Mirror Ball Trophy for first place. Hough is also one of Bruno Tonioli's panelists on "BBC One's DanceX," which is a reality team dance competition show in England. In addition to being a great dancer and singer, he has teamed up with his buddy Mark Ballas and formed a five-piece band, the BallasHough Band (BHB), at www.ballashoughband.com, where he plays guitar and is a lead singer. They released their first music album in 2009. He also has a website and invites people to participate in his dance learning routines at www.learning2dance.com, where dancers can learn "to dance with Derek." He also has appeared in TV films including: "Presenter in Real Lives," "Harry Potter and the Philosopher's Stone," and lead dancer in George Michael's "Round Here" video.

Indeed, he is a very busy and talented entertainer, just what the Ballas family had in mind when they took him and his sister under their loving wings and nurtured them to success in the music industry.

Lacey-Mae Schwimmer, at www.laceymaeschwimmersworld. com, was born in 1988 and is currently the youngest performer on DWTS; she predates Julianne by one month. Lacey was also born into a family of LDS (Mormons), in Moreno Valley, California. Her parents are Laurie Kauffman and noted West Coast Swing champion dancer, Buddy Schwimmer. She is the younger sister of Benji Schwimmer, winner of the second season in "So You Think You Can Dance." Lacey began competitive dancing at an early age and at seven-years-old, she danced in the 1995 U.S. Open Swing Dance Championships. At age ten, she placed first in the "Young American Division at the 1998 U.S. Open Swing Dance Championships." Some of her other titles include the U.S. Open Swing Dance Championship, 2000; Young American Division (6-14-year-olds) U.S. Open Swing Dance Championship, 2002; Young Adult Division (14-17-year-olds) U.S. Open Swing Dance Championship, 2004; Young Adult Division (14-17- year-olds) U.S. National Youth Latin Championship 2006; and World Swing Dance Championship, Classic Division, 2007, with her brother, Benji Schwimmer.

It seems that she will be a regular on DWTS as she is very popular with the TV audience, although she had not been successful with her partners Lance Bass (seventh season) of "N Sync" or former "Jackass" star, Steve-O in the eighth season. Lacey has expanded her career in TV, appearing on the Ellen Degeneres Show and in the movies, appearing with Adam Sandler in "Bedtime Stories." Much of her time is spent touring with the road show of DWTS and teaching master classes in ballroom dancing.

Louis van Amstel, at www.dancingwithlouis.com, was born in 1972 in Amsterdam and is a Dutch ballroom dance champion, professional dancer, choreographer and a DanceSport coach. He attended the University of the Arts in Amsterdam and won most of his prestigious titles with British dance partner, Julie Fryer. He is a seven times Dutch and three times world champion ballroom dancer, winning titles in Dutch Latin Championships in 1990 and 1991; World Amateur Latin Championships in both 1994 and 1995; European Amateur Latin Championship in 1995; Amateur Grand-Slam Winner in UK Champions, which included, British, International, European and World Championships. In the United States, he partnered with Karina Smirnoff in the year 2000 and won the U.S. National Latin Championship; Canadian-American DanceSport Gala-Canadian Open Professional Championship: they took 1st place in the Open Professional International Latin Division; the Japan International Dancing Championship, and first place in the esteemed, Emerald Ball DanceSport Championship Open Professional Latin Division.

He started dancing at an early age, concentrating on Ballet, Tap dancing and Jazz. He has expanded his career by producing, directing, and acting in such shows on Broadway at City Center as "Latin Fusion" and in Salt Lake City in "Latin Revolution." He has appeared several times on DWTS, but the prestigious trophy has eluded him. His experience and rare talent have led to his serving as creative director and choreographer on the popular pop culture phenomenon, DWTS.

Barbara and I recently saw one of the productions that he directed and choreographed, "Ballroom World Champion Tour 2008," at the Crest Theatre in Delray Beach, Florida, which played to a full house and included over 30 song and dance performances that were refreshingly entertaining. Watching the young talent test their mettle in the aerobic and subtle dance routines was enjoyable from the beginning, to the end of the show.

The dance professionals are constantly changing on DWTS so I just researched some of them, the others can be located on DWTS' website at www.abc.go.com. In the first season of 2009, the professionals that I did not list include Dmitry Chaplin, Tony Dovolani, Chelsie Hightower, Kym Johnson, and Jonathan Roberts. Each can be visited on ABC's website or on their individual sites.

In keeping with the athletic requirements of ballroom dancing, a DVD titled "Dancing with the Stars: Cardio Dance" was released in 2007 featuring Kym Johnson, Maksim Chmerkovskiy, and Ashly DelGrosso. The program contains cardiovascular workouts adapted from Cha-Cha, Paso Doble, Samba and Jive dance routines. A second DVD "Dancing with the Stars: Latin Cardio Dance" was released in 2008 featuring Maksim Chmerkovskiy and Cheryl Burke. The program contains cardiovascular workouts adapted from Cha-Cha, Merengue, Samba, and Mambo dance routines. After viewing and dancing to both DVDs, Barbara and I were reassured that ballroom dancing is absolutely an athletic event and is certainly a preferred way to exercise, as can be witnessed in the popularity of aerobic dance sessions at many gyms across America.

CHAPTER SEVENTEEN

Use It or Lose It:
Dancing Makes You Smarter

THERE IS NO DOUBT that dancing is considered physical activity, so much so, that it's expected to become an Olympic event in the near future. But little has been written about the effect that dancing has on one's mental condition. I came across an article by Richard Powers, www.Vintage@Stanford.edu, world-renowned scholar and an expert on American Social Dancing, that will hopefully set the stage for more people becoming aware of the intellectual advantages of dancing. With Richard Powers' permission, I'm presenting his thoughts; it's our hope that with mental enhancement thrown into the formula, more people will take up the challenge and enter the world of ballroom dancing:

Use It or Lose It: Dancing Makes Your Smarter, by Richard Powers.

"For hundreds of years dance manuals and other writings have lauded the health benefits of dancing, usually as physical exercise. More recently we've seen research on further health benefits of dancing, such as stress reduction and increased serotonin levels, with its sense of well-being.

Then, most recently we've heard of another benefit: Frequent dancing apparently makes us smarter. A major study added to the growing evidence that stimulating one's mind can ward off Alzheimer's disease and other dementia, much as physical exercise can keep the body fit.

You've probably heard about the New England Journal of Medicine report on the effects of recreational activities on the mental acuity in aging. Here it is in a nutshell:

The 21-year study of senior citizens, 75 and older, was led by the Albert Einstein College of Medicine in New York City, funded by the National Institute of Aging, and published in the New England Journal of Medicine. Their method for objectively measuring mental acuity in aging was to monitor rates of dementia, including Alzheimer's disease.

The study wanted to see if any physical or cognitive recreational activities influenced mental acuity. They discovered that some activities had a significant beneficial effect. Other activities had none.

They studied cognitive activities such as reading books, writing for pleasure, doing crossword puzzles, playing cards and playing musical instruments. And they studied physical activities like playing tennis or golf, swimming, bicycling, dancing, walking for exercise and doing housework.

One of the surprises of the study was that almost none of the physical activities appeared to offer any protection against dementia. There can be cardiovascular benefits of course, but the focus of this study was the mind. There was one important exception: the only physical activity to offer protection against dementia was frequent dancing.

> Reading – 35% reduced risk of dementia
>
> Bicycling and swimming – 0%
>
> Playing golf - 0%
>
> Dancing frequently –76%

That was the greatest risk reduction of any activity studied, cognitive or physical. Quoting Dr. Joseph Coyle, a Harvard Medical School psychiatrist who wrote an accompanying commentary: 'The cerebral cortex and hippocampus, which are critical to these activities, are remarkably plastic, and they rewire themselves based upon their use.'

And from the study itself, Dr. Katzman proposed that these persons are more resistant to the effects of dementia as a result of having greater cognitive reserve and increased complexity of neuronal synapses. Like education, participation in some leisure activities lowers the risk of dementia by improving cognitive reserve.

Our brain constantly rewires its neural pathways, as needed. If it doesn't need to, then it won't.

Aging and Memory:

When brain cells die and synapses weaken with aging, our nouns go first, like names of people, because there's only one neural pathway connecting to that stored information. If the single neural connection to that name fades, we lose access to it. So, as we age, we learn to parallel process, to come up with synonyms to go around these roadblocks. (Or maybe we don't learn to do this, and just become a dimmer bulb.) The key here is Dr. Katzman's emphasis on the complexity of our neuronal synapses. More is better. Do whatever you can to create new neural paths. The opposite of this is taking the same old well-worn path over and over again, with habitual patterns of thinking and living our lives.

When I was studying the creative process as a grad student at Stanford, I came across the perfect analogy to this: 'The more stepping stones there are across the creek, the easier it is to cross in your own style.'

The focus of that aphorism was creative thinking, to find as many alternative paths as possible to a creative solution. But as we age, parallel processing becomes more critical. Now it's no longer a matter of style, it's a matter of survival - getting across the creek at all. Randomly dying brain cells are like stepping stones being removed one by one. Those who had only one well-worn path of stones are completely blocked when some are removed. But those who spent their lives trying different mental routes each time, creating a myriad of possible paths, still have several paths left. The Albert Einstein College of Medicine study shows that we need to keep as many of those paths active as we can, while also generating new paths, to maintain the complexity of our neuronal synapses.

Why Dancing?

We immediately ask two questions: Why is dancing better than other activities for improving mental capabilities? And does this mean all kinds of dancing, or is one kind of dancing better than another?

The essence of intelligence is making decisions. And the concluding advice, when it comes to improving your mental acuity, is to involve yourself in activities which require split-second rapid-fire decision making, as opposed to rote memory (retracing the same well-worn path), or just working on your physical style.

One way to do that is to learn something new. Not just dancing, but anything new. Don't worry about the probability that you'll never use it in the future. Take a class to challenge your mind. It will stimulate the connectivity of your brain by generating the need for new pathways. Difficult and even frustrating classes are better for you, as they will create a greater need for new neural pathways.

Then take a dance class, which can be even better. Dancing integrates several brain functions at once, increasing connectivity. Dancing simultaneously involves kinesthetic, rational, musical and emotional processes.

What kind of dancing?

Let's go back to the study: Bicycling, swimming or playing golf – 0% reduced risk of dementia.

But doesn't golf require rapid-fire decision-making? No, not if you're a long-time player. You made most of the decisions when you first started playing, years ago. Now the game is mostly refining your technique. It can be good physical exercise, but the study showed it led to no improvement in mental acuity.

So, take the kinds of dance classes where you must make as many split-second decisions as possible. That's key to maintaining true intelligence.

Does any kind of dancing lead to increased mental acuity? No, not all forms of dancing will produce this benefit. Not dancing which, like golf or swimming, mostly works on style or retracing the same memorized paths. The key is the decision-making. Remember, Jean Piaget, influential philosopher and educator, suggests that intelligence is what we use when we don't already know what to do.

We wish that 25 years ago the Albert Einstein College of Medicine thought of doing side-by-side comparisons of different kinds of dancing, to find out which was better. But we can figure it out by looking at who they studied: senior citizens 75 and older, beginning in 1980. Those who danced in that particular population were former Roaring Twenties dancers (back in 1980) and former Swing Era dancers (today), so the kind of dancing most of them continued to do in retirement was what they began when they were young: freestyle social dancing – basic Foxtrot, Swing, Waltz and maybe some Latin.

I've been watching senior citizens dance all of my life, from my parents (who met at a Tommy Dorsey dance), to retirement communities, to the Roseland Ballroom in New York. I almost never see memorized sequences or patterns on the dance floor. I mostly see easygoing, fairly simple social dancing – freestyle leads and follow. But freestyle social dancing isn't that simple.

It requires a lot of split-second decision-making, in both the lead and follow roles.

When it comes to preserving mental acuity, some forms are apparently better than others. When we talk of intelligence (use it or lose it) then the more decision-making we can bring into our dancing, the better.

Who benefits more, women or men?

In social dancing, the follow role automatically gains a benefit, by making hundreds of split-second decisions as to what to do next. As I mentioned on this page, women don't "follow," they interpret the signals their partners are giving them, and this requires intelligence and decision-making, which is active, not passive. This benefit is greatly enhanced by dancing with different partners, not always the same leader. With different dance partners, you have to adjust much more and be aware of more variables. This is great for staying smarter longer.

But men, you can also match her degree of decision-making if you choose to do so. (1) Really notice your partner and what works best for her. Notice what is comfortable for her, where she is already going, which moves are successful with her and what aren't, and constantly adapt your dancing to these observations. That's rapid-fire split-second decisions making. (2) Don't lead the same old patterns the same way each time. Challenge yourself to try new things. Make more decisions more often. Intelligence: use it or lose it. And gentlemen, the huge side-benefit is that your partners will have much more fun dancing with you when you are attentive to their dancing and constantly adjust for their comfort and continuity of motion.

Dance often:

Finally, remember that this study made another suggestion: Recall that seniors who did crossword puzzles four days a week had a significantly lower risk of dementia than those who did the puzzle once a week. If you can't take classes or go out dancing four times a week, dance as much as you can. More is better.

And do it now, the sooner the better. It's essential to start building your cognitive reserve now. Some day you'll need as many of those stepping stones across the creek as possible. Don't wait – start building them now."

This article ends my dancealogue with the hope that my writings will encourage people to enter the world of ballroom dancing and become interested in this modern day popular phenomenon, that is not only an excellent physical activity that strengthens our bodies and builds confidence, but as the above studies point out, has a positive effect on our minds. Something to remember on a daily basis is that: "Smart people dance" or my preferred version: "Dancing makes people smart."

www.ingramcontent.com/pod-product-compliance
Lightning Source LLC
Chambersburg PA
CBHW030935150426
42812CB00064B/2917/J